D1600227

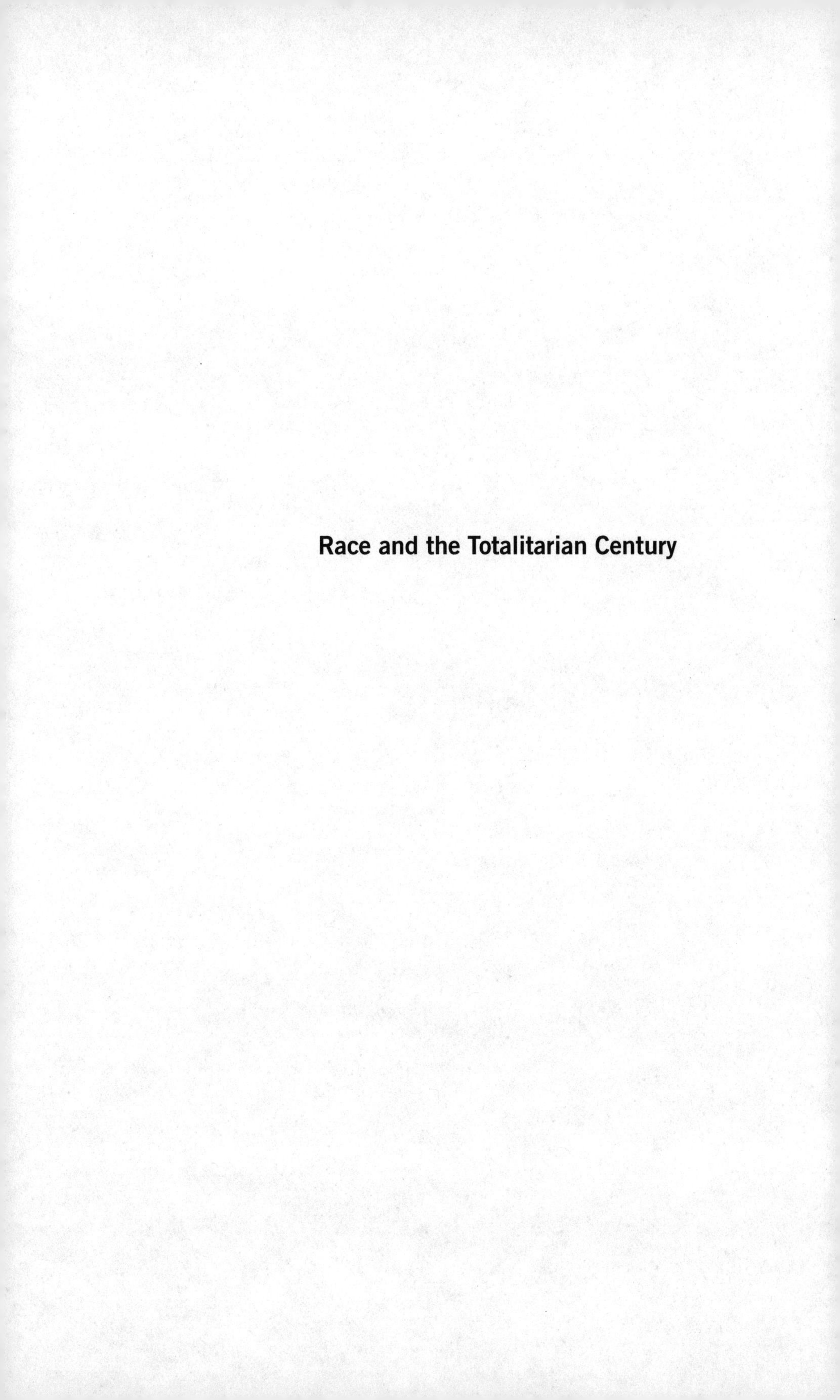

Race and the Totalitarian Century

Race and the Totalitarian Century

GEOPOLITICS IN THE BLACK LITERARY IMAGINATION

Vaughn Rasberry

Cambridge, Massachusetts
London, England 2016

Printed in the United States of America

Second printing

Library of Congress Cataloging-in-Publication Data

Names: Rasberry, Vaughn, author.
Title: Race and the totalitarian century : geopolitics in the Black literary imagination / Vaughn Rasberry.
Description: Cambridge, Massachusetts : Harvard University Press, 2016. | Includes bibliographical references and index.
Identifiers: LCCN 2016009529 | ISBN 9780674971080 (hardcover : alk. paper)
Subjects: LCSH: African American authors—Political activity—History—20th century. | African Americans—Politics and government—Philosophy. | Totalitarianism and literature. | Geopolitics in literature. | Racism—History—20th century. | Politics and literature—United States—History—20th century.
Classification: LCC E185.6 .R36 2016 | DDC 323.1196/073—dc23
LC record available at http://lccn.loc.gov/2016009529

To the memory of Dr. Lettie Jane Austin,
1925–2008

Contents

Introduction

FREE WORLDS

IF THE TWENTIETH CENTURY would witness, at the midpoint," writes Hortense Spillers, "the terrifying spectacle of the totalitarian regime, in which case *anything could happen*, as Hannah Arendt describes it, then we often think of its technologies of terror adumbrated in the long centuries of unregulated violence against black people." Reflecting on her landmark 1987 essay, "Mama's Baby, Papa's Maybe: An American Grammar Book," Spillers notes that in this context crisis could refer to the "collapse" or "clarification" of well-defined structures but in either case turns on the "moral and intellectual jujitsu that yielded the catachresis, person-as-property."[1] In just one scintillating detour of many, Spillers attaches racial terror of long centuries to the totalitarian regime of midcentury en route to a broader rumination on blackness and modernity. But this line of inquiry is worthy of pursuit.

As a step in this direction, it is worth recalling that Hannah Arendt's well-known analysis of imperialism in Africa in *The Origins of Totalitarianism* indicates that the subject of her study could not remain within a strictly European and Slavic provenance. Commentators disagree about the meaning and significance of Arendt's discussion of the Scramble for Africa[2] to her theory of totalitarianism. Does her work connect a prehistory of concentration camps, erected in southwestern Africa at the turn of the century, to the subsequent proliferation of modern camps in Europe and Russia? Or does her analysis replicate the colonialist mentality she criticizes? Is Africa instead adduced in her text mainly to convey the *discontinuity* between colonialism and totalitarianism? These questions remain a subject of debate, but it strikes me that her account probes the history of the Belgian Congo (and its literary evocation in Conrad's *Heart of Darkness*) in order to show how the sublimated effects of this colonial enterprise conduced, albeit elusively, and in ways that are difficult to explain historically, to the reduction of human life to superfluity in wartime Europe.

Until recently, though, very little of the vast literature on totalitarianism has followed the road opened by Arendt, and before her, by W. E. B. Du Bois—who viewed the First and Second World Wars as interimperialist rivalries fought in, and over, African territory—on the relation between modern racial terror and the onset of total war and totalitarianism. Subsequent chapters (particularly Chapter 1) review this scholarship in detail, but at this point it ought to be said that the critical literature does not bear Spillers out: theorists of totalitarianism scarcely include histories of unregulated violence against black people in their ideological coordinates. *Race and the Totalitarian Century* seeks to redress this deficit. This book argues that African American and Third World writers, drawing on an imaginative and rhetorical repertoire of desegregation and decolonization, activated an alternative global dialogue on totalitarian governance. In crucial situations described below, it was from this discursive space that writers like W. E. B. Du Bois, Shirley Graham, C. L. R. James, Richard Wright, and Frantz Fanon produced texts and collaborations designed to manipulate, maneuver, or assert agency within the very power blocs presumed to exercise control over subaltern actors. Inspired by the Third World strategy of nonalignment, these writers reconstitute official antitotalitarianism as an independent platform for Cold War geopolitical critique.[3] The book's orientation is meant to rebalance the Cold War so that the "Third World" achieves a symmetrical relation to the democratic and communist spheres in the world-historical framing of totalitarianism.

With respect to my use of the term *geopolitics*, this project is concerned with how black literary culture reframed pivotal geopolitical events (like the Suez Crisis or Hungarian Revolt of 1956) or foreign policy imperatives (like anticommunism) against the grain of official representations of antitotalitarianism.[4] But the term *geopolitics* designates a more capacious domain, even a philosophical one, as Martin Heidegger's occasional ruminations on the Soviet Union and the United States suggest.[5]

According to Heidegger, from the standpoint of Being, which unfolds in specific places and discloses truth in them, the hypermodernizing systems of the United States and the Soviet Union betray the same homogenizing and universalizing tendencies that eradicate place as such. Because these regimes compete to install technological and ideological regimes across the globe, the notion of place as a site for the disclosure of Being is ultimately, if not exclusively, a political question. "Actually," writes one commentator, "geography is politics for Heidegger insofar as truth is a sited, situation specific occurrence." And though the economic systems in both countries appear different or opposed in theory, "Heidegger contends that as exercised they are similar because they deny the question of being and, subsequently, ignore the hermeneutic situation to which all beings are tied. Disregarding the hermeneutic situation denies accord to the place and variation of the site of emergence of being. This leads to the dislocation of identity no less than the metaphysics of universal truths. The revolutions that gave rise to American destiny and Soviet world communism both mean the ideological spread of one way of life at the expense of other people and places, of the Other."[6] It is probably wise not to overstate this emphasis on the abstract "Other," but Heidegger's ruminations capture what is at stake in the geopolitical order taking shape at midcentury.

Heidegger's concern involves Europe after the Second World War, especially Germany, which he sees as caught "in the great pincers between Russia on the one side and America on the other," but for my purposes his reflections extend beyond the province of European historical pessimism.[7] Not only do we find in Heidegger's ontological conception of the geopolitical a dismissal of the Cold War superpower antithesis, not to mention a tacit rejection of the fascism-communism equation, but we can also locate in it a philosophical corollary to expressions of postcolonial melancholy: a sense that local spaces—particular dwelling places where authentic being is constituted—are being consumed by expansionist industrial-technological orders under which *Dasein* cannot survive.[8] "Russia and America," writes Heidegger, "seen metaphysically, are both the same: the same hopeless frenzy of unchained technology and of the rootless organization of the average man."[9] If the political register stresses how colonialism and then globalization infringe on Third World sovereignty and material resources, the metaphysical register underscores the ontological transformations wrought by an endlessly expansive technological regime.[10]

On this account, both Cold War America and Soviet Russia engender universal homogenization, exploitation of nature, eradication of difference, and diminution of the world's languages.[11] These reflections on modernity and technics bear on a key Third World dilemma: how to balance the imperative of modernization, a process indifferent if not hostile to the ontology of dwelling, and the accommodation and preservation of locality, which no postcolonial leadership could afford to ignore. As Richard Wright understood this paradox of postcolonial modernity, the Third World had little choice but to modernize (and to militarize), independently and rapidly, even if such efforts resulted in a period of authoritarian governance and dislocation of peoples. Otherwise the Third World, as Wright saw the matter, stood little chance of withstanding encroachments by advanced industrial powers.

"The African Sahara is only one kind of wasteland," writes Heidegger in his early 1950s lectures *What Is Called Thinking?* "The devastation of the earth," he continues, "can easily go hand in hand with a guaranteed supreme living standard for man, and just as easily with the organized establishment of a uniform state of happiness for all men."[12] What is meant by this passage? Readers of Heidegger will note in this sentence a key word in the philosopher's lexicon: *wasteland*. In the original German edition, Heidegger writes: "Die Sahara in Afrika ist nur eine Art der Wüste."[13] In his translation, J. Glenn Gray renders *Art der Wüste* as "one kind of wasteland," a term that also denotes desert, wilderness. (Eliot's *The Wasteland* was translated into German as *Das wüste Land*.)

In other works by Heidegger in which the word "wasteland" appears in English translation, he uses another word, "die Öde," which denotes wasteland as well as desert and barrenness. In Heidegger's usage, *wasteland* (die Öde) also describes metaphorical conditions, especially those states seemingly inimical to contemplation of Being, and those places in which Being as a question appears irrelevant. In certain states, such as despair or joy, it is natural to expect the question of why there are beings at all instead of nothing to take hold. But maybe these existentially charged states are not as conducive to thought as one might suppose. In the *Introduction to Metaphysics*, Heidegger writes: "The question is there in a spell of boredom, when we are equally distant from despair and joy, but when the stubborn ordinariness of beings lays open a wasteland [*eine Öde*] in which it makes no difference to us whether beings are or are not—and then, in a distinctive form, the question resonates again: Why are there beings at all instead of nothing?"[14] Heidegger's naming of the African Sahara as a wasteland does not single out this region as the quintessence of a primordial wasteland, a place devoid of civilization.

When in the early 1950s Heidegger referred to the African Sahara, perhaps as an afterthought, the punishing desert was transforming from an area of little interest to colonial powers to an industrial-extractive hub and quasi-colonial outpost of France. As the preceding passage indicates, the physical and mental spaces imagined as resistant to the contemplation of Being—the state of boredom, or life in the Sahara—are precisely those in which the question of Being intrudes so insistently. The "devastation of the earth" goes hand in hand with global homogenization of culture, norms of happiness, and the economy. Propelled by the teleology of modernization, these coeval processes seize power over the spirit (to use Heidegger's idiom) in dwelling places like the Sahara: an unexpected site for Being's disclosure.

Versus Heidegger's philosophical location of totalizing tendencies in America and Soviet Russia, the Cold War redefinition of the Soviet Union and Nazi Germany as the quintessence of totalitarianism persists. Despite the end of the Cold War, dramatically marked by China's Tiananmen Square protests and the fall of the Berlin Wall, the aftermath of September 11, 2001, has revived specters—in the guise of "Islamic totalitarianism" and resurgent nonsecular formations—that the collapse of international communism and the "end of history" were supposed to have laid to rest.

Few words evoke global memory of the twentieth century—of total war, genocide, political repression, ideological extremism, propaganda offensives; of gulags and concentration camps, secret police and surveillance agencies, atomic bombs and nuclear bluffs—more powerfully, if perhaps too capaciously, than the word *totalitarianism*. It is no secret that this word also forms the ideological core of narratives, across genres, about the twentieth century: from synthetic histories charting the rise and fall of fascism and communism, or the triumph of democratic capitalism, to memoirs and fiction conjuring damaged life under ultrarepressive regimes. Originating in the early 1920s, the term *sistema totalitaria* arises in connection with Italian fascism. Rejecting what they perceived as the political weakness, materialism, individualism, and spiritual degeneracy of liberal democracy, the fascist progenitors of the *sistema totalitaria* envisioned a total state defined by dictatorial control, ideological unity, ultranationalism, belligerent expansionism, and obliteration of the division between public and private spheres.

One of Mussolini's earliest opponents, the socialist Giovanni Amendola, invented the term, which referred to a foundational repressive act: Mussolini's successful effort to alter Italy's constitution and extant election laws in order to consolidate power for his fascist regime.[15] Only a few months later, Amendola was able to speak more expansively and presciently of a "totalitarian spirit" animating the fascist movement, one that over the years began to permeate continental politics.[16] Exuding total ideological commitment, the totalitarian spirit exalted collective valor against the stereotypically bourgeois traits of moral flabbiness, spiritual emptiness, political quiescence, and fear of violent death. Readers of Ernst Jünger's *On Pain* (1934), for example—which heralds a new machinelike subjectivity, cold and detached, to match the rise of terror-inducing torpedoes and airborne missiles—find in that text an exemplary expression of this ethos. For Jünger, a prominent voice in Germany's Conservative Revolution, the era demands the replacement of security, ease, and comfort with pain, destruction, and sacrifice.[17]

This subjectivity corresponds though is not identical with the imperatives of the totalitarian state, which likewise sought to obliterate the division between the public and private spheres and to subordinate the individual to the collective. It also exerted control over, and imposed congruence between, the economic and intellectual spheres. While the total state controlled the means of production, distribution, and exchange, what is more enduring in contemporary culture is the state's control of thought: what Élie Halévy in *The Era of Tyrannies* (1938) identifies as the negative regulation of ideas deemed unfavorable to the national interest, as well as the positive "organization of enthusiasm."[18] In the Soviet context, self-regulation—harkening to the French Revolution, whose revolutionaries coined the word *dénonciation*—emerged as perhaps the most impressive and startling phenomenon, as citizens policed themselves, publicly denouncing family members and friends as traitors of the state.[19]

The beginning of the Cold War marked a politically decisive redefinition of totalitarianism. Beginning in the interwar years and escalating in the post–Second World War era, the term came to refer, loosely, to dictatorships on the far left and right and to extremist ideological movements more generally. But after the defeat of Nazism and imperial Japan, communism emerged in democracy's crosshairs as the world's sole totalitarian threat. This Cold War redefinition returns the idea to its provenance in the Bolshevik Revolution, which fascist upstarts, according to analysts like Arendt, sought to emulate.[20] This mode of analysis codified a historical process ignited by the Nazi-Soviet Pact of 1939, the signal moment of disillusionment for American socialists and fellow travelers.[21] The postwar consensus on the evils of totalitarian (or even radical or utopian) politics produced a newly skeptical and chastened subjectivity that typically goes by the name of Cold War liberalism, but cognate terms like the "liberal imagination" (Lionel Trilling) or the "vital center" (Arthur Schlesinger) also circulated.[22]

For many commentators, including leftist critics of global capitalism and Western foreign policy, the totalitarian experience defines the twentieth century, imbuing the period from the First World War and the Bolshevik Revolution to the end of the Cold War with a macabre coherence. For other critics, however, such as Alain Badiou and Slavoj Žižek, totalitarianism is merely an ideological notion and an abuse of history invoked by defenders of capital in order to squelch radical initiative.[23] Badiou dismisses the idea of totalitarianism as emblematic of the "triumph of miniscule ideas," the "victory of Capital."[24] On this view, the idea capitulates to Churchill's alternately celebrated or despised quip that democracy is the worst form of government except all the others that have been tried. These critics rightly argue that, whatever the catastrophic failures of "Actually Existing Socialism" (Žižek), it nonetheless represents a universal desire for emancipation, whereas fascism represents a desire only for national and racial domination. Whatever similarities exist in the respective systems of Stalinism and Nazism, these philosophical projects are indeed radically opposed. Categorically, though, these critics insist that the very use of the term in critical discourse implies acquiescence in liberal democratic hegemony and the dim horizon of global capitalism. Yet by polemicizing against the misuses of a term that one might have expected to retreat from public discourse post-1990, these philosophers keep the debate alive.

For Badiou, the sequence that structures antitotalitarian discourse is an ideological, not a dialectical scheme. This "logical" sequence proceeds as follows: totalitarianism, whether from the left or right, incarnates political evil; only liberal democratic capitalism is equipped, and has risen to the occasion, to defeat this evil; as history teaches, any political formation in opposition to democratic capitalism is totalitarian, or potentially so; therefore, the proper aim of politics is to bolster democratic capitalism, and its values and institutions like human rights, tolerance, and humanitarian aid, which represent the political good—or the least evil—and to oppose totalitarianism in all its manifestations. To acknowledge that much of neoliberal thought embeds this illusory sequence is to concede, in large measure, the force of Badiou's critique.

This Cold War conflation of fascism and communism remains objectionable to certain factions on the left, whereas for other critics, especially survivors of communist repression, the equivalency is undeniable on structural and historical levels. An unacknowledged consensus, however, unites proponents and detractors of this normative conception of totalitarianism. After a century of vigorous debate on the subject, extant works continue to confine the academic study and literary representation of totalitarianism to Europe's collapse in the First and Second World Wars, to U.S. Cold War propaganda, or to historiographical comparison between the Soviet Union and Nazi Germany.[25] Employing the conventional markers of war and revolution, both antitotalitarian writers and their skeptics agree that the term names a chronologically specific crisis—or democratic capitalism's official *reaction* to crisis—that unfurled within the internal historical development, and exploded on the battlegrounds, of the Western world from 1917 to 1990.[26]

This historical and geographical locus reflects the prevailing sense among postwar observers and their chastened progeny that totalitarianism consummated all of the ills, dissatisfactions, and ruptures of European modernity since the Age of Enlightenment—from the terror of the French Revolution and the rise of nationalism and interimperial rivalry to the expanding iron cage of rationalization and the seemingly unstoppable spread of secularization, to the emergence of mass media technologies and the science of propaganda, and to the onset of industrialization and the crescendo of mechanized warfare. The confluence of these processes in European modernity permitted Max Horkheimer and Theodor Adorno famously to proclaim (too pessimistically, on the view of Jürgen Habermas): "Enlightenment is totalitarian." Perhaps these words are freighted with more historical weight than this sentence can bear. Enlightenment is totalitarian, in one sense, because any "intellectual resistance it encounters merely increases its strength."[27] In whatever sense *die Aufklärung* can be understood as totalitarian, the broader thrust of this text concerns how the array of progressive forces originating in Europe turned into barbarism. Equally significant for Horkheimer and Adorno is how liberal or "bourgeois" capitalist societies—and for these writers the U.S. "culture industry" was exemplary—perpetuate a hegemonic culture devoid of subversive possibilities: a threat more pervasive, and insidious, than the totalitarian apparatus of the communist world against which bourgeois society defined itself.

For these historical and other factors, genealogies of totalitarianism cluster around a European intellectual tradition, chiefly Germanic, stretching from Kant, Hegel, Marx, Nietzsche, Weber, Schmitt, Jünger, Horkheimer, Neumann, Adorno, to Arendt and beyond, in tandem with a broader continental corpus, including Koestler, Orwell, Sartre, Camus, Solzhenitsyn, Kolakowski, and Todorov, among many others. Cross-pollinating this intellectual history with an archive of decolonization, *Race and the Totalitarian Century* adopts a different point of departure. This story crystallizes in midcentury efforts by U.S. state actors to conscript black Americans and their colonial counterparts into the official antitotalitarian struggle. For critics then and now, these efforts either reoriented black political actors around U.S. liberalism or propelled them defiantly and misguidedly into the communist sphere. By contrast, this book shows how an array of black writers appropriated or deflected the appeals of liberalism and its antitotalitarian rhetoric in the service of a transformative vision of the postwar order. Their skeptical view of the wartime opposition of totalitarian slavery and democratic freedom, I argue, enabled writers to formulate what one critic calls a "writing of nonalignment," a stance independent of communism or liberal democracy but capable of manipulating both.[28]

Over the course of this argument, various chapters revisit the widespread claim that the Second World War and early Cold War transformed race relations on a domestic and global scale. *Race and the Totalitarian Century* reads the work of anticolonial writers who perceived the Allied war effort as symbolic of democracy's contradictions but also as a discursive field ripe for strategic manipulation. In situations in which black intellectuals of this era appear in postures of reaction to larger ideological forces—namely, U.S. liberalism or Soviet communism—this book instead reconstructs a complex counter-public activated by events like the Italian invasion of Ethiopia in 1935 and the Suez Canal Crisis and Hungarian revolt of 1956 to the Arab-Israeli War of 1967.

Though they constellate around a common set of midcentury themes and events, specific iterations of this critique vary over the course of my argument, which does not presuppose or describe a unitary black antitotalitarian front. To return to Spillers, if my argument draws on a common view (explicit in some texts and implicit in others) that terror exercised against blacks constitutes an unacknowledged mode of totalitarian domination, it does not then conclude that U.S. racial democracy or British liberal imperialism are basically equivalent in the repressive particulars to their illiberal counterparts. Even if continuities exist between democratic and totalitarian regimes along the axis of race, as many anticolonial writers argue, this point is one of departure, rather than a terminus, for the story told here. These literary intellectuals engage the geopolitics of totalitarianism in all the multifaceted and prolific ways that it operates at midcentury—and, important for my purposes, in ways that it does not. The work of C. L. R. James in the 1950s provides one case of the nonreductive, anticolonial critique of Cold War geopolitics I have in mind.

In his 2001 republication of C. L. R. James's *Mariners, Renegades, and Castaways,* Donald Pease observes that unlike celebrated works by James such as *The Black Jacobins* (1938) or *Beyond a Boundary* (1963), *Mariners* has posed an unusual interpretive challenge to scholars. Some critics have read the text as a forced rewriting of Melville that promotes a revolutionary agenda or, alternately, as an anticommunist apology for U.S capitalism.[29] Pease usefully reintroduces this neglected work as a Cold War allegory and reading of Melville's *Moby Dick* as a visionary antitotalitarian text. As James puts it: "Melville's theme is totalitarianism, its rise and fall, its power and its weakness."[30]

An adversary of communism, James adopts the conflation of Stalinism and Nazism ingrained in the postwar imagination: "Hitler was no sooner destroyed than Stalin threatened to overwhelm not only Europe but the whole of the world. The type is the same." For James and countless others, "Nazism and Communism" were dual symptoms of a broader European degeneration. James even presses the equation on the volatile terrain of racial domination. "Though they have sprung from such different origins, the Russian Communists are practicing today in the satellite states of Europe the Nazi doctrine of the master race with the thinnest of disguises. If Hitler had been successful and had survived, he would have been driven to adopt some form of the Communist plan."[31] But even this view, or some version of it, was widely held among anticommunists in the 1950s.

Mariners, Renegades, and Castaways unfolds into an idiosyncratic, antitotalitarian analysis of the Second World War. Like his contemporaries, C. L. R. James understood the Second World War as transformative yet in some sense abortive: a catalyst for decolonization but also a missed opportunity for global revolution. James "confesses frankly that it is only since the end of World War II that the emergence of the people of the Far East and of Africa into the daily headlines, the spread of Russian totalitarianism, the emergence of America as a power in every quarter of the globe, it is only this that has enabled him to see the range, the power, and the boldness of Melville. . . . In this no writer, at any time, has ever surpassed him."[32] Melville's achievement was not only to prognosticate the rise of totalitarianism; it was also to identify a complex weakness of the liberal state in the face of this threat.

Composed in 1952 while the author was detained in Ellis Island for six months by authorities from the Immigration and Naturalization Services, *Mariners* interprets Captain Ahab ("a true son of nineteenth century America") as the epitome of the charismatic totalitarian personality. "The crisis of Ahab," he writes, "is that of a civilization which has recognized that it is on the way to complete mastery of the arts and sciences of civilization."[33] James's characterization of Ahab, and thus of nineteenth-century America, imputes to Melville's protagonist a symbolism redolent of the dialectic of enlightenment. But how, James asks, was Melville able as early as 1851 to create a character that so clearly embodied the totalitarian movements of a century later? One might turn this question on its head and ask how James extrapolates a conception of totalitarianism from a singular nineteenth-century American novel.

"Fire, power, the civilization of material progress," James writes, "was a mighty creative force. But its creativity was mechanical. Mechanical is a word he will use many times. It is this which is destroying his life as a human being. And he will fight it." James reproduces a speech by Ahab in which he declares himself made of the "clear spirit" of fire, adding that "like a true child of fire, I breathe it back to thee."[34] Like Horkheimer and Adorno's evocation of Prometheus in *Dialectic of Enlightenment*, James sees in Ahab's conflagrant persona an embodiment of the dialectical struggle in a rapidly mechanized America. Melville's protagonist desires sovereignty over forces—"Fire, power, mechanical creativeness"—unleashed by the very industrialized order that is dehumanizing him, and against which he ultimately rebels.

In the chapter of *Renegades* titled "The Catastrophe," James wonders why the crew did not revolt against Ahab, whose megalomaniacal pursuit was hurling the *Pequod* toward disaster. James notes that Melville places responsibility for leading the revolt primarily on the crewman Starbuck, a character James describes as a brave, competent man of high moral principle, but also a "moral coward [who] is certain to fail before the concentrated purpose and force of character of Ahab."[35] Starbuck, a New Englander, symbolizes liberalism's response to the crisis of tyranny, personified in Ahab, who anticipates the charismatic fascists and communists of the future world. Starbuck's "story is the story of the liberals and democrats who during the last quarter of a century have led the capitulation to the totalitarians in country after country."

> On the night of the great storm, Starbuck, forgetting himself, shouts to Ahab before all the men, to turn back. He points to Ahab's harpoon which has caught fire from the magnetic flame on the mast. The voyage, he says, is doomed to disaster. For a moment, it seemed that Starbuck was saying what the men were thinking. They raise a half-mutinous cry and rush to the sails. One word from Starbuck and Ahab would be over the side. But Ahab seizes his harpoon and swearing to transfix with it any man who moves, tells them that he will blow out the flame and blows it out with one breath. His fearlessness, his skillful pretense of being able to command the mysterious, magnetic flame, terrify the men.[36]

On this reading, Melville intuits what becomes in the twentieth century the supposed paralysis of liberalism (Starbuck) before charismatic totalitarianism (Ahab). Ahab's mystical command of the emergency legitimates his complete authority, however irrational his behavior might appear to his subordinates.

Along with other anticolonial thinkers, James agreed that the liberal state proved inadequate to the task of resolving its racist contradictions. Writing as a target of the McCarran Act, which he read as "permeated with the doctrine of racial superiority," James was only too aware of U.S. racial contradictions in the 1950s.[37] But in this dramatic scene, James identifies a different weakness of the liberal state. Liberalism's commitment to procedural and deliberative methods, and even to law, betrays enfeeblement and a fundamental lack of resolve, against both totalitarian adversaries *and* its own illiberal tendencies. After multiple opportunities to take out Ahab, and thus to precipitate a revolt, Starbuck never does—why? Because for Starbuck "'there is no lawful way' in which to stop him," James explains (with some disdain for this attitude).

Yet isn't this masculine argument—that procedural, deliberative governance is weak and ineffectual compared to totalitarian governance—exactly how dictators on the right and left derided liberalism and taunted the United States?[38] On one level, James does seem to ground his reading in the antiliberal ethos he wants to critique. But on another level consistent with James's class politics, the problem involves just what kind of revolt liberalism (again, embodied overdeterminedly by Starbuck) is capable of producing. The racial and class composition of the crew—the mariners, renegades, and castaways—would appear to provide the perfect ingredients for a colonially representative rebellion, one with special resonance and foresight for the future wretched of the earth. Yet James astutely adds that Melville intentionally forecloses the possibility of Starbuck's having sparked a successful revolt, for a victory led by this character—who "hates the men and looks upon them as uncouth, barbarous sub-human beings"—would lead to nothing.[39] If they survived, James suggests, the crew's members would simply go on doing whatever they were doing before they set out for the white whale. The lives of these maritime proletarians, drawn from the colonized world, would not change, nor would their collective action possess any historical resonance. In what would have been a triumph of liberalism, their narratively stillborn revolt would have had little meaning beyond their own self-preservation.

As this distillation of James's *Mariners* indicates, my project parts ways with conventional accounts of twentieth-century world war and geopolitics in order to tell a strikingly different story. My hope is that the outcome of this approach is twofold: first, a renewed political imagination of totalitarianism from the vantage of colonial modernity, and second, a revisionist account of black cultural production that demonstrates its diverse, and often unexpected, engagements with the century's pressing dilemmas wrought by world war. This stylized approach, for all its inadequacies, provides another entrance to reconsider black writers whose careers apparently flagged during the 1950s, when they appeared creatively exhausted (Wright), politically doctrinaire and duped by communist propaganda (Du Bois), or disconnected from the energies of the civil rights movement (Wright, Shirley Graham, William Gardner Smith, Ollie Harrington) while luxuriating in the pleasures of exile. To tell this story, my project situates black literary culture in dialogue with European émigrés like Arendt and Frankfurt School thinkers, as well as with Third World intellectuals and leaders like Nehru, Memmi, Nasser, and Fanon who similarly sought to navigate perilous Cold War terrain via the strategy of nonalignment.

With respect to the temporal parameters of what I am calling the totalitarian century, this study finds its center of gravity in the post-1945 era before the advent of the black power movement and global rebellions of the late 1960s but registers at various points the Pandora's box opened in the First World War and the Bolshevik Revolution.[40] As Chapter 1 indicates, this earlier periodization underscores how colonial war intersects with world war and what this convergence meant for black politics across the diaspora. Woodrow Wilson, for one, signaled this significance in his anxious remark that the "American Negro returning from abroad would be our greatest medium in conveying Bolshevism to America."[41] To some degree, Wilson's concern was justified: Harry Haywood, an African American veteran in France during the Second World War, recounts in his autobiography that his new global awareness, exposure to European politics, and reaction to the Chicago race riot and Red Summer of 1919 precipitated his lifelong conversion to Bolshevism. Juxtaposed against such representations of the American Negro in the context of world war, Du Bois's study of the First World War, as I discuss in Chapter 1, led to his conviction that the conflict derived in some important sense from imperial rivalry in turn of the century Africa and the chaos it engendered beyond Europe's borders. Later commentators drew on Du Bois's insight, seeing in 1930s Europe a sinister element originating not only in the trenches of the First World War but also in the destruction of lives purchased so cheaply during the Scramble for Africa.

And what is the status of Wilson's dangerous "American Negro" and his global counterparts, geographically dispersed but sharing in the common drama of war, democratic struggle, and colonial subjugation? And given that all of the writers under discussion here cultivate diverse modes of literary and political internationalism, why foreground this figure of U.S. nativity and the archive clustered around it? As Brent Edwards and other scholars have demonstrated, black internationalism peaked in the interwar years, a period when writers generated a set of literary, political, and translational practices attesting to the appeal of diaspora collaboration, on the one hand, and to the domestic pressures forcing blacks to forge alliances and seek experiences beyond the nation-state, on the other.[42]

How did the historical confluence of the Cold War, decolonization, and desegregation transform black internationalism from the interwar practices of diaspora to a mode of transnational engagement shaped by the contest between communism and democratic capitalism? By the postwar era, internationalism had adapted to a geopolitical situation in which the U.S. state sought to enfold blacks within the sphere of liberal citizenship. At the same time that the state presented new opportunities to African Americans, the confiscation of passports held by black activists, some of whom were deposed before the House Un-American Activities Committee, reflects this attempt at political enclosure. For example, at the Paris Congress of Black Writers and Artists on September 19, 1956, Du Bois expressed his regret via telegram that he could not attend, since the State Department had revoked his passport. In James Baldwin's recounting, Du Bois then stated that any "American Negro travelling abroad today must either not care about Negroes or say what the State Department wishes him to say"—an applause-generating remark, Baldwin quips, that "very neatly destroyed whatever effectiveness the five-man American delegation then sitting in the hall might have hoped to have."[43] Anecdotes of this sort underscore the contrast between the relatively fluid terrain of black internationalism in the interwar years and the ideologically stultifying climate of the Cold War.

It is not as though similar impingements and opportunities did not exist in earlier decades, but they are far more pronounced at midcentury, with the consequence that U.S. nationality increasingly mediates, and constrains, black intellectual expression and political activity of this period.[44] This mediation precipitated formal shifts in black literary production at midcentury—a still-undefined interregnum (in the dual sense of "any period of freedom from the usual authority" and "any pause or interruption in continuity") between the canonized Harlem Renaissance and Black Arts movement—as writers experimented with "raceless" fiction, tempered earlier radical tendencies, and adopted various idioms of liberal individualism. One objection to this national focus is that it seems, prima facie, to perpetuate a U.S.-centric approach to global affairs or, as Paul Gilroy and others have argued, continues to situate African Americans as the advance guard of political struggle in the black diaspora.[45]

These criticisms have merit. Take, for instance, the claim that more so than New York, London was the headquarters—led by Africans and West Indians such as George Padmore, Jomo Kenyatta, and C. L. R. James—of the black diaspora's mobilization in defense of Ethiopia in the mid-1930s and other internationalist projects. Or consider the fact that the series of Pan-African conferences that spanned the years 1900 to 1945 began with mostly African American and West Indian leadership; during the interwar years included more balance between Africans and blacks in the West; and by midcentury were led mostly by African heads of state like Nkrumah and Kenyatta.[46] Indeed, part of the story of this book concerns African Americans' enhanced attention to African and Third World developments. This book tries to register these important distinctions but is not undone by them insofar as its focus is not the question of diaspora itself. Rather, it seeks to balance the centrality of national identity with the urgency of international concerns, on the premise that the theoretical revision enabled by close study of the black geopolitical dialogue with totalitarianism outweighs the risks of analogical and comparative analysis.[47]

In some cases, I read literary texts to pursue underexplored historical questions and sketch new narratives; in others, I read this history to pose new questions about (often underexplored) literary texts. Though some overlap exists in these two approaches, this dual method seems to me demanded by the archive itself, given my intuition that narrating how writers represent specific historical events enables me to show how subsequent writers worked out the tensions and unfinished business of history at the level of novelistic form.

In recent years, scholarship in American and African American Studies has highlighted the Cold War era as a pivotal moment in black literary culture and politics that catapulted the question of African American citizenship onto the global stage. Taken together, this research has questioned standard periodizations of the civil rights movement by locating crucial precedents in the 1930s and 1940s; reinvigorated discussion about the role of communism in the black freedom struggle; traced the continued resonance of popular front or social realist aesthetics, often in creative tension with modernist conventions; reexamined black literary experimentation with "raceless" fiction like the so-called novel of white life, once presumed to lift black cultural production into the sphere of universal expression; explored cosmopolitan and transnational affiliations at the nexus of desegregation and decolonization; reinstated the contribution of black feminism to radical political projects; measured the impact of Cold War pressures and opportunities for black activists; and demonstrated how postwar America's emergence as a global superpower forced the nation to confront, seriously, Jim Crow as an impediment to its hegemony.[48]

As it inserts the centrality of totalitarianism into black cultural production, this study builds on recent research that triangulates desegregation, decolonization, and Cold War politics into a coherent historical framework.[49] I regard the reinstatement of totalitarianism as a critical point of entry into this evolving body of scholarship. My project intercepts this incipient field at a moment when recent trends toward global intellectual history, in the face of sundry methodological challenges (linguistic, evidentiary, disciplinary), aspire to complement or supplant national, statist, or West-centered paradigms.[50]

This book is divided into two parts. Part 1, "Race and the Totalitarian Century," is thematically and geographically based, whereas Part 2, "How to Build Socialist Modernity in the Third World," is biographically based. The following chapter summary elaborates on this division of the book's structure.

Crystallizing the nexus of race, war, and totalitarianism, Chapter 1, "The Figure of the Negro Soldier: Racial Democracy and World War," sketches the figure of the Negro soldier in literature, film, and art from the First World War to the early Cold War. Representations of this figure provide an entry for thinking about how black engagement in world war summoned African American literary imaginaries of the totalitarian. During the Second World War, this figure of pathos and heroism, I argue, embodied the antitotalitarian struggle on multiple fronts: the Negro soldier and his chroniclers understood the fight to involve not only Nazism and fascism in Europe but also Jim Crow segregation in the United States and colonialism in Asia and Africa.

As a dual synecdoche for black militarization and citizenship, the meaning of the Negro soldier shifts, I argue, in the transition from the Second World War to the postwar era. The multiple antitotalitarian front (against Nazism, Jim Crow, colonialism) embodied by the Negro soldier assumes a different meaning after the defeat of Nazi Germany and imperial Japan, when the United States assumed its role as a superpower and bedrock of the democratic capitalist sphere. In this geopolitical situation, black soldiers who were greeted as liberators in Germany could be seen, only a few years later, as sympathetic but ambiguous agents of military occupation, as ironic emblems of U.S. dominance. I trace this historical arc of the Negro soldier across a range of texts, including *Journal of Negro Education* yearbook issues (1941, 1943) on the subject of blacks and other minorities in the First and Second World Wars; the propaganda film *The Negro Soldier* (1944), written by black filmmaker Carlton Moss with the support of Frank Capra and the

U.S. War Department; the wartime poetry of Gwendolyn Brooks in her collection *A Street in Bronzeville* (1945); Ann Petry's short story "In Darkness and Confusion" (1947); Leonard Freed's photograph *American Soldier* (1965); and the Rainer Werner Fassbinder film *The Marriage of Eva Braun* (1979), the first in his celebrated trilogy on the Federal Republic of Germany in the 1950s. A thread of interconnectivity for the book's argument, the symbolism of the Negro soldier illuminates three possible futures—global totalitarian rule, continued racial oppression, and democracy beyond the color line—available to blacks and other minorities in the international conflict.

Chapter 2, "Our Totalitarian Critics: Desegregation, Decolonization, and the Cold War," elaborates on the theoretical and historiographical intervention introduced above. Its aims are threefold: first, revisiting the characterization of the Second World War and Cold War era as a catalyst in global race relations, it revises the commonplace view that black writers were pawns of the larger forces of Soviet communism or U.S. liberalism, identifying how black writers manipulated the new field of Third World nonalignment and Cold War civil rights. The second aim is to excavate in readings of Douglass's *Narrative of the Life of Fredrick Douglass* (1845) and Wright's *Black Boy* (1945) a formal structure of totalitarian domination in narratives of slavery and Jim Crow. In subsequent chapters, I show how this structure reemerges in the rhetorical arsenal of black political actors and forms the basis for an independent geopolitical critique. Concluding with a critical survey of debates about totalitarianism, the chapter suggests directions for reconceptualizing the idea from within the frame of postcolonial modernity.

In an attempt to concretize this theoretical frame, Chapter 3, "The Twilight of Empire: The Suez Canal Crisis of 1956 and the Black Public Sphere," moves to black engagement with a situated conflict of the Cold War. When Egypt's president Gamal Abdel Nasser boldly nationalized the British- and French-controlled Suez Canal Company in July of 1956, African American and Third World observers championed this act of anticolonial defiance. This chapter probes unexamined archives to tell the story of the transnational black public sphere's response to the contemporaneous Suez Canal

Crisis and Hungarian revolt of 1956—the Third World's first major test of nonalignment but also an event that summoned the memory of Europe's near collapse in the context of postcolonial Africa. Though substantial research exists, for example, on the African American and black diaspora's response to the Italian invasion of Ethiopia in 1936 (a key precedent for the Suez invasion), very little scholarship has addressed the robust response to this event in the black public sphere.

My focus on the Suez Crisis enables me to delineate further how anticolonial writers and leaders employed nonalignment as a geopolitical tactic—but also to show how this tactic introduced another set of problems. In his poem "Suez," W. E. B. Du Bois celebrated Egyptian leader Gamal Abdel Nasser's audacious seizure of the Suez Canal—and praised Moscow's support for Egypt—but played down the Soviet Union's simultaneous crushing of the Hungarian uprising. In her obscure but fascinating 1972 biography of Nasser, Du Bois's wife Shirley Graham similarly employed a communist hermeneutic of the Suez Crisis. If Du Bois and Graham, avowed communists in the 1950s, could rationalize Soviet repression as the cost of a world without colonialism and capitalism, the convergence of Hungary and Suez raised thorny political questions for their contemporaries. For many black Americans and proponents of nonalignment, this quandary raised a broader question about anti-imperialism: What were the ethical and political consequences of black support for the Soviet Union, ostensibly a champion of the darker races? Should black activists extol a putatively anticolonial power like Soviet Russia that repressed countries within its own sphere of influence, to say nothing of its own citizens? What was the relationship between anti-imperialism and antitotalitarianism? How did the Suez crisis precipitate a discussion in the black public sphere about the U.S.-controlled Panama Canal, an imperial construction with a parallel history closer to home? This chapter explores these and other questions in the writings of Fanon, Du Bois, Graham, and a print archive of African American newspaper reports, alongside foreign policy documents and propaganda films.

Key events and strategies covered in Part 1—such as the Suez Crisis and Bandung Conference, or nonalignment tactics and propaganda battles—flow into Part 2, "How to Build Socialist Modernity in the Third World." As these keystones imply, and the chapters in Part 2 argue, many writers under discussion in this book were involved in a grand project to build socialist modernity in the Third World. In contrast to the bird's eye view attempted in the book's first half, the second half features condensed intellectual biographies of three figures—W. E. B. Du Bois, Shirley Graham, and Richard Wright—whose literary production and political activity embody the argument of this project. Yet as these chapters demonstrate, diverse iterations of antitotalitarianism framed or mediated Afro-Asian socialist modernity, often in surprising ways. As a frame of analysis, the totalitarian imagination renews critical inquiry of obscure or buried aspects of seminal literary production: Wright's concept of "terror in freedom," for example, emerges as an expression of the postcolonial condition in the nuclear age, whereas Graham's rhetorical partisanship and attempts at elite brokerage defy Western strictures but also manipulate newly formed alliances in the nonaligned and Soviet spheres. Whether they remain ebullient, wily, and constructive, like Du Bois and Graham, or balance solidarity with pessimism and ambivalence in equal measure, like Richard Wright, these literary inscriptions of Afro-Asian socialist modernity disclose an alternative discourse of the Cold War in the Third World.

If Du Bois's "Suez" poem leaves little doubt about his allegiances in the Cold War, other texts from this period tell a fuller story about Du Bois's political affiliations than previous accounts have allowed.[51] Chapter 4, "The Right to Fail: W. E. B. Du Bois and the Communist Hypothesis," interrogates these complex affiliations while extrapolating from his unpublished manuscript "Russia and America" and other writings a philosophy of history evolving from concrete geopolitical realities at midcentury: the advent of nuclear war, the rise of Afro-Asian solidarity, the limits of postwar liberal institutions, the continued aggressions by Western colonial powers, the anemic pace of desegregation and economic reform versus what appeared, from Du Bois's perspective, as the potentially superior program of the communist project.

Presumably aware of how public circulations of the "totalitarian threat" conflated Nazism and Stalinism, Du Bois noticeably refrains (as far as I can tell) from the use of this term altogether. When Frankfurt School theorists invoked totalitarianism, they tended to mean Nazism, which some viewed as a response to an all-encompassing instrumental reason or to the illusions of the culture industry and the malfunctions of capitalism. Du Bois adopted a similar view, but one that prompted study of how elements of Nazi Germany paralleled those of colonial democracies, not of communist states. The studied omission of *totalitarianism* from his postwar oeuvre suggests Du Bois's rejection of the dominant postwar equivalency of Nazism and Stalinism, or fascism and communism, as exemplary totalitarian regimes. During the Cold War, as Eric Porter notes, Du Bois "framed the current global conflict not in terms of a choice between freedom and totalitarianism as it was commonly put in the United States" but as a choice between socialism and colonialism.[52]

To put this point more strongly, Du Bois, employing a different calculus from antitotalitarian thinkers of the West, tallies the casualties of the Soviet experiment against the death tolls amassed by putatively liberal yet colonial regimes and sees a disquieting but nonetheless favorable comparison on the Soviet ledger. In light of this oppositional view, Du Bois sees experimentation, error, and even failure as intrinsic elements of a revolutionary situation. For this reason, Chapter 4 argues, Du Bois grounds his fidelity to communism in a belief that emergent nations—whether communist states like the Soviet Union or Maoist China or postcolonial nations gathered at Bandung—deserved what he calls "the right to experiment." In a revolutionary context, experimentation contains the possibility of failure, but also the prospect of breakthrough and discovery.

Commentators have noted the political influence of Shirley Graham, a communist writer, on her husband, W. E. B. Du Bois, but few works have studied her literary and political writings closely. The fifth chapter, "From Nkrumah's Ghana to Nasser's Egypt: Shirley Graham as Partisan," explores the obscure, prolific, itinerant career of Shirley Graham during the 1960s and early 1970s, when she first assumed a key position as director of television in Accra but then settled in Cairo after the overthrow of Nkrumah in 1966, where she wrote editorials for the *Egyptian Gazette* and other publications. Over these years Graham held passports from Tanzania and Ghana and other African countries, as well as a student visa in Egypt; she enjoyed diplomatic status in Nigeria and other countries, including China. As this chapter demonstrates, her residency in Cairo provided a privileged position from which to analyze Western foreign policy and events in Africa and the Middle East, particularly the 1967 Arab-Israeli war and its fallout.

Perhaps the neglect of Graham's political writing has to do in some measure with how it appears obviously beholden to leaders and larger ideological forces. On first glance, her essays in the *Egyptian Gazette* indicate a dogmatically Nasserist interpretation of international affairs, but closer inspection reveals pro-Soviet and subtly radical inflections at odds with official Nasserism and other state (or nonstatist) formations within her sphere of influence. Rather than a spokesperson for an official line, this chapter contends, Graham idiosyncratically rewrites Nasserism as a vanguard of Pan-African socialism that embraced a grander rapprochement between the communist states and the Third World than perhaps constituents in either sphere desired. As the astonishingly wide range of her diplomatic prestige suggests, Graham was not an intellectual who remained critically aloof from power and its blandishments; she gravitated to centers of power in the communist world and the Third World and used her mobile platform to shape a deeply partisan geopolitical discourse precipitating black power militancy.

In 1967, Kenneth W. Grundy, a political scientist with expertise in Third World affairs voiced a concern in the West when he published a journal article with the title, "Is Totalitarianism Taking over in Africa?" In his travel writings and essays on decolonization, Richard Wright anticipates this question but reverses its interrogative form. By synthesizing the history of totalitarianism in the West with the future of the postcolonial nation-state, Wright's work of the 1950s formulates the question in these terms: How can the newly liberated Asian and African nations, now subject to what Wright calls "terror in freedom," avoid the totalitarian catastrophes that marked Europe's recent past? Chapter 6, "Bandung or Barbarism: Richard Wright on Terror in Freedom," argues that Wright developed an affective repertoire comprising envy, fear, dread, and alienation to diagnose a postcolonial condition he called "terror in freedom": a worry among the colonized of resubjugation by industrialized, nuclear-equipped adversaries. In a reading of his 1953 novel *The Outsider*, I argue that Wright adapts this repertoire to the situation of his Chicago protagonist, Cross Damon, who embodies the terror in freedom of postcolonial subjectivity.

The conclusion, "Memory and Paranoia," finds in John A. Williams's neglected classic of 1967, *The Man Who Cried I Am*, a novelistic tour of the historical landscape and geopolitical imagination explored in this book's preceding chapters. Ostensibly a roman à clef with composite characters evoking Richard Wright, Malcolm X, James Baldwin, and Williams himself, this panoramic novel creates a peripatetic protagonist who discovers a CIA plot (the "King Alfred Plan") to corral and exterminate black dissidents. This totalitarian-style subplot clearly reflects the paranoiac mood of the 1960s—fostered by the state's reactivation of the McCarran Internal Security Act of 1950 to target African American dissidence—in a black public sphere still reeling from the succession of assassinations and uncanny deaths of prominent anticolonial and civil rights activists. More significant than this paranoid subplot, however, is the novel's memorialization of the twentieth century and the generation of writers who comprise the cast of *Race and the Totalitarian Century*. In this respect, the novel dramatizes the intersection of two grand narratives animating this book: the rise and fall of the global color line, on the one hand, and the battle between the "free world" and the totalitarian sphere, on the other.

I

Race and the Totalitarian Century

1

The Figure of the Negro Soldier

RACIAL DEMOCRACY AND WORLD WAR

During the First and Second World Wars, no figure embodied the contradictions of democracy and the ironies of the Allied war effort more poignantly than the Negro soldier. A figure of pathos and heroism, the American Negro soldier had a multitude of global counterparts. Colonial conscripts from the British and French empires confronted similar dilemmas and traumas, but also revelations and victories: the affective and corporeal price to pay for what the wretched of the earth imagined as rewards, or at least recognition, to be reaped after the war.[1] In the Second World War, the Negro soldier symbolized a struggle against "totalitarianism" on multiple fronts: Fascism and Nazism in Europe; Jim Crow segregation in the United States; and European colonialism in Africa and Asia. In 1942, the *Pittsburgh Courier* announced its Double Victory campaign—which advocated "Victory over discrimination at home/Victory over the Axis abroad"—prompting African American observers to expand upon and tease out the implications of this formulation. The *Courier* reported on one "militant" pastor of Brooklyn's Holy Trinity Baptist church, who articulated his own version of Double Victory: "I have not," he intoned, "and will not permit my congregation to pray for peace. I have thrown in the waste basket every bit of literature sent to me from white religious representatives asking for a 'day' of peace. I do not want the type of 'Victory Peace' that has been the outcome of previous wars. I want a 'DOUBLE VICTORY' even if it takes five or ten years for it to become a reality."[2]

No doubt many African Americans, particularly those inclined to stress economic and political advancements in African American life during the 1940s, viewed the war less in terms of the contradictions of racial democracy and more as an opportunity for broader incorporation into the nation's political, civic, and military spheres; no doubt many observers viewed the rise of Nazism as an apocalyptic threat that superseded domestic racial inequality. But it is also clear that for most writers in the black public sphere of the 1930s and 1940s, acidic memories of the First World War permeate responses to the Second. In the summers of 1941 and 1943, the *Journal of Negro Education* convened its special annual yearbook volume with titles such as "The American Negro in World War I and World War II" and "Racial Minorities and the Present International Crisis," respectively. Delineating an education agenda for African Americans who were ambivalent about the war effort, the 1941 yearbook defined its aims in the following terms: "first, to define these two worlds [i.e., the totalitarian and democratic] which are in mortal combat; *second*, to suggest what kind of a world is likely to result if Hitler wins, or whether Hitler wins; and *third*, to describe the stake which the Negro and other minorities have in the present conflict."[3] Triangulating three possible futures—a future of global totalitarian rule, a future of continued racial democracy, and a democratic future beyond the color line—the contributors to these and other wartime debates distill the concerns at the core of *Race and the Totalitarian Century.*

In what follows, I trace the figure of the Negro soldier—from the First World War to the early Cold War and the black power movement—in literature, film, and art. Representations of this figure suggest a point of entry for thinking about how black involvement in world war summoned African American literary imaginaries of the totalitarian.

Though unified in their emphasis on the war's grave racial implications, contributors to the *Journal of Negro Education* volumes disagreed substantially on what stance minorities, and blacks in particular, ought to adopt in this historical moment of crisis. Yet they intuited that the stakes of the present world conflict were much greater than its predecessor only two decades earlier. With a distinguished group of (predominantly though not exclusively) male contributors like W. E. B. Du Bois, historian Rayford Logan, political scientist and diplomat Ralph Bunche, president of the University of Chicago Robert M. Hutchins, historian Eric Williams, and sociologist Louis Wirth, both volumes adopted a cosmopolitan approach to the war. "I am particularly concerned," wrote the same editor, Chas. H. Thompson, in the 1943 volume, "that, as Negro youth go forth to fight or otherwise help to win this war, they fight for the freedom of oppressed peoples everywhere, at home and abroad; whether they are black or brown, yellow or white—whether it is the Jew in Poland, the untouchable in India, the Hottentot in Africa, the peasant in China, or the sharecropper in Mississippi. For only by establishing freedom for all peoples can we assure it for ourselves."[4]

The 1941 yearbook issue further sought to clarify differences between the First and Second World Wars, since many African Americans tended to view World War II as nothing "more than a clash of rival imperialisms" or as "just another struggle for power on an even larger and more devastating scale than World War I."[5] Estimates vary, but Europe and the United States mobilized some four million colonial and black American troops in the First World War. "In a grotesque reversal of Joseph Conrad's novelistic vision," writes Santanu Das, "hundreds of thousands of non-white men were voyaging to the heart of whiteness, as it were, to witness 'The horror! The horror!' of Western warfare."[6] Skeptics wondered if history would repeat itself with the Second World War; few believed that repetition this time would result in farce.

In 1945, one contributor to the *Negro History Bulletin* penned a "tribute to the Negro war correspondent" for his "courage and devotion . . . and willingness to face dangers and accept the sacrifices involved in the loyal and effective performance of [his] duties in war areas." These correspondents included figures like Roi Ottley, Ollie Harrington, and Thomas W. Young who wrote for the *Afro-American*, *The Pittsburgh Courier*, and *The Norfolk Journal and Guide*, among other black publications. "How well these [Negro soldiers] are performing their duty is best proved by the stories you read in the Negro press as reported by the Negro correspondent."[7]

Irrespective of the war's unpredictable consequences for Jim Crow and racial discrimination globally, the Negro soldier had earned a position at the vanguard of projects to realize democracy worldwide.

Yet by the onset of the Cold War, the figure of the Negro soldier—now an agent of a de jure (but not yet de facto) desegregated military, or military industrial complex, as Eisenhower later phrased it—acquires a more ambiguous significance, one consonant with the new social and political situation facing African Americans in the postwar era. As the next chapter describes, this period witnesses another mode of black conscription. While the Soviet bloc fomented alliances with the darker races, the United States responded with attempts to enfold African Americans within the bounds of liberal national citizenship and to garner their allegiance in the global struggle against communism—after the defeat of Nazi Germany and imperial Japan, the world's remaining totalitarian threat. I chart this historical shift with a focus on how world war shaped, and was shaped by, black literary and geopolitical imaginaries of racial democracy. In my use of the term *racial democracy*, I refer first to a political system and regime of governance within the nation-state (but operative in collaboration with likeminded nation-states) in which the rights, privileges, and affective dimensions of citizenship are distributed to or withheld from citizens on the basis of race; and second to a complementary network of disciplinary, punitive, and terroristic measures meted out to racial subjects by state and non-state actors alike. This term overlaps with but differs from the communist label of "bourgeois democracy," a term that encompasses more than the former but is perhaps less precise for that reason. World war compelled racial democracies to confront their strategies of exclusion and persecution with a new urgency, lest the Western world risk the perception of a preponderant affinity with its totalitarian adversaries. In the United States, the segregated military represented a powerful litmus test for the global legitimacy of American democracy.

Though the indignities of serving in a segregated army imbued the figure of the Negro soldier with pathos, the plight of these soldiers also lent itself to black humor and farce. In *Europeana*, his mock history of the twentieth century, the Czech writer Patrik Ouředník narrates the grisly absurdities of the era, linking Europe and America through the crucible of race, genocide, and total war. Employing a carefully calibrated, detached monotone, the narrative voice of *Europeana* sketches the century as an unrelenting burlesque of history. The first page of the text reads:

> The Americans who fell in Normandy in 1944 were tall men measuring 173 centimeters on average, and if they were laid head to foot would measure 38 kilometers. The Germans were tall too, while the tallest of all were the Senegalese fusiliers in the First World War who measured 176 centimeters, and so they were sent into battle on the front lines in order to scare the Germans. It was said of the First World War that people in it fell like seeds and the Russian Communists later calculated how much fertilizer a square kilometer of corpses would yield and how much they would save on expensive foreign fertilizers if they used the corpses of traitors and criminals instead of manure.[8]

If the height of the respective soldiers conjures the fascist cult of the body, and the destruction of those eight to ten million bodies in the First World War, the text's sly inclusion of "the Senegalese fusiliers"—who, as literal shock troops, frighten the Germans before falling to them—signals the colonial underpinnings of the war that echo in the next world conflict.

Might Ouředník's anonymous Senegalese fusilier belong to the ranks of the "unknown soldier" during the First World War? The ubiquitous trope of "the unknown soldier, the nameless," notes Ernst Jünger of Germany's Conservative Revolution, "lives not only in every capital but also in every village, in every family. The battlefields, the temporal goals, and even the peoples he has represented sink into the realm of the uncertain. . . . Yet the Unknown Soldier remains a hero, a conqueror of fiery worlds, who shoulders great burdens in the midst of the mechanical devastation. In this sense he is also a true descendant of western chivalry."[9] During the early twentieth century, Ouředník's "Senegalese fusiliers" would have been known by another name, the Tirailleurs Sénégalais, descendants of French colonial slaves in the 1850s who became conscripts, and in many cases volunteers, by the turn of the century.[10] A small but significant minority was made up of well-born Africans serving as intermediaries between French officers and African troops. In addition to their service in European theaters, the Tirailleurs Sénégalais also became part of an occupation force in the French Empire, including places like Morocco, Indochina, and the Levant.

The role of the Tirailleurs Sénégalais in the French Empire became a subject of intense debate, with General Charles Mangin and his 1910 book *La Force Noire* advancing the most vociferous defense of the African forces. This defense, alongside European counter-appraisals of African aptitudes, became an exercise in comparative masculinity, as military-ethnographic accounts attributed to groups varying physical endowments, capacities for discipline, and degrees of warlike zeal. Did West Africans possess a less-developed nervous system than Europeans, which rendered Tirailleurs Sénégalais less susceptible to pain? Could the sheer numbers of African conscripts rectify the demographic imbalance between the fertile Germans and the French of lower birth rates?[11]

Despite the racial indignities perpetrated against French African soldiers, a gallant image of these individuals and their units emerged in France following the First World War. But in the First and Second World Wars, France's decision to deploy colonial troops in European combat, and as occupying forces in the Rhineland after 1918, prompted a backlash from Germany. "In *Mein Kampf*," writes one historian, "Hitler railed several times against black Africans, whose presence in the French Army he saw as only the latest 'pollution,' or 'negrification' of the once pure Frankish blood of the French. . . . Rommel and other important officers in the Second World War considered it an insult to have to fight against such 'inferior' races."[12] Interpolating this history into a tableau of barbarism, Ouředník's *Europeana* compresses total war, colonial conscription, and racial purity doctrines into the genre of farce. Appropriately, the passage concludes with a parody of wartime fears about the intrusion of alien bodies—and dark imagery of corpses repurposed as a cheap, rationalized alternative to "expensive foreign fertilizers."

It is worth noting that the medium of African cinema—exemplified in Ousmane Sembène and Thierno Faty Sow's 1987 film *Camp de Thiaroye*—had the capacity to supplant or to challenge oral, collective, and largely heroic memories of the Tirailleurs Sénégalais preserved by West African griots.[13] In this film, Sembène and Sow employ tragedy as the affective register appropriate to the grotesque fate of a unit of Tirailleurs Sénégalais, survivors of Buchenwald, as they are slated to return to their respective homelands in French West Africa. Before the troops can return home, they are stationed temporarily at the Thiaroye "transit camp." Upon arrival, a French captain salutes the soldiers' valor in war. "You have been true," the captain declares, "to the reputation of your fathers in 1914–1918." He praises their "dedication to the fatherland, our dear France, betrayed, steeped in blood," but rising "from the ashes!" In a scene of foreshadowing, one soldier who has become mute after his experience in the concentration camps surveys the grounds of Thiaroye. He advances toward the barbed wire encircling the camp; he observes black guardsmen, armed with rifles, stationed at several watchtowers. As he runs his fingers along the barbed wire, a black sergeant approaches. The sergeant scoops some dirt into his hand, reassuring him that "here we are on African soil. Here you are no longer a prisoner." But a couple of troops, watching in the distance, note that the war has destroyed the mute soldier. "He is a bit cracked."

Based on the historical Thiaroye transit camp massacre of 1944, the film also distills, in the phrase of Richard Iton, a set of "diasporic negotiations in the area of comparative masculinities," performances animated by blacks in the diaspora jostling for control in the destabilized, and thus radically open, situation of the Second World War.[14] In *Camp de Thiaroye*, this arena of masculine control unfolds in an array of discrete interactions: between French officials and the Tirailleurs Sénégalais unit; between African troops from countries perceived to maintain an umbilical relation to France, like Senegal or Cote D'Ivoire, and soldiers from other countries, like Guinea, seen as defiant of the French Empire; and between an African American character—who exerts dominance in his Senegal post despite, or because of, his tenuous location within the U.S. military hierarchy—and the African captain Diatta, an increasingly assertive critic of the war-emasculated French. In the latter exchange, the African American soldier, on jeep patrol with other American G.I.s, questions Diatta's status and whereabouts; an altercation ensues, with the African American G.I. battering Captain Diatta. Later, the film heals this friction in a scene where the offending black American G.I. visits Diatta at Thiaroye to apologize. They listen to Charlie Parker while Diatta discusses his admiration of Langston Hughes, Paul Laurence Dunbar, and Marcus Garvey.

Educated, gallant, fluent in English and French, an embodiment of the French colonial mission, Diatta liaises between the African troops and the French officers. Yet in a conversation with the egalitarian-minded commanding officer, Captain Raymond, Diatta equates Nazi and Vichy atrocities with colonialism. "You can't compare Nazi barbarism with the excesses of our army," says Captain Raymond. Laconically, Diatta replies, "It's a colonial army. Same mentality." The two men change the subject to what ought to have been, from the standpoint of normative masculine sociality, a safer topic: the village bride that Diatta's family has proposed for him to marry. But even this tidy resolution is fraught. Captain Raymond admires the young woman, who waits demurely in the distance, as a bride for Diatta—but the African captain, it turns out, is already married to a French woman.

With American guardianship as a backdrop to the scene in Senegal, the French officers strip the African soldiers of their uniforms, donated by the U.S. army, in exchange for threadbare colonial outfits that they will wear for their repatriation. (This moment follows the serving of gruel to the African troops, while in separate barracks the French officers dine on meat.) If the film's emphasis on alternating French and American uniforms underscores the fungible character of colonial identity, this dual wartime scenario also dramatizes the formation of a rebellious African subjectivity: the process by which Africans learned to exploit France's fragility, as a nation vanquished by Nazism, in order to strike at colonial fascism.

Why were colonial subjects, African bodies, mobilized in this conflict of ostensibly European origin? In light of the affective ties that developed between European and non-European combatants, to say nothing of the ways in which colonial conscripts assimilated advanced Western technologies and disciplinary methods toward insurrectionary ends, the image of the African or Asian soldier as a tool of European imperialism's military aggression is at best incomplete. Yet as Marcus Garvey argued in Brooklyn in 1919, "[our] sacrifices, as made in the cause of other people, are many. . . . It is time that we should prepare to sacrifice now for ourselves. . . . Africa will be a bloody battlefield in years to come." As Garvey ominously implies: Were blacks—now armed with military knowledge and discipline—prepared to employ this experience in the service not of foreign liberation but of self-liberation? State awareness of this question inflects the muted but growing fear of the Negro soldier as a domestically threatening, but also internationally catalytic, embodiment of racial democracy's contradictions.

Representations of Negro soldiers and the anxieties elicited by them betray an obvious masculine normativity on either side of the color line. Yet war provided black soldiers and their champions more than an opportunity to reassert an abject manhood via the exercise of military valor. As Adrian Lentz-Smith argues, black soldiers saw the First World War as a situation prompting them to refashion their manhood in ways beyond, or in complex negotiation with, dominant masculine norms. Exposed to new countries and cultures yet attached to supporters back home, black G.I.s renegotiated their masculinity in relation to the ideas of black women activists, civilian communities, and interlocutors overseas. "Aware of their many audiences," Lentz-Smith writes, "black soldiers told their tales of transformed manhood through letters to the black press, in memoirs, and in fiction. Civilians spoke back to them through these same venues." But these soldiers did so under intense state surveillance. "The authority that African American men derived as uniformed representatives of the federal government posed a threat to Jim Crow at home, where they could inspire black civilians to push for their citizenship rights, and abroad, where foreigners might inspire them. . . . Black soldiers at war constructed their masculinity in the glare of an attentive, scrutinizing state."[15] As Bill Maxwell demonstrates in his revelatory account of the FBI's venture into African American literary criticism, this scrutiny reaches its apex during J. Edgar Hoover's control of that organization from 1935 to 1972, but he and other scholars have shown how bureaucratic surveillance of blacks dates to the First World War and the Bureau of Investigation (founded in 1908, the predecessor organization to the FBI).[16]

From 1942 to 1963, when he opposed war openly and eventually advocated communism, Du Bois amassed a hefty FBI file. His view of the First World War, however, defies bureaucratic classification: it balances interventionist politics with radical historical critique. In texts like "World War and the Color Line" (1914) and "The African Roots of War" (1915), Du Bois acknowledges the sacrifices made by black soldiers on behalf of European wars, but locates the origins of these conflicts in imperial rivalries spawned by the Berlin Conference of 1885 and subsequent Scramble for Africa—a Hobbesian competition for the continent's resources, marked by a partitioning that precipitates the global conflict of 1914 to 1918 and sets the stage for later antagonisms in Africa. For Du Bois, this competition among the colonial powers for primitive accumulation in Africa amplified over the turn of the century and erupted, finally, in the events of 1914 and beyond.[17] In this sense, Du Bois was the first analyst to identify an alternative causality, anchored in colonial plunder, of a catastrophic war that struck so many contemporaries as bewildering, meaningless, even devoid of a significant cause.

"There are those," writes Du Bois, "who would write world history and leave out this most marvelous of continents. Particularly today most men assume that Africa lies far afield from our present problem of World War. Yet in a very real sense Africa is the prime cause of this terrible overturning of civilization which we have lived to see; and these words seek to show how in the Dark Continent are hidden the roots, not simply of war to-day but of the menace of wars tomorrow."[18] Temporally between Conrad's *Heart of Darkness* and Arendt's *The Origins of Totalitarianism*, Du Bois's theory of imperialism and world war stands comparably prophetic in its linkage of the Scramble for Africa to the onset of totalitarianism in Europe.[19]

Retaining various degrees of hope in the promise of American democracy, or French universalism, or British liberalism, these subaltern soldiers and conscripts from New York and Mississippi, Dakar and Martinique, Bombay and Madagascar, served bravely, but on the assumption that their patriotism and valor would redound to racial equality and enhance black citizenship and dignity in their respective imperial centers. In the United States after the First World War, the precise opposite happened: lynching and racial violence intensified in those years, especially during the infamous Red Summer of 1919, when race riots erupted across the United States.

Many African Americans—not least those who heeded Du Bois's controversial appeal to blacks to "forget our special grievances and close our ranks shoulder to shoulder with our white fellow citizens and the allied nations that are fighting for democracy"—recalled the years after 1918 with cynicism and bitterness.[20] Among other nonwhite troops around the world, a common narrative takes shape: participation in world war elicits hope and opportunism, followed by betrayal and violence, and culminating in disillusionment. "In some of the colonies," writes Das, "there was also a conscious degree of political calculation: parties such as the Indian National Congress supported the [First World] war in the hope of greater political autonomy as a reward. However, for many of these colonies, the postwar period was deeply disillusioning."[21] In Jamaica during the First World War, a nascent national identity evolved in tandem with Pan-Africanism, and there "was an expectation that both would be invigorated by military service and post-war redemption would ensue."[22]

Having experienced the world, the war, international politics, respite from racial subjugation, and the intercultural and affective bonds that developed between European and non-European combatants, African Americans and colonial conscripts acquired a new militancy and determination to combat racism globally. In his autobiography, Harry Haywood, the black Communist and veteran of the First World War in France, describes his return to Chicago in 1919. Among the numerous race riots during that summer, the Chicago riot was the bloodiest. "The Chicago riot of 1919," he wrote, "was a pivotal point in my life. Always I had been hot-tempered and never took any insults lying down. This was even more true after the war."[23] The coincidence of this murderous postwar aftermath and the Bolshevik Revolution in 1917 led many black intellectuals in the United States and throughout the diaspora to Communism and other radical formations.

This radicalism manifested in popular art and literature of the period. In his cartoon "War Aims," African American political cartoonist and war correspondent Ollie Harrington captured the macabre but uncompromising tenor of black demands in the Second World War. The image foregrounds a skeletal black soldier clutching a rifle in one hand and a declaration of war aims—freedom not only for "ravished Europe" but also for the "oppressed colored people of Africa"—in the other; the text is "signed by the Negro youths who shall soon die on foreign battlefields." A ghoulish black soldier rising from alien European soil, this figure embodies the furious boomerang or "reverse shock" (Césaire's *Un Choc en Retour*) that anticolonial thinkers saw swinging back to the West if this aim went unmet.[24]

Famed for his 1930s cartoons chronicling the antics of his character "Brother Bootsie"—an endearing, tatterdemalion trickster who navigates the "hilarious chaos" of Harlem with slyness and buoyancy—Harrington's war cartoons project a darker political imagination.[25] In the 1940s, Harrington's work joined the ensemble of black writers and artists who analogized the persecution of blacks with the destruction of European Jewry. Liberal whites like Edward Embree, president of the Julian Rosenwald Fund and correspondent with Du Bois, rejected this analogy. On the same day, February 28, 1942, that *The People's Voice* published Harrington's "Sikeston, Missouri and Germany" sketch, *The Pittsburgh Courier* reported comments by Embree on Hitler's Germany versus segregated America. The philanthropist argued that Nazi terror is unlike that of Jim Crow persecution; the difference was less in kind than in the historical direction of each social order. Whereas Hitler has "crassly reversed the clock of civilization," Embree claims, "we in America have been slowly moving toward more tolerance" and greater opportunity for all people.[26] For many black Americans, too, this argument seemed sensible if hardly inspiriting.

Close inspection of this book's cover image by Harrington reveals a more intricate politics, and deeply personal component, than the analogy between black and Jewish suffering suggests. Employing gritty, chiaroscuro imagery, the drawing pairs an apparently anonymous woman slain under Nazism alongside a black man, Cleo Wright, who had been lynched in 1942 in Sikeston, Missouri, after assaulting a white woman in her home. After Wright's arrest, upon which he had been shot several times by police, a lynch mob wrested his dying body from jail, attached the man to a car and dragged him around black neighborhoods, and finally burned his flesh beyond recognition in front of a black church during Sunday service. In Harrington's picture, intriguingly, bullet holes appear on the wall against which the female victim of Nazism lay, but no visible bullet wounds mark Cleo Wright. Publishing his work one month after the lynching, Harrington would likely have known that police bullets riddled Wright's body *before* he was lynched. Does Harrington mean to transfer, symbolically, the bullets lodged in Wright to the scene of the unknown Nazi victim? Or by depicting Wright without bullet wounds did he intend to refute, graphically, the verdict returned by the grand jury: that no parties among the mob were guilty because Cleo Wright was effectively already dead? (Reportedly and astonishingly he was not, even until the moment before he was set aflame.)

As Domenic Capeci has shown, Sikeston encapsulated the racial divisions of wartime: working-class blacks and whites clashed in conditions of economic privation; in the mid-1930s, a group in Missouri called the Pacific Movement sought to promote Japan's image among blacks by issuing antiwhite propaganda and holding meetings in Southeast Missouri; in the wake of Pearl Harbor in 1941, some defenders of the mob justified its actions on the ironic grounds that antiblack terrorism supported American troops abroad. As the African American Press and the NAACP publicized this event, unrest gripped the state. Sikeston seized the national imagination. Unlike the thousands of lynchings that occurred in the United States in the previous half a century, the lynching of Cleo Wright "drew the Department of Justice into this area of civil rights for the first time," thereby establishing a precedent for the federal government in the prosecution of these crimes.[27] The *Pittsburgh Courier* noted that, thanks to the NAACP, the U.S. Department of Justice rediscovered its authority "to investigate lynchings where local police failed to protect the victim." The editorial lamented that this "ancient law was not dug up when the Administration took office in 1933, which would have been a real New Deal for us. Because of failure to find this law until the nation was attacked by Japan, over 100 Negroes have died at the hands of mobs confident they would never be investigated. But now that war has forced what peace was unable to bring about," the editorial concluded too optimistically, hope exists for justice in Sikeston as well as for legions of past victims of lynching.[28]

As the son of a Jewish mother from Budapest and an African American father, Harrington also evokes the duality of his identity in this sketch: the relation between totalitarianism and the color line, in my view the arch theme of Harrington's artwork, converged in his own family history and biography. Harrington's political aesthetic drew on his intimacy with the Second World War, his reportage on lynching in the U.S. South after 1945, and his expatriate experience in Paris and Berlin. His biography encapsulates the trajectory of numerous black intellectuals whose personal lives, artistic development, political affiliations and disaffiliations, and migration patterns and exilic tendencies were shaped by the tumult of the Second World War and the shifting geopolitics of the Cold War. Harrington grew up in the South Bronx; published as a freelance artist during the twilight of the Harlem Renaissance in the 1930s; reported on the war theaters of Europe and North Africa as a correspondent for the *Pittsburgh Courier;* returned to the United States to work in the NAACP's Public Relations Department at the invitation of Walter White; fled to Paris and its black expatriate community in the early 1950s after arousing suspicions from the FBI for his radical views; and finally traveled to East Berlin in 1961, during the construction of the Berlin Wall, where he remained for the following three decades as a contributor to East German publications like *Eugenspiel* and *Das Magazin.* "I'm fairly well convinced," he wrote, "that one is an exile only when one is not allowed to live in reasonable peace and dignity as a human being among other human beings." Though he returned periodically to the United States late in life, Harrington died in Berlin in 1995.

Also on the same date that saw the publication of Harrington's and Embree's texts, Horace Cayton penned an article for *The Pittsburgh Courier.* Sociologist, newspaper columnist, and co-author with St. Claire Drake of *Black Metropolis* (1945), Horace Cayton notes that a Philadelphia magistrate held a Negro in treason because he referred to the global conflict as a "white man's war." The statement was not treasonous, Cayton asserts; it was a statement of fact. The war was not a white man's war because its instigators were European, or because it displayed inter-imperial rivalry, or reflected a congenital western aggressiveness. World War II was a white man's war because, in the United States at least, blacks had been rigorously restricted from full participation and a meaningful stake in the conflict in accordance with the dictates of racial democracy. "The Negro is fighting on two fronts," Cayton asserts. "He is fighting (to the extent that he is allowed to fight) as soldiers in the armed forces and in the factories and plants as workers, to defeat the totalitarian states. But the Negro is engaged in a struggle to make this a peoples' war for democracy and not just a white man's war. In this latter task, it seems to me, Negroes are acting in the most patriotic fashion possible. Singapore is the hand writing on the wall. This war effort must include black Negroes, yellow Chinese, and all of the non-white races of the world and be a war for democratic principles and ideas. It must not continue, as it is, largely a white man's war."[29] Political expressions like Cayton's in the black public sphere relentlessly sought to expand the global meaning and democratic potential of the war.

The uniqueness of lived proximity to war theaters, however, did not inhibit other black writers and artists from engaging this subject. Chicago poet Gwendolyn Brooks imagined some of the most visceral representations of the black body and psyche scarred by war. Her "Gay Chaps at the Bar" poems, a sequence in her 1945 collection *A Street in Bronzeville*, drew inspiration from letters and poetry she received from black G.I.s on the war front.[30] Brooks's war poetry rewrites the entwined histories of black ambivalence about the war effort, on the one hand, and of damage inflicted upon war-ravaged minds and bodies, on the other. Given the resonance of these histories with the wider American public, Brooks's focus on the marginal but symbolically charged Negro soldier offers a litmus test for official wartime claims made on behalf of the liberal democratic order.

The publication of Brooks's modernist war poetry coincides with the production and dissemination of U.S. War Department films addressed to African American viewers. A prominent example is *The*

Negro Soldier (1944), written by the African American filmmaker Carlton Moss and produced by the War Department in tandem with Frank Capra's film unit.[31] Set in a black cathedral amid church bells and choir hymns, the film features a pastor whose sermon instructs the congregation on the evils of Nazism and stresses the urgency of the global crisis. Refuting antiwar arguments, he quotes passages from *Mein Kampf* and warns of the dangerous folly of pro-Japanese sentiment. "There are some who will tell you," the pastor intones, "Japan is the savior of the colored races"—before the scene cuts to explosive footage of the attack on Pearl Harbor.

Situating black Americans as the moral and spiritual core of American democracy, *The Negro Soldier* shows how blacks have fought honorably in virtually every American war, including imperialist conflicts like the Spanish-American War of 1898. During the American Civil War scene, no mention is made of slavery; nor does the film allude to segregation in the military. Against a panorama of the nation's historically black colleges, the pastor salutes Negro accomplishments in science, art, law, education, athletics, and medicine. Footage of Jesse Owens's triumph in Berlin and Joe Louis's knockout of Max Schmeling presented the now legendary symbolism of the superiority of U.S. democracy over German Nazism. The calculation underwriting the film is that imagery of black achievement would supersede or smooth over the erasure of slavery and segregation and the ambiguous role of blacks in U.S. imperialism.

The Negro Soldier bears the imprimatur of Capra, whose *Why We Fight* films, a seven-part propaganda series known for its dramatic case for interventionism, are a clear influence. It adapts the Manichean style of *Why We Fight*—where the Allied powers represent freedom and democracy, the Axis powers totalitarian slavery—to the historical experience of black Americans. Notably, *The Negro Soldier* concludes with an image of the letter *V* (for victory)—*not* an image of the "double V" that signified to black Americans the chorus of victory at home and abroad.

The proud G.I.s of *The Negro Soldier* stand in recto-verso relation to Brooks's maligned black veterans: in the former, the black soldier, ascending up the military ranks, appears all but fully integrated; in the latter, the black G.I. returns "from the front crying and trembling." How would these troubled veterans, black and white, fare in postwar America? Their reappearance from the war divided America's consciousness. "On the one hand," David Gerber writes, "the veteran's heroism and sacrifices are celebrated and memorialized, and debts of gratitude, both symbolic and material, are paid to him. On the other hand, the veteran also inspires anxiety and fear and is seen as a threat to social order and political stability." This second, "much less officially acknowledged response" derives from the public's repressed intuition about the consequences of removing young men from the stabilizing influences of family, employment, and educational institutions; of arming them with advanced weaponry and instructing them in how to destroy; of exposing them to horrific violence and injury; and of thrusting them back into the society they had previously known, inadequately supported, where they are now viewed as deranged or spectral presences. Supplementing forms of "advice literature" that instructed conscientious Americans on how to deal with disturbed vets, blockbuster films like *The Best Years of Our Lives* (1946), winner of seven Academy Awards, smoothed over these deep anxieties with upbeat reintegration scenarios and formulaic happy endings.[32]

In a *New Republic* article titled "Jim Crow in the Army" (1944), one journalist, Lucy B. Milner, anticipates the problem of reintegration but inflects it with an ominous racial undercurrent: "A new Negro will return from the war—a bitter Negro if he is disappointed again. He will have been taught to kill, to suffer, to die for something he believes in, and he will live by these rules to gain his personal rights."[33] No doubt Milner's observation captures the violence seething among dispossessed black veterans, but Brooks's "the progress," the final poem in the "Gay Chaps" sequence, limns more somber affective terrain.

> And still we wear our uniforms, follow
> The cracked cry of the bugles, comb and brush
> Our pride and prejudice, doctor the sallow
> Initial ardor, wish to keep it fresh.
> Still we applaud the President's voice and face.
> Still we remark on patriotism, sing,

Salute the flag, thrill heavily, rejoice
For death of men who too saluted, sang.
But inward grows a soberness, an awe,
A fear, a deepening hollow through the cold.
For even if we come out standing up
How shall we smile, congratulate: and how
Settle in chairs? Listen, listen. The step
Of iron feet again. And again wild.

The poem's first line keeps the ambiguity of "we" in play, but the adjective *still* refers unmistakably to the Negro soldier: for only this figure's uniform projects pathos and a tinge of obscenity; he betrays his humiliation by "still" donning an emblem of racial democracy. In the first half of the poem, each line conveys from the soldier's perspective the perversity of wartime patriotic appeals, reduced here to a desperate cacophony of salutes, "cracked" bugle cries, and ceremonial applause—a hollowness also felt by a nation spiritually exhausted and increasingly dubious about what it means to "rejoice / For death of men who too saluted, sang." Shaken by the traumas of war, Negro soldiers who could not remain in Europe are compelled to reenter a social order less hospitable than Nazi Germany.

The perverse double entendre of the line "For even if we come out standing up" undercuts dominant notions of "victory"—victory for whom, and for what?—but also conjures, with a stroke of black humor, the image of "disabled" veterans who will not come out of the war standing on two legs.[34] The rhyme scheme of the poem's first eight lines, it is important to note, slackens in the last five or six: a rhythmic interruption that mimics the soldier's shifting affective state from cynicism to "soberness, an awe."

The aforementioned representations of a humane reintegration process for the war's veterans parallel, strikingly, concurrent rhetoric about African American integration into the U.S. body politic. This rhetoric depicted American history as a redemption narrative in which the nation acknowledges its criminal past of slavery and racism before changing the subject to highlight the rapid "progress" achieved by black Americans in the 1940s. And yet "the progress" evinces a darker historical imagination than that of African American disillusionment about wartime promises reneged upon. Published in 1945, the year when Allied forces obliterated Dresden and the United States deployed atomic bombs in Nagasaki and Hiroshima, Brooks's vision in "the progress" asks how "shall we smile, congratulate" after meeting Axis attacks with incomparably greater acts of mass destruction. In her 2012 novel *Home*, Toni Morrison features protagonist Frank Money, a veteran of the Korean War, who returns to the United States not mute but minimalist, quietly battling "with his rage and his shame." Wandering the streets, he is drawn to the sound of a trumpet playing in a subterranean nightclub. "He preferred bebop to blues and happy-making love songs," says the narrator. "After Hiroshima, the musicians understood as early as anyone that Truman's bomb changed everything and only scat and bebop could say how."[35] Against Brooks's stress on the obscenity of progressive rhetoric in this moment, perhaps bebop stood in a closer relation to the truth about atomic destruction. Could poetry also say how?

"The destructive force of the Allies," notes one historian, "far outstripped that of the Axis powers. 74,000 tons of bombs were dropped on Britain, killing some 51,000. By contrast, the 2 million tons dropped by the Allies killed 900,000 in Japan, 600,000 in Germany, and 62,000 in Italy."[36] And after this conflagration, how do we "settle in chairs" and continue with administrative business as usual, buoyed by the self-satisfaction of victory? What could victory mean in this context? The imagery and timbre of the poem's final lines—"The step/of iron feet again"—conjure not the slogan of a war to end all wars but rather the incubus of perpetual war. To suggest that the poem merely defies official wartime rhetoric fails to capture the subversive, chilling effect of the repetition of "again" in the final line, with the lingering "wild" completing the poem. Compare this poetic vision with what theologian Reinhold Niebuhr famously described as the "irony of American History." Niehbur's interpretation of American history stressed how the use of mass violence to enforce a peace or to achieve democratic ends typically reflects an overestimation of the purity of one's motives: "The ironic tendency of virtues to turn into vices when too complacently relied upon." Placing the segregated military at the center of her war poems, Brooks foregrounds a different irony in American history. Turning

Niebuhr's theory on its head, the poem asks what if these ostensibly anti-fascist motives—coolly rationalized, in the case of Hiroshima and Nagasaki—turn out not to reveal an ironic historical logic, which presupposes a disjuncture between ideals and outcomes, but rather a military industrial logic, as Eisenhower predicted?

These questions invite another: why "*the* progress"? What kind of progress does the Allied victory represent? If the democratic motives said to characterize interventionism translate so smoothly into a colossus of militarization, then the question is what force will halt the march of "iron feet again," a sound, as the poem portends, that reverberates throughout postwar U.S. foreign policy. That nightmarish prospect, in a word: "wild." The determiner in the poem's title seems to refer, ironically, to the specific progress represented by the Allied victory over fascist barbarism, but it also signals modernity's supposedly inexorable telos toward enlightenment. These distinct articulations of progress are compatible. In 1944, Max Horkheimer and Theodor Adorno's *Dialectic of Enlightenment* triangulates these registers—enlightenment since the Greeks, the modern progress of the Enlightenment, and the eclipse of enlightenment witnessed by the rise of Fascism and the collapse of Europe—in order to show how progress, specifically the technological mastery of nature but also the overcoming of premodern or antimodern tendencies, summons concomitant barbarisms of varying degrees of intensity. And for many Marxist theorists, fascism originates from within the contradictions of liberal capitalism or, in Lenin's conception, belongs to the imperialist stage of capitalism—neither, in other words, as a spontaneous phenomenon spun out of the whole cloth of history nor as democratic capitalism's monstrous antithesis.

Because National Socialism had demonstrated to the world the combustible interface between scientific racism and mechanized warfare, the paradox of American racial democracy could no longer be avoided or repressed. "For the crime of their ancestry," Baldwin writes in *The Fire Next Time* (1963), "millions of people in the heart of Europe—God's citadel—were sent to a death so calculated, so hideous, and so prolonged that no age before this enlightened one had been able to imagine it, much less achieve and record it."[37] For Baldwin, the only event more frightening than the calculated destruction of

Europe's Jewry and other peoples deemed inferior was the civilized world's apparent indifference to it.

As Alan Wald has illustrated, several African American writers—including former Communist John Oliver Killens in his novel *And Then We Heard the Thunder* (1963), Ann Petry in "In Darkness and Confusion" (1944), Margaret Burroughs in "Private Jeff Johnson" (1944), and Chester Himes in "All He Needs Is Feet" (1943)—seized the symbolic potency of black soldiers from the urban North encountering Jim Crow–caliber conflicts during basic training in Georgia or other regions of the deep South.[38] Whereas Brooks engages this subject by interpolating the correspondence of an actual black veteran into her poetic text, Ann Petry introduces the war thematic with an obverse gesture: the black soldier's letter that has *not* arrived home. Depicting the volatile cityscape of wartime Harlem, her story "In Darkness and Confusion" centers on a black family made up of William and Pink, a married couple whose son, Sam, has been drafted into the war effort and deployed to Georgia for basic training, and their niece Annie May, whom Pink has taken in after the death of her mother Lottie.

A drugstore janitor, William invests in Sam his hopes for the family's future in terms resonant with the longstanding tradition of black uplift: Sam embodies the family's hope for a "new negro" who, unhampered by racial discrimination, will enter the professional ranks (William envisions Sam as a lawyer, doctor, or pharmacist), earn a dignified living, and uplift his family and community. Yet when Sam deploys to Georgia, William's dream appears to be deferred yet again. When the parents hear that Sam has been drafted, Pink's "huge body shook with her sobbing," and William "remembered that he had only felt queer and lost. There was this war and all the young men were being drafted. But why Sam—why did he have to go?" Born and raised in Harlem, Sam is unprepared for the racist mores of the South. "It was always in the back of [William's] mind. Next thing Sam was in a camp in Georgia. He and Pink never talked about his being in Georgia. The closest they ever came to it was one night when she said, 'I hope he gets used to it quick down there. Bein' born right here in New York there's lots he won't understand.'" But then "Sam's letters stopped coming."[39]

Later in the story, William remembers how "the very sound of the word Georgia did something to him inside. His mother has been born there. She had talked about it a lot and painted such vivid pictures of it that he felt he knew the place—the heat, the smell of the earth, how cotton looked. And something more. The way her mouth had folded together when she had said, 'They hate niggers down there. Don't you never none of you children go down there.'"[40] The subtext of his recollections of Georgia is the unspoken guilt that Pink and William repress for having failed to heed his mother's advice by preventing their son to "go down there." Sam's last few letters contain a refrain ("Ma, I can't stand this much longer") that foreshadows his eventual fate in Georgia.

In the absence of Sam's letters home, the narrative juxtaposes the presence of Annie May, who in the eyes of William has fallen from a respectful and respectable girl to a "Jezebel" who stays out all hours of the night. Old-fashioned but well-meaning, William visits Annie May's high school to enlist the principal's help in persuading his niece to return to school; but in response the principal spouts a tedious monologue, the only phrase William retains from which is her branding of Annie May as "a slow learner." "He left her office feeling confused and embarrassed," the narrative continues. "If he could only have found the words he could have explained that Annie May was bright as a dollar. She wasn't any 'slow learner.' Before he knew it he was out on the street, conscious only that he'd lost a whole afternoon's pay and he never had got what he'd come for."[41] Chiefly verbal, his confusion and frustration in the principal's office parallel his routinely thwarted efforts to move his family to an apartment in a better neighborhood. Only later in the story will William and his family find the words to express their discontent, although the fallout from this moment of enunciation is bittersweet.

The confusion he experiences here will transform into a measure of clarity when, in the following scene, he receives an update on Sam in the barbershop from a young soldier named Scummy. When asked about Sam, Scummy mumbles, "He's all right"—but then adds, ambiguously, "Was the las' time I seen him." William presses him and learns that Sam was "shot by a white MP. Because he wouldn't go to the nigger end of a bus. He had a bullet put through his guts. He took the MP's gun away from him and shot the bastard in the shoulder."[42] Consequently Sam was court-martialed and sentenced to twenty years at hard labor.

Sam's fate encodes a dual irony that grafts the personal and political impact of the war onto black life. William had done his best to shield Sam from the type of existence that he had led himself, namely, a life of "hard labor," and yet his son meets precisely this fate, and worse, at the judgment of his own regiment. The absurd but foreseeable character of the scenario permits William to renew his anger at Annie May and to wonder, "Why couldn't something have happened to her? Why did it have to be Sam?" (But "Then he was ashamed.") Later awakened from a nap by a woman and man arguing across the way, William peers directly into their room, "and he saw that they were half-undressed."

> The woman slapped the man across the face. The sound was like a pistol shot, and for an instant William felt his jaw relax. It seemed to him that the whole block grew quiet and waited. He waited with it. The man grabbed his belt and lashed out at the woman. He watched the belt rise and fall against her brown skin. The woman screamed with the regularity of clockwork. The street came alive again. There was the sound of voices, the rattle of dishes. A baby whined. The woman's voice became a murmur of pain in the background.

If this scene reprises the dictum that oppressed groups tend to reproduce violence internally, it also links such acts of domestic violence to the awakening—and the unsettling—of the community, intimating how this awareness might be mobilized politically.

Taking refuge from the sweltering heat in a bar and a cold beer, William "still had that awful trembling in his stomach, but he felt as though he were really beginning to think. Really think."[43] Next he witnesses an altercation between a black prostitute and a white policeman who is trying to remove her from the hotel lobby. Such a scenario is pedestrian enough in Harlem, apparently, as William watches in amusement and privately muses, "Better than a movie." His attitude changes when a black soldier, who reminds him of Sam

("Tall. Straight. Creases in his khaki pants. An overseas cap cocked over one eye"), comes to the woman's defense. As the officer approaches the woman, waving that preeminent authoritarian and phallic symbol—the nightstick—the soldier accosts him, twists the nightstick from his hands, and whisks it across the lobby. The policeman fires on the soldier, who drops and "fold[s] up as neatly as the brown-paper bags Pink brought home from the store, emptied, and then carefully put in the kitchen cupboard."[44] The brown-paper bag is an understated but powerful metaphor: the dead black soldier is similarly usable, disposable, pliable—but stored away for *future use.*

This scene closely resembles the sequence of events that scholars believe ignited the Harlem riot in August of 1943. Conjuring the phenomenological and psychological texture of the riot, Petry's story asks how the vanquished soldier might be "used" by the mass of black spectators who have witnessed his demise. How does an aggregate mass suddenly transform into an insurrectionary unity? For William (who, significantly, has begun to *think*), the spectacle of the slain soldier "was like having seen Sam killed before his eyes." As an ambulance arrives, the crowd begins to follow the dead soldier, spreading the news of what transpired among newcomers. Though he finds himself at the forefront of this movement, William "hadn't decided to go—the forward movement picked him up and moved him along without any intention on his part. He got the feeling that he had lost his identity as a person with a free will of his own. It frightened him at first. Then he began to feel powerful. He was surrounded by hundreds of people like himself. They were all together. They could do anything."[45] Annie May and Pink reemerge as volcanic agents of protest, their bodies no longer associated with inertia and obesity but with momentum and destructive force. Annie May seizes a slim mannequin and hurls it across the street, where the model's legs shatter and its head rolls toward the curb. Ordinarily abstinent from alcohol, Pink bursts through the gate of a liquor store for a group of young men who could not do so themselves. Meanwhile, William rethinks his previous deprecation of his niece, who "worked for young white women who probably despised her." Annie May, he realizes, was not lazy or irresponsible; she simply wanted more than "just the nigger end of things, and here in Harlem there wasn't anything else for her." Ultimately, the movement is disbanded, with Annie May hauled off to jail and Pink depleted and on death's edge. But the story's poignant portrayal of Sam's revelation about black female agency, sparked by his induction into the rebellious movement of history, constitutes one glimmer of hope in Petry's world of darkness and confusion.

As Brooks's poem and Petry's story suggest, the symbolism of the Negro soldier exceeds the polarity of insurrectionist or democratic aspirations. Moreover, ostensibly domestic and locally textured narratives drew on the interaction between domestic and international concerns. The extraordinary response among the black diaspora to the brutal Italian invasion of Ethiopia in 1935 remains an exemplary case. Many African Americans, poised to join the Ethiopian resistance, were said to be frustrated in this effort by a government prohibition on U.S. citizens engaging in a foreign army. Given the status of black citizenship, the irony of this prohibition must have smarted for Ethiopia's most ardent defenders, but black Americans supported the beleaguered nation—long idealized in the Pan-African imagination—in numerous other ways: through fundraising efforts, fomenting pro-Ethiopia opinion in the black press, and disseminating technical expertise via communication with Ethiopia. When blacks could not take up arms in Ethiopia's defense, as scholars have shown, a small but dedicated cadre of anti-Fascist blacks transferred their animus against Italian Fascism in East Africa to the Spanish Civil War, joining the Comintern's Abraham Lincoln Brigade and risking "life and limb to defend the Spanish Republic from a fascist takeover." Undoubtedly, as Robin D. G. Kelley observes, the more than eighty black men and one black woman who joined the Lincoln Brigade were motivated by a "political outlook that combined black nationalism and Pan-Africanism with a commitment to the Communists' vision of internationalism." To this extent they were not unlike American Jewish anti-Fascists who also joined the struggle in the Spanish Republic.[46]

What is startling in this historical sequence is the dedication of these figures to the century's unremitting demands. When the stresses of racial domination would seem to have encouraged resignation or cynicism in the face of yet another Western war whose proximity to global black interests seemed remote, the black literary imagination foregrounds the Negro soldier as a figure who answers the call of history in its multiple demands. This figure's literary inscription in war, into the call of history, constitutes an archive of the heroic that eludes or exceeds Double Victory. Philosophically significant, this heroic subjectivity also indexes an historical change: in the transition from the Second World War to the Cold War, this subject transforms from an agent of liberation to one of occupation, while the meaning of his tripartite assault on totalitarianism fades into the recent memory of Axis defeat.

For Badiou, the heroic figure of the soldier, mired in modernity's revolutions and total wars, is a figure of immortality: an emblem of humanity's capacity to exceed its limitations and create new possibilities. Heroism, he writes, "is the luminous appearance, in a concrete situation, of something that assumes its humanity beyond the natural limits of the human animal." This evocation recalls the biography of Frantz Fanon, who left Martinique to enlist in the French army during the Second World War, fighting in the battles of Alsace and earning the Croix de Guerre medal. In the misty space between biography and mythology, the narrative of Fanon's life turns on his disappointing discovery, as a young man in France, that he was not regarded as a French citizen. This revelation did not exactly precipitate his turn to anticolonial struggle, including his decision, years later, to join the Algerian Revolution as a military theorist and tactician. Yet later as a psychiatrist in the Blida-Joinville Hospital in Algeria, mediating between colonizer and colonized, Fanon reached a decisive point: To which side did he belong? Fanon remains buried in Algeria, where the people still ponder his life and role in their history.[47] For Badiou, we cannot relinquish the heroic figure of the soldier, even if it was borne of the cauldron of total war. Without an active agent of the heroic, on this view, social life devolves into a site of despair and disorientation, a nihilistic vacuum filled by late capitalism.[48] In some measure, even the twentieth century's ubiquitous, frenzied effort to create "a new world and a new man"—a plea Fanon recapitulates in his conclusion to *The Wretched of the Earth*—assumes an emancipatory form in the black soldier's subjectivity.

In *Mythologies* (1957), Roland Barthes could have been analyzing the younger Fanon in his semiotic analysis of the cover page of the magazine *Paris March*, featuring a picture of a black boy in French uniform. "On the cover," writes Barthes, "a young Negro in a French uniform is saluting, with his eyes uplifted, probably fixed on a fold of the tricolor. All this is the *meaning* of the picture. But, whether naively or not, I see very well what it signifies to me: that France is a great Empire, that all her sons, without any colour discrimination, faithfully serve under her flag, and that there is no better answer to the detractors of an alleged colonialism than the zeal shown by this Negro in serving his so-called oppressors."[49] In this image, we find a French analogue with *The Negro Soldier* film; in both productions, the patriotic zeal of the soldier, removed from any historical context of racial subjugation, vindicates American democracy and French universalism against its critics. But is it possible to differentiate cleanly between Badiou's figure of the heroic soldier and these propagandistic but celebratory representations of the Negro soldier in France and the United States?

This question comes into sharper focus in light of what I suggested at the outset as the historical shift in the Negro soldier's representation during the early Cold War. An image by the American photographer Leonard Freed illustrates this shift. Working in Germany in 1962, Freed noticed a black American soldier guarding the divide between East and West during the erection of the Berlin Wall. According to Freed's curator, it "was not the partition between the forces of communism and capitalism that captured Freed's imagination, however. Instead what haunted him was the idea of a man standing in defense of a country in which his own rights were in question."[50] The experience apparently prompted Freed to return stateside to document the civil rights movement, an effort that culminated in his 1967 collection *Black in White America*.

Notice, first, the title: *American Soldier*. Though the figure depicted in the foreground is black, he is not labeled a Negro soldier, which prompts the following question: Is the soldier's American identity as expressed through the title offered by Freed in defiance (the soldier has earned his American identity), or is it presented in accordance with official efforts to inscribe black Americans, by omitting the racial descriptor, within the Cold War mission? That answer is hard to ascertain, but it is not difficult to perceive in this image the absence of romantic or heroic attributes that characterize earlier

Leonard Freed, "American Soldier," *Black in White America* (New York: Grossman Publishers, 1967). (Leonard Freed / Magnum Photos)

representations of the Negro soldier—attributes that pit the soldier against the many-headed hydra of totalitarianism or include him within the province of U.S. citizenship. With slightly downcast eyes, a lackadaisical aspect marks his countenance. The soldier stands at attention but in isolation, flanked only by two fellow American soldiers in a jeep. In the background appears the famous sign posted by the U.S. Army, rendered in English, Russian, French, and German: *You are leaving the American sector.* This figure, the viewer can assume, is in charge of policing traffic between these international zones. His hands remain on his weapon and knapsack; he is a figure of occupation.

This posture of occupation is not without precedent among African American G.I.s, but the semiotic register of Freed's photograph contrasts sharply with representations of black occupation during the war's immediate aftermath. Twenty-one-year-old William Gardner Smith, a Philadelphia native and writer for the *Pittsburgh Courier*, was drafted into the occupation forces in Germany and published his first novel, *Last of the Conquerors* (1948), after spending eight months overseas. The novel's narrator, Hayes Dawkins, who falls in love with a German woman but is scheduled to return to the United States, attests to the feeling of those African American G.I.s who experienced racial and democratic freedom in postwar Germany—an ironic situation in two respects: first, the black G.I.s, accustomed to the experience of occupation themselves, now arrive in the role of an occupying force; and second, for many of these G.I.s, post-Nazi Germany was their first refuge from persecution.

In his essay "White Norms, Black Deviation," writer and World War II veteran Albert Murray writes: "It is a fact, for example, that Negro pilots of the 332nd Fighter Group who were captured during World War II preferred the treatment they received from the Nazis to that which they had endured at the hands of their fellow countrymen in Alabama [where, coincidentally, Jimmy Wilson was sentenced to death in 1958 for stealing less than two dollars], whose solicitude of German internees was beyond reproach!"[51] If Murray's remarks betray a disingenuous jab at Jim Crow—clearly Nazi officials, who destroyed Germany's black minorities alongside other targeted groups, nonetheless stood to gain by adequately accommodating captive African American G.I.s and thereby mocking American pretensions of equality—they also underscore the new international frame of reference for black activism.[52] Those black soldiers fated to return stateside departed with a diminished tolerance for racial degradation. "Do you know what it's like for a Negro to be among the 'conquerors' instead of the defeated?" William Gardner Smith asked in an interview in 1959. "We learned about it for the first time when we 'occupied' Germany and none of us ever got over it. We'll never go back to the old way again."[53]

Freed's American soldier, however, lacks either the heroic posture of the previous generation or the awakened militancy of Gardner Smith's African American G.I.s in Germany. Charged with serious international responsibility, this black figure of occupation appears to have surpassed his predecessors in the hierarchy of the U.S. armed forces establishment, but his status is even more ambiguous. This ambiguity did not escape the notice of other artists of the postwar era. In German director Werner Fassbinder's great BRD Trilogy

(*Bundesrepublik Deutschland*) on West Germany during its 1950s Wirtschaftswunder (economic miracle), for example, African American G.I.s make recurrent, beguiling appearances in each film: *The Marriage of Maria Braun* (1979), *Lola* (1981), and *Veronika Voss* (1982).

Though Fassbinder's films are well known for their focus on sexual desire as an instrument of power, and despite the fact that white military authorities relentlessly cautioned their European counterparts about the sexual depravity of blacks, the African American G.I.s featured in the BRD Trilogy are neither mere sexualized specters nor exotic seasoning in an otherwise monocultural tableau of West Germany. Are not Fassbinder's African American G.I.s, then, cinematic counterparts to Freed's lone American soldier guarding the Berlin Wall zone? The dislocation of these characters derives from the disjuncture between the vestiges of the Negro soldier's heroism in both world wars and his postwar role as part of an occupation force. These characters figure as an ironic embodiment of U.S. political, moral, and military control of postwar West Germany, as well as a teasing but serious gesture about the paradox of U.S.-led Allied control over a nation wrestling with (but at this moment mostly repressing) its own past of racial totalitarianism. In this respect, the trilogy casts a sly, critical glance at the Allied projects of reeducation and *Entnazifizierung* (denazification, a term first coined by the Pentagon in 1943) that accompanied Marshall Plan largesse and facilitated West Germany's sensational economic recovery. Nonetheless, "Germans loathed the hypocrisy and arrogance of the allied assumption of superiority," writes one historian of the denazification process.[54] In the BRD Trilogy, this resentment seethes beneath the surface of everyday West German life, as characters go about their uneasy domestic affairs while the radio, droning in the background, alternates between American pop music and reports on NATO, Radio Free Europe, and news of Adenauer-Eisenhower treaties.

In his transatlantic, cross-cultural imagination, Fassbinder draws on two historical convergences between the United States and Germany.[55] The first involves the paradoxical situation of the Second World War, when the ideological confrontation between liberal and illiberal modernity soon eclipsed and then obscured the common foundation of racial thinking between the two nations. The second concerns the political situation of the early Cold War, marked by U.S. supervision of a divided Germany.

In *The Marriage of Maria Braun*, the first and most celebrated film in the trilogy, the film opens with the heroine Maria—who later describes herself as "a master of disguises. A tool of capitalism by day. An agent of the working classes by night. The Mata Hari of the economic miracle"—on a steadfast search for her husband, Hermann, who has been a prisoner of war and is believed to be dead. Scarcely a beneficiary of the economic miracle herself, Maria (played by Hanna Schygulla) takes a position in a bar designated for U.S. soldiers stationed in Germany; most of the bar's denizens are African American G.I.s. Before Maria can begin her job, she needs a clean health certificate, so she visits her doctor, whom she reminds that, during her childhood, he used to kiss her on the forehead when she arrived. The doctor claims to have forgotten—"I've learned to forget," he says.

With a clean bill of health, Maria begins working at the bar, where one of the black G.I.s, a gentlemanly officer named Willie, fixes his eyes on her. Maria's female coworker advises her to take notice of the officer's attention. Against Maria's professions of love for her husband, her coworker counters that love is just "a feeling between your legs," and prompts her to go to Willie's table. After all, she says, Willie "is big and strong. He just happens to be black." And more important, she notes, "He's clearly not starving." Maria traipses over to Willie; they talk; they dance. Later, when Maria is informed that Hermann is dead, she returns to the bar, collapsing into Willie's embrace and blurting, "*Mein Mann ist tot.*"

Maria and Willie commence a love affair and she becomes pregnant.

Yet, as it turns out, Hermann is *not* dead, and when he returns home to discover Maria and Willie naked in the bed, the two men tussle. With an exquisite, nearly blasé intuitiveness, Maria cracks a bottle against Willie's head, killing him. During the military tribunal for his murder ("I was fond of Bill," Maria testifies, "I loved my husband"), Hermann takes responsibility for the killing and is sent, yet again, to prison. At the advice of her doctor, Maria decides to abort the baby, since life, after all, is hard enough. "I never said I wanted to have an easy life," Maria retorts. "But with a black child?"

the doctor asks. "Life would be hard for him and you, too. Now he's a little black angel." *A little black angel.* Maria says, "That's nice."

This scene is only one among a number of canny scenarios involving African American G.I.s in Fassbinder's BRD Trilogy. What to make of these representations? The trilogy reflects the historical situation in which the majority of African American soldiers serving abroad were stationed in West Germany—almost twenty million American military personnel have lived in West Germany since the Second World War, of whom about three million were African American—a fact that invariably marked the texture of quotidian West German life. "Germany retained its reputation," write Maria Höhn and Martin Klimke, "as a special place for black soldiers even after the American occupation ended in 1949 and the U.S. military took on the task of protector for the young Federal Republic. . . . Unlike black GIs elsewhere in the world, those stationed in Germany found allies among local civilians, who supported them in their fight for racial equality."[56] This description seems accurate, yet Fassbinder's films gesture toward a deeper, if more insidious and obscure, set of truths. As part of an occupying force, now the African American G.I.s, as Maria's coworker puts it, only "happen to be black," which is to say that these characters retain little of the tragic allure and none of the valor marking their previous wartime heroism, but are still anomalous, liminal, and above all, *visible.*

If occasionally drunk and philandering, Fassbinder's black characters betray little of the arrogance Germans associated with white American G.I.s. Yet their presence creates a symbolic tension in postwar Germany between the raw memory of that nation's racial past and the present humiliations of occupation by a nation, the United States, projecting a victorious moral authority but still hampered by its own racial past and present. In Fassbinder's narrative, occupied Germany's humiliation is mild, subtle, ironic, and injected with bleak humor. When Maria is having her hair done, she tells the stylist, "I look like a poodle." The hairdresser replies, "You think so? It's the latest thing." "I'll bet," says Maria. "The Americans are just crazy about poodles."

Had the film portrayed a historical moment only a decade or so earlier (that is, during wartime), it would have been difficult to depict Maria's killing of Willie in a similar affective register. In that context, the act of murder would have elicited a measure of pathos or indignation; viewers would likely presume the killer to be a Nazi. As a reenactment of the occupation years, however, there is neither pathos nor indignation. Maria murders Willie as a matter of course, and there is an exceedingly equivocal yet cathartic release in the faithful wife's ability to return (albeit through prison bars) to her husband Hermann. In Fassbinder's trilogy of postwar Germany, the presence of the Negro soldier reminds Germans and Americans alike of what they'd rather forget.

Over the next two decades, as the black power movement gained momentum, the phrase "black soldier" acquired a new, radical signification. Militant African Americans began to redefine the status of the black soldier on their own terms—not as a tragic or heroic symbol of democracy but as an agent and protector of his own community. Reprising Garvey's argument, many saw black participation in the military instrumentally, in terms of both self-interest and group interest: the training blacks received in the army or marines could serve them well against racist attacks and police brutality. In 1970, *The Negro Scholar* devoted an issue to the topic of the black soldier. An editorial note describes the travails of the intellectual Angela Davis who, at the time, famously, was a casualty of the Cold War, arrested by the FBI ("Angela Davis was a fugitive from **injustice,**" the editorial asserts, "from a vicious and systematic campaign to crush her spirit, her blackness, her right to earn her living as a college teacher"). A black soldier was now any militant who stood up against and defended her community—and black activists increasingly redefined their communities as "colonies"—from the repressive forces of the state. Black radicals now tended to characterize race riots as urban guerilla assaults against domestic white supremacy. "Angela Davis is indeed a black soldier," the article concludes.

One contributor to *The Negro Scholar* issue, an Air Force veteran and political scientist, distinguishes (as was common during this era) between the Negro soldier and the black soldier: "Simply compared," he writes, "Negro represents the Aframerican who strives for integration into Euramerican society, approximating as closely as he can the latter's values and lifestyle while black represents the Aframerican who strives for liberation from Euramerican values and ways as a prerequisite for learning, appreciating and pursuing his own. The Negro labels his objective 'equality' and the black calls his 'self-determination.'" Drawing on his inside knowledge of the military, this commentator argues for "ideological pluralism" within the armed forces, by which he means essentially separate and autonomous black and white units working in tandem when mutual interests coincide. The pluralism he advocates is "ideological" because of the assumption that blacks and whites have conflicting ways of life, a difference indissoluble under the military's requirement of unity and subordination to authority.

In the course of his argument, the writer and veteran notes that this pluralism "is the opposite of totalitarianism." The military necessitates total discipline, unity, and a rigid hierarchy. Yet "naturally the U.S. Armed Forces could not be pluralist in this sense of organizational pluralism," he concedes, "since any force capable of disciplined pursuit of war must be totalitarian."[57] For this commentator, the possibility exists that a racially "pluralistic" military could be both less totalitarian in structure and still retain the discipline and cohesiveness necessary for combat. The more ominous subtext in this analysis is that, for blacks, a measure of totalitarian discipline was far from detrimental, and indeed, might be necessary for mobilization in the event of large-scale (inter-) racial conflict.

Such separatist proposals were emblematic of black power. They reflect what Richard H. King characterizes as the substitution in minority discourse, only a decade or two later, of postwar universalism for racial particularism in the 1960s and 1970s—even if black power picked up the baton of earlier internationalisms in a more radical form.[58] From the Negro soldier closing ranks with racial democracy in the First World War to the black soldier espousing separatist views circa 1970, these shifting iterations of black identity in the context of world war mark the historical parameters of this book as it cross-pollinates the twentieth century's two grand narratives: the conflict between democracy and totalitarianism, on the one hand, and the rise and fall of the global color line, on the other.

2

Our Totalitarian Critics

DESEGREGATION, DECOLONIZATION, AND THE COLD WAR

FACING PRESSURE from Secretary of State Dean Acheson, who insisted that domestic discrimination against racial minorities was hampering U.S. foreign policy and constraining Cold War objectives, President Truman commissioned a 1947 report, *To Secure These Rights*, designed to advance civil rights initiatives and to enhance America's image abroad. "The international reason for acting to secure our civil rights now," the report claims, "is not to win the approval of our totalitarian critics."[1] Such action, the contributors noted, was consistent with the nation's democratic provenance, moral responsibilities, and economic objectives. Truman went public with some of the report's conclusions, addressing Congress and audiences in Harlem.[2] But the report's insistence on the dire foreign policy consequences of Jim Crow, whose exploits acquired a growing global audience during the Cold War, leaves little doubt that the committee's policy recommendations were calibrated in large measure to silence the nation's "totalitarian critics"—but not only these critics.[3] As many commentators have noted, the onset of the Cold War witnessed the contemporaneous rise of the Third World and the nonalignment movement, with onlookers from Asia and Africa paying close attention to discrimination against black Americans while adjudicating competing appeals from the communist and democratic spheres. Opinion in the Third World mattered decisively to the United States and the Soviet Union, as both superpowers identified vital material interests there and viewed these regions, containing the majority of the human population, as a critical battleground for the ideological contest between capitalism and socialism.[4]

Compared with his successor, John F. Kennedy, who made Third World affairs a touchstone of his administration, Dwight Eisenhower's presidency was less supportive of Asian and African aspirations for independence, but perhaps no less concerned about non-Western perceptions of the United States. For this reason, the Eisenhower administration viewed propaganda and psychological warfare as a principle means of victory in the Cold War. "As the focus of the Cold War competition shifted to the Third World in the 1950s," writes Kenneth Osgood, "so too did the propaganda war. The revolutionary and anti-imperialist messages of communism, as well as the Soviet track record of rapid industrialization and modernization, potentially held great appeal to the new states emerging from the throes of European imperialism."

The allure of communism led the Eisenhower administration to bolster its efforts to attract bourgeoning Third World states. "Yet contrary to what one might expect from an administration that tended to view the world through a myopic anti-communist lens, psychological warfare experts in the Eisenhower administration consistently labeled anti-colonialism and nationalism as greater threats to American influence in the Third World than communism—at least as far as international public opinion trends were concerned."[5] On this view, the president assumed that the power of ideas, words, and emotions, more than open military confrontation—though perhaps less than covert operations—could tilt the Third World balance in the direction of U.S. interests. For struggling, non-industrialized economies, however, words and images alone would not suffice. International trade and lending administrated through the World Bank, rather than direct foreign aid, was the preferred method for Eisenhower's strategists, except in situations in which "the national security threat posed by Moscow-directed communism justified the provision of aid to contain it."[6]

Concerns about Third World public opinion compelled Eisenhower, as it also compelled Kennedy, to address domestic race relations in a manner he would have rather postponed or avoided altogether. After the fallout from Eisenhower's enforcement of desegregation in Little Rock, Arkansas, as Mary Dudziak observes, a cadre of black activists including Roy Wilkins, A. Philip Randolph, and Martin Luther King Jr. addressed a joint statement to the president: "It is no secret that the foreign relations program of our nation has been hampered and damaged by the discriminatory treatment accorded citizens within the United States, solely on the basis of their race and color. In our world-wide struggle to strengthen the free world against the spread of totalitarianism, we are sabotaged by the totalitarian practices forced upon millions of our Negro citizens."[7] In these pronouncements, an image of the totalitarian threat mediates the State Department's translation of the significance of civil rights into the sphere of foreign policy; Truman's and Eisenhower's reluctant forays into desegregation policy; and the rhetorical pressure African American critics applied in opposition to the Jim Crow regime.[8]

This chapter proceeds in three sections: the first, "America's Totalitarian Critics," describes how conventional formulations of totalitarianism excise race and speculates about what the restoration of this category would mean for historical narrative of the postwar era. This description enables me to revisit the widely held view that the Second World War and Cold War era ushered in a global transformation in race relations, affording unprecedented political choices and opportunities for African American artists and activists—though often at the price of acquiescence in the antitotalitarian imperatives defining official U.S. policy. The second section, "Slavery, Jim Crow, and the Totalitarian Imagination," excavates in readings of Douglass's *Narrative of the Life of Fredrick Douglass* (1845) and Wright's *Black Boy* (1945) a formal structure of totalitarian domination in narratives of slavery and Jim Crow. In later chapters, I show how this structure reemerges in the rhetorical arsenal of black cultural expression during wartime. The third and final section, "Totalitarianism and Contemporary Intellectual Culture," sketches a brief, stylized intellectual history of this concept, setting the stage for the situated conflicts explored in the rest of the book.

America's Totalitarian Critics

As noted in the introduction, critics on the political far left recoil from the conflation of Nazism (or fascism) and Stalinism (or communism), largely on the grounds that these ideologies are fundamentally opposed: the former conceived as an ultranationalist, racial project and the former imagined (if not realized) as a universal, radically egalitarian project. Critics less persuaded by claims on behalf of the dissimilitude of Nazism and Stalinism still concede that the idea of totalitarianism functions by virtue of an implicit contrast with liberal democracy, and U.S. democracy in particular. "More often than not," write Michael Geyer and Sheila Fitzpatrick, "comparison of Stalinism and Nazism worked by way of implicating a third party—the United States. Whatever the differences between them, they appeared small in comparison with the chasm that separated them from liberal-constitutional states and free societies."[9] Though we might not be able to define a totalitarian regime with precision, the argument goes, we can recognize one by virtue of its stark contrast with liberal democracy. This focus crystallizes as negation: the former is defined by its antithetical relation to the latter, which is credited with attributes such as equality under the law, deliberative procedure, universal suffrage, and freedom of speech, press, and assembly, among others. After all, who would confuse the macabre paradigm of Stalinism with even the darkest hours of liberal democracy?

Tacit in some formulations and explicit in others, this mode of comparison relies on a liberal-progressive version of history in which democracy's entwinement with colonialism and the slave trade is downplayed, rationalized, or consigned to the dustbin of democratic history. Politically, this mode exonerates putatively democratic regimes from the infringements and repressive tendencies normally attributed to their illiberal counterparts. Yet from within the bounds of racial and colonial democracy, writers like Franz Fanon, Albert Memmi, Richard Wright, W. E. B. Du Bois, and Aimé Césaire translated colonial experience into fascist imaginaries as total war reverberated outside of Europe and beckoned the darker races to continental battlefields. "Every colonial nation" Tunisian writer Albert Memmi declares in *The Colonizer and the Colonized* (1957), "carries the seeds of fascist temptation in its bosom. . . . There is no doubt in the minds of those who have lived through it that colonialism is one variety of fascism. . . . This totalitarian aspect which even democratic regimes take on in their colonies is contradictory in appearance only."[10] This aspect appears contradictory, in other words, only to citizens whose proximity to democracy's self-mythology has shielded them from racial exclusions.

As far as fascism "proper" is concerned, colonialism remains not invisible but relegated to the parochial past of this or that fascist power and thus peripheral to synthetic narratives of the twentieth century. One objection to the remapping proposed here is that more comparison or analogical inquiry further dilutes the term's historical specificity or its usefulness as a category for political analysis—but most scholars agree that the term is no longer valid in either of these strict registers, if it ever was. In this remapping, the resources of the literary emerge unexpectedly, both by preserving the term's historical character and opening to view global narratives of totalitarianism that Cold War frames have obscured or demoted to the "periphery." This line of inquiry informs the 2003 French publication *The Black Book of Colonialism (Le livre noire du colonialisme)*, an eight-hundred-page volume of essays, modeled on the controversial bestseller *The Black Book of Communism* (1997), that span the history of colonization and its afterlives from the sixteenth to the twenty-first centuries.[11] This temporal and geographical scope contrasts with the abbreviated periodization and Eurocentric focus of the totalitarian twentieth century, with its conventional markers of war and revolution that impacted Europe most adversely. Asking explicitly whether colonialism is a form of totalitarianism, the *Black Book of Colonialism* analogizes the crimes of the former with those of the latter in chapters that reexamine Arab colonization of East Africa, American plantation slavery, and Japanese imperialism in East Asia, among several others.

Critics resist this conjoining of narratives (of the racial-colonial and the totalitarian) for the same reasons that some historians oppose the "continuity thesis" in twentieth-century historiography of Germany: namely, the claim that German colonialism in Cameroon, German Southwest Africa, Togo, and German East Africa constitutes, in the case of the Herero uprising, a form of genocide and—the more daring assertion—that these colonial episodes prefigure National Socialism and the Holocaust.[12] To be sure, disciplinary misgivings about the continuity thesis are warranted (as A. Dirk Moses suggests, it smacks of a "grand" historical theory). For many historians, such connections flatten out events and undermine the ability to make necessary historical distinctions. On the other hand, these misgivings often rest on the impression that the Nazi genocide and Stalinist crimes, taken together, represent a singular rupture in Western civilization. In place of this narrative of rupture, the possibility remains for Moses and scholars like Michael Rothberg that a comparative, transnational model that develops "links between Holocaust memory and memories of colonialism and decolonization" can achieve more than the mere conflation of historically disparate episodes of extreme violence.[13]

If these anticolonial interventions have rarely been taken seriously among scholars of the Cold War, the point is not to appeal for more recognition or inclusion within the official canon of antitotalitarian thought. My argument concerns a different epistemological view of the political history of the twentieth century. Fredric Jameson's remarks on "standpoint theory" help to tease out this epistemology. Derived from György Lukács, standpoint theory presupposes a structure in the social order with its own definite forms of oppression and exploitation in which, according to Jameson, "each group lives the world in a phenomenologically specific way that allows it to see, or, better still, that makes it unavoidable for that group to see and to know, features of the world that remain obscure, invisible, or merely occasional and secondary for other groups."[14]

For Jameson, Lukács's epistemological prioritizing of "group experience" over "abstract concepts such as class and production" remains the decisive move in *History and Class Consciousness* (1923). On this reading, the authentic legatees of Lukács's thought are less his Marxist descendants than certain representatives of feminist thought, who have appropriated this conceptual move for a political orientation named standpoint theory (after Lukács's own usage). Black intellectual culture adopts this conceptual move and like Third World feminisms links standpoint theory to global capitalism's career in the non-Western world. As it expands in the awareness of anticolonial writers in the twentieth century, this linkage between the histories of imperialist-capitalist accumulation and shared racial experience enlarges, proportionally, the role of geopolitical critique in black cultural production. "The black experience," writes Jameson, "has its 'priority' in something like a combination of both of these distinct moments of truth (that attributed to workers and that attributed to women), but a combination which is qualitatively distinct from both, including not merely an experience of reification deeper than the commodity form, but also the historic link, by way of imperialism and the plunder of what was to become of the Third World, with the older stage of capitalist accumulation." According to Jameson, "these kinds of unique epistemological priorities are surely presupposed in all black theory as it emerged from the 1960s and the Black Power movement, but their theoretical foundations lie in W. E. B. Du Bois's notion of '[double] consciousness' on the one hand, and Frantz Fanon's rewriting of the Hegelian Master Slave struggle for recognition on the other."

There is little to gainsay, although of course more to add, in Jameson's précis on the epistemology of "the black experience," but his more evocative remarks on the Jewish dimension of Marxism captures the phenomenological condition of fear that grounds any conception of marginalized group identity. "But this experience of fear," he writes, "in all its radicality, which cuts across class and gender to the point of touching the bourgeois in the very isolation of his town house or sumptuous Berlin apartment, is surely the very moment of truth of ghetto life itself, as the Jews and so many other ethnic groups have had to live it: the helplessness of the village community before the perpetual and unpredictable imminence of the lynching or the pogrom, the race riot."[15] Obviously class and geography among other factors shape the racial subject's degree of exposure to terror. Ralph Ellison describes how the contrasting geographies, but similar class backgrounds, between himself and Richard Wright—the former a product of a multiethnic and less severely racist Oklahoma and then college at Tuskegee, the latter a product of an intensely racist Mississippi and Tennessee and then industrial Chicago—shaped their thinking about black culture and literary aesthetics. They were "united by a past condition of servitude, and divided by geography. . . . Yet it was this very difference of experience and background which had much to do with Wright's impact upon my sensibilities."[16] Did Ellison have a reciprocal influence on Wright? Throughout Wright's fascinating imaginative and political evolution, the pervasive and multifaceted character of fear remains a dominant motif.

Freedom from fear remains central to the whole liberal tradition, from Thomas Hobbes and Jean-Jacques Rousseau to Franklin Roosevelt of the Four Freedoms, but this ideal of bourgeois security has rarely been available to dominated groups. The texture of social life has not insulated them from fear. A broken window, a bloodthirsty mob, a detonated bomb, a policeman's pounding at the door in the black of night: before these moments are seen or felt, they are often heard—sonic interludes in the soundtrack of subjugation. Jameson is right, then, to suggest that a phenomenology of fear unites minority experience in particular, for fear penetrates the Chicago ghetto just as ferociously as it intrudes, without warning, into the "town house or sumptuous Berlin apartment." This is why he interpolates without distinction the graphic signifiers specific to black and Jewish experience: the lynching, the pogrom, the race riot, and the insalubrious space called the ghetto.

The application of this standpoint to Cold War politics proved vital to black contestations of the state's representations of interracial progress. As Dudziak shows, by the late 1940s U.S. officials began "telling stories about race and democracy" in order to counteract the geopolitically explosive effects of communist propaganda, especially vis-à-vis the Third World. With the nation positioned as collective protagonist, these narratives—which measure the progress of the Negro at midcentury against an abject history, rather than against the normative socioeconomic status of whites—depict a modestly repentant U.S. power emerging from its dark racial past while proceeding toward a new interracial horizon.[17]

During the early Cold War, the United States could not credibly continue its posture as a beacon of freedom and democracy when the nation practiced its own version of totalitarian governance, writ small, against African Americans. Widely credited as a catalyst for desegregation and decolonization, the Second World War and Cold War era amplified this blotch on U.S. democracy's escutcheon but also empowered black intellectuals who perceived the war effort and its transformation after 1945 as an opportunity to leverage the liberal state—or to attack it at its weakest point.[18]

The social and political transformation wrought by world war presented unprecedented opportunities and political choices for black intellectuals, but in some cases these prospects amounted to a Faustian bargain: the state and its cultural institutions offered black activists, ministers, political leaders, writers, and other cultural workers access to the precincts of state power, institutional recognition, and opportunities in cultural diplomacy.[19] Beyond individual preferment, the nation's tangible strides toward desegregation created a horizon of racial equality and renewed hope in black citizenship. Yet the price of these opportunities involved black acquiescence in the Cold War imperative of antitotalitarianism, which now meant anticommunism. Heightened suspicion of anticolonialism followed.[20]

What were the imperatives of Cold War liberalism? Were these state imperatives or proscriptions advanced by liberal thinkers? Did these articulations converge? As Jan-Werner Müller notes, "There is no single coherent theoretical statement of anything called 'cold war liberalism'; and there remains the suspicion that, while the postwar western world might have seen a comprehensive 'liberalization,' this was a process of liberalization without liberal thinkers."[21] Whether a process of liberalization occurred after 1945 without liberal thinkers is debatable. At the same time, however, the experience of war inflected political theory to the degree that a certain liberal consensus subsumed other categories of thought. Liberals and realists, reformed socialists and theologians, isolationists and interventionists alike—most could agree after 1945 that tried, failed, extant, and future alternatives to liberal democracy were undesirable, even intolerable, if for no other reason than that they led to war.

For Isaiah Berlin, Cold War liberalism reflected a particular sensibility; it was a matter of temperament, one antithetical to the explosive, totalizing ambitions of communism or fascism. Skeptical and modest, this new liberalism sought to advance a conception of knowledge and human agency less given to grand projects than alert to political landmines. "For Judith Sklar," writes Müller, "it was a 'liberalism of fear'—a skeptical liberalism concerned with avoiding the worst, rather than achieving the best." Liberal thinkers like Isaiah Berlin, Raymond Aron, and Karl Popper "all shared what Sklar called a 'preoccupation with political evil'; their concern was to avoid a *summum malum*, not the realization of any *summum bonum*."[22] How this postwar liberal theory informed policy of the liberal state is unclear, but there's little doubt that a rhetorical congruence exists between the former's emphasis on fear and political evil and the latter's crusade against the totalitarian menace. Cold War liberalism's quest to root out agents of political evil meant that blackness acquired a new significance, one understood as a radical domestic and international threat. The introduction to this book notes Woodrow Wilson's worry, as early as the interwar years, that the Negro represented the greatest conveyor of Bolshevism to America. But with the right concessions and opportunities, as Truman and Eisenhower came to understand, he could also function as an asset in the Cold War struggle.

In his 1958 autobiography, *Here I Stand*, Paul Robeson discusses his own plight during the Cold War. Here he cites a passage from an unspecified columnist for the New York *Amsterdam News:* "Our government has been employing Negro intellectuals, entertainers, ministers, and many others to play the roles of ambassadorial Uncle Toms for years. They are supposed to show their well-fed, well-groomed faces behind the Iron Curtain as living proof that everyone is free and equal in the United States and the color bar is a myth." Coyly, Robeson suggests that it "is not my intention to engage in personal criticisms of any kind," and he acknowledges a "number of performing artists who went on these government-sponsored tours because they needed work and who were out to show the world, as they did, that the American Negro has talent and dignity deserving of respect anywhere. Yet it must be said that the Negro spokesmen who have set out to calm the clamor of world humanity against racism in America have done a grievous disservice to both their people and their country."[23]

Analyzing a cultural component of Cold War civil rights, Penny Von Eschen has shown how the Eisenhower administration sponsored delegations of jazz musicians and other cultural actors to tour Europe, Africa, and the Middle East in an effort to project images of black efflorescence and interracial collaboration, thereby countering (if not necessarily undermining) Soviet propaganda of America as a racist empire. Impressive as many of these performances undoubtedly were, these delegations—symbols of a triumphant American democracy—took flight, as Von Eschen points out, when the United States was still a Jim Crow nation.[24] For Brenda Gayle Plummer, "Government-sponsored tours by actors and musicians, artists and writers partook of a cheerful ambiguity: it was never entirely clear what their performances were meant to represent and on behalf of whom they addressed foreign audiences."[25] "The jazz ambassadorial projects," Richard Iton astutely observes, "also depended on the negotiation of a form of blackness that would serve the conflicting needs of the American state: a blackness that was in some sense credible and appealing to foreign audiences but at the same time would not disable the precise calibrations of the broader national mission. In other words, a blackness that traveled well but avoided the internationalist and diasporic paths laid out by Marcus Garvey, W. E. B. Du Bois, Robeson, James, and Jones, among others."[26]

Against critics like Robeson and Du Bois, many black delegates rebutted that they were free to speak the truth about racial inequality in the United States, and they hardly understood themselves as stooges of the U.S. government (although, as the scholars cited above note, Edith Sampson was one such intermediary who later regretted the role she played in these delegations). If this type of cultural diplomacy presented blacks with a cosmopolitan substitute for the internationalist formations of the 1930s and 1940s, it's unclear how to measure the success of these performances of liberal citizenship from the standpoint of the U.S. national mission.[27]

Cold War tensions mark the publication and reception histories of many postwar African American literary texts, most famously Ralph Ellison's *Invisible Man*. In *Wrestling with the Left*, Barbara Foley argues that Ellison abandoned, even excised, his earlier leftist affiliations, carefully revising *Invisible Man* in accordance with liberal anticommunist imperatives.[28] Ellison's biographer, Arnold Rampersad, credits the author's insistence that the Brotherhood is an invention ("no more the Communist Party than Invisible's college is Tuskegee Institute") but concedes that, "even so, it is the key metaphor Ellison uses to assail the totalitarian left in its dealings with blacks. The Brotherhood, which enters the text ominously, is never defended, much less rehabilitated."[29] By the early 1950s, communism and one's attachments to it was not a subject to be discussed publicly, and never to be championed. Alan Wald observes that when Ann Petry gained national attention with her bestseller *The Street* (1946), "she was straightforward about her radical convictions and activities, including her friendly attitude toward the Communist Party," but in interviews and autobiographical statements "after the onset of the Cold War, references to her engagement in the Harlem 'crusade' are sparse and entirely depoliticized."[30] As with many writers, however, her gravitation away from communism did not mean she relinquished her view of the novel as a form suited to critiquing racial and class inequality, even as she ventured into other modes of social criticism (for example, with the novel of "white life").

In 1950 Petry published the essay, "The Novel as Social Criticism," which defended a propagandistic notion of literature with an expansive view toward the troubling developments of the twentieth century but that cannily drew on ancient and biblical precedents. "Being a product of the twentieth century (Hitler, atomic energy, Hiroshima, Buchenwald, Mussolini, USSR)," she writes, "I find it difficult to subscribe to the idea that art exists for art's sake. It seems to me like all truly great art is propaganda, whether it be the Sistine Chapel, or La Gioconda, Madam Bovary, or War and Peace." Defending 1930s novels derided as "proletarian fiction," she questions the attribution of "the perfidious influence of Karl Marx" to these texts. Marx's thought forms part of the West's cultural heritage, she observes, but "whether we subscribe to the Marxist theory or not, a larger portion of it stems from the Bible." Obviously, the authority of the Bible was immune from censure in a way that even modest left-wing precepts were not, so a question emerges about whether Petry was arguing that these precepts formed tributaries, religious (biblical) and secular (Marxist), from one universal tradition within Western, Judeo-Christian culture? Or was her invocation of scripture a discursive maneuver intended to reauthorize, respiritualize, and thereby buffer radical critique from redbaiting? Even as Petry downplayed her earlier radicalism and distanced her fiction from the Marxian lineage, the aesthetic prescriptions outlined in this essay seem less an accommodation to Cold War liberalism than the construction of a discursive space for criticism of inequality within a hostile and reactionary climate.[31]

The point here is not to cast retrospective judgment on those figures who sought to cruise under the Cold War radar or to celebrate uncritically those dissidents, like Du Bois and Robeson, who defied state authorities by virtue of their radical commitments. This approach obscures the view "that black liberals," writes Carol Anderson, "were like stealth fighters who imbibed the strategy pronounced by the first African-American leader of the NAACP, James Weldon Johnson. He noted that 'the black man fights passively. . . . He bears the fury of the storm as does the willow tree.' That stealth resistance, to bend like the willow instead of taking the blows and snapping like an oak, has made it difficult to discern what role black liberals played at all in decolonization."[32]

Though this book primarily retraces the steps of the black literary left, Anderson's observation suggests the importance of incorporating black liberals into the narrative of decolonization, as subsequent chapters attempt by placing figures like Ralph Bunche alongside W. E. B. Du Bois, or J. Saunders Redding next to Richard Wright. To juxtapose these figures' approach to common problems is not to overlook the fact that postwar affiliations and disaffiliations had serious consequences for black dissidence—and this book tracks many of these consequences. But to adopt a binary approach to the politics of cultural production of this era is to reprise a story that has already been told. Ellison and Petry were not unlike many American writers who rejected their earlier radicalism in favor of postwar liberalism, a tendency Thomas Schaub dates from the Nazi-Soviet Nonaggression pact of 1939.[33] After this point, prevailing winds blew the pollen of American literary culture in conservative, centrist liberal, or Trotskyist directions.[34] As Irving Howe phrased the matter in his defense of Richard Wright against the broadsides of Baldwin and Ellison, these younger writers had succumbed to the "postwar zeitgeist," which violated "the reality of social life" taken so seriously in the 1930s for the "unqualified assertion of self-liberation" that "was a favorite strategy among American literary people in the fifties."[35]

Even Baldwin, for all his ostensibly liberal assertions about the priority of the individual and the autonomy of art, emerged as a pungent critic of liberalism at the intersection of race and the Cold War. More recently, Baldwin has even emerged as one of liberalism's prestigious critics, a reputation that might be gauged by his participation in the roundtable discussion, "Liberalism and the Negro," organized by the journal *Commentary* in 1964. In addition to Baldwin, participants included sociologist of race relations Nathan Glazer, Sidney Hook, left-wing philosopher at the time, and Gunnar Myrdal, author of *An American Dilemma*. Norman Podhoretz, editor of *Commentary* and the discussion moderator, began the roundtable with a distinction between two competing schools of thought within liberalism vis-à-vis the Negro problem. On the one side, Podhoretz says, liberals envision the gradual absorption of blacks into mainstream society; on the other side, many left liberals and radicals were beginning to demand preferential treatment for blacks as a social group; the first approach emphasizes the rights of individuals, the second stresses the priority of groups, and both presume the eradication of racist attitudes and discrimination. Baldwin, however, appears to reject both approaches and apparently any liberal paradigm.

Clearly, as the discussion proceeds, Baldwin's staunch refusal incurred the frustration, if not the ire, of his interlocutors. He repeatedly invokes what we might call a racial realpolitik—the notion that the government's civil rights concessions were designed to further larger geopolitical goals—that liberals only begrudgingly acknowledge. At several points in the conversation, the participants pin Baldwin in a corner, demanding his admission that the nation has progressed in the domain of race relations. Did not the conditions in the North pale in comparison with the stultifying racism of the South? Had the material conditions of blacks not improved substantially? Had the attitudes of whites toward blacks, on the whole, not also advanced?

Aside from the spiritual dimension in which Baldwin ultimately interpreted white supremacy, Baldwin concedes none of these points. Instead, he notes that as the nation's rapidly industrialized economy and acquisition of wealth soared at midcentury—the consequence of intensified mass production, technological acceleration, and comparatively minor human and infrastructural losses suffered in the United States during the Second World War—the material conditions of blacks rose accordingly, if not adequately. "As far as I can tell," Baldwin says, "the progress that has been made in the last twenty years has not been mainly due to the application of ethical principles but to the fact that the country has been extremely prosperous. When the economic level of the country as a whole rose, obviously the Negro level rose more or less proportionately with it."[36] Baldwin saw no diminution of white supremacy in the relative socioeconomic advancement of black America.

Accompanying the robust American economy and expansion of the middle class after the war, the U.S. effort to consolidate its global hegemony, as recent historiography explains, depended on addressing the problem of civil rights for black Americans. It became increasingly untenable for U.S. diplomats and state officials to extol the virtues of American-style democracy and freedom when blacks were routinely lynched and the nation subscribed to Jim Crow segregation. What precludes the sort of communicative ethics the conference hoped for, according to Baldwin, is a malfunction in language. Indeed, it becomes apparent in the course of the roundtable that Baldwin and his liberal counterparts are not speaking the same language. "What strikes me here," Baldwin intones, "is that you are an American, and I am an American talking about American society—both of us are very concerned with it—and yet your version of American society is very difficult for me to recognize." During the question-and-answer session, the black psychologist Kenneth Clark defends Baldwin with the observation that "so far as the Negro is concerned, the ethical aspect of American liberalism or the American Creed is primarily verbal. There is a peculiar kind of ambivalence in American liberalism, a persistent verbal liberalism that is never capable of overcoming an equally persistent illiberalism of action."[37] More succinctly, Baldwin referred to this disjunction as the price of the ticket: a moral injunction to relinquish the material privilege of whiteness. Baldwin did not specify what forms such abandonment ought to take, but he insisted that the eradication of whiteness as a form of social capital and manifestation of state power was a necessary precondition for the equality liberals defend rhetorically.

If the examples of Petry and Baldwin suggest the difficulty in assessing black writers' acquiescence in or defiance of Cold War liberalism, their cases also indicate the insufficiency of this approach. An alternative to this binary approach requires posing a different set of questions, the advantages of which come into focus in the career of a writer like Richard Wright, whose work frustrates the quiescence-opposition model.

After the Second World War, Richard Wright's writings, like his 1953 novel *The Outsider*, project a strong antitotalitarian flavor. Adopting the Cold War conflation of Nazism and Stalinism, *The Outsider* continues to insinuate (in terms more strident than *Invisible Man*) that communist interest in the Negro question reflects a perverse, even sadistic, form of domination. On the other hand, the novel's indictment of Western democracy and colonialism was hardly amenable to postwar liberalism. By the 1950s Wright turned his attention to the Third World, where he reported on Ghana's revolution in 1954 and the Bandung Conference in 1955, composed a series of lectures on the psychology of decolonization, and continued his investigation of totalitarianism in Europe with his 1957 report on Franco's Spain. Tinged by Wright's exposure to phenomenology and psychoanalysis in France, the result is a synthesis of theoretical reflection and travel narrative from which it is possible to extrapolate an original question: to what extent can the nascent Third World—in the grip of nonsecular traditions and the colonial psychology he called "terror in freedom"—avoid the perils that leveled Europe? What is less compelling, then, than Wright's entanglements in Western antitotalitarianism is his adaptation of Europe's collapse into barbarism to the global postcolonial future.

The postwar tableau sketched above provides only a glimpse of the broader narrative of how the totalitarian imagination mediates the interwoven developments of desegregation, decolonization, and Cold War geopolitics. Yet in order to take full stock of how black cultural actors operated within this configuration, it is necessary to examine precedents: earlier iterations of the totalitarian that black writers have employed, *avant la lettre*, to represent racial domination from slavery to segregation. On rare occasions, literary critics and historians have invoked totalitarianism to describe U.S. plantation slavery or the Jim Crow system, or have detected elements of this structure in African American literary texts, but it has not evolved into a category with implications for historiography of racial democracy.

That this category elides accounts of black political culture or U.S. racial democracy is not surprising: from the standpoint of most American observers, totalitarianism happened elsewhere, after all, during the inception of fascism in Europe or after the Bolshevik Revolution and the rise of the Soviet Union. At the same time, critics still debate whether totalitarianism accurately names an actual political regime or historical phenomenon. Walter Laqueur, for example, has asked, "Is there now, or has there ever been, such a thing as totalitarianism?"[38] Other commentators question whether it actually originates in the twentieth century, or in an earlier epoch like the Terror of the French Revolution. Opposing Arendt's claim that it originates in modern European dictatorships, one political philosopher highlights the paranoid despotism of Shaka's rule over the Zulu Kingdom in early-nineteenth-century southern Africa as a counter-example. Earlier still, Karl Popper identifies a germinal form of totalitarian thought in Plato's *Republic*.[39] In the American context, other scholars have investigated the processes and productions in which communism and fascism began to merge in the U.S. cultural imagination.[40] This complex genealogy will be taken up in the course of this chapter, but the next section suggests why totalitarianism is not as remote from racial democracy and the black literary imagination as dominant discourses suggest.

Slavery, Jim Crow, and the Totalitarian Imagination

Though scholars have long read the slave narrative as emblematic of racial terror, I want to suggest more specifically that this genre and certain historiographies of slavery furnish evidence of a totalitarian impulse at the heart of U.S. racial democracy. This impression informs Stanley Elkins's controversial study, *Slavery: A Problem in American Institutional and Intellectual Life* (1959), which adapts the experience of Nazi concentration camps to the study of U.S. plantation slavery. For Elkins, U.S. slavery approximated a totalitarian system not only because of the intensity of its violence and cruelty but because it functioned, like the twentieth-century totalitarianisms, as a "closed" system.[41] In contrast to slavery in Latin America (to say nothing of premodern forms of enslavement)—where "a system of contacts with free society" prevailed and "through which ultimate absorption into that society could and did occur with great frequency"—few such "contacts" existed in the U.S. context. (Subsequent scholars, beginning perhaps with Gwendolyn Midlo Hall, have challenged the idea that slavery in Latin America was relatively benign compared to North American plantation slavery.[42]) Elkins notes that an unexampled and robust legal structure buttressed the closed system of American slavery, further differentiating it from other slave systems. Whereas a West African slave might marry, own property, or himself own a slave, these rights were generally denied, through terroristic methods, to Africans delivered unto American enslavement. The experience of totalitarianism, on this view, is what makes the twentieth-century German camps a more apt comparison with American plantation slavery than, say, enslavement in nineteenth-century Brazil or ancient Greece or precolonial Ashanti society.[43]

Adopting the methods of psychoanalysis, Elkins's comparative study employs the idiom of "personality," specifically the type of personality deformed under extremely violent conditions. This approach, which mirrored contemporaneous studies of the dictatorial or authoritarian personality, dominated analyses of subjectivity in the aftermath of the Shoah.[44] What kind of damaged personality did plantation slavery produce?[45] For Elkins, the most vexing conundrum of American slavery was the existence—imagined or actual—of the figure called Sambo, a stereotype embodying the traits of shiftlessness, docility, childishness, and duplicity that constitute enslaved blacks as a "society of helpless dependents." Critics repudiated Elkins for accepting the Sambo figure as a historical product of total enslavement rather than as a figment of the racist imagination with little empirical basis and as a dangerous stereotype unworthy of consideration.[46] Alternatively, some critics proposed a dialectical conception of slave personality that strategically oscillated between multiple roles: Sambo also contained Nat Turner. Elkins contends that this stereotype has nothing to do with any natural or cultural traits of Africans and their American descendants and everything to do with the totalitarian system of plantation slavery. To support this claim, Elkins turned to writings by survivors of the Nazi camps (especially the 1943 essay "Individual and Mass Behavior in Extreme Situations," by Bruno Bettelheim, an Austrian psychoanalyst and survivor of Dachau and Buchenwald) that testified to the production of similar traits of immaturity, dependency, accommodation, and a disinclination to revolt in the camp structure. Totalitarianism, he concluded, had the power not only to enforce obedience but also to change personality.[47]

Elkins suggests that despite the diverse techniques employed in the concentration camps—to say nothing of the historical distance separating plantation slavery and the Nazi regime—the "basic technique was everywhere and at all times the same: the deliberate infliction of various forms of torture upon the incoming prisoners in such a way as to break their resistance and make way for their degradation as individuals."[48] Overawed by lethal authoritarian figures, the survivors of both regimes came to identify with their oppressors. "The closed system" of the camps, he concludes, "had become a kind of grotesque patriarchy."[49] Few today would accept Elkins's comparative theory of slavery without exception, but it contains important insights into the relation between racial slavery and totalitarianism that critics diminished on account of the text's determinism and recourse to sensitive racial stereotypes.

But a slave narrative like Douglass's *Narrative of the Life of Frederick Douglass* (1845) substantiates aspects of Elkins's theory. In the *Narrative*'s third chapter, Douglass constructs a scene redolent of the major themes articulated in the "slavery and personality" section of Elkins's study.[50] It opens with a description of a magnificent garden kept by Colonel Lloyd, owner of the large plantation inhabited by Douglass. The garden contains a variety of excellent fruit, which attracts the slaves. The colonel, in turn, devises "all kinds of stratagems to keep his slaves out of the garden." Finally, the colonel decides to spread tar over the fence surrounding the garden. After this last trick, "if a slave was caught with any tar upon his person, it was deemed sufficient proof that he had either been into the garden, or had tried to get in. In either case, he was severely whipped by the chief gardener. This plan worked well; the slaves became as fearful of tar as of the lash. They seemed to realize the impossibility of touching *tar* without being defiled."[51] Douglass dramatizes a paternalistic game of cat-and-mouse that culminates in a retelling of the "tar baby" myth of African American folklore and that dramatizes the "grotesque patriarchy" of Elkins's Master-Sambo relationship.

What leaps out in Douglass's account, though, is the overdetermined role-playing of the scenario: surely the wealthy Colonel Lloyd cannot be too troubled by the theft of a few apples and oranges? The intense regulation of slave conduct is a well-known feature of the archive of slavery. What is significant here is the perverse theatricality of the scene, the space it provides for performance and consolidation of the plantation's various roles. This type of performance is best understood as farce—a key ingredient in totalitarian governance, on display to varying effect in spectacles like the show trial or the sham election. In Douglass's scene, the element of farce emerges in the master's exploitation of a *petty* truth of the regime (stealing is forbidden and merits harsh punishment) in order to crystallize an *inner* truth of the regime (the authority of the master must be demonstrated, repeatedly and with increasing severity). The necessity of exercising control in this manner, however, simply highlights an essential weakness of totalitarian power, for if it could sustain its dominance by other means surely it would. That is why for a writer like Flannery O'Connor, a century later, the farce of black theft and white authoritarianism became grist for darkly comedic stories like the "The Displaced Person" from her 1955 collection *A Good Man Is Hard to Find.*

Recognition of this farcical element does not diminish the lethal or dehumanizing character of this mode of domination. Douglass's narrative is just as attentive to the more insidiously totalitarian procedure of manufacturing "truth," or aligning truth with the whims of the authoritarian slaveholder. To be sure, he registers cruelty through Colonel Lloyd's promiscuous use of the whip—and the whip, as Orlando Patterson reminds us in *Slavery and Social Death*, is an implement deployed in virtually all slave societies across time—but the text is more concerned with the slaveholder's methods of psychological manipulation and his effort to regulate the enunciation of truth. Douglass observes that the colonel fabricated countless and often contradictory complaints about the care of his horses as a pretext to exert his power. "To all these complaints," writes Douglass, "no matter how unjust, the slave must never answer a word. Colonel Lloyd could not brook any contradiction from a slave."

Douglass then recalls how the colonel, in disguise, met one of his slaves while in transit. The colonel "addressed him in the usual manner of speaking to colored people on the public highways of the south: 'Well, boy, whom do you belong to?' 'To Colonel Lloyd,' replied the slave. 'Well, does the colonel treat you well?' 'No, sir,' was the ready reply. 'What, does he work you too hard?' 'Yes, sir.' 'Well, don't he give you enough to eat?' 'Yes, sir, he gives me enough, such as it is.'" After ascertaining where the slave belonged, the colonel continued about his business. Not "dreaming that he had been conversing with his master," the slave "thought, said, and heard nothing more of the matter, until two or three weeks afterwards. The poor man was then informed by his overseer that, for having found fault with his master, he was now to be sold to a Georgia trader. He was immediately chained and handcuffed; and thus, without a moment's warning, he was snatched away, and forever sundered, from his family and friends, by a hand more unrelenting than death. This is the penalty of telling the truth, of telling the simple truth, in answer to a series of plain questions."

In a footnote to this passage, historian David Blight observes that "here Douglass portrays a structure of virtual totalitarianism in the master-slave relationship, similar to that offered in Stanley M. Elkins, *Slavery*." The subsequent paragraph, however, both extends and challenges Elkins's thesis. In response to these strategies, writes Douglass, "when inquired of as to their condition and the character of their masters," slaves "almost universally say they are contented, and that their masters are kind. The slaveholders have been known to send in spies among their slaves, to ascertain their views and feelings in regard to their condition. The frequency of this has had the effect to establish among the slaves the maxim, that a still tongue makes a wise head. *They suppress the truth rather than take the consequences of telling it, and in so doing prove themselves a part of the human family*" (my emphasis).[52] What might appear to be the Sambo role is actually a performance and survival strategy, as well as narrative means through which the slave subverts the process of neoteny—the slave's self-affirmation as "a part of the human family."

This logic of manufactured truth reemerges in the Jim Crow era as a narrative theme in the writings of Richard Wright and other twentieth-century black writers. Published in 1945, one century after Douglass's *Narrative*, Richard Wright's *Black Boy* embodies the perils and possibilities of one migration from the South to the North and the world in one remarkable life. *Black Boy* proceeds along the following plot lines: the protagonist ventures out from his rural Mississippi home in search not only of opportunity but survival; he educates himself in Western literature and social theory, but also receives a negative, and indeed more formative, education in "the ethics of living Jim Crow." He arrives in Chicago, where he enters communist politics, but like many of his contemporaries, grows disillusioned by the Communist Party in the United States of America and eventually communism as a whole. Where the narrative ends is where biography intrudes, since readers knew that along the way Wright had emerged as one of the most famous black writers, domestically and internationally, of his time—a climax emblematic of his archetypal yet extraordinary migration.

Black Boy blends the conventions of naturalism or social realism ("All my life had prepared me for the realism," Wright recalls, "the naturalism of the modern novel, and I could not read enough of them"); the symbolic and geographical registers of the black migration narrative; the tropes and moral aims of the bildungsroman; and the dark resonances of antitotalitarian literature. According to one of Wright's contemporaries, cited by Ellison in his 1945 essay "Richard Wright's Blues," *Black Boy* depicts a social context that reflects the "preindividual" status of Negro culture, in which "the stress is on the group. Instead of seeing in terms of the individual, the Negro sees in terms of 'races,' masses of peoples separated from other masses according to color." In response to this critic's observation, Ralph Ellison replies that this "pre-individual state is induced artificially—like the regression to primitive states noted among cultured inmates of Nazi prisons."[53] Connecting Wright's narrative, coincidentally, to Elkins's interpolation of the Nazi camps into American slavery, Ellison's remarks raise the question of whether Wright's narrative might be understood more profitably as a unique incarnation of the antitotalitarian novel.

In *Black Marxism*, Cedric Robinson was perhaps the first commentator to note that Wright's work, "with the stimulus of historical materialism and psychoanalysis, fell much closer to an emergent European literature (Sartre, Merleau-Ponty, Koestler, Lukács, Marcuse, Kolakowski) in the post-Second World War period than to any American fashion."[54] The postwar European literature Robinson has in mind might be designated as a literature of the totalitarian experience, and this experience has at least as much claim on Wright's literary imagination as does naturalism or Chicago School sociology.[55] Comparing Wright's project with a few remarks by Orwell helps to unpack the complex act of adaptation and translation at the heart of *Black Boy* and other texts. "One striking fact about English literature during the present century," writes George Orwell in a 1944 essay on Arthur Koestler, "is the extent to which it has been dominated by foreigners—for example, Conrad, Henry James, Shaw, Joyce, Yeats, Pound and Eliot. . . . It may be an exaggeration, but it cannot be a very great one, to say that whenever a book dealing with totalitarianism appears in this country, and still seems worth reading six months after publication, it is a book translated from a foreign language."[56] By writing *1984* and other texts, Orwell himself might have broken the streak of exclusively "foreign" antitotalitarian literature being published in Britain, but his subsequent remarks are worth teasing out.

He goes on to note that this surge of foreign-dominated literature reflects the turbulence of total war and political extremism in continental Europe—an experience mostly touching Britain indirectly, and certainly not on the scale of devastation marking the Soviet Union and continental Europe. And this lived proximity to totalitarianism and total war—its displacements and ruptures, gulags and concentration camps, secret police and repressive instruments, genocides and indiscriminate bombings—has produced what he calls "concentration-camp literature."[57] As this literature evolves largely from reportage of various kinds, notes Orwell, in Britain "there has been nothing resembling, for instance, *Fontamara* or *Darkness at Noon*, because there is almost no English writer to whom it has happened to see totalitarianism from the inside. In Europe, during the past decade and more, things have been happening to middle-class people which in England do not even happen to the working class." Britain lacks literary production of this type because the empire has been spared the worst of totalitarian excess. "To understand such things," he continues, "one has to be able to imagine oneself as the victim, and for an Englishman to write *Darkness at Noon* would be as unlikely an accident as for a slave-trader to write *Uncle Tom's Cabin*."[58]

Such an accident would have been strange indeed. But Orwell's inexact analogy (maybe an outside observer like de Tocqueville as imagined author of *Uncle Tom's Cabin* would have been a better example) furnishes an alternate entrance into the ideological basis of the antitotalitarian text. In other words, one might modify Orwell's concern about literary authenticity and instead ask: how adaptable or translatable is the experience of totalitarianism and its literary forms? If U.S. plantation slavery strikes Orwell as apposite to Europe's collapse into total war, then how might the history of totalitarianism look from the colonized world?

For Orwell and his contemporaries, concentration-camp literature articulates, though is not synonymous with, the subgenre of antitotalitarian literature. Called into being in the wake of the First World War, when collectivist ideologies outmuscled liberal individualism and engendered fears of social contagion, the concentration camp emerged as a global institution "predicated on the idea of a permanent state of war"—so that a literary geography of the camp might also encompass, for instance, texts produced under Franco's Spain, Maoist China, apartheid South Africa, French Algeria, British Kenya, North Korea, and so on.[59] Yet even a geography this capacious runs the risk of reinstating a Eurocentric history of the death camps and concentration camps, one in which National Socialism occasionally squints at its distant double: the camps erected at the turn of the century under Bismark's German southwest Africa, which some scholars view as having later functioned as blueprints for Nazi camps in Eastern Europe.[60]

To some degree, Orwell's problem about representing the totalitarian experience in literature—when one's immediate social context falls outside of this experience—belongs also to Wright. Wright has not experienced a concentration camp, but he has survived Jim Crow. In *Black Boy*, the formal tension centers on the text's adaptation of the literary conventions of the antitotalitarian narrative to the experience of Jim Crow, while balancing this essentially political choice with the moral and educational aims of the bildungsroman shown throughout *Black Boy*. Put simply, how can the text reconcile the story of *Bildung* with the system of Jim Crow?

One way is to rewrite the *Bildung* of Jim Crow as a mode of negative education. *Black Boy* recodes the regime of segregation—the crucible of Wright's education—as a system in which racial domination and terror fill the void denied knowledge and normative maturation. Accommodation to racial subjugation forms the most enduring component of Wright's negative education. "I had begun coping with the white world too late," young Richard reflects upon his arrival in Memphis. "I could not make subservience an automatic part of my behavior. I had to feel and think out each tiny item of racial experience in the light of the whole race problem, and to each item I brought the whole of my life."[61] In his recent study *The Death Bound Subject*, Abdul JanMohamed argues that in his fiction "Wright conducted, partly through a series of conscious and deliberate decisions, but partly through extremely sharp intuitive, often unconscious choices, a systematic and thorough archaeology of what I will call 'the death-bound-subject,' that is, of the subject who is formed, from infancy on, by the immanent and ubiquitous threat of death."[62] In these morbid terms, perhaps characterizing Wright's journey as a negative education understates the case, but as Ralph Ellison notes, Wright balances the hostility of segregated life with "the specific folk-art form" of the Negro blues. Ellison defines the blues as "an impulse to keep the painful details and episodes of a brutal experience alive in one's aching consciousness, to finger its jagged grain, and to transcend it, not by the consolation of philosophy, but by squeezing from it a near-tragic, near-comic lyricism."[63] By the time he wrote *The Outsider* in the early 1950s, Wright seemed to associate the blues with the demonic, imbuing this expressive form with an element obscenely at odds with the tragicomic lyricism Ellison celebrated in it.

Perhaps this earlier lyricism indicates how for the alternately dreamy and sullen protagonist of *Black Boy*, even a totalitarian system is navigable with sufficient cunning, imagination, and ingenuity. By necessity, young Richard had learned this system's rigid codes of discipline: "While standing before the white man I had to figure out how to perform each act and how to say each word. . . . In the past I had always said too much, now I found that it was difficult to say anything at all." Characteristically, Wright connects his own socialization with that of other black boys. "I began to marvel at how smoothly the black boys acted out the roles that the white race had mapped out for them," he writes. "Most of them were not conscious of living a special, separate, stunted way of life."[64] Though young Richard's nights are filled with readings of Conrad and Dostoyevsky, Kafka and Twain, Dreiser and Balzac, newspaper stories and Communist magazines, the text leaves no doubt that the discipline of Jim Crow comprises his compulsory education. Propelling the narrative forward, the tension between these two realms—aesthetic imagination and harsh lived experience—also propels the protagonist forward against impossible odds.

Though failure to adhere to Jim Crow's discipline risked the penalty of violence or death, Wright's autodidactic literary imagination—in a clearly intertextual, nearly umbilical connection to the slave narrative—also held the key to his emancipation. Oscillating between the panoramic and microscopic, the lyrical and sociological, Wright's depiction of a stultifying Mississippi and Tennessee is total and totalizing: its focus on the irrationality and intensity of intersubjective racism, abetted by a repressive apparatus for policing racial boundaries, harkens back to the slave narrative but also parallels the narratives of totalitarian experience proliferating contemporaneously in Europe.

In one scene, the narrator recalls a stint working in an optometrist's office, owned by a sympathetic doctor named Mr. Crane, who employed Pease and Reynolds, two characters bent on terrorizing young Richard. One day Pease and Reynolds confront Wright while Crane is out of the office, so that they can, in Wright's arresting phrase, "[turn] on the terror." As coconspirators, Pease and Reynolds trap him in an irresolvable situation. "'Richard, Reynolds here tells me that you called me Pease,' he said. I stiffened. A void opened up in me. I knew that this was the showdown. He meant that I had failed to call him Mr. Pease. I looked at Reynolds; he was gripping a steel bar in his hand." In a suspenseful and deftly crafted scene, Wright shows the futility of attempting a conciliatory response. "If I had said: No, sir, Mr. Pease, I never called you *Pease*, I would by inference have been calling Reynolds a liar; and if I had said: Yes, sir, Mr. Pease, I called you *Pease*, I would have been pleading guilty to the worst insult that a Negro can offer to a southern white man. I stood trying to think of a neutral course that would resolve this quickly risen nightmare, but my tongue would not move."[65]

Young Richard mumbles an apology and explanation, but these words only intensify their rage. Painting a perennial theme, this situation leaves him only one choice: to flee or risk injury and death. The encounter presents a classic double bind of totalitarian domination: facing two equally untenable courses of action, the young narrator replies unsteadily before fleeing the scene; he does not wait for his antagonists to "turn on the terror." Throughout *Black Boy*, scenarios like these replicate the conventions of antitotalitarian literature in the geography of the Jim Crow South. In the archetypal show trial (perhaps a questionable abstraction), the accused faces a line of interrogation for which no acceptable answers exist—none that will spare her life. On my reading, Wright's narrative portrays an analogous, localized structure in the Jim Crow order, in which ordinary citizens are permitted to conduct miniaturized "trials" in lieu of, or in collaboration with, the state. In this context, the nexus of state and privileged citizen aims at the expulsion of unwanted subjects and reinforcement of the regime's racial integrity.

The accusation of lying is a preferred method to effectuate this double bind since truth emerges as whatever the authority of the moment insists it is. This particular accusation is not really ironic, as its projection onto the accused reflects the debasement of truth under totalitarianism. As a tactic, false accusation corresponds with the falseness of the regime and the authority of those individuals and groups vested with power by a regime. As Leszek Kolakowski contends, the "virtue of the lie" is one of the singular imperatives of the totalitarian regime, a feature distinguishing this mode of mendacity from the blasé and generically different category of trivial lies and distortions used by political leaders throughout the ages. "The use of the lie," writes Kolakowski in the early 1980s, "is interesting not only politically but epistemologically as well. There is no applicable criterion of truth except for what is proclaimed true at any given moment. And so the lie really becomes truth, or at least the distinction between true and false in their usual meaning has disappeared. This is the great cognitive triumph of totalitarianism: it can no longer be accused of lying, because it has succeeded in abrogating the very idea of truth."[66]

Writing as a Polish former-communist dissident, Kolakowski's frame of reference is the Soviet Union. From this standpoint, the political and intellectual repression of the Soviet experience is not to be mentioned in the same breath as liberal democracy. For all of their fabrications and illusions, democratic regimes are thought to approach nowhere near the level of systematic mendacity found in the former Soviet bloc. What Wright constructs is a parallel structure that goes beyond the production of sheer terror to a deeper continuity, pace Kolakowski, at the epistemological level. Yet to grant the quasi-totalitarian character of Wright's milieu is not to obscure crucial differences between these repressive orders. To take only one difference, Wright showed how the dissolution of the public-private distinction typical of the ultrarepressive states in Europe operates differently in Jim Crow America, where the encroachment of segregation—sanctioned by but not restricted to the state—into the private sphere tended to manifest more symmetrically in its effects: as internalized racism and self-abnegation among blacks and as fanatical hatred and self-delusion among whites.[67] Shocked by the unremitting terror and violence portrayed in *Black Boy*, many of Wright's contemporaries questioned the veracity of his memoir. Against critics like Du Bois, Mary McCarthy, and Lionel Trilling, who asserted that *Black Boy* exaggerates the bleakness of Negro life or the acuteness of Southern racism (even as they acknowledged the narrative's power), Ellison argues that both "groups miss a very obvious point: that whatever else the environment contained, it had as little chance of prevailing against the overwhelming weight of the child's unpleasant experiences as Beethoven's Quartets would have of destroying the stench of a Nazi prison."[68]

Wright constructed a narrative that followed an individual not merely in tension with his society (per the bildungsroman) but in mortal and intellectual combat with it. Self-conscious, however, of oppositions like fact and fiction or experience and imagination, Wright emphasizes the moral or "emotional" rather than factual truth of his autobiography.[69] In one scene, he recounts a rumor he had heard of a black woman whose husband had been seized and killed by a lynch mob. Vowing to avenge her husband's death, she "took a shotgun, wrapped it in a sheet, and went humbly to the whites, pleading that she be allowed to take her husband's body for burial." Granted access to her dead husband's body, so the legend goes, the woman then unsheathes the gun and slays "four of them, shooting at them from her knees." Tales like these make up the cultural inventory that Wright calls the ethics of living Jim Crow. "I did not know if the story was factually true or not," Wright admits, "but it was emotionally true because I had already grown to feel that there existed men against whom I was powerless, men who could violate my life at will. I resolved I would emulate the black woman if I were ever faced with a white mob. . . . The story of the woman's deception gave form and meaning to confused defensive feelings that had long been sleeping in me."[70]

What I've argued is Wright's reimagining of Jim Crow as a totalitarian regime connects intertextually to his famous first novel, *Native Son* (1940), the story of a poor black teenager in a Chicago slum who murders a white woman and his black girlfriend. "What happens," JanMohamed asks, "to the 'life' of the subject who grows up under the threat of death, a threat that is constant yet unpredictable?"[71]

What happens, Wright suggests, is that among other consequences this subject grows susceptible to the illiberal ideological currents sweeping the world of the 1930s and 1940s. In his 1940 essay, "How 'Bigger' Was Born," Wright observes: "I felt that Bigger, an American product, a native son of this land, carried within him the potentialities of either Communism or Fascism." Wright sketches various incarnations of his infamous protagonist Bigger Thomas, profiles suggesting a composite figure stretched between extreme marginalization and authoritarianism. Rebellious above all against the Jim Crow system, this figure manifests a lust for exacting humiliation, appropriating material objects, and enforcing obedience from other blacks less defiant than he. A century removed from slavery, he no longer identifies with his oppressor in the manner of Elkins's Sambo figure; he now identifies with the authoritarian personality.[72]

As one commentator notes, "Bigger is the prototypical 'mass man,' hardly necessary to anyone, and is 'superfluous' in somewhat the sense that Hannah Arendt characterized the victims of totalitarian regimes. . . . Put another way, *Native Son* is about the process whereby Bigger ceases to be superfluous to others and to himself."[73] Arguing that millions of Negroes like Bigger Thomas inhabited the nation's ghettos, Wright saw an immediate connection between his character's combination of defiance and authoritarianism and the sphere of global politics. "I've even heard Negroes," he writes, "praise what Japan is doing in China, not because they believed in oppression (being objects of oppression themselves), but because they would suddenly see how empty their lives were when looking at the dark faces of Japanese generals. . . . They would dream of what it would look like to live in a country where they could forget their color and play a responsible role in the vital process of the nation's life. I've even heard Negroes say that maybe Hitler and Mussolini are all right; that maybe Stalin is all right."[74] On this subject Wright spoke with authority: he, too, had been what the Chicago School sociologists labeled "marginal man," and one who also grew enamored of illiberal modernity. Wright understood that black attitudes about world war and the international crisis exceeded the bounds of the Double V campaign's precise, if limited, formulation of victory at home and abroad.

Totalitarianism and Contemporary Intellectual Culture

As the historical and cultural landscape surveyed thus far indicates, the multiple and conflicting representations of the totalitarian experience suggest that the concept is as much a literary as a strictly political or ideological construct—even if, to some degree like liberal democracy, it was a political fiction from the start. Even the diplomat George Kennan, author of "The Sources of Soviet Conduct" (1947), formulated the term's meaning in literary and psychological terms. After noting that the Soviet Union and Nazi Germany—together "a source of sorrow and suffering" that has "overshadowed every other source of human woe in our times"—were so different that the concept itself verged on incoherence, Kennan articulated its true meaning in the symbolic domain:

> When I try to picture totalitarianism to myself as a general phenomenon, what comes into my mind most prominently is neither the Soviet picture nor the Nazi picture as I have known them in the flesh, but rather the fictional and symbolic images created by such people as Orwell or Kafka or Koestler or the early Soviet satirists. The purest expression of the phenomenon, in other words, seems to me to have been rendered not in its physical reality but in its power as a dream, or a nightmare. Not that it lacks the physical reality, or that this reality is lacking in power; but it is precisely in the way it appears to people, in the impact it has on the subconscious, in the state of mind it creates in its victims, that totalitarianism reveals most deeply its meaning and its nature.[75]

Kennan does not belabor this point, but his stress on the nightmare switches the emphasis from the features of the dictator or total state to the subjectivity of literature's incarcerated Everymen, who are subjected in some cases to physical imprisonment and in other instances held, in Czeslaw Milosz's phrase, as "captive minds."[76] On this view, literature becomes the site for comprehending totalitarianism as history rather than the reverse procedure, which establishes historical context to interpret antitotalitarian texts.

Kennan's literary and symbolic focus resurfaces when, for instance, Werner Sollors, in his study *Ethnic Modernism*, asks, "Was modernism antitotalitarian?" Despite the fact that some individual modernists flirted with totalitarian movements and ideologies, U.S. modernism in this account was generally antitotalitarian, insofar as both Nazi and Soviet authorities denounced and banned modernist productions like jazz and abstract expressionism as cultural emblems of spiritual pollution, sexual and racial degeneracy, and individualist or antistatist tendencies. On the communist view, modernist productions abdicated the social and artistic responsibility to produce objective knowledge of the world, advance the class struggle, and emancipate humanity; only socialist realism could rise to this challenge. It's unclear, albeit easy enough to infer, what aesthetic properties of modernist literature were intrinsically antitotalitarian: linguistic play, indeterminacy, bourgeois interiority, epistemological "unknowing," and so on.[77]

Admittedly, a literary redefinition of the totalitarian is unlikely to satisfy aforementioned critics for whom the term remains a scandal. Any invocation of totalitarianism signals a posture of resignation or pacification. Against this supposed resignation, Alain Badiou retrieves, bracingly, the "passion for the real" as the governing logic of twentieth-century subjectivity. Rather than a betrayal of—or "negative discontinuity" with—the nineteenth century, twentieth-century subjectivity constitutes an unprecedented effort to transform into reality what the previous century conceived as the Imaginary (nineteenth-century utopian ideals) or the Symbolic (what the nineteenth century produced as doctrine, what it thought and organized). The conventional view that the revolutionaries of the century, whether fascists or communists, "accepted horror in the name of a promise, in the name of 'glorious tomorrows,'" ignores the possibility that the century's actors harbored few illusions about their individual fate or that of their grand political projects. "On the contrary," writes Badiou, "I am convinced that what fascinated the militants of the twentieth century was the real. In this century there is a veritable exaltation of the real, even in its horror." He is aware of the limits of the century's passion for the real and its irrepressible will to destruction. Though the century's will to destruction constitutes one of its strengths—"after all, many things deserve to be destroyed"—it also marks its limits, for "purification is a process doomed to incompletion, a figure of the bad infinite."[78]

With respect to the deep desire of the revolutionary subject to purge impure elements, subtraction rather than destruction remains the road considered but seldom taken during the twentieth century. An antidote to the regime of pacification wrought by history's end, this passionate enactment of the real embodies a truth procedure in Badiou's terms: the process by which a subject ushers something new and universal into the world, often committing grave errors along the way, but errors from which the subject learns and "keeps going."

Despite acknowledging that both fascists and communists incarnated this passion for the real, Badiou is obviously not enamored of the rightist, mystical destructiveness valorized by the likes of Ernst Jünger but rather of the capacity of twentieth-century militants to invent and to exercise "an absolutely new and concrete reality" that can claim victory over the deliberative and procedural, yet "savage" and "nihilist," reign of liberal democracy. On my reading, it is the intimation of victory—"the transcendental motive that organizes even the defeat"—that almost always complements his disdain for "parliamentary" democracy. For Badiou, invoking Lenin, ultimate victory must be total, the outcome of "total war." As Etienne Balibar puts it, "*there is only one philosophical moment in Lenin, and it is precisely war that determines it*" (emphasis in original).[79]

This emphasis on total war and total victory suggests the need at this point to disentangle seemingly overlapping terms like *total war*, *totalitarianism*, and *totality*.[80] Attention to the various permutations of the concept of totality in Western Marxism would take this study too far afield, and has already been magisterially done by scholars like Martin Jay, but it is useful here to distinguish totality from totalitarianism with some assistance from Jameson's reappraisal of Lukács.[81] First, to confuse totalitarianism with totality is something of an embarrassment, a telltale sign of internalized Cold War residua. "The enthusiastic republication in France today," he writes, "of the hoariest of American Cold War literature, such as James Burnham, awakens the suspicion that at least a few of the most strident of the anti-totality positions are based on that silliest of puns, the confusion of 'totality' with 'totalitarianism.'" For Jameson, the idea of totality is an indispensible contribution of Marxist thought, principally owing to Lukács's forceful articulation in *History and Class Consciousness.*

Part of Lukács's enduring, but for many readers doctrinaire, fascination with nineteenth-century European realism inheres in this fiction's capacity to "think totality" within a novelistic aesthetic of social interrelationships. Above all, this aesthetic requires both the nineteenth-century and even the modernist novelist to render "the complexities of urban and industrial totalities—in a situation in which they have become ungraspable, and in which the sheer simultaneity of unrelated destinies in the city, the sheer contingency of random meetings and chance intersections, suggest deeper interrelationships which constitutively escape individual experience and the 'point of view' of any individual actor or participant."[82] Yet contemporary theory, exhausted by any pretenses to totality or totalizing knowledge, has routinely found this aspect of Lukács's aesthetics to be antediluvian or symptomatic of his allegiance to "socialist realism."

Indeed, more damning than the Cold War confusion is the critique advanced by postmodernism and poststructuralism, which Jameson adjudges to have launched a "war on totality." However, some overlap exists between the Cold War and postmodern critiques of totality. It is unnecessary to rehearse this critique, but we find even in Michel Foucault's usage some slippage in the meaning of these terms. "For the last ten or fifteen years," Foucault says in one of his 1976 lectures at the College de France, we have witnessed "the immense and proliferating criticizability of things, institutions, practices, and discourses; a sort of general feeling that the ground was crumbling beneath our feet. . . . But alongside this crumbling and the astonishing efficacy of discontinuous, particular, and local critiques, the facts were also revealing something that could not, perhaps, have been foreseen from the outset: what might be called the inhibiting effect specific to totalitarian theories, or at least—what I mean is—all-encompassing and global theories."

Foucault concedes that all-encompassing theories like Marxism and psychoanalysis continue to provide "tools" that can be used at the local level, but only when "the theoretical unity of their discourse" is turned inside out or ripped to shreds, caricatured and theatricalized—a necessary procedure since "the totalizing approach always has the effect of putting the brakes on."[83] Foucault makes clear that his usage involves the constraints of grand theories versus the merits of localized knowledge, and that his use of "totalitarian theories" really means something like "totality" or "totalizing theories" (as he then indicates). But these theories nonetheless revealed an "inhibiting effect." Was Cold War discourse effective in discouraging even oppositional intellectuals from thinking in terms of totality, broadly understood?[84]

This postmodern skepticism seems responsive to a previous generation of intellectual discourse that married the concepts of totality and total war. As the earlier reference to Lenin indicates, total war acquires an electrifying charge in Badiou and other philosophers, whereas historians tend to characterize total war in terms of a comprehensive rupture. This historical rupture, precipitated by the collapse of liberal democratic orders throughout Europe, in Japan, and across Latin America in the interwar years (threatened to a greater extent by the ideological right than the left), witnessed mass destruction on a scale in the Second World War that eclipsed the First World War. If the deployment of more sophisticated implements facilitated this heightened scale of carnage, what stands out in retrospect is the erosion of former distinctions enshrined in war: between combatants and civilians; rural and urban combat; wartime casualties and organized mass murder.

As commentators have noted, historical actors of the Second World War harbored vitally different intentions from their precursors'. Despite its unprecedented scale of devastation, Gerhard Wedinberg argues, the First World War remained "quite traditional in its aims," with neither side intending the epochal changes that resulted from the state's ability to mobilize its vast industrial, material, and human resources in a total war. In the Second World War, however, the "*intent* was different from the start. A total reordering of the globe was at stake from the very beginning, and the leadership on both sides recognized this. . . . This was, in fact, a struggle not only for control for territory and resources but about who would live and control the resources of the globe and which peoples would vanish entirely because they were believed inferior or undesirable by the victors."[85] With respect to the question of intentionality, this summation strikes the right chord, but seems to imply that the frenetic effort to regulate desirable resources and undesirable peoples belonged principally to the illiberal sphere.

Unlike the (Marxist) concept of totality, the concepts of total war and totalitarianism are closely linked. They share an umbilical connection from which interwar advancements in military technology—especially aerial bombardment—along with new intentions to reorder the globe gave birth to the antiliberal aspirations espoused by the likes of Mussolini and Giovanni Gentile in Italy as well as by sophisticated thinkers like Jünger and Carl Schmitt in Germany. Ira Katznelson dates "total war" as a designation from 1921, when a Mussolini supporter and "prophet of strategic bombing," Giulio Douhet, believed that in the future, "war from the air could most effectively decimate civilian areas," and "wrote that 'the prevailing forms of social organization have given war a character of national totality—that is, the entire population and all the resources of the nation are sucked into the maws of war. And since society is now definitely evolving along this line, it is within the power of human foresight to see now that future wars will be total in character and scope.'" (In this usage, we see "totality" invoked from the ultraright, and in a way consonant with the idea of the totalitarian state rather than the Marxist concept.) Douhet's argument was adopted by interwar British and American military theorists who, according to Katznelson, "believed it could be possible to force an enemy to sue for peace by directing massive air attacks to destroy its industrial capacity and transport links and demoralize its densely concentrated" and vulnerable urban populations. In his 1930 text *Krieg und Krieger*, Jünger's notion of "Die total Mobilmachtung" circulated the idea of total military mobilization "into wider discourse."[86]

Yet as Sven Lindvqist emphasizes in his brilliant experimental work, *A History of Bombing*, the conception and realization of aerial bombing originates in a colonial encounter in the early twentieth century, when Italy deployed the air bomb in Tripoli in 1911. During the interwar years, Britain targeted Egypt, India, Iraq, Afghanistan, and Palestine beginning in 1919, and Spain tested the Moroccan village of Chechauouen in 1925. "Modern war is total," writes Lindqvist, "in the sense that it touches the lives and souls of every single citizen in the warring countries. Air bombardment has intensified the concept, since the entire area of the warring country has become a theater of war. 'The total war is a struggle of life or death and therefore has an ethical justification that the limited war of the 19th century lacked,' writes Ludendorff [who wrote *Der Total Krieg* in 1935]. Colonial wars were total for the tribes and peoples fighting for their lives, but for the enemy who could easily and painlessly crush them, these raids were 'immoral acts that do not deserve the exalted name of war.'" As the compilation of colonial episodes in *A History of Bombing* demonstrates, the still-widespread notion that colonial bombardment eludes the classic definition of total war provides the rationale for Lindqvist's reinterpretation of this history.[87]

In "Antinomies of Total War," Takeshi Kimoto reorients this phenomenon within the Asia Pacific theatre and the intellectual milieu of the Kyoto School of philosophy.[88] These thinkers articulated their aims and principles in a series of deliberations that took place just before the bombing of Pearl Harbor. Kimoto notes that this discussion did not center on the world war in general, but on the "greater East Asian war," which constituted a "war of worldviews." The unique status of total war did not derive from advancements in military technology, but rather from "the entire historical transformation of social structures, state regimes, worldviews, and technology. 'In short, total war represents the overcoming of modernity,' as Suzuki [Shigetaka] declares."[89] Some critics have seen the Kyoto School as galvanized by antiracist aims, but for Kimoto the eradication of white supremacy was at best subordinate to a broader ambition to surpass or "overcome" modernity. Kimoto stresses the world historical component of the Kyoto School's idea of total war, an "indignant" conception meant "ultimately [to] overcome Western modernity and lead to the construction of a new world order."[90] Overcoming modernity signified the transcendence of capitalism and imperialism; it meant capsizing the entire order the West has imposed on the non-Western world, which includes not only the economic sphere but also the (economically determined) imposition of derivative cultural styles, shallow materialism, mimicked aesthetics, and modernity's endless fascination with newness, which many Japanese thinkers saw as eroding stable and eternal values.[91]

But what kind of order, according to these thinkers, would follow from total war? For different reasons this answer is difficult to discern, not least of which involves the Kyoto's school's nullification of the very idea of a postwar world. Like their European counterparts, Kyoto thinkers negated ordinary social divisions during the war's unfolding, even obliterating temporal and spatial distinctions such as those between peacetime and wartime, war and postwar, the frontline and the home front. Total war was "indeterminate, endless."[92] Such negations of spatiality and temporality were necessary because, in the normal course of warfare (which entails a sequence of declaration of war, conflict, and eventual resolution), consideration *in the midst of war* of a peaceful postwar order would threaten to restore the very conditions that total war sought to overcome.

The Japanese context is relevant here because of that nation's anti-imperialist stance against the West and its ambiguous relationship to African American and anticolonial struggle—a relationship that arguably grew more ambiguous with the ascension of Hirohito in imperial Japan. Du Bois, who wrote dozens of articles on Asia, and several on Japan in particular, certainly saw Japan's world historical role as anti-imperialist, an alternative modernity bursting across the color line. One signal moment of convergence was the Paris Peace Conference of 1919 convened by the League of Nations.

Albeit with different motives and levels of influence, both the Pan African Congress of 1919 in Brussels and the Japanese delegation to the Paris Peace Conference of the same year appealed to the League to affirm the absolute equality of nations. Japan enjoyed representative parity with the major Western Allies (Britain, France, Italy, and the United States), with five seats in the conference plenary.[93] (Japan's proposal was approved by the majority of member nations but ultimately overturned by the League, chaired by Woodrow Wilson.) Yet what would happen to this Afro-Asian confluence of interest and feeling after the rise of Japanese imperial aggression? Notably, Du Bois's first trip to China was in 1936, in the midst of the national crisis of Japanese military aggression that would escalate until 1945. Though Japanese militarism conquered vast portions of the Pacific and the Asian mainland, with China and other major targets within the empire's crosshairs, this rapidly unfolding expansionism struck Du Bois as categorically different than Western imperialism.[94] European colonialism was one thing, Japanese anticolonial imperialism another.[95] Controversially, and stubbornly, he defended Japan's ambitions despite its ravages throughout Asia (as Du Bois later gravitated to Mao's China, he would be called upon to answer for this judgment).[96] He also seemed to countenance the view that Japan's success in industrialization—which enabled it to defeat a semi-European nation, Russia, in 1905, thus winning it pride of place in the anticolonial imagination—earned Japan the right, or at least placed the nation in the historical *role*, of a force that could realize an "Asia for the Asiatics" and inspire the Darker Races worldwide.[97]

The cross-historical tableau of totalitarianism sketched thus far might rankle some critics concerned with methodology and the analytical rather than imaginative purchase of concepts. Underscoring constitutive and temporally specific features of the totalitarian across history, culture, politics, and geography, some critics infer on the basis of this heterogeneity that the idea lacks precision and therefore eludes the grip of historiographical rigor. On this view, totalitarianism has the paradoxical status of being an ahistorical concept that historians employ all the time. But even if no perfect totalitarian regime exists, and even if none of the exemplary regimes achieved "the ideal of the absolute unity of leadership and of unlimited power," to concede this point does not mean that the concept is useless.[98] Following this logic, one might as well draw the same conclusion concerning the liberal democratic state, or any other state archetype for that matter. Whether one views the concept as indispensible or useless, progressive or reactionary, *some* idiom seems necessary to describe the politically extremist and destructive turn of events marking the century. Among contemporary thinkers, Tzvetan Todorov has emerged as perhaps the most eloquent interpreter of "the totalitarian experience," which he locates primarily in the Soviet bloc of which he has intimate knowledge. Unlike most antitotalitarian, anti-Soviet critics, however, Todorov has written on Western colonialism (in *The Conquest of America*), and stated elsewhere that one's perspective on the century depends on one's national or ethnic identity. "What counted most in the twentieth century—what allows you to make sense of it—depends of course on who you are," he writes. "For an African, for example, colonization and decolonization must presumably be the decisive political events of the past hundred years."[99] Similarly, since Western European countries were occupied by Nazi Germany and not by the Soviet Union, they "have direct scores to settle with Nazism, Fascism and Francoism but not with Communism."[100] And in noting a Manichean turn in U.S. culture, both in the market ethos of "ultraliberalism" (what most refer to today as neoliberalism) and military adventurism conducted in the name of human rights, Todorov detects a totalitarian shadow over U.S. foreign and domestic policy in the twenty-first century.[101]

Nonetheless, figures like Badiou and Todorov remain politically and philosophically opposed on the validity of the totalitarian experience. It's worth noting, however, that they share an affinity for the individual or collective heroic figure who emerges from that experience: in Badiou's general sense, the heroic figure is one who, propelled by fidelity to a truth, overcomes the normal limits of human possibility and in the event becomes a subject. In Todorov's specific sense, the heroic subject is the "figure . . . of the rescuer (sometimes called the Righteous). . . . Such people who, at the risk of their lives, help persecuted Jews or other victims of totalitarian terror." And yet their valorization of these respective figures betrays a crucial difference. Todorov celebrates a figure like Germaine Tillion, the anthropologist of Algeria who, during an outbreak of war, refused to take the side of either warring party in a moment that would have required her "to kill one to save the other."[102] It is less clear in Badiou's ethics that in a concrete situation of war such as Todorov recounts, one can avoid taking sides.

It is easy to be seduced by the dramatic flair and unabashed romanticism in the portrayal of Badiou's generic insurrectionists: "The sailors who threw their officers to carnivorous fish, the utopians of solar cities who opened fire in their territorial outposts, Quechua miners from the Andes with an appetite for dynamite! And the successive tidal waves of African rebels sheltering behind flaming leopard-skin shields in the colonial stench! Not forgetting the lone man who took down his hunting rifle and, like a suspicious wild boar, began to resist the aggressor in the forests of Europe."[103] Brazen in its identification of heroic insurrection with primordial masculinity, the imagery of this tableau foregrounds the fundamental difference in how each thinker sketches the picture of "political evil." Todorov is concerned with the capacity of ordinary and powerful individuals alike to commit atrocious acts in extreme or ultrarepressive social conditions. For Badiou, it seems that such actions are symptomatic of the blasé evil that resides within the human animal, anywhere and in all epochs. Redirecting attention away from practices of barbarism, his philosophy defines evil as the dereliction of individuals to transcend this limitation of the human and to rise to the occasion of subject-hood; to embrace this subjectivity in a perilous and righteous situation defines the good. In contrast to Todorov's scenarios, Badiou locates evil in the system of liberal capitalism and its defenders, not in the perpetrators of sadistic acts underwritten by a grand ideology. Political evil, on this view, is an inhumane and destructive regime that has enthroned itself as the best of all possible worlds.[104]

Influenced by Arendt and by Wolfgang Sofsky's classic *The Order of Terror: The Concentration Camp*, Giorgio Agamben's definition of the camp as the paradigmatic state of exception and symbol of totalitarianism points in another direction. Agamben defines "modern totalitarianism" (by which he generally means Nazism, but includes also democratic regimes) "as the establishment, by means of the state of exception, of a legal civil war that allows for the physical elimination not only of political adversaries but of entire categories of citizens who for some reason cannot be integrated into the political system."[105] In principle and in history, the state of exception, embodied by the proliferation of the camp, constitutes a pillar of modernity's exclusionary strategies and forms the basis of a universal history.

There is a sign posted to a road not quite taken in Agamben's representation of the camp as a state of exception. Noting the debate about modernity's first bona fide camps, namely the Spanish *campos de concentraciones* in Cuba in 1896 or the English concentration camps designed for the Boers at the turn of the century, Agamben writes: "What matters here is that in both cases one is dealing with the extension to an entire civilian population of a state of exception linked to a colonial war."[106] But as Agamben's postcolonial critics have observed, despite his emphasis on "the camp as the 'nomos' of the modern," the philosopher largely ignores colonialism, even Italy's production of bare life during its colonial heyday.[107] Implementing spatial control, surveillance, and mass violence, Italy's concentration camps in interwar Cyrenaica (present-day Libya) manifest all the features that define bare life for Agamben, but these institutions elude his representations of the camp as state of exception. A fog cloaks Mussolini's brutal invasion of Ethiopia, an event that has never figured prominently in the narrative of the Second World War, despite the dark preview it presented of fascist belligerence on the horizon.[108] (Incidentally, it is in this context that the NAACP, after the Second World War, leveraged the United Nations to prevent Italy from regaining its former colonies in Libya, Somalia, and Eritrea.)[109] If the omission of these presumably peripheral iterations of the totalitarian "promulgates the myth of the *Italiani brava gente*—of the Italians as 'good' and 'decent' colonisers"—it also forecloses a truly universal account of the camp as the fundamental biopolitical space of modernity that Agamben gestures toward.[110]

On the other hand, Agamben's rhetorical dissolution of the strict boundary between totalitarianism and democracy merits attention. It is not so much that Agamben identifies democracy with repression as much as he obscures the clean opposition between the two, imbuing a quasi-mystical affinity between fascist and democratic regimes (he is noticeably reticent, as other commentators have observed, about the communist regimes). This rhetorical maneuver is not a mystification, however, since it is grounded in modalities of biopolitics common to the United States and Germany (especially eugenics), or the proliferation of the "concentration camp universe" endemic to colonial democracy.[111] The difference, it seems, for Agamben is one of form and perhaps scale, as the following remarks suggest: "The contiguity between mass democracy and totalitarian states, nevertheless, does not have the form of a sudden transformation. . . . Before impetuously coming to light in our century, the river of biopolitics that gave *homo sacer* his life runs its course in a hidden but continuous fashion."[112]

Agamben's use of the word *hidden* is significant for registering continuities and discontinuities between liberal and illiberal modernity. "While democratic liberalism continually reimagines fascism as its monstrous Other," argues Nikhil Singh, "fascism might be better understood as its doppelganger or double—an exclusionary will to power that has regularly reemerged." For Singh, this reemergence manifests in "zones of internal exclusion within liberal-democratic societies (plantations, reservations, ghettos, and prisons); and . . . those sites where liberalism's expansionist impulse and universalizing force has been able to evade its own 'constitutional restraints' (the frontier, the colony, the state of emergency, the occupation, and the counterinsurgency)."[113] Clearly, these antidemocratic elements within democracy contrast sharply with the oft-repeated claims articulated during the 1960s concerning the quasi-totalitarian aspects of mass culture marking the consumerist and technologically advanced United States. Few today would countenance the 1960s idea that the mass-mediated, "soft" totalitarian culture of late capitalism threatened to transmogrify into anything like the systems enforced by the likes of Stalin. And yet the possibility of a symbiosis exists between the Frankfurt School notion of the "wholly administered society" and the sites of exclusion, enslavement, and incarceration that reflect what Domenico Losurdo calls the "soi-disant" character of liberalism: its emancipatory self-image crafted in the twilight of transatlantic slavery.[114]

As U.S. democracy sought to recreate its self-image following the military defeat of the Axis powers in World War II, "'totalitarianism' began to be defined as a Soviet and implicitly anti-Western phenomenon, [and] the origins of fascism within the political culture of Western liberalism became obscure."[115] If it is reductive, or even false, to insinuate that little more than ideology differentiates liberalism from totalitarianism, then there is also little doubt that the Allies' victory and postwar reconstruction initiatives tended to shield the former from mainstream associations with the latter. As the Cold

War gained momentum, U.S. presidents moved from insouciance to opposition to the old-style European imperialisms' clinging, desperately, to power at midcentury. If postwar America's ideological makeover distanced the nation from its secret sharers in colonial fascism, the writers featured in subsequent chapters of this book sought to restore this buried rapport to discourse in the international arena.

3

The Twilight of Empire

THE SUEZ CANAL CRISIS OF 1956 AND THE BLACK PUBLIC SPHERE

REGARDED BY MANY CRITICS as Langston Hughes's most original and enduring literary creation, the character of Jesse B. Semple—known colloquially as "Simple"—originates in an influential African American newspaper, the *Chicago Defender*, during the early 1940s. Born from the paroxysms and contradictions of world war, Simple embodies a working-class, uncensored, and irrepressible persona who repudiated anticommunism and U.S. racial democracy while ventilating for readers his romantic and quotidian problems.

Speaking freely on domestic and world events, Simple signified on the ironies of official pronouncements of American freedom and democracy in a streetwise idiom that resonated with Hughes's predominantly black readership. One reviewer for *The Chicago Defender* noted that Simple represented "millions of urban Negroes who have been largely voiceless in our short stories, novels and plays."[1] Though Simple's attacks on Jim Crow and Allied war rhetoric are well known, his commentary on geopolitical events apparently remote from African American interests has elicited less critical attention. Yet in a series of columns in the 1950s, Hughes employed the literary dialogue among other genres as a form in which to translate international politics into the Harlem vernacular and rhythm of black metropolitan life. During this period, the international event that claimed the attention of Hughes, and numerous other writers in the black public sphere, was the Suez Canal Crisis of 1956.

A legendary aura enshrouds the drama at Suez. In most accounts, the sequence of events unfolds in a rapid succession of scenes of daring decision making, elite power brokerage, passionate speech making, nuclear bluffing, military mobilizations, and intramural squabbles on all sides. As the story goes, the match that set Suez aflame was Egyptian president Gamal Abd al-Nasir's nationalization of the Suez Canal Company on July 26, 1956. In an unprecedented act of anticolonial defiance, al-Nasir (hereafter "Nasser") reclaimed the Canal Zone for Egyptian sovereignty, wresting the prized international waterway from British and French control. Despite worries about the consequences of nationalization, Egyptian citizens, Nasser's admirers in the Arab world, and Third World observers viewed this action as legitimate and an assault on the colonial order. Repossession of Suez was understood to reorient Egyptian history from colonial and neocolonial subjugation to a future of total independence and sovereignty. "We shall eliminate the past," Nasser announced, "by regaining our right to the Suez Canal."[2]

Nasser regained the right to the Suez Canal, but eliminating the past was a different story—at least that part of the past consequential for the present crisis. After Nasser's seizure of the canal, Britain and France, with Israel's cooperation, closed ranks when commercial and maritime interests were at stake, and in that way resurrected a formidable colonial past for operationalization in the present. In a dramatic action that struck even the Eisenhower administration as redolent of old-fashioned European colonial adventurism, Britain, France, and Israel colluded in a tripartite invasion of Egypt from late October to early November 1956, in a desperate, and ultimately failed, effort to regain control of the Suez Canal.

"Even American Negroes," writes Horace Cayton, "are affected by the plight of Egypt and stimulated by the dramatic, and dangerous, maneuvers of Nasser. A brilliant and talented painter with whom I lived this summer greeted Nasser's seizure of the canal with the same enthusiasm that he had for the Montgomery bus strike. And this man was not an unsophisticated man politically. A Negro political thinker in New York, who had devoted his life to a fight for civil rights said, perhaps in half-jest but with an undercurrent of deep emotional identification, 'If Nasser wants volunteers, I'm willing to take the first boat.'"[3] Despite this passage's fervent tone, its meaning and implications are far from clear. What were the sources of this "deep emotional identification"? Why did this apparently remote affair elicit as much "enthusiasm" as a national event, the Montgomery bus strike, with direct consequences for domestic racial politics? Did a critical mass, rather than a few zealous individuals, exist to mobilize on Egypt's behalf? Were other voices less sanguine about Nasser's "dangerous diplomacy"? Or were these sentiments simply emblematic of the broader anticolonial Zeitgeist marking the postwar era?

As the previous chapter indicates, one point of entry into Cayton's remarks is the historical precedent of the Italian invasion of Ethiopia in 1935, which animated the transnational black public sphere of that era. But Suez in 1956 was not Ethiopia in 1935. To be sure, many commentators analogized the crises in Ethiopia and Egypt, but the more precise context of these responses involves what Brenda Gayle Plummer calls the "two parallel processes in world history and Afro-American history [that] became evident by 1956." The first process, according to Plummer, reflected the dissatisfaction among Afro-Asian independence movements with the slow pace of decolonization, as well as the impatience among black Americans with desegregation; the resultant process witnessed acceleration on both liberation fronts.[4]

In what follows, I argue that literary texts like Hughes's dialogues—premised on the translatability of complex international events into ostensibly "simple" vernacular forms—make up part of a robust counter-discourse on the Suez Crisis in the black public sphere. Whereas Western officials deployed a set of containment strategies for the Third World—often reinventing the language of totalitarianism to fit the needs of imperialism—the black public sphere framed the crisis within an alternative geopolitical context, one that linked European aggression against Egypt with domestic attacks on black militancy, for example, or situated the conflict within a longer genealogy of the Scramble for Africa. Whereas Western officials cynically compared Egypt's leader to Mussolini and Hitler, black writers countered with alternately measured and hagiographic portrayals of

Nasser. My claim is not that the Suez Crisis impacted African American politics, domestically conceived, in any significant way. But the event did capture the literary and political imagination of African Americans, reigniting internationalist energies and highlighting the creative possibilities of nonalignment that were operational in the domestic struggle against segregation. As the black public sphere assimilated the lessons of Suez, this internalization also refracted outward, opening the public discourse to a more expansive terrain of geopolitical analysis. To substantiate this claim, this chapter shows how events at Suez precipitated black engagement with an array of often interconnected postwar dilemmas, from nuclear testing in the Sahara to the contemporaneous Hungarian Revolt to imperial projects closer to home such as the U.S.-controlled Panama Canal.

Like many African American representations of Africa, the black public sphere's response may shed little light on Egyptian or African history (which in any case is not my claim). The generally pro-Nasserist sentiment among black Americans, moreover, marks a tension with Egyptian interpretations of Nasser over the last half century—particularly for those who suffered under his repressive regime. But my conviction is that this counter-public discourse does reveal much of significance to black involvement in foreign affairs. This involvement formed part of a broader effort among blacks to pressure the U.S. state to sever its historical rapport with European allies on Suez. When Eisenhower rebuffed Anglo-French entreaties in support of this military adventure, and then threatened the British with financial sanctions, the president did so "out of concern that the United States would be associated with colonialism, either British or French."[5] The Eisenhower administration's unanticipated opposition to the Suez War must be understood in the context of mounting global public opinion in favor of Nasser and in disfavor of the tripartite invasion—a shift in perception that the black public sphere helped to engineer.

With Suez as a case study, this chapter delineates what kinds of global agency were possible for subaltern actors of this era, as well as what limits constrained their initiative. But the fact that subaltern actors managed to exercise significant agency *at all* vis-à-vis the superpowers is one of the more underappreciated aspects of the international situation of the 1950s. In an interpretive essay on the Cold War in Asia, Immanuel Wallerstein rejects a conventional narrative in which the superpowers are seen, indomitably, as ventriloquizing Third World actors and events. The underlying assumption of this narrative is that "anything important that happened in all those years was initiated by the US or by the Soviet Union." This assumption held that in order to understand what was going on anywhere in the world at any given time in the 1950s and 1960s, one had only to examine what the "US and/or the Soviet Union were doing and why they were presumed to be doing it." With this information, one could explain the geopolitical situation just about anywhere. But this narrative, according to Wallerstein, is "largely a fantasy" because it overlooks a counter-narrative that tended to upset the bipolar logic of the Cold War. In some cases, subaltern agency frustrated the desires of the superpowers or compelled them to enter conflicts they would have preferred to avoid. For Wallerstein, the example of the Cuban Missile Crisis—in which Castro's takeover of the Cuban Communist Party obliged the Soviet Union, reluctantly, to aid in its defense—is an exemplary case in point.[6] The Suez Crisis is another such case.

An experiment in historiography that traverses and intersects multiple events—U.S. desegregation, the Suez Crisis, the Hungarian Revolt—this chapter demonstrates how a pivotal year, 1956, stimulated diverse modes of black literary production that applied pressure to imperial and totalitarian formations in the democratic and communist spheres. If this chapter's experimental approach to periodization accords with recent initiatives devoted to global and transnational inquiry, it acknowledges that the transgression of national and other boundaries is not necessarily a satisfying end in itself.[7] If this end reflects how globalization shapes contemporary thought in ways scholars often fail to acknowledge, then a transnational approach, minimally, ought to demonstrate the conceptual or historical knowledge foreclosed by conventional periodization and national paradigms.[8] For this chapter, a transnational approach is necessary to show how the Suez Canal Crisis was not simply a European colonial affair, a flashpoint in the narrative of French and British imperial decline, as accounts of this event typically suggest: it reverberated far beyond the principle European and Middle Eastern actors involved, marking a crucial chapter within the history of decolonization as well as within the intellectual history of totalitarianism.

In the "whirlpool" of the Cold War, as Frantz Fanon astutely observes, "the statesmen of underdeveloped countries keep up indefinitely the tone of aggressiveness and exasperation in their public speeches which in the normal way ought to have disappeared."[9] Fanon's insight suggests that the celebrated defiance of Nasser's announcement implies that he did not move in a multilateral situation in which Egypt enjoyed equal status with the principal national actors involved. Rather, Egypt inhabited what we might call, adopting Alain Badiou's conception of membership and inclusion, a *singular* position in this geopolitical playing field. Badiou distinguishes the *singular* position from the *normal* and *excrescent* positions. In *Homo Sacer*, Giorgio Agamben crisply summarizes this formulation: "Badiou defines a term as *normal* when it is both presented and represented (that is, when it both is a member and is included), as *excrescent* when it is represented but not presented (that is, when it is included in a situation without being a member of that situation), and as *singular* when it is presented but not represented (a term that is a member without being included)."[10] Somewhat schematically, the United States and the Soviet Union can be understood as *excrescent* in this situation: though these nations are not present among the principal actors at Suez, their interests are disproportionally represented and shape the outcome of the entire crisis. The positions of France and Britain are *normal*, in the sense that they are both present in the situation and their interests are represented. In the singular role, Egypt is *present*—a member—but it is not represented on par with the interests of more powerful national actors.

But this geopolitical field of play was more fluid than this schematic arrangement suggests. The Third World innovation of nonalignment, of which Nasser proved to be an adept practitioner, held the potential to scramble these coordinates.[11] Empowering non-Western actors to capitalize on Cold War tensions, nonalignment enabled Nasser to level the field by maximizing Egypt's degree of representation on the world stage and by delegitimizing his country's aggressors.[12] This new measure of agency notwithstanding, few observers standing in solidarity with Egypt underestimated the significance of the Suez Crisis and the challenges Nasser faced.

The Suez Crisis, the Cold War, and Decolonization

In one *Defender* column, "Simple's World of Black and White," Hughes opens with Simple's expression of gratitude to "the Lord for making Negroes" and concomitant wish that "He had not made white folks." The first-person narrator replies that there are many races in the world beyond black and white, and "many more white folks in it than just the American variety." "You don't really want to wish white people out of existence, do you?" the narrator asks. "For example, the English, what have they ever done to you?"

With this question Hughes sets the stage for Simple's interpretation of the meaning of the rise of Egyptian leader Gamal Abdel Nasser and the Suez Canal Crisis for Western imperialism. Simple responds: "Tried to take my canal away from me."

> "Your canal?"
>
> "The Suez, which is the same as mine, since it belonged to my boy Nasser who is the Adam Powell of Egypt. Also, was it not the English which kept India down all them two or three hundred years until [Gandhi] fasted himself [*sic*] to death to get India free? No, do not talk to me about the English."

Simple's companion then asks him about the French—"white people" also, but hardly akin to the Dixiecrat variety. "Have you ever heard any Negro," the narrator continues, "say he did not love Paris?"

"Negroes might love Paris," replies Simple, "but ain't you ever seen that picture about French Guiana? I would hate to be black or white down there." Though he does not name this "picture," Simple is likely referring to the 1944 blockbuster film, *Passage to Marseilles*, set in the notorious penal colony named Devil's Island in French Guiana. Debunking the idea of a resplendent French civilization, egalitarian and hospitable to blacks, Simple's allusion to this film alerts readers to the reality of penal colonies like Devil's Island (where Alfred Dreyfus, coincidentally, was sentenced to life imprisonment following his conviction of treason), that were hidden from Western view in tropical colonial outposts. Simple then adds:

> "And what about them Arabs in Algeria, lots of them colored as me—and the French are running them ragged, chasing down their caravans with jeeps and tanks, and bombing their villages from the air. Some of my kin folks might be Arab."
> "Hardly likely," I said.

In this exchange, the narrator functions as a necessary counterpoint to Simple's proclivity for racial mythmaking: the idea that the Suez Canal in some way "belongs" to Simple, or that his ancestry might include Arab peoples. But were Simple's imagined kinships so preposterous? The dialogue form enables Hughes to introduce a skeptical alternative to Simple; by the conclusion of the dialogue, each has moved closer to the other's position, culminating in a reconciliation between racially passionate and dispassionate assessments of the crisis.[13]

For contemporary readers, Simple's reference to the Suez as "the same as mine" might suggest a questionable point of entry, though his remark's basis in a distant kinship was not uncommon at the time: Hughes was among several commentators who noticed a resemblance between Nasser and New York congressman Adam Clayton Powell (who also attended the Bandung Conference in 1955). For other readers, Simple's response might evoke a folksy Pan-Africanism that had been a powerful current within African American culture for at least the previous half century, or century and a half on some accounts.[14] But Hughes, employing his column as a pedagogical tool, employs rhetoric of racial kinship and solidarity to impress upon readers a more decisive lesson: the interface between racial and Cold War politics has created an opportunity to accelerate the processes of desegregation and decolonization.

If the West sought to convince the world that Nasser was Hitler reincarnated, black writers told very different stories about the audacious Egyptian leader. For all observers in the mid-1950s, Gamal Nasser appeared as a bold new contender in the international arena. Writers in the black press perceived that Nasser interrupted the seemingly intransigent logic of empire and set a fearless example for black America and the colonized world. His nationalization of the Suez Canal Company also sent a warning to the West; one of the first orders of business was the removal of the statue of Suez entrepreneur Ferdinand de Lesseps—for Egyptians, a sort of negative talisman—from the entrance of the canal. Thus Nasser was able to voice his oft-quoted slogan: "Lift up your head, brother, the age of subjugation is over."[15]

In this respect, Nasser's action represented as much an *ethical* as a *political* procedure. Irrespective of the economic and political consequences of nationalization—since these were, as his closest advisers stressed, unpredictable and potentially disastrous—Nasser insisted on the symbolic and ethical dimension of Suez: its seizure was meant both to restore national dignity and to precipitate Egypt's entrance into postcolonial modernity. Nasser's discourse concerning Suez was racially tinged—a necessary ingredient in decolonization, as Fanon pointed out ("Decolonization unifies that people by the radical decision to remove from it its heterogeneity, and by unifying it on a national, sometimes a racial, basis")—but there was a universal dimension in his demonstration to the Third World of a new mode of global agency.[16] This meaning of Suez resonated for many, but not all, writers in the black public sphere.

In my use of this term, I draw on Michael Warner's account of publics and counter-publics, especially his observation about gossip as a unique genre of public discourse. There is no shortage of print evidence on the subject of Suez, as the hundreds of black-authored newspaper reports, journal articles, fictions, and poems on the crisis attest; but this print culture also fomented a public dialogue in the genre of gossip, which the press both recorded and facilitated—even if print could not capture the varied meanings of a genre that by definition eludes codification.[17] Many accounts in the African American press, for example, allude to debates, lectures, and rumors about the crisis that were conducted in intimate spaces like the church or in social networks like the neighborhood uplift organization.

Part of this gossip, both oral and textual, included debates about the Soviet role in Suez. It was a subject ripe for impassioned discord among African Americans, especially in light of the Soviet Union's widely publicized crushing of the Hungarian Revolt that coincided with events in Egypt. The literary response to this crisis of Shirley Graham and W. E. B. Du Bois constellates many of the prickly issues surrounding the meaning of totalitarianism for the global anticolonial movement. For many black observers the simultaneity of these events provoked the following questions: Does the Soviet Union's support for decolonization outweigh what the West justifiably assailed as its totalitarian tendencies, dramatically in evidence with the repression of the Polish and Hungarian rebellions? Can the Communist bloc be understood as an anti-imperialist force given its occupation of east and central Europe, with whose plight many African Americans sympathized?

The debates this crisis fomented among African Americans are more illuminating, in my estimation, than a unified narrative of protest against colonialism, and a concrete situation like Suez furnishes a complex case study in expressions of solidarity and dissension, translation and misrepresentation, propaganda and counter-propaganda. But it is important to note at this point that the black American response to Suez was not, on the whole, dialogical with Egyptian actors—that is to say, though expressions in the black public sphere dovetailed in critical ways with Egyptian political sentiments, and diverged in others, these expressions nonetheless represent a discourse *on* Africa more than a dialogue *with* Africa.[18] But given the realities of geographical and cultural distance, to say nothing of the powerful American and European forces arrayed against transnational projects, it is remarkable that African American anticolonialism during the Cold War managed to form at all.[19] "In the absence of nation-state power and territorial sovereignty," writes Michael Hanchard, "Afro-Modern political actors have often utilized a combination of domestic and international institutions to redress situations of inequality for specific African-descended populations, much in the way that Jewish transnational political actors have operated on behalf of Jewish populations throughout the world."[20]

Moreover, the U.S. black public sphere's response reveals a significant historical shift in, if not a reversal of, what Paul Gilroy identifies in *The Black Atlantic* as a critical tendency toward African American exceptionalism. With bold efforts led by figures like Kwame Nkrumah and Nasser, the diaspora at midcentury shifts to developments on the continent, which black Americans observed with admiration and pride. Consider, for example, one commentator in the *Baltimore Afro-American:* "With the increased importance of Africa in the world and the UN, those of us who are of African descent can now take justifiable pride in the continent from which our forbears came. From now on we should refer to ourselves as Africans, rather than colored people or Afro-Americans or 'Negroes' when such designation becomes necessary."[21] In some instances, this admiration led African Americans to join postcolonial nation-building efforts in Africa, and in others, it renewed desegregation initiative domestically. For many black Americans, Africa's political efflorescence rendered previous brooding about their identification with the continent—often expressed in tones of ambivalence, loss, and estrangement—largely irrelevant.[22] One way to chart this evolution is to track how African American literary representations of Africa evolve from ambivalence about and occasional endorsement of colonization around the turn of the century to unqualified enthusiasm about decolonization by midcentury.[23] In light of the unequivocal character of black anticolonialism at midcentury, however, the response to Suez is compelling because of the nuance in geopolitical analysis made possible once colonialism is unambiguously repudiated.

During the nation's Red Scare, the United States identified certain forms of anticolonial nationalism and internationalism as imbued with the same radical energies of communism, and therefore as dangerously susceptible to Soviet appeals. Consequently, U.S. officials sought to apply more insidious, less outwardly antagonistic strategies of containment to the Third World.[24] These approaches were necessarily less hostile than those applied to international communism, since the United States, as the previous chapter discusses, also sought to recruit Asia and Africa to the liberal capitalist sphere. Since their national interests often conflicted, American and European officials shared no common agenda with respect to management of decolonization, but they did agree on certain containment strategies.

One of these strategies drew on the "historical lesson of the 1930s," otherwise known as the Munich syndrome: the notion that the liberal democratic bloc, after once capitulating to Hitler's demands, can "never again" appease totalitarian initiative. At midcentury, European officials reshaped this lesson in accordance with imperialist foreign policy and Cold War objectives. Rhetorically, these efforts were desperate, indicative of imperial power on the wane. Mass media genres like documentary film and political cartoons portrayed Nasser as a volatile dictator, perhaps with imperial ambitions of his own in the Arab World and Africa, edging perilously close to the Soviet sphere. Other depictions showed Nasser playing the Americans and Soviets off each other whenever the opportunity presented itself. Yet these images of Nasser merely reflected broader anxieties about the swelling ranks of increasingly defiant Third World leadership. Would the West be able to manage these upstarts? When confronted with conflict in the Third World, European and American officials characterized Egypt's Gamal Nasser, Ghana's Kwame Nkrumah, Algeria's Ben Bella, and the Congo's Patrice Lumumba as (African) incarnations of the totalitarian spirit—generally presumed to be imbibing this spirit from Soviet agents, though more often than not Third World leaders sought to resist Moscow's influence.[25]

Outraged by what they perceived as the Egyptian leader's intransigence and recklessness, the governments of England and France painted the event with apocalyptic imagery. Prime Minister Anthony Eden, French premier Guy Mollet, and other officials and media outlets sought to shape public opinion and garner majority support for the invasion by comparing Nasser to Mussolini and Hitler.[26] To be sure, many Egyptian victims of Nasser's repression saw his regime as authoritarian, and for those who suffered imprisonment and torture, a prison outside of Cairo is presumably little different from a camp in Europe or a Soviet gulag. Though set in sixteenth-century Egypt, contemporary Egyptian novelist Gamal al-Ghitany's celebrated 1974 novel *Zayni Barakat*, for example, is read by critics as an allegory for Nasser's turn toward authoritarianism and an expression of "postcolonial disappointment" for a promising revolution sliding into totalitarian rule. As a prisoner under Nasser's regime, al-Ghitany knew this dark experience from the inside.[27] In his novella *That Smell*, originally published in Arabic in 1966, Egyptian writer Sonallah Ibrahim, who joined the Egyptian Communist Party in 1954, depicts a surreal social order under Nasser, who persecuted the country's communists while simultaneously developing closer Soviet ties. In these two prominent literary cases, we see one fissure between the black literary left's valorization of Nasser and the works of Egyptian communists and other dissidents that tell a starkly different story of the celebrated leader's internal governance.

The image of Nasser's totalitarian legacy, then, is not unfounded, yet the European campaign waged against him in the 1950s was not aimed at the leader's domestic repression. Nor was it merely a rhetorical expression of frustration with Nasser's steadfastness; it was apparently calculated to garner Western (mainly U.S.) support for the reacquisition of the Suez—and when that support was not forthcoming, to justify the tripartite invasion by France, England, and Israel of Egypt in late October of 1956. "So it was as early as 1956," Badiou recalls, "in order to justify the Anglo-French invasion of Egypt, some Western political leaders and the press did not hesitate for a second to use the formula: 'Nasser is Hitler.'"[28] U.S. officials saw Nasser as a troublesome instigator, but employed less vituperative language in the public domain to describe the Egyptian leader.

Beyond the instrumental function of this propaganda campaign, does not the exaggerated characterization of Nasser as Hitler expose the West's denial and repression of the totalitarian governance it exercised in its own colonies? Despite more dispassionate reports to the contrary, for figures like Eden and Mollet, Nasser was immune to reason and negotiation. To this extent, the resilient trope of native irrationality renders the Egyptian leader a "native" in Fanon's specific sense of that term. "As if to show the totalitarian character of colonial exploitation," writes Fanon, "the settler paints the native as a sort of quintessence of evil. . . . The native is declared insensible to ethics; he represents not only the absence of values, but also the negation of values. He is, let us dare to admit, the enemy of values, and in this sense he is the absolute evil."[29] In this passage,

Fanon intuits the repressed guilt of exploitation projected onto the native. This inscription of the native leader legitimates the suspension of what is called normal diplomatic relations and international law, since the leader in question, a negation of values, is said to belong outside the sphere of rational intersubjectivity.

That European officials would mobilize propaganda against Nasser is not surprising, but the cultural and media productions themselves command attention. Throughout the late summer and fall of 1956, a time when newspaper reading in Britain reached its apex, the British government launched an intense propaganda campaign designed to capture "the moral high ground" in advance of any military intervention against Egypt. Nasser "was presented as a fanatic nationalist, and the autocratic nature of his regime was emphasized. He was a second Hitler whose 'plunder' put the world 'at his mercy' and who therefore could not be 'appeased.'" But as the Suez Canal Company, historian Tony Shaw notes, "was registered as an Egyptian company under Egyptian law and Nasser had indicated that he intended to compensate the shareholders at ruling market prices, the cabinet admitted that 'from the strictly legal point of view, his action amounts to no more than a decision to buy out the shareholders.' . . . And yet, if Nasser had not even technically broken the law, how could the British government brand him as an international criminal whose act merited the strongest retaliatory measures, even armed force outside of the United Nations?" Eden's solution was to manage (if maladroitly) the British press—inducing it to portray Nasser as a menace to world order and commerce and British imperial integrity—while the government concealed its true agenda, insisting "that its only objective was to 'restore' international control of the Suez Canal. This called for media manipulation of the highest calibre, not to mention Machiavellian nature."[30] In its campaign, Eden's administration sought to address publics beyond the British, and among these the U.S. public garnered the highest priority. Nasser's provocative arms deal with Czechoslovakia in September of 1955—negotiated before the United States and the United Kingdom humiliated Nasser by reneging on their loan to Egypt for the construction of the Aswan Dam—fanned the flames of these propaganda initiatives.[31]

Though the association of all manner of phenomena with Hitler or Nazism has become banal and even kitsch in recent years, in the 1950s this association exploited the most potent historical memory available in global consciousness. Wary of Nasser's Pan-Arabism and support for the Algerian Revolution, French Prime Minister Guy Mollet unequivocally adopted the comparison of Nasser with Hitler.[32] He labeled Nasser's manifesto *The Philosophy of the Revolution* the Egyptian version of *Mein Kampf*.[33] Mollet's position was extreme, and calibrated with an eye toward the raging French-Algerian War, but as the conflict gathered momentum the Nasser-as-Hitler equation saturated British and French media.[34] For his part, Nasser skillfully deployed his own propaganda (Nasser was among the first leaders in the region to use the mass power of radio, launching the Voice of the Arabs station in 1953) to assail imperialism—and appropriately for this genre, apparently exaggerating Egyptian civilian deaths from the Anglo-French aggression.

Even as astute an analyst of the postwar scene as Karl Jaspers describes Nasser's anticolonial assertiveness as a dangerous species of totalitarianism. Though conceding that European colonialism had no legitimate place in the global postwar order, and deriding Europe's pronouncements about its "inviolable economic demands" ("Europe absolutely needs Middle Eastern oil"), Jaspers nonetheless appears to conflate Hitler's expansionism with Nasser's reclamation of the Suez. Arguing for Western democratic solidarity in the face of new totalitarianisms, he saw the Soviet and American pressure on Britain and France to withdraw from Egypt as "the most foolish and most disgraceful moment of contemporary Western politics," the first time that America, under Eisenhower, "had made herself independent of British and French Asian policies!"[35] "It has been claimed," he later writes, "that localized force is not aggressive, that atrocities, terror, violations of foreign rights within territories recognized as sovereign do not affect world peace. What a mistake! It means to permit the growth on foreign territory—as in Hitler's Germany or Nasser's Egypt—of realities and attitudes bound to lead some day to external aggression. By restricting our own use of force we would breed another, threatening force, protecting its borders until it was ready to cross them." In this instance, the United States' departure from Europe's "Asian policies" was a categorically different move in foreign policy than Jaspers's general characterization of colonialism as unacceptable in the postwar world. On this theory, major power aggression against a minor nation is justified if that action will prevent a new totalitarian threat, like Nasser, from gaining legitimacy and expanding his political and territorial sphere of influence.

In order to justify British actions at Suez to the nation's citizens and the world, a series of informational films on Suez appeared shortly after the conflict. Three short films in particular—*Suez in Perspective* (1957), produced by the Central Office of Information, in London, together with two other short films, *The Facts about Port Said* (1956) and *Report from Port Said* (1956)—defined the Middle East's strategic importance while exonerating Britain, retroactively, for any presumed malfeasance in the war's aftermath. Displaying a map of the region's vital air and sea routes, the narrator of *Suez in Perspective* stresses that the region is the most "vital source of oil in the whole world." Only five years before the Suez affair, Iran's Muhammad Mossadegh in 1951 nationalized the Anglo-Iranian Oil Company—then the world's largest oil refinery—evicting its British employees from Abadan Island.[36] Many observers of the Suez affair saw in the actions of Mossadegh, who was overthrown in a coup organized by the United States and Britain in 1953, an inspiration to Nasser.

The narrator proceeds to a capsule history of the Palestine-Israeli conflict as the backdrop for Suez. Omitting Britain's colonial encroachments in the region, the narrator portrays the beleaguered empire in a thankless role: as guardians of the British mandate in war-torn Israel. After the 1948 war between Israel and Egypt, which concluded with an armistice that "never blossomed into peace," a revolution followed in Egypt, "and before long Nasser became dictator." Deftly, the film combines a portrayal of Britain as a dutiful presence in the region, bound to its former semi-colonies by an imperial noblesse oblige, with an ominous narrative of revolutionary Egypt as a fledgling postcolonial nation on the brink of mass repression: the latter story a consequence of Egypt's hasty and unceremonious rupture with the imperial center. The film then reenacts the Czech arms deal as the pivot of Egypt's drift into the communist sphere: "a significant visit to Egypt was paid by Mr. Shepilov, Russia's new Foreign Minister," the narrator intones. "It seemed certain that a bargain was being struck between Nasser and Shepilov, and so it proved to be." If *Suez in Perspective* constructs a narrative of Nasser's rise as a transition from spontaneous authoritarian to Soviet puppet, the film also betrays the need felt among the government to disseminate a defensive, ex post facto account of the event for a confused public still licking its wounds: the Suez Crisis, after all, hastened the end of the British Empire, and one function of films like these was to furnish meaning and narrative coherence in the wake of British imperial diminution.

Adapting the durable conflation of fascism and communism to the Egyptian crisis, *Suez in Perspective* connects Soviet encroachments in Egypt with the memory of Nazi Germany, foreshadowing Nasser's regime as the next installment of political terror in the strategically vital Middle East. Against the backdrop of menacing horns and dark images of a Nasserist cult of personality on the streets of Cairo, the narrator continues: "Cairo in 1956 reminded many of Berlin in 1939. Warlike signs in the streets and violent radio propaganda starkly reveal the mood of Egyptian defiance. Nasser himself created and sustained the uncompromising and bellicose attitude. He had made no secret of his intentions. He had already seized the Canal. What next?" If the scene's imagery and the acoustics of *Berlin in 1939* blared the historical lesson of the 1930s, some viewers might also have connected the film's juxtaposition of Nasserism and Nazism with the encroachments of Hitler's regime into the Middle East during the 1930s and 1940s, when the Nazis distributed pamphlets and broadcasted propaganda over shortwave transmitters in Egypt and throughout the region.[37] If this campaign eluded viewers, many would remember when Nazi Germany, aware of the canal's vital importance to British imperial strategy, bombed Suez in March 1941, halting maritime traffic for several days.

Along with corporate sponsors like British Petroleum and the Imperial Tobacco Company, the British government produced a series of films in the 1950s and 1960s highlighting a moderate, transitional path to independence—one that sustained the umbilical connection between center and periphery through economic interdependence. In these productions, Nigeria—by avoiding the temptations of communism and the antics of Nasserism—appears to embody the model for African independence. Films like *Three Roads to Tomorrow* (1958), *Giant in the Sun* (1959), and *Nigeria—The Making of a Nation* (1960) highlight the west African nation as a fledgling postcolonial state successfully negotiating modernization and tradition.[38]

Whereas the Suez documentaries were filmed in black and white (the better to project the Manichean struggle between democracy and totalitarianism), *Three Roads to Tomorrow* is filmed in Technicolor, ostensibly to capture the vibrancy and vividness of Nigerian life.[39] In this film, three young Nigerian men—Reuben, an Igbo from the eastern coast; Moyo, a Yoruba from Lagos; and Ado, a Muslim Hausa from northern Nigeria—embark on a journey from their respective locales to enroll in Ibadan University. "This is a short tale of three long journeys which changed three lives," the British narrator announces against the backdrop of a map of Nigeria. "Modern transport and oil power have changed the lives of all Nigeria and that is part of our theme. The rest of our theme is where these journeys lead." Sponsored by the British Petroleum Company (formerly the Anglo-Iranian Oil Company, before Mossadegh nationalized its operations in the early 1950s), *Three Roads to Tomorrow* shows the new friends socializing in a co-ed dancehall near campus where they chat against the backdrop of a band playing highlife music.

Taking one last ride down the river ("forever the haunt," says the narrator, "of unpredictable habits") with his father before departing for Ibadan, Reuben's canoe collides with a boat in the river, which causes him to miss the bus that will take him to Ibadan. Luckily, a green and yellow British Petroleum truck is nearby, whose driver is happy to give him a lift. In precolonial times, the film suggests, it would be very difficult for men from remote regions of a vast country like Nigeria to come into contact. But "you can go places in Nigeria these days," thanks to the installation of modern systems of communication and transportation ("cars, buses, power boats, diesel trains, aircraft"). Figuratively you can go places, too, since the nation's commitment to higher education promises upward mobility and opportunity. When the friends alight from a plane to Ado's village in northern Nigeria, a multidirectional sign at the airport indicating the distance to several world metropolitan centers—Nairobi and Sydney, Natal and Lima, Dakar and Los Angeles, Rio de Janeiro and Buenos Aires, Mecca—confirms Nigeria's status as a global hub and lodestar of postcolonial modernity.

The Idea of a Suez Canal

Though the idea of a canal connecting the Mediterranean and Red Seas has roots in antiquity, the project of a modern Suez Canal was the brainchild of Claude-Henri de Saint-Simon (1760–1825), the exponent of a so-called Christian socialism and prophet of the scientific organization of industry and society. Experiencing a philosophical epiphany in the wake of the American and French Revolutions, Saint-Simon helped to found the famed École polytechnique, an institution premised on the Enlightenment belief in the perfectibility of humankind. This institution aspired to establish a religion of science and industry, "with Newton as its patron saint," that would usher in an era of "limitless prosperity, universal peace, and international harmony." Saint-Simon soon garnered an energetic retinue of scientists, philosophers, and engineers eager to actualize his philosophy. At the turn of the nineteenth century, according to Zachary Karabell, his apostles "began to spread the gospel of Saint-Simon, one of whose tenets was that the world should be linked by canals. The passion for canals was part of an overall philosophy of industrialization."[40]

One of Saint-Simon's most influential disciples, Barthélemy-Prosper Enfantin, continued the master's intellectual projects after his death in 1825. One of Enfantin's priorities was the creation of the Suez Canal, the meaning of which is embodied in a poem he (or one of his followers) composed:

> It is we who will make
> Between ancient Egypt and old Judea
> One of the two new routes from Europe
> To India and China

Later, we will pierce the other
At Panama

Suez
Is the center of our life's work
There, we will do something
That the world will witness
In order to confess that we are
Males[41]

With its blend of romanticism, enlightenment progressivism, capitalist imperatives, and orientalist imaginaries, this poem distills complex gender geopolitics. The verb "to confess" in the poem's strange denouement points to Saint-Simon's doctrine of "New Christianity" that emphasized a widening chasm between the masculine and feminine, a cleavage just as indicative of anxieties about French imperial masculinity as of the orientalism surrounding the canal's construction. Beset by such doubts, the creators of Suez assumed that the magnitude of the venture would force the world to "confess" that the Saint-Simonians were, indeed, "males."

But the successful completion of the canal would also manifest momentous, even world historical, implications that were conceived in curiously gendered ways.[42] In Karabell's interpretation, the engineers, poets, and designers of the canal imagined Egypt and Suez as the "nuptial bed" in a symbolic union of East and West. Perhaps it is an overstatement, but not by much, to say that this vision of the canal constituted nothing less than a cosmic solution to the divisions of East and West, the culmination of a long-sought-after geopolitical unity based on Enlightenment ideals and ancient oriental traditions. "A canal through the Isthmus of Suez would consummate the marriage," Karabell writes, "because then the waters of the Mediterranean would mingle with those of the Red Sea. The Mediterranean was the sea of the West, of the male Occident. The Red Sea was of the female Orient. Once the canal was cut, the two seas, representing the two eternal forces of life, would join, and the duality that had sundered the planet would be no more."[43]

Drawing on similar Orientalist tropes, other observers created poetry of doubt about the Suez venture. In 1869, the British periodical *Punch* published a poem that responds directly to the dream of the canal as a union of East and West:

> What of this piercing of the sands?
> What of this union of the seas?
> This grasp of unfamiliar hands,
> This blending of strange litanies?

Here, the language of union and blending, the grasping "of unfamiliar hands," signals interracial or intercultural anxieties common to Victorian England, but the poem's concluding stanza strikes a menacing chord that has less to do with the threat of racial amalgamation:

> Answer in vain the Sphinx invites;
> A darkling veil the future hides:
> We know what seas the work unites,
> Who knows what sovereigns it divides?[44]

Suez could also be imagined as reversing the flow of an earlier, decisive historical moment: the intellectual traffic between the Muslim world and Europe in the multicultural, religiously plural context of al-Andalusia, or Islamic Spain, when the diffusion of enlightenment crossed cultures in complex ways but emanated from the south. In the Enfantin poem cited previously, notice the poem's allusion to a future time when "we" will "pierce" another canal, this one in Panama. Constructed with an intricately segregated labor force at the turn of the twentieth century, the history of the Panama Canal mirrors the history of the Suez Canal. Years later, the fallout of Suez prompted the black public sphere to interrogate the United States' own imperial waterway in central America.

If Saint-Simon conceived the modern idea of a Suez Canal, historical memory then and now credits Ferdinand de Lesseps as the project's modern progenitor (precolonial Egyptian history records previous attempts to create such a canal). A French diplomat in Egypt descended from a line of distinguished French diplomats in Egypt, Lesseps (1805–94) intercepted Saint-Simon's ecumenical vision of a world connected by canals.[45] Among his many challenges was convincing European investors of both the moral significance of this project (its meaning for world enlightenment) and its enormous potential for profit, both for individual shareholders and for Europe as a whole. At the same time, he had to satisfy Egyptian leadership who suspected its country would fare ill in the deal, Ottoman officials who largely controlled Egypt, and Islamic authorities who perceived this project as an affront to Islam.

Lesseps pursued this vision indefatigably, over decades, until the canal's completion in 1869. Invariably, once the canal was operational, Lesseps's resolve at Suez enshrouded the diplomat in a mythical aura that led subsequent observers to cast him in the role of a romantic hero.[46] Lesseps wanted to register his own heroic efforts, and to acknowledge the contributions of certain continental supporters, in undertaking the colossal project against all odds. A tribute to German proponents of the endeavor, a document by Lesseps indicates a broader continental understanding of Suez. In his preface to a German-language text published in 1859, Lesseps confidently asserts: "The old idea of piercing the Isthmus of Suez has become a practical one. Europe is itching to bring competition to this enterprise; the time for theoretical persuasion has passed, the time for positive execution commenced."[47] For helping to realize this enterprise, Lesseps thanks the German press profusely: "Now is the time for me to express . . . the important role undertaken by the German press in these preliminary struggles. It has ceaselessly supported, defended, and explained our project; it has unmasked malevolent adversaries and convinced benevolent spirits; it has exposed the immense utility of a canal connecting two seas for civilization, for the future, and for social [relations] of the whole world. These distinguished publicists have defended our cause with passion [*chaleur*, 'heat'], with enthusiasm, with spirit and sagacity." In his tribute, Lesseps praises Germany's cosmopolitanism compared with other nations that are more concerned about special interests than about "the general interest of humanity."[48]

The Saint-Simonians, and their descendants like Lesseps, sought to achieve their vision of a world shrunken by canals and other engineering projects. A French variant of what Saree Makdisi calls (the predominantly British project of) "romantic imperialism," this imagining of Suez coincides with a multinational order of colonization in nineteenth-century Egypt marked by a new disciplinary regime instantiated by French, British, and Ottoman officials who shared governance of the country, often from afar.[49] In a Foucauldian analysis of the colonization of Egypt, Timothy Mitchell shows how the country became subject to a foreign military regime defined by surveillance, confinement, forced conscription, and other disciplinary methods "administered by French and Egyptian military engineers and scholars, many of whom had been trained at the École polytechnique in Paris, including several disciples of Saint-Simon and of his secretary Auguste Comte." In the second quarter of the nineteenth century, Mitchell writes, "the people of Egypt were made inmates of their own villages. A government ordinance of January 1830 confined them to their native districts, and required them to seek a permit and papers of identification if they wished to travel outside. . . . The village was to be run like a barracks, its inhabitants placed under the surveillance of guards night and day, and under the supervision of inspectors as they cultivated the land—and surrendered to the government warehouse its produce."[50] On this account, Egypt's nineteenth-century disciplinary regime and the Suez Canal project share an intellectual foundation in Saint-Simonian tenets of progress, industry, science, and prosperity. At the same time, in contrast to this conventional Enlightenment narrative, a mystical element infuses the literary imagination of Suez. This mysticism pervades the assortment of European poetic hymns to Suez as well as the private thoughts of Lesseps himself, who sought confirmation of his mission in the cosmological world of ancient Egypt. "In his journal entries," notes Mia Carter, "De Lesseps read Egyptian meteors and ancient texts as evidence that he, and he alone, was destined to build the canal." Other critics warned that Lesseps, by cutting a strait through the isthmus, was creating a battlefield where wars of the future would be waged.[51]

"The fundamental event of the modern age," writes Martin Heidegger, "is the conquest of the world as picture." In its essence, *world picture* does not refer to a picture of the world but the world conceived and grasped as picture. The phrase *to get the picture* "throbs with being acquainted with something, with being equipped and prepared for it."[52] For the picture of the colonial world, the map was a primary technology of conquest. As he wrote to the British consul general in Egypt, Lesseps spoke of the necessity of the Suez Canal as self-evident to anyone concerned with progress who bothered to look at a map.[53] Thanks to elaborate reenactments and representations of Egypt like those on display at the Paris World Exhibition of 1889, the material map interacted with a mental map already fixed in the European imagination. One effect of these representations, writes Mitchell, "was that the Orient more and more became a place that one 'already knew by heart' on arrival. . . . [Théophile] Gautier, for his part, wrote that if the visitor to Egypt 'has long inhabited in his dreams' a certain town, he will carry in his head 'an imaginary map, difficult indeed to erase even when he finds himself facing the reality.' "[54]

Lesseps infused his own mental maps in the construction of Suez, but his remarks also underscore the material map's imaginary significance to global commerce that Joseph Conrad portrayed so memorably in *Heart of Darkness*. "Now when I was a little chap I had a passion for maps," Marlowe recalls. "I would look for hours at South America, or Africa, or Australia, and lose myself in all the glories of exploration. At that time there were many blank spaces on the earth, and when I saw one that looked particularly inviting on a map . . . I would put my finger on it and say, 'When I grow up I will go there.' " As Marlowe matures, he realizes that spaces on the map are no longer "blank," but he also comes to understand that these spaces are yet to be filled with commerce, specifically the trading companies powered by industrial steamboats and buttressed by European capital. Marlowe is especially captivated by "a mighty big river, that you could see on the map, resembling an immense snake uncoiled, with its head in the sea, its body at rest curving afar over a vast country, and its tail lost in the depths of the land." This river, of course, is the Congo River, and Marlowe "remembered there was a big concern, a Company for trade on that river. Dash it all! I thought to myself, they can't trade without using some kind of craft on that lot of fresh water—steamboats! Why shouldn't I try to get charge of one? I went on along Fleet Street, but could not shake off the idea. The snake had charmed me."[55] If Lesseps was naïvely committed to the gospel of progress, *Heart of Darkness*, with its visionary undercurrent of rapacity and violence belying colonial projects in Africa, imbues the dialectic of enlightenment into the "blank" or naïve space of the French diplomat's mapping of Suez.

Writing with echoes of Conrad, Richard Wright highlighted the negative dialectic in the enlightenment project of canal construction in the Third World. "I passed those famous canals," he reports from Bandung,

> which the Dutch, for some inexplicable reason, had insisted upon digging here in this hot mudhole of a city. (Indeed the site of Jakarta itself must have been chosen for its sheer utility as a port and with no thought of the health of the people who had to live in it.) I saw a young man squatting upon the bank of a canal, defecating in broad daylight into the canal's muddy, swirling water; I saw another, then another. . . . Children use the canal for their water closet; then I saw a young woman washing clothes only a few yards from them. . . . A young girl was bathing; she had a cloth around her middle and she was dipping water out of the canal and, holding the cloth out from her body, she poured the water over her covered breasts. . . . A tiny boy was washing his teeth, dipping his toothbrush into the canal.[56]

If Wright's graphic imagery anticipates what by now have become stock representations of global capitalism gone awry in the Third World, his description's intrusion of warped human bodies into a landscape of lapsed modernity produces a jarring juxtaposition with nineteenth-century European projections.

Before the dark perceptions of Conrad and Wright, many observers valorized Lesseps's herculean efforts. "The story of the Suez Canal," wrote one British historian in 1876, "together with that of its persevering projector, who has finally succeeded in triumphing over all obstacles and all opposition, has ever seemed to contain something romantic, and to be worthy of being made the subject of a regular narrative."[57] Fitzgerald's wish for a romantic narrative of the canal's construction and the heroism of its architect was realized cinematically, in 1938, with the American film *Suez* starring Tyrone Power in the role of Lesseps (though in a portrayal so liberally fictionalized that Lesseps's descendants were rumored to have sued the film's producers, unsuccessfully, for libel).[58] In any case, it is easy to imagine how Lesseps's unflagging pursuit of his dream adapted easily to melodramatic cinematic conventions and the American mythos of rugged individualism.

The film pairs de Lesseps with a love interest, Toni Pellerin (played by French actress Annabella, born Suzanne Georgette Charpentier), who faithfully buoys Ferdinand against his doubters and enemies. During a trek through the Egyptian desert, Ferdinand and Toni take refuge from a brief storm near an ancient ruin. When the showers clear, they find a rainbow on the horizon; Toni recalls the adage about a pot of gold lying at the other end. Ferdinand then notices that one end of the rainbow pours into the Mediterranean, the other into the Red Sea. "What a pot of gold for the world," he muses, "if they could be joined, the Red Sea and the Mediterranean." He points to water in an old gulf, "just as it was centuries ago when the Phoenicians sailed through." Whimsically, he wonders aloud: "Can you imagine ships sailing right through here where we're standing?" He pictures modern ships and steamers sailing a short trade route through the East. "It could be done." Ferdinand's destiny has arrived. "I was looking for a way to serve France," he says. "And . . . I think I found a way to serve the world."

When Ferdinand informs the viceroy of Egypt of his aim to form a stock company in Paris in order to finance the construction of the canal, he asks for his "Highness's assurance that Egypt will lease to us the necessary strip of territory." Chiding Ferdinand for his youthful brashness, the viceroy replies: "The wisdom of age will teach you the folly of tampering with the work of Allah." "What man can accomplish," Ferdinand replies, "is also the work of Allah."

The villain of *Suez* is Louis Napoleon (played by Leon Ames), who uses Ferdinand as a pawn to consolidate his power and squelch nationwide riots. In this subplot, Napoleon prevails upon Ferdinand to convince his father, a powerful player in France's opposition faction, to relent in his subversive activities for the security of the nation; in exchange, Napoleon promises to give the "canal project my full support." Aware that this deal might betray his father and comrades, Ferdinand reluctantly agrees to the exchange. Later, Napoleon divulges to his wife, Countess Eugenie (played by Loretta Young), that he intended only to use Ferdinand as a political expedient. "No, you don't understand," she pleads, "his family and his honor, they mean so much to him." Suddenly a mouthpiece for the totalitarian spirit sweeping the 1930s, Louis Napoleon intones: "In a crisis the individual is unimportant. The state is everything. The state—France, foundering in the fallacy of democracy, its industries idle, its army weak, crippled by the poisonous doctrines of the republicans and the socialists—has called me, to save it from anarchy and ruin. I had to act swiftly, ruthlessly—but act. If I have used young de Lesseps badly, it was for a great end." The countess replies, "You have used me too, Louis." In the film's dramatic weaving of plot and subplot, *Suez* manages to valorize colonialist enlightenment in the Americanized figure of Ferdinand *and* to assail totalitarianism in the figure of Louis Napoleon.

Naturally, Ferdinand overcomes these various challenges to proceed apace with the canal project. When construction begins, the scene portrays the *corvée*, the Egyptian peasant laborers or fellahin contracted to dig the sand by hand. In nineteenth-century Egypt, the *corvée* (the French expression "*Quelle corvée!*" translates as "What a chore!") was a mass of forced peasant laborers whose equivalents can be found throughout history as the labor pool in such grand construction projects as the pyramids of Giza or the Great Wall of China, but who were differentiated from previous indentured servants as subjects of colonial Egypt's new disciplinary regime. Neither the property of the state nor of the private companies contracting their labor, the fellahin who made up the *corvée* were nonetheless recruited and forced to work under the threat of violence.

In the film, the *corvée* appear (racially) differentiated, with the dark-skinned laborers clothed only in pants, and the lighter-skinned laborers fully clothed and donning a fez. In one scene, an assistant informs Lesseps that "Arab raiders" captured a shipment of blasting powder from Port Said. "*Arabs*," Lesseps replies, quizzically and with eyes downcast, before ordering another shipment from Marseilles. In the next scene, the "Arab" raiders, stealing into the night, plant bombs along the banks of the canal, which they detonate the following day during the peak of construction. The explosion kills or maims mostly the *corvée*. As agents of a racialized terrorist plot, the nameless and faceless Arab raiders are deprived of motive, backstory, or any substantial integration into the narrative. Do they see the canal as an affront to Allah, as the viceroy implied, or as a project of imperialism? Did Ottoman leaders—who objected to the idea from the start—order the attack? Rhetorically, this differentiation constructs a native Egyptian simplicity that accepts modernization without question versus a foreign Arab insurgency whose recourse to terrorism, without any specified motive, leaves this action intelligible only as a response to the encroachment of modernity. The film quickly leaves this episode behind, which is meant to symbolize one trial in a succession that the mythical hero must overcome to realize his ambition. Yet this scene's enactment of racialization depicts the Arabs as foreign agitators to be distinguished from the native fellahin, who are enthusiastic about the construction of the canal; they are told and believe the canal will reap untold benefits for Egypt and the world.

These benefits redounded mostly to Britain and France, even though many nations, East and West, profited from this massive undertaking. Constructed under French direction, the Suez Canal moved closer to British control toward the close of the nineteenth century, an acquisition enabled by Disraeli's purchase of a 44 percent stake in the Suez Canal Company in 1875 as well as by the British occupation of Cairo in 1882. In addition to increasing global commerce and flows, especially the transport of oil, the canal shortened the distance between England and India by thousands of miles (to Bombay by 4,543 miles, to Calcutta by 3,667 miles, and to Melbourne by 645 miles) and facilitated the transport of British troops and warships to and from India and the Far East.[59] British prime minister Anthony Eden declared the Suez Canal "Britain's life-line," and it became known, alternately, as "the spinal column" and "the jugular vein of the British Empire."[60] At the Bandung Conference in 1955, Indonesia's president Sukarno located the Suez Canal at the center of what he designated the "Life-line of Imperialism" stretching from the Strait of Gibraltar to the Sea of Japan.[61] The prospect of Britain relinquishing control of the canal to an upstart like Nasser unnerved the empire's leadership. "During the past few weeks," Clarissa Eden remarked in a scintillating metaphor, "I have sometimes felt that the Suez Canal was flowing through my drawing room."[62]

Nasserism and the Black Public Sphere

Anticolonial leaders and intellectuals articulated their own "lessons" from the Second World War. They, too, emphasized the catastrophic possibilities of global conflict in the nuclear age and drew on the raw historical memory of genocide, racial subjugation, and total war. Arguably, in few crises of the 1950s was this memory more resonant than during Suez, a conflict observers from East and West believed had the potential to combust into a third world war. Deeply cognizant of this potential, African Americans writers and publics identified with Nasser's defiance but tempered their support with respect for imperialism's capacity for military retribution.

Langston Hughes's dialogues are just one example among many texts produced by black writers alert to the Suez Canal crisis, a Cold War crucible insufficiently acknowledged among postcolonial critics for its role in emboldening Third World activists and accelerating the global anticolonial movement. Whereas for Western foreign policy officials Nasser's nationalization of the canal constituted a rupture in international order and a threat to global commerce, for many (though by no means all) writers in the black public sphere, the Suez Crisis represented a watershed in the unfolding drama of decolonization. Inspired by Nasser's boldness and the implications of nonalignment, African American observers published running commentary on the Egyptian leader's risky maneuvering at Suez. In 1956 Du Bois published a poem, "Suez," rhapsodizing about the moment when "Young Egypt rose and seized her ditch/And said 'What's mine is mine!'" Writing on the eve of Nasser's death in 1970, the playwright, historian, and second wife of Du Bois, Shirley

Graham, wrote a two-part article, "Egypt Is Africa," before publishing a full-length biography of Nasser.

In leading African American newspapers like the *Pittsburgh Courier*, the *Baltimore Afro-American*, and the *Chicago Defender*, writers and public figures such as George Schuyler, Horace Cayton, Benjamin Mays, and Marguerite Cartwright published running commentary on the meaning of Suez for American diplomacy, black political interests, and the global anticolonial struggle. The black press was central not only in reporting on developments at Suez but also in connecting readers with churches, universities, and community centers where they could attend lectures by experts and visitors to the region.[63] In this respect, the black press helped to instantiate what Dominick LaCapra (drawing on Hans Blumenberg) refers to as a "concept of 'reoccupation,' whereby sites and even conceptual or imaginary spaces that were formerly invested by religion (a chapel or church, for example) may come to acquire 'secular' functions that nonetheless remain imbued with sacral dimensions."[64] Yet it was unnecessary for African Americans to reinvest religious spaces with worldly concerns, since the black church had always blended the political and spiritual, the sacred and secular meanings of liberation.

In these middle-class spaces, one name everyone would have known is Ralph Bunche. The central role in Suez of the African American diplomat Bunche—who organized the United Nations' first peacekeeping force, charged with securing the withdrawal of the invading British, French, and Israeli forces from Egypt—heightened attention to the crisis in the black public sphere. Bunche, who brokered a difficult 1949 armistice between Israel, Lebanon, Egypt, Syria, and Jordan that earned him a Nobel Peace Prize in 1950, was the subject of numerous reports in the African American press. As a Howard University professor, diplomat in the State Department, and then permanent U.N. Secretariat, Bunche provided African Americans with a familiar figure and compelling personal narrative through which to enter discussions on Suez. His role in the crisis also brought to the fore fissures within black public discourse.

Bunche's role symbolized the broader, if ambiguous, incorporation of African Americans into the U.S. political structure during the historical convergence of desegregation, decolonization, and anticommunism. If the State Department in the 1950s supported interracial delegations of writers, jazz musicians, and artists to project a positive image of U.S. race relations on the global stage, then Bunche, the genuine diplomatic article, could be upheld on either side of the color line as proof of black assimilation and integrity within the precincts of U.S. foreign policy: as the highest-ranking U.S. official of the United Nations, tasked with resolving the most explosive problems in the Middle East and Africa, Bunche also advocated for racial equality and full citizenship for African Americans. "For those who sought to defend the United States against the challenges of communist ideology," writes Charles P. Henry, "Bunche was proof that American democracy was superior to Soviet and Chinese totalitarianism."[65]

For thinkers like Du Bois, however, American democracy in the 1950s was not clearly superior to Soviet and Chinese totalitarianism. In the December 1956 issue of *Masses and Mainstream*, a left-wing magazine published from 1948 to 1956 (and successor to the defunct *New Masses*, published from 1926 to 1948, the "principle organ of the American cultural left"),[66] Du Bois published his poem "Suez." The poem begins:

> Young Egypt rose and seized her ditch
> And said: "What's mine is mine!"
> Old Europe sneered and cried: "The bitch
> Must learn again to whine!"
>
> The British lion up and roared
> But used his nether end
> Which raised a stink and made men shrink
> As world peace seemed to rend.
>
> Dull Dulles rushed about the world,
> His pockets full of gold
> Ike sadly left his game of golf
> And talked as he was told:
>
> "Lord God! Send Peace and Plenty down
> And keep on drafting men

Send billions east and so at least
No income tax shall end."

Adlai essays with polished phrase
To say the same thing less
And prove without a shade of doubt
Both parties made this mess.[67]

Amid the confusion, fear, propaganda, and private discussions following the tripartite invasion of Egypt in late October, it was difficult to know what parties were responsible for this prelude to war. Yet many observers of the Suez invasion, on both sides of the Atlantic, in the British Parliament and in the Eisenhower administration, suspected "collusion" between Britain, France, and Israel.[68] In "Suez," Du Bois also suspects collusion—but principally between the United States and Britain ("Both parties made this mess").

It is easy to imagine how, in the absence of reliable information, an anti-imperialist like Du Bois would suspect British and American collusion: recent history had already suggested an Anglo-American rapprochement in covert operations in the Third World. But on my reading, the poem articulates with a socialist hermeneutics of suspicion more than it exposes an uninformed perspective (however knowledgeable Du Bois may have actually been).

After pitting "Young Egypt" against "Old Europe" and the "British lion" in the poem's first two stanzas, the third stanza shifts, significantly, to American culprits: John Foster Dulles, Dwight Eisenhower, and Adlai Stevenson. Note that these U.S. officials are named, whereas the principle British and French actors—even the notorious Anthony Eden—are not. The seventh stanza of "Suez" situates Israel in the affair.

Young Israel raised a mighty cry:
"Shall Pharaoh ride anew?"
But Nasser grimly pointed West,
"They mixed this witches' brew!"

A supporter of Israel since the nation's inception, Du Bois cautions the new state—precariously located in the Afro-Asian world—against becoming a pawn of imperialism:

Israel as the West betrays
Its murdered, mocked, and damned,
Becomes the shock troops of two knaves
Who steal the dark man's land.

Du Bois, as Melani McAlister observes, "refused to posit Nasser as the ruler of a metaphorical 'Egypt of colonialism and imperialism.' Instead, Nasser points toward the West, where the 'witches' brew' of the Suez invasion has made Israel into a pawn for colonial power." In 1948, the year of Israel's founding, Du Bois wrote articles recalling the "supertragedy" of the Holocaust ("a slaughter so vast and cruel that we will not be able to realize what happened to six million human beings in Eastern Europe during the Second World War until years have gone by"), affirming the legitimacy of the nascent state, and calling on President Harry Truman to aid in its establishment.[69]

Israel's role in the Suez Crisis elicits a stern reproof from Du Bois. In the poem, Israel's collusion with Britain and France has "betrayed the suffering of the Jews, its own 'murdered, mocked, and damned.'"[70] The impression conveyed, however, is cautionary, not condemnatory: Du Bois warns the vulnerable new state to resist the temptations of imperialist collaboration. Yet what stands out in the previous stanzas is the poem's insinuation that the United States—not Britain and France—was the principle instigator of the invasion. This rhetorical move raises questions: Did he believe that U.S. officials, contrary to their public statements, in fact orchestrated the invasion? Or did his commitment to communism lead Du Bois to misrepresent the American role in Suez? And given the poem's concluding encomium to the Soviet Union, did ideology also lead Du Bois to dismiss the Hungarian Revolt as an event choreographed or "bought" by American interests? And was this insinuation meant to neutralize or divert attention from the Soviet quashing of the revolt in Budapest? In Badiou's philosophy, one measure of a subject's relation to a truth procedure, particularly in emancipatory politics, involves her response when thrust into a decisive situation or "point." For Du Bois, might the conjuncture of the Suez and Hungarian crises constitute one such decisive point?[71] If so, what is the status of truth in this procedure, as the poetics here foregrounds an ideological and political rather than empirical truth?

Du Bois was unique among prominent writers in embracing an explicitly propagandistic definition of art. "We have raised Propaganda to capital 'P' and elaborated an art," writes Du Bois in the interwar years, "almost a science of how one may make the world believe what is not true, provided the untruth is a widely wished-for thing like the probable extermination of Negroes, the failure of the Chinese Republic, the incapacity of India for self-rule, the failure of Russian Revolution."[72] Whereas Du Bois previously believed that knowledge was the solution to racism, which he viewed as a problem of ignorance, later in life he seemed invested in propaganda as a form to counteract reactionary politics.

To take Du Bois at his word that all art is, and should be, propaganda, is to read "Suez" as exemplary of this genre, a text mobilized during an intense anti-Nasser campaign executed principally by Britain, but with much aid from France and Israel.[73] Du Bois sought not only to propagate a pro-Nasserist interpretation of Suez but also to extol the virtues of the Soviet Union and international communism, especially in light of Nikita Khrushchev's support of Nasser. At this historical moment, many of Du Bois's contemporaries on either side of the color line resisted the binary logic of the Cold War by adopting one or another position on the anti-Stalinist left or the stance of nonalignment. Immune to the anticommunist effluvium of the era, Graham and Du Bois resisted a noncommittal approach. Why? Chapter 4 takes up this question in more detail, but at this point we can note that although many commentators view Du Bois's communist poetics and politics in terms of negativity—as a gesture of defiance or resignation from the receding promise of American democracy—another approach is to ask how this affiliation enabled him to read the geopolitical scene in a manner foreclosed by liberalism, nonalignment, or the anti-Stalinist left positions. Even Du Bois's misidentification of the agents of the invasion sheds new light on how anticommunism shaped developments at Suez.

Reputedly, the catalyst for suspicions of U.S. involvement was Dulles's unceremonious withdrawal of America's offer to help fund Egypt's Aswan Dam project—a factor widely cited in Nasser's decision to nationalize the canal.[74] (In his meeting with Nasser, Nehru reportedly agreed that the tone of this announcement displayed the "arrogance" of "these people.") Du Bois's portrayal of Dulles is ambiguous: Is the poem meant to depict the secretary of state, who "rushed about the world" with his "pockets full of gold," as a globe-trotting robber baron or war profiteer? Or was the gold in his pockets meant to suggest that Dulles promiscuously used the nation's wealth in order to pay off certain actors, reshaping the postwar order in accordance with U.S. interests?[75]

"Suez" remains ambiguous on this point, and certainly the matter of U.S. entanglements in the crisis was more complex than the poem's denunciatory language suggests. But in light of the anticommunist foreign policy marking the "special relationship" between Britain and the United States, the suspicion of these governments as collaborators was not entirely wrongheaded—for the same reason that the Eden regime was shocked that the Eisenhower administration refused to support war on Egypt. To be sure, the British and American positions differed during the Suez talks: Eden had already considered overthrowing Nasser, whereas Eisenhower and Dulles apparently sought only to keep him outside of the Soviet sphere. If "Egypt finds herself thus isolated from the rest of the Arab world," Eisenhower noted in his diary, "and with no ally in sight except Soviet Russia, she would very quickly get sick of that prospect and would join us in the search for a just and decent peace in that region."[76] Britain and America differed on other objectives in the Middle East: the Baghdad Pact, which the United States refused to join, or on relations with Saudi Arabia, for example. Despite these disagreements, "the United States and Britain could co-operate on an immediate programme of seeking to put pressure on Nasser and weaken his influence."[77] More significant, the fact that both nations, as recently as 1953, colluded in a coup of Iran's daring leader Mohammed Mossadegh, provides some justification for Du Bois's suspicion that "without a shade of doubt / both parties [Britain and America] made this mess."

Ultimately, of course, it was Eisenhower's administration that publicly criticized the aggression and doused the fire of world war with the threat of economic sanctions on Britain. Suez demonstrated that U.S. economic power could both ignite and extinguish a geopolitical crisis: in the first instance, by revoking aid for the Aswan

Dam and thus humiliating Nasser; in the second instance, by withholding economic support for Britain that in turn forced the military withdrawal of this U.S. ally from Egypt.[78] With respect to the latter scenario, America demonstrated the scope of its power, perhaps *the* measure of imperial sovereignty in the mid-twentieth century: the ability of one empire to dictate to, and then financially to undermine, the world's previously dominant empire.[79]

In *Epic Encounters*, Melani McAlister identifies four major foreign policy concerns that shaped U.S. involvements in the Middle East after the Second World War: a "military and strategic" concern about the region's susceptibility to communist domination—a threat amplified by the Middle East's position at the nexus of trade routes and communication lines connecting Asia, Africa, and Europe; a sense of religious attachment to the region; U.S. support for the new state of Israel; and concern about "access to Middle Eastern oil at favorable prices."[80] To this last concern it is worth adding that U.S. policy sought not only to keep this commodity available to the West but also to deny the Soviet Union access to it.[81] Among these four overlapping concerns, anxiety about the encroachment of communism combined with a quasi-missionary imperative to "save" vulnerable countries from the Soviet scourge, imbuing this foreign policy objective with a special moral force.

This heightened emphasis on Middle Eastern affairs, historians have noted, marks a sea change in U.S. foreign policy during the 1950s and beyond. In 1941 political relations between the United States and Arab countries were minimal, but by late 1956, notes Salim Yaqub, "American officials believed that only the United States could keep the region from falling under Soviet domination."[82] During Truman's administration (1945 to 1953), Middle Eastern affairs were not a major priority in foreign policy, despite the nation's increased involvement in the region during the Second World War and Roosevelt's late effort to cement ties between the United States and Saudi Arabia. The Middle East remained a priority for European, and especially British, strategic interests; European economies relied on Middle Eastern oil during the immediate postwar years, but the U.S. economy was not yet dependent on that oil. Whereas the Truman Doctrine, oriented around communist encroachments in Europe, declared that it "must be the policy of the United States to support free peoples who are resisting attempted subjugation by armed minorities or by outside pressures," what became known as the Eisenhower Doctrine seemed to shift geographic focus from Europe to the Middle East and other Afro-Asian countries with a strong communist presence, like Indonesia. "Whatever else Suez had shown, President Eisenhower drew the conclusion that the Middle East had become a major arena of action, and in March 1957 he secured a joint resolution from the U.S. Congress permitting him to intervene with U.S. military forces if need be. Ike's mandate, soon termed the Eisenhower Doctrine, aimed squarely at the pan-Arabist appeal of Nasser."[83] Syria had recently joined Egypt in forming the United Arab Republic, but Eisenhower hoped to prevent other countries, like Lebanon and Iraq, from aligning with Nasser. This hope motivated Eisenhower's decision, in 1958, to send Marines into Lebanon with the aim of reinforcing pro-American, anti-Nasser factions in that country. In addition to deploying covert operations, Eisenhower's foreign policy also "aimed at discrediting Nasser's neutralist program by forging a coalition of conservative Arab regimes willing to side openly with the United States in the Cold War."[84] Though such coalitions did emerge briefly, they could not withstand the popularity of Nasserist sentiment in the region.

With his speech's focus on the communist threat, Eisenhower's allusion to the Suez Canal Crisis downplays the heightened attention accorded to the region in the 1950s. But where exactly was the region? The European effort to demarcate territory previously known as the "Orient," as Edward Said observed, originates in the early-fourteenth century, but the calibrations of postwar U.S. foreign policy necessitated tortuous efforts to define anew what came to be known as the "Middle East."[85] Writing in the wake of the Eisenhower Doctrine, commentators in journals like *Foreign Affairs* spoke to how geographical quandaries intersected, and conflicted, with political priorities. In 1958, one veteran U.S. envoy to western Asia noted that the "Middle East" is "not a clearly defined geographical term; it exists chiefly in the minds of diplomats." As evidence, he cites the publication in the *New York Times* of four maps of the Middle East "as defined by Secretary Dulles, the British Foreign

Office, and two leading dictionaries. Each of them encompassed a different area; in none did the borders coincide."[86] In 1960 a historian of Ottoman Turkey, Roderic H. Davison, asked rhetorically, "Where Is the Middle East?" What exactly, these commentators wondered, constitute the unifying elements—language, culture, religion, ethnicity, geography—of this regional designation? Did any unifying logic exist, or did the definitions simply shift to accommodate British or American interests at given points in time? Not until the Second World War does the "Middle East," notes Davison, become a "strategic concept imposed from without by British interests."[87] By the mid-1950s, the "Middle East" was a coinage of recent vintage in U.S. foreign policy; previously the State Department contained only an Office of Near Eastern Affairs.

In addition to reaffirming the anticommunist stance, Eisenhower sought to distance the nation from the nakedly colonialist adventurism typified by the Anglo-French-Israeli invasion of Egypt, which had been conducted without the consent or knowledge of U.S. officials. In his second inaugural address on January 21, 1957, Eisenhower spoke on the theme, "The Price of Peace," recalling the previous year's tumult in Egypt and Hungary. "From the deserts of North Africa to the islands of the South Pacific," Eisenhower intoned, "one third of all mankind has entered upon an historic struggle for a new freedom; freedom from grinding poverty. Across all continents, nearly a billion people seek, sometimes almost in desperation, for the skills and knowledge and assistance by which they may satisfy from their own resources, the material wants common to all mankind." In what by the late 1950s had become a de rigueur pronouncement, the president said, "The divisive force is International Communism and the power that it controls." But a "fierce and mighty force" of dissidence is sweeping across the Soviet bloc, he added.

"Budapest is no longer merely the name of a city; henceforth it is a new and shining symbol of man's yearning to be free." Beyond the "general resolve" needed to defeat international communism, history had summoned the United States to an expansive, resplendent role in global affairs, one that embraced conflicts from the grandest to the minutest scale. "We are called to act a responsible role," Eisenhower asserted, "in the world's great concerns or conflicts—whether they touch upon the affairs of a vast region, the fate of an island in the Pacific, or the use of a canal in the Middle East. Only in respecting the hopes and cultures of others will we practice the equality of all nations."[88] If Eisenhower's emphasis on the nation's heroic role in history appears continuous with American exceptionalism, crises like Suez forced the United States to break, at least provisionally, with European colonial aggression.

Though Eisenhower's second inaugural address makes no mention of domestic race struggles, a subject he addressed in numerous other speeches, the president and his cabinet were fully aware of desegregation's reciprocal impact on international and particularly Third World affairs. In September of 1957, Eisenhower was embroiled in the crisis at Little Rock, Arkansas, where he had reluctantly ordered federal troops to enforce court-ordered integration measures in the public schools. The president's decision to send troops to Little Rock sparked a famous confrontation between Eisenhower and the governor of Arkansas, Orval Faubus. Exploited by the Soviets and Communist China, the Little Rock crisis, lamented Dulles, "was ruining our foreign policy. The effect of this in Asia and Africa will be worse for us than Hungary was for the Russians." Though Eisenhower sympathized with the Southern opposition to desegregation and held conventional views about race, his administration could not risk the international blowback that capitulation to the Dixiecrats would have entailed.[89]

Despite the Eisenhower administration's stand in the Suez affair, the Soviet Union nonetheless appeared, undoubtedly from the perspective of anticolonial critics, to take the lead in Egypt's defense. Meanwhile, the administration's efforts to depict the Soviet Union as an imperialist power to the Third World largely foundered. In his "World at Large" column, Horace Cayton points to race as the elephant in the room of Suez. For Cayton, though "it is obvious—an inescapable fact—that the Western colonial nations are white and the people they dominate in the Middle East, in Asia and in Africa are not white, this reality is glossed over for fear of the frightful thought of the world rising up in wrath and in turn dominating the whites."[90] Seizing another opportunity to exploit Western vulnerability in the Third World, the Soviet Union, according to Cayton, implored the Bandung nations to reconvene to discuss the Suez affair.[91]

In 1953 Hughes had already endured a hearing before the House Un-American Activities Committee and wanted no more attention from this commission. But the Soviet Union's crushing of the Hungarian Revolt and other contemporaneous crackdowns made demurral on Soviet support a legitimate response for former black fellow travelers. It had become difficult for an anti-imperialist of any stripe to laud the Soviet role in Suez while the Khrushchev regime crushed uprisings in Poland, East Germany, and Hungary. The simultaneity of these dramatic world events raised thorny questions not only about the Soviet Union's status as a champion of the darker races but also about the meaning of anti-imperialism itself: Could the Soviet Union be viewed as an anticolonial ally when it brutally colonizes its own Eastern European neighbors? Could anticolonial thinkers who valued Soviet backing in the nuclear age ignore the plight of Hungary and Poland? However they imagined the anticolonial bona fides of the Soviet Union, communist and leftwing activists of color could not ignore these questions. But thinkers like Frantz Fanon shifted the terms of debate.

In *The Wretched of the Earth*, Fanon highlights the colonial massacres of the 1940s and early 1950s that supposedly went unnoticed, but then argues that the Cold War changed this state of affairs: colonial aggression in the non-Western world was now globally visible, thanks in large measure to the communist sphere—a claim that does not hinge on the credibility or stoutness of Soviet anticolonialism. "In 1945," writes Fanon, "the 45,000 dead at Sétif could pass unnoticed; in 1947, the 90,000 dead at Madagascar could be the subject of a simple paragraph in the papers; in 1952, the 200,000 victims of the repression in Kenya could meet with relative indifference." By highlighting these tallies, Fanon critiques the liberal tendency to enumerate and memorialize the victims of fascism and communism while ignoring the West's own colonial victims. But rather than attributing this indifference to racist devaluations—whereby the lives of the colonized merit less representation and security than European lives—Fanon ascribes this disproportion, somewhat elliptically, to "international contradictions" that "were not sufficiently distinct." However, Fanon's meaning becomes clearer when, abruptly, the text switches from a discussion of earlier colonial wars to the proxy wars being fought in Asia and the events in Hungary and Egypt: "Already the Korean and Indo-Chinese wars had begun a new phase. But it is above all Budapest and Suez which constitute the decisive moments of this confrontation [between liberal democracy and communism]." With the Korean and Indo-Chinese wars representing a "new phase," Fanon's allusion to "international contradictions" seems to refer to the emergence of proxy wars as the emblematic Cold War battleground.

But why did Budapest and Suez "constitute the decisive moments of this confrontation"? Were these events analogous or simply contemporaneous? Fanon does not clarify the difference, as he sees it, between the state repression of Hungarian protestors and the colonial adventurism of Suez. But the difference between the colonial wars of Sétif and Kenya and the proxy wars then being fought in Asia and Africa involves the magnifying effect of the Cold War rivalry. "This competition [between capitalism and socialism] gives an almost universal dimension to even the most localized demands," he writes. "Every meeting held, every act of repression committed, reverberates in the international arena." Fanon's use of the word "repression" (*répression*)—which he uses largely in reference to colonial struggle but in this context includes Soviet power ("Budapest")—is intriguing. This ambiguity suggests, somewhat perversely, that repression perpetrated by the Soviet Union, no less than imperial aggressions committed by European powers, redounds to the Third World: it keeps the Cold War contest alive. In contrast to what Fanon imagines as earlier colonial massacres trapped in the margins of global consciousness, even "localized" Third World conflicts transformed into universal expressions of a grand ideological struggle; reciprocally, the colonial dimension imbues the struggle between capitalism and socialism with a planetary, world historical character. Fanon does not specify how each moment "reverberates in the international arena," but no doubt the growth of media technologies like the newsreel and television—Anthony Eden, for example, sought to control the BBC's tenacious reportage on the Suez Crisis—amplified this ripple effect.[92]

"Strengthened by the unconditional support of the socialist countries," Fanon continues, "the colonized peoples fling themselves with whatever arms they have against the impregnable citadel [*la citadelle inexpugnable*] of colonialism. If this citadel is invulnerable to knives and naked fists, it is no longer so when we decide to take into account the context of the Cold War."[93] Allowing for Fanon's use of hyperbole, I don't think that this passage naïvely regards the support of socialist countries as "unconditional." But by this act of inscription, does Fanon not issue the socialist countries a challenge, and with it a solemn (and perhaps unwanted) reminder of obligation? This reminder was consistent, after all, with Khrushchev's public sacralization of national liberation struggle in 1961. I expand on the political implications of this maneuver in Chapter 5, on Shirley Graham Du Bois, who develops this logic into a rhetorical strategy, but for now want only to note that what might appear as political naivety actually represents a tactic of nonalignment. What this tactic could not circumvent, as Fanon well knew, was the kind of covert procedures—as opposed to full-scale war, which commanded global attention—that the CIA undertook across the nonaligned world, including in the Congo, where Fanon's friend Patrice Lumumba was assassinated by political rivals supported by Belgium and the United States.[94]

Between the Eisenhower administration's desire to win the propaganda war and the actuality of covert operations, nonaligned actors often relied on Soviet reinforcement. Previously restricted to "knives and fists" in the face of Western industrial weaponry, the Third World could now, minimally, leverage the threat of Soviet technology, even its nuclear arsenal. In addition to its public condemnation of the tripartite invasion, the Soviet Union, via Czechoslovakia, outfitted Egypt with over $200 million in advanced weaponry in 1955. Though such reinforcement was alarming from the U.S. and British point of view, it is worth noting Nasser's skillful exercise of the nonalignment principle, which enabled his access to arms and other support while remaining more than nominally independent of Soviet control. In a chilling private communiqué to Britain, France, and Israel, Soviet premier Nikolai Bulganin intimated that the USSR was prepared to attack Britain if the Suez War continued. "In what position would Britain have found herself," the communiqué stated, "if she herself had been attacked by more powerful states possessing every kind of modern destructive weapon? And there are countries now which need not have sent a navy or air force to the coasts of Britain but could have used other means, such as rocket technique."[95] Although this note was later seen as a nuclear bluff, the notion that such military backing by the communist sphere was an illusion (held by the Third World) or self-serving (of the Soviet Union) is beside the point. Western regimes, as the black public sphere understood, could not ignore these actions.

Writers like Fanon and Cayton champion the Soviet role at Suez and in the Third World but remain within the discursive frame of nonalignment. This frame permits tribute to the Soviet Union, and to putatively communist regimes, but resists affiliation. By contrast, Du Bois's aggrandizement of the Soviet Union leaves no doubt about his stance in the Cold War. (Suez and Hungary followed months after Khrushchev's shattering "secret speech" to the Communist Party's Twentieth Congress of February 24, 1956—published in the *New York Times* on June 5, 1956—that revealed Stalin's immense crimes and denounced the cult of personality surrounding his reign.)[96] After cheering "that great black hand / Which Nasser's power waves," Du Bois's poem ends with a panegyric to the Soviet Union.

> The Soviets in blood and tears
> Have made their socialism strong
> The West quite frantic in its fears
> Has tried to stamp it to the ground.

Again, it is easy to infer that "Suez" furnishes further proof that Du Bois had become a dupe of the Soviet Union, but that reading forecloses the possibility that he was propagandizing in a specific way, nudging the communist sphere in a Third World direction. This prodding entailed a mutual obligation: black glorification of the socialist project that would thrive but for the determined depredations of the West.

At the same time, other observers of the confluence of Suez and Hungary contended that the U.S.S.R. exploited, or even welcomed, the Suez Crisis since it diverted attention from the Hungarian Revolt. On Hungary, Du Bois's poem ventures a riskier proposition:

> This cannot be, it's but the sight
> Of private capital's sad plight.
> Fear makes America feel free
> To buy revolt in Hungary.

For observers who viewed Budapest as an authentic expression of rebellion, the poem's insinuation that "private capital" purchased revolt in Hungary contained an inadvertent irony: supporters of Hungarian resistance impugned the United States for instilling false hope—over the airwaves of Radio Free Europe—that should the people rebel, the U.N. would step in with military assistance.

In "Suez," Du Bois parts ways with African American and Third World observers who praised Eisenhower's break with European colonial aggression. By the mid-1950s, Du Bois could justly claim that anticommunist hysteria had taken its toll not only on him personally but on American democracy generally. The alliteration in the paradoxical formulation "Fear makes America feel free" lyricizes what was for Du Bois a dispiriting state of affairs: anticommunist anxieties strangled the imagining of any socioeconomic order outside the boundaries of liberal capitalism. Yet the poem's suggestion that America's "fear" fomented rebellion in Hungary is surprising insofar as it attributes too much agency to U.S. intervention in this circumstance and shows little compunction about the Soviet government's repression of the uprising. Du Bois, then, goes beyond the Bandung position on the Soviet sphere, which held roughly that the occupation of Eastern and Central Europe is disturbing and warrants criticism but does not belong in the category of modern colonialism, which was a white supremacist practice imposed on the darker nations. As Dipesh Chakrabarty notes, Ceylon's prime minister, Sir John Kotelawala, caused some consternation in the conference's "Political Committee—and shocked Nehru—when on the afternoon of Thursday, April 21, 1955, referring to the Eastern European countries he asked, 'Are not these colonies as much as any of the colonial territories in Africa or Asia? . . . Should it not be our duty to declare open opposition to Soviet colonialism as much as Western imperialism?' " The committee compromised by crafting language denunciatory of "colonialism in all its manifestation" rather than "the form of the colonialism of the Soviet Union."[97]

As Chapter 5 explores in depth, "Suez" raises the question of whether Du Bois subordinates the ethical question of Soviet repression to his own philosophy of history, a vision that synthesizes colorblind communist modernity, African communal values, and Third World solidarity as a superior and geopolitically realizable alternative to the Western democratic capitalist order.[98] "Suez" detects a glimpse of this grand historical vision in Egypt's unexpectedly successful operation of the canal after European departure. "With whites withdrawn," the poem continues in the ninth stanza,

> the traffic runs
> As it has run before
> But white folk fumed and pointed out
> Red pilots from the shore.

Whereas Hughes equivocates on the "whiteness" of Russians, Du Bois clearly opposes "red pilots" and "white folk"—and the difference here is not ethnic but moral. As Kate Baldwin argues in her account of encounters between black Americans and the U.S.S.R, the Soviets' "refusal to be 'white' " grounds Du Bois's fidelity to the Communist project.[99] What defines "white folk" in this instance is an inability to envisage Egyptians managing the canal without European supervision, and it is precisely this development that African American commentators championed.[100] Over the next decade, commentators on either side of the color line acknowledged the advent of what Western skeptics deemed impossible: Egyptian success in running the Suez Canal, apparently more efficiently than its former European managers. "Incidentally," writes George Schuyler, "officials of the old Suez Canal Company now concede they were wrong in predicting the canal would flop under Egyptian control. Actually it is doing much better than ever."[101]

In his columns, Langston Hughes continued to translate the meaning of these events into black vernacular understandings. In a 1958 *Defender* column, "Simple Discusses Rocks," Hughes's character riffs on the "world's three most famous rocks": the Rock of Gibraltar, the Rock of Ages, and Little Rock. When asked to explain, Simple replies: " 'The Rock of Gibraltar is the biggest rock sticking up out of the ocean anywhere on earth. The Rock of Ages is the oldest rock because it is eternal. And Little Rock is the dirtiest rock because it is the [devil's] and was put on earth to try men's souls and keep the President from playing golf in peace. Them is the three most famous rocks.' " Simple's companion adds that Gibraltar " 'is a powerful British fortress guarding the entrance of the Mediterranean Sea. In the old days when cannons were powerful, Gibraltar permitted Britain to dominate that part of the world, control the Suez Canal, and protect her power in the Middle East.' 'That power is gone now,' said Simple, 'and them cannons do not amount to doodledy-squat.' "[102] (For John Stuart Mill, incidentally, Gibraltar represented one of the "small posts . . . held only as naval or military positions" for the British Empire.)[103] Simple then evokes the biblical resonance of the Rock of Ages, a symbol that allows Hughes to draw on the moral authority of the black church—Simple recalls singing the spiritual "Oh, rock of ages, cleft for me" in Sunday school—against the imperial and racial associations of Gibraltar and Little Rock.

Versus politically mainstream representations of "good" (or moderate) and "bad" (or defiant) modes of decolonization, African American newspapers tended to adopt the Nasserist perspective, even though opinion varied on his leadership. Most black newspapers carried snippets from Nasser's famous speech announcing nationalization, such as the following excerpt in the *Baltimore Afro-American:* "The Suez Canal belongs to us. It was built by Egyptians, and 120,000 Egyptians died building it. Thirty-five million Egyptian pounds ($100,000,000) have been taken from us every year by the Suez Canal Company. We shall use that money for building the High Dam. We shall rely on our own strength, our own muscle, and our own funds."[104] Among African American newspapers, the *Baltimore Afro-American* seems to have covered the Suez affair most extensively. On August 18, 1956, it reported Jawaharlal Nehru's response to Nasser's nationalization. "The terms of the nationalization itself, under the laws of Egypt, are within the province of that government," the paper quotes Nehru, speaking in the Indian Parliament before his departure for an international conference on Suez.[105] Nehru's views, as historians have noted, were especially meaningful to African Americans. During the Bandung Conference, Nehru concluded his speech by characterizing the transatlantic slave trade of Africans as the "infinite tragedy." Colonial rule in Asia was deleterious, "but I think that there is nothing more terrible . . . than the infinite tragedy of Africa in the past few hundred years."

> When I think of it everything else pales into insignificance, all that we have had in Asia. That infinite tragedy of Africa ever since the days when millions of them were carried away in galleys as slaves to America and elsewhere; the way they were treated, the way they were caught, the way they were taken away, 50 percent dying in the galleys. We have to bear that burden, all of us. We did not do it ourselves, I mean, but the world has to bear it. We talk about this little country and that little country in Africa or outside, but let us remember this Infinite Tragedy.[106]

Nehru's moving statement at Bandung symbolizes the reciprocal engagement of Indians and African Americans in their respective struggles, but it also indicates Nehru's acumen in facilitating the moral and affective atmosphere of the fledgling nonalignment movement.[107] Ever alert to ideological and psychological tensions at Bandung, Richard Wright's *The Color Curtain* underscores Nehru's flexible and pragmatic approach, particularly with respect to the specter of communism looming over the proceedings. Noting the hostility of Afro-Asia toward communism—Zhou En-Lai, Wright observes, listened "to all arguments with patience . . . turning the other cheek when receiving ideological slaps"—*The Color Curtain* portrays Nehru as a skilled arbitrator between Mao's China (which fell outside of the nonalignment camp but saw itself as part of the colonized world) and the nonaligned nations. Citing China's ability to adapt its ideology to the Bandung situation, Wright showed how Nehru and Zhou En-Lai skillfully managed religious and ideological differences among participant nations toward the end of Afro-Asian unity.

The *Afro-American* article placed in bold print Nehru's reproof to Britain and France regarding Suez. The recourse to military resolutions, said Nehru, "does not belong to this age and it is not dictated by reason. It fails to take account of the world as it is today and of Asia today."[108] His characterization of European bellicosity as anachronistic and irrational signals the public confidence—privately Nehru had his doubts—that Third World leaders drew from their new stance. Alternatively, it suggests the moral obligations that Bandung imposed on its participants. One of the great advantages of this strategy was that it allowed Third World nations, generally, to avoid the vortex of war and in some cases to reap material benefits from Western powers. But the Suez crisis, as one commentator observes, "was the first major international test of non-alignment,"[109] since the event marked the first military confrontation between a Third World nation and the Western powers over an issue central to global commerce.

Initially, Nehru, the most powerful mediator between the Western powers and Egypt, as well as the most skilled practitioner of nonalignment, had no advance warning about Nasser's intention to reclaim the Suez and thus acted cautiously, unwilling to alienate himself from Britain or to embroil India too deeply in the conflict. Rather improbably, Nehru wanted to defuse the threat of war, maintain solidarity with Egypt, allow for the continued operation of the canal, placate Western interests, and preserve India's distance from the conflict. But after the invasion of Egypt on October 29, Nehru denounced this act of aggression and voiced his unqualified support for Egypt. On November 17, 1956, the *Afro-American* published the full text of Nehru's reaction to the invasion. Though privately Nehru questioned Nasser's decision-making process, and even his aptitude as a leader, publicly he affirmed his support for Nasser and excoriated the British, French, and Israelis. "Egypt, which has suffered from Israeli aggression, has, in addition to suffer grievously by the Anglo-French invasion of her territory," he said. In the earlier address, Nehru acknowledged his nation's alliance with Egypt after the Bandung Conference and noted India's own stake in the crisis, since "she is a principle user of this waterway and her economic life and development" relied on its continued operation.[110] Accordingly, Nehru spoke from a position of vested interest when he rejected the "argument that this invasion is meant to protect the Suez Canal and to ensure free traffic," since the first consequence of the invasion was to halt its traffic.[111]

Though Nehru saw Nasser's actions as hasty and provocative, the Egyptian leader's defiance resonated throughout Africa and western Asia, especially in Ghana, Iraq, and Syria. Commenting on oil-rich Kuwait ("How I'd like to live to there, I thought"), journalist J. A. Rogers observed that the country had recently witnessed social and political unrest. "The cause? Well, it's a British protectorate and the English get a half of the oil revenue. But Kuwait, like most lands today, wants self-rule. Nasser and his doctrine of Arab unity is very popular. . . . Kuwait also wants something else: Democracy."[112] The heightened global attention on Suez prompted black observers to interrogate the economics of oil extraction and global finance underlying the crisis. "With all this talk about the Suez Canal," asked the *Afro-American*, "just how much oil bound for America goes through the canal?"[113] "The oil in the Middle East," another commentator writes, "is one of the richest prizes on earth and it is vital to the welfare of Europe. Practically all the oil is in the hands of the Arab peoples. The British and French imperialists feel it would be suicidal to lose that oil."[114] Reporting from Nigeria, a staff writer for the *Courier* spoke of the "unbalanced trade" between Africa and the West, "the rule rather than the exception in practically all countries whose economies are tied, hand and foot, to colonialism. One of the key factors in this state of affairs has been European control of banking and enterprise, which prior to the rise of Gamal Abdel Nasser of Egypt had been, in practice, a monopoly of either European or American whites. . . . Nasser's Egypt gave some indication of the thinking throughout Africa on the subject of finances when sweeping decrees were issued in January which seized all British and French banks, commercial houses and insurance firms."[115] The *Courier* writer probably overstates the number of "sweeping decrees" being issued, but his emphasis on the chain reaction of Suez aptly registers Nasser's impact on the continent.

By playing the United States and Soviet Union against each other, Nasser also demonstrated acumen in the manipulation of Cold War politics. "Nasser has proved both an able and wily chess player in the game of diplomacy," the *Chicago Defender* asserted, "in which he has managed to outmaneuver and outthink the striped pants department. Since Bandung last year, his stature has steadily grown." The editorial also lauded Nasser's idiosyncratically modest style, which avoided "the mistake common to most dictators of ruthlessly seizing power and permitting corruption to flourish through a spoils system. Instead, Nasser has insisted on honesty in government and has set an example by living plainly and frugally himself."[116] If Nasser's slide into authoritarianism overshadows this early portrait, it was a legitimate observation in 1956 and has some currency in contemporary iterations of Egyptian public memory. The image of Nasser as a frugal, incorruptible populist is certainly the version of the leader portrayed in director Mohammad Fadil's blockbuster 1996 film *Nasser 56*, which set unprecedented attendance records in Egypt and sparked a national discussion about Nasser's legacy.[117]

Whereas U.S. officials and the mainstream press worried about Nasser's apparent drift into the Soviet sphere, commentary by figures like Horace Cayton, Benjamin Mays, and George Schuyler adopted contrarian views. Writing in the *Pittsburgh Courier* in 1959, Cayton, whose frequent columns on Suez balanced support for Nasser with sympathy for Israel, referenced the seventh anniversary of the Egyptian Revolution, an event he compared with the French Revolution in its significance for the Arab world.[118] Cayton also rejects the image of Nasser as a Soviet puppet. On the contrary, according to Cayton, Nasser used this occasion to highlight Soviet intrigue as the cause for the growing rift between Egypt and Syria, on the one hand, and tensions between Egypt and Iraq, on the other; Soviet meddling also seemed responsible for disrupting relations between Cairo and London, as well as for recent outbreaks of violence in Mosul and Kirkuk. "These hardly sound like statements," he continues, "of a 'dupe of the Kremlin,' as Nasser was so widely described and cartooned just a year ago. Nasser is not Khrushchev's man. It is time for the West to realize that Egypt's revolution of 1952 was as much a revolution against the imperialism of the West as it was against

King Farouk."[119] In a column from the previous year, Cayton warned that the U.S. decision in 1958 to install troops in Lebanon undermined American prestige in the region, vitiating rather than advancing anticommunist objectives there.[120]

Many representations of Nasser in the black public sphere drew on racial structures of feeling and longstanding inquiries about the status of Egypt in African civilization.[121] Newspapers featured numerous articles about African American students visiting or studying in Egypt (in some instances with the support of Nasser's government), stories that invariably remarked on the ability of black Americans to "pass" or blend in as Egyptians.[122] This interplay between diasporic and cross-cultural identification led to numerous comparisons of Nasser with African American figures like the New York Congressman Adam Clayton Powell and Supreme Court Justice Thurgood Marshall.[123] Beyond these comparisons, however, African American observers underscored the element of race in the Suez drama that foreign policy officials studiously avoided. "There is a desperate effort," argued Cayton in another column, "on the part of the Western nations to make the present world crisis, particularly the Suez Canal affair, seem to be devoid of racial implications."[124]

The Chicago Defender suggested how the multiplicity of views on Nasser opened new racial and class fissures in the United States. The paper indicted the prominent American labor union leader "Walter Reuther's blast at Nasser as the aggressor against Israel in the Middle East crisis with a pledge that the UAW [United Automobile Workers] would do all it could to force Egypt to open the Suez to Israel"—a statement that "had a lot of people wondering where this puts his union on the matter of colonialism and aggression against the dark-skinned people of Egypt."[125] Several commentators wondered in print why the United States did not invite Nasser to Washington for talks.

Against the grain of prevailing black opinion, other commentators viewed the Egyptian leader skeptically. If most black commentators saw Nasser in this redemptive capacity, others questioned his tactics. Marguerite Cartwright was one such skeptic. A journalist, actress, and civil rights activist with a doctorate in sociology, Cartwright covered international events from the Arab-Israeli conflict to the 1951 Zagreb Conference in Yugoslavia to the Bandung Conference.[126] Throughout the 1950s, she interviewed and wrote profiles of figures like Nasser, Zhou En-Lai, Nehru, Kwame Nkrumah, and Israel's Golda Meir. In a series of "Essays on Nasser" for the *Pittsburgh Courier*, Cartwright begins with her first impressions of the colonel at Bandung, who looked "extremely handsome" in his "white suit." She mentions his speech at the conference, and "wondered why he felt that the United States should be prominent in his list of imperialist nations." After this reference to U.S. imperialism, "Colonel Nasser lost his smile, and I noted he was less handsome than I first thought." If Cartwright seemed to have little problem with Nasser's charisma, or even the idea of charismatic leadership, her initial attraction to him did not cloud her skepticism about Nasser and her concerns about Israel's security in light of the protracted struggle between the two nations.

"Taking refuge in what I hoped would be mutual admiration," Cartwright then broached the subject of Ralph Bunche, by then an established Middle East diplomat. "The former mediator," she writes, "had expressed his fervent hope for the success of the conference, and I reported this to Colonel Nasser. 'Ralph Bunche, Ralph Bunche,' Colonel Nasser repeated twice, as though he were trying to decide whether he'd admit to having ever heard his name. It became apparent that he did not admire Bunche, who, he said, 'served imperialist interests.' At this point I became another not admired by Colonel Nasser, for he strode away, leaving me standing there alone."[127]

Cartwright projects, initially, a sense of equanimity in the exchange. In previous interviews with Golda Meir, Israel's Foreign Minister—who had negotiated, tenaciously, with Bunche over the Arab-Israeli armistice—Cartwright signaled her support for the young state of Israel, which by the time of her exchange with Nasser had just led the tripartite invasion of Egypt. She concludes with her conversation with Colonel Henry Byroade, the U.S. Ambassador to Egypt, and his staff. They defend Nasser as an essentially "reasonable, moderate" leader who harbors "only understandable fears of enemies who were very real to him." Nasser was concerned primarily, they insisted, on "raising the standard of living of his people and preserving their hard-won independence." In Cartwright's account,

Byroade and his staff describe Nasser as a sensible, fair-minded modernizer who held balanced views on the Israeli-Palestine conflict. In a 1988 oral history interview, Byroade recalls his impressions based on extensive interactions with Nasser: "Nasser was the most sensible Arab leader on the subject of Israel; this is in the beginning before Suez and our later troubles with Nasser. In the beginning Nasser was trying to rebuild a different kind of Egypt; he thought a better Egypt."[128] Like many leaders, Nasser seemed to project different faces to various individuals and constituencies. But Cartwright's reports latched onto the demagogic face of Nasser prevalent in the western press.

During intense meetings on Suez, with Nasser's physiognomy on full display, Bunche was struck by his perception of the Egyptian leader's suspicious, nervous, and tireless character. "Clearly [Nasser] has a feeling of personal insecurity," Bunche wrote in his journal, "which accounts for his frequent smile and giggle, which noticeably becomes less frequent as he becomes better acquainted and more at ease. Basically suspicious, his thinking is all in political terms." One week later in March 1957, Bunche recorded that "Nasser has weird eyes—a wild and rather furtive look, half smile, half smirk. He frequently broke into the nervous laugh or giggle, especially in the early stages of our discussion. Once or twice it was semi-hysterical . . . he has a habit of sitting forward on the edge of his chair, leaning forward in a semi-crouch, with his massive shoulders and big head giving him a powerful and rather monstrous appearance."[129] Revealing is Bunche's observation that Nasser, "suffering from his sinuses," nonetheless "made no effort to close the meeting," which "might have gone on endlessly" had Dag Hammarskjöld not closed it. It is difficult to read Bunche's description without recalling Fanon's typology of the beleaguered Third World leader, whose tenuous position manifests in nervous bodily excesses: composure is an unaffordable luxury; he expresses political precariousness through his body and mannerisms. During speeches, this leader, pace Fanon, continues a "tone of aggressiveness and exasperation . . . which in the normal way out to have disappeared."[130]

With Bunche as a fault line between Nasser and Cartwright, the latter continued her series from Alexandria, where she had arrived from Beirut. "This was how I happened to be one of the some 200,000 souls who sat in Al Tahrir (Liberation) Square and heard the not-soon-to-be-forgotten speech which proved to be of such consequence that it reverberated in nearly all of the capitals of the world." She recalled a conversation she struck up, before Nasser's speech, with an Eastern European figure who with "obvious relish . . . described the glories to be when 'democratic socialism' came." This mysterious socialist signaled to Cartwright the encroachment of Soviet agents in Egypt. "I had occasion to recall the conversation later," she writes, "when I saw the Czech-built T 36's, the jets, tanks, anti-aircraft weapons, and the Russian-built Ilyushin bombers."

Cartwright says that she understood none of Nasser's speech in Arabic, but "not knowing the language actually worked somewhat to my advantage. I was not distracted by the content, and found time to concentrate on the wildly cheering audience and the colonel, himself." She describes the scene as an "orgiastic frenzy," with Nasser gesticulating with clenched fists and rousing the passions of the audience in "emotionally charged, vituperative Arabic." (Presumably Cartwright imputed a "vituperative" quality to Nasser's Arabic after reading English transcriptions of the speech, but her report does not indicate any lag in her impressions.) In response to Nasser's refrain—"The canal belongs to us. It will be run by Egyptians. Egyptians, Egyptians"—Cartwright notes: "The effect was one of mass hypnosis. . . . Unquestionably, the colonel rates this aspect of this campaign highly, for I later learned that some of the enthusiasm was imported from as far away as Beirut, and paid for." Like Du Bois on Budapest, Cartwright assumes the inauthenticity of an insurrection that must have been "paid for." By evoking the image of "mass hypnosis" and stripping the political content and context from his performance, Cartwright perpetuates the image of Nasser as a charismatic demagogue that had become a staple of European officialdom.[131]

"Is Nasser the glamorous hero," Cartwright asks in the final essay, "the man of destiny, the true leader of the Arab world for whom they have waited?" Drawing on infantilizing tropes, Cartwright's profile interprets Nasser's nationalization not as a political act but as an unwarranted provocation: "What does Nasser hope to gain by the act of defiance, the ill-considered outpourings and needlessly humiliating provocation? Prestige is vital to him, but so also is it important to the West in an age of crumbling empires. Was it merely a hurried act of childish bad temper, or a passing gesture of vengeance, due to a smoldering sense of wounded pride?" The reference to the West's humiliation is ironic. If Nasser's speech emphasized how European control of Suez humiliated the Egyptian people, Cartwright suggested that the power to humiliate the West now belonged to Nasser. Her contrarian view sought to temper uncritical black adulation of Nasser, but her portrait also tried to distance African American interests from diaspora and anticolonial currents.[132]

With respect to Nasser, Shirley Graham can be viewed as Marguerite Cartwright's doppelgänger during the Suez affair. Graham lived in Egypt during Nasser's reign and published a fascinating biography, *Nasser: Gift of the Nile,* on the eve of her subject's death. In this biography and a two-part essay, "Egypt Is Africa" (1970), Graham reimagines the geography of Egypt, Africa, and the Arab World in light of Nasser's revolution. Removing Egypt from the foreign policy discourse of "strategic interests," Graham locates the famed Nile River (the "ideal disciplinarian—neither too stern nor too lenient") both within the country's African past and in relation to the geopolitical fallout of Suez. By situating Egypt within Africa rather than in Europe, the Mediterranean, or the Arab world, Graham, on first glance, appears simply to reproduce the Pan-Africanist relocation of Egypt from a Eurocentric to an Afrocentric paradigm.

Yet Graham's rebuttal to Western claims on Third World space indicates a more complex moral geography.[133] Her reading of the Aswan Dam project, at the time the world's largest civil engineering project, exemplifies this moral geography but also highlights the ambiguities of anticolonial solidarity. This ambiguity pivots, for example, on the mapping of actual geographical space.[134] Graham accedes to the Nasserist position that the United States and the United Kingdom, by reneging on the Aswan Dam loan, forced the Egyptian leader's hand, obliging him to seek alternative revenues. But writing in 1970, several years after the Suez crisis, Graham sees the Aswan Dam in terms grander than its stated purpose of fostering Egyptian industrialization. "Once the Aswan Dam is completed," writes

Graham, "not a drop of water from Lake Tana, at one source, or Lake Victoria, at the other, will reach Resetta or Darmietta, where the sea pushes back into the river. The Nile waters, entirely canalized, redistributed, employed, passed through turbines and filtered through dams, will be absorbed into Sudanese and Egyptian soil. Thus, Egypt definitely turns her back on the Mediterranean and Europe, folding in on her river and Africa."[135] Industrialization, on this analysis, is not an economic or modernizing end in itself; it is the means to cultivating an integral geographical unity within Africa. It is not clear, however, that Graham's vision of the Aswan Dam comported with Nasser's objectives or Egypt's national interests, but this ambiguity reveals a diaspora vision worth reconstructing.

In her biography of Nasser, Graham historicizes the Suez Crisis within the various chapters of imperial control of Egypt by multiple regional actors. Mussolini's concurrent expansionism in northeast Africa, as one commentator notes, posed a threat to the British presence in the region and thus forms part of the backdrop of the Anglo-Egyptian Treaty. But the problem that the British government faced in 1936 was not Egyptian independence as such but, as a speaker in a House of Commons Parliamentary debate phrased it, "to reconcile the principle of Egyptian independence with that of safeguarding the vital interests of the British Empire in the line of communications through the Suez Canal."[136] Graham describes the state of affairs in Egypt after the signing of the Anglo-Egyptian Treaty of 1936, which nominally granted Egyptian independence but continued British occupation of the region. The treaty still permitted the British Royal Air Force to control Egyptian air space, while the canal remained garrisoned by British troops. In this arrangement, she argued, the British relinquished neither land nor cotton nor the canal. Most important, the balance between Egyptians and numerous foreign residents in the country continued to favor Europeans.

Graham notes that the Anglo-Egyptian Treaty marginalized the vast majority of Egyptians. In the decade preceding postwar legislation protecting stateless and displaced persons, in Egypt in "1936 there were distinct advantages in being a foreigner," writes Graham, "or even stateless in Egypt. . . . Cypriots, Greeks, Italians, Maltese,

Rumanians, French, English, Austrians, Germans and European stateless Jews lived in Egypt as permanent residents. And by their arrogance, extravagance and ignorance these prosperous European communities were a constant irritant and shame to the Egyptians. Jews fleeing from Hitler were freely admitted to Egypt, were allowed to work and establish businesses. Being European and mostly middle-class, they were contemptuous of poor Arabs and poor Egyptian Jews alike."[137] She portrays a colonial version of the "open" society, long controlled from within and from without, but that absorbed elements from its various foreign occupants to create an irrevocably hybrid culture.[138] Yet these very intrusions, over time, also called an indigenous leader like Nasser into being—what he referred to in his manifesto as the role in the Arab world wandering aimlessly in search of a hero.

Though Graham demurely professes a lack of expertise in Middle Eastern and international politics, her narrative captures the historical dynamics shaping postwar developments in the region with impressive sweep. With respect to the encroachments of Nazi Germany in 1930s Egypt, Graham notes that Germany, exploiting the language of anti-British sentiment, garnered some attention from a progressively rebellious population looking for formidable allies. She recounts one harrowing episode in the style of the political thriller:

> Meanwhile, the British were certain that some Egyptians had been involved with the two they had now identified as Nazi spies. . . . When this was reported to Winston Churchill he ordered that the two be brought before him. He promised that their lives would be spared if they answered questions, and thus, managed to elicit from them the names of Egyptians whom they said had been in a conspiracy to aid Germany against the British. Among those named was Lieutenant Anwar el Sadat. He and the others were immediately picked up and sent to a concentration camp near Minieh. These were the blackest days for the Allies. . . . The British were defeated in Libya. Germans were masters of the skies. And Egyptians believed that very soon the British would be forced to evacuate Egypt.[139]

But as it turned out, "soon it became very clear that Egypt was not to be liberated with German help. Within months the war was virtually over for Egypt; and for the majority of Egyptians in town and country, life had become more difficult."[140] Graham's narrative indicates no plaudits for Nazi Germany's cynical "anti-colonial" intrusions, but she underscores the fact that Egyptian resentment enabled Germany to insinuate itself within Egyptian political discourse in the first place. In Graham's account, Churchill and his officers appear to the Egyptians as symbols of a total commitment to imperial rule. For Graham, there was no ideological or political affinity between Germany and Egypt; some Egyptians simply found in Germany a Western power speaking the language of resistance and expressing a willingness to aid in Egypt's expulsion of the British.

Graham saw Nasser's rise—he was the first indigenous Egyptian Head of State in more than two millennia—not primarily in the terms of anticolonial nativism but in terms of the diaspora project of reinstating Egypt as an African nation. Articles in the black press tended to reinforce Graham's view. The *Pittsburgh Courier*, for instance, adopted Nasser's interpretation of events following the creation of the United Arab Republic: "He described the Suez crisis in 1956 as the turning point in the 'African war of liberation,' adding that the recent Casablanca Conference had proved Africa was no more to be divided into Arab and Black Africa."[141] Subsequent to G. W. F. Hegel's infamous suturing of Egypt from what he calls "Africa proper," northern Africa had been regarded in the Western imagination as an extension of Europe or essentially Mediterranean.[142] Describing the aristocratic class of Egyptians whose identity increasingly shifted toward Europe, Graham depicts the emergence of Nasser as a break with the mentality of the nineteenth-century Egyptian ruler Khadive Ismail (Isma'il Pasha), said to have claimed that "This country is no longer Africa; we are now part of Europe."[143]

For Fanon, certain factions within Africa perpetuated this division. "Colonialism will set the African peoples moving," he writes, "by revealing to them the existence of 'spiritual' rivalries. In Senegal, it is the newspaper *New Africa* which week by week distills hatred of Islam and of the Arabs. . . . The missionaries find it opportune to remind the masses that long before the advent of European colonialism the great African empires were disrupted by the Arab invasion. There is no hesitation in saying that it was the Arab occupation which paved the way for European colonialism; Arab imperialism is commonly spoken of, and the cultural imperialism of Islam is condemned."[144] These reconfigurations of Africa north and south of the Sahara comprise a moral geography articulated across various spaces within the black diaspora, from Fanon to Du Bois and Shirley Graham to Senegalese writers Leopold Senghor and Cheik Anta Diop.[145]

Yet this dream of African reconciliation is more fraught than Graham's analysis suggests. In "Egypt Is Africa" and in her biography of Nasser, Graham cites statements in the Egyptian leader's manifesto, *The Philosophy of the Revolution* (1955), as evidence of his commitment to reincorporating Egypt into Africa and to supporting decolonization on the entire African continent. One of the central passages from *The Philosophy of the Revolution* is the following:

> Can we ignore that there is a continent of Africa in which fate has placed us and which is destined today to witness a terrible struggle for its future? Can we ignore that there is a Moslem world to which we are tied by bonds forged not only by religious faith but also by facts of history? I have said that fate plays no tricks. It is not in vain that our country lies in the northeast of Africa, a position from which it overlooks the continent wherein rages today the most violent struggle between white colonizers and black natives for possession of its most inexhaustible resources. It is not in vain that Islamic civilization and the Islamic heritage, which the Mongols ravaged in their conquest of the old Islamic capitals, reverted to and sought refuge in Egypt, where it found shelter and safety. . . . We are the Guardians of the continent's northern gate.[146]

But how did this Pan-African vision comport with Nasser's own project of Pan-Arabism? One commentator in *Foreign Affairs*, Arnold Rivkin, writing in 1959 on Israel's growing rapprochement with the Afro-Asian world, portrayed Nasser's ambitions in Africa in imperialist terms: "The role President Nasser envisages for Egypt in Africa is set forth in his book on the Egyptian revolution. It expresses a latter-day version of the 'white man's burden,' complete with references to Egypt's 'manifest destiny' and 'civilizing burden' in the 'interior of the Dark Continent.' " In support of this claim Rivkin cites a passage from *The Philosophy of the Revolution:* "The peoples of Africa will continue to look to us, who guard their northern gate, and who constitute their link with the outside world. We will never in any circumstances be able to relinquish our responsibility to support, with all our might, the spread of enlightenment and civilization to the remotest depths of the jungle." This missionary zeal, according to Rivkin, has resulted in Egyptian interference, via appeals to "Moslem unity," into the internal affairs of the Maghreb and Horn of Africa.[147] Though this writer falsely attributes to *The Philosophy of the Revolution* an idiom of European imperialism—the "white man's burden," "manifest destiny," "the Dark Continent"—that misconstrues Nasser's text, his characterization of the Egyptian leader's ambition was not entirely off base.

As Philip Muehlenbeck observes, Nasser undertook efforts to establish Egypt as a hub of African liberation activity. Establishing several diplomatic missions throughout Africa, Egypt "trained sub-Saharan military officers at Kulliat al-Harbia military college, and invited black Africans to complete their university studies in Egypt. Nasser made a concerted effort to frequently meet with black African leaders. In fact, some Egyptians saw it as their nation's 'Manifest Destiny' to lead the rest of the continent."[148] This kind of pan-African collaboration, it is easy to see, corresponds with Graham's vision of Egyptian leadership in the continent. And as a secular intellectual, Graham did not envision appeals to "Moslem unity" as problematic and tended instead to interpret Western indictments of Islam as disruptive of Pan-African unity. "In Africa," she writes, echoing Fanon, "we do not speak of the 'conquest of Egypt' by the Moslems."[149]

Nonetheless, Graham *does* excise this passage from *The Philosophy* in her writings on Egypt and Nasser. In fact, Graham's citation of Nasser is carefully, indeed intrusively, crafted: in the ellipses between the phrase "shelter and safety" and "We are the Guardians of the continent's northern gate," Graham skips approximately fifteen pages of Nasser's text. The concluding sentence of the cited passage ("We are the Guardians . . .") actually derives from a sentence found in the later, ostensibly incriminating passage (referring to Egypt's civilizing role in Africa). Graham also omits the second part of Nasser's sentence, which contains the remark that Egypt represents the continent's "connecting link with the world outside."[150]

It is unsurprising that Nasser's antagonists and his hagiographer would cite *The Philosophy* selectively. In the text's English translation, it is not clear whether its evocation of "enlightenment" and "civilization" suggests a paternalistic attitude toward Africa south of the Sahara ("the jungle"), though such an attitude does seem to inflect the manifesto, especially in the context of its overall positioning of Egypt within the African continent. But Nasser clarifies his notion of enlightenment in the conclusion of his text: "I shall continue to dream of the day when I see in Cairo a great institute for exploring all parts of this continent, arousing in our minds an enlightening and real consciousness and contributing with others in the different centres of the world, towards the progress and prosperity of Africa."[151] The mistranslation of this sentence into English, however, obscures the meaning of Nasser's vision.

In the 1950s, *The Philosophy of the Revolution* was translated from Arabic into English, in a series of similarly rendered versions, but appears not to have been translated since. Readers of Arabic may take issue with many aspects of the English translation, but I want to highlight one significant mistranslation—or substitution—in the English language version. In the previously quoted passage, the phrase "arousing in our minds an enlightening and real consciousness" substitutes the word "real" for "Africa" in the original Arabic. Another English version renders the Arabic sentence more accurately: "to create in our minds an enlightened *Africa* consciousness." The original text includes the Arabic word for "Africa" (أفريقيا) to describe the enlightenment Nasser envisions. Here, and in at least one other instance in the Arabic text, the word "Africa" is either omitted or mistranslated (as in "real" versus "Africa" or "African" consciousness). Few if any of the English translations contain proper attribution. The version containing the correct translation of this sentence appears to have been published by a government printing office in Cairo.[152]

Nasser describes Egypt's location as occupying the center of three concentric circles: the Arab world, Africa, and the global Muslim community, in roughly that order of priority. In her own geography, Graham adopts the same circular coordinates but shifts their priority so that Africa occupies the central position in Egyptian identity. Writing for an African American readership in *The Black Scholar*, Graham most likely omitted the passage on enlightenment lest her readers interpret these references to "enlightenment" and "civilization" vis-à-vis Africa as paternalistic. In her reconstruction of Nasser's image, Graham produces what might be called an anticolonial hagiography—a genre associated with W. E. B. Du Bois, but one that Shirley Graham mastered in biographical treatments (in the tradition of history's "representative men") of Nasser, Paul Robeson, Du Bois, Julius Nyrere, and Frederick Douglass.

In her biography, Graham recalls that when "the United States dropped atom bombs on Hiroshima and Nagasaki after the Allied victory was assured, [Nasser] said to a friend: 'That's a warning to us! Submit, or be destroyed! Only when we take matters into our own hands will Egypt save herself.' "[153] But how would Third World nations, outfitted with yesteryear's or last century's weaponry, defend themselves in the nuclear age? Among his contemporaries, Wright understood better than most how the nuclear age amplified what he called the condition of "terror in freedom" latent in the newly independent Third World. While many in the non-Western world celebrated a postcolonial horizon free from Western domination, Wright was one of the few analysts to diagnose how, in a sad irony of history, a "native" totalitarianism could take root in the Third World, a potential Wright attributed to what he called "Post-Mortem Terror": "A state of mind of newly freed colonial people who feel that they will be resubjugated; that they are abandoned, that no new house of the heart is as yet made for them to enter. They know that they do not possess the necessary tools and arms to guarantee their freedom. Hence, their terror in freedom, their anxiety right after their liberation is greater than when under the domination of the superior Western power."[154]

In an essay cited earlier, Wallerstein notes that since the United States and the U.S.S.R. both developed nuclear weapons by 1949, "these institutions faced each other in what was called a balance of terror,'" a phrase that refers "to the presumption that neither side would be the first to launch nuclear weapons, because a response was certain, and the damage to both sides would be too dangerously high."[155] In the popular Cold War imagination, this balance of terror is known as mutually assured destruction.

But what about the minor postcolonial nations being mined for resources that did not possess this technology? What leaps out in Wright's passage is his evocation of the latent affective state, the embryonic feeling of terror and insecurity, attending but rarely spoken of in decolonization. Fond of Stalin's dictum that the side with the most iron wins, Wright frames his pessimism about the prospects for the Third World in terms of its relative dearth of industrialized iron. And Wright (who also wrote "The machine gun on the corner is the symbol of the twentieth century") might have been familiar with Trotsky's observation, in 1933, that "all the distinctive traits of the races fade before the internal combustion engine, not to speak of the machine gun." It seems Wright would have approved of Trotsky's view of the insignificance of racial difference in a situation of war, but this statement only underscores the vast industrial disparities stratifying races and nations in the postcolonial era. Nasser angered the West by securing an arms deal with the Soviet Union, but what did technologies of guns and combustible engines mean in the nuclear age?

In *The Color Curtain*, Wright investigates this state of affairs by asking the Bandung delegates whether a "nation [is] ever justified in using the atom or hydrogen bomb as a military weapon?"[156] None of the delegates believed that nuclear warfare was ever justified (he quotes Iraq's representative as calling for "ideological disarmament and moral rearmament"), yet what is clear is that none possessed this technology or the capacity to deter nuclear-endowed nations from deploying it.

During the late 1950s, the French anthropologist (and author of the classic 1955 ethnography, *Daily Life of the Aztecs*) and later colonial administrator Jacques Soustelle began publicizing French economic activity in the Sahara for a U.S. readership. In the July 1959 issue of *Foreign Affairs*, Soustelle's article, "The Wealth of the Sahara," describes French economic exploration and activity in the region from "the Atlantic westwards to Libya, from Algeria south to the frontiers of Nigeria . . . 1,650,000 square miles of what we call the French community." The wealth of the Sahara, he notes, includes enormous deposits of manganese, iron, coal, oil, and gas, among other extractable resources. In this essay he announces that on June 12, 1956, "the first drilling at the now famous field of Hassi-Messaoud [Blessed Well] struck oil at a depth of 10,800 feet" in oil fields owned by two French companies, supported "with exclusively French public capital."[157] Preceding Egypt's nationalization of Suez by only one month, this splendid discovery transpired against the backdrop of Nasser's support of Ben Bella's Algerian *Front de libération nationale* that so infuriated French prime minister Guy Mollet.[158] Soustelle cleanly excises the grisly Algerian Revolution from his publicity campaign in *Foreign Affairs*, but a *Time* magazine feature on Soustelle ("The Visionary") alludes to the conflict briefly, portentously: "The F.L.N. rebels, insisting that the French Sahara is an inseparable part of Algeria (although most Algerian Moslems fear the Sahara and have traditionally avoided it), swore to destroy any oil the French tried to move out of the desert, proclaimed that the rebel government would automatically consider void any Sahara concessions that foreign oil companies negotiated with the French government."[159] But the article returns quickly to Soustelle's expansive vision, being carried out "despite the F.L.N."

Proposing that the Sahara has the potential to be to France what California became to the United States (but with the Sahara's punishing climate, the article wryly notes, "comparison with any part of California except Death Valley seems ridiculous"), Soustelle constructs a once barren and barely habitable Saharan landscape, plagued by slavery and theft, that is presently, thanks to French administration, a link between Europe and Africa and an engine of Mediterranean prosperity. Buoyed by an entrepreneurial ebullience, Soustelle's discourse betrays a strain of Lockean liberalism that would seem anachronistic in the era of decolonization. In Locke's liberalism, as David Harvey observes, a "territory is depicted as empty and open for settlement by those colonists who could justify their rights to property by mixing their labor with the land in a true Lockean fashion."[160] In Soustelle's Sahara, this problem is sidestepped to the degree that the desert is so punishing that its inhabitants can scarcely survive, let alone mix their labor with the land; its geography conduces to brigandage and slavery. "The Sahara had to wait until the second half of the twentieth century before Westerners," writes Soustelle, "helped by technology, began to have some success in overcoming the immense difficulty of penetrating the desert with modern industry and offering its benefits to the inhabitants."[161] Though ostensibly neocolonialist in its framing of the Sahara, Soustelle's language is better understood as an instantiation of the post-1945 development paradigm and its promulgation of mimicry: the idea that the most developed states could provide a model for less developed states, "urging the latter to engage in a sort of mimicry, and promising a higher standard of living and a more liberal government structure ('political development') at the end of the rainbow."[162]

In its equation of enlightenment with technological mastery of nature, Soustelle's language echoes the Saint Simonian discourse draping the Suez Canal's conception. But in the 1950s, the advent of nuclear testing added a different dimension to Soustelle's enlightenment project. As the *Time* profile notes, among Soustelle's "responsibilities" were the testing of "atomic energy ('but not the bomb')" in the Sahara; the implication is that these initiatives were to be understood, in the language of Eisenhower, as "atoms for peace."[163]

As an architect of Algerian independence, Fanon, characteristically, limns the negative dialectic of these projects. "Between the violence of the colonies and that peaceful violence that the world is steeped in," he writes in *The Wretched of the Earth*, "there is a kind of complicit agreement, a sort of homogeneity. The colonized peoples are well adapted to this atmosphere; for once, they are up to date." For Fanon, this period of violent stasis represents the actual situation of "neutralism," which can be distinguished from, or seen as the drawback of, nonalignment as a means of tactical agency. Whereas many commentators, according to Fanon, equate neutralism "with a sort of mercantilism which consists of taking what it can get from both sides," he is careful to circumscribe the limits of this gamesmanship for the colonized world.[164]

Wallerstein's insights are an important corrective to calcified accounts of Cold War domination—proxy wars and the like—of the Third World. Despite the ability, however, of anticolonial leaders like Nehru and Nasser, and later Mao and Castro, to manipulate the superpowers toward their own objectives, this strategy had limitations that Third World leadership invariably confronted. Fanon balances an awareness of this postcolonial agency with a sense of Wright's notion of postmortem terror. In a passage worth quoting at length, Fanon writes: "In fact, neutralism, a state of affairs created by the cold war, if it allows underdeveloped countries to receive economic help from both sides, does not allow either party to aid underdeveloped areas to the extent that is necessary."

> Those literally astronomic sums of money which are invested in military research, those engineers who are transformed into technicians of nuclear war, could in the space of fifteen years raise the standard of living of underdeveloped countries by 60 percent. So we see that the true interests of underdeveloped countries do not lie in the protraction nor in the accentuation of this cold war. But it so happens that no one asks their advice. Therefore, when they can, they cut loose from it. But can they really remain outside it? At this moment, France is trying out her atomic bombs in Africa. Apart from the passing of motions, the holding of meetings and the shattering of diplomatic relations, we cannot say that the peoples of Africa have had much influence, in this particular sector, on France's attitude.[165]

This last sentence might have struck an ironic note were it not for the melancholic admission that "the peoples of Africa" have neither the ability to "remain outside" the Cold War nor the power to repulse nuclear testing, attack, or the extraction of materials for nuclear production—a relation between industrialized and nonindustrialized nations, or corporations and governments, that scholars have recently called nuclear colonialism.[166] Contrary to Soustelle's assertion in *Time*, French atomic testing efforts were well under way by the late 1950s; France exploded the first bomb in the Sahara in 1960.

The Suez Crisis, according to one scholar, "had exposed French weakness relative to the Great Powers, and had finally convinced the leaders of the Fourth Republic of the necessity of speeding up its nuclear development program."[167] French officials, consequently, began to deliberate about appropriate sites—the Sahara and French Polynesia emerging as the preferred locations—for testing the atomic bomb. These atomic incursions, as Kevin Gaines notes, did not go unchallenged by Africans and their diaspora collaborators. He describes the efforts of Pan-Africanist Bill Sutherland, then resident in revolutionary Ghana, and his Sahara Protest Team that "successfully lobbied the Convention People's Party [the ruling party of Ghana] to back an international team that would attempt to stop the nuclear test with an audacious plan to drive across the Sahara to the test site in Algeria." Comprising an international coterie of peace and antinuclear activists, the Sahara Protest Team caravanned through northern Ghana, staging open-air rallies, collecting donations, and mobilizing support—even cycling from Paris to Moscow to protest nuclear proliferation, and garnering headlines along the way.[168]

That the Third World cannot conduct its affairs "outside" of Cold War imperatives, especially the nuclear arms race, signals the condition of "terror in freedom" theorized by Wright. Yet for Third World actors and onlookers inspired by the Bandung moment and Suez, nonalignment represented a site for creative and perilous geopolitical maneuvering and syntheses of anti-imperialist and antitotalitarian critique.

From Suez to the Panama Canal

The previously cited poem about Enfantin's conception of the Suez Canal concludes with the divination that "Later, we will pierce the other / At Panama." The author of this verse did not realize his later ambition in Central America, but his words were visionary nonetheless. In a "Tale of Two Canals," Egyptian journalist and writer on Pan-African politics, Gamal Nkrumah (son of Kwame Nkrumah and Fathia Rizk), describes the parallel histories of the world's two most important canals, Suez and Panama. The backdrop of this capsule history is both states' twenty-first century, multibillion-dollar commitment to expanding their respective canals (which can no longer accommodate larger ships) and thereby fulfilling their obligation to strengthen their national economies and bolster the engine of global commerce. "For seven years," in Nkrumah's summation, "Panamanian crews under American technical supervision laboured day and night in the blistering heat of the tropical jungle and torrential rain to build the Panama Canal, blasting immense mountains, hauling huge boulders, and suffering mountainside avalanches until their mission was accomplished. By every measure, the Panama Canal was rightly regarded as one of the seven wonders of modern times." But just as laborers in the Canal Zone fell to tropical disease, the dearth of water in the Egyptian desert contributed to the thousands of lost lives at Suez. On this version of events, the Canal Zone and the wider region—after surviving a devastating earthquake that rocked Panama City but left the canal intact, tropical diseases like malaria and yellow fever, and mudslides—increasingly came under U.S. control, which bred resentment among Panama and neighbors like Columbia. Before this control, the U.S. military possessed minor naval strength but evolved into a superpower in the Southern Hemisphere as the "Caribbean metamorphosed into an American lake and a new era was ushered in with the monumental engineering feat of the Panama Canal. Latin America was unceremoniously relegated into the subservient status of America's backyard."

Though he suggests that the Suez Canal possesses certain strategic advantages relative to the Panama Canal, thus making the Egyptian waterway in principle a more attractive route for foreign shippers, Gamal Nkrumah concedes that the former, unlike the latter, has functioned as a recurrent scene of international conflict since 1956. "No major armed conflicts have taken place in Panama, whereas in Egypt many battles have been fought on the banks of the Suez Canal." A decade later, Gamal Nkrumah notes, much of the combat operations in the Arab-Israeli War of 1967 (a topic explored in Chapter 5) occurred around the Suez Canal, which remained closed until June 5,

1975. "Wreckage from this conflict remains visible along the canal's banks," he writes.[169]

Nkrumah is right to suggest that the Suez Canal, in comparison to its central American counterpart, has emerged as a crucible of conflict in the world's most war-torn region. For the African American public sphere, however, the Panama Canal represented another racially inflected project subject to international conflict, and the fallout of Suez prompted many writers to turn their attention to this imperial construction closer to home.

In 1926 the young Caribbean writer Eric Walrond published his short story collection, *Tropic Death*, to wide acclaim among the literary circles of Harlem, drawing comparisons with Jean Toomer's 1923 masterpiece, *Cane*, and catapulting the author to Harlem's political and cultural elite. Despite its positive initial reception, however, *Tropic Death* has for decades remained obscure, though renewed critical interest in Walrond's work has begun to reinstate its place not only within Harlem's cultural ferment in the 1920s but within a black internationalist network centered in the Caribbean. Among *Tropic Death*'s many innovations, the collection's imagining of the U.S.-controlled Panama Canal Zone—cosmopolitan yet segregated, vibrant but insalubrious, a vortex of meager opportunity and a destination for death, an emblem of U.S. imperial prowess and black diaspora agglomeration—uniquely foreshadows, for the purposes of this chapter, how the fallout of Suez reverberated in the Americas.

Born in British Guiana, Walrond moved to Barbados and then to Panama, where his father was a laborer in the Canal Zone. Written from Harlem, where the completion of the canal in 1914 led record numbers of Caribbean migrants to New York, including the nineteen-year-old Walrond who arrived from Panama in 1918, the stories in *Tropic Death* traffic between Barbados, the Panama Canal Zone, British Guiana, and a ship headed from Barbados to the Canal Zone. One story set in the Canal Zone, "Wharf Rats," begins with the following tableau: "Among the motley crew recruited to dig the Panama Canal were artisans from the four ends of the earth. Down in the Cut drifted hordes of Italians, Greeks, Chinese, Negroes—a hardy, sun-defying set of white, black and yellow men. But the bulk of the actual brawn for the work was supplied by the dusky peons of those coral isles in the Caribbean ruled by Britain, France, and Holland." When the long workday ended, these men, "exhausted, half-asleep, naked but for wormy singlets, would hum queer creole tunes, play on guitar or piccolo, and jig to the rhythm of the *coombia.* It was a *brujerial* chant, for *obeah*, a heritage of the French colonial, honeycombed the life of the Negro laboring camps. Over smoking pots, on black, death-black nights, legends of the bloodiest sort were recited till they became the essence of a sort of Negro Koran. One refuted them at the price of one's breath."[170] Each story concludes with a death: a shark attack, a child dying from a mysterious illness, a man burning alive in his blazing storefront, a Negro laborer being shot by a Marine.

But en route to these fatal denouements, the narrative texture of Canal Zone life—with its uncongenial climate, familial antagonisms, Barbadian and Jamaican rituals, interrupted love affairs, scuffles with white bosses, encounters with chiggers and centipedes, struggles with yellow fever and malaria—generates Walrond's most mesmeric prose. Like the fish "lured onto the glimmering ends of loaded lines" that "snarled gutterally, for release," while leaving "crescents of gills on green and silvery hooks," the men and women from Jamaica, Barbados, and other islands of the Caribbean in these stories set sail for Panama, also lured by glittering silver pieces, and like the captured fish leaving parts of their flesh behind in the pursuit. For Walrond, writes Jennifer Brittan, "problems of narrative form, most fundamentally between the singular (death) and the communicable (the event), are linked to problems of geography. Whereas a travel narrative accumulates, *Tropic Death* records attrition, whether of body parts (like an ear, part of a toe, a foot) or the capacity for narrative itself."[171] Despite the celebration of communication, capital flows, and mobility enabled by the canals in Panama and Suez, for Walrond the Panama Canal Zone represents a point of termination, a macabre impasse.

In the anonymous poem by one of Saint-Simon's disciples cited above, the author expresses an intention that belonged to Ferdinand de Lesseps himself: after constructing the Suez Canal "we will pierce the other / At Panama." Lesseps, as it turned out, would not realize this vision in Central America. Following the bankruptcy of the Compagnie universelle du Canal Interocéanique, the French abandoned the project in 1889 "due to mismanagement, devastating disease, financial problems, and engineering mistakes."[172] In 1904 Theodore Roosevelt, in defiance of some domestic antiexpansionist opposition, assumed the task, the completion of which he regarded as one of his signal achievements. One decade later the Panama Canal opened to a tremendous celebration, demonstrating U.S. global leadership and progress at a moment when Europe was embroiled in war.

If the philosophy underwriting the Suez Canal derived from Saint-Simonian ideas about industrialization as the route to human perfectibility, the U.S. progressive movement of the early-twentieth century—which combined an optimistic belief in progress and science with rigid notions about government-enforced discipline and social order—furnished the ideological foundation for the Panama Canal. "This strain of progressivism," writes Julie Greene, "focused on racial segregation, disenfranchisement of African Americans and immigrants, new forms of judicial and prison discipline, vagrancy laws, and moral sanitation efforts such as the temperance movement." As was the case with the Suez Canal, one of the major challenges of the Panama Canal's construction involved finding and managing a cheap labor pool to build the waterway. The resultant labor force—an assortment of white Americans, African Americans, but mostly Caribbean migrants mainly from Barbados as well as Jamaica, Grenada, Martinique, and St. Lucia—found itself subject to "progressive" disciplinary measures, especially those pertaining to racial segregation. Organized according to a quasi-Jim Crow logic, the Isthmian Canal Company segregated virtually all spheres of Canal Zone life, from hospitals and housing to a dual pay scale that compensated the various racial and national laborers in different currency, and in varying amounts, conveying the impression of a "gold" and "silver" standard on the basis of race.[173]

Yet to "many, the genius of the Panama Canal lay precisely in the fact that it seemed unconnected to imperialism; instead, it was seen as a display of America's *domestic* strengths in a world setting. In its triumph, the Panama Canal articulated American expansionism as a positive, humane, and beneficial activity, one equally valuable to world civilization and to American national identity. Emerging as the apparent antithesis of empire, the Panama Canal ironically helped make American empire possible."[174] In the years following the Panama Canal's construction, Americans generally took for granted the waterway as an integral component of U.S. commerce and influence in the Western hemisphere. During the Second World War, Hollywood movies like *Panama Patrol* (1939) and *South of Panama* (1941) showed how the Canal Zone furnished an ideal setting for plots of intrigue and espionage but also conveyed to viewers how security of the canal constituted an urgent national interest.

In the World War II film *The Negro Soldier* discussed in Chapter 1, one African American G.I. mentions to a fellow soldier that, after he helped "clean up in Cuba," he was headed to Panama for a "little job." During the Second World War, U.S. officials regarded the inviolability of the Panama Canal as seriously as the British perceived the Suez Canal a decade later. But the threat of fascist expansionism into the Americas prompted commentators to reiterate the importance of the Canal Zone to the U.S. sphere of influence. Writing in opposition to propaganda like *The Negro Soldier* that sought to incorporate American blacks into U.S. imperialism and the war effort, Eric Williams, author of *Capitalism and Slavery* (1944) and the first prime minister of Trinidad and Tobago from 1956 until his death in 1981, provided an anticolonial analysis of U.S.-Caribbean relations during World War II.

In his contribution to the *Journal of Negro Education* symposium on "Racial Minorities and the Present International Crisis," Williams begins with an historical anecdote. "In 1940," he writes, "the American public was informed of a deal by which, in return for fifty destroyers, the United States Government was granted by Great Britain a chain of naval bases in the British Caribbean colonies. That deal . . . made Americans acutely aware of the existence of these islands and their strategic importance vis-à-vis the Panama Canal. This strategic importance has received its due emphasis in the American press." Stripping the conflict of any ethical inflection, Williams locates the United States' investment in the war's outcome not to any possible totalitarian takeover by the Axis but in more plausible interruptions in economic and strategic interests in the Caribbean.

"The Panama Canal, that artery vital to the United States, would be gravely endangered were the Nazis installed in any harbor of the Caribbean. In addition the oilfield of Trinidad, the oil refineries of Curacao and Aruba, are a temptation to Fascists notoriously short of strategic war materials." Though this sequence of events, according to Williams, has awakened the American public to the Panama Canal's "strategic importance," it has not occurred to this public that West Indians themselves might have a say in "the transfer of parts of the areas they inhabit." (Writing in the same volume as Eric Williams, the Chicago School sociologist Louis Wirth notes: "We must not overlook the fact . . . that we have overseas possessions and commitments, including Hawaii, the Philippines, the Panama Canal, and our outposts in the Far East and in the Caribbean.")[175] Williams assumes that his American readers are aware of the significance of the Panama Canal and the region surrounding it to U.S. interests. But are they aware of the consequences of U.S. dominance of this commercial waterway for Latino and West Indian sovereignty and the ordinary inhabitants of the region? Williams issues a special warning to his African American readers. "The American Negro," writes Williams, "will continue to treat these 'racial brothers' with the indifference of the white folks only at his peril. Trinidad may be far from Texas, Martinique may have no apparent connection with the problem of Mississippi, but what happens in the Caribbean will influence, one way or another, the situation of the Negro minority in this country (and vice versa)."[176] For Williams, the analogy between the Caribbean and American Negro reflects more than "a mere academic test of racial solidarity"; it symbolizes the major geopolitical and economic interests, rooted in black labor and land, that the global crisis has brought to the fore.

On January 4, 1958, the *New York Times* reported a U.S. company's announcement that the "strife" in Suez of 1956 resulted in a boon for the Panama Canal. "During the fiscal year of 1957," the article notes, "the Panama Canal collected about $3,000,000 in additional tolls as a result of the closing of the Suez Canal in October of 1956."[177] But for the Eisenhower administration, concern over the implications of the Suez Crisis for the Panama Canal outweighed the additional revenue gained by the temporary closure of Suez. In correspondence between Dulles and Eisenhower during Suez, the secretary of state alluded to rumors of a dialogue between Panama and Egypt. "I mentioned to the President that there was some indication that Panama was getting into contact with Egypt. The President indicated considerable annoyance and stated that if we left the Panama Zone we would take the locks with us. He again reverted to a suggestion that he had made once or twice before that we should consider the desirability of building an alternative route in Nicaragua so that we would not be subject to blackmail."[178] In Eden's memoirs he recalls the ignominy of Suez but does not miss the opportunity to take a swipe at the Eisenhower administration's management of the affair. "The dispute over Nasser's seizure of the canal," Eden writes, "had, of course, nothing to do with colonialism, but was concerned with international rights." Eden adds—touché—that "if the United States had to defend her treaty rights in the Panama Canal, she would not regard such action as colonialism."[179]

The global attention focused on Suez awakened interest among African Americans in the Panama Canal. A 1961 capsule editorial in the *Afro-American* takes issue with a *U.S. News and World Report* article that posed the missionary question: "Will Cuba Be Rescued?" "But we have long been convinced that Cuba," the *Afro-American* editorial retorts, "doesn't want to be 'rescued' at least not by the American interests which had foisted upon it a one-crop economy and starvation wages while keeping tight control of its banks, telephones, electricity and most of its arable land." Anticipating the Cuban Missile Crisis that transpired one year later, the next sentence reads: "Yet we don't want any Soviet spies within 90 miles of our shores, nor Russian missile bases so close to the Panama Canal and Cape Canaveral."[180] It's worth noting that the first-person plural *we* employed in these two sentences conceals a productive ambiguity: in the first sentence, the "we" seems to refer to the collective opinion of the *Baltimore Afro-American* newspaper and perhaps to the broader black counter-public sphere—a *we* that is distinct, then, from dominant interpretations of international events. In the second sentence, the "we" invokes the mainstream perspective of anticommunism and U.S. national security interests.

In some instances, arguably, this oscillation creates a wider space for critique than is possible within the unambiguously communist or U.S. mainstream points of view, where the use of first-person plural is either politically untenable, in the first instance, or quiescent, in the second. Consider the first-person-plural pronouns employed in the following passage: "Moreover, the United States does not have the best reputation when it comes to dealing with colored countries. We took Panama from Colombia and by force ran a canal through their territory. Then years later to redeem ourselves we prevented England and France from conquering Egypt to regain possession of the Suez Canal. We also expressed our opposition to France's treating Algeria as a colonial territory." Persisting in the theme of legitimacy and consistency in U.S. foreign policy—"we have condemned Russia for gobbling up Poland, Hungary, and East Germany," as the previous paragraph reads—this passage moves from a collective (and obviously rhetorical) identification with U.S. imperialism to an acknowledgment of U.S. state resistance to colonial governance, as demonstrated by Suez and Algeria.

In "Suez and Panama," the *Afro-American* in 1956 addressed the diplomatic efforts of John Foster Dulles, who speaks of "peace and justice" but fails to grasp that "justice requires us to recognize that the Suez Canal is in Egypt; that the Suez Canal Company must operate under Egyptian law; that the Egyptian government had a legal right to take up its charter and pay off its stockholders and operate the canal, and that the agreement which Egypt signed with the Suez Canal Company 97 years ago, was made under duress when Egypt was an occupied country." After Suez, critics began to rethink the legitimacy of treaties and negotiations conducted under colonialism and whether such agreements should survive at all in the postcolonial era. The article concludes with the remark that "the United States should make no demands upon Egypt for the operation of the Suez Canal that Uncle Sam would not accept for America in the operation of the Panama Canal."[181]

In a wryly titled article, "Rev. Mr. Dulles," P. L. Prattis in his "Horizon" column for the *Pittsburgh Courier* lampoons the secretary's garishly moralistic persona on the world stage ("Does . . . Mr. Dulles know how ludicrous he appears lugging the Holy Bible around and playing the role of diplomat?") when observers saw American foreign policy at midcentury as grounded in political realism more than religious idealism. Prattis notes Dulles's return from fruitless discussions concerning Suez in London, where the secretary of state "refuses to face the possibility of a failure of the prospective Suez Canal conference of the maritime powers which Great Britain and France are calling while oiling their guns."

> Mr. Dulles does not believe that President Nasser of Egypt will be able to prevail against the MORAL forces in the world which will be arrayed against him. . . . It is clear that, except for Western Europe (a part of it) the MORAL forces of the world are WITH rather than AGAINST Nasser. And who are we to prate about morality? There is going to be more and more talk about our iron-handed, single-handed control of the Panama Canal. Of course, we have been very decent in our management of the canal except that we took the color line and jim crow to Panama and even had one kind of money for whites and another for blacks.[182]

Prattis then recalls the use of what was perceived as "gunboat diplomacy" in Panama.[183]

With Panama increasingly on the radar, the theme of gunboat diplomacy permeates black antiexpansionist discourse on Central and Latin America. In 1959 the *Afro-American* referred to a "showdown in Panama," in which the present conflict over control of the waterway is rendered as a dense footnote in the history of Jim Crow and empire. "The U.S. put a pistol to the head of little Panama 56 years ago and took their land because it would provide the quick[est] and best shipping route to the Pacific."

> We then set up the jim crow policies that are still prevalent in the United States. We then sent troops to occupy an area adjacent to their land "to protect it." And we built military bases and air fields. Until July 29, 1955, in hiring Panamanians, we paid

> them on a so-called "silver" standard which was a fraction of what we paid white Americans for doing the same work. Merely because their skin was white, we placed American workers on a so-called "gold standard." The British did the same thing to the Egyptians, who three years ago rebelled and took over the Suez Canal.[184]

On January 9, 1964, riots broke out along the border between Panamanian cities and the U.S.-run Canal Zone, resulting in the deaths of twenty-one Panamanians and four U.S. soldiers, as well as substantial economic and political damage on both sides. (Seen as the culmination of a long struggle to win the canal, this event is still memorialized in Panama today as *El Día de los Mártires*, or Day of Martyrs.)[185] On January 25, the *Afro-American* published a blunt editorial, "Get Out of Panama," echoing earlier racial themes but now insisting on transfer of the canal to Panama.

> Of course the Canal and its locks were built with American money and American engineering skills and Jamaican laborers. But the canal is on Panama territory and we took advantage of a weak little country to sign them up to a long term lease, at a low annual rental. Further, we regarded the Canal Zone as a Southern state and set up jim crow schools, restaurants, housing and wage rates such as we have in Alabama and Mississippi. . . . The day Mexico confiscated our oil wells, and Egypt's Nasser took over the Suez Canal from the British only one question remained—how long could we stay in Panama.[186]

In 1977 Benjamin L. Hooks, civil rights activist and eventual director of the NAACP, applauded President Jimmy Carter's decision to sign the controversial Panama Canal Treaty, which transferred control of the canal and the Canal Zone from the United States to Panama.[187] "To blacks," writes Hooks, "other minorities, the poor and women, ending our shameful control of a slice of property that demonstrably belongs to another nation is a worthy issue to be supported wholeheartedly. For our foreign policy cannot, as Martin

Luther King Jr., said of U.S. involvement in the Vietnam War, be one thing abroad and another at home." Drolly, he concludes with a quip by the linguist and U.S. senator S. I. Hayakawa encapsulating the British and American mentality on these grand canal projects: "It's our canal. We stole it fair and square."[188]

II

How to Build Socialist Modernity in the Third World

4

The Right to Fail

W. E. B. DU BOIS AND THE COMMUNIST HYPOTHESIS

PHILOSOPHER LESZEK KOLAKOWSKI recounts a joke about a schoolgirl in Poland who is assigned an essay on the topic, "Why I love the Soviet Union." Unsure of what to write, she consults her mother. "Love the Soviet Union!" her mother gasps. "What are you talking about? Why *nobody* loves the Soviet Union! *Everyone* hates the Soviet Union!" Then she consults her father. "Father, why do I love the Soviet Union?" "Who's asking you such rubbish?" he snarls. "Soviets troops are occupying our land, they're our oppressors. Moreover, the whole world despises them." Dismayed, she asks the other adults in the neighborhood, who uniformly express contempt for the Soviet Union. Finally she decides to write: "I love the Soviet Union because nobody else does."

A champion of Stalin and Mao, W. E. B. Du Bois seemed to love the Soviet Union at a time when no one else did. The combination of defiance, love, and naivety in the schoolgirl's punch line, I want to suggest, captures the spirit of these curious attachments. From the late 1940s until his death in 1963, Du Bois developed a synthesis of communism and Pan-Africanism that, for critics then and now, presents serious interpretive challenges.

Until recently, most scholars have elided this beguiling period of Du Bois's intellectual biography.[1] The prodigious years stretching from the publication of *The Philadelphia Negro* and *Souls of Black Folk* at the turn of the century to *Darkwater* and the novel *Dark Princess* in the interwar years, *Black Reconstruction* in the 1930s, and *Dusk of Dawn* and *The World and Africa* in the 1940s—to name only the best-known works and to say nothing of marginal or unpublished material—have bequeathed students of Du Bois with a daunting reservoir for scholarly research. Yet the relative neglect of his late work seems difficult to explain, except as a devaluation or excision inherited from the Cold War era. Eric Porter charges scholars of Du Bois with a tendency to ignore his late career; those who take his post-1940 texts seriously, he suggests, do so only to the extent that they illuminate earlier writings or events. On the other hand, Porter notes, "there does seem to be a point after 1952 where his criticism becomes significantly less nuanced. His take on communist states and leaders, for example, seems increasingly driven more by hagiography, wishful thinking, and a refusal to acknowledge disturbing facts than by analysis."[2] Other critics have found in Du Bois's communist poetics and politics a gesture of Cold War defiance or resignation; a betrayal of his supposed commitment to liberalism; evidence of an ethical deficit or secret affinity for authoritarian rule; or another embarrassing example of a prominent intellectual's seduction by the delusions of Soviet propaganda.

There is also the question of the celebrity status and elite conviviality that Du Bois and his second wife, Shirley Graham Du Bois, enjoyed in communist and nonaligned nations.[3] The editor of the venerable journal *The Crisis*, according to biographer David Levering Lewis, "would attain the incommensurable status in 1959 of both political pariah in his native land and venerated elder savant among the leaders of postcolonial Africa and the Communist rulers of Eastern Europe, Russia, and China."[4] Venerated elder to the rulers of the Communist sphere, indeed, but how did his pro-Soviet stance appear to the dissidents and ordinary citizens of Eastern Europe or Maoist China who imagined that they and Du Bois were on the same side of freedom?

Critics have questioned how Du Bois, who spoke as a Stalinist, could "gesture toward" but fail to name the "shattering truths" of Stalinism, ranging from the Moscow trials and the Great Purge of 1936–1938 and the Nazi-Soviet nonaggression pact and Soviet invasion of Poland and Finland in 1939 to the staggering disruptions and suffering wrought by collectivization, systematic liquidation or incarceration, and state-sanctioned anti-Semitism conducted under Stalin's regime.[5] Recalling his youthful adulation for Germany's Bismarck, Du Bois wrote in *Dusk of Dawn:* "This choice in itself showed the abyss between my education and the truth in the world."[6] In print or in personal communications, Du Bois appears not to have acknowledged a gap between his understanding of the Soviet experiment and the truth about Stalinism.[7]

Can we read Du Bois's allegiance to the Russian Revolution, asks Kate Baldwin, as anything other than a breakdown or a personal tragedy? "Because the Soviet Union did not achieve its promise of global democracy," she writes, "must Du Bois's commitment to the aspirations of the Soviet promise also be read as an ultimate indicator of the failure of one of the twentieth century's most influential thinkers?"[8] I want to highlight the word *failure* in Baldwin's question, since the collapse of the Soviet Union is bound up with a sense of Du Bois's failure, as a critical intellectual and humanist, to rebuke Stalinism. Drawing on Du Bois's unpublished manuscript, *Russia and America*, this chapter ventures an alternative conception in which experimentation and failure constitute intrinsic elements of a revolutionary situation.

In order to understand Du Bois's fidelity to this experiment, it is worth reconsidering the surprisingly noninstrumental aspect of the relationship between the communist sphere and the African diaspora, despite the acknowledged gains motivating the superpower rivalry in the Third World described in this book's pages. Why were communists, both in the U.S. Communist Party and in Moscow, so deeply invested in the Negro problem when the benefits of this investment seemed disproportionate to its expenditures? Why did the Soviet Union sponsor an entire research and strategic apparatus devoted to the Negro problem? Why were antiracism and the rejection of white supremacy so central to Soviet propaganda? No doubt the existence of antiblack persecution in the United States provided crucial evidence for the communist argument; clearly representations of Western racism formed a strategic component in the Soviet Cold War arsenal. Yet it's not clear that Cold War strategy alone answers these questions.

Nor is it difficult to imagine how these aspects of Soviet domestic and foreign policy would impress Du Bois during his sojourns in the USSR. These efforts represented more than mere ideological jousting. In Du Bois's historical imagination, the Soviet Union's radical approach to racial equality, if nothing else, had to be recognized as a genuine transformation of subjectivity and society: the emancipatory face of the totalitarian ambition to create a "New Man."[9] "It is easy to dismiss [Du Bois] as a Stalinist," James Baldwin writes, "but it is more interesting to consider just why so intelligent a man became so disillusioned." Perhaps it is even more interesting to consider what *illusions* Du Bois projected onto the communist experiment and inscribed in his postwar writings. In what follows, I argue that Du Bois interprets the Soviet Union as a social order in process of victory over the twentieth century's most intractable problem: the global color line, a construction that the USSR apparently managed to dismantle in its own society before preaching antiracism and anti-imperialism to the West. This victory alone was insufficient for the triumph of world socialism, but from Du Bois's point of view the Soviet achievement on racial equality represented an auspicious beginning that counterbalanced the economic disasters and repressive techniques of Stalinism. The cost of this exhilarating glimpse of history's daybreak, however, was the subordination of known suffering among Stalin's victims to a prospective vision: the restitution of racially subjugated groups and an globally egalitarian social order.

Like those of Du Bois, the later writings of György Lukács were dismissed as politically doctrinaire and conceptually impoverished, stale. But this dismissal of Lukács, as Frederic Jameson argues, unwittingly adheres to a spurious "biographical myth" that divides a subject's life into discontinuous "periods" and pits different intellectual phases against one another. Yet what if the earlier works "proved to be fully comprehensible only in the light of the later ones? What if, far from being a series of self-betrayals, Lukács's successive positions proved to be a progressive exploration and enlargement of a single complex of problems?"[10] A biographical myth of Du Bois congeals along the following plot lines: the young, idealistic intellectual dedicates his life to the eradication of racism, the attainment of full citizenship for black Americans, and the inclusion of blacks within the wider American society and the progress of modernity in general; throughout his long life the United States and its Western allies fail to make adequate progress on any of these political aims; by the time the nation appears to be rescinding its commitment to de jure segregation, Du Bois comes under increased state surveillance and emerges as a full-fledged casualty of the Cold War; exhausted and disgusted, Du Bois abandons hope in American racial progress and cynically adopts Stalinism before expatriating to Ghana—once his confiscated passport becomes reinstated after six years—at the age of ninety-one. Yet what if Du Bois's theory of the global color line comes to light fully in relation to his attachment to the Soviet experiment?

In his recent study of Du Bois, Bill Mullen traces Du Bois's evolving and adaptive commitment to world revolution to the era of the First World War and Russian Revolution. "World War I thus produced something like a *class* of political refugees from the old capitalist-colonial order," writes Mullen, "who over the next forty years found themselves in new mutual relations via compulsory dedication to revolutionary thought and practice. Du Bois was a citizen-subject of that class. Inspired particularly by the Russian Revolution of 1917 and the formation of the Communist International in 1919, revolution replaced reform in the shared consciousness of diasporic international subjects; self-determination replaced national belonging; a tacit commitment to an idea of permanent revolution—the global liberation of humanity from both capitalism and colonialism—became the leitmotif of their shared political work and political lives."[11] Yet by the 1950s, the chronological focus of this chapter, Du Bois was one of the very few remaining citizen-subjects in that class—insofar as the communist vision remained indispensible to its original orientation.

As noted in Chapter 3 on the Suez Crisis, February 24, 1956, marks the delivery of Nikita Khrushchev's famous "secret speech" during the Twentieth Party Congress, where the Soviet leader unleashed details about "Stalin's horrendous crimes against the Party (but not those against Soviet people as a whole)," including "the purges between 1935 and 1940 alone [when] nearly two million people had been arrested for anti-Soviet activities, 700,000 of whom had been shot." Four to six hours in length, Khrushchev's secret speech was rumored to have induced illness in many of its auditors, including possibly Polish Communist leader Boleslaw Bierut, who died of "heart complications" in Moscow about two weeks after the speech (though he was also rumored to have been poisoned).[12] The CIA acquired a copy of the speech, and the *New York Times* published excerpts from it on June 4, 1956.

Khrushchev's speech forms the backdrop of Aimé Césaire's "Letter to Maurice Thorez," dated October 24, 1956. "Khrushchev's revelations concerning Stalin," Césaire writes, "are enough to have plunged all those who have participated in communist activity, to whatever degree, into an abyss of shock, pain, and shame (or, at least, I hope so)." Though addressed specifically to the French Communist Party, Césaire's letter conveyed the dilemmas—the unknown legions of tortured and executed, the scope and intrusiveness of state power, the immiseration of the proletariat in both communist and capitalist nations—and evoked the affective states—failure, humiliation, disappointment, hope—common to narrative genres of communist apostasy. In a phrase tucked away in one dispirited paragraph, Césaire expresses hope for "something like the Communist Party founded a second time," observing that, even now, "Communist parties are stirring: Italy, Poland, Hungary, China." This last rustling of coals smolders but does not quite die out. After questioning whether communism "in practice" is compatible with the aspirations of colonized peoples, Césaire's criticisms did not lead him to renounce the communist idea in this text; his hope was to re-constitute the project with blacks in a vanguard and autonomous rather than subaltern role.

Césaire then proceeds to add "a certain number of considerations related to my position as a man of color." "Let us say it straight out," he intones, before referring parenthetically to "the shameful anti-Semitic practices that have had currency and, it seems, continue to have currency in countries that claim to be socialist." Here the parenthetical statement leaps out: the remarks contained within call the entire subject of Soviet universalism into question. Just as Irving Howe characterized the effect of inserting political events into a novel—namely, like hearing a gunshot in a movie theater—the poet's parentheses stiffen the reader's spine. A decade after 1945, it was difficult to downplay these developments as merely reactionary echoes of the chronic state-supported anti-Semitism marking pre-Bolshevik Russia.

Like Fanon, who was famously told by his Antillean philosophy teacher, "When you hear someone insulting the Jews pay attention; he is talking about you," Césaire wrote in *Notebook of a Return to the Native Land:*

> As there are hyena-men and panther-men, I would
>   be a jew-man
> a Kaffir-man
> a Hindu-man-from-Calcutta
> a-man-from-Harlem-who doesn't-vote

Césaire highlights what was a stretch of state-sanctioned and unofficial anti-Semitic practices of greater or lesser intensity marking the postwar moment, from the "anti-cosmopolitan" campaign of 1948–1949 targeting Jews to Stalin's paranoid persecutions in the early 1950s of the Jewish Anti-Fascist Committee and purges of Jewish doctors charged with involvement in insurrectionary plots.[13]

Césaire's willingness to confront, in print, anti-Semitism in late Stalinist Russia punctures the balloon of Soviet antiracism that Du Bois and other black fellow travelers had helped to inflate. Césaire's expression of dissonance between international communism (the Soviet Union, certain Eastern Bloc regimes, the French Communist Party) and anticolonialism exemplifies a position Brent Edwards has identified in black internationalist currents of the 1930s, a discourse "that is once inside communism, fiercely engaged with its ideological debates and funneled through its institutions," yet at the same time adjudicating race-specific appeals. This negotiation, which became a tension, often took the form of opposing the Comintern's insistence on subordinating racial struggle to, or enfolding it within, the supposedly broader class struggle.[14] By 1956, however (two decades after figures like George Padmore and Garan Kouyaté were officially expelled from the Comintern), Césaire's letter was a textual severance of ties between the Third World and the Soviet Union.

Unlike Césaire, Du Bois generally refrains from public discussion of anti-Semitic practices under Stalin or within the wider socialist world. When Du Bois does address aspects of Stalinist repression, or the disasters of collectivization, he employs a different political calculus than that used by liberal antitotalitarianism. Du Bois, as Eric Porter notes, "framed the current global conflict not in terms of a choice between freedom and totalitarianism as it was commonly put in the United States" but as a choice between socialism and the racial project of colonialism. Porter is correct on this score, but it is important to unpack precisely what this rejection of official antitotalitarianism entails. What alternative rationale did he employ? In his slender 1945 volume *Color and Democracy: Colonies and Peace*, Du Bois acknowledges that

> above all, Russia was condemned for murder—not only for the complete wiping out of the degenerate imperial family, but for purging a group of its own revolutionary officials; and one of the leaders in this pharisaical attack was the British, who in 1919 in Amritsar, India, killed 379 persons and wounded 1,200 others in order to keep India in subjection and avoid "being laughed at," as General Dyer explained. . . . The United States, which was also a leader in anti-Russian propaganda, had lynched 1,047 Negroes in thirty-five years, and in 1917 was still lynching over 50 a year and refusing to take effective legal steps to stop this lawlessness.[15]

It is true that Du Bois understates the magnitude of Soviet repression, but the crucial point is that his balance sheet accords as much ethical weight to the devalued colonized subject as to the European dissidents who command the attention of Western officials and their publics.

Du Bois's position resembles a transatlantic or, more accurately, Francophone intellectual style asserting itself in the postwar period. Unlike their American counterparts, French intellectuals did not acquiesce in a choice between political realism and a renovated liberalism. From the European standpoint neither option was attractive, but French intellectuals tended to highlight liberal hypocrisies over and against communist atrocities. As Maurice Merleau-Ponty writes in his 1946 treatise *Humanism and Terror*: "Communism is often discussed in terms of the contrast between deception, cunning, violence, propaganda, and the respect for truth, law, and individual consciousness—in short, the opposition between political realism and liberal values. Communists reply that in democracies cunning, violence, propaganda, and *realpolitik* in the guise of liberal principles are the substance of foreign or colonial politics or even of domestic politics. . . . A regime which is nominally liberal can be oppressive in reality. A regime which acknowledges its violence *might* have in it more genuine humanity."

Merleau-Ponty's argument does not solely allege liberal hypocrisy but underscores "that all regimes are criminal, that Western liberalism rests upon the forced labor of the colonies and twenty wars, that from an ethical standpoint the death of a Negro lynched in Louisiana, or a native in Indonesia, Algeria, or Indochina is no less excusable than Rubashov's death . . . that communism does not invent violence but finds it already institutionalized."[16] Few critics today would accept without qualification Merleau-Ponty's division of political violence into progressive or self-perpetuating tendencies. But his rejection of the opposition between "political realism" and liberal values implies that nominally democratic regimes conceal racial violence by virtue of a tacit devaluation of colonized lives. In a postwar France possessed of a large socialist constituency and a robust Communist Party, arguments like Merleau-Ponty's were more permissible in France than in the United States, where Du Bois's censure of colonial democracy over communist totalitarianism elicited official scrutiny and alienated mainstream black activists.

To return to the question posed at the outset—why did Du Bois love the Soviet Union? Here it is instructive to posit a corollary question: *Why did the Soviet Union love black people?* Why did the American Negro, according to David Levering Lewis, "become the subject of intense Kremlin discussions and resolutions" by 1928 and beyond? "As formulated personally by Stalin at the Sixth Congress of the Communist International," he writes, "the American Negro was defined as a special case—a 'peculiarity . . . not only in view of the prominent *racial distinctions*' but as an 'oppressed nation' whose eventual self-determination in the Black Belt would be followed by integration into the working class and final liberation as a constituent of the triumphant proletariat." Even as a succinct distillation of this position, this passage glides over what is by no means an ordinary geopolitical situation, illustrated by the unexpected fact that the Soviet leader would see to it that his personal formulation of the American Negro problem prevails in the Sixth Congress. Even though it may have been true that to "sophisticated people of color, all this seemed to amount to little more than a preposterous inspection of the American South through the lens of Uzbekistan or Soviet Mongolia," this conclusion leaves untouched the utter quirkiness of these deliberations.[17] In retrospect, the idiosyncrasies of Soviet policy seem too easily taken for granted, attributed to the eccentricity of Leninism-Stalinism or the intensity of the superpower competition for the darker races. But intriguing questions remain about the meaning and legacy of these efforts: the self-determination thesis in Soviet foreign policy; or the Comintern's doctrinal permutations on the Negro problem; or the stream of state-supported research on black political movements and social conditions (even if this research, according to Allison Blakely, was marred by confusion of terminology and misunderstandings about the particulars of and sociological data about black life).[18]

In other words, it was one thing for the Soviet Union to condemn racism, to support the aspirations of colonized peoples, and to codify its beliefs in constitutional documents. It was quite another to establish a formal apparatus for policy centered on the American Negro—as though intense scrutiny of the political situation of U.S. blacks were an ordinary matter of governance for a foreign state, even a rival superpower.[19]

This point is not to minimize reciprocal efforts conducted by the U.S. government concerning Soviet Russia's own occupied countries, or to downplay the advent of area studies, Radio Free Europe, and related formations as American analogues to Soviet initiatives. But these international efforts between rival powers are not exactly comparable, for several reasons, but primarily for the sheer asymmetry between U.S. interests in the Soviet sphere of influence and the USSR's interests in the Negro problem. The latter no doubt possessed strategic value, but nothing on the scale of Soviet control over vast swathes of Europe and Central Asia. To complicate further this asymmetrical analogy, Soviet energies invested in the Negro, as can be seen in a work by Claude McKay, seem disproportionate in relation to their real or perceived benefits.

Soviet policy on the Negro problem entailed the worldwide dissemination of anti-imperialist, antiracist propaganda alongside a steady production of academic works about black political movements. Though attention to the Negro problem fluctuated over time, in accordance with historical vicissitudes, the subject remained on the Soviet agenda even into the decade of détente from 1969 to 1979. As an index of this continued interest, Allison Blakely, a historian of relations between Russia and the African diaspora, was able to conduct a literature review in 1979 of recent Soviet scholarship on the Negro question.[20] Referring to a number of intellectual texts spanning the 1960s and 1970s, he predicted that the Negro question would continue to preoccupy Soviet writers "for the foreseeable future." This research and policy apparatus was distinct from, though ideologically consonant with, the Soviet support for colonized groups worldwide. (Indeed, Soviet scholars, in Blakely's account, differed on whether American blacks constitute a persecuted minority, a nation within a nation, or an internally colonized population.) But taken together and in hindsight, the Soviet commitment to decolonization and to desegregation represents a productively eccentric geopolitical stance.

Commentators have explained the Soviets' establishment of this formal apparatus in familiar Cold War terms. Insofar as the United States has remained capitalism's citadel, and thus an obstacle to the triumph of world communism, the Soviets have probed American society for flaws that they could exploit. No doubt the Soviet spotlight on these aspects of U.S. racial capitalism made up part of a comprehensive effort to undermine social stability in the United States and to alienate nonaligned countries from the democratic-capitalist sphere. "The predicament of the American Negro," writes one scholar in 1966, "would seem to provide an ideal basis on which to incite unrest at home and revulsion toward the United States abroad.

The Russian Communists have indeed utilized the problem for these very purposes, though at times they have not fully apprehended the magnitude of the opportunities occasioned by the issue's existence."[21] Even if this conventional explanation stands the test of time, it's worth pausing over this latter, somewhat awkward phrase. What is the "magnitude" of the opportunities that the Soviets have supposedly failed to apprehend? Another way to phrase this question is to ask how the scale of Soviet attention to the Negro problem *exceeded* instrumental concerns or strategic priorities to become, ultimately, an end in itself: the culmination of what Claude McKay, a fellow traveller to the Soviet Union in the 1920s and a later apostate, called the "love affair" between Communists and blacks.

By the early 1940s, McKay identified this puzzling, noninstrumental aspect of the Soviet-Negro connection in his 1941 novel *Amiable with Big Teeth: A Novel of the Love Affair between the Communists and the Poor Black Sheep of Harlem*, a manuscript recently discovered by Jean-Christophe Cloutier and authenticated with Brent Edwards.[22] Against the backdrop of the Italian invasion of Ethiopia in the mid-1930s, *Amiable* lampoons the Communist Party's irrepressible desire for intrigue in the streets of Harlem. The emergency of Ethiopia brings together a motley cast of politicos, tricksters, race men, socialists, and socialites. The racial and ideological composition of the characters is accordingly representative, with black anticommunists, West Indian militants, "white friends of Ethiopia," and Ethiopian delegates alongside American Negroes passing as Ethiopians. This eclectic, multiracial backdrop furnishes the ideal setting for the novel's satirical treatment of communism.

Certainly, internationalists like McKay and George Padmore had good reason to reject communism after the invasion of Ethiopia. As Bill Mullen notes, the Soviet Union's decision to outfit Italy with material provisions throughout its invasion of Ethiopia was just one factor among several that "hastened Padmore's retreat from international communism."[23] *Amiable* reads like an anticommunist satire; readers would have recognized in this unpublished novel familiar caricatures of the Communist Party, particularly those pertaining to black Americans. Yet McKay's satire raises a question that the narrative tries to resolve but cannot: how to comprehend communism's inexplicable and irrepressible involvement in black affairs in the first place.

Maxim Tasan, a high-ranking Communist and mysterious leader of the White Friends of Ethiopia, is the story's memorable villain. Pablo Piexote, the novel's protagonist, wonders why the communists, and Tasan in particular, are so solicitous of African American support, so eager to regulate African American sympathies, and so invested in black politics. What, Piexote wonders, could possibly be in it for the Communists? For Soviet Russia? McKay writes:

> But he [Piexote] was puzzled by the situation. He saw what the "White Friends" using Newton Castle [secretary of the Hands to Ethiopia and friend of Tasan] as their instrument, were aiming at—the control of his organization. But he could not understand why they should seek such control, why they should be expending so much energy and subterfuge to obtain their ends. *For he could not see the colored group as an effective asset in furthering the policy of Soviet Russia.* If it were to win the colored people over to the Communist Party, their tactics were absurd, he thought, for political converts are not made by that type of propaganda. (*Amiable with Big Teeth*, 131, my italics)

The Communists' interference is imagined as noninstrumental, that is, neither disruptive of U.S. social stability—that ground had long been unstable without outside interference—nor of any appreciable benefit to the Comintern.

If the energies expended by communists in support of black enfranchisement were vastly disproportional to any imagined benefits, then what was the point, strategically speaking? In the passage from McKay quoted, the key words are *instrument*, *control*, and *ends:* the novel foregrounds the absence of a coherent or meaningful relationship among them. Even if the Soviet-Negro connection originates in politics, McKay's novel suggests that the relationship has morphed into a nonpolitical entity—a love affair—because it has relinquished the instrumental function crucial to political mobilization. And politics, on one crucial definition, presumes some form of instrumentality—an articulation of means and ends—and requires some proportion between its causes and effects.[24]

McKay's manuscript does not resolve the question of why the Comintern invests so much energy into the Negro problem. Yet the question's centrality to the narrative destabilizes its own anticommunist critique, which unfolds in the genre of farce, and gestures toward a more profound insight. Symbolized by the enigmatic Tasan, the Communist International accrues a certain appeal by virtue of its noninstrumental relation with black people. The communist "love affair" with the African diaspora is striking precisely because there is so *little*, politically speaking, to be gained by it. To contend, as many commentators have, that Soviet crusades against racial injustice served a useful political function—bolstering the assault on capitalist democracy and enhancing the appeal of the communist sphere—is an inadequate explanation, as McKay's novel slyly suggests. Maxim Tasan utterly confounds Piexote because he can understand neither his motives nor his political objectives; he seems irrationally, even supernaturally driven.

In turn, as John Henrik Clarke notes in his review of Harry Haywood's autobiography *Black Bolshevik*, black Americans on the left have comprised the "true believers" in the communist experiment. Clarke notes that Haywood joined the American Communist Party in 1925 and was expelled in 1957. But after his expulsion, he remained a Marxist and continued his activity in leftist political movements in hope of the triumph of world socialism. "This pattern in the life of a black Marxist is worth some comment," writes Clarke. "A large number of the whites who are expelled from the American Communist Party, or leave, become reactionaries, professional soreheads, and sometimes, informers for the FBI. Most of the blacks who are expelled, or leave, remain committed to the political left and to world socialism. In the political and religious affiliations of black people, down through the years, we have been the true believers."[25] While U.S. state agencies propagated progress narratives about race and democracy during the Cold War, black communists like Haywood and other African American sojourners in the Soviet Union told stories about race and socialism that were difficult to ignore, even for skeptics of the USSR.

In the Soviet Union, Haywood explains in *Black Bolshevik*, "remnants of national and racial prejudices from the old society were attacked by education and law." He explains that the Soviet state criminalized the conferral or reception of "direct or indirect privileges," as well as the exercise of discrimination on the basis of race or nationality. "Any manifestation of racial or national superiority was punishable by law and regarded as a serious political offense, a social crime." He then relays an anecdote worth quoting at length:

> During my entire stay in the Soviet Union, I encountered only one incident of racial hostility. It was on a Moscow streetcar. Several of us Black students had boarded the car on our way to spend an evening with our friend MacCloud. It was after rush hour, and the car was only about half filled with Russian passengers. As usual, we were the objects of friendly curiosity. At one stop, a drunken Russian staggered aboard. Seeing us, he muttered (but loud enough for the whole car to hear) something about "Black devils in our country." A group of outraged Russian passengers thereupon seized him and ordered the motorman to stop the car. It was a citizen's arrest, the first I had ever witnessed. "How dare you, you scum, insult people who are the guests of our country!" What then occurred was an impromptu, on-the-spot meeting, where they debated what to do with the man. I was to see many of this kind of "meeting" during my stay in Russia.

Haywood witnesses what amounts to a citizen's arrest. The group decides to take the culprit to the police station, where "they hustled the drunk out of the car and insisted that we Blacks, as the injured parties, come along to make the charges." Initially the injured parties demurred, "saying that the man was obviously drunk and not responsible for his remarks. 'No, citizens,' said a young man (who had done most of the talking), 'drunk or not, we don't allow this sort of thing in our country. You must come with us to the militia (police) station and prefer charges against this man.'" As he is being dragged into the station, the drunk man sobers up and apologizes, swearing that he was angry about another matter and that he holds no "race prejudice against those Black *gospoda* [gentlemen]." The black men take pity on the man and accept his apology. "We didn't want to press the matter," writes Haywood. " 'No,' said the commandant, 'we'll keep him overnight. Perhaps this will be a lesson to him.' "[26] What Haywood highlights in this anecdote is what we might call a moment of antiracist totalitarianism. By no means, the moral of this story makes clear, can this offense be resolved in the aristocratic tradition of an apology and a handshake: the police must get involved, the assailant punished. Even if Soviet enforcement of racial equality stretches credulity in Haywood's account, the lesson of the drunken belligerent also presents a lesson to American readers: a social study of diametrical contrasts in racial attitudes, crystallized in a startling episode of Soviet-style, *citizen*-led, and state-sponsored reeducation.

For a true believer like Haywood, who knew better than Du Bois about Soviet society and politics from the inside, his ability to generate such forceful narratives of racial reeducation distinguished him from black political commentators who lacked first-hand knowledge of Soviet Russia. Perspectives from black left intellectuals tended to attribute less significance to Soviet race narratives, which they denuded as propaganda equivalent to U.S. propaganda. Some African American skeptics of the Soviet experiment nonetheless corroborated the racial milieu depicted in Haywood's autobiography, whereas other black visitors derided the Soviet Union and insisted that life there was inferior to American life, even for the Negro.[27]

In June 1950, Du Bois drafted but never published a manuscript, *Russia and America.* In Levering Lewis's estimation, Harcourt and Brace did Du Bois's legacy a favor by declining to publish this manuscript, which the biographer finds replete with "venom and plain bad taste," especially in those passages dealing with Trotsky. Khrushchev's secret speech, which occurred six years after the composition of *Russia and America*, "left [Du Bois] publicly unmoved."[28] It is true that passages in this study adopt a surprisingly illiberal tone. But the manuscript's title conceals a larger, if unrealized, ambition: to develop a global history of modern nation states entwined in an emergent world system marked by continuous war and revolution. In addition to the United States and the Soviet Union, the other national actors in this drama include Germany and Italy, Britain and France, China and Japan. Alternating between macroscopic and microscopic analyses, *Russia and America* treats the gamut of social, economic, and political topics: industrialization, organized labor versus corporate interests, propaganda, race and national minorities, revolution, education, socialism versus capitalism. Drawing on sources like Sidney and Beatrice Webb's *Soviet Communism: A New Civilization* (1935 or 1936) and *Russia Today: The Official Report of the British Trade Union Delegation Visiting Soviet Russia and the Caucasus* (1925), Du Bois devotes most of his analysis to detailed descriptions of Soviet labor conditions, union organizing, education initiatives, historical advancements over Russia's czarist regime, government structures, and entanglements with foreign states and corporate interests.

"Thousands of Americans visited Russia in the early 1930s," writes Melvyn Leffler, "and many returned home with favorable accounts. Ignoring or discounting the human toll of collectivization, they regarded the rational planning of a command economy as superior to the vagaries and hardships of a private marketplace economy and a free enterprise system."[29] Leffler could well be describing *Russia and America*, except for the fact that Du Bois composed his study in 1950, in advance of certain shattering developments—Stalin's paranoid plot against Russian Jews, for example, or Khrushchev's secret speech of 1956—but well after the onslaught of collectivization and repression that marked the intervening years, decades when Du Bois visited the Soviet Union in 1926, 1936, and 1949. Du Bois made his fourth and final trip in 1958.[30]

In 1932, as one historian notes, André Gide—like so many of his contemporaries who characterized their belief in communism in religious terms—wrote that his "conversion is like a faith" and, in light of the "deplorable state of distress of the modern world," the plan of the Soviet Union seems "to point to salvation." Gide projected a willingness to give his life to ensure the success of the Soviet Union. But his attitude, Archie Brown observes, would change after a visit on the invitation of the Soviet Union's official writers' organization in 1936. Whereas other foreign authors in the delegation relished the lavish hospitality, André Gide "was repelled by being offered 'all the prerogatives and privileges which I abhorred in the old world,' since he had not failed to observe the widespread poverty of the USSR. He also discovered that the officially approved 'criticism and self-criticism' was a sham."[31] Recording this narrative of conversion in the edited volume *The God That Failed* (1949), Gide joins a coterie of writers across the Atlantic who inscribed what Michael Denning calls "melodramas of commitment," narratives of ideological disavowal and rightward migration by former radicals of the late 1930s to the 1950s.[32]

It is in this international context of renunciation and migration that Du Bois's miscellaneous pro-Soviet writings, especially the 1950 manuscript *Russia and America*, appear altogether anachronistic.[33] "I may be partially deceived and half-informed," Du Bois announces in *Russia and America*, "but [if] what I have seen with my eyes and heard with my ears in Russia is Bolshevism, I am a Bolshevik."[34] During his first trip to the USSR, he was under no illusion "that in 1926, Russia was a picture of happiness and success. It was not. There was stark poverty. I remember the hordes of incredibly dirty, ragged and wild children of war and famine who were hiding in sewers and stealing like beasts through the streets at dusk. I remember the long lines of ragged people, waiting to buy a loaf of bread" (19). Still, it is easy to consign much of Du Bois's analyses to the Communist Party catechism which, in the words of one American fellow traveler, holds that the USSR represents "a world in which there is no racism or national discrimination, no oppression of man by man, no bitterness and futility and despair."[35] To some degree, Du Bois did submit to this catechism because, unlike in the United States, racial equality in the Soviet Union was constitutive rather than aspirational, the core of the social experiment rather than an ideal poisoned by the past.

As a self-conscious outsider, Du Bois's impressions of Soviet Russia may have been less scrupulous than he imagined, but the focus of this chapter is not the disparity between his perception of Soviet life and the reality. Accordingly, this chapter avoids the temptation to measure Du Bois's analysis against the historical record of the Soviet Union. My interest, rather, centers on his conception of failure and experimentation in the communist project: namely, the right of political movements to fail, sometimes massively, en route to a genuinely emancipatory sequence. "What amazed and uplifted me in 1926," Du Bois writes, "was to see a nation stoutly facing a problem which most other nations did not dare even to admit was real. . . . *It might fail, I knew; but the effort in itself was social progress and neither foolishness nor crime*" (48). After surviving long centuries of serfdom, a total revolution, and the staggering losses of the Second World War, the Soviet Union, on Du Bois's view, had earned the right to fail.

This combination of political conviction and self-consciousness about the limits of his knowledge shapes the narrative form of *Russia and America.* As Du Bois compares Russia's past, present, and future with America and other industrial powers, the text oscillates between a sense of credulity and skepticism: credulity, because Du Bois supports communist ideals and admires what he sees in Russia, but also because he must overcompensate for his own mis-education about Soviet Communism from Western and Trotskyist propaganda with a disciplined receptivity to new ideas and developments; skepticism, because he is all too aware of the barriers to unvarnished knowledge of the Soviet Union. "I was long grasping this intricate story and I essay its outlines now with a certain trepidation" (58). This interplay prompts a form of critical reportage that, on first glance, resembles communist apologetics but actually constitutes a form of prolepsis: Du Bois anticipates objections to his analyses not necessarily to disprove them but to reposition them discursively from the sphere of liberal-humanism into the problem space of the communist hypothesis. Badiou defines the Communist hypothesis as "the imaginary operation whereby an individual subjectivation projects a fragment of the political real into the symbolic narrative of a History. It is in this sense that one may appropriately say that the Idea is (as might be expected!) ideological." It is life lived in accordance with the Idea, versus life resigned to "contemporary democratic materialism," which "commands us to live without any Idea."[36]

In *The Communist Hypothesis*, Badiou opens with a preamble, "What Is Called Failure?" that reflects on the waning of the so-called Red Decade of revolutionary movements, concluding, ruefully, that the mid-1970s witnessed "a resigned surrender," a capitulation to democratic capitalism or the "Western" order and its "conviction that to want something better is to want something worse." This state of affairs updates American anticommunism of the 1950s by charging, yet again, that socialist regimes are nothing but despotisms and dictatorships, despised and ensanguined. "At the level of the state, this socialist 'totalitarianism' must be contrasted with representative democracy which, while it is of course imperfect, is by far the least bad form of government" (2). Here, Badiou reformulates Churchill's famous assertion that democracy is the worst form of government except all those other forms that have been tried. With the collapse of the Soviet Union and its clients in the early 1990s, a consensus among liberals and conservatives emerged that the communist project was, in the final analysis, an abject failure; this consensus went by other names, such as "the end of history" (Francis Fukuyama) or the "end of ideology" (Daniel Bell). In fact, it was Churchill who, in his speech to the Scottish Unionist Conference in 1948, proclaimed: "We are oppressed by a deadly fallacy. Socialism is the philosophy of failure, the creed of ignorance and the gospel of envy." But what is a philosophy of failure? Is it any politics external to liberal capitalism, in which the conception of the "Good is never anything more than the struggle against Evil, which is tantamount to saying that we must care only for those who present themselves, or who are exhibited, as the victims of Evil"?[37]

After the First World War and the Russian Revolution, Du Bois was "bewildered at what was happening and tried for ten years to withhold final judgment." He wondered whether "Marxian Communism" was "possible or a wild, perverted dream? I again relapsed into silence; but I did believe that the *Russian people had a right to experiment* and the United States ought to recognize the new government. We had certainly recognized worse in the past" (11, my emphasis). Du Bois's insistence that Russia had a right to experiment—to construct a genuinely new social order—implies that the socialist federation also had the right to fail, for failure also contains the possibility of discovery, of a breakthrough. Du Bois was not so uncritically devoted to communism that he was unable to recognize grave errors committed in its name; in a dialectical conception of history, errors were to be expected. As John Roberts writes, "Modern dialectics begins here in the notion of truth as a kind of wandering *through error*, as opposed, that is, to the notion of the error as parasitic on truth, as the incorrigible realm of the mistake."[38] What might it mean to regard Du Bois's communism as a wandering through error?

And what exactly is meant by *failure*, writes Badiou,

> when we refer to a historical sequence that experimented with one or another form of the communist hypothesis? What exactly do we mean when we say that all the socialist experiments that took place under the sign of that hypothesis ended in "failure"? Was it a complete failure? By which I mean: does it require us to abandon the hypothesis itself, and to renounce the whole problem of emancipation? Or was it merely a relative failure? Was it a failure because of the form it took or the path it explored? Was it a failure that simply proves that it was not the right way to resolve the initial problem?[39]

Because any incipient political movement is bound to encounter obstacles that determine the outcome of the whole project, Badiou adumbrates failure in politics via his notion of a "point," which he defines as "a moment within a truth procedure (such as a sequence of emancipatory politics) when a binary choice (do this *or* that) decides the future of the entire process" (38). At certain points, revolutionaries may succumb to the temptations of power, or to excessive violence, but such errors neither disprove the validity of the hypothesis nor constitute grounds for resignation, since valuable lessons may be gleaned from these points. For Badiou, the ethical imperative remains: to "keep going."[40]

This imperative was the lesson, according to Shirley Graham, that Mao told Du Bois over tea. In a revolutionary situation, mistakes were inevitable, though mistakes were not failures; failures prompt the subject to give up. Addressing a group of young Pan-Africanists, Graham spoke of the errors and misjudgments that her generation, her audience's elders, committed en route to independence and continental unity. "Speaking of mistakes," she writes,

> I am reminded of a conversation my husband had some years ago with the Wise Old Man of China. It was spring in the heart of China and we were having tea in a garden fragrant with peach and cherry blossoms. My husband spoke of mistakes he had made in carrying forward his work and how he regretted them. The Wise Old Man shook his head and said: "The only deplorable mistake a man makes is when he lies down and lets the enemy walk all over him. As long as he stands on his feet—as long as he continues the struggle—even if knocked down—every mistake is a stepping stone whereby he may climb higher and higher. Now, from your elevated place you may look back and call out warnings and advice to those who come behind. For you are able the better to see where the enemy is hiding."[41]

If she knew, Graham does not divulge what mistakes weighed on Du Bois's mind.

Since the characterization of the USSR as a totalitarian regime repeats a judgment of failure, or what today might be called a "failed state," Du Bois scrupulously avoids any reference to the totalitarian and its typologies. (North Korea, for example, is regarded as perhaps the world's remaining, vestigial totalitarian regime; it is also called "a failed state.") As Bill Mullen asks, what does Du Bois mean by democracy in "Russia and America"? In a portion of the manuscript devoted to comparison of the political systems of the United States and the Soviet Union, Du Bois "rejects democracy as electoral polity or parliamentary rule." What is truly democratic in Du Bois's view is "localized political activity" in which citizens debate matters of vital interest—wages, working conditions, living accommodations—that are then represented via soviets in cities, farms, and villages.[42]

What Du Bois saw in Soviet Russia was extraordinary promise.

> It is October, 1936, I am in Russia. I am here where the world's greatest experiment in organized life [is being made], whether it fails or not. Nothing since the discovery of America and the French Revolution is of equal importance. And yet, this experiment is being made in the midst of unexampled hostility; amid deep-seated bitterness and recrimination, such as men reserve

> usually for crime, degeneracy, blasphemy. . . . Yet can one doubt the sincerity of Russia? *Can one question for a moment the gain to civilization if it were proven possible to make human welfare rather than profit the chief end of industry? Even if Russia fails to accomplish this, or accomplishes it only in part, what a stupendous adventure, what a search magnificent, and at a cost so far less than that of any similar revolution in world history, if perchance there ever was such an effort on such a scale.* (104)

Even if Du Bois situated the Soviet Union in a sweeping expanse of human history, his reiteration of the point about the relatively low "cost" of the Russian revolution suggests, proverbially, that he doth protest too much. For many readers, the characterization of the Soviet experiment as "a stupendous adventure" and "a search magnificent" will sound anachronistic and perverse, even for his time.

For victims of Stalinist repression, especially, Du Bois's language will remain wrongheaded or worse. But recent reappraisals question whether a liberal pornography of violence must always be summoned in discussions of the legacy of communism. Is it necessary to revive the violence of history's communist regimes as a means to indict, prima facie, communist thinkers like Du Bois? Are there alternative ways to conceive this violence than anticommunist bromides consistently serve up? Nearly unexampled among black intellectuals after World War II, Du Bois's radical overidentification with Stalinism—who else dared to eulogize Stalin's death in 1953?—parallels the logic of overidentification at the heart of Communist excesses. Slavoj Žižek unpacks this logic via reference to Heinrich von Kleist's 1810 novella *Michael Kohlhaas.* A decent and reasonable horse trader, Kohlhaas is stopped on the estate of a corrupt nobleman, Baron von Tronka, because he cannot produce a permit. Kohlhaas leaves the estate to obtain a permit, which was not actually required for his entry, but he returns to find that his servant and two horses have been abused. After calmly pursuing justice in the courts, his case is rejected and eventually dismissed—per the intervention of von Tronka's high-ranking relatives.

Incensed by this display of corruption, Kohlhaas takes the law into his own hands, unleashing a campaign of violence, burning a series of castles and towns in pursuit of von Tronka. At the same time, he insists that he wants nothing more than to rectify this minor injustice. Sentenced to death, our hero is nonetheless satisfied because his horses are returned in full health and the Baron von Tronka is sentenced to two years in prison. "In a paradigmatic dialectical reversal," writes Žižek, "Kohlhaas's very unconditional sticking to the rules," his "*law-preserving violence* turns into *law-making violence* (to use Walter Benjamin's classic opposition)." This process constitutes a reversal of the standard sequence: "it is not the law-founding violence which, once its rule is established, becomes law-preserving; on the contrary, it is the very law-preserving violence which, brought to its extreme form, turns into the violent founding of a new law."[43] *Michael Kohlhaas*, then, can be read as an allegory of communism's worst "excesses." Bordering on the comic absurd, the narrative's portrayal of total allegiance to the moral law, on Žižek's reading, furnishes a superior template for understanding communist extremism than the dominant liberal paradigm. Contesting the "liberal democratic vision of Stalin as a perverse Master systematically pursuing a diabolical plan of mass murder," Žižek suggests the opposite was closer to the truth: Stalinism instead represented "a total incapacity to govern the country through 'normal' authority and executive measures." Stalinism's failure "to master and regulate events, to get the situation under control" implicitly acknowledges his regime's impotence.[44] If it is possible to credit the notion of Stalin's failure of mastery, then this idea helps to explain why the Soviet leader felt compelled to regulate a problem as ostensibly remote as American Negro policy.

Like contemporary philosophers on the Western European left, Du Bois was able to relativize the Soviet cataclysms by inverting the death tallies employed in Western formulations of the totalitarian. The premise underlying this approach is that liberal democracies—whose targets of repression were racialized minorities or colonized subjects in remote peripheries—cannot remain exempt from the clear-eyed historical reckoning applied to Communist regimes. If mass death tolls, concentration camps, and repressive techniques measure the relative success or failure of a political regime, then the liberal democracies, Du Bois insisted, must likewise be regarded as failures, as indeed he began to believe they were.

In one chapter, "I Gird the Globe," Du Bois describes the fate of Russia's kulaks in the context of Soviet repression. "The Kulaks had the mentality of capitalists," he writes, "enforced by ignorance and custom. The opportunity to cheat and coerce the poor peasant was broad and continuous. Stalin knew the kulak; his fathers had been their slaves for generations. He did not hesitate. He broke their power by savage attack. This revolution was more radical than in 1917, and Stalin knew it." Then he adds in hagiographic language: "He walked the Giant's Causeway almost without halt or rest. Behind him were tramping the myriads of weary, and bleeding Russian feet'" (76).

Tellingly, in this manuscript Du Bois begins writing but then crosses out a passage: "There were a million kulak families in Russia in 1928, [but] 25,000,000 peasant families, and the State proceeded to break their power. The proceedings involved force and cruelty. The kulaks reduced agricultural output, stirred up revolt and slaughtered animals, so as to bring a crisis in 1928 to 1932. But the state persisted. Large numbers were banished to Siberia and the struggle was won by 1934" (77). The phrase "the struggle was won" leaves little ambiguity about not only his allegiance to the Soviet regime but also to the cost of revolutionary progress: the liquidation of large segments of a population, one that is counterrevolutionary by virtue of not only its class position but also its historical character. But if the French or American Revolutions manifested similarly bloody upheavals alongside liquidations of African-descended lives in the course of democratic evolution, Du Bois asks, then why ought communist revolution not be permitted similar excesses? Few antitotalitarian writers question the massive costs of a democratic capitalist system that is said to represent the best of all possible worlds. Obviously, however, his deletion of this passage suggests that Du Bois thought better than to highlight this cracking of kulak eggs in the preparation of the revolutionary omelet.

Subsequent passages adopt a more sensitive tone. "We may ask whether or not the Russian Revolution might have not been carried through with less blood and cruelty, with less appeal to brute force. We may believe that with all the gain from the efforts of Lenin and Stalin, most of it might not have been accomplished at lower cost to the decent instincts of mankind. But Russia answers and has right to answer, that this revolution cost less in life and decency than the French Revolution, than the Protestant Reformation, and than the English Civil War." Whether the violence of these previous revolutions in Europe equates to the Bolshevik Revolution is debatable, but then Du Bois lapses into apologetics with the following proposition: The "chief guilt for the high cost of communism was not the fault of Russia but of Europe and America which silently condoned the slavery of Russians for centuries and then at fabulous cost tried for ten years to [reenslave] them to the degenerate Czars and filthy priesthood. If the cost of revolution was excessive and revolting, the fault is certainly not with Russia alone" (78).

In the picture that follows, the Western powers, threatened by the prospect of world socialist revolution, reverse course after 1945 and collaborate in official and unofficial ways in an effort to contain and then defeat the Soviet Union. Du Bois attributed the Soviet repression of dissent and free expression to Western incursions. In the course of his argument, Du Bois's sense of the freedoms associated with liberal democracy straddle between the Western and the Soviet view: freedom of assembly and press were desirable but subordinate to material and other priorities: mass literacy, employment, housing, gender equality, decolonization, industrialization. To the extent that individual and political rights harmonized with the aims of Soviet revolutionary egalitarianism, these rights acquire a future or prospective temporality.[45]

Du Bois never quite demurred from the Soviet line that progress required the elimination of reactionary classes, but as Mullen observes, the text's equivocation on the fate of Russia's kulaks introduces doubts about the Soviet experiment.[46] Du Bois rues the deployment of violent repression but never condemns it. "In the Soviet Union," he writes, "following the liquidation of the kulaks, began a Five Year Plan which proceeded with its industrialization and included collective farms and the development of heavy industry in coal, oil, electricity, blast furnaces, automobiles and machines." Notice that the phrase "liquidation of the kulaks" tucked away in this passage does not call attention to itself. But it does signal the increasingly illiberal flavor in Du Bois's prose. Ultimately, for Du Bois, these unfortunate measures facilitated outstanding achievements, like Russian advancements in literacy and education. "On a scale never before seen in this world," he writes, "Russia in a generation turned millions of illiterates into a nation with ninety per cent literacy" (78).

The sheer velocity and scale of Soviet modernization deeply impressed Du Bois. Between "1917 and 1935, Russia carried through the revolutions which took the attention of Western Europe from 1500 to 1900." These revolutions involved principally three sectors: the reformation of religion; rationalization of industry and agriculture; and the transformation of the state into an "authority of the mass of people." The problem with Soviet modernity, like that of the newly independent Third World nations, was temporal: the Bolsheviks sought, and felt the urgent *need*, to accomplish in one generation what Western Europe achieved in three or four centuries. "No one can compute the sum of human suffering caused by this triple revolution over so vast an area, in so brief a time. . . . The total cost was less than Western Europe paid. Whether the result was better or not, Time must tell" (79). In the meantime, Du Bois saw no reason to gainsay the Soviet experiment for its determination to accelerate history, even if the human toll of velocity was massive. On this logic, given the level of technological advancement of its Western adversaries, the Soviet Union had little other choice.

Yet the tragic consequence of Soviet hyperindustrialization was one thing; the issue of Stalin's mass repression was quite another. On the latter question, passages in *Russia and America* extend the text's illiberal tone. "In the summer of 1936," writes Du Bois, "the Soviets began to strike hard. . . . They started the first of the celebrated Moscow trials and sentenced 16 to be shot. . . . The trials were fair and the testimony overwhelming" (82). Later in the text, Du Bois agrees that "in the face of world militarism and new nationalism, Russia, intent on her internal tasks, must put down Trotskyism with ruthless hand, lest the armed world smash in blood the hopeful beginnings of a state seeking to replace private profit with public welfare" (126). In Du Bois's interpretation, the liberal-capitalist, rather than the communist, order was "armed" and soaked in blood; the Soviet Union is an underdog encircled by powerful enemies and infested with traitors to the revolution.

Du Bois's understanding of the fallout of the First World War shapes his interpretation of the Soviet Union at midcentury. Du Bois displays a keen sensitivity to the Soviet Union's fragile position in the emergent world system brought to a crisis after the war. But his Communist hermeneutics of suspicion sometimes overstates the conspiratorial machinations of Russia's enemies. The Western powers "crystallized a world-wide opposition to the Revolution; an opposition all the more powerful and persuasive, because it was based on real suffering and sincere conviction that this blasphemous revolt against divine right, was something so inherently hideous as to merit any kind of suppression" (64–66). Besieged on all sides, the Soviet Union faced a diverse barrage of threats: multinational corporate interests; Western propaganda and political intrigue; U.S. anticommunism; Trotsky's "betrayal" and crusade for power; and the constant menace of Germany, to name only the most prominent forces.

Presumably because he was shielded from Soviet repression, and indeed feted throughout the communist bloc, what matters more to Du Bois than the Soviet Union's shortcomings is what he perceives as its outstanding accomplishments in the domains of education, social equality, labor organization, and racial equality. Not surprisingly, education in the Soviet Union is most impressive to Du Bois. He describes the Communist University for Eastern Peoples (attended by figures like Ho Chi Minh, Deng Xiaoping, and the African American Communist Harry Haywood); he visits Moscow's Chinese University, otherwise known as Sun Yat-sen University. He visits Lenin's School for abandoned children, orphanages, and homes for the elderly.

Whatever Du Bois misunderstands about the particulars of these Soviet institutions, his interpretation is based on, and intelligible only as, a comparison with U.S. racial democracy. He writes:

> If anyone doubts . . . the planning for democracy in this nation, the system of Soviet education would seem a sufficient answer.

> If a mass of people are to be misled and used by others for selfish and anti-social interests, they must not be educated save in limited ways. This explains why black slaves in the United States were denied by law the right to learn to read and write; it explains the determined limitation of native education in all colonies. But in Soviet Russia from the beginning, the Revolution stressed education. . . . It is a universal compulsory education free of expense, not only for literacy but for life; with no restrictions of race, sex, color, or creed. (113)

He then cites the transformative increase in literacy achieved, over a brief span of time, in the Soviet Union; the expansion in college enrollment within less than a decade; classrooms made up mostly of peasants and working-class students; and a dramatic rise in newspaper circulation. Everywhere in mid-1930s Russia, Du Bois notes, one saw the schoolhouse.

As Du Bois saw the matter, appraisals of the Soviet Union ought to rely less on anecdotal experience—namely, on personal accounts of what life is like in Communist countries—and more on boldness of experimentation. As Du Bois somewhat awkwardly phrases his position: "We are thinking beyond experience and our only appeal is not to logic but to experiment: if increasingly exact and long continued observation and measurement of human action, reveals an inexplicable and irreducible element of the Unpredictable, or as exact science would put it, Change; then scientific hypothesis must say, here lies evidence of that miraculous freedom of action which is the Uncaused Cause of a certain human deed and of development of human life and, perhaps, of other manifestations of Life" (87). Another way to phrase the matter is that the problem with revolution is its fundamentally unpredictable nature, especially its potential for chaos. But in this respect, it is not much different from the scientific hypothesis. This is why Du Bois's idiom changes registers from history to science. Is it possible to understand the communist hypothesis in terms of the scientific hypothesis, in which discovery and epistemological breakthrough presuppose experimentation and failure? The point here is not to imagine Marxism and its political instantiations as grounded in rigorous science, or even as dogmatically committed to dialectical materialism as a supposed science of history, but rather to preserve the experimental spirit and the assumption of failure as a precondition of new knowledge.

It is clear that the climate of Cold War antitotalitarianism foreclosed the possibility of conceiving the communist hypothesis in these terms. With respect to the human toll of the Soviet experiment, Du Bois would appear to be either seriously misinformed or unsympathetic to the suffering wrought by collectivization or other Stalinist initiatives. Though he only hinted at state crimes and surveillance, Du Bois's own reports suggest that he was reasonably well informed about and favorably disposed toward collectivization. He denied witnessing state crimes, though he lamented that revolution could not have been achieved with less human toll, a cost that he repeatedly attributed to Western interventionism and protection of capitalist interests. The argument that colonial democracies over centuries also committed totalitarian-scale atrocities did not, by itself, exonerate Soviet repression, so how did Du Bois justify his commitment to a regime of social disruption and suffering?

And if the communist hypothesis can be understood on the analogy of scientific experimentation, then what kind of disciplinary knowledge does this enterprise demand? What kind of discipline can explain what Du Bois calls the "inexplicable paradox," namely the limitations placed on human agency by nature and the "duty of man to change conditions of life"? Du Bois writes: "Here lies the task of Sociology, which the Western World shirks and which only the Soviet Union and its followers have assumed on a scale adequate to real scientific advance in the paradox of human deed" (87–88). On the surface, Du Bois appears to have named the opposite state of affairs: sociology emerged from Enlightenment protocols in the nineteenth century and became institutionalized as an academic discipline in the twentieth-century West; the Soviet Union, by contrast, tended to dismiss sociology as a bourgeois discipline associated with public policy and middle-class normativity.

What is not clear in Du Bois's analysis, however, is the extent to which fidelity to the communist hypothesis overwhelms the exploratory model of scientific inquiry. What are the limits of failure? When is the time right to immobilize the injured but enraged Kohlhaas?

Here, the analogy with the scientific hypothesis encounters difficulty, insofar as normative science retains the possibility of relinquishing the hypothesis altogether or replacing it with another, fundamentally different, hypothesis. What possibilities exist for modification of the communist hypothesis to prevent it from *abject* failure? Du Bois's account rejects the premise of this question on the conviction that the Soviet government, by virtue of its own supposedly stringent forms of self-criticism, has rendered the deliberative public sphere of liberal democracy nugatory: there is little of substance that either internal or external critique can contribute that the party leadership has not already considered. "The Soviet system at present," he writes, "consists of a series of compromises, most of them in constant change. One of the most striking characteristics of the present regime is its readiness to recognize failure. Should a Communist theory fail to give the required results it is scrapped for all practical purposes as ruthlessly as any Tsarist tradition. On the other hand, should ideas of institutions or individuals associated with the old order prove useful instruments there is no hesitation in using them" (45). In Du Bois's imagining, the Soviet leadership was far more open, deliberative, spontaneous, and self-critical than its antagonists ever allowed.

If anything, Du Bois relishes the inability of the Western powers to asphyxiate the Soviet experiment, which demonstrates the resiliency and ultimate historical destiny of communism. "It was a cold, hard trip back to Moscow," he recalls in one of his visits, "but with it went the thrill of realizing how near the West had come to conquering Russia and stopping the crucial effort to make socialism work, and how completely it had failed" (33). Meanwhile, he continues, "Russia is at work. God how these officials work!" For Du Bois, in what seems like a counterintuitive deduction, the way to ensure a more peaceful transition to world socialism is not to hinder but to promote Soviet industry, despite its losses. For "if Russia fails, reason in industry fails. If Russia succeeds gradually every modern state will socialize industry and the greater the Russian success, the less revolution" (37). In a familiar rhetorical move, Du Bois recodes socialism as democracy, with the implicit revision of capitalist democracy as universal inequality—or what Du Bois calls in the concluding hymn to *Darkwater* (1920) the "anarchy of empire."

Du Bois was pleased to see that Russia's beneficiaries of the czarist era, representatives of "polite culture and grace of high society and wealth," were banished in exile. He had nothing but scorn for these members of the old regime who bore false witness "against Soviet Russia in places of influence throughout the world" (37–38). In hindsight, some symmetry existed between these Russian exiles and Eastern European dissidents welcomed in the West and black Americans embraced by the communist sphere. In Moscow and East Berlin, or London and Washington, tales of the horror of collectivization, on the one side, competed with tales of Jim Crow terror, on the other, as both groups (exiled Russians and persecuted blacks) sought sympathetic audiences and resources outside their native lands.

In *Russia and America*, Du Bois articulates his own communist hypothesis, but unlike conventional Marxist genealogies, his version removes Europe as its sovereign subject and point of origin. It seeks out the communal elements found in non-Western cultures—from China's synthesis of Confucianism and Marxism, to Japanese Shintoism and so-called vertical clan traditions, to African communal spirituality and to Gandhi's and Tagore's philosophical revolutions—to combine with Soviet modernity in a world revolution that as yet knows no name, except in its negation of Western democratic materialism. The dialectical accretion of these elements, which will incorporate the best aspects of liberalism even as it transcends this political philosophy, results in a synthesis that Du Bois calls a "democracy of the spirit" (151).

In order to reeducate his readers, Du Bois highlights his own miseducation about Russia and the Soviet Union. "In college, I remember reading George Kennan's articles in the Century magazine," he writes. (Du Bois refers to George Kennan [1845–1924], the American explorer noted for his travels in the Russian Empire and cousin of George F. Kennan, author of "Sources of Soviet Conduct"). "These stories of cruelty and injustice connected with banishment to Siberia stirred me greatly: the long trek across a quarter of the world; the tearing apart of families; the insensibility of human suffering. I never quite outlived the impression which these stories made upon me." Kennan's accounts left in Du Bois's "mind the current impression of Russia as semi-civilized" and tyrannical (9). "All of this was of passing interest until Russia and Japan went to war in 1904–1905. I admired the temerity of one of the Darker peoples daring to wage war against a great white power." Later in the text he writes, "The Sino-Japanese War perplexed me. . . . I was really uplifted by the Japanese defeat of Russia in 1904, and saw in this event the beginning of the overthrow of white supremacy" (126). What impressed Du Bois about both powers was their respective rejection of white supremacy, even as both Japan and Russia mastered the technological acumen of Euro-American modernity.[47]

Expanding his conception of whiteness and white supremacy in *Russia and America*, Du Bois reiterates his long-held belief in America's missed opportunity after slavery, a pathway cleared but swiftly blocked. Here Du Bois tells a familiar tale, updated for the Cold War. In the Reconstruction era and during the instantiation of the Freedman's Bureau, the nation "made a great start toward real democracy and incipient socialism in the United States, without color caste and with full economic opportunity." Compromise between North and South, however, rendered this effort stillborn. During Reconstruction, this bargain allowed Northern control of industry and commerce in exchange for Southern license to dominate blacks with impunity. "This bargain was consummated in 1876," writes Du Bois, "after a decade of struggle, when the temporarily enfranchised Negroes put up a tragic and hopeless struggle to enter modern democracy as free men, despite their handicap of ignorance and poverty. Their effort did not wholly fail. It succeeded in many ways. This success doomed it" (160). What were the consequences of this doomed success?

What Du Bois seems to suggest is that the incorporation of a small contingent of blacks into this compromised socioeconomic space meant, in the long term, that U.S. racial democracy could sustain itself without substantially enfranchising the black majority. In other words, the "success" of a small portion of postemancipation blacks paved the way for the economic and ideological stratification of black Americans generally, as well as the consolidation of a racial democracy capable of minor adjustments but not of substantial reform. In the eve of his own long lifetime, Du Bois was disturbed by the widening social, economic, and political stratification among blacks.

This shift explained why black Americans in the McCarthy era shunned the once universally beloved Paul Robeson, whose fate suggested that increasing numbers of African Americans had made peace not only with postwar liberalism but with the American creed of industry and commerce, a reconfiguration Du Bois designates as the fresh face of "white supremacy."[48] Notably, this redefinition of white supremacy had no need to engage with the racial science marking the century's first half, since the ethnic genocides of World War II had effectively discredited scientistic discourses on race. The postwar challenge of white supremacy necessitated not the replacement of ignorance with knowledge, as Du Bois previously supposed; it required mobilization against the hegemony of liberal capitalism; it invited testing of the communist hypothesis.

The Soviet rejection of whiteness coincided with the view among some U.S. officials that Russia, in any case, was *not* white—a racialization of Russian identity that shaped the U.S. foreign policy of containment. In his famous "Long Telegram" sent from the U.S. embassy in Moscow to the State Department in 1946, George Kennan ascribes the Soviet tendency toward despotism to Russia's partially Asian identity, consummated over its "century-long contact with Asiatic hordes." The inscrutability of Soviet leaders reflected an "attitude of Oriental secretiveness and conspiracy."[49] The Bolshevik Revolution, in Thomas Borstelmann's summation of Kennan's telegram, "had stripped away 'the westernized upper crust' of the old czarist elite, revealing Russians in their true form as 'a 17th-century semi-Asiatic people.' It was Asia and 'Asia-ness' that had done so much to corrupt the healthier, 'European' elements of Russian life and character, according to Kennan, and that now made it imperative to contain the USSR within its own boundaries."[50] In an effort to align itself with the wretched of the earth, Stalin embraced an "Asiatic" image of Russia.

At the Bandung Conference, Richard Wright asked his interlocutors their opinion of "Stalin's identifying Russia with Asia." Most respondents, if they took the Soviet leader's remarks seriously at all, seemed to think "Stalin used such a phrase [i.e., 'We Asiatics . . .'] because he felt that it benefited the policies of his country at that moment." He concluded that from "a strictly Stalinist point of view, such a gathering as this was unthinkable for it was evident that the Communists had no control here."[51] Wright was probably astute in his judgment that the nonaligned leadership saw through Stalin's identification of Russia with Asia. But Du Bois seemed to view the Soviet rejection of whiteness—from Lenin's analysis of colonialism in 1928 to the 1936 Soviet constitution's prohibition of racial discrimination to Khrushchev's early 1960s talk of sacred wars of national liberation—as transcendent and irreducible to the Cold War rivalry.

In a 1953 eulogy for Stalin published in the *National Guardian*, Du Bois lauded Stalin's leadership and his country's sacrifices during World War II, which he saw as irrefragable proof of Soviet antifascism. Du Bois's hagiographic tone leads to some embarrassing homilies ("For his calm, stern leadership here, if nowhere else, arises the deep worship of Stalin by the people of all the Russias"), but Du Bois wanted to highlight the meaning, as he understood it, of a momentous historical sequence led by Stalin: first, the Soviet Union's dismantling of the color line destabilized the Allied balance of power, which was consolidated, tacitly, by white supremacist consensus; second, World War II was preeminently a global race war with grave implications for the darker races, who, whether they realized or not, were thus indebted to the Soviet Union; and finally, the Soviet Union triumphed over Nazism at an enormous cost, one seldom recognized but that dwarfed the losses sustained by the Allies.[52] Stalin "risked the utter ruin of socialism in order to smash the dictatorship of Hitler and Mussolini," Du Bois contends, before gruesomely adding: "After Stalingrad the Western World did not know whether to weep or applaud. The cost of victory was frightful. To this day the outside world has no dream of the hurt, the loss and the sacrifices."[53] Historians of World War II have confirmed Du Bois's sense of the scale of Soviet losses relative to the Allies, especially the United States. Whereas some 40,000 U.S. military personnel gave their lives in combat against the Axis powers, the numbers represent about 2 percent of the casualties amassed by the Soviet Union. The war left some 25 million dead in the USSR, another 25 million homeless, 6 million buildings destroyed, and much of its industrial and agricultural sectors decimated.[54]

At the same time, Du Bois was relatively quiet about the Nazi-Soviet Pact of 1939, which he seems not to have experienced as the profound betrayal it undoubtedly was for other fellow travelers. In the few months after August 1939, writes David Levering Lewis,

> Du Bois all but enjoined the Negroes of America to adopt a plague-on-all-houses attitude. Notwithstanding his loathing of Hitler's regime and increasing disenchantment with Stalin's excesses, he was undeceived by what he divined as the real significance of Munich—the plot of western capitalists to redirect Nazi Germany eastward into a good-riddance war between fascism and communism. As the Battle of the Atlantic raged during the winter of 1939–1940, Du Bois explained what was at stake to his people. Because he was an expositor of the history of the future—because he was Du Bois—he stated the case for U.S. abstention from the war in accents that brooked no compromise.[55]

One is tempted to speculate that Du Bois, a master of suspicion of Western foreign policy, downplayed the Nazi-Soviet Pact because of his sense that weak Allied support drove the Soviets to such a measure but also because of his stated conviction that democratic capitalism's deeper desire was to destroy Communism.

The Soviet Union might not have suffered such tremendous losses, Du Bois reminds readers, or have felt compelled to align with the Third Reich in 1939 had its supposed allies responded more robustly to repeated requests for assistance against Nazi incursions. Du Bois envisioned Soviet Russia's military front against Nazism not only as an urgent mobilization for national self-preservation, which it was, but also as a heroic response to the call of history—a call that the United States answered belatedly, after Pearl Harbor, with a segregated military defending Jim Crow democracy. "Someone once said that the best punishment for Hitler would be to paint him black and send him to the United States," he wrote in an article titled "The Real Reason behind Robeson's Persecution," published (also in the *National Guardian*) the month after his Stalin eulogy. A principled figure whose outspoken praise of the Soviet Union earned him persecution by authorities and derision from former fans, Robeson emerges in this narrative as a casualty of anticommunist hysteria and a hero as tragic as any he had embodied on the stage. Robeson never attacked the United States, according to Du Bois, and loved the Soviet Union because he was revered there as a great artist and discriminated against in his country of birth.[56]

In the view of Americans of the early Cold War, his love of the Soviet Union "was Robeson's crime. He might hate anybody. He might join in murder around the world. He might lie and steal. But for him to declare that he loved the Soviet Union and would not join in war against it—that was the highest crime that the United States recognized." The idea that Robeson's persecution did not rest on criminal acts of aggression, murder, treason, or theft simultaneously submits a sly verdict on America's own past. More revealing, perhaps, is Du Bois's disappointment with many African Americans, who in his view had surrendered to McCarthyist pressures or succumbed to opportunism in their abandonment of Robeson. Robeson "believed that every black man with blood in his veins would with him love the nation which first outlawed the color line." Instead, "his own people, American Negroes, joined in hounding one of their greatest artists."[57] Robeson had fallen into pariah status, and the USSR a pariah federation.

Other African American writers, like J. Saunders Redding, sought to challenge Soviet inroads in the Third World.[58] In 1952 the State Department invited Redding to represent the government on a tour of India, five years after that nation's independence and during a moment when Asia's largest democracy was intensely focused on America's Negro problem.[59] If Redding, according to Lawrence Jackson, "admitted his cynicism at being selected to go to India as the representative of a rather coy U.S. liberalism,"[60] he resented more deeply the assumption among his Indian hosts that they shared, or ought to share, an anti-Western solidarity.[61]

When referring to the United States, its diplomatic aims and overseas personnel, military and state apparatuses, Redding consistently employs the first-person plural pronouns *we*, *our*, and *us* (for example, "George Mann, at that time our second-ranking officer in Calcutta") as he measures his impressions of India against U.S. national interests.

When he refers to black Americans, Redding employs third-person pronouns. Unlike, say, James Baldwin—who, depending on his audience, oscillates between first-person plural and third-person plural in reference to the nation, or employs "we" alternately to include himself within the fold of either black America or white liberalism—Redding's usage signifies a straightforward identification with the national mission, which his narrative projects as a commitment to anticommunism, gradual racial integration via procedural or peaceful methods, and modernization and development in the Third World. Though Redding is careful to register regional, religious, and ideological differences throughout the vast subcontinent, what is so puzzling to him is why his Indian interlocutors cannot grasp the mutual benefits of America's sensible foreign policy and the virtues of its capitalist system. At every gathering and speaking engagement, he is confronted with a muscular, if paranoid, hermeneutics of suspicion concerning U.S. affairs—one fueled by what Redding sees as fatal inaccuracies generated by Soviet propaganda. Because of this propaganda, Indians seem convinced that in America, capitalism requires war to survive, democracy necessitates the subjugation of blacks, and the legal system thrives on bribery, corruption, and racial injustice. Like a shadow boxer, Redding rebuts each claim at the risk of embarrassment or worse.

On the whole, however, the view emerging from Soviet Russia was an image of a genuinely colorblind society, almost suspiciously hospitable to blacks. "In some cases, a dark face in Moscow has as much advantage as it would have disadvantage in Mississippi," writes William B. Davis in a 1960 travel essay, "How Negroes Live in Russia," for *Ebony* magazine. A U.S. Treasury agent reputedly fluent in Russian and five other languages, Davis was one among four blacks out of a total of seventy-five Americans selected to serve as guides at the American National Exhibition in Moscow. Davis profiles several black American expatriates to Russia, all of whom are employed, well integrated into Soviet society, involved in interracial marriages, and mostly free from the experience of racial discrimination.[62]

As a U.S. representative abroad, Davis naturally finds fault with many aspects of Soviet society: voting is a sham; Russians are grievously misinformed about American life, including the status of blacks;

the state restricts mobility and foreign travel, to say nothing of political and expressive rights; citizens work long hours with modest pay and meager accommodations. But the Soviet construction of a racially egalitarian society, he concedes, is far from an illusion or geopolitical pretense. Davis profiles several black Americans, including one Robert Robinson, an engineer who in 1930 left a job at Ford Motor Company for a position in the Soviet Union, where he continued his education and trained young Russian engineers. A "Negro of wide and varied experience," in the phrase of Davis, Robinson eventually became involved in Soviet political affairs when in "1934 he was elected to the Moscow City Council where he sat with Joseph V. Stalin, Khrushchev, Molotov, Kaganovich, Bulganin and others." Robinson reportedly gained Soviet citizenship in 1937 and later published an autobiography, *Black on Red*, about his forty-four-year sojourn there.[63]

"The Russians, who happen to be among the world's best propagandists," writes Davis, "would be sure to gain the favor of many Africans if they sent Robinson to one of the African countries as an engineer representing the Soviet Union." But Davis then observes that the Soviet Union was also cultivating its own African contingent of engineers and other specialists, with remarkable provisions for African students in Moscow: stipends, bonuses, and travel funds that exceeded the salaries of ordinary Russian workers. Most African students were enrolled in courses of study that required six years to complete.[64] "The African students are grateful for the opportunity to study in Moscow. The Russians are leaving no stones unturned in their attempt to make reliable friends in Africa. It is reasonable to assume that the best educated Africans will be key figures in their native governments in the future. Many of these best educated Africans will have been students at Moscow University."

Davis was right to characterize the Russians as "among the world's best propagandists," particularly where Western racism and imperialism were concerned. Versus American productions replete with demeaning portrayals of blacks, the Soviet Union showcased propaganda films depicting a radically colorblind society bound by solidarity. Films like the grim 1933 animated short *Black and White* depicts a system of plantation slavery set to Paul Robeson's singing of "Sometimes I Feel Like a Motherless Child." The two-and-a-half-minute film opens with a vignette: a corpulent overseer in blackface slicing a pineapple; the plantation owner poised to dig in to the massive pineapple; and two sullen black workers looking at the literal fruit of their labor. Punctuating the sequence, a question mark forms on the screen. The question mark unravels into a winding thread, which then morphs into a straight line; finally the line ties into a knot before spinning like a phonograph record or an auto wheel.

The overseer parades along the plantation paths waving a cross and berating two field hands, one black and the other white. When not cruising in his automobile, a buffoonish master surveys the plantation, gesticulating and brandishing his whip. When one laborer protests against his mistreatment, the master—with comic exaggeratedness—strikes him unconscious and dashes off in the car. In the rear-view mirror a black body dangles in reflection. The scene shifts to a bird's-eye view of the car zooming along a highway lined with tall trees on either side before cutting back to the dangling body in the mirror. Then there is a new picture of the highway: the trees have been replaced by electric poles connected by wire, from which dozens of black men are hung.

By the film's end, this enigmatic image makes sense, as it achieves a grim symmetry with another image of black men, shrunken and in lockstep, being herded into prisons. A succession of inmates settles into an electric chair. The film's interweaving of caricature with grim racial violence lends this avant-garde production a surrealist quality, one that evokes the horror, fear, and determinism of the 1930s but also the era's ominous sense of radical possibility. At the close of film, the name "Lenin" appears on the screen, untying the knot and answering the question mark that opens *Black and White.*[65]

Over the decades, other Soviet propaganda films like *Mister Twister* (1963) drew on a recognizably modernist visual aesthetic to assail U.S. commercialism, racism, overconsumption, and arrogance symbolized in the film's eponymous main character. Mister Twister, a rich Chicago industrialist, decides to take his family on a vacation to Soviet Russia. When Mister Twister checks into his hotel, he is startled by the presence of an elegant black man who is clearly not a member of the hotel staff.

> "Lord," cried the foreigner, suddenly scared.
> Mister Twister looked up in despair.
> Staying next door in room 193,
> Down walked a black man as big as a tree.
> His dark hand relaxed on the balustrade bright.
> Calmly the black man was smoking a pipe![66]

With his face turning red and contorting in disbelief, Mister Twister succumbs to delusions as these nattily dressed, pipe-smoking, black men multiply by the dozens before his horror-stricken eyes. Apoplectic, Mister Twister complains to the hotel manager about its interracial policy. The hotel manager explains that there's nothing he can do—the Soviet Union does not discriminate against blacks (or, the same thing, privilege wealthy whites). But once he sends the rich American off, the manager calls the other area hotels to warn them of this American troublemaker who fails to understand the Soviet Union's colorblind society. The other hotel managers conspire to deny Mister Twister accommodations until, finally, he and his family have nowhere to go. By this point, the Chicago industrialist is compelled to return to the first hotel, which, to his further astonishment, welcomes guests from all races and nationalities. Beleaguered and desperate, Mister Twister is forced to accept this fact of Soviet life and, coming full circle, settles into the hotel that first denied him. In the film's denouement, Mister Twister's reeducation about racial equality is complete. Drawing on modernist visual tropes of hallucination, surrealism, and the comic absurd, Mr. Twister represents aesthetically the ideological, antiracist regime the Soviets sought to project to its citizens and the world.

In this context, it is worth remembering Richard Wright's recollection of what historian Terry Martin called the "affirmative action empire," a massive effort among Soviet leadership to engender a multinational, multiethnic empire opposed to Russian nationalism and committed to the reenfranchisement of ethnic minorities—albeit a policy that backfired in ironic ways, as it encouraged resentment among Russians and the eventual promotion of reactionary policies to neutralize the progressive effort.[67] But for African American observers like Richard Wright, it was the initial, progressive effort—at least as Soviet literature portrayed it—that ignited the imagination. In *Black Boy*, he recalls his first encounter with Stalin's *The National and Colonial Question.* "Stalin's book showed how diverse minorities could be welded into unity," he writes, "and I regarded it as a most politically sensitive volume that revealed a new way of looking upon lost and beaten peoples."

> Of all the developments in the Soviet Union, the method by which scores of backward peoples had been led into unity on a national scale was what had enthralled me. I had read with awe how the Communists had sent phonetic experts into the vast regions of Russia to listen to the stammering dialects of peoples oppressed for centuries by the czars. I had made the first total emotional commitment of my life when I read how the phonetic experts had given these tongueless people a language, newspapers, institutions. I had read how these forgotten folk had been encouraged to keep their old cultures, to see in their ancient customs meanings and satisfactions as deep as those contained in supposedly superior ways of living. And I had exclaimed to myself how different this was from the way in which Negroes were sneered at in America.[68]

For Wright, the party's mismanagement of black politics, among other factors, eventually dissipated its radical appeal. For Du Bois, by contrast, the more he understood the nature of the Soviet opposition to racism and commercialism, the stronger his fidelity to communism grew.

In *Russia and America*, Du Bois notes that his experience in Germany had already inclined him toward socialism and made him critical of Czarism. "After that I followed from afar the Russians' struggle for emancipation and drew parallels between Russian peasants and American Freedmen, emancipated at nearly the same moment and both kept in slavery by denial of land. I read of the pogroms against the Jews and likened them to our lynchings, which were ominously increasing" (10). Invoking the Slavic linguistic origin of the word *slave*, Du Bois links the status of subjugated Russians and blacks by referring to the former as "slaves" rather than the conventional "serfs." Stalin, for example, "was the son of a shoemaker and grandson of a Georgian *slave* and knew the workers of the Russian Caucasus had their problems, because he was one of them."[69]

A major problem the text confronts is epistemological, in a very localized sense: how do outside observers and fellow travelers acquire knowledge of the communist project in the midst of relentless propaganda efforts perpetrated by the Soviet Union's enemies? How do critical intellectuals sustain their fidelity to the communist idea while trying to pierce through the veneer of Soviet officialdom—to glimpse the secret life lurking in distant factories, collectivized farms, and remote gulags? And how do they develop their interpretation of Soviet life from this liminal and limited epistemological space?

Du Bois signals his awareness of the limits of his understanding with passages like the following: "My reasoning may be strained," he writes, "but whether the reader agrees or not, I am sure he can understand the impact which Russia had upon me in 1926. I was not naïve enough to think I had visited Utopia." What he saw was not a workers' paradise but a functioning socialist society, itself an astonishing development. "I did not see the Russia of war and blood and rapine. I know nothing of political prisoners, secret police, and underground government. . . . I have seen only a small part." He realizes that his hosts have shielded him from this repressive apparatus; just because he has not witnessed the workings of the secret police does not mean they do not exist. "But I have seen something. . . . I have looked into the faces of its races—Russians, Ukrainians, Jews, Tartars, Gypsies, Caucasians, Armenians, and Chinese. . . . I have seen schools, universities, factories, stores; printing establishments, government offices, palaces, museums, summer colonies of children, libraries, churches, monasteries, Boyar houses, theatres, cinemas, day nurseries and cooperatives. I have seen some celebration—200,000 youth marching on Youth Day" (18).

Du Bois was especially keen to learn how the Soviet Union's "plans would affect the Negro peoples, not simply in the United States but in Africa; and I wanted to know what part Russia and Communism would play in the coming change." But in order to arrive at this knowledge, he had to concede that like "all Americans of that day, I was tremendously influenced by Leon Trotsky and the propaganda he was loosing on the world. . . . I knew only too well what the Americans and the European press could do with facts, when they related to black folk or to brown and yellow; or to any unpopular or threatening minority" (80). Though elsewhere Du Bois lauded the idea of art as propaganda, here he writes, "The greatest single invention of World War I was propaganda: the systematic distortion of the truth, for the purpose of making large numbers of people believe in anything authority wishes them to believe." The most poisonous form to emerge from the post–World War I era was Nazism's anti-Semitic propaganda. Nazi Germany's propaganda apparatus "said that the whole oppression of Germany by the world was caused by Jewish emigrants. Every misfortune of the world is in whole or in part blamed on Jews: the Spanish rebellion, the obstruction of world trade, and so on" (96). As Chapter 3 has shown, Du Bois was enamored of propaganda; his propensity was to counter imperialist with socialist propaganda.

Ever since his first visit to the Soviet Union in 1926, Du Bois maintained his interest in the socialist republics and "was increasingly disturbed by the news" about the region. "I did not, however, place reliance on the American Press, as I had formerly. For instance the reports of famine and trouble with the peasants did not alarm me. I did not expect miracles in Russia. I knew that she had embarked upon a momentous and revolutionary social program and that from its inherent difficulties and those deliberately placed in its path by the Western world, she was bound to have a difficult path. . . . I knew that few persons criticizing Russia had any idea of her utter prostration from ten awful years of foreign and civil strife" (57–58). Few of his American contemporaries appreciated the enormous sacrifices made by the Soviets in defeating Nazi Germany; fewer still grasped, or even questioned, why the Western powers abruptly unified in opposition to the USSR, their erstwhile ally, after the Second World War.

During his trip to India, one of the most common questions J. Saunders Redding received was precisely why the United States turned so suddenly on the Soviet Union, its ally against fascism. In a series of relentless interrogations, his Indian acquaintances query him about various aspects of America's domestic and geopolitical situation: the question of development aid, the Korean War, the condition of the Negro, the fairness of the legal system, the antagonism with the Soviet Union, America's use of "germ warfare." Why, at least two interlocutors ask, did the U.S. sustain an alliance with the U.S.S.R. during World War II but promptly reverse course after the war, entering a Manichean struggle with that nation? Why was communist activity repressed in the United States? Facing skeptical, often hostile audiences, Redding constructs a narrative self often caught off guard, frazzled, inarticulate, beleaguered, and embarrassed. Redding notes that some "of the questions shocked me," and many "of them revealed the false or faulty information behind them." But the act of writing about his travels affords Redding the chance to reconstitute his inundated self by showing how these questions simply reveal India's misguided assumptions about America.

In Redding's account, these suspicions reflected the assumption that U.S. capitalism necessitates war, broadly conceived. Redding was prepared to answer this question, at least, confidently. "'I do not think that the premise is valid,' I said at last, 'though it has been repeated many times since Marx first said it quite a long time ago.'"

> "Since that time, if you except a civil war we had which does not count because it destroyed the economy of one half of my country—if you except that, and although you include the Spanish-American War which lasted about three months, you will see that my country has been in three wars for a total of less than eight years." There was restless movement, murmuring, but, raising my voice a little, I went on. "For about ninety-two per cent of the time since the middle of the nineteenth century, my country has been at peace. In the face of this, does it not seem strange to suggest that the American economic system survives because of wars?"[70]

Du Bois did not frame the relation between capitalism and war in such a dogmatically causal fashion, but he did envision capitalist nations as driven, sometimes inadvertently, and other times ruthlessly, toward imperialist war. On this view, the socialist nations, except when aiding African and Asian countries engaged in national liberation struggles, were militarily defensive and essentially peaceful. On the other hand, Soviet leadership was also convinced, and prepared for the event, that history ordained war between the Communist and capitalist spheres.

Like his analysis of the First World War, which he saw as driven by imperialism, Du Bois's interpretation of the Second World War shaped his later understanding of communism and capitalist democracy as competing economic and geopolitical orders—but also as *competing forms of life*. In 1941 Du Bois contributed his views on war, imperialism, and capitalism in the previously noted yearbook symposium of the *Journal of Negro Education*, titled "Racial Minorities and the Present International Crisis." With the notable exception of Du Bois, most contributors accepted the basic characterization of the global struggle as a conflict between democratic freedom and totalitarian slavery, but many also undermined that division by questioning the status of democracy and its complex relation to fascism. Analysts who advanced economic interpretations of fascism argued that this phenomenon—a regression in civilization—emerged from the intrinsic problems and "contradictions" within capitalist democracy. Other critics stressed the racial and imperialist parallels between fascism and democracy. For some commentators, the term *fascism* meant Nazism, whereas for others it signified the Axis powers generally.

Though most essays staked out some position on the war—if not necessarily within the dominant binary of interventionism or noninterventionism—contributors tended to eschew polemical arguments in favor of historical, ideological, economic, and sociological approaches.[71] On the whole, contributors were less concerned about the ultranationalist, white supremacist, and expansionist tendencies of fascism as an *external* threat to the darker peoples than about similar tendencies rooted in U.S. and Western democracy.

Is the United States presently, or has it ever been, a democracy? Conceding the noxiousness of the totalitarian systems, Robert M. Hutchins notes that with respect to "democracy, we know that millions of men and women are disfranchised in this country because of their race, color, or condition of economic servitude" (438). He cites Roosevelt's "Four Freedoms" address of January 1941—in which the president envisions "a world founded on freedom of speech, freedom of worship, freedom from want, and freedom from fear"—as, at best, prospective rather than descriptive terms. In no way, according to Hutchins, do these fundamental freedoms exist in contemporary America, a society afflicted by staggering want, fear of ideological persecution, racial subjugation, and suppression of speech and action deemed incongruent with the national mission. For Hutchins, entrance into the war will only hamper further the attainment of these freedoms. "The four freedoms must be abandoned if they interfere with winning a war," he states, laconically. "In the ordinary course of war most of them do interfere." Why? According to Hutchins, the war will exacerbate existing tensions and suspicions, resulting on infringements on democratic freedom.[72]

Though prointerventionist, Ralph Bunche's position was more complex. Bunche, who had begun his career as a Marxist-influenced political scientist studying colonialism in French West Africa, moved closer to the political center in the 1940s and beyond. In his essay, "The Negro in the Political Life of the United States," Bunche compares the political situation of blacks in the South and the North with an emphasis on voting rights, remaining somewhat agnostic about the war effort and highlighting the "tragically ironical" fact that subjugated blacks are now entreated "to throw in their brain, toil and sweat, and even their blood for the defense of the nation and its cherished democratic ideals." Ultimately, however, he reaffirms the double victory approach, rebuffing those "who say that it is of little consequence to the Negro whether this country maintains its pseudo-democratic institutions or becomes nationalistic and totalitarian. This is dangerous advice for the Negro; it is an insidious type of defeatism."[73] This kind of attitude was not even tenable for Africans, for whom the stakes of the war were inestimably high. Speaking as a social scientist with fieldwork in Africa, Bunche elaborated on Du Bois's theory of war and imperialism, suggesting how Africans had both tremendous opportunities for emancipation, given the sudden weakness of their war-devastated colonial masters, *and* prospects for devastation, since these wars were being conducted on continental territory with African soldiers.

In an earlier essay, "Africa and the Current World Conflict" (1940), Bunche observes that the continent has functioned as a crucial but often overlooked battleground of the First and Second World Wars. These wars, he writes, are "never of the African's making; the black man has no desire for it, and no voice about it. Nor is he permitted to stay out of it. He is given a gun and a uniform and ordered to fight on one side or the other—and he is usually fighting against other Africans who are similarly controlled." Africans and African Americans faced a similar conundrum with respect to Allied war rhetoric and the actuality of colonial democracy. "We are not permitted to share in the full fruits of democracy, but we are given some of the peelings from the fruit." Even the peelings, however, include freedoms not permitted in totalitarian societies—"freedom of speech, press, assembly and religion," the right to "let the American public and world public know of the abuses we suffer"—and for Bunche, the exercise of these rights "form the foundation upon which our hopes for the future are erected." But he notes that the outcome of the war had graver implications for Africans, since the continent's "strategic geographical location" covered much of the conflict's battleground.

For Bunche, the current world conflict must not boil down to a choice for Africans between fascist imperialism and democratic imperialism. Nazism, he grants, is certainly the boldest and most noxious form of racism the modern world has ever known, "more formal, more deliberate even than that to be found in our own deep South." Yet in his projection of an Africa ruled by Nazism, Bunche adopts, ironically, the familiar scenarios and idioms of Jim Crow. "Africans, under fascist domination," he writes, "would have no rights that any German or Italian would be expected to respect." Was there a more common axiom in America to describe black life under segregation? Granting that fascism destroys individual liberties, even for whites, he then notes that in Nazi-occupied France, "French Negroes, who formerly were able to walk as men in France, who knew nothing of Jim Crow in Paris," now "find Nazi-dictated signs barring them from cafes, hotels, and even prohibiting them from buying railroad tickets."[74] By employing the language of Jim Crow to describe a Fascist-ruled Africa, Bunche undercuts his claim about the specificity of Nazism.

In contrarian fashion, Du Bois begins with an analysis of Germany, based on his personal study and travel in that country over four decades, and rather than emphasizing the global threat posed by Nazism he notes the ostensible *advances* Nazism introduced, successes that partially explain Hitler's sensational rise. Surprisingly, his analysis of Nazism deemphasizes the regime's fanatical white supremacist ideology in favor of an explanatory framework rooted in economics. Du Bois goes so far as to speculate that should Nazism conquer Europe, the attitudes of the French, Dutch, and Scandinavian peoples might well acquiesce in this new order, provided that they, too, benefit from Germany's sophisticated "technocracy." What Du Bois does have to say about the racial implications of war seems nearly an afterthought. "Of course," he adds, "the exaggerated and childish theory of race could not long stand and there would be little reason why it should; in the long run economic reasons will be decisive."[75] Compared with Du Bois's other writings on Nazism and the Second World War, what leaps out in this essay is its apparent agnosticism, even detachment.[76] But it was precisely this detachment, or distance from the subject, that enables Du Bois to produce the kind of counterintuitive critical analysis that Hortense Spillers likens to the Frankfurt School. In her essay "The Idea of Black Culture," Spillers elaborates an "interlocutory occasion" between Du Bois and certain representatives of the Frankfurt School, especially Herbert Marcuse, without overstating the convergence of their respective endeavors. In the context of World War II, what makes this interlocution particularly apt is the formation of a critical theory of society by black and Jewish intellectuals whose thought crystallizes under conditions of crisis or duress, fugitivity and exile.[77]

Like his Frankfurt counterparts, Du Bois understates the alarming, sensational rise of Nazism, or its rabid anti-Semitism, in order to attend to the latent elements of industrial capitalist nations that incline toward the fascistic. "Most Americans," he writes, "think of the future only in terms of Hitler's extravagance—his theories of race, delusions of grandeur, his cruel oppression, imprisonment and murder. But with this must go his leadership of a development of economic planning on a world scale which rivals and even exceeds the plans of Russia." Du Bois frames the global conflict not in the prevailing terms of freedom versus totalitarianism, or as racial chauvinism versus democratic universalism, but as an opposition between economic rationalization—which produces equality, even if substandard in some areas relative to wealthy Western nations—and an ethos of possessive individualism endemic to liberal capitalism.[78]

Unless England and the United States, writes Du Bois, "follow the footsteps of Germany, they can never expect to rival her in technical production and distribution. But, of course, such revolutionary procedure could not have gone on in Germany without a corresponding revolution in the minds of men" (383). Yet this revolution in the minds of men, Du Bois concedes, transpired via a massive agglomeration of racial propaganda, mythologizing of an ancient Germanic militarism, consolidation of dictatorial power, and attacks on institutions (churches, political rivals) that were deemed unfavorable to the national (or National Socialist) interest. Did Du Bois believe it was possible to engender in England and the United States such a revolutionary transformation in national attitudes without the correspondent techniques of repression witnessed in the Soviet Union and Nazi Germany?

Du Bois equivocates on this question, but his elusiveness seems to reflect an unwillingness to characterize the Neuropa as *fundamentally* antithetical to the Western democracies—especially with respect to race and colonialism. To be sure, Du Bois in several publications registers the threat of Nazism, especially its persecution of European Jewry, and is unequivocal in his imperative that Hitler must be vanquished. Du Bois was especially impressed by the rationalization of Germany's economy and astounding advancement in industrialization under National Socialism, which grounded Germany's vulnerable middle class under the Weimar era within the new regime. Moreover, the National Socialist regime organized farmers and peasants into the nation's industrial planning apparatus. The result was a planned economy dominated by the state—and not without considerable gains, like full employment, universal health care, affordable housing, vacations, travel, and recreation in Germany.

Though he does not phrase the matter so explicitly, his essay clearly intends to critique liberal democracy and capitalist inequality *through* an ironic appraisal of Nazism's economic and industrial achievements. Though his attitude toward Nazism would evolve over the course of the war, and his sense of its threat would amplify, by 1941 he appeared unconvinced that Hitler's racial regime posed a serious global threat and persuaded that the democratic bloc was susceptible to similar convulsions based on its own internal contradictions. From Du Bois's perspective, Germany, Italy, and the Soviet Union were not the only dictatorships on the world stage: "The so-called democracies—England, France, and America—have become lands where . . . a façade of political 'freedom,' [conceals a] dictatorship under the guise of economic anarchy" (385). Unchecked, this anarchy could lead democracies to self-destruction. By the mid-twentieth century, Du Bois seemed content to allow the so-called democracies to commit suicide in order to create space for the future socialist world order.

Du Bois dedicated *Russia and America* to his second wife, Shirley Graham Du Bois, an important writer who some scholars believe influenced Du Bois's gravitation toward the Communist sphere. For Du Bois, as for Graham, the genre of literary propaganda—apparently, but not necessarily, a contradiction in terms—constituted a crucial tool for intellectuals to intervene in the geopolitical currents of their time. This story continues in Chapter 5 on Shirley Graham, who employed propaganda en route to her own synthetic vision of socialist modernity in the Third World.[79]

5

From Nkrumah's Ghana to Nasser's Egypt

SHIRLEY GRAHAM AS PARTISAN

In a July 17, 1958, letter to Shirley Graham Du Bois, P. L. Prattis, the editor of the *Pittsburgh Courier*, expressed his hope that as Shirley Graham and W. E. B. Du Bois embarked on their world tour, they would be able to contribute articles on their travels and international affairs to the *Courier*. Suavely, Prattis concludes with his wish that he could join them on their journey. After all, someone needed to record the pomp and splendor awaiting the couple in Moscow. "You ought not," he writes, "to have to tell with what grace Nikita kissed your hand."[1]

Yet Prattis's stipulations for publication in the *Courier* were direct. "I think you would want me to be clear and [unequivocal] on one point: the political coloration of any articles you may write." In his three-page, single-spaced letter, the editor outlines his own political perspective and the status of his newspaper, with a nod to Cold War surveillance of the black press. "I think that the Negro's fight," Prattis writes, "is against his oppressor wherever he finds him . . . in Africa or in the Western Hemisphere. This is the man with whom he lives everyday. I think Negroes must be unrelenting in their fight against this man. I think they must hold their ground as Americans (or Africans) and fight in the most effective ways possible for their rights and their heritage. Further, we must remember always that this is

OUR HOME and OUR COUNTRY. We must protect and promote its welfare because it is OURS."

Prattis highlights an opportunity to exploit opposed factions of white America: those who promoted racial equality versus those who fought it. "Deep within me," he writes, "it seems the part of wisdom to divide and conquer our enemy on the basis of the justice of our cause and the unassailable virtue of our tactics." The divide-and-conquer tactic is not typically associated with virtue, but from the editor's viewpoint, in trying Cold War circumstances, it was a pragmatic and effective tactic, legitimated by history, "wisdom," and the "justice of our cause."

Yet for Prattis there is one major obstacle preventing the successful deployment of this tactic. This obstacle, he reminds Graham, concerns the persistent involvement of communism ("of whatever brand") in black affairs. Though Prattis believes "a change in the social order is inevitable," "I am horror-struck by the methods employed by Communist regimes." Aside from his views on Communist states, his personal attitude or position, he reassures Graham, is not important; he could not bear an anti-communist-led unraveling of "our best and most important newspaper."

Invariably, however, his personal convictions and sense of political realism inform his editorial protocols. "What is important is the fact that most people in OUR COUNTRY reject Communist, and even Socialist, doctrine. That is the climate of thinking today. Most Americans believe that Communist doctrine is evil, conspiratorial, and would destroy our country." Prattis then articulates his own approach, in his role as an editor and an agent in the struggle. "We Negroes must preserve what little strength we have. And we must comport ourselves that we can win friends from the enemy camp [that is, white Americans in general]. We cannot do these things if we give the enemy the slightest pretext for pinning the Communist label upon us." Then he adds: "This is not a matter of being afraid or of lacking courage. It is a matter of being tactically smart." Drawing on unabashedly but suitably divisive techniques within the democratic system, Prattis's articulation of tactical agency sought to manipulate liberal anticommunist support and to ignite another civil war among whites. Abandoning the struggle to reconstitute racial democracy, Graham, by contrast, defined a model of communist partisanship that sought to buttress—and to manipulate—various power blocs (Soviet Communism, Pan-Africanism, Arab Nationalism, Maoism) in opposition to the democratic capitalist sphere.

In the Cold War Crucible

In his letter to Graham, Prattis goes on to note that he has known practically "all the Communists and so-called fellow travelers during the last forty years" but has conducted himself in such a way that he is immune, he believes, to anticommunist smears. "I think this fact gives me strength. I think I am in a position to scout the enemy's ranks, to find weak positions and to take prisoners (friends)." This position, he says, also defines the editorial stance of the *Courier.* Prattis recalls the Paris Peace Conference of 1946, when Du Bois "did not follow the 'line,' as apparently defined by [former leader of the French Communist Party Maurice] Thorez and [Italian Socialist leader Pietro] Nenni." He acknowledges the "great respect and regard which you and Dr. Du Bois have for both me and the Courier. I am positive that neither of you would want to see it weakened in its effectiveness as an instrument in the fight for justice in our lands. I am glad that the smearers can't smear me and I am determined that they shall not smear The Courier."[2]

With a stroking of egos necessary for his delicate but firm request for ideological moderation, Prattis affirms Du Bois as "the greatest thinker and scholar we have produced in the last century," a visionary whose every breath "has been drawn in behalf of me and of all of his people." Consequently, it "would be unfortunate indeed" if the *Courier* "were not open to this modern apostle. This great American has a right to speak (and write) and where perforce should there be a better place than in this newspaper?" The *Courier,* then, functions as a bastion of African American free speech, though one like every other publication that had to calibrate carefully its proximity to communism if it hoped to survive the Cold War.

That said, Prattis was requesting not only detachment from communist ideology but also honest and "balanced" reportage of their sojourn, irrespective of their sympathy or antipathy for a particular regime. "I want you to write about what you see, but I want you to write about the good and the bad, whether it be in England, France, Russia, China, or Ghana. What you write will be authoritative, without doubt, but what I am asking for is balance." Prattis was not "ruling out political observations (even in Russia and China)" but suggests that "our readers will be interested in the social, and economic conditions in the countries you visit, and particularly in color as a factor in world affairs." And of course readers would "be interested in all honors bestowed on you and Dr. Du Bois and any evidence which shows the esteem in which your are held wherever you visit." It was a fair request, at least under the volatile conditions in which writers and publishers were compelled to operate in this era. In closing, Prattis adds: "I hope you will be able to use a double byline: By W. E. B. and Shirley Du Bois."

The *Courier* editor's hope for dual bylines by W. E. B. and Shirley Graham Du Bois suggests the collaborative nature of the work in which the couple was engaged during these years and thus the need to study their projects in tandem. On the surface, this collaboration seemed in perfect consonance, but this chapter attends also to the ways in which Graham undertook literary and political commitments that parted ways with those of Du Bois and, indeed, of the diminishing black literary left (eventually supplanted by the black power and Black Arts movements). For example, as she gravitated toward Maoism in the wake of the Sino-Soviet split—initiated largely after Khrushchev's 1956 speech on Stalinism at the twentieth congress, which Mao viewed as negatively consequential to his own leadership—she adopted the view of Soviet détente as "revisionist."[3] To take another crucial example, whereas Du Bois long defended the state of Israel and the Zionist movement, Graham excoriated Zionism, assailed U.S. support for Israel, and advocated Palestinian armed resistance in the wake of the 1967 Arab-Israeli War.

In what follows, I reconstruct the mélange of communism, Pan-Africanism, Nasserism, and Maoism defining the cultural production of Graham's late career. After sketching the Cold War milieu in which Graham maneuvered, this chapter examines two discrete phases and projects in Graham's late career, both marked by instability, itinerancy, and ideological persecution: her position as Ghana's first director of television and her relocation to Egypt and subsequent adoption of Nasserism and her new persona as a critic of Middle East politics and propagator of Arab-African unity.

The reconstruction of this eccentric ideological trajectory, I argue, reveals an ambitious project to inscribe and instantiate a geopolitical power bloc—socialist modernity in the Third World—arrayed against the adversarial forces of racial liberalism and anticommunism. What is more surprising, however, is the degree to which Graham's writings also "revised" official doctrines among her putative nonaligned and Communist allies in directions more congruent with her own geopolitical vision. In other cases, Graham's valorization of communism represents an insidious and tactically clever attempt to hold this sphere accountable for its anticolonial commitments. In this respect, an element of play accompanies her commitment to an ostensibly masculine geopolitics of heroic transformation characterized by revolutionary, charismatic leadership.

Nonetheless, certain dilemmas flow from her commitment to this vision. The hagiographies and encomia she wrote of Gamal Abdel Nasser, Paul Robeson, Du Bois, Mao Zedong, Julius Nyerere, and others foreground at least two difficulties: first, with respect to her treatments of actual revolutionary leaders, it is easy to dismiss Graham as a pawn, a mouthpiece of a regime, a "useful idiot" in this or that situation. Second, despite Graham's concern, for example, about the location of women in Egyptian and Chinese society, her adulation of male charismatic leadership seems incongruent with narratives of black feminist internationalism. Both her advocacy of socialist modernization and her fidelity to narratives of masculine individual transformation implicate her in the belief that "Nations develop in a teleological manner according to modernization and Marxist theories alike," as one commentator puts it, and in this process "men are the bearers of the modernizing gene."[4]

Graham's version of partisanship, dramatized in the narratives of heroic male leaders and in the promulgation of wars of national liberation, implies a normatively masculine and nondemocratic tradition. In *Charisma and the Fictions of Black Leadership*, Erica R. Edwards challenges what she sees as the valorization of charismatic, predominantly male authority at the center of African American culture and politics. Black political formations, according to Edwards, have typically produced violent models of charismatic leadership that foreclose alternative and potentially more democratic political arrangements. Edwards argues that "charisma is founded in three forms of violence: the historical or historiographical violence of reducing a heterogeneous black freedom struggle to a top-down narrative of Great Man leadership; the social violence of performing social change in the form of a fundamentally antidemocratic form of authority; and the epistemological violence of structuring knowledge of black political subjectivity and movement within a gendered hierarchy of political value that grants uninterrogated power to normative masculinity."[5] In this account, charisma constitutes at once a mythology (constructed around male charismatic leaders like Martin Luther King Jr. and Malcolm X) and a political fiction (the idea that such leadership is necessary for black political progress) but also, more insidiously, a form of desire: the yearning among many African Americans for a redemptive politics that a charismatic leader is presumed to shoulder.

But in the postwar era, when so many of Graham's anticolonial contemporaries—finding themselves suddenly on the wrong side of the Cold War divide—were assassinated or overthrown, it is important not to dismiss the affective and concrete political transformations enabled by charismatic authority, particularly since this authority was so intimately tied with the aspirations of sundry individuals, mass publics, and transnational collectivities. "As the 1960s and 1970s progressed," Ann Douglas notes, "colonialism gave way not to independence, but to neocolonialism, and many of the charismatic leaders and intellectuals of the 1950s and 1960s were systematically assassinated, deposed, or died young, sometimes in mysterious circumstances. I think of Felix Moumié, Patrice Lumumba, Amilcar Cabral, Kwame Nkrumah, Richard Wright, Frantz Fanon, Che Guevara, Jacobo Arbenz Guzmán, Malcolm X, Martin Luther King, and even John and Robert Kennedy." Douglas suggests that the consequences of these extinguishments are difficult to calculate and impossible to overstate, insofar as the hopes and transformative possibilities invested in the likes of Malcolm X, Nkrumah, and Fanon also perished along with these figures. It "is hard to imagine or to overestimate the effect of such losses," Douglas continues. "Independence in Africa is 'represented by certain men,' Fanon wrote in his impassioned elegy for his friend Lumumba. We should not be too quick to deconstruct or disbelieve his statement."[6]

For Graham, whose own fate was tied to these leaders, history assumed the character of quicksand: the moment or sequence of events when what seemed like relatively stable political ground begins to shift beneath one's feet. When a postcolonial government confidently appoints a comrade to a significant position on one day, the possibility exists that on the next day this government might be overthrown, its leadership assassinated or drawn into war. The quicksand of history—from the ouster of Nkrumah, which prompted Graham's departure from Ghana, to Nasser's death, which precipitated her exit from Egypt, to U.S. anticommunism, which alienated her from the United States—compelled Graham to adapt to constantly shifting geopolitical circumstances, from which she characteristically emerged in positions of remarkable influence.

The story of Graham's conception of a Third World socialist bloc begins in postcolonial Ghana. Shirley Graham and W. E. B. Du Bois joined a relatively small but diversely talented group of African Americans and other blacks in the diaspora, contributing to the establishment of a continental forerunner in decolonization. According to Kevin Gaines, the formation of this diaspora community in Ghana represented less a renunciation of the promise of U.S. integration than a commitment to "Ghana's progressive vision of freedom" that "placed in sharper relief [E. Franklin] Frazier's critique of a postwar American liberalism compromised by antilabor and segregationist reaction and the stifling of dissent." A proponent of African decolonization who excoriated American racial liberalism, Frazier was disturbed by the sense that "integrationism under Cold War auspices was predicated on the renunciation of an independent group consciousness."[7] This collective consciousness, however, was not something to be found in West Africa, ipso facto, and ready for absorption among the sojourners to Ghana; like any project of modernity, it had to be built.

If an independent group consciousness indeed took root in Ghana, it required construction on multiple fronts, especially in the cultural sphere. The projects of W. E. B. and Shirley Graham Du Bois were integral to the construction of this cultural front. Du Bois had long dreamt of completing his Encyclopedia Africana project under Nkrumah's patronage. He died before realizing this dream; Nkrumah was overthrown before Shirley Graham could complete hers.

Cold War rivalries threatened the flowering of an autonomous Pan-African or anticolonial consciousness described by Gaines and exemplified by intellectuals like Prattis and Frazier. Unlike these figures, however, who supported decolonization but rejected communism, Graham repeatedly lauded Soviet power in the Third World, at least until the 1970s—years after the Sino-Soviet split that began brewing in 1956—when she belatedly adopted Mao's anti-USSR position. During these intervening years, a time of hostility between Beijing and Moscow, her voice contributed to the pressure communists felt to live up to their anticolonial commitments. Were the African wars of national liberation, as Nikita Khrushchev famously declared, truly "'sacred wars' that merited assistance and would probably require violence to succeed"?[8]

Despite such scintillating pronouncements, however, Soviet officials (like their U.S. counterparts) sought to avoid embroilment in Third World wars, conflicts that anticolonial leaders frequently escalated, in some moments promiscuously, as the case of Nasser's Egypt during Suez (1956) and the Arab-Israeli War (1967) indicates. The notion, then, that writers like Graham functioned as a pawn or a mouthpiece of international communism fails to consider the discursive pressure that she and her biographical subjects were able to exert on the reluctant Soviet big brother. For Graham, Soviet support counterbalanced Western power, especially in the context of colonial or asymmetrical war, and accelerated modernization processes necessary to constitute an autonomous Third World power bloc. Though hindsight suggests the remoteness of this latter prospect, in what follows Graham's cultural and political activities create an imaginative space for a geopolitical configuration on this scale.

Stained by the experiments by Communist states like the USSR and China in collectivization, great leaps forward, persecution of real or imagined dissidents, and the debasement of language associated with these acts, the phrase "building socialism" might seem perverse or anachronistic. But in the political imagination of Graham, the idea of building socialism assumed a very different form, a path delineated but not taken. A synthesis of Afro-Asian communalism and socialist modernity and a quest for rapprochement between the Third and Second Worlds, her vision was neither utopian (it heralded no future classless society) nor predicated on the constitution of a "new man" endemic of the totalitarian movements or Fanonian decolonization.

Yet in order to stand a fighting chance against liberal capitalism, a power bloc on this scale required the healing of divisions that characterized relations among multiple regional factions: between Africans north and south of the Sahara; between Muslims and Christians; between "moderate" and "radical" postcolonial actors; between the Second and Third Worlds. As Chapter 3 discussed, Graham's 1970 essay, "Egypt Is Africa," furnishes one example of Graham's reconciliatory project. "In Africa," she writes, "we do not speak of the 'conquest of Egypt' by the Moslems."[9] Sidestepping the fraught history of Islam in Africa, Graham's stentorian yet ambiguous first-person plural voice constructs a selective historical narrative that exploits, if not aggrandizes, the momentum of Arab and black African collaboration during decolonization. Broad in scope, her historical imagination sought to reverse the divisions opened by the Hegelian philosophy of history and the Scramble for Africa.

Graham mobilized an uncommonly diverse and idiosyncratic array of literary, political, commercial, technological, and media resources at her disposal to create a blueprint for socialist modernity in the Third World. Yet given "her notoriety and attainments," Graham's biographer wonders why his subject has been ignored by recent scholars and criticized, often harshly, by her contemporaries. Some of her associates regarded Graham, especially as she assumed roles of increasing influence in Ghana, as haughty and officious—an impression that likely accounts for the shrillness of their criticisms.[10] Her marginalization in recent scholarship is more difficult to explain. Where her work is mentioned at all, it remains peripheral in studies of the black literary left, the Afro-Asian (or Afro-Arab) analogy, the global decolonization movement, and black internationalism.

On the other hand, this neglect is unsurprising insofar as Graham was a writer of propaganda, a genre that many literary critics tend to overlook or to regard as unworthy of sustained critical attention.[11] For some critics, propaganda elicits interest as a historical artifact but as little more. Since overtly propagandistic texts are easily taken at face value, these works seem to diminish the role of literary critics who are trained in what Sharon Marcus and Stephen Best call "symptomatic reading," "an interpretive method that argues that the most interesting aspect of a text is what it represses." From this perspective, Fredric Jameson deduces that "interpretation should therefore seek 'a latent meaning behind a manifest one.'"[12] As Jameson's work demonstrates, the effort to locate latent meanings necessitates a muscular mode of close reading.[13]

With propaganda, however, there is apparently no repressed or latent meaning for the critic to excavate. Consequently, Russ Castronovo and Jonathon Auerbach seek to reorient the field of propaganda studies by acknowledging the residual opprobrium attached to the term following the First and Second World Wars but also by insisting that as "a cultural practice, propaganda concerns nothing less than the ways in which human beings communicate, particularly with respect to the creation and widespread dissemination of attitudes, images, and beliefs." In an excellent introductory synthesis, Castronovo and Auerbach distill thirteen propositions about propaganda, of which the following few observations are especially relevant. The root word of propaganda originates in response to a biblical injunction, and orators "in classical antiquity certainly addressed audiences, but they did so without the aid of megaphones, the printing press, radio signals, or the networks of the Internet."[14] On this view, what was most modern about Pope Gregory XV's propagation initiative in 1622 was a provision that the Vatican's post office would handle dissemination of the true faith.

But by the twentieth and twenty-first centuries, propaganda is conceived *as* propaganda only to the degree that it finds expression through, and can manipulate, modern media technologies and the information networks they create. Outside this network of mediation and dissemination, the singular propaganda text ceases to be propaganda as such, since the novelty of modern propaganda, at least in some circumstances, resides less in its content (ideas, narratives, beliefs, and so on) than in the new and influential modes of transmission—from political pamphlets in taverns to radios in villages to newspapers in cities—that rendered these messages more widely available, especially in rural and illiterate populations. This expansion of propaganda networks does not mean, however, that its reach is total (its effects can be partial, no matter how stringent the enforcement of propaganda), or that audiences remain passive recipients.

"People can actively use propaganda and are not simply passive dupes used by it," Castronovo and Auerbach note. "Propaganda does not necessarily spread from the top down." As the authors rightly note, scholarship on twentieth-century propaganda emphasizes the pliability of target audiences, populations "easily shaped and molded by master manipulators."[15] This presumed sense of manipulation, for one thing, is often disrupted by an array of factors, from technical glitches and radio signal failures to plain distraction. More important, audiences—or to use the phrase adopted in previous chapters, publics and counterpublics—also reinterpret and reactivate the propaganda they consume. But the case of W. E. B. and Shirley Graham Du Bois is exemplary because they can be described not merely as opponents or even reinterpreters of dominant Western propaganda but rather as master counterpractitioners themselves who deployed the genre's deconstructive and constructive capacities: by taking apart, in the first instance, the claims of the capitalist sphere and by imagining, in the second, alternative geopolitical futures and pathways toward them.

This dual tendency is understandably easy to overlook, since Graham's polemics often seem doctrinaire: the West is unambiguously, even villainously, imperialist; the Soviet Union is a friend of the darker races and super-agent of peace. Yet as Du Bois's or Graham's writings suggest, the propaganda genre betrays surprising, sometimes strenuous, modes of redaction, revision, and reinterpretation that these writers employed in the discursive field of Cold War geopolitics.

From her expatriation to Ghana in 1961 to her death in China in 1977, Shirley Graham led a peripatetic existence straddled between the Communist and nonaligned Afro-Asian spheres. Communist, pan-Africanist, Nasserist, and Maoist articulations and affiliations—in roughly that chronological order—mark her literary and political activities of these years. In light of this eclecticism, it is reasonable to conclude, as her biographer asserts, that beyond developing a vague "sort of 'left nationalism,'" she "floundered ideologically" after her husband's death in Accra in 1963.[16] Reviewing her intellectual productions of this period, one is tempted to surmise that denunciation of liberal capitalism, a phrase synonymous for Graham with imperialism, represents the only ideological consistency of these years. Taking for granted that the priority on ideological consistency is uninteresting at best and chimerical at worst, it is still worth asking whether Graham's legacy represents merely a scattershot style of negative critique, a radical anti-imperialism sprinkled with whatever ideological orientation that was available to her at the time. This chapter, by contrast, ventures an interpretation grounded in her constructive vision.

In the cultural battlefield of the Cold War in the Third World, the Communist bloc did seem to enjoy a competitive edge, at least in the estimation of certain African Americans abroad. As J. Saunders Redding notes in his *An American in India*, the Soviets had made impressive inroads into this crucial nonaligned nation via the propagation of Russian culture. Redding worried less about the penetration of Soviet spies and agitators into the nonaligned countries than he did about the proliferation of Russian literature and propaganda films. Soviet officials appeared to grasp that Russian high culture complemented the dissemination of propaganda. Early in his narrative, he ominously records a group of Indian military personnel exiting a movie theater, where they had just watched *The Fall of Berlin*, the state-sponsored film that valorizes Stalin's collectivization schemes and leadership in the defeat of Nazi Germany. But as he takes stock of the Soviet presence in India, Redding notices that beyond explicitly propagandistic materials, India's bookstores display handsome, affordable editions of Russian literary classics, whereas the American offerings consisted only of overpriced dime novels and Hollywood films that offended Indian sensibilities. One of Redding's companions assails "those vicious writers whose obscene books are in our stalls! You have not considered the immoral moving pictures which are shown in our cinemas! Why? Why do the Americans send such vulgar and worthless books and pictures to us?"[17] Redding coolly counters with free market logic: if Indians did not consume America's culture industry, then it would not be exported there.

But Redding, who defended—sometimes with comic ineffectualness—the supremacy of the American capitalist system to skeptical Indian audiences, was forced to concede the superiority of the Soviet position in the culture wars. For the United States to prevail in the non-Western world, the government would have to invest not only in the military or economic spheres but also in "high" culture. Over the next decade, CIA-funded organizations like the Congress for Cultural Freedom, the Asia Foundation, and the National Students Association expanded America's cultural and ideological presence in India and elsewhere, but the exposure in 1967 of the CIA's involvement in a series of assassination and subversion plots of foreign leaders—described by one Democratic senator, Frank Church, as akin to "a rogue elephant on a rampage"—only increased South Asia's distrust of U.S. penetration.[18]

Graham capitalized on these suspicions in the Third World, but her work also constructed didactic models that aimed to globalize the African American uplift tradition. Reviewing Graham's *There Was Once a Slave* in 1947 for *The Nation*, James Baldwin read her fictionalized biography of Frederick Douglass, rightly, as race propaganda. Baldwin opined that this text was devoid of "dignity and humanity alike," an insufferable attempt to "Uplift the Race."[19] To one degree or another, most of Graham's later work was propagandistic, but many African American writers in the first half of the twentieth century—particularly those associated with "social realist" fiction—defended, and defined, art as propaganda, even as they differed on whether literary production ought to follow in the traditions of racial uplift, naturalist portrayals of the decayed black metropolis, or graphic indictments of racial violence.

For Ann Petry, all art is propaganda because all "truly great art" constitutes a form of social critique; the novel is simply one formidable form for this task. Therefore, dismissals of social realist fiction as mere propaganda forget that the function of all serious art is propagandistic, which in this context is understood not as a buttress to the state but as a critique of power. But this transhistorical conception of propaganda smudges the distinction between art or the novel in general and the specific forms of propaganda that proliferate in the First World War era and beyond, a context to which Petry alludes in the framing of her remarks on twentieth-century developments ("Hitler, atomic energy, Hiroshima, Buchenwald, Mussolini, USSR").[20]

The theory and praxis underwriting Graham's work suggests a different intention: to synthesize a *negative* critique of Western imperialism with a *constructive*, idiosyncratic, yet cohesive vision of socialist modernity in the Third World. Indeed, the strident and often repetitive character of Graham's assailment of imperialism—what most recollections by her contemporaries tended to emphasize—can overshadow the didactic function of her historical and biographical narratives. If hagiographic, these narratives are also didactic in a specific sense: they are meant to demarcate paths to socialism and to inspire and instruct readers, especially younger audiences, in techniques of Cold War defiance.

Versus determinist representations of black life associated with Petry's or Wright's social realism, Graham's fictional and historical works portrayed individuals and collectivities triumphant over subjugation: U.S. plantation slavery, British colonialism, or anticommunist persecution. That many of these heroic figures were state actors committed to Arab, African, and Chinese socialism—and thus viewed by Western officialdom as figures of authoritarianism or totalitarianism—would appear to implicate her project in the type of socialist aesthetics that dissidents in the Eastern bloc derided so vigorously.

In contrast with Petry's social realism there is what Eastern dissidents derided as "socialist realism," defined by Czeslaw Milosz not only as an aesthetic but also as a "philosophy, too, and the cornerstone of official doctrine worked out in Stalin's days. [Socialist realism] is directly responsible for the deaths of millions of men and women, for it is based on the glorification of the state by the writer and artist, whose task is to portray the power of the state as the greatest good, and to scorn the sufferings of the individual."[21] Under the pseudonym "Abram Tertz," one writer in late Stalinist Russia noted that all works of socialist realism, however varied in style and content, betray fidelity to the "Purpose": they "are panegyrics of

Communism, satires on some of its many enemies, or descriptions of life 'in its revolutionary development,' i.e., life moving toward Communism."[22] The Stalinist atrocities tied to socialist realism found no equivalent of scale in the Third World. But even without the deadly eye of Stalinist supervision, Graham's work was similarly purposeful, emphasizing social processes of "revolutionary development" and buttressing the cult of personality that identified her postcolonial protagonists so intimately with their respective nation-states as well as with the global anticolonial movement.

It is not accidental, then, that the figures who capture Graham's imagination—Robeson, Nasser, Nyerere, Du Bois, Mao—embody various iterations of Third World socialist modernity. Graham's vision of socialist modernity parts ways with the strategic liberalism adopted by many black intellectuals in favor of the radical moves made by internationalists of the decolonization movement. Countering the prestige critics attribute to Fanon's notion of revolutionary violence, Carol Anderson, as discussed in Chapter 2, defends the strategic forms of black liberal resistance that critics downplay in favor of Fanon's militancy.[23] And yet the literary partisanship displayed by Graham—a rejection of the stealthy liberal strategies deployed by Prattis—has equally eluded the attention of contemporary criticism. Combined with her roles as Ghana's director of television, editorial writer in Egypt, and liaison between Africa and Asia (and, until the Sino-Soviet split, between Asia and the USSR), Graham's own authorship, I want to argue, itself embodies a model of literary and political *partisanship* integral to her didacticism.

In Carl Schmitt's theory of the partisan, the significance of armed combat against an enemy, especially in the context of a war of liberation, remains indispensible; otherwise, the partisan devolves into metaphor. Because "the term *partisan* defines specific historical figures and situations," metaphorical usage of the term, Schmitt suggests, enables different commentators to describe the partisan, on the one hand, as a militant opposed to the "nihilism of a thoroughly technologized world, the last defender of species and soil," and, on the other, as "precisely the opposite, i.e., a figure of modern nihilism" encompassed by all classes and professions ("the priest, the peasant, the scholar, and, in this way, also the soldier"). For Schmitt, the necessary criteria for his conception of the partisan include "irregularity, increased mobility of active combat, and increased intensity of political engagement."[24]

Though Schmitt does not emphasize this fact, it is worth noting that his paradigmatic embodiments of the partisan derive from the Communist sphere, and specifically from anticolonial revolutions of which Mao's China is foundational. The "partisan struggles during World War II and the years thereafter in Indochina and other countries, well identified by the names of Mao Tse-tung, Ho Chi-minh, and Fidel Castro, indicate that the tie to the soil, to the autochthonous population, and to the geographical particularity of the land—mountain-ranges, forests, jungles, or deserts—are topical even today. . . . For as at least as long as anti-colonial wars are possible on our planet, the partisan will represent a specifically terrestrial type of fighter."[25] To distill a concept of the partisan from Graham's writings is to risk the kind of metaphorization that Schmitt opposes, but his location of the partisan in the exemplary historical context—the anticolonial war of national liberation—makes his usage apposite for Graham: a writer of national liberation whose advocacy of armed combat and guerilla warfare in the Palestinian intifada, in Vietnamese resistance, or in African American struggles anchors her within this tradition of militant partisanship.

During the early Cold War, a cloud of mystery if not intrigue enshrouds Graham's biography. Official documents and statements by Graham list different dates of birth (a confusion, Gerald Horne notes, that dates from earlier in her life).[26] Her canceled U.S. passport states November 11, 1899; the "certificate of identity" issued for her Tanzanian passport states the same month and day but records the year as 1906. Her Republic of Guinea passport, which also records the November 11, 1906, birthdate, states her nationality as "Guinean." In November 1960, the Government of Nigeria invited her to honor Nnamdi Azikiwe in his governor-general's "Ceremony of Taking the Oaths of Office" of his country. As few black Americans were as well connected among African elites as Graham, these affiliations with nonaligned radical leaders only increased suspicion among U.S. intelligence officials.

Some newspaper coverage, such as a 1970 *Le Monde* report, recognized that Graham held Ghanaian citizenship, but few seemed aware that she also held Tanzanian and Guinean passports—to say nothing of her long-term residency in Egypt (where her records indicate she studied Arabic), a geographical position that enabled her to publish wide-ranging commentary on African, Egyptian, and Middle Eastern affairs. U.S. State Department documents assert that she renounced her U.S. citizenship and joined the Communist Party; Graham rejects both charges, though her denial of Party membership was false.

In its May 1970 issue, the French paper *Le Monde* featured the following headline: "Mme W. E. B. Du Bois interdite aux États-Unis." The article notes that in his 1952 memoir, *In Battle for Peace—The Story of My 83rd Birthday*, W. E. B. Du Bois, "écrivain noir américain et 'père du panafricanisme,'" "described his struggle against the McCarthyite tribunal [*la lutte . . . contre les tribunaux maccarthystes*]." The article continues: "This book was accompanied by '*Commentaires*' by the second wife of Du Bois, Shirley Graham. It is this last part that has prompted the Department of Justice, in spite of the Department of State's contrary recommendation, to refuse her access to United States territory, thereby forbidding her to speak at Fisk University, and to visit members of her family. Since 1963, like her husband, Shirley Graham—today aged seventy-one years old—has assumed Ghanaian nationality."[27] In *Battle for Peace*, Shirley Graham interspersed Du Bois's chapters with "comments," supplementary personal insights intended for the reader's delectation, she explains but then adds the following: "the title may also be looked upon as the French '*Comment*' which with the addition of the question mark is best translated into everyday English as 'How come?'"[28] According to the *Le Monde* report, Shirley Graham "was 'affiliated with some subversive organizations' that the spokesman of the Department of Justice 'has refused to identify.'" [Shirley Graham serait 'affiliée a des organisations subversives' que le porte-parole du department de la justice "s'est refusé à identifier."] This interdiction followed a 1970 investigatory commission, presided over by Spiro Agnew, Ronald Reagan, and one Sol M. Linowitz, ambassador of the Organization of American States and director of Xerox, two months earlier concerning sources of "agitation" in American universities.[29]

PASSPORT

These are to request and require in the name of the President of the Republic of Ghana all those whom it may concern to allow the bearer to pass freely without let or hindrance and to afford him or her every assistance and protection of which he or she may stand in need.

Given at ACCRA *this* 9TH *day of* OCTOBER 1963

1

This Passport contains 32 pages.
Ce passeport contient 32 pages.

PASSPORT.
PASSEPORT.
GHANA

No. of PASSPORT / No. du PASSEPORT: 26894

NAME OF BEARER / NOM DU TITULAIRE: MRS. SHIRLEY GRAHAM DU BOIS

~~ACCOMPANIED BY HIS WIFE~~ (Maiden name) / ~~ACCOMPAGNÉ DE SA FEMME~~ (Neé): GRAHAM

and by / et de ... children / enfants

NATIONAL STATUS / NATIONALITÉ: CITIZEN OF GHANA

2

DESCRIPTION — SIGNALEMENT

	Bearer—Titulaire	Wife—Femme
Profession / Profession	TELEVISION EDUCATIONAL DIRECTOR	
Place and date of birth / Lieu et date de naissance	INDIANAPOLIS, U.S.A. 11.11.1906	
Residence / Résidence	GHANA	
Height / Taille	5 ft. 4 in. 5	ft. in.
Colour of eyes / Couleur des yeux	BROWN	
Colour of hair / Couleur des cheveux	BLACK-GREY	
Special peculiarities / Signes particuliers		

CHILDREN — ENFANTS

Name-Nom | Date of birth-Date de naissance | Sex-Sexe

Usual Signature of Bearer / Signature du Titulaire: Shirley G. Du Bois

Usual Signature of Wife / Signature de sa Femme

3

Bearer (Titulaire)

Wife (Femme) (Photo)

Shirley Graham Du Bois's Ghanaian passport. (Papers of Shirley Graham Du Bois. Harvard University, Radcliffe Institute for Advanced Studies, Schlesinger Library.)

Appealing to the attorney general and other U.S. State agencies, several friends tried to intercede on her behalf. One of her advocates was Phillip Burton of the U.S. House of Representatives, who on May 27, 1970, received a response to his appeal from Raymond F. Farrell, commissioner of Immigration and Naturalization Services under the U.S. Department of Justice. "The basic law under which the Service operates is the Immigration and Nationality Act of 1952," the department letter explains. "The United States, as a matter of sovereign right, exercises control over aliens seeking to enter, pass through, or remain in this country."

> The purpose of the controls is to protect the national interest and the continuing good order and well-being of the nation. These controls have been spelled out by the Congress in the Immigration and Nationality Act. Aliens may, because of their political activities, or because of membership in or affiliation with certain organizations, render themselves ineligible to receive visas and subject themselves to exclusion from the United States under Section 212(a) (28) of the Immigration and Nationality Act, 8 U.S.C. 1182. A United States Consular Officer of the Department of State, in Cairo, Egypt, found Mrs. Du Bois to be ineligible for a visa under that section of the law when she applied to visit the United States in February 1970.

The Department of State's decision was based, Farrell continues, "on her activities in the Communist movement and her affiliation with Communist organizations." The letter goes on to explain that although a provision exists in the law "whereby under certain conditions the temporary admission of such an alien into the United States may be authorized, a decision was made that the exercise of this extraordinary authority in the case of Mrs. Du Bois would not be in the best interests of this country." The committee decided that Graham's stated purpose of speaking at American colleges "did not outweigh, from a national interest view, the factors in her background which compelled the initial denial of the visa. Mrs. Du Bois, a native of Indianapolis, Indiana, voluntarily renounced her United States citizenship at the American Embassy at Accra, Ghana, on October 4, 1963. She has been affiliated with over thirty Communist-controlled organizations, in many of which she held leadership positions, and there is no evidence of any change in her views."[30] Though this report likely exaggerates the extent of Graham's involvement in international communist activities, it underscores U.S. officials' perception of Graham as a radical with global influence.

Graham addressed these charges in correspondence with Dr. Richard P. Stevens of Lincoln University's Department of Political Science. A newspaper article by an African American woman elicited second thoughts from Graham about her U.S. visit. "After reading the enclosed article, written by a Black Woman for the *San Francisco Examiner*," she wrote, "I am having second thoughts. . . . Would you understand and not feel annoyed with me if I say that this article makes me doubt if I want to come to the United States at all?" That this *Examiner* writer was a black woman signaled, for Graham as it did for her husband, that black Americans were in the grip of Cold War political quiescence. "Were this written by a white person—I could shrug it off—but this is the type of thing a black woman throws at another!" (Yet as her biographer shows, censures of Graham by black women were not uncommon: Dorothy Hunton, Maya Angelou, Alice Walker also deprecated her work and personality.)[31] If black liberals, for Graham, were now too close to the enemy, younger militants like the Black Panther Party and the Student Nonviolent Coordinating Committee gave her cause for hope. Believing the time had come for armed resistance, she was encouraged by black militants who, finally, were laying nonviolent struggle and liberal accommodation to rest.

"This writer," Graham's letter continues, "knows as well as you and I do that my husband was never a 'Communist leader'—we did not leave the United States in 1963, and he never 'renounced' any citizenship. The reason he did not, however, was that when the U.S. Embassy, having read the enthusiastic account of his having become a citizen of Ghana, in the *Ghanaian Times*, wrote him to come to the embassy and renounce his U.S. citizenship, in order that any other citizenship 'be valid,' he simply ignored the order. I remember him saying that he was '[too] busy'!" As far as her political convictions were concerned, "I certainly will never deny, nor deplore my 'association' with Du Bois and I certainly am in 'opposition to racism, neo-colonialism, and apartheid.' Nor do I at this point feel in the mood to explain that I never joined the Communist Party."[32] As one judge in W. E. B. Du Bois's arraignment suggested, when confronted with the charge of supporting communist subversion, the venerable race leader demurred, arrogating the right to define communism and his affiliation with it on his own terms.[33]

Graham also demurred on the question of her precise communist attachments, when she did not ignore such probing altogether. For contemporary readers, whether she was a "card-carrying" Communist is probably the least interesting aspect of her late career. Graham did not bother with ideological consistency or the status of her projects in the eyes of official monitors: her efforts to build Third World socialism consisted in a set of overlapping and sometimes competing practices, of which her activities in Ghana represent a crucial, if uncompleted, initial phase.

Ghana Television: Shirley Graham's Unfinished Project

During the March 1957 inaugural celebration of Ghana's independence, attended by vice president Richard Nixon, Du Bois had been denied a visa and was prevented from attending. But on July 1, 1960, Graham and Du Bois boarded a flight to Accra, Ghana, where they were scheduled to attend ceremonies commemorating the independent republic.[34]

Graham's new role as Ghana's first director of television provided the institutional structure to propagate her vision of African and Third World socialist modernity. The ambition of Ghana Television was to construct an alternative to the Western culture industry and mass media: an entity capable of consolidating national and continental identity via Africa-centered and cosmopolitan programming and communal spectatorship. But the logistics of constructing an infrastructure to support this technology in a largely nonindustrialized country consumed much of Graham's energies. In order to "bring television to villages that barely had electricity," Horne writes, "let alone television, she intended to set up 'television viewing centers' powered by generators until electricity came on line. In an updating of the African tradition of the 'griot,' there would be 'traditional story tellers' present to explain in local languages what was taking place on the screen. Her ambitious plan was to insure that '85% of the material shown' would be 'produced right here' in Ghana; 'this rules out entirely the type of television which is being imposed by the West on the people of Nigeria,' she boasted."[35] What she envisioned was not the commercial or privatized experience of Western television viewing but rather a communitarian model with programming presumably administered by elites like Graham.

To realize this vision Graham developed partnerships with Sanyo Corporation and other Japanese interests. In a letter to one Sanyo representative, she expressed regret for the delay in her reply, the consequence of the "pressure under which we are working here in Ghana. The African Summit Conference opens in Accra 21st October," she explained, and already "the Foreign Ministers are here as well as thousands of newsmen, observers and visitors. Our new Television Service has a tremendous responsibility and must, under difficult circumstances, give first class coverage as well as carry all African programmes." After conveying her gratitude for Sanyo's dispatch of 100 twelve-inch portable televisions, she exonerated Sanyo personnel of any responsibility for the actual distribution of the sets. Who would respond to the repair needs of these imports? Ghana Television would be responsible for any technical support, Graham assured a representative from the African division of Sanyo, as would Ghana Sanyo when its factory operations commenced.

In search of alternatives to Western mass cultural production, Graham traversed the global to meet with diplomats, corporate executives, and technology experts.[36] The FBI observed her new position, which took her to Japan, where she met with corporate and government officials to learn the newest techniques for televisual production and to consolidate commercial partnerships with the Sanyo Corporation and the Ghanaian government.[37] In her "Radio Report to Japan," dated March 14, 1964, she writes from Tokyo:

> Three weeks ago I arrived in Japan with two technical assistants to study Japanese television. Ghana is planning its first television system and last fall I made a survey and study of television

> in Europe—remaining several weeks each in Great Britain, France, Czechoslovakia and Italy. I also attended UNESCO's International Conference on Educational Television which met in Paris, November 10th–14th. On my return to Ghana I submitted a report, including observations on television in the United States, which I know very well. The report closed with certain recommendations to the Ghana government. One recommendation was: "That the alleged excellence of Japan's Television be considered. We are convinced it would be a mistake to start television in Ghana without first hand knowledge of Japan's contributions in this field."[38]

Japan was the natural choice for her research mission, since the prosperous East Asian nation that had once sought to mimic technological innovations originating in the United States now appeared to surpass the West in the realm of electronics.

Recent history taught that funding for modernization projects by Western powers came with strings attached or portended unsavory consequences. When the U.S. government unceremoniously reneged on funding for the Aswan Dam, Gamal Nasser responded by nationalizing the Suez Canal Company. As Chapter 3 discussed, Nasser wanted to fund the dam with revenue from the canal but also, according to some observers, to retaliate for what he perceived as America's casually arrogant withdrawal of financing. Mohamed H. Heikal, a prolific journalist and close advisor to Nasser, describes a scene in which Nasser hears the news of the "American action" on the radio of a plane carrying him and Nehru back from the island of Brioni in Yugoslavia, where they had conferred about the future of the Third World with President Tito. Upon arrival in Cairo, Nasser reads the full text of the U.S. memo. "He realized immediately that this was something much more than a financial blow which threatened Egypt's entire development programme. That blow he had already anticipated. But the studied offensiveness of the language made it clear that Dulles' action was also a deliberate snub, a political challenge to Egypt's dignity as well as to her aspirations."[39] Chapter 3 describes the prehistory and fallout of this moment. From the 1950s to the 1970s, Graham's aversion to what she and other anticolonial thinkers perceived as humiliating and aborted transactions prompted her to seek geopolitical, intercultural, and economic exchanges largely outside of the West.

As Graham well knew, Kwame Nkrumah encountered a similar dilemma concerning his proposed construction of the Volta Dam project. Years before John F. Kennedy agonized over whether to fund Ghana's Volta Dam, Richard Wright counseled Nkrumah: "Beware of a Volta Project built by foreign money. Build your own Volta, and build it out of the sheer lives and bodies of your people!"[40]

Graham's reports from Japan betray confidence that Asian and African modernization could proceed apace with minimal Western intercession. Instead of relying on aid from Western partners, Graham saw Japan as an avant-garde modern power from within the ranks of the darker races. Indeed, Japanese companies appeared to be producing high-quality equipment less expensively than their Western counterparts and training unskilled laborers who eventually joined the ranks of skilled professionals. "We know that Japan's television was patterned after the United States and that your first equipment came from the United States," she writes. "Now you are manufacturing your own equipment and shipping equipment to the United States. This is a real achievement!" There was little reason to believe that such methods could not be replicated in a nation like Ghana.

Japan's approach was attractive not only because it reduced production costs by sidestepping Western intermediaries and training their own laborers; Japanese companies invested in their workforce in a way that provided obvious lessons for a newly independent nation like Ghana. In electronic plants owned by Sanyo and Toshiba throughout Japan, "we learned why your companies can produce equipment of high quality to sell cheaper than similar equipment produced in other countries: You take unskilled workers, train and educate them and give them the opportunity to join the ranks of skilled workers. Through cooperative effort the [workers'] earning capacity is increased. Ghana, where more of its workers are unskilled, can learn from you." Graham recalls witnessing "an impressive and beautiful demonstration of stage lighting with music . . . and saw the traditional artistry and sensitivity of the Japanese people being transmitted by electronics."[41] The visual and audial potential of television, she felt, was ideal for projecting the sensuousness of West African culture.

Graham conceived of Ghana Television not only as an alternative to the Western culture industry but also as a vehicle of mass pedagogical and communitarian nation building. In her "Radio Report to Japan," dated March 14, 1964, she writes from Tokyo: "Television is now being planned as an aid to Ghana's rapidly expanding educational system. Knowledge of the symbols of learning, knowledge of the world in which one lives, of demands and potential resources are essentials for exercising citizenship and assuming responsibilities as free men and women." In addition to promoting democratic citizenship, television had the unique potential to transform industry and agriculture, since "every sort of visual aid speeds up mass education. And television, because it is essentially visual, is the most effective medium of communication yet devised by man."[42]

What effects, for Graham, did this "essentially visual" medium produce? What effects did she want Ghana TV to produce? Since Nkrumah's removal from power left her project unfinished, these questions are difficult to answer, but it is possible to distill from Graham's biographical works her approach to postcolonial pedagogy and to speculate about what she sought to instantiate in Ghana TV. For Graham, the function of biography, hagiography, or young-adult literature involves the production of states like *enthusiasm* and *inspiration* and the contravention of dispositions like *cynicism*, *apathy*, and *disillusionment*. In her posthumously produced play of the early 1960s, *Les Blancs*, Lorraine Hansberry portrays a character, Tshembe, who returns to his fictitious Zatembe after years spent abroad in the United Kingdom and the United States. Combining elements of the Congo, South Africa, and Ghana, the composite country Zatembe is engaged in a bloody revolutionary struggle, toward which Tshembe adopts an aloof attitude: contemptuous of his brother Abioseh's aspirations to Catholic leadership, to say nothing of his scorn for European missionaries, he also deflects appeals from revolutionary actors who implore him to join the anticolonial resistance. And as novels like Ayi Kwei Armah's *The Beautyful Ones Are Not Yet Born* suggest, disillusionment about the postcolonial future—surrealistically sketched in this classic 1968 dystopian narrative of post-Nkrumah's Ghana—was already in evidence by the decade's end. Graham sought to intercept this burgeoning pessimism with heroic stories, tinged with an oracular Maoism, of individual and collective agency.

In the narrative tradition of ordinary, often downtrodden, individuals rising above modest circumstances or prevailing over a class enemy, Graham's biographies adapt this structure to the masculine drama of "representative men," figures who change the course of world history by sheer willpower, charisma, and endurance. These heteroglossic texts combine elements of nineteenth-century hagiography, racial uplift narrative, revisionist African historiography, and young adult literature. In Graham's biographies, the potential antagonism between the ordinary figure of socialist realism, the peasant or proletarian, and the representative man of nineteenth-century romantic heroism resolves itself when the former soon discovers his destiny to become the latter: a trajectory marking the mythical rise of figures like Nasser, Nyrere, Nkrumah, and Mao.

Her creation of idealized portraits of heroic representatives (of a nation, tribe, continent) reflects a specific political commitment expressed in anachronistic literary forms. Neither the forms of modernist aesthetics nor the philosophically informed poetics of negritude served her purposes. Uniquely, though, Graham's treatments of postcolonial leadership combine the genre of romantic biography with elements of what she understood as an integral African communalist tradition. This hybrid form enables Graham to elide, if not to render irrelevant, the mid-twentieth-century priority on a protagonist's individual interiority, his relation to the public-private dichotomy, or his projection of complex psychological dynamics. The pedagogical solution for Graham was not, as it was for Soviet comrades, to arraign the literary forms of bourgeois liberalism but rather to imagine an alternative to liberalism's priority on individualism. When anticolonial intellectuals succeed in eradicating the "superstructure" built by "the bourgeois colonialist environment," writes Fanon, then the erosion of colonized subjectivities will follow: "Individualism is the first to disappear."[43]

The substitution of individualism for collectivism was crucial to the success of Graham's enterprise, and Japan provided an exemplary case of a non-Western nation engaged in collective nation building following the devastation of World War II. Just as significantly, Japan was weaning itself from postwar reconstruction aid from the United States and even outpacing Western modernity in technological endeavors. "Only a determined people," she writes, "fully alive to all the potentialities of television could have made the progress in this field which Japan has made in the past ten years." She visited research laboratories that exposed her to "experiments and developments of original ideas. We examined the Separate Luminance Color Camera which will be introduced at the Olympic Games and which may well revolutionize television everywhere. I am sure it will bring color television to Ghana much sooner than we had dared hope."[44]

In her capacity as director of television, Graham corresponded with representatives from the United Nations regarding educational programming, short films, and other programs for purchase in Ghana. She reported directly to Nkrumah. On June 30, 1965, Graham writes to the Ghanaian leader (whom she addresses "My dear Osagyefe"): "May I come in at your earliest convenience to discuss the disposition of your television receiving sets? Sanyo wants to make a presentation of the colour television cabinet together with a color camera. They are now in our studio awaiting your pleasure. Also, we wish to place television receivers where you can easily view them—perhaps in your office and at The Castle. . . . Everybody is cooperating beautifully in a mighty effort. Your visits to Television inspired the determination to overcome all obstacles." She signs off, "Sincerely yours, Director of Television."[45]

Graham received encouragement from her hosts in Japan and other interested observers. A message of congratulations on Ghana TV's inception came from BBC Television in Scotland (July 30, 1965). After Graham's visit, the president of Sanyo Electric wrote Nkrumah to strengthen the partnership between his company and Ghana, offering "heartfelt congratulations to the [ever]-growing development in the country of Your Excellency." W. Baideo-Ansah, the ambassador to the Embassy of Ghana in Japan, wrote to Graham:

"There is no doubt that this Corporation can be regarded as your 'baby' and I hope to see it grow to contribute its share to the educational, cultural and industrial advancement of Ghana." In his letter, Baideo-Ansah included clippings of Japanese newspaper coverage on the signing of the agreement between Ghana and Japan. "In looking over the August 11, 1965 issue of Ghana Today," wrote one James H. Robinson in a letter to Graham, "I came across a story of Ghana's television for education and edification which I had overlooked in passing these magazines around among my staff. It brought back all the wonderful memories of the people we met, the studios we visited, the young men in training whom we saw in preparation, the equipment, the sets which were going to be used in many parts of the country to provide opportunity where people could not purchase them and to develop a community focal point for viewing." Lauding Ghana TV's emphasis on "education" and "edification," Robinson commends Graham's project as an alternative to "popular programs, interspersed with large doses of commercialism," produced by the Western culture industry. "More power to you," he concludes.[46]

In a letter dated May 13, 1965, the chief of United Nations Television, one Michael Hayward, wrote to Graham after hearing word of her "valuable participation in the recent Editors Roundtable in Dakar." "Since you will, no doubt, soon be concerned with programming about International Cooperation Year on Ghana Television, I take the liberty of outlining some material which we have available." He refers to a brochure on "our television series *International Zone*. . . . All the film for the 1964 series of *International Zone* has been specially shot by three camera crews working on location in Asia, Africa and Latin America—each equipped with newly designed highly mobile camera rigs and radio microphones, employing the 'living camera' style."[47] He notes that one program in the series, "Spreading the Word," focused on Ghana's literacy campaign.

Correspondence between Graham and her international partners emphasizes cutting-edge technologies: mobile cameras and microphones, color television sets, and programs employing the latest audio-visual innovations. This emphasis disregards the conventional dilemma of Afro-modernity, which highlights a vast chasm separating

Africa from the modern world. Like many of her contemporaries, the lawyer and poet Pauli Murray expressed doubts that Africa dared to accomplish in one generation what Western modernity required centuries of "civilizational development" to achieve.

Early in 1959, Murray received an advertisement in the *London Times* for a faculty position in the newly established law school in Ghana, and she leapt at the opportunity. With an "interest in the emerging movements for African independence" spurred by conversations with leaders like Tom Mboya and Julius Nyerere, Murray saw this position as a chance to "satisfy a nagging curiosity about the African component of my ancestry."[48] Her autobiography recounts a moment when, docking for a couple days in Monrovia, Liberia, Murray borrows a car and drives into the countryside. "Nothing I had read or heard prepared me for the contrast between the opulence of a wealthy nation like the United States and the overwhelming poverty of the masses of people I saw everywhere in this African city—"

> The mildewed dilapidation of the few stores on the main street; the flies and insects swarming over the smoked fish sold on the ground in the native markets; the naked children with protruding stomachs wading through the cesspools of muck; a child with large tumors growing out of his neck begging in the street; the furnitureless mud shacks with dirt floors and roofs of straw pieced together with old tarpaulins or discarded fragments of rusty tin; the mangy, half-starved dogs creeping along the gutters; the ragged dockworkers in westernized shirts and trousers, their bodies glistening through the tatters; and the half-comatose, scurvy-ridden old people dozing in the sun and looking like breathing corpses.[49]

This kind of landscape "was a fairly common sight in Africa." In a letter home, Murray writes that any traveler to Ghana will be struck by "the turmoil of a country trying in one generation to leap over several centuries of painfully evolved human development. One also has the feeling at times of looking at the entire range of problems encountered in human history from the beginnings of the human race to the mid-twentieth century."[50] The temporality invoked here epitomizes the unmistakably historicist tone adopted by many black American sojourners to independent Africa.

No one views " 'late capitalism' as a system whose driving engine may be in the third world," writes Dipesh Chakrabarty, "though its impact on the rest of the globe is never denied."[51] How did African Americans in Ghana comprehend and represent this impact? Though Richard Wright also conjured imagery of bodies and landscapes disfigured by poverty, his travel writings on Ghana tend to situate the economic realities of West Africa within the paradigm of what is called uneven development, a product of the convergence of colonialism and global capitalism. If Wright's work shows how capitalism assumes astonishing forms in the Third World, Murray's reflections naturalize the distressing socioeconomic situation she encounters.

Murray was coauthor of an important text on Ghana's constitution and government, but the West African experience depicted in her autobiography reaffirms her commitment to U.S. liberal democracy and the pursuit of African American citizenship, while diminishing any identification with Africa she might have felt before arriving in Accra. "America is 'home' to me, however alienated or disinherited I have felt at times." Murray drew on the resources of her own family history, one irrevocably tied to U.S. national history, as opposed to what she perceived as an imagined kinship with Africa. "I discover that without knowledge of personal antecedents the African past exists in a great vacuum. I haven't the slightest notion of who my particular ancestors were, what region or tribe they came from, whether they were traders, fisherfolk, herdspeople, or farmers, what their customs were or what language they spoke. There is no African village to which I can make a sentimental journey."[52] She finds herself "unable to conjure up some vicarious identity and [I] can do little more than relate to the people I meet on the basis of our common humanity."

For Graham, on the other hand, a combination of cultural imagination, entrepreneurship, and powerful international alliances sufficed to instantiate a workable, if not utopian, modernity on the continent. Like Du Bois, Graham viewed liberal democracy's codification of individual and political liberties (freedom of expression, of assembly, of the press) as an unnecessary ingredient in this version of postcolonial modernity. What mattered was that other democratic and populist elements prevailed: mass literacy and education, economic enfranchisement of the poor, and modernization of village life. By all accounts, Graham labored indefatigably to inaugurate Ghana Television as both a mass pedagogical tool for the nation and a beacon of Afro-Asian partnership in practice.[53] Yet Nkrumah's ouster in 1966 meant that Graham's vision for this Pan-African media enterprise went largely unfulfilled.

In her review of Nkrumah's *Africa Must Unite* (1963) for the journal *Freedomways*, Graham observes that when the nation achieved "full independence" on March 6, 1957, and "Ghanaians sat down to draw up their own constitution, they wrote it as *Africans*, not merely as Ghanaians." Nkrumah's treatise, Graham notes, underscores the significance of enshrining the principle of Pan-African unity into Ghana's constitution. Then Graham notes an extraordinary passage tucked away in the Ghanaian constitution: "That the independence of Ghana should not be surrendered or diminished on any grounds *other than the furtherance of African Unity*." "This, I believe," Graham writes in her review, "is the first time that an independent, sovereign state has voluntarily offered to surrender its sovereignty for the sake of unity." What this remarkable concession of sovereignty meant in practice is unclear, but what mattered for Graham was its supposed ripple effect on the continent: she observes that Ghana's constitutional instantiation of Pan-African unity led to "similar provisions" being "written into the Constitutions of Guinea, Tunisia, Mali and the U.A.R."[54]

After Nkrumah was overthrown, Graham defended the Ghanaian leader against his detractors, many of whom, to her consternation, were leftists or members of the Communist Party worldwide. If Nkrumah's rule devolved into autocracy, Graham rationalized this turn as the cost of revolutionary progress. This familiar line of argument demarcates one limit of Graham's political imagination.[55] "Despite her high-level post in Ghana and her often inflamed revolutionary rhetoric," writes Horne, "Graham Du Bois was not as politically sophisticated as she appeared to be. But one thing she did believe firmly: the Nkrumah regime was a boon and his downfall was a bane for Africa."[56]

Graham in Cairo: Partisan of Nasserism

In the years between her departure from Ghana and her death in Beijing, Shirley Graham resided mostly in Cairo, a location that afforded her the opportunity to witness and write about events in Africa and Western Asia from an enviable vantage point. Writing from and for Egypt empowered Graham to discuss explosive subjects in international affairs without the constraints and pressures that journalists experienced in the United States. In 1956 the *Pittsburgh Courier* issued a statement addressing efforts by advocates of Israel to thwart free discussion of the Arab-Israeli conflict. "We are distressed to learn that there are Jewish groups keeping tabs on our columnists and interpreting the opinions of our columnists as the policies of this newspaper." Defending its neutrality and right to free expression, the text then reads: "For the sake of the record, let it be said that, generally speaking, The Courier is a pro-Jew, pro-Semitic, pro-minority, pro-underdog, pro all those classes of human beings who suffer proscriptions and overlordship because of race, color, religion or descent." At the same time, and despite "the provocations suffered by Israel, there are many persons of integrity who question the wisdom of Israel's attack (or counter-attack) on Egypt." The statement concludes with the suggestion that proponents of Israel undermine their own advocacy of the Jewish state by attempting to stifle criticism and "free expression by imputing strong anti-Semitism to individuals who might differ strongly with them about Israel."[57] By opting out of the United States and gaining entry into the Egyptian public sphere, Graham was able to elide such strictures.

Resident in Cairo for approximately a year before the Arab-Israeli War, Graham kept a diary and set of notes about the war's effects upon the city. In an unpublished essay, "Cairo—Six Months after the Blitzkrieg," she described her experience of the war's fallout for Egypt and the region. After the war, according to Graham, the streets continued their frenetic activity, while cars of "all sizes and vintage are driven at breakneck speed" alongside horse-drawn carriages, bicycles, and the occasional camel. (But "in the eighteen months I have lived in Cairo," she notes, "I have never seen a traffic accident.")

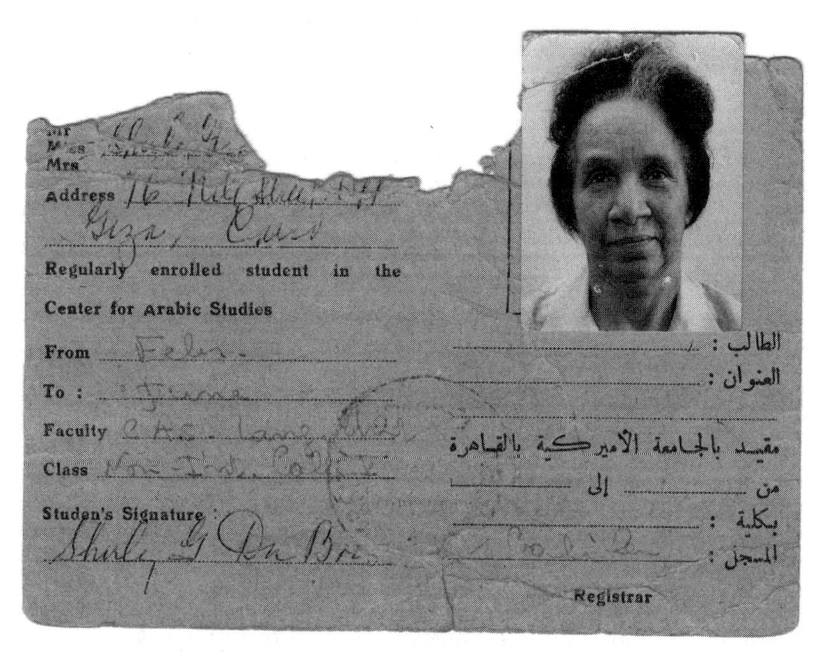
Mr
Miss
Mrs
Address
Regularly enrolled student in the
Center for Arabic Studies
From
To :
Faculty
Class
Student's Signature : Shirley G Du Bois
Registrar

الطالب :
العنوان :
مقيد بالجامعة الأمريكية بالقاهرة
من الى
بكلية :
المسجل :

Shirley Graham Du Bois's registration card, in Center for Arabic Studies, Cairo. (Papers of Shirley Graham Du Bois. Harvard University, Radcliffe Institute for Advanced Studies, Schlesinger Library.)

Boutiques, cafés, and restaurants remained busy; haggling continued at the markets; lines formed at the cinemas. On the bustling surface, everyday life in Cairo appeared relatively unaffected by the war. But then, after a several weeks' absence, Graham grew "conscious of qualitative change." Fewer loiterers and beggars were shadowing the streets, whereas everyone else "is going somewhere with brisk determination." More palpably, the built environment had changed. All of a sudden, "brick barricades, surrounded by piles of sandbags, have mushroomed and a shooting gallery across the Square from my hotel, which I had never noticed before, seems to be doing a thriving business."

"The blitz last June was my first experience of being in a bombed city," she continues. "Particularly distasteful to me was being huddled into the [improvised], hotel air-raid shelter, there in the quivering darkness to hear the muffled crash of bombs, while realizing that every night raid was aimed at Cairo's towering Broadcast Station where my son was only one of the hundreds at work in that Station. During those nights I saw my first total blackouts." She records a passage from her diary from June 6th:

> Last night I stood at my 10th floor window and looked out at a phantom city. Below me the wide Al-Tahrir Square lay in total darkness, with its surrounding buildings dimly outlined against the sky. In the distance I could distinguish the top of [Shepard] Hotel and a mosque with its delicate minaret. Across the Nile, on previous nights I could see the glittering bracelet of the Kars el Nile Bridge and skyscrapers in Giza. Last night I could see the pale waters of the Nile, but no lights. Buildings rose out of the darkness like ghosts. On the ground a red bug scampered . . . occasionally there was the rumble of a heavy vehicle, accompanied by a dim, moving light, but no outline could be seen. Things seemed to float in the darkness. Then, the rising moon touched the whole with silver. Far away I could see the tip of a pyramid.

Then, after the typescript page is left blank as if to fill in a later thought, Graham enigmatically concludes the diary entry with the fragment: "and all was a dream of peace."[58] Her diary and other writings record a country wracked and humiliated by the war, but also, like the proverbial phoenix, resilient and rising under the leadership of Gamal Nasser and the reliable fortification of the Soviet Union; increasingly aware of the global economic significance of the oil industry and the influence the Arab world can wield as a power bloc; and determined to reclaim the territories occupied by Israel after 1967.

During these years, Graham analyzed developments on the entire African continent: from Uganda, Tanzania, Sudan, and Ethiopia in the East, to Egypt and Algeria in the North, to Nigeria, Ghana, and Guinea in the West, to the Congo in the center, and to Lesotho and Mozambique in the South. Yet this location also prompted Graham to channel her radical energies into new international arenas: Middle East and Afro-Arab politics. In retrospect, Graham's symbolic migration across the desert appears uncannily consonant with a set of affiliations then developing north and south of the Sahara. In the early 1960s, as Pan-Africanists sought to define and instantiate a continental agenda, radical leaders like Nkrumah formed closer alliances with Arab North African leaders, who increasingly represented a vanguard of decolonization. For their part, Arab anti-imperialists, and Nasser in particular, made increasing overtures to sub-Saharan Africa. Under Nasser, Egypt hosted and provided scholarships for African students as well as support for "militant insurrectionists from places like Cameroon, Kenya, and South Africa."[59] Nasser also developed closer ties to Nkrumah, his counterpart in West Africa.

As Graham entered these arenas via domestic and international print cultures (in publications like the *Black Scholar*, *Freedomways*, and the *Egyptian Gazette*), Graham embraced Nasser's synthesis of anti-imperialism, socialism, Pan-Arabism, and Pan-Africanism. If one credits her writings of the late 1960s as evidence, Graham emerges as an unlikely *partisan*—in Schmitt's sense of the term referenced earlier and elaborated below—of Nasserism and the Palestinian struggle.

In the spirit in which the Tunisian intellectual Albert Memmi asked of Fanon—*Why Algeria and the Algerian Liberation Movement?*—one might pose the question of Graham: *Why Egypt and Nasserism?* Perhaps Graham's motivations were practical and personal: her son, David Graham, was already resident in Cairo and editor of the *Egyptian Gazette*. Moreover, as her biographer suggests, other possible post-Nkrumah locales—she considered Mexico, East Germany, Tanzania, France, and Algeria—intrigued Graham but presented obstacles to relocation.[60] Horne recounts conversations between Graham and Nkrumah after his overthrow, when the two apparently became even closer, and as the deposed leader struggled to adjust to his new life in Guinea. Graham possessed a Tanzanian passport, but Nkrumah advised her against relocating there, for "East Africa at the moment is filled up with American agents—CIA and so forth. I don't trust these 'guys.'"[61] Whatever her motivation, however, she chose Egypt and adopted Nasserism with an ideological fervor that exceeds practical or even self-preservationist considerations. This section elaborates the interplay between Graham's commitment to and creative manipulation of Nasserism in light of her broader imagining of Third World socialist modernity.

Before exploring Graham's adaptation and revision of Nasserism, it is important to review recent scholarly descriptions of this term. Historians Elie Podeh and Onn Winkler have categorized Nasserism, a phenomenon spanning roughly the years 1952 to 1970 (from the Egyptian Revolution until Nasser's death), into five dominant interpretations. The first considers Nasserism as an ideological movement, less systematic than liberalism, socialism, or communism, but one that encompasses a set of ideas about anti-imperialism, Pan-Arabism, and Arab socialism. The second centers on the charismatic personality of Nasser himself, his leadership style, vision, rhetorical powers, and authoritarian mode of governance; this interpretation gave rise to Weberian analyses of Nasser and comparisons of the Egyptian leader with Turkey's modernizer Kamal Ataturk.[62] Overlapping with but distinct from the previous interpretation, the third views Nasserism as a modernization movement with strong secularizing connotations. The fourth regards Nasserism "primarily as a protest movement against Western colonialism and imperialism, which appeared following a significant period of crisis or disorientation." The fifth and most recent interpretation attempts "to equate Nasserism with populist leaders and movements, mainly found in Latin America during the first half of the twentieth century."[63] Taken together, these categories suggest the following distillation: Nasserism denotes an anti-imperialist and Pan-Arab vision of socialist modernity embodied by a charismatic, populist leader.

This useful categorization omits one comparatively minor but significant dimension: the Pan-African element that Nasserism included within its historical and geopolitical coordinates. Though it is wise not to overstate the significance of Pan-Africanism to Egyptian politics, it is equally important not to overlook this component that was deeply meaningful to Nasser and his Pan-African colleagues, including Nkrumah and Graham. By reinscribing Egypt's location within Nilotic Africa, Nasser broke with vestigial nineteenth-century colonial and Hegelian traditions that relocated the ancient country to the Mediterranean basin and thus closer to European civilization. In retrospect, this widely imagined relocation, betrayed in advance by an African-influenced Greek antiquity—a classical age "which was seen not merely as the epitome of Europe," writes Martin Bernal, "but also as its pure childhood"—played an outsized role in generations of historiography depicting a racially integral European civilization propelled by an oft-interrupted but steady progress of enlightenment.[64]

During these years of crisis in the Middle East and Vietnam, Shirley Graham began writing a column for the *Egyptian Gazette*, an English-language newspaper that her son, David Graham Du Bois, edited after expatriating to Cairo in the early 1960s. Contributing dozens of articles over an approximately three-year span (from 1967 to 1969), Graham's column is informed by the watershed 1967 Arab-Israeli (or Six-Day) War, an event that shifted the military and geopolitical balance of power in Israel's favor in the Middle East and severely diminished the stature of Nasser's Pan-Arabism. Ilan Pappé signals a shift in U.S. foreign policy toward Israel as early as the Jewish state's foundational first years of existence. "By the spring of 1949," writes Pappé, "American policy had already been reoriented onto a conspicuously pro-Israeli track, turning Washington's mediators into the opposite of honest brokers as they largely ignored the Palestinian point of view in general, and disregarded in particular the Palestinian refugees' right of return."[65] For most commentators, however, the consolidation of ties between both states truly strengthens in 1967. Scholarship on the Six-Day War agrees that this conflict inaugurated the "special relationship" between the United States and Israel, so this event merits more attention from scholars of American Studies than it typically receives.[66]

Scholars identify a diverse range of factors that prompted Israel to attack Egypt, but one catalyst involved a bold set of actions initiated by Nasser from May 13 to the first days of June: on May 13, Egypt heard reports from Soviet, Syrian, and Lebanese sources that Israeli troops were amassing on the Syrian border, so Egyptian forces countered by mobilizing in Sinai; next, Nasser ordered the withdrawal of the UN Emergency Force, a peacekeeping unit that some actors perceived as a pillar of stability in the region but which Nasser viewed as an infringement of Egyptian sovereignty; finally, and perhaps most fatefully, Egypt closed the Straits of Tiran, which Israel interpreted as a direct assault. The Egyptian leader and his advisers underestimated the strength of Israel's military capacity and were devastated, physically and emotionally, by Israel's powerful military showing, especially its rapid obliteration of Egypt's air force. Historical memory marks this defeat as *the* moment of humiliation of Egypt and of the broader Arab world. Nasser offered to resign but remained in power after a groundswell of Egyptian supporters clamored for his continued leadership. As ardently as she defended Nkrumah after he was overthrown, Graham amplified her support for Nasser following the Six-Day War.

Precipitated by geopolitical vicissitudes, or what I've called the quicksand of history, Graham's swift adaptation to this complex arena raises questions. By operating within a nexus of simultaneous or overlapping networks, affiliations, and ideological commitments, was Graham's attachment to so many formations ultimately a commitment to nothing in particular? Does her array of leftist attachments suggest that she was manipulated or seduced by sundry and sometimes competing ideological regimes? Closer inspection of Graham's textual and political operations, I argue, reveals a writer less duped by larger forces than one who sought to realign these regional politics with her own vision of Third World socialist modernity. This section elaborates this claim by focusing on three critical aspects marking Graham's engagement with Nasserism: her celebration of the Soviet role in Egypt; her analysis of the Arab-Israeli War and its fallout, especially the controversial UN Resolution 242; and her interpretation of Nasser's *Philosophy of the Revolution* in light of incipient Afro-Arab alliances.

As Carl Schmitt reminded readers in the early 1930s, one may bemoan but cannot deny the fact that nations continue to organize themselves according to a friend-enemy antithesis or grouping [*Freund und Feind gruppieren*], which appears in twentieth-century modernity as both an "atavistic remnant of barbaric times" and an undeniably constitutive feature of international politics. "[Rationally] speaking," Schmitt argues, "it cannot be denied that nations continue to group themselves according to the friend and enemy antithesis, that the distinction still remains actual today, and that this is an ever present possibility for every people existing in the political sphere."[67] Adopting the idiom of friend and enemy in her analyses—with the West portrayed as an unambiguous enemy, the Communist world a friend—Graham both reported on and contributed to an atavistic politics.

In the Cold War crucible, Graham adapted the friend-enemy grouping so that both poles of the antitheses encompass supranational rather than national entities. For example, since the Soviet Union aided Nasser during crucial confrontations with the "West," mainly during the period from the Suez War to the Six-Day War, Graham unabashedly entwined communism and Nasserism, representing both as interdependent constituents of a global socialist modernity. In an *Egyptian Gazette* column, "Friends and Enemies," of October 23, 1967, Graham refers to a full-page advertisement in the *New York Times*, featuring "a grim-visaged, be-medalled, unidentified Soviet officer saluting." Graham launched into this new arena of propaganda and counterpropaganda.

This ad "was not a public relations effort by the Soviet Armed Forces, but rather it was a sabre-rattling attempt of a well-heeled group of Americans, ironically calling themselves Americans for Permanent Peace in the Middle East, Inc., to convince the American people that armed aggression against the Arab peoples of the Middle East is the only solution to guaranteeing US interests in the area." In Graham's account, these kinds of organizations ("interest" groups, in contemporary parlance) portray the Soviet Union as "fanning the flames of Arab hatred in order to achieve their own ends: total control over the flow of oil in the Middle East." Graham does not specify what, beyond a putative ideological commitment to decolonization, defines Soviet interests in the region, but implies that Arab-Soviet relations were mutually beneficial and a crucial bulwark to Western concerns, which could only remain exploitative. "Indeed, the balance of world power is changing," she contends. "The Arab people can no longer be frightened into submission at the threat of imperialist military might. Nor can the Arab people any longer be a pawn of any great power. Arab policy is a policy of genuine independence and friendship with all those nations which respect Arab right to independence and sovereignty."

It's unclear that actors on either side of the Arab-Soviet collaboration viewed this relationship in precisely these terms: Nasser, for example, had reason to fear Soviet domination even as he relied on

Communist reinforcement to counterbalance Western power; for their part, and despite earlier avowals of colonial wars as "sacred wars," the Soviets were loath to be conscripted into a conflict in the Middle East. Smoothing over these political realities, Graham concludes her article firmly: "Beyond this point, we neither explain nor apologise for those we recognise as our friends or our enemies."[68]

Graham was able to elide these realities because the Western powers *were* animated by what looked like an increasingly cozy relationship between the Arab world and the Soviet sphere. In another article, Graham responds to American and British consternation over the upsurge of Soviet naval units in the Mediterranean. "From the period of the creation of the USSR up to the present," she writes, "the imperialist West, and particularly the USA, has attempted to represent the Soviet Union as a serious threat to the security and sovereignty of all other nations of the globe, but particularly to developing nations and peoples."[69] Yet as national liberation movements gained momentum after the Second World War, "and particularly as the peoples of Africa and the Middle East, following the example of the pioneering Revolution of Egypt, won victory after victory," the "subterfuge" of imperialism exposed itself, supposedly motivating the Third World to turn to the Soviet Union for assistance. To this appeal, "the Soviet Union responded generously." She reports Nasser as having said that the Soviet Union and Egypt share "one object in common, namely to combat imperialism."

Graham claims that the Soviet naval fleet in the Mediterranean poses no threat to the nations of the region; it remains there only to ensure that "the Mediterranean Sea does not become 'an American lake,' under the control of the US Sixth Fleet, which is already acting as 'a strategic reserve of Israel' in its capacity as outpost and protector of imperialist interests in the Middle East. It is for this reason that President Nasser proclaims: 'I say that all free countries of the area welcome the presence of the Soviet Fleet in the Mediterranean.'"[70] For Graham, the meaning of Nasser's remarks is clear—or rather she renders these remarks with polemical clarity. Western depredations necessitate the "balance" provided by Soviet power, which, on this analysis, will erode in proportion to the diminution of imperial activity in the region. If this logic seems naive, it ought to be interpreted as part of her effort to conjoin Arab and Soviet interests in a manner more strident than either side was comfortable with.

Nowhere was Graham's suturing of these interests more evident than during the Arab-Israeli War, which distracted world attention from what was supposed to be the glorious semicentennial anniversary of the October Revolution. Undeterred, Graham impressed upon readers the significance of this event for Egypt and the Third World. "Fifty years of Soviet power," she writes, "have proved that the October Revolution faithfully expressed the will of the people and the victory of the people's struggle for the realization of liberty and progress." Riskily, Graham then ventures: "The Egyptian people have watched with deep interest Soviet power bring the Soviet society to the vanguard among peoples and societies in development, science and creative expression"—despite the supposed efforts of imperialism to distort or conceal these achievements.

In case her *Gazette* readers were unconvinced, Graham reminds them that the "Egyptian people have been a party to the bright and pioneering example set by the Soviet Union in the sphere of international relations," as well as in the establishment of a cooperative, peaceful social order. How, exactly, were Egypt's citizens the beneficiaries of Soviet power? The Aswan Dam, a project that the Eisenhower administration decided not to fund, supposedly to disastrous effect, was a key example. "The Aswan High Dam," Graham intones, "will forever stand as a shining example of Soviet aid and a symbol of unconditional cooperation between the UAR [United Arab Republic] and the Soviet Union. The Soviet Union's unswerving support of the Arab peoples' efforts to liquidate the consequences of the imperialist-aided Zionist aggression [against] the Arab peoples is an example of the Soviet Union's determination to support justice and right against the forces of imperialism. The great October Revolution made all this possible."[71] Yet this imagined interdependence was far from apparent to the leadership of these respective power blocs, to say nothing of perceptions among their citizens. Tellingly, Graham never mentions the well-known displacement and relocation of thousands of Egypt's Nubian population as a consequence of the construction of the Aswan Dam—an uprooting for which former Nilotic inhabitants and their descendants continue to seek redress.[72]

Because the meaning of the Bolshevik Revolution and Soviet-Egyptian interdependence was unclear or obscured by imperialist powers, Graham tried to neutralize potential, existing, or imagined fissures between Nasserism and the Soviet Bloc: a tactic meant to offset, in Schmitt's terms, the "intensification of internal antagonisms" within the socialist bloc and thereby reduce "the effect of weakening the common identity vis-à-vis another state."[73] Graham's reconciliatory efforts, I want to emphasize, conform neither to Nasserist doctrine nor to the Egyptian leader's actual intentions or views; nor did they necessarily dovetail with Moscow's aims and what amounted, historically, to tentative Soviet support for Nasser and other radical actors in the Arab world. I argue that Graham's partisanship performs an affirmative, ostensibly hagiographic, role in relation to the state yet also works to massage official doctrines in accordance with her own geopolitical vision. The cultural production that results from this kind of partisanship, I argue, constitutes a logic of *instigation*, defined here as the application of discursive power on reluctant political actors in a context of war.

During the 1960s, Graham began to anticipate, and to some extent to call for, armed resistance in liberation struggles, from the black power to the Palestinian liberation movements. In one article, she applauded Nasser's decision to award medals of honor to the Egyptian naval officers who had sunk an Israeli destroyer, the *Eilat*, on October 21, 1967. Rebutting condemnations of Nasser's decision in the British press, Graham asks: "Has he [the editor of the *London Evening Standard*] forgotten that a state of war exists between the United Arab Republic and Israel? Has he forgotten that Israeli forces occupy territory of the United Arab Republic, Jordan and Syria, and, by their presence on the east bank of the Suez Canal, they constitute a constant threat to the security of the United Arab Republic? Has the editor of the Standard forgotten that for the people of the UAR Israel is the enemy, and that it is the duty of the men of the UAR armed forces to protect the security of the people and the territory of the UAR from enemy attack?"[74] As we will see, Graham's partisanship of Nasserism and concomitant anti-Zionism contrasts sharply with her husband's earlier defense of Israel.

On the whole, Graham was careful to calibrate her prose so that it expressed hostility not to Jews but to the Israeli state and distinguished between Zionism and the Jewish people—though then as now that distinction did not always hold. A revealing letter she wrote to a Lincoln University political science professor highlights Graham's mentality in this perilous edge of critique. She had sent a paper on the Arab-Israeli conflict to an organization that was pleased with it; the group distributed copies. But she felt compelled to write the organization "expressing deep regret of one phrase in that paper. Although I know it is too late to eradicate anything, I feel I should register this regret: I referred to 'the Jew, Disraeli, making a gift of the Suez Canal to Queen Victoria'. I should have said, 'Disraeli, the arch-imperialist'. The phrase I used does smack of anti-Semitism, which I do not feel and should be extremely careful to avoid. The Palestinians repeatedly point out that they are not fighting Jews—but imperialist Zionism! I'm sorry about this."[75]

In his 1948 article, "The Case for the Jews," W. E. B. Du Bois asks: "What is there right and wrong in the question of Palestine, which today faces not simply the United States but the whole world? It is not a difficult question. There is something terribly simple about it." In Du Boisian fashion, he presents a capsule history of the region, shaped from antiquity to modernity by an invading "succession of peoples and empires." The simplicity of the question reflects what Du Bois deems to be universally acknowledged fragments from history: "Every child knows that ancient Jewish civilization and religion centered in Palestine." Jewish indigenousness, on this argument, overrides competing claims by other dwellers, including the Arabs, whose history and religion are not seen as comparably rooted in Palestine's geography. An elementary survey of the region's cities, rivers, and places—"Jerusalem, Bethlehem, Damascus, Jordan, Galilee and a hundred others"—testifies to this truth. Beyond dispute for Du Bois was the "way in which the history of the Jewish religion is wound about Palestine." From this tributary, centuries of Jewish dispersals into the world constitute a narrative "thread" that "runs through modern history."[76]

In his case for Israel, Du Bois has little to say on behalf of the region's Arab inhabitants, or their own religious, historical, and affective ties to the land. What he does write is unsympathetic: "Among the million Arabs there is widespread ignorance, poverty and disease and fanatic belief in the Mohammedan religion, which makes these people suspicious of other peoples and other religions." Another oblique but telling reference is to the "overthrow" of the Jews in Palestine "by Islam." For Du Bois, the intrusion of Islam into Palestine represents yet another tidal wave of history, further displacing and dispersing the Jewish people. He concludes his article with a plea to the United Nations (an institution "apparently helpless" in the case of Palestine) and to the world. "In the meantime," he writes, "a million displaced Jews are begging to be allowed to migrate to Palestine, where there is room for them, where there is work for them to do, where what Jews have done already is for the advantage, not simply of the Jews, but of the Arabs."[77]

If Du Bois's characterization of Palestinian Arabs leaves little doubt about what group he envisaged as the intellectual and economic forerunners of the new Israel, his view that the Jewish diaspora's legitimate claim to residence and right to construct a nation-state did not equate to "ownership" of the land. "*When, therefore, it comes a question of original possession and ownership there is no final answer for any people*," Du Bois writes with emphasis. "*After all, as Americans ought to know, the question of a land is in the long run the question of the use to which the land is put.*"[78] If he undermines the idea of *final* land possession by any one group, Du Bois's vaguely Lockean formulation leaves unclear how, precisely, the lesson of American colonization ought to apply to the situation in Palestine. But it does seem to imply, unwittingly and without irony, that Zionism resembles settler colonialism.

Du Bois's views were not wholly idiosyncratic among black writers in the nineteenth and twentieth centuries. They can be situated within an African American genealogy of orientalist discourse on Palestine/Israel, one that acknowledges to varying degrees the legitimate claims of Arabs and Jews on the land but tends to attribute backwardness onto the former group and modernity onto the latter. As Alex Lubin demonstrates, this genealogy stretches from the mid-nineteenth century to 1948 and includes writers such as Edward Blyden, Adam Clayton Powell Sr., and Dusé Mohamed Ali, a mysterious figure who claimed Egyptian nationality while resident in London. The nineteenth-century black interpreters of Palestine wrote in an era in the United States captivated by the fate of the Holy Land; twentieth-century observers linked concern with the region with the emergence of Zionism, the historical parallel between this movement and Pan-Africanism, and the horrors of Nazism.[79]

Du Bois remained a staunch, if occasionally critical, supporter of the incipient Jewish state. Three visits to the Warsaw Ghetto impressed upon Du Bois "not so much clearer understanding of the Jewish problem in the world as it was a real and more complete understanding of the Negro problem."[80] The American drama of slavery and emancipation was not as unique as Du Bois had previously supposed; nor was the problem of race "principally a matter of color and physical and racial characteristics" but rather a phenomenon of "cultural patterns, perverted teaching and human hate and prejudice." The "ghetto of Warsaw helped me to emerge from a certain social provincialism into a broader conception of what the fight against race segregation, religious discrimination and the oppression by wealth had to become if civilization was going to triumph and broaden in the world." Du Bois's reawakened cosmopolitanism notwithstanding, it is not difficult to imagine how these experiences in Warsaw and earlier travels in Nazi Germany profoundly reinforced his identification with the Jewish diaspora's desire for a national homeland.[81]

But it is equally difficult to ignore that his juxtaposition of a resourceful, resilient Jewish diaspora—and its vast contributions to "modern civilization, not only in banking and finance, but in the arts, in the fineness of his family life, in the magnificent clearness of his intellect"—with a primitive and fanatical Arab population implies that only one people is poised to make productive use of "a land largely of plateaus, mountains, and deserts, sparsely inhabited."[82] The central issue going forward, Du Bois writes, "was a question of young and forward-thinking Jews bringing a new civilization into an old land and building up that land out of ignorance, disease, and poverty into which it had fallen; and by democratic methods erecting a new and peculiarly fateful modern state." For Du Bois, European Jews were uniquely qualified to inaugurate a modern democracy in the

Middle East; the Arab system of "family and clan despotism," by contrast, makes "effective use of democratic methods difficult."

In the unfolding tragedy of Palestine, Du Bois, whose own brief remarks drew on Orientalist schemas, did not seem to perceive Arabs as increasingly racialized subjects or as an occupied population. His support for Israel, however, was not unqualified. In his later ruminations on the Negro and the Warsaw ghetto, written during the Korean War, he indicts American blacks who are "selling their souls to those who want war and colonialism" in order to join the ranks of the ruling class. Somewhat obliquely, Du Bois juxtaposes these recreants, who "encourage their sons to kill 'Gooks,'" with Jews who may be tempted to betray their own heroic traditions. "Among Jews there is the same dichotomy and inner strife," he continues, "which forgets the bravery of the Warsaw ghetto and the bones of the thousands of dead who still lie buried in that dust."[83] If his "Suez" poem is any indication, by 1956 Du Bois amplifies his admonition to Israel. As we have seen, "Suez" not only valorizes Nasser and the Soviet Union but also reproves the Jewish state for colluding with European imperialism.

Unlike Graham, Du Bois did not live to see the staggering consequences of the Six-Day War. If Graham lacked Du Bois's sensitivity to the emergency situation of European and diaspora Jewry, her editorials capture the sense of crisis experienced in the Arab world after 1967. This sense of crisis precipitated increased militancy that the west portrayed as terrorist. According to historian of Israel Ilan Pappé, 1967 ushered in a discursive regime that crystallized an image of the Palestinian as synonymous with terrorism. A synthesis of academic research, media representations, public policy, and military intelligence, this production of knowledge about the Palestinian coincided with a mounting sense of alienation simultaneously *experienced* by Jewish Israelis and *imposed* on Palestinian Arabs by Zionism. "The experience of alienation," writes Pappé, "—both in the sense of feeling alien in the Arab world and depicting the Arabs as hostile aliens—became more institutionalized after 1967 through discriminatory legislation, governmental policies, and official conduct."[84] Graham was one of the very few black intellectuals of her time to oppose this portrayal of the Palestinian Arab as terrorist—a representation previously applied to the Algerian resistance fighter—and to rewrite the Palestinian struggle as a national liberation movement and its agents as legitimate militants.

Though phrases like "ethnic cleansing" or "crimes against humanity" had emerged by the time Graham penned her polemics against the Zionist state, these concepts were less pervasive in public discourse and codified in international law during the period when she wrote than they are today. Instead she draws on an incendiary repertoire of terms associated with the totalitarian experience: the state of Israel, Graham argued, engaged in *terrorism and extermination* and *military offensives* against the Palestinians in some episodes and *aggression*, *expansionism*, *occupation*, and *expulsion* in others. Taken together, this vocabulary evokes a combustible militarized reality in Palestine that commentators like Pappé now identify with the concept of ethnic cleansing.

Her commitment to Palestinian resistance reflects her perception that Israel had come to embrace white supremacy. "Surrounded as they are by an ocean of sun-tanned peoples, Israel has repeatedly, defiantly and arrogantly asserted its superior 'whiteness.'"

> Dark-skinned Jews who lived peacefully with Arabs in Palestine before the Zionists took over have always and consistently been treated with a condescending, if not contemptuous, attitude much like the over-all treatment accorded Afro-Americans in the United States. These original inhabitants of the land were given to understand that the new "socialist" state had been set up for immigrants—not for them. But Jews who migrated to Israel from Africa, Asia, South America or the South Pacific found, to their dismay, that they were not welcomed to "the Promised Land." They had to accept a status far below that of white Jews who came from Europe and America. And as for "black Jews" from the United States—Well! Nobody was allowed to forget that the State of Israel belonged to the dominant, "enlightened" *white* world. (Abba Eban is from South Africa!)[85]

What made this "attitude of innate racial superiority on the part of Israel" "particularly tragic" was the notion that "Jews were originally

Semites and therefore have closer genetic affinity to Arabs," to say nothing of the common foundations of Judaism and Islam manifested in shared holy spaces. Graham could have been responding to Du Bois's remarks from 1948 when she scorned how "frequently and glibly have Middle East experts written about the disunity of Arabs, with their monarchies, feudal lords, dictators, religious fanatics and illiterate, slothful nomad peoples!"[86]

Graham tended to attribute Palestinian militancy, among other reasons, to the failure of the UN to enforce measures formulated by its Security Council.[87] After citing a litany of Israeli attacks condemned by the UN, including those on the Jordanian towns of as-Samu' in November 1966 and Karameh in March 1968, she asks rhetorically why it has proved so difficult for the Security Council to arrive "at an agreed upon formula" in response to this aggression. The obvious but unacknowledged reason, according to Graham, is the unwillingness of "the United States and her 'allies' to throw their weight behind 'more serious actions' against Israel. And this weight is considerable, but it is subject to Zionist pressure." Like many anticolonial intellectuals, Graham initially saw the UN as an auspicious forum for adjudicating Third World affairs but came to view the organization as hamstrung in the face of U.S. imperatives. In this respect a striking reversal had occurred: whereas Du Bois, in his 1948 defense of Israel, could refer to the United Nations as an institution "apparently helpless" in its capacity to assist the nascent state, Graham, two decades later, lamented the same body's inability to enforce its mandate on Israel.

But in her *Gazette* editorials she emphasized, repeatedly and forcefully, the UN Security Council's adoption of the infamous Resolution 242, a document produced in the aftermath of the 1967 war that expresses "continuing concern with the grave situation in the Middle East" and highlights "the inadmissibility of the acquisition of territory by war and the need for a just and lasting peace in which every State in the area can live in security."[88] Since 1967 a touchstone for negotiations between Israel and its neighbors, the deliberately vague text invited competing interpretations. If Resolution 242 represented, in the words of one commentator, "a masterpiece of British ambiguity and obfuscation," for Graham the document was sufficiently clear, at least on one—or rather *the*—principle point and outcome of the conflict: the status of Palestinian territories seized by Israel in the war.

Much of the ambiguity of Resolution 242, drafted by British ambassador to the UN Lord Caradon, hinged on the infamous deletion of the definite article "the" before "territories" (so that the revised text read "territories" rather than "*the* territories") from the original draft of the text. The resolution passed after Lord Caradon omitted the determiner before the phrase "territories occupied in the recent conflict," "thereby making the resolution minimally acceptable to the Israelis and by offering something other than total defeat to the Arabs."[89] The translation of the text into the official United Nations languages exacerbated the ambiguity. The resolution "*Affirms* that the fulfillment of Charter principles requires the establishment of a just and lasting peace in the Middle East which should include the application of both the following principles:

> i. Withdrawal of Israel armed forces from territories occupied in the recent conflict;
>
> ii. Termination of all claims of states of belligerency and respect for and acknowledgment of the sovereignty, territorial integrity and political independence of every State in the area and their right to live in peace within secure and recognized boundaries free from threats or acts of force."

To some degree, the ambiguity of the phrase "territories occupied" was mitigated by the resolution's previous pronouncement on "the inadmissibility of the acquisition of territory by war," even if the exact territory under question remained unclear. Resolution 242 also referred to Article 2 of the UN Charter, the fourth point of which states that "All members shall refrain in their international relations from the threat or use of force against the territorial integrity or political independence of any state. . . ." Clearly both sides contravened the charter's mandate to refrain from threats or deployments of force, but Graham argued that Israel's spoils of war—namely, the newly gained territories in the Gaza Strip, the Golan Heights, and the West Bank—violated the territorial integrity of the formerly

Arab-controlled regions. For Graham and partisans of the Arab struggle, what else could the document mean?

Unlike the English version, translations of Resolution 242 into official UN languages Spanish and French employed definite and indefinite articles, respectively, before the word "territories" (*territorios, territoires*). The Spanish text reads: "Retiro de las fuerzas armadas israelíes de los territorios que ocuparon durante el reciente conflicto"; the French version reads: "Retrait des forces armées israéliennes des territoires occupés lors du récent conflit."[90] As Wm. Roger Louis asks, which "version should prevail, 'territories' or '*des territoires*'?" In the French and Spanish versions, *des* and *los* both translate into idiomatic English as "the," but in French the phrase in question can be translated as "the territories," "some territories," or simply "territories."[91] And what was the status of subsequent translations into Arabic, Russian, and Chinese, the other official UN languages? Caradon settled the matter by asserting that since Resolution 242 was "a British resolution it is of course the British text which prevails."[92]

"The Arabs," Louis observes, "later believed they had been betrayed. They assumed that 'occupied territories' meant every inch of land taken by the Israelis during the course of the war. Caradon certainly did not misrepresent the draft wording, but neither did he emphasize the significance of dropping the definite article 'the.'"[93] In her numerous references to Resolution 242, Graham always speaks of "*the* occupied territories" in a context that implies not only the return of war-captured lands but also, it seems, the removal of Israel from "the Arab homeland." Revisiting the interpretive ambiguity of Resolution 242, recent scholarship draws on new archives to argue that British and U.S. diplomats phrased the document in such a way as to leave open the possibility of future negotiations between the Palestinians and Israelis.[94] Graham, however, defended the dominant interpretation of the text in the Arab world. Evoking the sense of betrayal among Arabs following 242, Graham sought to invest the resolution with clarity that it did not possess and was not meant to possess.

From Graham's point of view, the Arab political leadership abided by United Nations mandates, especially Resolution 242, whereas

Israeli leadership continued to flout international law. "There is not a hint of a suggestion that Israeli ruling circles are giving the slightest attention to the Security Council's resolution of November 22 calling upon Israel to withdraw her troops from the occupied Arab territories." Of course, Graham's insertion of the determiner *the* before "occupied Arab territories" casually revises what had been the grammatical bone of contention in the document's language. But Graham was expressing a widespread view in the Arab world that the resolution signified that the territories seized by Israel were to be returned. The resolution also emphasized the "necessity" of "guaranteeing freedom of navigation through international waterways in the area" (a reference primarily to the Straights of Tiran and the Suez Canal) and "achieving a just settlement of the refugee problem." On these points, Graham demanded nothing less than the full right of return of Palestinian refugees, the restoration of occupied territory, and Israeli evacuation of the Suez Canal Zone.[95]

In an article on preparations for the Suemed oil pipeline, a construction designed to run from the Gulf of Suez to Alexandria on the Mediterranean Sea, Graham fashions Nasser's management of the Suez Canal from 1956 to 1967 into a postcolonial narrative of progress interrupted by Israeli aggression and U.S. foreign policy, stretching from the Eisenhower administration's withdrawal of funding for the Aswan Dam in 1956 to the Lyndon Johnson administration's support for Israel in the late 1960s. "From the moment President Gamal Abdul Nasser announced the decision of the revolutionary government to nationalize the Suez Canal in 1956, the Egyptian administration of the Canal has been one of continual, [wide-scale] work to improve facilities in the Canal and to increase the Canal capacity for ever larger and larger ships and tankers." Echoing the adulatory African American response to Nasser's success in running the Suez Canal after 1956, Graham depicts this achievement as a postcolonial blow to imperialist morale.[96]

Her analysis culminates in the interruption of this progress narrative by implying that disruption of Suez rests on Israeli, not Egyptian, actions. Israeli encroachments on Egyptian sovereignty—and concomitant disruptions of the Suez Canal—impede this progress. With the advent of supertankers for the transport of oil, she writes, which the canal could not accommodate, the necessity arose "for shipping companies to plan the routing of the larger tankers around the Cape of Good Hope, double the distance to the European markets, thus double the cost." The major point is that Israel's actions undermine not only Egyptian interests but also global commerce and the crucial passage of oil. "As has already been evident from the temporary closing of the Canal resulting from the June, 1967 aggression by Israel against the UAR, the effect of the use of the Cape route is higher prices to the consumer for this vital source of energy." This free-market language of the "consumer" and "this vital source of energy" signals both the sly disingenuousness of her remarks and a willingness to couch Israeli policy in a financial idiom the West understands.

The implication was clear: if consumers and global commercial interests fulminate at the prospect of skyrocketing oil prices, they ought to point at Israel, not Egypt. "It seems hardly necessary," she writes, "to point out the striking comparison of the positive role of the UAR in its constant efforts to facilitate transport through the Suez Canal . . . and the negative role of Israel and those who stand behind her in obstructing that transport, at the moment shown in Israel's refusal to withdraw from the east bank of the Canal despite the UN resolution of November 22 calling for this withdrawal." Egypt, she argued, had lived up to its responsibility in operating, modernizing, and allowing passage through Suez, but it could not be expected to capitulate to foreign pressure for unrestricted access to the canal—or cessation of armed resistance—without fulfillment of any Arab demands.

Like the Indian delegates to the United Nations, whose proposal during Security Council deliberations was thought to be "more Arab than the Arabs," Graham's positions exceeded Nasser's demands, if not his rhetoric.[97] Did her uncompromising advocacy of Nasserism mean that she was merely a mouthpiece of the UAR regime? It is easy to see the role of Graham, a recent transplant to Cairo and a neophyte in Middle East politics, as tantamount to that of the "useful idiot" of Stalinism. Graham was a quick study, however, and her famous work ethic and adaptability enabled her to grasp regional complexities in a remarkably short period of time. The point, however, is not about whether she was knowledgeable or ill-informed about history and current events or about whether she was a Nasserist dupe. My concern involves the textually subtle ways in which Graham managed to repackage while appearing merely to propagate Nasserist doctrine.

Graham attributed Israel's "refusal" to abide by the terms of Resolution 242 to the Johnson administration's "unqualified support for Israel," a commitment that is supposedly "causing more and more US voters to demand a change in the US policy in the Middle East."[98] In the pages of the *Egyptian Gazette*, Graham uses her column to highlight this support, which she viewed as cynically motivated in the Johnson administration's effort to secure a crucial "East Coast Jewish vote" in a tight election season. "Israel's insistence upon a condition she knows is utterly unacceptable to the Arabs is only possible because of the support and encouragement of the US government, a support which is occasioned by the determination of the Johnson Administration to maintain the support of the powerful Zionist lobby in anticipation of a rough time ahead over the Presidential nomination and elections."[99] She believed that Israel and the United States were trying to submit Egypt to "blackmail": forcing Nasser to accede to direct negotiations with Israel without resolving, in advance, the question of the occupied territories, especially Islam's holy sites.

In this judgment she was not alone, at least in her reportage of events. In the unpublished "A Letter to My Brothers in America," dated February 25, 1974, she reported on the Islamic Summit in Lahore (covered in "so limited, stupid, and distorted" a fashion in the Western press), where the "Islamic world showed itself as fully matured and as facing its responsibilities in the last half of the Twentieth Century." She cites the opening remarks from Pakistan's prime minister Zulfikar Aly Bhutto as the following: "Let me make it clear from this platform that any agreement, any protocol which postulates the continuance of the holy city under, or the transfer of the holy city to, any non-Moslem or non-Arab sovereignty will not be worth the paper it is written on."[100] In order to posit Christian-Muslim unity against the common Zionist enemy, she cites the expression of fraternity and support by one patriarch of Christian Churches in the Middle East.

Graham was convinced that the Johnson administration had no intention of alienating Jewish voters by withdrawing aid to Israel.[101] "So once again the fate of peace in the Middle East," she laments, "the lives of innocent Arab civilians on the East Bank of the River Jordan and, indeed, the very prestige of the United Nations Organization are being compromised for the sake of an election victory for the Democratic Party in November." Without economic sanctions leveled by the United States against Israel, she argued, no peace is possible between Israel and its neighbors.[102]

Johnson was far less disposed to a preemptive Israeli strike than Graham's analysis permitted, but she did intuit the consolidation of a "special relationship" between the United States and Israel in the wake of the Six-Day War. Before the war, Johnson was preoccupied with his Jewish American constituency and calibrated public relations with Israel accordingly. "Though he was not blindly supportive of Israel," writes one historian, "Johnson's initial sympathies were buttressed by a much greater sensitivity to criticism of his policies than was seen in the Eisenhower or Kennedy eras, particularly once he intensified American involvement in Vietnam during 1965."[103]

In his 1968 State of the Union address, Johnson informed the American public: "During the Arab-Israeli War last June, the hotline between Washington and Moscow was used for the first time in our history. A cease-fire was achieved without a major power confrontation." The president's address sidesteps the foreign policy shift that resulted from U.S. involvement in the prewar situation. In the tense atmosphere preceding the conflict, the central political problem for Israel, according to historian Avi Shlaim, involved securing U.S. support in the event of a full-blown war. "Everyone remembered that in the aftermath of the Suez War," Shlaim writes, "President Dwight Eisenhower had compelled Israel to pull out its troops from Sinai and few politicians were willing to risk another crisis in U.S.-Israel relations."[104] Historians differ regarding whether, or to what degree, Johnson backed Israel's decision to use military force.[105] But as a president concerned about upcoming elections and also, apparently, a sincere supporter of Israel, Lyndon Johnson—who proudly recalled his opposition to Eisenhower's management of the Suez Crisis—shaped a foreign policy in the Middle East that continues to structure contemporary events. If Palestine's cycle of violence was more complex than Graham's polemics allowed, her analysis was visionary in at least two respects: it identified both the creeping paralysis of the UN and the formation of a "special relationship" between the United States and Israel post-1967.[106]

If dogmatic, Graham's articles limn an expansive map of the fallout of 1967, from the development of closer ties between the United States and Israel to the cataclysms following Israel's occupation of the Gaza Strip, the Golan Heights, and the West Bank (territories previously controlled by Egypt, Syria, and Jordan, respectively). Graham underscores electoral politics as a primary force in Johnson's foreign policy in the Middle East, but her analysis elides—or misrepresents—the probability, for example, that the president's disinclination to enter war paralleled the Soviet Union's hesitancy to join on the side of the Arab nations.

In Graham's polemics, it is hard to distinguish between situations or events she misunderstood and those that she willfully misrepresents for partisan purposes. But her propensity for exquisite partisan redaction is expressed, for example, in her treatment of Nasser, especially her parsing of his *Philosophy of the Revolution*. In other words, when she carefully constructed the statecraft and charismatic persona of Nasser it is unlikely that she was unaware, for example, of the Egyptian leader's own set of provocations toward Israel—actions that were less attributable to imperialist depredations than to internal pressures within the Arab sphere. In Graham's writings, no mention is made of what seemed then and now to be a set of bold actions instigating a war that Egypt was ill equipped to wage. In one article, Graham celebrates Jordan's offensive against Israel and reaffirms the Nasserist line of the "imperialist-Zionist threat." Then she refers to the "Arab people of the entire Arab nation" joining in salute of the heroic Jordanian forces under King Hussein's leadership—though relations between King Hussein and Nasser were tense and unequal. The fiction of a unified Arab nation rested mainly on pro-Palestinian sentiment.

Even as she defends Arab resistance and efforts in the diplomatic sphere, her partisan commitment demands that actors from Arab nations appear in postures of reaction to Zionist or imperialist aggression. But Graham's literary partisanship implies that beyond retaliatory and defensive actions—which define her primary terrain for postcolonial assertiveness—Arab actors remain deprived of more complex forms of agency, even of the right to fail or the chance to miscalculate in volatile situations. Consequently, in Graham's accounts, these actors are denied an adequate role in shaping events, in both generative and deleterious ways.[107] The war's displacement of Arab populations prompted Graham to portray the foundation of Israel as a continuous act of state terror, one that was bound to initiate a cycle of (legitimate) resistance activities and reprisals from Arabs and (illegitimate) calls for "national defense" and counterterrorism from Israel, emboldened by U.S. support.[108] One week later, in another article, she refers to the "Nazi-like oppression of the Israeli occupation authorities," "Zionist terrorist gangs," and the "Israeli usurpers." Attacks launched by Palestinians and Arabs were "resistance activities of the people who are suffering the occupation."[109]

In a draft essay, "Morality of Militarism," intended for the *Gazette*, Graham assails Abba Eban for "[legislating] in one way for Israel, and in another for the rest of the world." During an address to the British Immigrants' Association held in Jerusalem, the Israeli foreign minister, according to Graham, "told his audience that any international Middle East resolution which does not condemn what he dubbed 'terrorism' would be 'morally worthless and politically mischievous.'" Needless to say, Graham did not view Israel's precondition for negotiation—official condemnation and desistance of all terrorist activities—as equivalent to the Arabs' demand for the return of occupied territories and the repatriation of refugees.

"The people whom Mr. Eban would wish the world to condemn and proscribe as 'terrorists' are, of course, the Arab men and women engaged in resistance work to clear their land of an unwelcome invader and occupier—the Israelis. And almost every day there is news of a new resistance group being formed amongst the Palestinian Arabs, or certain groups, getting together for organizational and military purposes." She argues that the Arab resistance organizations are based on principles "similar to those of the African freedom fighters opposing racist governments in South Africa, Rhodesia and

Portuguese-ruled Africa, and similar to the famous maquis of France and other underground resistance groups which fought the forces of Hitlerian imperialism in occupied Europe during World War II." Referring to Sami Hadawi's *Bitter Harvest* (1967), a history of Palestine, she highlights the author's comparison between contemporary Arab militias and the Zionist underground movements during the British mandate era in Palestine. Not surprisingly, there was a signal difference between these underground movements: "The Zionist groups were organized to wrest a country from its original inhabitants using political intrigue, influence and pressure abroad and brute force, massacres, expulsions and dispossessions in Palestine. The objectives of the Palestinian Arabs, on the other hand are to regain possession of their rights and property and to liberate their homeland from the invader."[110]

Though clear-sighted in its arraignment of Zionist displacements during the nation's inception, this binary analysis shields the exercise of historical agency by the various inter-Arab rivalries that intensified the atmosphere of war in the late 1960s.[111] Despite the reportorial advantages her Cairo location afforded Graham, as signaled by the command she displays of complex regional affairs, it is difficult to gauge the extent of her awareness of the Arab disputes that compelled Nasser to adopt a firmer, and ultimately fatal, stance toward Israel. Whether or not these particulars were available to Graham, however, her omission of internecine tensions is consistent with what I have argued is Graham's mode of narrating events in alignment with her own geopolitical imagination.

The main areas of historical contention involve precisely the reasons why Nasser initiated these risky moves (especially when his army was then bogged down in the Yemen War, which impeded Egypt's ability to engage Israel militarily) and why Israel felt compelled to respond with a surprise military attack, which enabled the seizure of territory in the West Bank and Gaza that reconfigured Israel's political geography and expanded its territorial sovereignty. Israel's incursion into Palestinian-occupied territory also confirmed to observers in the Arab world what they had long perceived as Israel's ambitions for colonial expansion.[112] On this highly contested subject, some commentators believe that Nasser forced Israel's hand, whereas others view the Egyptian leader's actions as a response to credible intelligence he received from multiple sources (Soviet, Syrian, Lebanese) concerning an impending Israeli attack on Syria. Other commentators stress the regional nature of the conflict: namely, the pressure Nasser felt from other Arab regimes (especially the rhetorically belligerent Syrians) to confront Israeli military encroachments.[113] At various points in the fortnight leading to war both sides seemed unclear about whether their respective militaries were preparing for a defensive or an offensive war.[114]

In keeping with historical tradition, both Israeli and Egyptian (among other Arab) regimes in this conflict demonized the other, and in this case, as commentators have noted, these representations conceivably influenced foreign policy decisions and military strategy. If Israel represented an outpost of imperialism reinforced by the world's dominant superpower, and if U.S. interventionism had led to the demise or endangerment of anticolonial leaders in the Congo or Cuba, then how could Egypt afford not to call on the Soviet Union to protect its sovereignty and to rise to the occasion in the Palestinian struggle? Conversely, if Nasser, Radio Cairo, and Syria blasted anti-Zionist rhetoric, and if Nasser aspired to domination of the Afro-Asiatic world, then how could a geographically imperiled Israel afford to risk another Shoah?

These questions suggest that the production, dissemination, interpretation, and reinterpretation of texts mediated critical decisions in the crucible of war. The Second World War taught, especially to Israel, that foreign policy necessitated taking seriously the enemy's manifestos, propaganda, and speeches, even when realistic assessments of the geopolitical situation suggested the unlikelihood of imminent attack. What follows describes Graham's involvement in these politicized hermeneutics and modes of textual revision. When Israeli leaders sought to mobilize public support for a preemptive war by casting Nasser's *Philosophy of the Revolution* as an imperialist screed, Graham reinterpreted that text—indeed, the very same passages—as an anti-imperialist tract calibrated less to restore an imagined Afro-Arab historical bond sundered by colonialism than to forge a new unity.

Graham's biographical writings, as noted earlier, drew heavily on Nasser's *Philosophy of the Revolution*, a manifesto in which political geography is a central theme. Describing his treatise as akin to a "reconnaissance-patrol" rather than a philosophical system, Nasser endeavors "to discover the pattern of our environment so that we should know that we do not live on an isolated island surrounded with water on every side." If Egypt's northern seaboard functioned as the continent's commercial and cross-cultural gate to the world, the reality was that the country's borders limned an intimate connection both to the Arab and Islamic world and to "black" Africa. Nasser employed the metaphor of concentric circles to describe this complex geography. He made clear that among the three concentric circles—the Arab world, Africa, and Islamic civilization—in which "fate" positioned Egypt, the Arabic sphere claimed priority: "There is no doubt that the Arab circle is the most important and the most closely connected with us. Its history merges with ours."[115] In accounts of Nasserism, to say nothing of Middle East affairs in general, Egypt's centrality to the Arab world is impossible to overstate, but the charismatic leader's relocation of Egyptian history within a parallel narrative of African liberation merits closer attention.

Nasser realized this vision in multiple forms of Pan-African collaboration. In 1964 and 1965, he served as the second president of the Organization of African Unity (OAU), led also by Nkrumah; before this tenure, he was a founding member of the Casablanca Group, a precursor to the OAU made up of Egypt, Algeria, Ghana, and Morocco. Anti-imperialist in orientation, the Casablanca Group competed with the "moderate" Monrovia Group, led by Nigeria and Liberia, until both merged into the OAU, which in 1964 convened its first summit in Cairo (following a reconciliatory meeting in Addis Ababa in 1963). Establishing diplomatic relationships throughout Africa, Nasser, as noted previously, invited sub-Saharan Africans to study in Egypt and to train in the nation's military college.[116] His regime even hosted seemingly smaller numbers of African American university students.[117] Graham sought to restore and amplify the Pan-African element in the Egyptian leader's vision.

The following passages from *The Philosophy of the Revolution* furnished Graham with evidence for her Africanist interpretation. "Can we ignore," Nasser asks, "that there is a continent of Africa in which fate has placed us and which is destined today to witness a terrible struggle on its future?" Nasser emphasized the Nile River, the "artery of life of our country" that "draws its supply from the heart of the continent." Finally, there "remains the Sudan, our beloved brother, whose boundaries extend deeply into Africa and which is the neighbor to all the sensitive spots in the centre of the continent."[118] Geography is fate, wrote Ralph Ellison, in a rewriting of Heraclitus's well-known dictum. For Nasser this dictum resonated with his individual destiny and with the fate of the nation. "It is not in vain that our country lies to the south-west of Asia close to the Arab world, whose life is intermingled with ours. It is not in vain that our country lies in the north-east of Africa, a position from which it gives upon the dark continent, wherein rages today the most violent struggle between white colonisers and black natives for the possession of its inexhaustible resources."[119] Egypt, he insisted, could ill afford to turn its back on this struggle.

Yet what, precisely, would Egypt's role in African liberation entail? "If we direct our attention after that [that is, the Arab circle] to the second circle," Nasser continues, "the circle of the continent of Africa, I would say, without exaggeration, that we cannot, even if we wish to, in any way stand aside, from the sanguinary and dreadful struggle now raging in the heart of Africa between five million whites and two hundred million Africans." In strident, even proleptic language, this passage anticipates resistance to the idea that Egypt ought to assume a vanguard role in decolonization in sub-Saharan Africa. The significance of Egyptian leadership in the Palestinian or Algerian struggles was evident to all observers. But were the colonial wars of Kenya or Ghana or Mozambique really an Egyptian concern?

Nasser insisted that Africa's colonial wars were indeed an Egyptian concern, but the exact nature of this concern was debatable, since his language also included a tutelary inflection that evokes historically asymmetrical relationships between Arabs and black Africans.[120] "We cannot [turn our back on the continent] for one principle and clear reason," Nasser asserts, "namely that we are in Africa. The people of Africa will continue to look up to us, who guard the northern gate of the continent and who are its connecting link with the world outside. We cannot, under any condition, relinquish our responsibility in helping, in every way possible, to diffuse the light of civilization into the farthest parts of that virgin jungle." As noted in Chapter 3, ambiguities and awkward phrasing mark the various English translations of Nasser's treatise. One translation replaces *in every way possible* with the phrase *with all our might; the light of civilization* with *the spread of enlightenment and civilization;* and *virgin jungle* with *the remotest depths of the jungle.* I note in Chapter 3 how certain key passages in one English translation omit or mistranslate the word "Africa." As I argue, also in that chapter, Graham carefully redacted Nasser's treatise—omitting or deemphasizing the text's evocation of a master-client relationship—while endorsing Nasser's vision of Egypt as a Pan-Arab and Pan-African cultural, political, and intellectual hub.

As Graham's writings in the late 1960s and early 1970s for the *Egyptian Gazette*, *Freedomways*, the *Black Scholar*, and other publications indicate, the role of Israel in Africa applied pressure to Afro-Arab solidarity. From its inception, Israel cultivated strong economic relationships with several sub-Saharan African nations, including Nkrumah's Ghana.[121] Israel also had longstanding ties with the apartheid regime in South Africa. Over time, this latter alliance prompted some erstwhile African allies to distance themselves from the fledgling Jewish state—an outcome that Arab leaders had sought at Bandung. "The entire Arab world," Wright reports, "headed by Egypt's Nasser, would be seeking to air its direct grievance against Israel and its indirect case against France."[122]

To be sure, Wright's phrase "entire Arab world" obscures ideological and geopolitical fissures within this sphere—particularly the aforementioned rivalries among Egypt and Syria's radical Pan-Arabism, Jordan's anti-Nasserism, Iraq's secular Baath'ism, and King Saud's U.S.-backed conservatism—that had already manifested by the mid-1950s. Yet what struck Wright was how Israel (a "direct grievance") had superseded French colonialism (an "indirect case") as the Arab sphere's arch concern on the global stage. Wright recalls the moment when Nasser "struck at Israel as hard as he could." As Wright quotes Nasser: "Under the eyes of the United Nations and with her help and sanction, the people of Palestine were uprooted from their fatherland, to be replaced by a completely imported populace. Never before in history has there been such a brutal and immoral violation of human principles. Is there any guarantee for the small nations that the big powers who took part in this tragedy would not allow themselves to repeat it again, against another innocent and helpless people?"[123] Though factions within the Arab world diverged ideologically during the 1950s, over time—especially during the 1967 Arab-Israeli War—they proved capable of closing ranks on the question of Palestine.

Moving toward solidarity with Palestine in allegiance with the Arab North, Nkrumah embraced this mounting anti-imperialist and continental unity. "As Nkrumah became more radical," writes Ali A. Mazrui, "he was less inclined to recognize the Sahara as a legitimate political divide. Symbolically, Nkrumah even married an Egyptian woman to emphasize the solidarity of the African continent. . . . Nkrumah and Nyerere genuinely regarded Algerians, for example, as fellow Africans." In 1961 the Ghanaian leader participated in a conference at Casablanca with Guinea, Mali, Morocco, and Egypt, whose leadership were said to represent a radical faction on the continent.[124] The conference produced a final communiqué describing Israel as a "tool of neo-colonialism."[125] Even if sub-Saharan actors were not as vociferous in opposition to the Jewish state as Arab militants would have preferred, the status of Israel in Africa continued to mediate Afro-Arab politics. As part of this fledgling alliance, Nkrumah and other African leaders eventually had to come to grips with their Arab counterparts' animus toward Israel.

Whereas Du Bois spoke of the overthrow of Palestinian Jews by Islam, Graham regarded Islam as a benign, perhaps unifying, force on the continent and between Africa and western Asia. "In Africa," she writes in 1970, "we do not speak of the 'conquest of Egypt' by the Moslems."[126] Like Fanon's use of the first-person plural "we" in Algeria (as in the statement, "We Algerian patriots . . ."), Graham's use of the first-person plural pronoun not only carves out an inclusive space for an outsider-comrade like herself. It also asserts that the "we" who do not speak of Muslim conquest want to construct a capacious African subjectivity that invariably conceals divisions befitting the enormous diversity of the continent.

These years of Afro-Arab rapprochement coincide with Frantz Fanon's Algerian phase, perhaps the era's most striking individual embodiment of Pan-African theory and praxis. In the forms of mutual misrecognition characterizing Fanon's Algerian years, we also detect the ambiguities and cleavages marking this moment of solidarity. In the "Impossible Life of Frantz Fanon," the Tunisian writer Albert Memmi emphasizes the unprecedented, eccentric, and truly audacious nature of Fanon's commitment to the Algerian struggle of independence from France, a grisly conflict that lasted from 1954 to 1962. Perhaps more than any other commentator on Fanon, Memmi is sensitive to the profundity and novelty of Fanon's identification with Algeria, one that far exceeds—politically, physically, and existentially—more conventional modalities of Third World solidarity.[127]

For Fanon sought not only to aid the Algerians in their struggle: he dedicated, perhaps even sacrificed, his life for this cause; via his writings on Algerian military strategy, he added another credential—war theorist—to his impressive resume. "The extraordinary Algerian phase of Frantz Fanon's life," writes Memmi, in a highly stylized if not fictionalized account, "has been accepted as a matter of course. Yet it is scarcely believable. A man who has never set foot in a country decides within a rather brief span of time that this people will be his people, this country his country until death, even though he knows neither its language nor its civilization and has no particular ties to it. He eventually dies for this cause and is buried in Algerian soil." Fanon often repeated the phrases, "I am an Algerian" and "We Algerian patriots," and he meant them. When he concluded *The Wretched of the Earth* with his famous invocation "to start over, to develop new thought, and to try to create a new man" [Pour l'Europe, pour nous-même et pour l'humanité, camarades, il faut faire peau neuve, développer une pensée neuve, tenter de mettre sur pied un homme neuf], Memmi believed that Fanon's own transformation into an Algerian militant, enabled only by an extraordinary reconfiguration or revaluation of identity, concretized this beguiling injunction.

But why, the Tunisian writer asks, Algeria and the Algerians? For Fanon, according to Memmi, the Algerian War was certainly just, and the Antillean psychiatrist was indeed a militant. "But he went further and made of Algeria the center of his existence, of his thought and of his work. Why did he believe it necessary to join so totally in the struggle that he thought himself transformed into an Algerian and consented to die for Algeria?" (14–15). Apparently, Fanon's relocation to Algeria was to some degree accidental; after his decision to leave France, where he no longer felt at ease, Fanon initially considered seeking employment in sub-Saharan Africa—though apparently not out of any particularly political or diasporic connection with the continent. He might well have followed in the footsteps of his former teacher Aimé Césaire and returned to his native Martinique to undertake the project of nation building there.

But he opted for Algeria—perhaps for no more profound reason, as some commentators have surmised, than that he was offered a position there. He did not, however, identify with Algerians from the outset. Upon assuming his position at the Blida-Joinville Psychiatric Hospital in Algeria, Fanon initially employed the first-person plural pronouns *us* and *we* to refer to himself and the French, thereby distinguishing himself from the Algerians, whom he rendered as *them* or *these men;* even after his famous resignation from the Blida-Joinville hospital in 1956, he still identified with the French and assailed their treatment of Algerians on universal humanitarian grounds. Yet as an editor of the Algerian nationalist newspaper *El Moudjahid* in 1957, he had reversed his previous usage, employing the pronouns *us* and *we* in reference to himself and the Algerians. When referring to people of the West Indies, Memmi observes, even (or perhaps especially) of those who had been killed in moments of social unrest, he used the pronouns *you*, *your*, and *they*. To Fanon's mind, if not necessarily to the minds of all his comrades in the liberation struggle, he had become an Algerian.

If Graham never quite "became" an Egyptian, she crafted a strident rhetorical voice that purported to defend the nation's domestic and international interests in the face of Cold War and regional pressures. Like the secular humanist Fanon, however, the Communist Graham had to adjust to the various cultural and religious differences that separated her from her new compatriots. How did Graham negotiate her secular orientation with her entry into the region's nonsecular public sphere?

When it came to ancient Egyptian spirituality, Coptic Christianity, or modern Islam, Graham's secular orientation did not preclude her from pronouncements like "man's religion is the core of his being" and "the religious beliefs and observances of Egypt ran parallel in form and expression to the early religions of deepest Africa."[128] Perhaps these ruminations reflect her adaptation to a deeply religious society; on the other hand, a slight ethnographic inflection in her prose suggests a measure of distance from the spirituality she describes. In any case, Graham's thought on Islam seems calibrated to counter Cold War enemies who sought to keep Africans divided. In her own capsule history in "Egypt Is Africa," Graham narrates the dissemination of the Arabic language, from the Persian Gulf to the Atlantic shores of Africa, alongside the proliferation of Islam, an Old Testament–derived "religion with little pomp and ritual, which revived the zeal and devotion of early Christians." But unlike Western Christianity, global Islam "made no distinction in color or class, tribe or clan—a religion which, far more realistically than Christianity has ever done—created a Brotherhood of believers. . . . The essence of that Brotherhood remains in Africa today so that the *larger part of Africa is Islamic*."[129] On the involvement of Arabs in the African slave trade—the abolition of which the British used, ironically, to justify expanding colonial interventions in Africa—Graham is largely silent.

She castigated authorities who, in failing to see the unity in diversity among Africans, wrote extensively about " 'Africa, South of the Sahara,' 'Africa, North of the Sahara;' of 'Black Africa' and 'Arab Africa,' as if there are long dividing and confining walls stretching in every direction. I must tell you that there are black peoples all over Africa; and reluctantly, I must add—there are white people all over Africa."[130] Whereas other accounts, like Ali Mazrui's, stress the master-slave, client, or otherwise asymmetrical relationship between Arabs and black Africans, Graham inverts this paradigm by inscribing Africans in the Muslim conquest of—or perhaps, as Graham would have it, *victory* over—North Africa. In the seventh-century battle of Carthage between Mohammed's forces and the "Roman plunderers," by "the time the victorious Muslim armies reached the Atlantic Ocean they could hardly be described as 'Arabians.' So many Africans—from north, east and west, had been added to their ranks and leadership that the *color of the forces* had become much darker." In opposition to conventional accounts about the religion's conquest of Africa, Graham narrates the *Africanization* of an Islam that, in the eighth century, brought enlightenment to Europe via Spain and southern France.[131]

For Graham, the word *Egypt* names not only a sophisticated, ancient civilization but also extrinsic forms of desire alternately or concurrently esoteric and economic: to learn the secrets of ancient Egypt or the feats of Muslim expansion; to exfoliate the surface of successive imperial influences and penetrate the African layers of Kemet; to employ the country's transcontinental nexus as an engine of global commerce; to symbolize Afro-Arab and Third World collaboration. What else can explain why all "peoples have come to the Valley of the Nile—the Assyrians, the Phoenecians, the Persians, the Mongols, the Turks, the Greeks, the Romans, the Arabs, the British"? For Herodotus, she reminds the reader, Egypt was the "gift of the Nile"—the subtitle Graham uses for her biography of Nasser.[132]

If, as Michael Latham argues, the intellectuals of the Kennedy administration betrayed vestiges of Manifest Destiny ideology in their ambitions of global modernization, especially in Africa, for his part Nasser also envisioned Egypt's destiny as manifest in the continent.[133] Commentators analogized Egypt's task in Africa with the United States' role in the Americas. Some "Egyptians saw it as their nation's 'Manifest Destiny' to lead the rest of the continent," writes Philip Muehlenbeck. In 1953 "the government-affiliated periodical *Al-Akhbar* editorialized, 'We look for a power which will protect Africa and play the same role as the United States *vis-à-vis* the American continent. We see no one but Egypt. It is the greatest African power with a personality that is universally recognised. It is necessary for Egypt to pursue one African policy, the enfranchisement of the Continent.'"[134] The idea of Egypt as an *African* power reflects, in part, Nasser's efforts to shape a national and international consciousness with anti-imperialism at its core. Graham championed this role. In addition to his support of other African leaders and his willingness to render Cairo a center of Pan-African and Afro-Asian collaboration, Nasser's effort to remap Egypt within Africa encouraged

Graham to focus her attention on the intensifying situation of war and imperialism in the Middle East. But she entered this arena on her own terms, and with her own priorities, leaving behind a singular archive that sought not only to destabilize Western imperialism but also to construct a viable socialist alternative in Africa and the Third World.

6

Bandung or Barbarism

RICHARD WRIGHT ON TERROR IN FREEDOM

FOR READERS of Richard Wright's literary explorations of the Third World, his commitment to secular enlightenment and modernization in Asia and Africa presents a paradox. On the one hand, his advocacy of secularization, rationalization, and industrialization as a necessary antidote to non-Western spiritual and economic traditions appears to deny the viability of African and Asian societies and their multiple ways of being in the world. If Wright paid tribute to the aesthetic and religious traditions that affirmed African humanity, he also insisted that the realities of the postwar order necessitated the replacement of ancient traditions by modern subjectivity and its institutions: secular democracy and the rule of law, industry and technological progress, bureaucratic order and rationalized living spaces. As a champion of Third World modernity, Wright was not, of course, unique among his colleagues, but his apparent endorsement of military discipline and the use of dictatorial means to implement these aims suggested his willingness to promote modernization at an intolerable and somewhat perverse cost.[1]

On the other hand, his focus on the negative dialectic of colonial enlightenment leaves scant room to imagine how these processes, at least in the short run of history, would take root in the postcolony. This conclusion is not necessarily surprising, since many commentators during Wright's time and since have argued that certain practices of modernity lead to catastrophic consequences. Consider two contrasting but compatible arguments: the idea that secular modernity unleashes a rootless mass society, untethered to traditional mores or religious injunctions, that lubricates the production of sociopathic subjects (like infamous 1920s University of Chicago student murderers Leopold and Loeb, for instance, who happen to make a cameo appearance in Wright's *Native Son;* these figures also appear to have been incorporated into the composite protagonist of Wright's *The Outsider*); or the idea that the disciplinary nature of instrumental reason and the "wholly administered society" represses irrational urges or produces social conditions amenable to mass violence. These ideas saturate Wright's literary imagination, but his engagement with the Third World obliges him to adapt or jettison these notions and invent new ones in light of a startling set of realizations on the actual terrain of decolonization.

To be sure, at times Wright enthusiastically expresses faith in the enlightenment project. The "spirit of the Enlightenment," he declaims, "of the Reformation, which made Europe great, now has a chance to be extended to all mankind!"[2] But in Wright's imagination, what eclipses this occasional ebullience is a darker story, a fragmentary but grand narrative about the globalization of enlightenment. From the constellation of ideas evoking modern enlightenment, many midcentury thinkers reduced the term's multiplicity, equating rationalization and secularization with human freedom and agency, if not necessarily with human flourishing or virtue.[3] This equation of rationalization and secularization is certainly what Wright and official modernization theorists (that is, those employed in government or advising capacities) had in mind. As many critics have noted, reified terms like "enlightenment" or "the Enlightenment project" are as reductive as an undifferentiated "Africa," "Asia," "Third World," or binaries like "tradition versus modernity." Wright was not alone when he failed to spell out what he meant by a key term like "industrialization," instead conveying his meaning by example or imagery, like his valorization of the figure of the engineer ("Where is the engineer," he asks, "who can build a project out of eighty million lives, a project that can nourish and sustain them?").[4] Yet these concepts constitute the discursive traffic of the mid-twentieth century and evoked a common historical imagination among their proponents.

If abstract or facile in conception, these terms were not always as reductive as retroactive judgments suggest. By the postwar era, iterations of the Enlightenment project included fewer Age of Reason clichés and more of the searing critiques (internal to Enlightenment thought itself) advanced by members of the Frankfurt School and other theorists. Writing at "a time when the end of the National Socialist terror was in sight," Max Horkheimer and Theodor Adorno traced the latent barbarism of the Enlightenment—which in its determination to evacuate the realm of mythical thought produced its own self-mythology—without abandoning the era's universal provenance in the sovereignty of reason. In an alternative to the Marxian frame of analysis, Max Weber, on whose ideas the Frankfurt theorists drew, famously described the rationalization of the world as an iron cage.[5] As Achille Mbembe argues, modern political theory alongside the philosophical discourse on modernity have enshrined a "distinction between reason and unreason (passion, fantasy)" in which "late-modern criticism has been able to articulate a certain idea of the political, the community, the subject—or, more fundamentally, of what the good life is all about, how to achieve it, and, in the process, to become a fully moral agent. Within this paradigm, reason is the truth of the subject and politics is the exercise of reason in the public sphere." The exercise of reason, on this view, is equivalent to the exercise of freedom itself and forms the basis of conceptions of individual autonomy, collective sovereignty, and politics generally. Yet this genealogy of the sovereignty of reason, according to Mbembe, elides populations subjected to necropolitics, "those figures of sovereignty whose central project is not the struggle for autonomy but *the generalized instrumentalization of human existence and the material destruction of human bodies and populations.*"[6]

Yet if Wright shared with thinkers in this tradition a sense of the intrinsic barbarity of enlightened industrial modernity, he also expanded the scope of this lineage by synthesizing the collapse of Europe with the future of the postcolony. It is worth nothing that for theorists like Horkheimer and Adorno, the dialectic of enlightenment is intrinsically totalitarian (though their use of *totalitarianism* referred to National Socialism, or to a lesser extent the "culture industry," but not to communism), or at least potentially so, insofar as its quest for domination of the natural world and the rationalization of human subjectivity plants its own seeds of barbarism—a potentiality that originates in Greek antiquity and reaches its apotheosis in the mid-twentieth century.

If Wright spoke more positively about the Enlightenment project, his emphasis on the terror and barbarism of the twentieth century suggests an affinity with this theoretical tradition. Though contemporary critics may rue the disappointments of the postcolonial era, seeing in them so many failures or tragedies, as anthropologist David Scott characterizes them, I contend that Wright's travel narratives, fiction, and anticolonial phenomenology offer an alternative conceptualization of this era, even if this picture leaves intact extant accounts of the Third World project as either a partial victory or a tragic failure, a disfigurement or an unrealized vision of the enlightenment.[7] In what follows, however, I argue that Wright's notion of postmortem terror absorbs but transcends the dominant narrative of postcolonial failure in its effort to resolve the paradox of Third World enlightenment.

For Wright, the main obstructions to the enlightenment project in the Third World are both external and internal: externally, the geopolitical situation of the Cold War, if it affords the Third World a measure of agency via nonalignment and internationalist solidarity, also renders this bloc vulnerable to superpower intrusion or aggression; internally, the imposition of secular and rationalist modes of discipline in the largely nonsecular nations of Africa and Asia portend an affective and spiritual maelstrom, characterized by "unrest, violence, and an astounding emotional thrashing about as men seek new objects about which they can center their loyalties."[8] As a corollary to his emphasis on rationalization, Wright limned the affective sphere of decolonization, the structures of feeling that will sustain the postcolonial nation once the colonists have withdrawn their flag and the disciplinary mechanisms of modernity have taken root.

Wright encapsulates this affective sphere in his notion of "terror in freedom," or what he also calls "postmortem terror": a postcolonial condition induced by the desire to keep pace with Western modernity and the concomitant fear of resubjugation by nuclear-equipped powers. "The psychological agony that Indonesia suffers,"

Wright observes, "was created by a situation compounded of fear of the return of Western technical expertise which they feel they need, which in their hearts they adore; yet, how can they have the cooperation of the West and at the same time fend off what they feel to be the desire of the West to dominate?" At Bandung, Wright notes, many Indonesians were willing to forego the benefits of Western technology, "but they know that in doing so they are leaving themselves open to re-enslavement."[9] Many in the Afro-Asian world had internalized Stalin's motto during the Second World War—"the side with the most motors will win"—but constructing a mechanized, industrial society in such a compressed time span defined a quintessential postcolonial dilemma: the achievement of this level of technological prowess in a preindustrial society seemed impossible without soliciting the support of external actors who may wind up as agents of domination.

However, Wright alludes to how history's ironic moments provide signposts to rectify this geopolitical and technological imbalance. In his discussion with Indonesia's first premier, Sutan Sjahrir, Wright records the leader's description of the role of the brutal and industrially muscular Japanese forces in Indonesia's independence movement against Dutch rule. According to Sjahrir, the Dutch cowered before the Japanese invaders. And if the colonizers were so terrified by an Asian power, he explains, then why ought the Indonesians to fear the Dutch?

In 1967 an American political scientist with expertise in African affairs posed a question in the journal *Africa Today:* "Is Totalitarianism Taking Over in Africa?" This question verbalized what worried onlookers in the West detected as the rise of charismatic Third World leadership eager to concentrate power and repress freedom. In this respect, as in others, Wright appears alternately visionary or prescriptive: he either anticipated the rise of totalitarian-style dictatorship in the Third World or provided a blueprint that subsequent leaders enacted. This chapter adopts a different interpretation. During the 1950s, Wright imagined a synthetic vision of decolonization and modernization against the backdrop of totalitarianism. The idea of terror in freedom, I argue, constitutes an imaginative resource for theorizing the confluence of these historical forces.

U.S. journalists covering the Afro-Asian Conference, Wright felt, "had no philosophy of history with which to understand Bandung." This chapter reads his fiction, travel writings, and anticolonial essays in order to reconstruct his conception of a philosophy of history appropriate to decolonization. The following questions guide this inquiry: how can the newly liberated Asian and African nations, now subject to terror in freedom and the inevitable dilemmas of secularization and modernization, avoid the totalitarian catastrophes marking the West's recent past? And how would the barbarisms that plagued Western enlightenment in the twentieth century elude the geopolitically fraught Third World?

Enlightenment, Secularization, Totalitarianism

Generally, criticism of Wright's defense of enlightenment and modernization in the Third World points in two opposite directions. In "Third World of Theory: Enlightenment's Esau," Henry Louis Gates Jr. argues that Richard Wright's unflagging commitment to Enlightenment protocols prompted him to concede the superiority of Western rationalism and to characterize European colonialism as a lamentably destructive but ultimately advantageous benefit to the non-Western world—a world asphyxiated, in Wright's view, by tradition and the nonsecular.[10] "We have to admire his courage," Gates writes, "for Wright's chief argument was that colonialism was the best thing that had ever befallen the continent of Africa."[11]

For Manthia Diawara, by contrast, Wright courageously countenanced secular enlightenment—what he saw as a universal paradigm betrayed by the West—and industrialization as the only guarantor of Third World independence, which would otherwise remain vulnerable to Cold War and neocolonial depredations. Diawara contends that Wright—whom he deems undoubtedly "*for* Africa"—did not merely endorse colonial mimicry of Western enlightenment. This observation finds support in Wright's complaint that the person "who would question, with all the good faith in the world, whether the philosophical ideas and assumptions of John Stuart Mill and John Locke are valid for all times, for all peoples, and for all countries with their vastly differing traditions and backgrounds, with the motive of psychologically freeing men's minds so that they can seek new conditions and instrumentalities for freedom, can be indicted as an enemy of democracy."[12] The question was not whether all Third World countries, however massively differentiated, ought to blaze the path of modern democracy; the question was whether the Western powers were capable of recognizing nonaligned modernity (what commentators now call "alternative modernities") as legitimate and not merely the ventriloquism of Moscow. In this context, "psychologically freeing men's minds" did not mean decolonizing the mind; it meant liberating the intellect from superstitious and irrational habits. Yet Wright clearly did not believe that all countries had to mimic the intellectual and cultural lineage of the West in order to modernize.

Rather, he projected a vision in which Asian and African societies, strengthened by twentieth-century disciplinary techniques, could forge their own idiosyncratic versions of postcolonial modernity. Diawara recalls a conversation with one Abdoulaye Ly, a retired Senegalese history professor and Second World War veteran who explained how commonly the term "militarization" was used in the 1940s and 1950s. People employed the term not only in the "communist sense of creating a proletarian army, but also in the sense of educating the African people, creating fraternal bonds beyond tribal groups, and forming disciplined militants for the Pan-African cause of decolonization and modernization of Africa. He reminded me that in French the words *militaire* and *militant* had the same root, the Latin *militis*, which means disciplined and committed to an ideal, ready to fight for a cause."[13] In its combination of idealism and realism, Wright's notion of militarization draws on his communist understanding of this term, while anticipating Third World revolutionary modalities that outlived the author, who died in 1960.[14]

In the communist usage, the meaning of militancy was not primarily about creating a proletarian army; above all, militancy involved the production of new subjectivities. In his influential 1954 study *The Appeals of Communism,* Gabriel Almond extrapolates two figures of the militant from the thought of Marx and Lenin. "The image of the socialist or Communist militant in Marx was of a leader, guide, and organizer of the proletariat, of an individual who educated the working class in its function of conquering political power." A rational calculator of means and ends, the Marxist militant was conceived as a *scientific socialist* acting with "full knowledge of the laws of history and the social process." But he was also schooled in a "dialectic of progress that emphasized the persistent conflict between progress and reaction, in which progress triumphed but only with costs."[15] The Marxian horizon of utopia was not naïve but realistic and earned—and all the more attractive for that reason. On this account, the Marxist model overlapped with the Leninist and Stalinist models but differed in the crucial sense that the Marxist militant, though working in a vanguard role, was not sharply stratified from the broader proletariat. Over time but invariably, history in the form of a victorious proletariat would erode the distance in position and class-consciousness between vanguard militant and rank-and-file proletarian.

In the thought of Lenin, by contrast, "the Communist militant was viewed as a very special kind of person, a member of a kind of aristocracy, sharing in an esoteric knowledge not assimilable by the average proletarian during the era of the bourgeois dictatorship." This militant also manifests the spirit of radicalism specific to Russia in the latter half of the nineteenth century. For Almond, Leninism can be "understood as a marriage of Marxism with this extreme Russian revolutionary current," producing a hybrid figure unforgettably imagined in Dostoyevsky's character Sergei Nechaev in *The Possessed* ("perhaps the most extreme example of the nihilistic revolutionary terrorist of the 1860's and 1870's").[16]

Blending quantitative and qualitative methods, *The Appeals of Communism* employs a wide range of evidence: formulations from the Marxist-Leninist-Stalinist classics of theory, ideas found in communist print culture, case studies, and the results of interviews conducted among four national communist parties: the French, Italian, British, and American. From this data, Almond distills characteristics of the archetypal communist militant that I read against the characters, fictional and historical, portrayed by Wright.

This distillation results in a multifaceted set of profiles, compilations and analyses of data, and composite sketches of members of the four national parties. Overall, the study described what drew people to communism and what these members were like: what properties they did or did not share in common across national or educational or class lines; how they perceived communism in society; and how and what they learned about this movement and its politics. What was their family background? Were they immigrants, and if so did they tend to reject their parents' values and behavior even as they felt rejected by the dominant American culture? Were they exposed to childhood religious influences? Did they speak one language at home and another in the world? Did they experience family or personal suffering during the war, or fascist occupation, or a strike or labor disorder? What were their employment prospects? Did they perceive a disparity between their career aspirations and expectations? How old were they when they first engaged in radical activity? What qualities did they associate with party leaders, and how did their perceptions change as leaders moved up the party ladder? Responses to these questions are predictably diverse, but the study extrapolates from this data a few relevant continuities discussed below.

Though taking for granted like other midcentury intellectual productions the gravity of the communist threat, *Appeals* impressively constellates the features of communist doctrine, establishes its coherence, and shows its capacity to resolve internal tactical dilemmas or ideological tensions. For example, "a careful reader of the Leninist and Stalinist classics might conclude that while the party has a theory, the right to be 'theoretical' . . . is carefully located in the central organs of the party, and all that is left to the echelons below is the power to expound, and perhaps, within limits, to explain."[17] At the same time, *Appeals* distinguishes between the thematic tendencies of each master-theorist, Lenin and Stalin: whereas the "Leninist classics emphasize the themes of rational calculating behavior," the Stalinist texts stress organization and especially "centralized direction, discipline, and loyalty"—a doctrinal difference that reflects Stalin's transformation of the communist movement into a far more centralized and disciplined apparatus than its predecessor organization under Lenin.[18] To put the matter a bit too schematically, Wright's fiction—especially *The Outsider*—evokes the Leninist image of an intellectual aristocracy, possessed of esoteric knowledge, whereas

Wright's anticolonial nonfiction adopts the Stalinist inflection of disciplined regimentation. Part of the aim of this chapter is to place these two tendencies in dialogue.

In order to juxtapose these tendencies, it is instructive to note Almond's observation concerning a number of intriguing differences in "non-political perceptions of the party" among the four national groups of respondents. The seductively subversive allure of communism motivates members across national borders. All four national groups, the study finds, identify the party as antiauthoritarian, rebellious, exciting, and unconventional. A sociologically significant finding, however, divides the European from the Anglophone countries. Data showed that the "perception of the party as a means of solving problems of loneliness and isolation was far more frequent among the American and British cases than among the French and Italian." Why did more Americans and British—in numbers twice or thrice that of their French and Italian counterparts—register isolation as the problem to which the party was the solution? One explanation, Almond avers, involves the disproportionate number of minorities, immigrants, and other outsiders in the British and American Communist Parties. "Members of minority groups are confronted with a serious problem of conformity and assimilation to the dominant society," he writes. "Feelings of vulnerability and of isolation are often associated with this social status, particularly among the more socially mobile elements." Since many of the rights and benefits afforded the dominant ethnic group are unavailable to minorities, it is no surprise that they should perceive the party "as a way of coping with feelings of vulnerability and isolation."[19] Obsessed by the literary figure of society's outsider, Wright was a specialist in this nexus between deracinating social affects and radical politics. One way to read his literary production of the 1950s is as a series of doomed coping strategies conjured to fill the void previously occupied by organized radicalism.[20]

As much as Wright derived his sense of militancy from his communist training, the onset of decolonization also prompted him to adapt these conceptions to the Afro-Asian world of nonsecular militancy. Competing elements in Wright's conception of militarization and rationalization destabilize the crisp set of connections with communism sketched above. For Wright's imagination exceeds his investment in the disciplinary, fraternal, and enlightened elements of militarization. He is equally attuned to the kernel of barbarism latent in militarized, industrial organization.

This latter concern suggests another point of entry with respect to Wright's iteration of the Enlightenment project. What these interpretations overlook is Wright's attention to the fragility of secularization and industrialization processes—and, more important, to the tenacity of nonsecular formations to resist these processes and to search for ideological alternatives to liberal modernity. "In particular," writes Guy Reynolds, "Wright realized that race and religion were still animating, vital forces across the globe, even as cold war imperatives boiled geopolitics down to the military-ideological struggle against Communism."[21] One might phrase this relevance more strongly: Wright's intuition about the dilemmas of tribalism and the nonsecular strike at the core of contemporary anxieties about global signs of reenchantment. When Wright covered the Bandung Conference in *The Color Curtain*, what fascinated him about Islam in Southeast Asia was the religion's apparent imperviousness to Western missionary or secularizing influences: here was a vast swathe of the colonized (or semi-colonized) world that had managed to remain relatively autonomous, if not politically at least culturally and religiously; the essential elements of the "Moslem mind" had endured intact. Though Wright draws on orientalist clichés in this text, the key point of his encounter with Islam is what he sees as visceral evidence of the religion's unifying power and insulating fortitude. What intrigues him about this religion and civilization is the model it provides for other Third World cultures. How could this strength be mobilized, this cultural integrity harnessed?

Impressed by Islam's capacity for cultural resistance while also suspicious of powerful religious formations, Wright then observes that because missionaries had failed to "tamper" with the Muslim's beliefs, "he was, therefore, outside of the western world, objective about it in a way that no Jew, Gypsy, or refugee could ever be; he could hate, that is, he could reason passionately toward the aim of destroying a loathsome enemy." Since he was less prone to mimic Western normativity, the Muslim's "objectivity" was rooted in the imagined firmness of his identity, which supposedly was not bifurcated like Wright's own or like the identities of other subjects inadequately integrated into the West (precisely the opposite dynamic, it's worth noting, than today's talk about "Islam and the West," which imagines the divided identity of Muslims as the source of their alienation in, and failure to acclimate to, the modern world.) As Reynolds observes, another American writer and longtime expatriate in Morocco, Paul Bowles, also admired Islam for what he perceived as its resistance to historical change and hermetic enclosure from the modern world, but for reasons obviously different than Wright's. He simply wanted Morocco to preserve its historical character and unique culture for his and the world's delectation. Bowles, however, underestimated the modernizing impulse of decolonization; he assumed that the onset of independence in North Africa signaled a resumption of "the old manner of life" that preceded French occupation.[22]

Wright drew a different conclusion from Islam's insularity. Because of this characteristic, according to Wright, the Muslim was "totalitarian-minded, but without the buttress of modern Communist or Fascist ideology; he did not need any, for his totalitarian outlook was born of his religious convictions. Allah was his dictator."[23] He spoke with Mohammed Natsir ("I found him alert, friendly, open, relaxed, with a ready smile"), a scholar of Islam regarded as an architect of modern Indonesia. In his exchange with Wright, the Indonesian premier appears hopeful about the prospect of a modern Muslim state: democratic in orientation, rooted in Islam, and free of communist domination. In talking to Natsir and other Indonesians, Wright observes, "concepts like Right and Left, and ideologies in general, did not figure decisively in his thinking. I had the feeling that the Indonesian Moslem had a personality that was intact, poised, healthy, and largely free from neurotic conflicts. These eighty million Indonesians, 90 per cent Moslem, had not been tampered with too much by missionaries as had all too many Africans. There was none of that uneasy shifting backward and forward between two worlds of values and two spheres of psychological being."[24] Wright's construction of this integral personality, which apparently contrasts so sharply with types in other parts of the colonized world, suggests an enhanced ability to steer clear of the gravitational pull of Cold War ideology and, by extension, to resist superpower domination.

The foundation of an integral personality also meant the possibility of restoring dignity. "Centuries of abject submission to foreign rulers," Natsir continues, "have destroyed the prestige of the Moslems the world over as well as their sense of self-respect. Nevertheless, the Western world having once experienced the power of the sword of Islam has never lost sight of the potentialities contained in the Moslem world." Natsir asserts that Muslim efforts in the nineteenth century to resurrect a Pan-Islamic movement threatened Western imperial power and its control of "precious indispensible raw materials" (525). Both interlocutors register the West's anxieties about an Islamic resurgence but understand that U.S. foreign policy subordinated concern for this religious bloc to the greater evil of communism: when pressed to ally with a radical Pan-Arab movement led by Nasser versus other conservative (and hence anticommunist) currents of Pan-Islam, U.S. officials opted for the latter.

Like his understanding of Afro-Asian religiosity, Wright's perception of Islam reflects his often-dogmatic secular orientation. Still, his encounter with Islam is characteristically prescient. Just "what kind of social structure," Wright asks, "would a Moslem state have?" "'There will be no need for Communism in Moslem countries,' [Natsir] said. 'Pan-Islam will represent a world force, socialistic in nature, keeping a middle ground between Communism and Capitalism.' It was obvious to me that, if you tried to make this man choose between Communism and Capitalism, he'd feel that you were pushing him out of his natural mental orbit. He was more pro-Islam than anti-Communist or pro-Capitalist." When he read Natsir's Karachi declaration in 1952, Wright "learned that a Moslem state is not a state run by priests or a religious hierarchy. A Moslem state is a state for Moslems, but this does not mean that such a state is a theocracy. Moslems draw sharp distinctions between their kind of religious state and, say, a state in which a king rules by divine right. Every Moslem is a kind of priest; there is no separate church in a Moslem state, hence, there is no question of a separation of church and state. Again I was impressed by the firm rejection by the Asian mind of a division between the secular and the sacred" (525–527). If Islam's rejection of this secular-sacred division rebuffs Wright's own prescription for the postcolonial liberal state, he is nonetheless impressed by the religion's internal fortitude: an affirmative and historically powerful alternative to Western secularism.

In Wright's philosophy of history, as in sundry versions of historicism, monotheism outmuscles polytheism in the progressive movement toward secular rationalization.[25] Polytheism, on this (commonplace) view, conduces to mythical thought and tribalism and is therefore vulnerable to imperialist or crusading adversaries; it is also imagined as incapable of responding internally to modern problems (poverty, illness, governance, and bio-politics).[26] At the same time, Wright recognized that Christianity gained traction in Africa and Asia not only because colonized subjects "had pretended to accept it to stave off attack, to receive petty favors," but also because there "was too much in that Christian religion that the Asian and African had believed in long before the Christian religion ever came to their shores," since it was from the Afro-Asiatic world that monotheism's ensemble of myths, symbols, and rituals had originated.[27]

Richard H. King phrases the matter rather baldly, but there's little gainsaying his "conclusion that Wright had little feeling for African or any non-Western cultures."[28] It is also true that Wright hardly tolerated what Wole Soyinka celebrates as the "invisible" African religions overshadowed by, but that mediated between, the rival monotheisms.[29] Though he argued forcefully for the diminishment, if not outright eradication, of these nonsecular formations, he also insisted that, because the colonized world had been "two time victims—victims of their own religious projections and victims of Western imperialism—my sympathies are unavoidably with, and unashamedly for, them. For this sympathy I offer no apology." Notably, he was more sensitive than most when he listened to his African and Asian interlocutors describe the effects of modernity's deracination of tribal life.

Wright cites the remarks of one African scholar who explains that tribal life, if characterized by "deadly boredom," is nonetheless clean, orderly, regimented, and obedient to authority. But, this scholar continued, "when Europeans yank a tribal man out of his tribe, shattering his orientation of the world, and inject him suddenly into a new and completely different sphere of living with other assumptions, that tribal man becomes emotionally confused, finds himself acting upon a wide range of conflicting values." The actions of this subject become "erratic," since he finds himself thrown into the ordeal of fusing these "disparate elements into an impossible whole": all under the condescending eye of colonial masters whom he seeks to please while struggling "to keep peace in his own torn heart."[30] Wright infused his own literary production with an acute sense of how this internal division, if not replaced by a more formidable ideology, religion, or worldview, would precipitate the violence and spiritual unrest associated today with the idioms of terrorism and extremism. When he contends that "the ultimate effect of white Europe was to cast millions into a kind of spiritual void," and that this void "suffused their lives with a sense of meaninglessness," it is impossible not to hear resonances with contemporary discourses on global terror and the reenchantment of the world.[31]

It is in this context that Wright theorizes secularization and the role of Islam in the Afro-Asian world. In the same way that capitalism formed a necessary historical phase on the road to socialism, so too did monotheism constitute a step on the path to secular enlightenment: the desired and inevitable world-historical teleology. This concession to monotheism, however, points multidirectionally, since Wright locates Islam and Christianity very differently in the Afro-Asian world. "God," James Baldwin quipped in *The Fire Next Time*, "going north, and rising on the wings of power, had become white, and Allah, out of power, and on the dark side of Heaven, had become—for all practical purposes, anyway—black."[32] Islam belonged to the Third World; it was apparent enough to Baldwin, Wright, Shirley Graham, and other observers how the religion's energies could be harnessed for anti-imperialism.

For the arch-secularist Wright, Islam possessed an identity sufficiently powerful to resist the tendency among the Bandung world to define itself in relation to Western normativity. In his 1957 essay "The Psychological Reactions of Oppressed People," Wright adapted Nietzsche's idea of a "perspective from below" or "frog perspective" (*Froschperspektive*) to describe this tendency. The frog's perspective, on this adaptation, refers to the psychological distance that marks "someone looking from below upward, a sense of someone who feels himself lower than others," despite the fact that "physically they all live on the same general, material plane." Ever attentive to capitalist schisms between North and South, Wright obviously does not imagine that the nonaligned world dwells on the same material plane, in the economic sense, as its former colonial rulers. They simply inhabit, and are similarly constrained and sustained by, the same material world. Given this basic fact of existence, Wright is struck by how the *imagined* distance between the colonizer and colonized remains so vast. This distance produces a worrisome ambivalence—the postcolonial subject's definition of self and other betrays a "certain degree of hate combined with love"—that does not dissolve with the surrender of colonial rule. Peering upward from below, this subject "loves the object because he would like to resemble it; he hates the object because his chances of resembling it are remote, slight." This dynamic, he argued, was on full display among the leadership at Bandung.

Carlos Romulo of the Philippines, says Wright at the conference, proposed that the Third World could regain confidence in the recognition that white supremacy was finally discredited, an admission of Europe's own weakness. Once cognizant of this weakness, newly independent peoples the world over, according to Romulo and other leaders, "could and would reassert [themselves] as men." Yet it "is quite clear," adds Wright, "that it is against the dominance of the white man that Romulo measures the concept of manhood. . . . Once more we are confronted with the problem of distance, a psychological distance, a feeling that one must regain something lost."[33] That Wright viewed Islam as capable of overcoming that distance can appear, from today's vantage point, as alternately visionary or misguided. But in the context of the mid-1950s, Wright's sense that Islam possessed a global appeal to rival the century's grand ideological systems is undoubtedly prescient—even, or perhaps especially, if the religion's oppositional stance suggests a quasi-totalitarian character (the Muslim's "totalitarian outlook was born of his religious convictions. Allah was his dictator"). But during the peak of decolonization, what Wright perceived as the totalitarian impulses in the Third

World were scarcely limited to political Islam, as a plurality of ideological regimes adopted militarization alongside modernization in the 1960s and beyond. In order to elaborate Wright's conception of this interplay, the next section explores his application of modernization theory to the Afro-Asian world.

Wright and Modernization Theory

"There is an autobiographical dimension to Wright's affinity for the idea of modernization," notes Kevin Gaines. "Wright understood the trajectory of his own intellectual development in terms of a migration from tradition to modernity."[34] And given Wright's well-known studies in sociology, professed (but habitually questioned) anticommunism, and commitment to rational subjectivity, it is not surprising that his idiom of tradition and modernization, progress and industrialization resembles the language employed by modernization theorists of the 1950s.[35] "As a social scientific theory," writes Michael Latham, "modernization represented an interdisciplinary attempt to define a universal model of global change." By uniting various branches of social scientific analysis, figures like Gabriel Almond, Talcott Parsons, Lucian Pye, and Walt Rostow sought "to define the essential stages through which all societies traveled from traditional to modern conditions. They also claimed to do so in a rigorously scientific fashion, even when they attempted to provide knowledge that they expected would be of great utility to U.S. policymakers seeking to comprehend a world in tremendous flux. Modernization theory, in this regard, always had a strong normative component."[36] This normativity typically, if not exclusively, translated into a form of anticommunism that appealed to John F. Kennedy, whose cabinet comprised many distinguished modernization theorists.[37]

In works such as Pye's *Guerilla Communism in Malaya* (1956), Daniel Lerner's *The Passing of Traditional Society: Modernizing the Middle East* (1958), and Rostow's *Stages of Economic Growth: A Non-Communist Manifesto* (1960), these theorists argued that modernization, supported by the United States in the form of technical and development aid, constituted the best means to foreclose social revolution or to intercept communist subversion in the Third World.

But these theorists would have taken heart from Wright's conclusion at Bandung that communism, beyond a begrudgingly admitted China, found scant enthusiasm in the Afro-Asian world. In an effort to gauge Bandung's incipient articulation of nonalignment, Wright took the temperature of communism in the Afro-Asian world in slier ways, with questions grounded in a tacit racial understanding. He asked his interlocutors, for instance, about their opinion of "Stalin's identifying Russia with Asia." Most respondents, if they took the Soviet leader's remarks seriously at all, seemed to think "Stalin used such a phrase [that is, 'We Asiatics . . .'] because he felt that it benefited the policies of his country at that moment." Wright opined that, from "a strictly Stalinist point of view, such a gathering as this was unthinkable for it was evident that the Communists had no control here."[38]

These and other figures who eventually shaped Kennedy's foreign policy in the early 1960s developed initiatives like the Alliance for Progress and the Peace Corps, programs focused on those developing nations, especially in Latin America, that seemed to occupy a "transitional" phase between tradition and modernity. Designed to facilitate these nations' transition to the modern democratic capitalist order, as well as to serve U.S. economic interests abroad, these initiatives sought to project U.S. global engagement, good will abroad, and even the idea of American cooperation and unity between North and South.[39] For these theorists, modernization entailed more than large-scale industrialization and development projects. This process required non-Western peoples to replace their "traditional" values with "modern" values. As Latham notes, the question of cultural values became increasingly significant for these theorists, at least since Talcott Parsons—a forerunner of modernization theory—defied conventional wisdom about social structures in his *The Structure of Social Action* (1937), which downplayed determinants like the economy, the environment, and innate human drives, instead calling attention to the influence of culture and ideology.

Modernization theorists, Latham observes, associated traditional values with fatalism, superstition, emotionalism, stagnancy, romanticism, inertia, and apathy; they identified modern values as industriousness, rationalism, cleanliness, self-discipline, orderliness, and efficiency. Moreover, they hoped that the distinctively "American" traits of empathy, altruism, entrepreneurialism, idealism, and ingenuity would demonstrate the superiority and benevolence of U.S. foreign policy and rub off in the developing world. Figures like the political scientist William Nisbit Chambers and the sociologist Seymour Martin Lipset believed that America's history of revolution against British colonial rule would appeal to the Third World and encourage these newly independent societies to follow an imagined U.S. model of moderate, pragmatic strides toward democracy and development.[40] Incidentally, the planners of the Bandung Conference, as Dipesh Chakrabarty points out, deliberately held the event on April 18, which they recalled as a pivotal moment in the American Revolution: the date when "a young patriot named Paul Revere rode at midnight from Boston harbor to the town of Concord, arousing the spirit of opposition to British troops . . . It was clear that 18 April 1775 was an historic day for the American nation in their struggle against colonialism. Why should we not link these two events, the date of which was the same, the spirit of which was the same, only the years were different?"[41] On this account, the replication of U.S. advances in industry, infrastructure, and freedom in the Third World depended on the ability of Afro-Asian actors to cultivate modern (American) habits, values, and modes of conduct.

Buoyed by a sense of U.S. commitment to the developing world, these narratives tended to project a relatively smooth revaluation of culture outside the West, but a forerunner of modernization theory like Talcott Parsons understood that this process could easily go awry, as in the case of Weimar Germany. Drawing on Weber's theory of rationalization (which Parsons studied as a doctoral student at Heidelberg and later translated), his 1942 essay "Democracy and Social Structure in Pre-Nazi Germany" asks why Germany, which exhibited many of the historical and "structural elements" of other Western societies, traveled the path of totalitarianism rather than liberal democracy. Historically, Germany shared with the United States a rapid, high degree of industrialization, among other commonalities, but politically the two nations diverged on the path to liberalization. He concedes that several factors—the punishment and mortification of Germany following the Second World War, economic dislocation, political instability, and the class struggle—contributed to Germany's transmogrification into "the most radical anti-liberal and anti-democratic movement of modern history." But the most compelling explanation, he argues, involved Germany's extraordinarily difficult adaptation to rationalized, bureaucratic life.

On this account, what distinguishes Weimar from the rest of the West was a German population culturally and—though Parsons does not use this word, *spiritually*—unsuited to the unrelenting force of rationalization, a process that fostered a proportionally high degree of *anomie*. The social impact of anomie, writes Parsons, has been more severe in Germany relative to Western Europe and the United States because that country "has been more 'conservative.' Hence the impact of science, industrialism and such phenomena has been more unsettling and has led to more drastic extremes of attitudes." German conservatism signifies an affective response—"a good deal of free-floating aggression, a tendency to unstable emotionalism and susceptibility to emotionalized propaganda and mobilization of affect around various kinds of symbols"—to the reign of instrumental reason in all spheres of life.

Instead of accepting the reality of rational bourgeois subjectivity, Germans were said to lapse into idealism and escapism, a "romanticism" hostile to the rationalist intellectual traditions of France and England. Consequently, liberalism was not allowed to flourish; the only political rationalism to be found in Germany was "the extreme rationalistic radicalism" of Marxism, "the obverse of the predominant 'conservative' tendencies." National Socialism, he concludes, succeeded in mobilizing the "extremely deep-seated romantic tendencies of German society in the service of a violently aggressive political movement, incorporating a 'fundamentalist' revolt against the whole tendency of rationalization in the Western world, and at the same time against its deepest institutionalized foundations."[42]

For Wright, this question acquired renewed significance for the nonaligned movement. How were the social structures of the Afro-Asian world similarly susceptible to illiberal or antiliberal forces? If Germany and other industrialized nations took a fatal turn in their passage to modernity, then what did history presage for Asian and African societies that Wright imagined as characterized by a more profound antirationalism than that exemplified by the German Romantic tradition? By 1967, one political scientist formulated the question in the language of an epidemic when he asked "Is Totalitarianism Taking Over in Africa?"

"The last five years," Kenneth Grundy writes, "have seen the rise of military regimes and single-party systems all over Africa." Certain journalists and politicians "maintain the African revolution is becoming increasingly totalitarian." The most frequently mentioned states include Kwame Nkrumah's Ghana, Gamal Nasser's Egypt, the Republic of South Africa, Sékou Touré's Guinea, and Ahmed Ben Bella's Algeria. With the interesting exception of South Africa, what these African states supposedly had in common was a preponderance of regimes marked by single-party rule and centralized power, a cult of personality-style leadership, repressive political techniques, "or maybe the ideological or verbal similarities with Fascist or Communist doctrines." Presumably South Africa fit under the category of racial totalitarianism of the kind practiced by the Western empires.

As two different but related phenomena, totalitarianism "may appear to be an ideological phenomenon or an empirical one, or both. As a political ideology totalitarianism is the bringing about and *rationalizing* of 'the extension of permanent governmental control over the totality of social life.' Empirically it refers to a state where such thorough governmental control is a reality."[43] Grundy stresses the root word *total.* Acknowledging that it is impossible for any given regime to exercise total control over its subjects, the dimension of totality is nonetheless what distinguishes totalitarianism from its milder and less tentacular cousin, authoritarianism. In general, dictatorial or authoritarian regimes do not enjoy a complete monopoly on mass communication, armed combat, police control, and the deployment of terror. Tucked away in the political theorist's formulation is the element of rationalization he cites as the process through which ideology manifests into an empirical reality. In his distillation of totalitarianism, Grundy draws on the European experience, so that rationalization as a precondition for the total state could be taken for granted; rationalization simply intensifies as a historical process that had been under way for centuries in the West. Since Wright did not take for granted a parallel trajectory in the Third

World, his inquiry seeks to identify what forces in the Afro-Asian sphere will determine whether rationalization proceeds along the path of secular democracy or of nonsecular totalitarianism.

Under certain social, economic, or governmental conditions, any dictatorial or repressive regime can give way to totalitarian governance. Yet despite mounting talk of totalitarianism in Africa, Grundy asserts that neither the ideological nor empirical criteria for this phenomenon are being met on the continent—even under Nkrumah's regime, widely targeted in the West as dangerously illiberal ("Although some facets of Nkrumah's ideology served to rationalize a growing concentration of power," he writes, "actual control never approached totalitarian proportions"). But he suggests that empirical criteria constitute only one way of defining the phenomenon. One possibility relevant to Africa, he writes, "is that totalitarianism can perhaps evolve or grow as a series of little responses to various problems facing the government of the day, thereby yielding a heightened concentration of power. Viewed in this framework, totalitarianism could conceivably be the outgrowth of numerous authoritarian responses to the twin desires of keeping peace and order and maintaining oneself in power." In other words, dictators may find themselves, "slowly, pragmatically, almost accidentally" sliding into totalitarian governance, "as the choice of alternatives becomes more limited and the policies designed to keep a certain group in power more pernicious."[44]

Grundy's account of prospective African totalitarianism is useful because it reorients the phenomenon away from charismatic personalities and radical ideologies to the material, state-administrative, internecine conflicts, and economic dilemmas that can give rise to these formations in a non-Western context. These problems derive from the particularities of postcolonial politics: fissures and disunities—grounded in the arbitrary partitioning of the continent by fin-de-siècle colonial powers—along lines of internal ethnic, linguistic, religious, and religious diversity; a shortage of high-skilled operatives and managerial personnel capable of managing the economy and realizing the regime's goals, which turn out to have been unrealistic; the difficulty of fostering a "different philosophical outlook" among the people once the target of their animus, the

European colonizer, has departed; and the tenuous position of the party leadership, once the people's champion and consolidator of the independent nation, now thrust into the role of state disciplinarian. This mode of analysis reconfigures the dominant imaginary of the totalitarian dictator as a figure of ruthless and extraordinary willpower, on the one hand, but also paranoiac about rivals and given to haphazard repressiveness, on the other. Rather, on this account, the African leader is a figure of vulnerability, eager to consolidate power to be sure, but whose control often sinks into the quicksand of authoritarianism.

What I want to underscore in this analysis is the paradoxical relation in Africa of modernization to totalitarianism. Arguing that totalitarianism, strictly speaking, does not, and likely will not, exist in Africa, Grundy concedes that undeniably "there have been tendencies in the direction of greater control of social life. But such developments need not be linear or one-directional." Then he concludes with the observation that modernization, should it proceed apace in Africa, can stem the totalitarian tide: "With further modernization this tendency may well be slowed, arrested, and even reversed. Although totalitarianism is more easily achieved in a modern, technically developed society, the modernization process creates such destabilizing forces that rigid control of all forms of social life is unlikely in transitional societies."[45] Akin to Marx's contradictions within capitalism, Grundy's formulation attributes to modernization the capacity both to inhibit or to reverse totalitarianism as well as to destabilize societies in such a way that total control is difficult to exercise. This view of modernization suggests a trajectory distinct from the West's history of totalitarianism, where precisely these disruptions created social vacuums necessary for totalitarian power to insert and assert itself. But even if totalitarianism, on this definition, seems unlikely in Africa, the conditions for the production of democratic norms seem equally inauspicious: "Civil chaos, apathy, and stagnation are more the clear and present dangers to Africa than is totalitarianism."[46]

If Wright was anxious about the threat of totalitarianism taking root in the Third World, then why would he countenance militarization, a precursory and necessary element of such governance?

When viewed in light of the continent's recent history, this injunction appears counterintuitive, perverse. But Wright is careful to delineate precisely what he means by this term, and his explanation suggests why it was possible for him to countenance militarization as a *means* for the Third World to avoid the traps of totalitarianism. The statement "AFRICA MUST BE MILITARIZED!" appears in *Black Power*'s concluding letter to Kwame Nkrumah, after which Wright adds: "not for war, but for peace; not for destruction, but for service; not for aggression, but for production; not for despotism, but to free minds from mumbo-jumbo."

> I'm not speaking of military dictatorship. . . . I'm speaking simply of a militarization of the daily, social lives of the people; I'm speaking of giving form, organization, direction, meaning, and a sense of justification to those lives. . . . I'm speaking of a temporary discipline that will unite the nation, sweep out the tribal cobwebs, and place the feet of the masses upon a basis of reality. I'm not speaking of guns or secret police; I'm speaking of a method of taking people from one order of life and making them face what men, all men everywhere, must face. What the Europeans failed to do, didn't want to do because they feared disrupting their own profits and global real estate, you must do.[47]

Grounding these measures in a realistic assessment of Africa's geopolitical situation, Wright admits that his language sounds "gratuitously hard, cruel"—"*You must be hard!*" he implores Nkrumah—but these prescriptions distill temporal anxieties of the kind evidenced by his insistence that "Our people must be made to walk, forced draft, into the twentieth century."[48] The Cold War situation presented the newly liberated nations with copious offers of aid, from both ideological blocs. But Wright, like Fanon, implored postcolonial leaders to resist the temptation to accept offers of foreign capital or expert personnel: strings will always be attached.

In the 1950s and 1960s, examples abounded of the quandaries involved with foreign aid. As Chapter 5 discusses, in 1961 John F. Kennedy confronted a seemingly peripheral but highly symbolic foreign policy dilemma: whether to finance Ghana's Volta River Project, a massive dam construction designed to generate electricity, promote modernization, and diversify Ghana's economy. The project was similar in conception and scope to the 1933 Tennessee Valley Authority, which proponents lauded as a success story that could be replicated in the non-Western world.[49] In 1960, Eisenhower had pledged $30 million toward construction of the dam but soon reneged on the offer when the assassination of Nkrumah's Congolese protégé Patrice Lumumba—whose elimination the CIA had plotted if not executed—soured relations between Washington and Accra. As previous chapters note, many observers viewed the withdrawal of financing for Aswan as a provocation of Nasser and a catalyst for the Suez Crisis. Kennedy did not want to repeat the geopolitical errors of his predecessors, especially where anticolonial sentiment and foreign aid to Africa were concerned. Ultimately Kennedy decided to fund the Volta project.

Years before the JFK administration, however, agonized over whether to fund Ghana's Volta Dam project, Wright counseled Nkrumah to beware of foreign aid and to build the dam from the labor and ingenuity of his own people.[50] Yet most African leaders found such counsel difficult to put into practice. Wright seemed aware of this tension when he observed about the Third World: "Stalin's World War II motto of: 'The side with the most motors will win' has sunk home in their hearts, but they find as yet no humane method of arming themselves with the necessary motors."[51] Where were the necessary motors to be found? Wright knew that his advice highlighted rather than addressed the fundamental problem of how, or where, to acquire the engines of modernity. His repetition of the word *heart* in these texts captures his sense of where this profound postcolonial dilemma resides.

In lieu of foreign capital and other resources, Wright championed, perhaps naïvely in retrospect, the Third World's immense human resources, which in his view could only be harnessed effectively via militarization. The "military is but another name for fraternalization, for cohesiveness. And a military structure of African society can be used eventually for defense. . . . It is the one and only stroke that can project the African immediately into the twentieth century!"[52]

Wright believed that militarization "can replace, for a time, the political" and that it "contains its own form of idealistic and emotional sustenance" that can substitute for ideology. But the main rationale for this mode of social organization—and this point is crucial—lay in its capacity to repulse "the domination of foreigners."

Wright articulates some of these views, and his own biases shaping them, in a delicately worded but forcefully argued address that was later adapted, according to Richard King, into "The Psychological Reactions of Oppressed People." To an august cast of attendees—including Aimé Césaire, Leopold Sédar Senghor, Cheikh-Anta Diop, Frantz Fanon, James Baldwin, George Lamming, Jean Price-Mars, and Jacques Alexis—Wright posed the question: "Might not the vivid and beautiful culture that Senghor has described not been—I speak carefully, choosing my words with the utmost caution, speaking to my colleagues, hoping that you will understand my intentions—might not that beautiful culture have been a fifth column a corps of saboteurs and spies of Europe? . . . The ancestor cult religion with all of its manifold, poetic richness that created a sense of self-sufficiency . . . did that religion help the people to resist fiercely and hardily and hurl the Europeans out? I question the value of that culture in relationship to our future. I do not condemn it. But how can we use it?"[53] For Wright, the idea of culture, however poetically rich, has an instrumental function; it needed to serve political and economic, not only spiritual or communitarian, ends. In an audience where a number of figures were not only reclaiming African civilizations but also forging "new 'weapons of theory' out of negritude, Marxism, psychoanalysis, [and] African communalism," Wright's views must have been exceedingly difficult to announce.[54]

Astutely, Gates observes how Wright, constantly checking his watch during the proceedings, announces that "the hour is late and *I* am pressed for time," and "Ladies and gentlemen, I shall be as brief as possible: the hour is late." Maybe Wright had better things to do that evening, but as Gates suggests, "perhaps the hour *was* late, historically speaking—too late for Richard Wright. His vision of Africa doesn't seem any kind of advance on that of, say, nineteenth-century pan-Africanist Edward Blyden; it's still a place, as Blyden put it, 'in a state of barbarism.'" And what did Wright's negation of religion—a surrogate here for culture writ large—mean in a context in which no boundary exists between "religious practices and ordinary life"?[55] Rather than question the feasibility of African culture, Wright might have been expected to assail foreign involvements in pervious, nonindustrialized countries. But his pledge to articulating openly a version of realpolitik in Africa—what we might call speaking truth to powerlessness—precluded such a posture.

Gates goes on to note, however, that his concern is not primarily with Wright but with the author's legacy for "all of us diasporic intellectuals." If for Wright there's a Bigger Thomas inside all blacks of his era, then for Gates there's a Richard Wright in every intellectual of the black diaspora. Gates juxtaposes Wright's commitment to the universalism, secularism, and rationalism of the eighteenth century with another figure, Edmund Burke, often dubbed the "father of modern conservatism" but whose indictment of British imperialism and Enlightenment arrogance anticipates postcolonial criticism.[56] Similarly, political theorist Uday Singh Mehta recuperates the contrarian Burke, whose profound humility in the face of Indian alterity distinguished him from the sense of superiority displayed by a colonial liberal tradition associated with John Locke, James Stuart Mill, and Jeremy Bentham.[57]

If intellectuals in the black diaspora are indeed the legatees of Wright's rationalism rather than Burke's conservative pluralism, then the former's inheritance seems linked to the persistence of temporal concerns ("the hour is late and I am pressed for time") alluded to earlier. According to Michael Hanchard, a pervasive consciousness of temporality—what he calls "racial time"—underwrites the theory and practice of Afro-modernity, and not least Wright's diaspora politics. From black nationalism and Pan-Africanism to anticolonialism and civil rights, the entire repertoire of black discourses and movements produces various but overlapping responses to the progressive temporality of modernity. Afro-modernity refers to the ways in which Africa's descendants have incorporated the "technologies, discourses, and institutions of the modern West" in order to create not a "mere mimicry of Western modernity" but a distinctive, innovative, and relatively autonomous modernity. "Dialectically," Hanchard writes, "Afro-Modernity can be seen as the negation of the idea of African and African-derived peoples as the antithesis of modernity."[58]

On this account, Afro-modern political actors, bereft of nation-state power and territorial sovereignty, sought to form a supranational, imagined community demarcated not by geography but by a shared sense of Western oppression experienced by African-descended peoples. This sense of oppression originates in plantation slavery, an institution in which temporality shaped the lives of slaves in specific ways. Versus the relations between serfs and lords under feudalism or between labor and capital in the modern age, in New World slavery relations between slave and master constituted a "struggle for the appropriation of time, such as the relative freedom" for slaves to "tend gardens on Saturdays or to shop independently at Sunday markets. Resistance to forced labor and time could be seen in work slowdowns, for example, by African-New World slaves." As Hanchard notes, "free time," or time unaccounted for by slave labor, had political consequences—especially after the Haitian Revolution, when slave owners across the Americas exercised a firmer grip on slave time in both work and leisure. The totality of this control is said to distinguish the temporality of slavery from the relation between time and labor under normal capitalist relations.

Sustaining this supranational, Afro-modern community necessitated the development of alternative political and cultural networks—of the kind, say, delineated in Brent Edwards's *The Practice of Diaspora* or in Kevin Gaines's *American Africans in Ghana*—across nation-state boundaries.[59] One feature of such networks involved "an explicit critique of the uneven application of the discourses of the Enlightenment and processes of modernization in the West, along with these discourses' attendant notions of sovereignty and citizenship." Accordingly, Afro-modern political actors identify alternative models of sovereignty and citizenship not exactly beyond the nation-state but—like other diaspora populations the world over—in a manner that leverages both domestic and international institutions.[60]

Infused with a deep consciousness of history and temporality, the practices of Afro-modernity typically project a desire to approximate or to "catch up" to Western modernity. Yet this historical consciousness often manifested as an anxiety about a time lag in Third World development—a sense that whatever progress newly independent nations achieved, they would nevertheless continue to lag behind advanced industrial powers. Seemingly expressed more by diaspora fellow travelers than by Africans themselves, this anxiety reflected both an awareness of Africa's vulnerable geopolitical situation and an effort to counteract representations of black cultures as ahistorical.

In his discussion of "violence in an international context," Fanon sketches with precision the postcolonial dilemma Wright describes. In underdeveloped countries, Fanon writes, "the political leader is constantly calling on the people to fight: to fight against colonialism, to fight against poverty and underdevelopment, and to fight against debilitating traditions." He employs a militaristic vocabulary of a chief of staff: he speaks of *mass mobilization, the agricultural front, the illiteracy front, defeats suffered, victories won.* "During its early years the young independent nation evolves in the atmosphere of a battleground. This is because the political leader of an underdeveloped country is terror-stricken at the prospect of the long road that lies ahead." Telling his people to roll up their sleeves and get to work, the leader and his nation, gripped in creative frenzy, plunges "into action of a hugely disproportionate nature. The agenda is not only to pull through but to catch up with the other nations as best one can."[61] For Fanon as for Wright, the need to catch up, taken for granted as a precondition of meaningful independence, could only find expression in the language of militant mobilization.

The innovative projects of Afro-modernity could not overturn the conventional impression that, versus the progressive and productive time of Western modernity, an empty, non-historical time prevailed in Africa and its diaspora. In this "temporal disjuncture," writes Hanchard, as "African and African-derived peoples had to sophisticate themselves through their relation to Western ideals and civilizations, they had to do so only after the West had. They could either 'catch up' with the West by assuming certain practices and behaviors, or forever look across a civilizational chasm, stricken with a constitutional, genetic inability to forge societies that the West would stare upon with awe." From an existential standpoint, the "temporal consequences of racial inequality were to be experienced and felt," Hanchard asserts, "across the African diaspora wherever a person defined by his phenotypic proximity to the indigenous peoples of sub-Saharan African inhabited the same territorial realm with whites." Conjunctures of disparate racial temporalities, such international scenarios structure relations between and within both dominant and subordinate groups and determine the access of each to the intellectual and material resources of modernity.[62]

A measure of this temporal conjuncture mediates the interaction between Nkrumah and Wright, as described in the latter's account. Wright's counsel to Nkrumah complicated the matter of modernization further by introducing the idea that any bold, autonomous initiatives in the Third World (namely, any major action or project that was not supported by the Western allies or even the Soviet sphere) courted scrutiny and sometimes intervention by Western powers. "He who would invoke," Wright asserts, "as sanction for experimental political action, a desire to seek the realization of the basic ideals of the Western world in terms of unorthodox and as yet untried institutional structures—instrumentalities for short-cutting long, drawn-out historical processes—as a means of constructing conditions for the creation of individual freedom, can be branded as being 'emotionally unstable' and having tendencies that *could* lead, therefore, to Communism."[63] Put differently, Wright suggests that any newly independent country, irrespective of its ideological orientation, looked dangerously unaccountable and unpredictable when experimenting with new ways of accelerating modernization—especially projects undertaken without Western intercession and guidance. Yet Wright does not specify what these "instrumentalities" might look like. What shortcuts to history did he have in mind?

By the midcentury, the experimental history of communism had suggested the catastrophic consequences of such short cuts. Writing in the 1950s, in the wake of Soviet collectivization and on the cusp of Mao's Great Leap Forward, Wright had internalized communist efforts to increase the velocity of industrialization. Though referring to the Third World's unspecified instrumentalities as of "yet untried," Wright suggests that (noncommunist) alternatives to accelerate modernity might exist for the postcolony. But it's not clear what these methods entail and how they differ from the century's previously fatal grand projects. In order to approach this question, part of the interpretive task here involves reconstructing Wright's literary imagination of totalitarianism as one intertextual link with his literary imagination of postcolonial modernity. In the next section, I explore how Wright's commitment to modernization articulates with the illiberal or totalitarian movements with which he was intimately familiar.

The Outsider and Illiberal Modernity

In the opening pages of *Pagan Spain*, his 1957 account of Spanish society under General Franco's authoritarian regime, Wright describes his reluctance to cross the border into Spain from France, where he had been living in self-imposed exile for a decade. "I wanted to go to Spain," he writes, "but something was holding me back. The only thing that stood between me and a Spain that beckoned was a state of mind. God knows, totalitarian governments and ways of life were no mysteries to me. I had been born under an absolutistic racist regime in Mississippi; I had lived and worked for twelve years under the political dictatorship of the Communist party of the United States; and I had spent a year of my life under the police terror of Peron in Buenos Aires. So why avoid the reality of life under Franco? What was I scared of?"[64]

Despite the signature tinge of self-dramatization in this passage, one ought to take Wright's question seriously: what was he scared of? Like his contemporaries—not only Cold Warriors but also European émigrés to the U.S. and American intellectuals comprising the anti-Stalinist left—Wright employs the term "totalitarianism" frequently in his writings of the 1950s. On the surface, Wright's usage resembles that which had come to define a Cold War consensus on totalitarianism described in earlier chapters of this book. In contrast to earlier deployments of the term in the 1920s and 1930s, this consensus conflated communism and fascism, united dictatorships on the left and the right, and exalted centrist liberalism as the antidote to extremist ideologies across the political spectrum. But it's important to note that, in Wright's list of totalitarian regimes, Jim Crow occupies the first position. By incorporating the "absolutistic racist regime in Mississippi" into this ideological matrix, Wright upsets liberal capitalism's default status as the political norm defined in opposition to fascism and communism.

In Part 1, "Race and the Totalitarian Century," I describe a totalitarian structure in U.S. plantation slavery and the Jim Crow order via readings of Frederick Douglass's *Narrative* (1845), Richard Wright's *Black Boy* (1945), and Stanley Elkins's *Slavery* (1959). In that discussion, I emphasize a few points. In my juxtaposition of Douglass's *Narrative* and Wright's *Black Boy*, separated by publication dates one century apart, I show how both narratives describe a complex scenario of surveillance, performance, and spying in order to highlight the production of truth—that is, the truth of power relations under slavery—in the context of racial democracy. The social logic of manufactured truth, as Leszek Kolakowski notes, happens to be one of the central ingredients of a totalitarian regime. ("When inquired of as to their condition and the character of their masters," Douglass writes, slaves "almost universally say they are contented, and that their masters are kind. . . . *They suppress the truth rather than take the consequences of telling it, and in so doing prove themselves a part of the human family.*") Similarly, in *Black Boy*, a confrontation with two vicious racists compels Wright's protagonist to abide by the racial wisdom offered by Douglass. Though Wright has not experienced a concentration camp or a totalitarian regime from the inside, he has survived the system of Jim Crow. Wright's aim, however, was not only to configure what he called the ethics of living Jim Crow into a narrative of totalitarian experience. This reconfiguration, as we will see, enabled him to expand his conception of the totalitarian into the sphere of geopolitics, particularly the intersection of the Cold War and decolonization. To understand this reconfiguration it is helpful to excavate Wright's idiosyncratic investment, as a communist intellectual, in *illiberal* modernity.[65]

Now we return to the question Wright posed in *Pagan Spain:* what was he scared of? "The fate of Spain had hurt me, had haunted me," he writes. "I had never been able to stifle a hunger to understand what had happened there and why. Yet I had no wish to resuscitate mocking recollections while roaming a land whose free men had been shut in concentration camps, or exiled, or slain. An uneasy question kept floating in my mind: How did one live after the death of the hope for freedom?"[66] This question, I want to suggest, refers not only to the "fate of Spain." Wright is also posing this question to himself, as well as to those of his contemporaries similarly invested in the projects of illiberal modernity. How does one reconcile the accumulated, and indeed, extinguished hopes in the grand narratives of emancipation and regeneration defining the century?

In a brief unpublished essay titled "There Are Still Men Left," Wright confesses that "the most meaningful moments of experience I have gotten from this world have been in either making an attempt to change the limits of life under which men live, or in watching with *sympathy* the efforts of others to do the same. For that reason I am a card-carrying Communist. . . . Communism to me is a way of life, . . . an unusual mode of existence." Exposing a fragment of political ontology, this passage suggests that this *way of life* supersedes ideology or the permutations of party politics. It would be inexact, however, to suggest that among the century's radical alternatives to liberal capitalism, Wright has only communism in mind. For then he adds parenthetically: "(sometimes I feel myself most deeply attracted to it when most people are repelled—that is, for instance, when the USSR signed the pact with Nazi Germany)." Wright was by no means alone among black leftists in expressing a similar sentiment, but the confessional and affective quality of this statement stands out. In his study *Ethnic Modernism*, Werner Sollors observes that, "by implication, Wright spoke not only about Communists but also about Nazis when he concluded: 'They are men who are used to seeking, not comfort, security, *individual* happiness, equality, but *meaning*, meaning in terms of feeling and knowing in its most concrete and literal sense.' "[67] This fragment conveys as clearly as any Wright's rejection of bourgeois normativity and his embrace of—no, yearning for—the collective energies and structures of feeling summoned by illiberal modernity.

A revealing glimpse into Wright's political unconscious, this moment also registers the seductiveness of an event that disillusioned American leftists from the Soviet experiment. By August of 1939, as

Thomas Hill Schaub observes, many left liberals, socialists, and communists distanced themselves from Stalinism, developed loyalties to Leon Trotsky, fomented alternatives such as the anti-Stalinist left, or renounced socialism and communism altogether. Sober and skeptical of human nature, these figures awakened and adapted to the geopolitical realism of their time.[68] Of course, Wright, too, would eventually relinquish his membership in the Communist Party, publishing his essay "I Tried to Be a Communist" in the 1949 volume, *The God That Failed.* But as Brenda Gayle Plummer notes, "Although Richard Wright renounced communism in the early 1940s, he appears in later FBI records as 'unwittingly' supporting Red aims in France by 'flirting with Titoism and Sartre-ism' and by writing for 'neutralist publications.'"[69] His disengagement from communism, then, transitioned into an extended meditation and critical self-reflection on this period and therefore a valuable contribution to Marxist intellectual history.

In light of Wright's complex political ontology, how do we read his attraction to the promises of illiberal modernity? Alain Badiou's philosophy of history, *The Century*, provides a way to think productively about Wright's own recalcitrant romance with totalitarianism. For Badiou, what defines the logic of the century is what he calls, in Lacanian terms, a passion for the real—an unprecedented effort to transform into reality what the previous century conceived as either the Imaginary (nineteenth-century utopian ideals) or the Symbolic (what the nineteenth century produced as doctrine, what it thought and organized). The twentieth century represents less a betrayal or what Badiou terms a "negative discontinuity" with the previous century than an unremitting passion to make the century real, at whatever cost.[70]

Put another way, Badiou questions the conventional idea that the "barbarity of the twentieth century was a consequence of the fact that its main actors—be they revolutionaries or fascists—accepted horror in the name of a promise, in the name of 'glorious tomorrows.'" This notion implies that the century's actors either harbored grand illusions of the century or renounced its promise. "On the contrary," writes Badiou, "I am convinced that what fascinated the militants of the twentieth century was the real. In this century there is a veritable exaltation of the real, even in its horror."[71] This passion for the real defines what Wright understood by "meaning" in its "most concrete and literal sense."

What we see in this passage by Wright—an admission, perhaps, against his better historical judgment—is a barely submerged exaltation of this real, one defiant of or indifferent to official wartime appeals. But for Wright this passion for the century's real was not merely personal, or a passion shared by his fellow communists; indeed, he identified this tendency within the black proletarian majority, as well as within the dispossessed masses of the emergent Third World.

In his 1940 lecture, "How 'Bigger' Was Born," Wright limns the totalitarian features of Jim Crow and urban industrial society in the manner I suggest earlier, but in this text he also speculates on the kinds of subjectivities—rebellious, authoritarian, rootless, with little to lose—produced by such a social order. Wright notes that blacks identified with the extremist movements of the century (Stalinism, Nazism, Japanese Imperialism) not out of any comprehension of world history or its leaders but rather "because they felt that these men 'did things,' a phrase which is charged with more meaning than the mere words imply. There was in the back of their minds, when they said this, a wild and intense longing (wild and intense because it was suppressed!) to belong, to be identified, to feel that they were alive as other people were, to be caught up forgetfully and exultingly in the swing of events, to feel the clean, deep, organic satisfaction of doing a job in common with others."[72] Despite the body of commentary on the epochal *Native Son*, what Wright describes does not fit comfortably within established paradigms of black political imaginaries or cultural production. In this respect, the tenor of Wright's thought is best understood in terms of the century's experience of the real, which is also the experience of horror. The name for this horror is the twentieth or totalitarian century.

Wright's internalization of this horror finds its fullest expression in his 1953 novel *The Outsider*, the story of Cross Damon, a twenty-six-year-old postal worker, would-be philosophy student at the University of Chicago, alcoholic, and eventual murderer. Via the novel's intrusive narrative voice, *The Outsider* intersperses ruminations on the history of totalitarianism—of Stalinism, Nazism, colonial and racial terror, industrial alienation—throughout the text. Blending elements of naturalism, existentialism, phenomenology, and noir genres, *The Outsider* aspires to be a novel of ideas, a kind of philosophical judgment on the recent past. Few of Wright's contemporaries considered this literary experiment a success.

Wright was not exceptional among African American writers in his tendency toward literary experimentation in this period. During the 1940s and 1950s, many black writers were seen by their contemporaries as having fundamentally shifted or "deviated" from the aesthetic formulas and political principles that defined their early success. Yet even in light of this development, one still wonders about Wright: At a time when African Americans are propelling the civil rights movement forward, *after* the defeat of Nazism, and several *years* after Wright's own denunciation of communism, why is he still so obsessed with the specter of totalitarianism?

In her review of *The Outsider*, Lorraine Hansberry praises Wright's ability in *Native Son* and *Black Boy* to deploy a "stark and terrible realism" in the service of exposing "the filth and sickness of white supremacy." But with the publication of *The Outsider*, she argues, Wright has abandoned his previous commitment to realistic portraiture of the black experience and sunk to concocting scenes of gratuitous violence peppered with philosophical nihilism. A decade has passed since the publication of the early works, she notes, and "Richard Wright has been away from home for a long time." The product of Wright's exile in France, *The Outsider*, Hansberry writes with some justification, "is a story of sheer violence, death and disgusting spectacle, written by a man who has seemingly come to despise humanity."[73]

Embroiled in a set of domestic, romantic, and financial troubles, Cross seizes an opportunity to escape Chicago and begin life anew: as the sole survivor of a train crash, he hatches the idea to switch clothes and identification with a dead passenger. Armed with the alias "Lionel Lane," Cross flees to New York, where he takes refuge with a communist couple, Gil and Eva Blount, who happen to live in an apartment building owned by Langley Herndon, an outspoken fascist. Cross's arrival completes the totalitarian configuration Wright has in mind: the narrative positions Cross Damon between the communists Gil and Eva and the fascist Herndon—symbolically, Cross inhabits Wright's own self-professed stance as an outsider in "the middle of that most fateful of the world's centuries: the twentieth century."[74]

When Herndon—whose name alludes to Angelo Herndon, the Depression-era black labor organizer and leading critic of the Scottsboro case—discovers that the communists are permitting a black man to lodge in his building, the fascist confronts Gil after threatening to kill Cross. In Gil's apartment, an argument between the communist and the fascist escalates into a brawl. But then, inexplicably, Cross sneaks into the apartment and kills Herndon *and* Gil—thereby slaying the totalitarian systems they represent. This scene recalls Jean-Paul Sartre's observation, in his preface to Fanon's *The Wretched of the Earth*, that "to shoot down a European is to kill two birds with one stone, to destroy an oppressor and the man he oppresses at the same time." But Wright's text inverts this principle: killing the two figures (fascism and communism) achieves the destruction of the One (the behemoth of totalitarianism). What motivates this inversion is the brawl's allegorizing of the Nazi-Soviet Pact and eventual battle of Stalingrad.[75] By naming the fascist character *Herndon*, however, Wright slyly injects the memory of black communism into this symbolic struggle.

Later Cross encounters a salacious newspaper article inaccurately reporting the killings, with the rather improbable headline: "DOUBLE TOTALITARIAN MURDER." Cross reads the caption beneath the sketch:

> Hardened Metropolitan police circles were rocked and stunned late yesterday by the Greenwich Village sensationally freakish double murder of a Communist by a Fascist and of a Fascist by a Communist. . . . These men's diseased brains had been poisoned by the dangerously esoteric doctrines of communal property advocated in the decadent writings of the notorious German author Karl Marx, and the Superman ideas sponsored by syphilis-infected German philosopher Friedrich Nietzsche who died in an insane asylum. These two rowdy agitators, Gilbert Blount

> and Langley Herndon, clashed bloodily in a quarrel regarding racial amalgamation theories and both died of their mutually inflicted wounds.[76]

Reading this lurid coverage in the press, Cross begins to wonder if he might have slain the wrong enemy. Whereas the propaganda apparatuses of totalitarian regimes were straightforward, Cross seems to sense that the illusions of liberal democracy, like the supposedly free press, were more insidiously repressive. He ponders aloud, "But this is a kind of inverted pro-communist and pro-nazi propaganda. They've so distorted their psychological types. . . . A Gil or a Herndon might be working at the City Desk of the Daily News this very moment. . . . What kind of people make up these papers? There couldn't be a better way of disguising totalitarian aims than this."[77] This question leads him to wonder that if newspapers like this one can pass for a medium of democratic enlightenment, then totalitarians stood a chance of victory in the long run of history.

Also repulsive to Cross is the caricature of Nietzsche and Marx, the novel's not so subtly evoked intellectual forefathers of totalitarianism. For Cross, Nietzsche and Marx unleashed ideas that merit the fiercest criticism, ideas that were likely complicit in the century's catastrophes, but only a desiccated and pacified society could afford to treat these thinkers so glibly. As this revelation sinks in, Cross has a change of heart about his victims. He contemplates that Gil and Herndon, or the ideological systems they represent, "were so much more intelligent than the men who had written the news story that it was pathetic."[78] Indicative of the manipulations of the capitalist order, the newspaper article vindicates, ironically, democracy's illiberal competitors.

For Hansberry, the novel's protagonist appears to represent less a recognizable social type than a figment of Wright's own disfigured psyche. "Cross Damon is someone you will never meet on the Southside of Chicago or in Harlem," she writes. "For if he is anything at all, he is the symbol of Wright's new philosophy—the glorification of—nothingness."[79] There is no contradiction between Hansberry's focus on the novel's nihilism and the idea that Cross represents the dangerous detritus of industrial capitalism, what Hannah Arendt called superfluous humanity.[80]

But I would add that this protagonist is also meant to embody what Wright imagines as the totalitarian impulses latent in the postcolony. Cross Damon contains the duality of what Wright called the tragic marginality of the postcolonial elite and the totalitarian tendencies he identified in Bigger Thomas—who, again, was created as a figure of global dispossession, comprising the wretched of the earth *and* the masses of illiberal modernity: all embodied, unexpectedly, in one black boy on Chicago's south side. "It was my conviction," Wright asserts, "that the twentieth century was throwing up these mass patterns of behavior out of the compulsive nakedness of men's disinherited lives." In the way he connected Bigger to the masses seduced by fascism, Wright also linked the "outsider," Cross Damon, to those figures whom he regards, in his dedication to *White Man Listen!*, as "the westernized and tragic elite of Asia, Africa, and the West Indies—the lonely outsiders who exist precariously/on the cliff-like margins of many cultures." Unlike Bigger, Cross is an aspirant to the intellectual elite because Wright believes that the "acute unrest" in the colonized world, "this thrashing about for a new security, is mainly confined to the elite" that wishes to "break the force of religion and tradition" but is aware of an accusatory West that "stands looking critical at this new elite and warns: 'Don't act like fascists toward your own people!'"

The newly liberated nations of Africa and Asia, according to Wright, "are more profoundly upset, filled with more fear and unrest than obtained even when the colonizing power was there in all of its brutal glory." Wright called this condition "post-mortem terror," or "terror in freedom," by which he means "a state of mind of newly freed colonial people who feel that they will be resubjugated; that they are abandoned, that no new house of the heart is as yet made for them to enter. *They know that they do not possess the necessary tools and arms to guarantee their freedom.* Hence, their *terror in freedom*, their anxiety right after their liberation is greater than when under the domination of the superior Western power."[81]

These remarks are easy to reduce to some notion of colonial dependency. Wright suggests as much, in passages of *The Color Curtain*, when he notices that in Indonesia "almost every item in the home in which I was staying had been imported from faraway Europe. There is a nervous kind of dependence bred by imperialism: not only are the people taught Western law, ethics, and finance; but they are encouraged to develop a taste, yea, a need, for goods which are only to be had from the European mother country. Then, when the natives rise and make a revolution in the name of the values of the West, they find themselves trapped, for they cannot build even a modern house without Western aid."[82] Wright is clear that he is not suggesting any notion of colonial dependency here. "Many people have misread this phenomenon [of postmortem terror] and said that the people were unhappy because the Western white man had gone. How silly." Third World "unrest," he continues, "stems from a fear that the white man will come back, and from the cold void in which they are suspended."[83] Writing in the thermonuclear age, during the balance of terror known as mutually assured destruction, Wright's earlier allusion to "arms" is significant here. In *The Color Curtain*, Wright emphasizes how the Afro-Asian leadership's robust moral opposition to nuclear arms concealed latent anxieties about the fact that none possessed this technology. These anxieties came to the fore when France, newly equipped with nuclear weaponry, sought appropriate sites outside of its own national borders to test this technology; in 1960, the year of Wright's death, France selected the African Sahara as an ideal site for nuclear testing. As discussed in Chapter 3, the selection of the African Sahara prompted Africans and blacks in the diaspora, under the leadership of Pan-Africanist Bill Sutherland, to form the Sahara Protest Team, which "successfully lobbied the Convention People's Party [the ruling party of Ghana] to back an international team that would attempt to stop the nuclear test with an audacious plan to drive across the Sahara to the test site in Algeria."[84] This movement mobilized support and reaped headlines, but as Wright might have put it, it did not possess the necessary tools and arms to guarantee African sovereignty and to fend off these incursions.

Fond of Stalin's dictum that the side with the most iron wins, Wright frames his analysis about the prospects for the Third World in terms of its relative dearth of industrialized iron. Wright might also have approved of Trotsky's observation, in 1933, that "all the distinctive traits of the races fade before the internal combustion engine, not to speak of the machine gun." Uttered in the late 1950s, this statement only underscores the industrial disparities stratifying races and nations in the postwar order. What did access to technologies of guns and combustion engines mean in the nuclear age?

In the archive of decolonization, the language of velocity and acceleration appears frequently in statements of Third World development. Because Wright imposes a teleology of secular modernity on the Third World, it is easy to overlook his sensitivity to the profound consequences of industrialization—and the processes we now call globalization—for nations that could not afford the centuries of historical development available to the West's passage to modernity.

On my reading, *The Outsider* constitutes a fictional response to what Wright perceived as the condition of "terror in freedom" afflicting the postcolony. Refusing at *any* cost to surrender to the continuation of enslavement by other means, Cross reveals himself as capable of producing the violence that he fully understands to be the hallmark of the twentieth century. Cross defends himself late in the narrative: "The real slaves of the Twentieth Century are not those sharecroppers who wince at the stinging swish of a riding boss's whip; the slaves of today are those who are congenitally afraid of the new and the untried, who fall on their knees and break into a deep sweat when confronted with the horrible truth of the uncertain and enigmatic nature of life."[85] Behind the existential bravado of Cross's monologue is an insight about those emancipated subjects who are no longer "afraid of the new and untried." The consequences of the death of hope for freedom—this is what Wright feared in Franco's Spain, what he depicted in America's industrial cityscapes, and what he intuited among the newly independent nations of Africa and Asia.

Bandung versus Barbarism

After "about a hundred and fifty years of secular decline," Eric Hobsbawm writes, "barbarism has been on the increase for most of the twentieth century, and there is no sign that this increase is at an end." In this context, he understands "barbarism" to signify two things:

> First, the disruption and breakdown of the systems of rules and moral behaviour by which *all* societies regulate the relations among their members and, to a lesser extent, between their members and those of other societies. Second, I mean, more specifically, the reversal of what we may call the project of the eighteenth-century Enlightenment, namely the establishment of a *universal* system of such rules and standards of moral behaviour, embodied in the institutions of states dedicated to the rational progress of humanity: to Life, Liberty and the Pursuit of Happiness, to Equality, Liberty and Fraternity or whatever. Both are now taking place and reinforce each other's negative effects on our lives.[86]

In this first form of barbarization, Hobsbawm identifies a resonant symbol in the Bosnian wars of the 1990s. Referencing *Blood and Belonging*, Michael Ignatieff's narrative of that conflict, he notes "that in the stateless society of Kurdistan, every male child reaching adolescence gets a gun. Carrying a weapon simply means that a boy has ceased to be a child and must behave like a man. 'The accent of meaning in the culture of the gun thus stresses responsibility, sobriety, tragic duty.' Guns are fired when they need to be." For Hobsbawm, the period after 1945—when the "state enjoyed a legitimate monopoly of violence"—later gave way to an "all-is-permitted" and "semi-sexual, semi-pornographic" culture of the gun.[87]

Wright limns this territory—a thicket of authoritarian masculinity, indiscriminate violence, and normalized barbarism—during the immediate postwar era itself, in the Third World. In *The Color Curtain*, Wright analyzes the divisions between rich and poor in Indonesia. Speculating about what he is told of the "mystery of the Indonesian bandit," Wright "suspected that during the nighttime a good part of the population, resentful of the *status quo*, took to the byways with guns to get what they felt society owed them."[88] Upon his arrival to Bandung with his Indonesian guide, Wright surveys "stout, squat, white-helmeted troops" lining the clean streets, "holding Sten guns in their hands and from their white belts hand grenades dangled. . . . The faces of those troops were like blank masks, and they looked at you with black, cold, unresponsive eyes."

At the sight of these troops, Wright's companion asks: " 'Horrible, isn't it?' 'Not so horrible,' I said. 'You see, I've just come from Spain where you live under the muzzles of machine guns every hour of the day. You get used to it. The machine gun at the street corner is the trademark of the twentieth century. Open force is better than swarms of plain-clothes men. You know where you are with a machine gun' " (535). These recollections suggest a world-weary cynicism or, alternately, furnish evidence of Wright's insistence on Third World militarization. But it is also possible to glean from this passage the paradox that what the Third World needs for its security is precisely what threatens the slide into barbarism that enlightenment norms, for Hobsbawm and other critics, are supposed to prevent. Upon the entrance of the Vietnamese delegation, a few pages later, Wright notes parenthetically that he "spied an Indo-Chinese friend I'd known years before in Paris and he seemed unchanged despite his background of war and suffering and revolution."[89] It is hard not to see in these blank-faced figures, hardened revolutionaries, or simply blasé young men strapped with guns and explosives, the predecessors to Hobsbawm and Ignatieff's duty-bound militants of the Balkans. The omnipresence of the machine gun symbolizes the normalization of barbarism that Hobsbawm identifies at the close of the twentieth century: *Guns are fired when they need to be.*

Yet this situation of inadequate weaponry or asymmetrical warfare was not irreversible, as the case of imperial Japan illustrated. In a revealing passage, Wright records a conversation with Sutan Sjahrir, the first premier of Indonesia, a "Socialist, patriot, intellectual, and one of the country's ablest students of Western political thought," who refused to collaborate with Japanese invaders during the course of his country's independence movement.

> "The Japanese were not loved here," he told me quietly. "We killed more Japanese than we did Dutch. One of the most decisive

> factors in the Indonesians' winning of independence is something that is not well known abroad, not at all. And that was how the Dutch behaved when the Japanese came in. They caved in. The Dutch were scared; they bowed; they wept; they all but crawled. . . . And we Indonesians said to ourselves: 'If the Dutch are that scared of the Japanese, then why ought we be scared of the Dutch?' Dutch fear of the Japanese was a powerful psychological element in our resolve to fight the Dutch for our freedom."[90]

Like his interest in Islam's autonomy, Wright's attention to how Japanese domination prompted Dutch humiliation underscores a key aim of *The Color Curtain*: to probe not only psychological maladies of colonization but also Afro-Asian sources of strength.

"In the early and difficult days of the Russian Revolution," Wright observes, "Lenin had dreamed of a gathering like [Bandung], a conglomeration of the world's underdogs, coming to the aid of his hard-pressed Soviets, but that dream had been a vain one indeed" (537). Not only vain, since Bandung's stance of nonalignment—even the inclusion of Maoist China was a subject of controversy—reversed the Leninist dream: these representatives gathered to assert their autonomy from the Cold War superpowers, even if awareness of the roles of the United States and the Soviet Union permeates the proceedings.[91] In contrast to the Leninist moment, the historical juncture of Bandung witnessed the ascendency of the Soviet Union as a nuclear power vying for the Third World's allegiance—not the other way around. Many Third World leaders desired the aid and technological assistance the Soviets could provide but refused to relinquish the sovereignty such alignment could entail. Yet in light of Moscow's expression of support for Bandung, whose planners invited China but not Soviet Russia, was it possible for the Third World to ignore the idea of Soviet protection altogether, if only as a counterbalance to Western technology?

In *The Color Curtain*, Wright interviews Asian and African delegates along with ordinary observers about their views on the nuclear threat. His interlocutors agree that atomic weaponry is immoral and barbaric and unworthy of human civilization. In Wright's narrative, the unanimity of these responses produces the effect of a refrain, one that reveals a set of unspoken, largely subtextual implications: that none of Bandung's participant nations possesses this technology; that the Bandung strategy of nonalignment, along with the force of its moral authority and diplomatic efforts in the United Nations, was incapable of interrupting the development or application of nuclear technology (at Bandung, Carlos Romulo of the Philippines noted that "if the United Nations has been weak and limited in its progress toward these goals [of peaceful change and development], it is because the United Nations is still much more a mirror of the world than an effective instrument for changing it");[92] and that despite an apparent consensus on the nuclear threat, none in the Third World could afford to ignore this technology's consequences. Beyond the threat of nuclear attack, the development of these technologies of war signaled other impingements on Third World sovereignty: the presence of uranium for nuclear production in the Congo, for example, or atomic testing by the Soviets in Kazakhstan in 1949 and by the French in the Sahara and Polynesia in the late 1950s.

Wright's selection of quotations from Bandung's delegates is instructive. In Sukarno's opening address to the Bandung Conference, Wright's report reproduces excerpts from the Indonesian president's speech that capture the flavor of the Third World geopolitical situation. "We are living in a world of fear," Sukarno asserts. "The life of man today is corroded and made bitter by fear."

> Fear of the future, fear of the hydrogen bomb, fear of ideologies. Perhaps this fear is a greater danger than the danger itself, because it is fear which drives men to act foolishly, to act thoughtlessly, to act dangerously. . . . And do not think that the oceans and the seas will protect us. The food we eat, the water that we drink, yes, even the very air that we breathe can be contaminated by poisons originating from thousands of miles away. And it could be that, even if we ourselves escaped lightly, the unborn generations of our children would bear on their distorted bodies the marks of our failure to control the forces which have been released on our world.[93]

For Wright the central question persists: What sources of strength among African and Asian nations were capable of counteracting this state of affairs? Wright was not deaf to the force of Bandung's moral imagination, but he also wanted to create, out of the congeries of opinions and observations he accumulated in Bandung and elsewhere, a theory of the existential situation of the postcolony and a kind of blueprint for its modern independence.

Continuing this existential and geopolitical thematic, Wright excerpts the speech of Sir John Kotelawala, prime minister of Ceylon: "When the great powers of the West talk peace," Sir John intones, "their chances of agreement are weakened by the fact that each suspects the other's strength. We by contrast come to the conference table weak and relatively unarmed. We have no thermonuclear bombs in our pockets, no weapons of chemical or bacteriological warfare up our sleeves, no plans for armament factories or blueprints for ever more deadly methods of genocide in our brief cases" (544). The "old heresy dies hard," Sir John laments, that in order to secure peace one must prepare for war, but the actuality of an interconnected world meant that even the most localized disputes threaten to engulf a globe characterized by vastly uneven military distributions.

Wright cites the address of Egypt's Gamal Nasser, who continued the theme of nuclear annihilation: "All over the world there is a growing sense of insecurity. The fear of war has been aggravated by the development of mass-destructive weapons capable of effecting total annihilation. The stakes are high in terms of the very survival of mankind." Wright then notes that Nasser, slyly, uses the uprooting of Palestinians during the establishment of Israel ("Never before in human history has there been such a brutal and immoral violation of human principles") as a lesson for other Third World peoples. "Is there any guarantee," Nasser asks, "for the small nations that the big powers who took part in this tragedy would not allow themselves to repeat it again, against another innocent and helpless people?" (545). Nasser's intention to delegitimize Israel is clear, but as the Suez Canal Crisis unfolded the following year—when his own nation succumbed to the incursions of powerful nations—his point about international power politics resonated around the world.

For generations, Sukarno announces, the "voiceless" peoples of Asia and Africa "have been the unregarded, the peoples for whom decisions were made by others whose interests were paramount, the peoples who lived in poverty and humiliation. . . . What can we do? The peoples of Asia and Africa wield little physical power. Even our economic strength is dispersed and slight. We cannot indulge in power politics. . . . Our statesmen, by and large, are not backed up with serried ranks of jet bombers." Wright notes that Sukarno defines the strength of the Bandung gathering in terms of sheer population: with delegates representing nations comprising over 1.4 billion people, far more than half of the world's population, the nonaligned nations wield the power to mobilize the "*Moral Violence of Nations* in favor of peace." Similarly, Iraq's delegate called for "ideological disarmament and moral rearmament" as the outcome of the conference. Not every Bandung participant nation, however, could rely on moral rearmament or afford to stand apart from the super powers: Wright records the remarks of Thailand's Prince Wan, who admitted that his country felt obliged to join the Manila Pact, a Western-backed defense treaty designed to obstruct communist infiltration into Southeast Asia. But for those nations committed to nonalignment, where, Wright asks, would this moral violence come from?

Sukarno's answer fascinates and troubles Wright. "Religion is of dominating importance particularly in this part of the world," Sukarno continues. "There are perhaps more religions here than in other regions of the globe. . . . Our countries were the birthplace of religions." The other unifying force among the conference participants was, of course, the "common experience . . . of colonialism" (540–541). Against Western military dominance, Sir John similarly appealed to the shared heritage of colonialism and spirituality in the Third World, grounded in "that traditional respect for the spiritual values of life and for the dignity of the human personality which is the distinguishing feature of all their great religions" (544–545). What this meant for Wright is that, in the face of Cold War and nuclear dangers, the Third World appeared poised to draw on "race and religion, *two of the most powerful and irrational forces in human nature.* Sukarno was not evoking these twin demons; he was not trying to create them; he was trying to organize them. The reality of race and religion was there, swollen, sensitive, turbulent" (540–541). For all of his stress on the advancements made by the Protestant Reformation and the Enlightenment, and on how these intellectual revolutions require absorption in the Third World, on my reading Wright's encounter with the Afro-Asian world disturbs rather than reinforces his secularism.

Whether seeking to alleviate Western anxieties about Third World retaliation or, alternatively, to foment anticolonial resistance, other U.S. commentators interpreted the theme of racial consciousness at Bandung in accordance with varying ideological or political objectives. African American journalist Marguerite Cartwright, writing in the *Pittsburgh Courier*, suggested that at the conference "it soon became clear that color faded in the face of more relevant issues of social, cultural, economic and ideological import: Few speakers mentioned color as such. . . . In the end a positive contribution had been made toward democratic development and partnership with the West." In the *New York Times*, a reviewer of Wright's *The Color Curtain* wrote that Bandung was not "a manifestation of solidarity and resurgence of the colored peoples of the world against the whites. (Many of the participants, indeed, were white and many who were brown, tan and yellow had few complexes and resentments either about the color of their own skins or the skins of others.)"[94] Even modestly impartial observers recognized in Bandung more than an occasion merely to ventilate racial grievances or to conspire against the West, but some commentators went too far in their attempt to purge Bandung's environment of racial awareness.

At the opposite end of the racial spectrum, Malcolm X interpreted Bandung pedagogically, as an example of unity from which black America could learn. The participants of Bandung, he told the Northern Negro Grass Roots Leadership Conference in Detroit of 1963, comprised Muslims and Christians, Buddhists and atheists, communists and capitalists, but one feature defined the landmark gathering: "The number-one thing that was not allowed to attend the Bandung conference was the white man. He couldn't come. Once they excluded the white man, they found that they could get together. . . . And these people who came together didn't have nuclear weapons, they didn't have jet planes, they didn't have all of the heavy armaments that the white man has. But they had unity."[95] Exclusion is not exactly unity, however, and if Wright understood that recognition of a common racial consciousness formed a point of departure rather than an end in itself, he also saw the very premise of the gathering as an indictment against the Western world.

As I suggest earlier, Wright was doubtful about the "moral violence" of which Sukarno and other representatives spoke. Yet as one revealing anecdote in *The Color Curtain* illustrates, there was another type of moral violence capable of grounding an industrial prowess worthy of respect. As the ironic case of imperial Japan illustrated, the situation of inadequate industrialization or asymmetrical warfare was not irreversible. In a previously cited conversation with Sutan Sjahrir, the first premier of Indonesia, Wright notes that Sjahrir refused to collaborate with Japanese invaders in the course of Indonesia's independence movement, but Sjahrir learned a valuable lesson from the East Asian power.

His refusal to collaborate with Japan distinguishes the first premier from his country's colluders, but Sjahrir had to concede that the Japanese invasion empowered Indonesia to oust the Dutch. The example of industrial Japan as a hybrid formation of anti-Western colonialism and illiberal modernity suggested the prospect that non-Western nations were able not only to surpass the West in technological acumen but also to strike fear in empire's heart. In the late twentieth century, the ascendency of former colonies such as Malaysia, Singapore, and South Korea—countries that African philosopher Olúfémi Táíwò claims "were much farther behind some African countries in terms of their potential for success in the development race on the eve of independence"—attested to the power of industrialization to counterbalance the existential condition of terror in freedom.[96]

In light of his travel writings' reliance on discredited ethnographic modes of representation, his endorsement of militarization on a continent that tragically came to be wracked by dictatorial rule, or his departure from the explosive realism that defined his early success, it is not difficult to see why critics once (though fortunately no longer) neglected Wright's work in the 1950s. As the twenty-first century witnesses a resurgence of concerns about terrorism, secularism, and reenchantment in the non-Western world, Wright's postwar literary imagination, apparently anachronistic in his last and most productive decade, seems strikingly contemporary.

Conclusion

MEMORY AND PARANOIA

In the spring of 1963, the journal *Freedomways*, edited by Shirley Graham, hosted a symposium on the topic "The Assault on Civil Rights." Two contributors—journalist William Worthy and lawyer Benjamin J. Davis—warned of the pernicious effects of the Internal Security Act of 1950, widely known as the McCarran Act, on American democracy and its black critics.[1] In "McCarranism and a Free Press," Worthy narrates how he wound up in the crosshairs of the law after reporting on "the numerous positive developments" of the Cuban Revolution and signing a declaration with thirty "other Negro citizens opposing and *promising to resist* any invasion of Cuba."[2] Charged with "illegal re-entry" under the McCarran Act, Worthy's court trial in Miami ensued. "For a black man," Worthy wrote, a fair trial in a Miami "crowded with hate-filled seething" émigrés is unlikely; in that atmosphere, "a fair trial for any anti-colonial individual is out of the question." His request to transfer the case to another city or to recalibrate the jury selection was denied.

The veteran Communist lawyer Davis described the "McCarran Concentration Camp Act [as] the greatest threat to the struggle for Negro rights since the Fugitive Slave law more than 100 years ago." Though the law purports to target only communist-identified individuals and organizations, Davis argued, its vague and "irrational provisions" empowered the state to persecute virtually any organization, "no matter the political philosophy of its members."[3] Yet as these essays made clear, this piece of anticommunist legislation had been redirected toward the suppression, surveillance, and censorship of *black* activism.

During the 1950s, this legislation impacted Caribbean intellectuals who lacked the advantage of a U.S. passport. As Bill Mullen recounts, on December 7, 1955, officials deported Claudia Jones from the United States to London after seven years of state surveillance and numerous arrests, upon which she was "charged with violating both the Smith Act and the McCarran-Walter Internal Security Act." "On the day of her deportation, more than three hundred people gathered at Harlem's Hotel Theresa to bid her farewell. W. E. B. Du Bois and Shirley Graham Du Bois, traveling, sent a telegram. Just two years earlier, the United States had also deported C. L. R. James, ostensibly for overstaying his visa." Interned on Ellis Island, James set to work on *Mariners, Renegades, and Castaways*, a study of Herman Melville and an allegory on Cold War anticommunism.[4] In the early 1950s, James collected notes for his posthumously published *American Civilization*, another Cold War–inflected text that highlighted U.S. cultural fluidity as a bulwark against the nation's totalitarian undertow.

In the 1960s, heightened state scrutiny and persecution of anticolonial radicalism conjured a paranoid milieu in the transnational black public sphere. Paranoia found its basis and symbolic expression in the decade's honor roll of African revolutionaries, civil rights militants, and critical intellectuals who were assassinated or who died mysteriously. As for the leading lights of nonalignment, Jawaharlal Nehru died in 1964, Kwame Nkrumah was overthrown in 1966, and Gamal Nasser was diminished by defeat in war in 1967 and died in 1970. Giving voice to the decade's depressing vicissitudes, James Baldwin wrote in 1963 that every American Negro "risks having the gates of paranoia close on him," a remark following his interview in Chicago with Elijah Muhammad and the Nation of Islam, whose beliefs struck him as folly but whose "emotional tone is as familiar to me as my own skin."[5]

This paranoid milieu elicited new textual exercises in the hermeneutics of suspicion.[6] In what follows, I conclude with a reading of John A. Williams's neglected classic of 1967, *The Man Who Cried*

I Am, with the aim of extrapolating two tendencies in this and other texts: the first involves *paranoia* about repressive or even genocidal plots supposedly under way in the 1960s; the second concerns historical *memory* of the midcentury internationalism that gave rise to worries about state suppression in the first place. The capaciousness of the novel genre enables Williams to stake out multiple, ambitious itineraries at once. *The Man Who Cried I Am* is at once an extended obituary on the literary life of Richard Wright, an evocation of black expatriate life in Europe and Africa, an inquiry into colonial history, and a meditation on race, war, and totalitarianism.

"Wright was an American phenomenon," cartoonist Ollie Harrington wrote in remembrance of the author of classics like *Native Son*, *The Color Curtain*, and *The Outsider*. "Lenin, during the Russian Revolution, looked at the jubilant former serfs who'd changed the course of history. Wouldn't he be thinking also of one like this one when he dreamed of creating a new man?"[7] In two articles on the death of Richard Wright, Harrington (a frequent contributor to *Freedomways*, among other international publications) chronicles the curious demise of his close friend, one-time artistic collaborator, and fellow expatriate. In his 1961 article "The Last Days of Richard Wright," Harrington lovingly paints his colossal subject but only hints at ominous details surrounding his death. In his 1977 essay, "The Mysterious Death of Richard Wright," Harrington renders more explicit his sense that Wright was assassinated. It is possible that Harrington, like Wright, appears in composite form as a character in *The Man Who Cried I Am*. In fiction and nonfiction, respectively, both Williams and Harrington hinted at foul play in Wright's death.

My argument is that even as political developments of the 1960s warranted a measure of paranoia among blacks, the effort in Williams's novel to imagine impending totalitarian scenarios—a contrivance that functions to reactivate history, as it were—compensates for a sense that internationalist engagement, in its zenith in the century's first half, was on the wane. This conclusion seems counterintuitive, even wrongheaded, given the resurgence of various Pan-Africanisms in the 1960s. Journals like *Freedomways* and *The Black Scholar*, for example, attest that Pan-African ideas remained vital to black intellectual discourse in the 1960s. Williams evokes this heady atmosphere in the following passage: "Black fever. Harlem streets revealing more and more Negroes in African dress—kentes, agbadas, shamas—these days without laughter. Minister Q filling Harlem Square, pounding home the lost lessons of black empires. Marcus Garvey recalled. Negro papers filled with statements from African leaders who had studied in America."[8] The narrator observes that every day, several black faces could be found boarding Pan American flights to Africa. For all of this Africanist energy, however, there is an overwhelming sense in Williams's novel that the spirit of romantic, expatriate defiance defined by Frantz Fanon and Wright, or the earlier cosmopolitanism of Du Bois and Nehru, was on the wane.

Temporality is key to the juxtaposition of these terms. Whereas memory evokes a past, paranoia imagines a future, even as each modality draws on and refracts the other. This interactivity between memory and paranoia, past and future, is congenial for my purposes here, as each modality distills elements of the story told in *Race and the Totalitarian Century*.

Given the paranoia aroused by what seemed like the reorientation of national security enforcement around black radicalism, it is not surprising that a novel like John A. Williams's neglected 1967 classic, *The Man Who Cried I Am*, adopts the conceit of the "King Alfred Plan," an FBI scheme to exterminate black dissidents, one by one, and then in mass quantities, in the event of a major African American insurgency. The King Alfred Plan represents the most extreme project conceived in a coalition of Western nations, the "Alliance Blanc," whose European members seek to reclaim control of African resources not with naked conquest but in accordance with the insidious postwar paradigm of Third World development, international cooperation, and foreign aid.

This subplot suspends the novel's realism and realigns the narrative, in certain instances, with conspiracy theory or political thriller genres. But it is worth recalling how for contemporaneous readers, the King Alfred Plan could appear plausibly like the logical extension of resurgent, McCarran-style reaction. As awareness of the novel grew, rumors circulated among black communities that the King Alfred Plan was not a wholly fabricated fiction but an actual conspiracy under way. Critics of the time underwrote that view. "The plot," writes one critic from the early 1970s, "similar in many ways to Nazi Germany's 'final solution,' employs enough facts from everyday life to give the reader an uneasy feeling that perhaps this section of the book is not pure fiction: only slightly disguised, James Meredith, Malcolm X, Martin Luther King, Richard Wright, and James Baldwin all appear in the novel; so do numerous black organizations ranging from the Urban League to the Black Muslims (the Black Panther Party had not yet come to prominence at the time Williams was writing the book)." In light of what this critic identified as "the recent furor over detention camps still in existence and the growing suspicion of the CIA and the FBI," it is understandable how readers mistook Williams's fictions for fact. Current events generated paranoid interpretive communities.[9]

Yet it is equally difficult to avoid the conclusion that the Alliance Blanc and King Alfred subplot is a conceit necessary to resuscitate a romantic history that—in the world eulogized in Williams's novel—is fading, being snuffed out, assimilating into political mainstreams, or migrating into new radicalisms with mixed success. A novel of four hundred pages, *The Man Who Cried I Am* does not divulge much about the King Alfred Plan until the very end of the story, with only a few suspense-building snippets sprinkled into the narrative along the way. The majority of the plan's details do not emerge until pages 362 to 376, divulged in the form of a long letter from Harry to Max—the contents of which are so explosive that its bearer, Max, is told to expect certain assassination, a cause for consternation were he not already expiring from cancer. If the macabre mystery of King Alfred functions to expose a totalitarian conspiracy in the heart of U.S. democracy while propelling a story otherwise bereft of plot, it is clear that the narrative's orientation is retrospective rather than prospective. The main plot unfolds, apparently, over only a few days in the life of Max Reddick, but the bulk of the narrative dwells in memory, which in the universe of the novel is potentially infinite as it unfolds in the particulars of the hero's subjectivity. In this respect, the novel is far more concerned with memorializing black agency in the twentieth century's grand projects than with prognosticating a future marked by new racial genocides.

This memorial traverses the determined internationalism occasioned by the century's world wars and its fateful triad of fascism, communism, and liberalism. Despite the continued efforts of older and younger generations of black activists to sustain the internationalist momentum spanning the interwar through the Bandung years, the novel's nostalgia for this period invariably underscores the distance between that era and the novel's setting in the late 1960s, when successive waves of anticommunism, liberal consensus building, and clandestine Third World operations bludgeoned but did not extinguish the *live* ethos of internationalism.

The novel centers on Max Reddick, a New York-based writer and foreign correspondent who is dying of rectal cancer—the disease a symbol of American industrialization, the rectum an allusion to the location of blacks within this order—and seeking to reconnect with friends and lovers in Europe.[10] The story pairs Max with his friend Harry Ames, a character modeled on Richard Wright. On a return trip to Leiden, Max, expiring himself, learns that Harry has just died in Paris from a heart attack.

All the characters with a public persona in the novel are composite characters. Max and Harry evoke Wright, Baldwin, and perhaps Williams himself, in the same manner that the novel's Minister Q, for example, splices Malcolm X and Muhammad Ali. Readers immediately recognize Wright in Harry Ames, though, because the fictional character embodies a self-identified, rootless outsider who nonetheless happens to be the world's premier black writer and literary father figure to younger generations. Other aspects of Harry's characterization recall Richard Wright. In a distillation of Wright's own Cold War entanglements, the narrator notes that "the Spanish Government managed to let Harry know that it wasn't at all happy about the series of articles he had written on the Franco regime" (an allusion to Wright's 1957 travel narrative, *Pagan Spain*) and that a "number of West Africans had started to cut Harry dead because of what he said about them." We learn that his convivial residency in Europe is in jeopardy, since "the Communists of Europe distrusted him" after Harry quit the U.S. Communist Party and spoke publicly and "wrote about all of them."[11]

The novel conjures the imagery—Amsterdam's canals, cafes on the Left Bank filled with smoke and debate, martinis and witticisms among New York's literati—that inscribe the black expatriate narrative as a romantic genre. In his youth, Max "wanted to do with the novel what Charlie Parker was doing to music—tearing it up and remaking it; basing it on nasty, nasty blues and overlaying it with the deep overriding tragedy not of Dostoyevsky, but an American who knew of consequences to come: Herman Melville, a super Confidence Man, a Benito Cereno saddened beyond death."[12] But his illness, along with more quotidian pressures such as earning a living, relaxed those ambitions.

The idea that cancer is a symptom of industrialized society is not lost on Max, whose lived experience and sense of the disease as uniquely historical colors his own view of history. With his body's leaks, pangs, convulsions, and effluvia of decay, all manifesting in the most inconvenient (sexual) encounters, and requiring the regular consumption of drugs for relief, Max's confrontation with death provides a narrative opportunity for the protagonist to introspect on his existence and to meditate on history writ large, as he has lived it and as the past dwells in him. As though to inhabit Max's morphine-soaked consciousness, the narrator itself is at times inebriated, delivered to eccentric punctuation and syntax, with rapid alternations between the third-person and second-person points of view—and momentary, italicized interjections of first-person streams of consciousness revealing the protagonist's darkest moments. These alternations enable the narrator to zoom in and out of Max's consciousness but also back and forth in history. Reversing the notion of black particularity as provincial, the novel wants to inscribe *all* the grand narratives of the twentieth century, and many of the not so grand, in one black body contemplating its own ontology in time.[13]

In its insistent inscription of the body and history in a mutual teleology of disease, the novel reiterates the idea that blacks remain in a fundamental sense alien to Western and especially American society. But happily for the characters in Williams's expatriate narrative, this view provides the perfect rationale for pursuing the pleasures of exile. And perhaps it was the black exile's intellectual pleasures, above all, that so exercised certain observers. During his time in Paris, Harrington recalls "a tight band of Americans who never tried to cloak their outright hatred" of Richard Wright, whom they would attack "in the most insulting manner, referring to his books and his opinions with contempt. They hurled the term 'expatriate' at Wright with a venom which shocked the listening French and other European intellectuals."[14] In Harrington's remembrance of Wright and Williams's portrait of Harry Ames, both figures embrace the expatriate as an American term of derision.

Were Wright and other fellow travelers expatriates or exiles? Probably they were both: seeking refuge from Jim Crow and trading their *patria* for more hospitable, politically energetic, or cosmopolitan forms of attachment. In this context, what often made the real difference between the two, the exile and the expat, involved how state actors dealt with the nationality or restricted the mobility of those who sought other modes of citizenship.

In Williams's novel, what the exilic consciousness yields is a more voluptuous and esoteric historical imagination than what U.S. national scripts allow. In a letter to Max describing the machinations of Alliance Blanc, Harry concludes by reiterating a key point: that despite Europe's record of internecine struggles and protracted wars, intracontinental prejudices and animosities, the European continent has nonetheless enjoyed "an amazing historical rapport in Africa" and will never fail to close ranks "where the black man is concerned." ("That rapport in plundering Africa never existed and never will when it requires the same passion for getting along with each other in Europe.") And finally: "How goddamn different this would have been if there had been no Charles Martel at Tours in 732!"[15] Reading this last sentence returns Max to a memory of a road trip with Harry across France, when they stopped in the city of Tours en route "to Carcassonne to buy smuggled Spanish shotguns." Minus a few encyclopedia entries, Max thinks, the meaning of Tours "had been lost in history, perhaps intentionally." Thus he muses: "Somewhere between Tours and Poitiers, Charles Martel had halted the Moors driving up from Spain in, the encyclopedias said, 'one of the decisive battles in history.' There was a stinging clue, Max thought, as they were taking lunch in a café along the

Loire. Otherwise how white would Europe be? Or America, for that matter?" (222).

What follows is the kind of historical conjecture that seeks clues of blackness in premodernity and their erasure in modernity. "Why couldn't they tell you straight out who was a Moor? They told you a Moor was a Berber, a Saracen, an Arab, anything to keep you from knowing that Berbers, Saracens, and Arabs were often black. But the Spanish knew; how well they knew." He learned this lesson during a trip to Madrid when the Spanish, upon seeing Max, began to "whisper loudly to each other . . . *'Mira! Mira! Un moro!'* Max had heard the history resounding in their voices" (222–223). In that voice, Max hears a signifying chain of histories and denials of history: the memory of Al-Andalusia, when Africa occupied Europe; counter-factual speculations of a different outcome at Tours, from which "modernity" might have taken a radically different turn, if what is conventionally understood by modernity emerges at all; and the knowledge that in the European consciousness, this African path of civilization not taken must remain subliminal, excised from canonical history but not to be forgotten. "What they wouldn't do," Max thinks, "the white folks, to keep you from having a history, the better, after all, to protect theirs" (223).

Walking along the Loire, Max "felt empty" and "even felt stupid," as he tries to make sense of the pieces of an historical puzzle that even if fitted together properly might not complete the picture. What language or esoteric wisdom would be necessary to round out the picture, to imagine another form of life? The English language, though exquisitely and eccentrically enriched by imperialism, as Richard Wright observed at Bandung, alone is insufficient. "English is limiting but it's all we know well," Max says to himself early in the novel. The black vernacular was a powerful resource but provided no access to alternate life-worlds in the same way afforded by native intimacy with Amharic or Farsi or Kikuyu and other languages sustained throughout processes of decolonization, dispersal, and diaspora.

As sociologist E. Franklin Frazier argued with relentless clarity in *The Negro Family in the United States*, black Americans across the generations possessed nothing more than "forgotten memories" of

Africa. It was true, he conceded, that numerous Africans who were presumed to lack literacy spoke and sometimes wrote in Arabic, transmitting that language into the new world, as numerous colonial and first-person Arabic sources attest.[16] If evidence of funereal rites, dances, prayers, songs, and other African-derived practices survived in the New World, they evolved in geographically disparate and disproportionate ways. For Frazier, as for sociologist Robert E. Park or historian Stanley Elkins, enslaved Africans transported to the West Indies or South America stood a better chance to preserve and reconstitute such linguistic and other cultural connections than did those fated for North America. In what became the United States, decisively different conditions of bondage were said to prevail. "Probably never before in history," Frazier writes, "has a people been so nearly completely stripped of its social heritage as the Negroes who were brought to America."[17]

Frazier, as Williams's character Max would have admitted, was probably correct in his assessment, but Max cannot help but wonder about distant life-worlds and cultural traffics, buried in obscure pasts. "There was so much he wanted to know," Max laments, "but never would know." "How wonderful it would be to be able to read Arabic; what answers would come from that! Or classic Chinese to understand what had happened to the great Chinese navies and find a clue, perhaps, to the presence of black people in the Melanesian islands of the Pacific. How did they get there? What immense traffic in goods and people took place between China and Africa, and in which dawn of which history?" (223).

In some measure, Max's romantic desire to be able to read Arabic ("what answers would come from that!") might appear as bound up in what Edward Said taught us was a colonial tradition in which the "exaggerated value heaped upon Arabic as a language permits the Orientalist to make the language equivalent to mind, society, history, and nature."[18] Yet Max's linguistic desires limn a more esoteric domain: language is the medium by which he would gain access to an alternate historical imagination—in which Africa conquers Europe—deprived him by the English language. "Caught up in the spin of history," Max's divination about elusive, recondite knowledge, however, does not achieve narrative realization.

Though English has significant limitations, there were occasions "when it should be used, such as when describing how Harry died."[19] What the protagonist has in mind is not describing his actual decease, or even understanding the suddenness of his death, but expressing why he, Max, recoils from an invitation to participate in the banal ritual of Harry's cremation. Max "had seen enough men cremated in tanks, the bodies curling and snapping and frying in their own juices. He wasn't going to sit in anybody's anteroom and wait for Harry to be cooked down to ashes."[20] This parallel may sound tendentious, but Williams has a point to make: How did language enable Max to see cremation as anything other than industrialized death? Or the rush to cremate Harry as anything other than destruction of the evidence of his body? In this context, what Max needs linguistically is not access to alternate or premodern life-worlds but a certain vocabulary of modern experience. English remained indispensible, among other reasons, to reshape via writing the society that called the language of generalized barbarism into being.

More often, however, his reveries return him to the Western world that has produced him, and for Max as for his generation, the formative experience remains the Second World War. It is no surprise, then, that memory tends to cluster around this predominantly masculine arena, but it operates in the novel in unexpected ways. Memory filters through the (male) narrator—better characterized as unmoored than unreliable—whose voice aligns with Max's thoughts and perceptions but speaks beyond them. As with many of the male characters, the narrator injects testosterone into the story as promiscuously as Max pumps morphine into his body. Max isn't taking morphine principally to get high (sometimes, when combined with alcohol and Librium, the effect is a pleasant and desperately needed numbness, but morphine is not his drug of choice) but to relieve the agony of his pain—as his body, emitting odors during sex, humiliates his ever-libidinous self.

The compensatory fantasy indulged in the novel—in which the expatriate black artist, beloved and unburdened, learns European geography in part through sexual conquest—is graphically undone by Max's illness and consequent emasculation. His sexuality is ultimately desperate and tinged with sadness, awkwardness. The sexual fantasy is compensatory in another sense because Max, as the reader learns, is portrayed as having never recovered from a failed romance with Lillian, a young African American woman who desires something from Max that he cannot provide: financial security and a bourgeois life. When Lillian becomes pregnant, she aborts the child against Max's wishes, and dies during the botched operation. Years later, when Max receives a lucrative offer to write for a prestigious magazine, he says to himself: "(Lillian, look. Look at it, Lillian, the money. Look! Goddamn it!)" (239). At the same time, this characterization of Lillian continues a tradition that grounds black women's desire in economic and bourgeois normativity. By associating Lillian with this form of normativity, which the reader understands is unavailable to the strapped young writer Max, the novel renders the hero a sympathetic figure—forever haunted by the lover who wronged him for all the wrong reasons. But it's difficult not to read this plot as a conveniently masculine resolution of the tension between the black male intellectual's irrepressible urge for globetrotting engagement with the world and his simultaneously desired role of paterfamilias.

But this fantasy is arguably a proxy for another kind of male drama that involves Max and Harry, one that turns on the meanings of the figure of the Negro soldier. Both writers are black expatriates whom the publishing industry has tried to set against each other for the title of Preeminent Negro Writer. "Goddamnit, Harry, Max thought in the silence, it's not *me* against you; it's you against them working out of your bag and me against them working out of my bag; us against the bad guys" (226). Though his literary authority is never seriously challenged by the succession of upstart Negro writers who must seek his help, Harry jealously guards his vaunted status. His relationship with Max, however, upsets this gendered politics of recognition and literature's economy of prestige—at least in Harry's mind. As it turns out, what equalizes the relationship between Harry and Max is their relationship to the Second World War, in which Max has fought and Harry has not. In this respect, the novel leaves largely intact certain norms clustered around war and masculinity. But as Max observes, blacks did not choose these circumstances, even if by necessity they internalized Cro-Magnon norms of war. This logic applies even more viscerally to decolonization. "But why think of [Africa] in terms of wars? Why?" Max wonders. "Because that's just the way the white folks spelled it out" (98).

As Max prepares for duty, he consoles himself with the thought that serving "in the army was to be an experience. How much worse could life be?" Then he contemplates: "Armies are like the societies that produce them. Max knew that. But the confrontation with that fact, logically, had to be harsher than the suspicion. The society expected, nay *demanded*, that every black soldier within its ranks die as he had lived—segregated, deprived, discriminated against. That is, to die if ever permitted to be in a situation where that was possible. The honor of dying, on the whole, was reserved for white soldiers."

It would be hasty to dismiss this "honor" as merely the expression of a primordial and gladiatorial masculinity. What this view overlooks is the degree to which blacks maintain, or fail to maintain, control of the narrative of their own death or survival. For proponents of the social death view of black subjectivity, for example, soldiers who perish in war have only sacrificed their lives in a conflagration orchestrated by imperialist actors. On the other hand, should they fight and survive to tell the tale, the meaning of that tale redounds to the ideological imperatives of Allied victory.

The U.S. Army, Max reflects, would not make the same error in the Second World War that it had made in the First: "detaching Negro soldiers to fight with the French and accumulate all those *Croix de Guerre*." From the vantage point of white segregationists, the valor displayed by Negro soldiers in French battlefields in 1918 had, unexpectedly and unacceptably, enhanced the image of black humanity on the world stage. This ironic effect, Max notes, prompted the War Department, "with help from the French military mission, to issue a paper on 7 August 1918: *Secret Information Concerning Black American Troops*. The usual, official, vicious stuff."[21] The right to die—honorably, in battle—is inscribed here as the masculine privilege that a segregated army denies a person like Max. But Harry understands that even these paradoxes are grist for powerful literary material—and the war is an experiential dimension that the world-famous Harry envies in the neophyte Max.

Actually, it was his service in the war that emboldened Max, still a novice writer, to critique Harry's work in the first place and thus to command the elder's respect. "Perhaps it was being in the Army, sheltered," Max reflects, "that made Max [write about Harry's novel]. Where else would he have gotten the nerve to discuss Harry Ames's work?" For his part, "Harry envied Max the experience. It was true there was no moral equivalent for war. . . . Being a man was still tied to being at war" (78). Harry's intuition is correct, since after the war Max is aloof, chastened, and less solicitous of Harry's attention; Harry senses, rightly, that Max's war experience will translate smoothly into literary authenticity and thus enhance his stature as a writer. And to Harry's mind, the enlargement of Max's stature threatens the diminution of his own.

Yet Harry's envy extends beyond the literary authenticity and rewards that Max will eventually reap. Again sexuality mediates interracial and intraracial perceptions: for many Europeans, including the character Margrit, Max's Dutch love interest, the Negro soldier symbolizes liberation and American largesse. After seeing Max again after a prolonged absence, she admits to herself that she is still attracted to him—*but* her attraction to Max is tied to an image of blackness that she recalls from her youth, when a squadron of Negro soldiers liberated her town of Groningen. "Perhaps in a way the reason for [Margrit's continued attraction to Max] *was* because of that big, ponderously walking Negro who led a column of liberating black Americans through the streets of Groningen."

> He had walked, Margrit remembered, with a wide step, and there was a grin on his face and chocolate bars were sticking out from his pockets. She had broken loose from her parents and, with a group of other small children who waved the tiny American flags their parents had kept hidden, had raced into the street. The big black man picked her up and laughed, gave her candy and put her down again. Max had said, once when she talked about that day, "Well, the world starts whirling for different people for different reasons and at different times. I'll thank that guy if I ever see him." (27–28)

The phallic imagery of chocolate bars "sticking out from his pockets" encodes a glimpse of social disruption intimated in the next sentence: along with the other neighborhood children, Margrit had "broken loose from her parents" in full and joyous stride toward their black liberators. Would Europe's exuberance about emancipation from Nazism, and the U.S. role in continental liberation and reconstruction, break or reinforce intergenerational taboos about interracial sex? In a different register, as the novel suggests, the sexual tension between (male) African Americans and (female) Europeans revealed an unexpected symmetry, since both segregated blacks and wartime Europeans dwelled with the ubiquity of violent death. "On a continent where life marched evenly with the tread of armies," writes Williams, "the European was attuned to death, expected it in a way, [Max] supposed, and avoided the first suggestion of its coming. So many of them were Negroes in that respect, and didn't know it" (388). Europeans may not have known they were akin to blacks in this way, but after the war the continent was also populated by "people who said they were Jews when [Margrit] knew they were not," because there "was something about wanting to belong to and be a survivor of the worst of the Continent's history" (342).

The image of the black liberator in Europe returns to my previous discussion of William Gardner Smith's *Last of the Conquerors.* In Chapter 1, I cited Smith's remarks from an interview in 1959. "Do you know what it's like for a Negro to be among the 'conquerors' instead of the defeated?" For Smith and others, this experience marked a turning point: never would they return to the "old way again."[22] Max is less sanguine about the catalytic effect of this moment. Years later, his editor asks him to report on the Korean War, since it required a Negro perspective to take full measure of "Harry Truman's integrated Armed Forces" taking "the field against the North Koreans." Clearly, by the early 1950s, the symbolic and geopolitical meaning of black involvement in world war had shifted: the enemy is no longer Nazism or fascism, but a homogenized communism, and Max can see through America's military desegregation to discern Korea as a racial war "called something else. The Russians understood the hell out of that. They carried the blood of the Khans and the Timurids. Thus tinged they were the least white of all the major Allies in War II—and suffered most" (194).

"Besides," Max thinks, "when the white Americans called out 'Gook!' it sounded awfully like nigger" (194). His white editor "had enough sense to know that any Negro really aware of his position in American society in the year 1950, if given the chance to refuse to go to a real fighting war and still remain economically and socially solvent, would refuse." In previous wars, though, the Negro had not refused; why would he in 1950? In Williams's imagination, he refused not because life was improving stateside but because he sensed a volte-face: black soldiers were no longer agents of the multiple antitotalitarian front described in Chapter 1 but after 1945 were increasingly figures of occupation, or worse, of racially inflected aggression. That is one reason why the novel's King Alfred's Plan includes a component to liquidate the nation's minorities by using them as cannon fodder in war.

The racial norms that shaped the U.S. war effort in the 1940s—wherein blacks are denied the right to an honorable death—shift in a perverse way a decade later during the Korean and then Vietnam wars. Toward the novel's end, a detail tucked away in Harry's account of the King Alfred plan reveals the following: "Since the Korean War, this Department [of Defense] has shifted Minority members of the Armed Forces to areas where combat is most likely to occur, with the aim of eliminating, through combat, as many combat-trained Minority servicemen as possible. Today the ratio of Minority member combat deaths in Vietnam, where they are serving as 'advisers,' is twice as high as the Minority population ratio to the rest of America" (375). While this scenario advances the plan's overall aim to reduce or destroy the nation's African American population, its ingeniousness ensures the elimination of trained black soldiers—in other words, those best equipped to lead the supposedly forthcoming insurrection the King Alfred plan is designed to squelch.

In one war memory, Max recalls his time aboard a ship on the verge of capsizing. He remembers thinking, "How in the hell did we get like this? In a time when we fight for the things we can't have." Max then recalls what Harry, who had not served, told him once: "maybe we'll do the war unloading ships and trucks." Harry's consolation was no doubt a piece of Jim Crow wisdom—stay alive at all costs—but Max cannot abide by that code. "Military humiliations could be forgiven under a military code," the narrator intones, "but racial humiliations dealt under a military code never could be forgiven." Yet with mass destruction all around, was not survival—even if that meant taking refuge in menial, racially relegated tasks—the better part of wisdom? Yes, that "would be survival," Max thought, "but would that be enough?"

Notes

Introduction

1. Hortense Spillers, "Mama's Baby, Papa's Maybe: An American Grammar Book," in *Black, White, and in Color: Essays on American Literature and Culture* (Chicago: University of Chicago Press, 2003), 19–20.

2. See Volker Langbehn and Mohammad Salama, eds., *German Colonialism: Race, the Holocaust, and Postwar Germany* (New York: Columbia University Press, 2011), iv–xxxi.

3. As Chris Goto-Jones contends concerning the exclusion of non-European philosophy from the history of philosophy, this tendency rests on an assumption that, in context, "the history of ideas can teach us something about *our own* intellectual, philosophical, moral, or political predicament." The study of political thought, he writes in a critique of Charles Taylor, must remain Eurocentric because only then will it enable "us" to recognize "our" own dilemmas in the present. Other traditions have a place on the byways, but European philosophy remains the highway. But as Goto-Jones contends, "The highways, not the byways, appear to be the problem. The insistence on Europe's centrality looks increasingly like a conservative reaction to the emergence of a world in which Europe is no longer the center." Goto-Jones, "The Kyoto School, the Cambridge School, and the History of Political Philosophy in Wartime Japan," *Positions* 17, no. 1 (Spring 2009): 13–42, especially 14–20.

4. Because of the massive scope of the world wars, and the constraints inherent in treating their particularities with due complexity, I've had to choose the historical events, geographical areas, and political or ideological dilemmas of interest very selectively—generally on the basis of how powerfully they illuminate the connection between race and totalitarianism. That

means other conflicts and events are necessarily left out. For example, despite their obvious significance, some colonial or wartime events, such as African American criticism of the U.S. occupation of Haiti or involvement in the Cuban Revolution or experience in the Korean and Vietnam Wars, I neglect because they either have been capably studied, have less bearing on the intervention proposed here, or simply exceed the scope of this study.

5. See also Fredric Jameson, "Globalization as a Philosophical Issue," in *Valences of the Dialectic* (New York: Verso, 2010), 435–455.

6. Dean Lauer, "'America and Russia Are the Same': Geopolitics in Heidegger's *Seinsfrage*," *Telos* 132 (Fall 2005): 132–150.

7. It is important to note, however, that Heidegger amends his earlier statement about Europe's position within the "pincers" of Russia and America: "We said: Europe lies in the pincers between Russia and America, which are metaphysically the same, namely in regard to their world-character and their relation to the spirit. The situation of Europe is all the more dire because the disempowering of the spirit comes from Europe itself and—though prepared by earlier factors—is determined at last by its own spiritual situation in the first half of the nineteenth century." Martin Heidegger, *Introduction to Metaphysics* (New Haven, CT: Yale University Press, 2014), 50. On my reading, Heidegger's point is that Europe's vulnerable position between America and Russia reflects the geopolitical situation of the Cold War, when Europe still reeled from the war's immediate aftermath, but that both of these superpowers, and the spiritual impoverishment they symbolize, derive from Europe's own fateful historical development in the nineteenth century. In the sphere of geopolitics, then, Russia and America are not fundamentally different from Europe, either, simply more powerful contestants.

8. This aspect of the philosopher's thought informs Dipesh Chakrabarty's appropriation of Heidegger in *Provincializing Europe*, which produces "affective histories" of India against the secular, universalizing—but also necessary—analytical categories of Marxism. See Chakrabarty, *Provincializing Europe: Postcolonial Thought and Historical Difference* (Princeton, NJ: Princeton University Press, 2000), 18–22 and Part 2, "Histories of Belonging."

9. Heidegger, *Introduction to Metaphysics*, 41.

10. During the Second World War years in America, as Mark Grief notes, a period when German émigrés were altering the U.S. intellectual landscape, "the German discourse to take deepest root in America was the conflict over 'technics.' We would only say 'technology' today. That word does appear to predominate in America in the 1930s, too, but American technology remained, then and now, primarily industrial or mechanical, in the engine, the drill, the dynamo. Where one finds 'technics' as a term in English in the '30s and '40s, there is a good chance it is a sign of penetration from or interchange with the Continental and usually German discourse, from *die Technik* (or, more rarely, *la technique*, the cognate term in French)." In the German and then American usage, "Technics meant something more all-embracing than the machine." Increasingly, technics named not only mechanization but also

"organizational technics that embraced purely social ways of remaking and regimenting man, what we might call 'social technique,' organization, or simply government." Greif, *The Age of the Crisis of Man: Thought and Fiction in America, 1933–1973* (Princeton, NJ: Princeton University Press, 2015), 47.

11. On this last point concerning language and difference, however, one might differentiate Soviet Russia from America, since the former at least attempted, with characteristic overambition and mismanagement, the enfranchisement of Russian minorities and their many languages—a project tantamount to what one scholar felicitously calls an "affirmative action empire." Terry Martin, *The Affirmative Action Empire: Nations and Nationalism in the Soviet Union, 1923–1939* (Ithaca, NY: Cornell University Press, 2001). However misunderstood by black observers, this component of the Soviet experiment struck many African American communists, like Harry Haywood and Richard Wright, as an inspiring contrast with America's persecution of minorities.

12. Martin Heidegger, *What Is Called Thinking?* (New York: Harper and Row, 1968), 11.

13. Martin Heidegger, *Was Heisst Denken?* (Tübingen, Germany: Max Niemeyer Verlag Tübingen, 1954), 11.

14. Heidegger, *Introduction to Metaphysics*, 2. ("In einer Langeweile is die Frage da, wo wir von Verzweiflung und Jubel Gleichweit entfernt sind, wo aber die hart-näckige Gewöhnlichkeit des Seienden eine Öde ausbreitet, in der es uns gleichgültig erscheint, ob das Seiende ist oder ob es nicht ist, womit in eigenartiger Form wieder die Frage anklingt: Warum ist überhaupt Seiendes und nicht vielmehr Nichts?")

15. See Abbott Gleason, *Totalitarianism: The Inner History of the Cold War* (Oxford: Oxford University Press, 1995), 13–30.

16. For an account of the fascist momentum in continental Europe, see Mark Mazower, *Dark Continent: Europe's Twentieth Century* (London: Allen Lane, 1997). Though Mazower does not explore colonialism in Europe's twentieth century, it inflects his sense of Europe's collapse: "Precisely because the Nazi utopia of a dynamic, racially purified German empire required a war for its fulfillment, and because that utopia was also a nightmarish revelation of the destructive potential of European civilization—turning imperialism on its head and treating Europeans as Africans—the experience of fascism's New Order (and its short-lived allure) was forgotten as quickly as possible after 1945." Mazower, *Dark Continent*, xiii. For the "totalitarian spirit" as "spiritual leprosy," see Tzvetan Todorov, *The Totalitarian Experience* (London: Seagull Books, 2001), 35.

17. See Ernst Jünger, *On Pain* (New York: Telos Press, 2008). This ethos, according to Susan Sontag, long outlived the fascist regimes themselves, albeit in late-twentieth-century kitschy forms—SS uniforms and faux Nazi regalia, sadomasochism, occultism, "Third World camp-following," and so on—that Sontag dubs "fascinating fascism," a rejection of materialist and rationalist orientations that recuperates "the ideal of life as art, the cult of beauty, the fetishism of courage, the dissolution of alienation in ecstatic feelings of

community; the repudiation of the intellect; the family of man (under the parenthood of leaders)." The occasion for her essay is a counterrevisionist analysis of Leni Riefenstahl's career, which, according to Sontag, perpetuates the aesthetic appeal of (proto-) Nazism's emphasis on "unlimited aspiration toward the high mystic goal" (embodied, for example, in the ubiquitous metaphor of mountain climbing in German film). See Sontag, "Fascinating Fascism," in *Under the Sign of Saturn* (New York: Picador, 1980), 73–105. For a scholarly volume inspired by (and critical of) Sontag's essay, see Jeffrey T. Schnapp, "Fascinating Fascism," in "The Aesthetics of Fascism," ed. Jeffrey T. Schnapp, special issue, *Journal of Contemporary History* 31, no. 2 (1996): 235–244.

18. Élie Halévy, *The Era of Tyrannies* (Garden City, NY: Doubleday, 1965), 266.

19. See Sheila Fitzpatrick, "Signals from Below: Soviet Letters of Denunciation from the 1930s," in *Accusatory Practices: Denunciation in Modern European History, 1789–1989*, ed. Sheila Fitzpatrick and Robert Gellately (Chicago: University of Chicago Press, 1997), 85–120.

20. "The Nazis," writes Hannah Arendt, ". . . used to comment contemptuously on the shortcomings of their Fascist allies while their genuine admiration for the Bolshevik regime in Russia (and the Communist Party in Germany) was matched and checked only by their contempt for Eastern European races. The only man for whom Hitler had 'unqualified respect' was 'Stalin the genius.'" See Arendt, *The Origins of Totalitarianism* (San Diego, CA: Harcourt, 1973), 309–310.

21. Yet as Melvin P. Leffler and other historians have shown, "Stalin and his new foreign minister, V. M. Molotov, opted for the Nazi-Soviet Pact at the last moment and quite grudgingly. The Kremlin had sought assistance and guarantees from the West." The West reneged on their wartime assurances. "'We would have preferred an agreement with the so-called democratic countries,' Stalin conceded to his closest associates, and 'we entered negotiations with them, but Britain and France wanted us to be their hired hand . . . and without pay.'" See Leffler, *The Specter of Communism: The United States and the Origins of the Cold War, 1917–1953* (New York: Hill and Wang), 26.

22. See Arthur M. Schlesinger Jr., *The Vital Center: The Politics of Freedom* (New York: Transaction Publishers, 1997), and Lionel Trilling, *The Liberal Imagination* (New York: New York Review Books Classics, 2008).

23. "Throughout its career," Slavoj Žižek writes, "'totalitarianism' was an ideological notion that sustained the complex operation of 'taming free radicals,' of guaranteeing the liberal-democratic hegemony." Žižek, *Did Somebody Say Totalitarianism? Five Interventions in the (Mis)Use of a Notion* (New York: Verso, 2001), 2–3. For a critique of Žižek on totalitarianism, see Julia Hell, "Remnants of Totalitarianism: Hannah Arendt, Heiner Müller, Slavoj Žižek, and the Re-Invention of Politics," *Telos* 136 (Summer 2006): 76–103; and Alain Badiou, *The Century* (Cambridge: Polity Press, 2007), 7–8.

24. Badiou, *Century*, 3; and Christoph Cox, Molly Whalen, and Alain Badiou, "On Evil: An Interview with Alain Badiou," *Cabinet*, no. 5 (Winter 2001–02). More recently Badiou has written: "Lumping together Stalin and

Hitler was already a sign of extreme intellectual poverty: the norm by which any collective undertaking has to be judged is, it was argued, the number of deaths it causes. If that were really the case, the huge colonial genocides and massacres, the millions of deaths in the civil and world wars through which our West has forged its might, should be enough to discredit, even in the eyes of 'philosophers' who extol their morality, the parliamentary regimes of Europe and America." Alain Badiou, *The Communist Hypothesis* (London: Verso, 2010), 3.

25. One notable exception to this scholarly tendency is a recent, frequently polemical invocation of "Islamic totalitarianism" that stretches across the ideological spectrum, from neoconservative to liberal and leftist circles, but also among some critics within the Muslim world. "The terrorist attacks of September 11, 2001," writes the historian Anson Rabinbach, "and the debate over the American war in Iraq, revived talk of totalitarianism among liberals and leftists thinking about radical Islamists and Middle East dictatorships." See Rabinbach, "Totalitarianism Revisited," *Dissent Magazine* 53, no. 3 (2006): 77–84. On the failure of the Islamic totalitarianism argument to gain traction in the mainstream public sphere, see Richard Shorten, "The Failure of Political Argument: The Language of Anti-Fascism and Anti-Totalitarianism in Post–September 11th Discourse," *British Journal of Politics and International Relations* 11, no. 3 (2009): 479–503. In different ways, some Muslim scholars, such as Bassam Tibi, Abdullahi Gallab, and Abdullahi Ahmed An-Na'im, endorse a view of the contemporary jihad as a form of mimicry of the totalitarian state and an altogether foreign importation into the religion. See Bassam Tibi, "The Political Legacy of Max Horkheimer and Islamist Totalitarianism," *Telos* 148 (Fall 2009): 7–15; Abdullahi A. Gallab, "The Insecure Rendezvous between Islam and Totalitarianism: The Failure of the Islamist State in the Sudan," *Arab Studies Quarterly* 23, no. 2 (Spring 2001): 87–108; and Boualem Sansal, "There Are Parallels between Islamism and National Socialism," *Qantara*, June 19, 2009, http://en.qantara.de/wcsite.php?wc_c=9075.

26. Whereas some might regard this focus as patently necessary (where else did totalitarianism evolve, or reach its apex?), others might object to this characterization on the grounds that certain narratives of totalitarianism occasionally venture into, or focus on, non-Western geographies. This point may be true, but the tendency in these cases is to highlight autochthonous totalitarian movements, such as Imperial Japan or Maoist China, or in other instances to detour into colonial or strategic war theaters, such as North Africa.

27. Max Horkheimer and Theodor W. Adorno, *Dialectic of Enlightenment: Philosophical Fragments* (Stanford, CA: Stanford University Press, 2002), 3–4. On Habermas's critique of *Dialectic of Enlightenment*, see Jürgen Habermas, *The Philosophical Discourse of Modernity: Twelve Lectures* (Cambridge, MA: MIT Press, 1990), 106–130.

28. On "writing of nonalignment," see Guy Reynolds, *Apostles of Modernity: American Writers in the Age of Development* (Lincoln: University of Nebraska Press, 2008), 105.

29. Donald E. Pease, introduction to *Mariners, Renegades, and Castaways: The Story of Herman Melville and the World We Live In*, by C. L. R. James (Hanover, NH: Dartmouth College Press, 2001), vii–xxxiii.

30. Ibid., 54.

31. Ibid., 14–15.

32. Ibid., 19.

33. Ibid., 10.

34. Ibid.

35. Ibid., 17.

36. Ibid., 51.

37. Ibid., 13.

38. For an account of illiberal disparagement of U.S. liberalism, see Ira Katznelson, *Fear Itself: The New Deal and the Origins of Our Time* (New York: W. W. Norton), especially 5–57.

39. James, *Mariners*, 51.

40. On the significance of the period 1917 to 1941 in the formation of the Cold War, see Leffler, *Specter of Communism*, 3–32. For an account that gestures toward a longer view of mounting tensions between Russia and the United States, see Gordon S. Barrass, *The Great Cold War: A Journey through the Hall of Mirrors* (Stanford, CA: Stanford University Press, 2009).

41. Quoted in Leffler, *Specter of Communism*, 14.

42. See Brent Edwards's *The Practice of Diaspora: Literature, Translation, and the Rise of Black Internationalism* (Cambridge, MA: Harvard University Press, 2003). See also Aric Putnam, *The Insistent Call: Rhetorical Moments in Black Anticolonialism, 1929–1937* (Amherst: University of Massachusetts Press, 2012). For a critique of diaspora discourse centered on its "necessary misrecognitions," see Kenneth Warren, "Appeals for (Mis)recognition: Theorizing the Diaspora," in *Cultures of U.S. Imperialism*, ed. Amy Kaplan and Donald E. Pease (Durham, NC: Duke University Press, 1993). For a critique of the historical scope and coherence of the Black Atlantic, see Kenneth Warren, "Taking Measure of the Black Atlantic," in *States of Emergency: The Object of American Studies*, ed. Russ Castronovo and Susan Gillman (Chapel Hill: University of North Carolina Press, 2009), 116–123. In light of these debates, it's worth noting that even the transnational black writers of Caribbean origin I consider—figures such as C. L. R. James, George Padmore, and Claudia Jones—all spent significant time in the United States and wrote substantially about American culture and politics; others, like Fanon and Césaire, left an indelible imprint on African American culture. By no means do I intend to subsume these figures under the umbrella of a putatively U.S. identity or to drain the cultural specificity of their respective geographies; but I do want to underscore this shifting historical terrain and its implications for black geopolitical critique.

43. "Hanging in the air," Baldwin continues, "as real as the heat from which we suffered, were the great spectres of America and Russia, of the battle going on between them for the domination of the world." James Baldwin, "Princes and Powers," *Encounter*, January 1957, 52–53.

44. For an account of black international literary and ambassadorial activity in the late-nineteenth and early-twentieth centuries, see Brian Russell Roberts, *Artistic Ambassadors: Literary and International Representation of the New Negro Era* (Charlottesville: University of Virginia Press, 2013).

45. See W. E. B. Du Bois, "The Conservation of Races," in *The Oxford W. E. B. Du Bois Reader*, ed. Eric J. Sundquist (Oxford: Oxford University Press, 1996). For his critique of African American exceptionalism, see Paul Gilroy, *The Black Atlantic: Modernity and Double Consciousness* (Cambridge, MA: Harvard University Press, 1994). Regarding globalization and trends toward global analysis, Frederick Cooper notes: "It is salutary to get away from whatever tendencies there may have been to analyze social, economic, political, and cultural processes as if they took place in national and continental containers; but to adopt a language that implies that there is no container at all, except the planetary one, risks defining problems in misleading ways. The world has long been—and still is—a space where economic and political relations are very uneven. . . . Structures and networks penetrate certain places and do certain things with great intensity, but their effects tail off elsewhere." Cooper, *Colonialism in Question: Theory, Knowledge, History* (Berkeley: University of California Press, 2005), 91–92. For the purposes of this study, there are two contrasting points to be drawn from this claim. First, the continued centrality of the nation state, which here functions as the arena in which battles over black citizenship are waged and the space from which black writers claimed special authority to contest U.S. wartime and foreign policy. Second, the historical period analyzed here marks a moment when African American and Third World intellectuals sought, with some success, to equalize the uneven playing field of the Cold War through nonalignment, collaboration, and a robust international print and literary culture. One measure of the efficacy of this literary culture, especially the African American press, is the increased surveillance and response it elicited from U.S. officials—even if its "effects tail off elsewhere."

46. See John Cullen Gruesser, *Black on Black: Twentieth-Century African American Writing about Africa* (Lexington: University Press of Kentucky, 2000), 12–13.

47. On the African American–Third World parallel, Michael Hanchard writes: "Though much maligned for its analytic—as opposed to its analogical—limitations, the parallels between colonialism in the Third World and racial oppression in the United States converge on the roles of violence and temporality. Violence, meted out by the state and by those whom the state vests with qualitatively superior citizenship, structures the process of temporal inequality. In both the colonial and postcolonial contexts, racial difference was the premise for maintaining inequality between U.S. whites and blacks, as well as between Africans and Europeans." Hanchard, "Afro-Modernity: Temporality, Politics, and the African Diaspora," *Public Culture* 11, no. 1 (1999): 266.

48. As Laura Friedman summarizes the state of the field: "The histories of the domestic Cold War and the twentieth-century African American

freedom struggle have both been undergoing dramatic revision in recent years. Scholars of post–Second World War politics and society have increasingly substituted a focus on contradiction and undercurrents of change for the traditional emphasis on consensus and conformity while historians of race and reform have traced the contours of a 'long civil rights movement' that reaches back to the prewar years and encompasses new groups and individuals." See Friedman's review of Dayo F. Gore, *Radicalism at the Crossroads: African American Women Activists in the Cold War*, and Erik S. McDuffie, *Sojourning for Freedom: Black Women, American Communism, and the Making of Black Left Feminism* (Durham, NC: Duke University Press, 2011). Several recent studies include Kate Baldwin, *Beyond the Color Line and the Iron Curtain: Reading Encounters between Black and Red, 1922–1963* (Durham, NC: Duke University Press, 2002); Thomas Borstellmann, *The Cold War and the Color Line: American Race Relations in the Global Arena* (Cambridge, MA: Harvard University Press, 2003); John C. Charles, *Abandoning the Black Hero: Sympathy and Privacy in the Postwar African American Novel* (New York: New York University Press, 2013); Carol Boyce Davies, *Left of Karl Marx: The Political Life of Black Communist Claudia Jones* (Durham, NC: Duke University Press, 2008); Kevin Gaines, *American Africans in Ghana: Black Expatriates and the Civil Rights Era* (Chapel Hill: University of North Carolina Press, 2007); Dayo Gore, *Radicalism at the Crossroads: African American Women Activists in the Cold War* (New York: New York University Press, 2012); Cheryl Higashida, *Black Internationalist Feminism: Women Writers of the Black Left, 1945–1995* (Urbana: University of Illinois Press, 2011); Lawrence Jackson, *The Indignant Generation: A Narrative History of African American Writers and Critics, 1934–1960* (Princeton, NJ: Princeton University Press, 2011); Richard H. King, *Race, Culture, and the Intellectuals, 1940–1970* (Baltimore: Johns Hopkins University Press, 2004); Erik S. McDuffie, *Sojourning for Freedom: Black Women, American Communism, and the Making of Black Left Feminism* (Durham, NC: Duke University Press, 2011); Stacy I. Morgan, *Rethinking Social Realism: African American Art and Literature, 1930–1953* (Athens: University of Georgia Press, 2004); Toni Perucci, *Paul Robeson and the Cold War Performance Complex: Race, Madness, Activism* (Ann Arbor: University of Michigan Press, 2012); Eric Porter, *The Problem of the Future World: W. E. B. Du Bois and the Race Concept at Midcentury* (Durham, NC: Duke University Press, 2010); and Nikhil Pal Singh, *Black Is a Country: Race and the Unfinished Struggle for Democracy* (Cambridge, MA: Harvard University Press, 2005).

49. Abbott Gleason, *Totalitarianism: The Inner History of the Cold War* (Oxford: Oxford University Press, 1995), 3. For a precise formulation of the relationship between desegregation, decolonization, and Cold War politics through the work of St. Claire Drake and Claudia Jones, see Kevin Gaines, "Locating the Transnational in Postwar African American History," *small axe* 13, no. 1 (March 2009): 193–202.

50. It is important, however, not to assert the priority of globalization naively, since many commentators have noted that conceptions of the global long predate modernity or postmodernity; or that the present emergence of

a global consciousness is itself a phenomenon to be historicized; and that, inadvertently, various modes of transnational inquiry (for instance, on global cultural flows) appear symptomatic of processes of late global capitalism itself. Subsequent chapters work out this issue in greater detail, but Samuel Moyn and Andrew Sartori helpfully articulate the methodological space in which this project moves:

> A global intellectual history might compare intellectuals or intellectual practices or ideas or concepts geographically or chronologically. In such an enterprise, the point might be to elaborate on processes or tendencies that developed on a global scale or to use comparison to elaborate on the different processes or tendencies that developed in different parts of the world or in different eras. Indeed, a minimal conception of the idea of a "global intellectual history" might be seen as merely a call to create a more inclusive intellectual history that respects the diversity of intellectual traditions and broadens the parameters of thought beyond the narrow limits defined by the traditions institutionalized in the Western or Eurocentric academy. In other words, it would be a call to attend to non-Western intellectual histories with a rigor commensurate with the scholarship on Western intellectual histories. (Moyn and Sartori, "Approaches to Global Intellectual History," in *Global Intellectual History*, ed. Samuel Moyn and Andrew Sartori [New York: Columbia University Press, 2013], 7)

As I indicate in what follows, my emphasis involves not only inclusivity as such but also an epistemological claim grounded in my revision of the intellectual history of totalitarianism. That said, Moyn and Sartori are alert to the possibility "that historically specific forms of connectedness provide an epistemological foundation for specific kinds of comparison." Ibid., 8.

51. Recent scholarship, however, proves that the tendency to dismiss or repudiate Du Bois's late writings about the Soviet Union and Mao's China is changing. I treat this revisionist scholarship in Chapter 3 but want to acknowledge here one recent effort: Bill V. Mullen's *Un-American: W. E. B. Du Bois and the Century of World Revolution* (Philadelphia: Temple University Press, 2015).

52. Porter, *Problem of the Future World*, 156.

CHAPTER 1 The Figure of the Negro Soldier

1. Of course, not every colonial subject who fought in the wars was a conscript in the strict sense of that term. My usage draws on David Scott's notion of "conscripts of modernity," namely, blacks in the diaspora (especially the Caribbean) who, conscripted into the modern Western order, are both subjects and objects of history whose thwarted stories of rebellion against this order can be told—following C. L. R. James in his revised 1963 version of *The Black Jacobins*—through the form of tragedy. See Scott, *Conscripts of Modernity: The Tragedy of Colonial Enlightenment* (Durham, NC: Duke University Press, 2004).

2. "No Peace until Double Victory," *Pittsburgh [PA] Courier*, May 2, 1942, 5.

3. "Editorial Note: Racial Minorities and the Present International Crisis," *Journal of Negro Education* 10, no. 3 (July 1941): 305. "Since it has been deemed necessary to resort to a process of sampling," the editor, Charles H. Thompson, described their collective definition of "racial minorities" to include "as typical of minorities in the Eastern Hemisphere: the African native as typical of Africa; and the European Jew, of Europe. In the Western Hemisphere, our sampling includes: the Indian and Negro in South America, the Negro in the Caribbean area, and the Negro and Jew in continental United States." Ibid., 308.

4. "Editorial Note: The American Negro in World War I and World War II," *Journal of Negro Education* 12, no. 3 (Summer 1943): 267.

5. "Editorial Note: Racial Minorities and the Present International Crisis," 306.

6. Santanu Das, introduction to *Race, Empire, and First World War Writing*, ed. Santanu Das (Cambridge: Cambridge University Press, 2011), 4.

7. Ethel L. Williams, "A Tribute to the Negro War Correspondent," *Negro History Bulletin* 8, no. 5 (February 1, 1945): 110.

8. Patrik Ouředník, *Europeana: A Brief History of the Twentieth Century* (London: Dalkey Archive Press, 2005), 1.

9. Ernst Jünger, *On Pain* (New York: Telos Press, 2008), 21.

10. "Until the First World War," writes Myron Echenberg,

> the *Tirailleurs Sénégalais* was essentially a mercenary army. It was composed of volunteer soldiers attracted by a variety of incentives, whose numbers were supplemented by partial conscription through the terms of the Conscription Law of 1912. The First World War changed the *Tirailleurs Sénégalais* forever. Not only did French officials themselves admit that wartime recruitment was conducted by coercive methods reminiscent of the repudiated era of the slave trade. Even more dramatic was the decision of the Clemenceau government in 1919 to maintain and expand a conscript rather than a volunteer army by the introduction of universal peacetime conscription in FWA. (Echenberg, *Colonial Conscripts: The* Tirailleurs Sénégalais *in French West Africa, 1857–1960* [Portsmouth, NH: Heinemann Books, 1991], 42–43)

11. Ibid., 42–46.

12. Ibid., 2.

13. Joe Lunn, "France's Legacy to Demba Mboup? A Senegalese Griot and His Descendants Remember His Military Service during the First World War," in Das, *Race, Empire, and First World War Writing*, 118–119. As Lunn observes in his essay's postscript, the descendants of First World War veteran Demba Mboup differ on the meaning of his service and that of other Tirailleurs Sénégalais. One daughter stressed Mboup's acquisition of French nationality and the material benefits of his service, which enabled him to provide well for his family; a grandson, though proud of his grandfather's heroism, rejects the version of the past preserved in oral histories—largely on account of his viewing Sembène's film, *Camp de Thiaroye*. "Three points," writes Lunn,

> exemplified French injustice toward the former soldiers in his view: the "inequality" of the Senegalese veterans' pensions compared with those of their French counterparts; the "killing of many" of the returning African POWs in 1944 at Thiaroye by the colonial authorities—a collective memory significantly transmitted in his case through Ousmane Sembène's film *Camp de Thiaroye* instead of through oral traditions as among earlier generations; and the denial of admission into France to "the sons" of Senegalese veterans who fought to defend the country against German aggression during the two world wars. Although he felt pride in the courage exhibited by his grandfather, he was indignant that he had been used by the French in such a way. (19)

14. See Richard Iton, *In Search of the Black Fantastic* (Oxford: Oxford University Press, 2008), 261–262.

15. Adrian Lentz-Smith, *Freedom Struggles: African Americans and World War I* (Cambridge, MA: Harvard University Press, 2009), 8.

16. William J. Maxwell, *F.B. Eyes: How J. Edgar Hoover's Ghostreaders Framed African American Literature* (Princeton, NJ: Princeton University Press, 2015); and Mark Ellis, *Race, War, and Surveillance: African Americans and the United States Government during World War I* (Bloomington: Indiana University Press, 2001).

17. As Alain Badiou explains the connection between the Scramble for Africa and the onset of total war,

> Well before the war of 1914, there is Africa, delivered over to what some rare witnesses call an upright conquering savagery. . . . After two or three centuries of the deportation of human meat for the purposes of slavery, conquest managed to turn Africa into the horrific obverse of European, capitalist, democratic splendor. And this continues to our very day. In the dark fury of the thirties, in the indifference to death, there is something that certainly originates in the Great War and the trenches, but also something that comes—as a sort of infernal return—from the colonies, from the way that the differences in humanity were envisaged down there. (Badiou, *The Century* [Cambridge: Polity Press, 2007], 7–8)

18. W. E. B. Du Bois, "The African Roots of War," *Atlantic Monthly*, May 1914, 711.

19. As Robert B. Pippen points out, "At the heart of Conrad's *Heart of Darkness* is not a universal truth about 'unbridled' or 'uncivilized' man as he is in himself, despite the way the novel is commonly read. At the 'Heart of Darkness' Marlowe finds an outpost of modern European commerce and the most efficient ivory-trading company employee in history, a completely consistent and so mad representative of 'all Europe.'" Pippen, *Modernism as a Philosophical Problem: On the Dissatisfactions of European High Culture* (Oxford: Blackwell, 1999), 39–40. On Arendt's account of the role of the Scramble for Africa in the making of totalitarianism in Europe, see Hannah Arendt, *The Origins of Totalitarianism* (San Diego, CA: Harcourt, 1973), 185–221. Chapter 2 considers the critical reception of Arendt's argument on colonialism.

20. W. E. B. Du Bois, "Close Ranks," *The Crisis* 16 (July 1918): 111. See also Mark Ellis, "'Closing Ranks' and 'Seeking Honors': W. E. B. Du Bois in World War I," *Journal of American History* 79, no. 1 (June 1992): 96–124. Exploring the coincidence between Du Bois's "accommodationist" editorial and his application for a captain position with the Military Intelligence Branch, "an antiradical agency of the United States Army General Staff," Ellis notes: "Du Bois was to recall World War I with a mixture of shame and bitterness for the next forty years." For a response to Ellis, see William Jordan, "'The Damnable Dilemma': African-American Accommodation and Protest during World War I," *Journal of American History* 81, no. 4 (March 1995): 1562–1583.

21. Das, *Race, Empire and First World War Writing*, 17. Das continues: "But did the war experience radicalize the soldiers and workers who actually served? While it was not always possible to draw a direct trajectory between war experience and anti-colonial resistance, several essays [in this edited volume] indicate that the war significantly raised levels of self-confidence and political, national or racial awareness among different groups."

22. Richard Smith, "'Heaven Grant You Strength to Fight the Battle for Your Race': Nationalism, Pan-Africanism, and the First World War in Jamaican Memory," in Das, *Race, Empire and First World War Writing*, 267–268. Ironically, pro-war sentiment among Jamaicans, who believed that a Prussian victory would reintroduce slavery, often took the form of a defense of British imperialism.

23. Harry Haywood, *A Black Communist in the Freedom Struggle: The Life of Harry Haywood* (Minneapolis: University of Minnesota Press, 2012), 72.

24. On Césaire's notion of *Un Choc au Retour* in dialogue with Conrad and Arendt, see Michael Rothberg, *Multidirectional Memory: Remembering the Holocaust in the Age of Decolonization* (Stanford, CA: Stanford University Press, 2009), 33–107.

25. "Luckily, not much imagination was needed for the job," Harrington says of his first position as a cartoonist for the *Amsterdam News* in the 1930s. "I simply recorded the almost unbelievable but hilarious chaos around me and came up with a character." Eric Page, "Oliver Harrington, Cartoonist Who Created 'Bootsie,' Dies at 84," *New York Times*, November 7, 1995.

26. "'Nazi Treatment Unlike U.S.,' Embree," *Pittsburgh Courier*, February 28, 1942, 3.

27. Dominic J. Capeci Jr., "The Lynching of Cleo Wright: Federal Protection of Constitutional Rights during World War II," *Journal of American History* 72, no. 4 (March 1986): 859; and Capeci, *The Lynching of Cleo Wright* (Lexington: University of Kentucky Press, 1998).

28. "Doing Something about Lynching," *Pittsburgh Courier*, February 28, 1942, 6.

29. Horace Cayton, "White Man's War, But Negroes Are Fighting on 2 Fronts for Democratic War," *Pittsburgh Courier*, February 28, 1942, 13.

30. In "Gay Chaps," writes one critic, Brooks "displaces both the site and meaning of war, and in her hands it becomes a civil struggle, one fought on the

terrain of white racism. . . . She rewrites 'war' as a complex tissue of meaning and signification; the battlefield exists simultaneously on foreign fronts, in the trenches, on Chicago streets, even at home." Ann Folwell Stanford, "Dialectics of Desire and the Resistive Voice in Gwendolyn Brooks's 'Negro Hero' and 'Gay Chaps at the Bar,'" *African American Review* 26, no. 2 (1992): 197–198.

31. See Thomas Cripps and David Culbert, "*The Negro Soldier* (1944): Film Propaganda in Black and White," *American Quarterly* 31, no. 5 (Winter 1979): 616–640.

32. David A. Gerber, "Heroes and Misfits: The Troubled Social Reintegration of Disabled Veterans in *The Best Years of Our Lives*," in *Disabled Veterans in History*, ed. David A. Gerber (Ann Arbor: University of Michigan Press, 2000), 71–72.

33. Lucille B. Milner, "Jim Crow in the Army," *New Republic* 110 (March 13, 1944): 339.

34. As Jennifer James notes, Brooks reprises the figure of the "disabled" black vet in the closing chapters of her novel *Maud Martha* (1953). See Jennifer C. James, *A Freedom Bought with Blood: African American War Literature from the Civil War to World War II* (Chapel Hill: University of North Carolina Press, 2007), 232–259.

35. Toni Morrison, *Home* (New York: Vintage, 2012), 108.

36. Ira Katznelson, *Desolation and Enlightenment: Political Knowledge after Total War, Totalitarianism, and the Holocaust* (New York: Columbia University Press, 2003), 20.

37. James Baldwin, "The Fire Next Time," in *The Price of the Ticket: Collected Nonfiction, 1948–1985* (New York: St. Martin's Press, 1985), 52–53.

38. Alan M. Wald, *Trinity of Passion: The Literary Left and the Antifascist Crusade* (Chapel Hill: University of North Carolina Press, 2007), 62–66.

39. Ann Petry, "In Darkness and Confusion," in *Miss Muriel and Other Stories* (New York: Kensington, 2008), 258.

40. Ibid., 262.

41. Ibid., 265.

42. Ibid., 268.

43. Ibid., 277–279.

44. Ibid., 280.

45. Ibid., 282.

46. See Robin D. G. Kelley, *Race Rebels: Culture, Politics, and the Black Working Class* (New York: Free Press, 1996), 123–160. See also John Cullen Gruesser, *Black on Black: Twentieth-Century African American Writing about Africa* (Lexington: University of Kentucky Press, 2000), 94–119; Aric Putnam, *The Insistent Call: Rhetorical Moments in Black Anticolonialism, 1929–1937* (Amherst: University of Massachusetts Press, 2012), 97–118; and Mark R. Scott, *The Sons of Sheba's Race: African-Americans and the Italo-Ethiopian War* (Bloomington: Indiana University Press, 1993). Ichiro Takayoshi writes: "'In 1935, Italian troops invaded Ethiopia,' notes a later historian, 'and, in the eyes of black observers the world over, inaugurated World War II.' With the outbreak of the new African conflict, American prewar writers, most notably

those of African descent, began producing works that explored the meaning of the world crisis to their country with an altogether unprecedented degree of urgency and seriousness. To put this all rather dramatically, the Fascist invasion of the oldest sovereign nation in the horn of Africa gave birth to the prewar literary culture." Takayoshi, *American Writers and the Approach of World War II, 1935–1941: A Literary History* (Cambridge: Cambridge University Press, 2015), 45.

47. On contemporary memory of Fanon in Algeria, see the documentary film by Cheikh Djemaï, *Frantz Fanon: une vie, un combat, une œuvre* (New York: ArtMattan Productions, 2001).

48. Since few wish to reprise the twentieth century's catastrophes, writes Badiou, the challenge is "to create a new paradigm of heroism beyond war, a figure that is neither that of the warrior nor that of the soldier." But in the absence of *any* heroic figure, we are left with the resurrection of reactionary forces, of "old dead gods," and the "strict inhumanity of technological murder and the bureaucratic surveillance of all aspects of life. . . . In fact, without an active figure involving an element of creative value, we have only a formless conflict between the old religious sacrifice and the blind will of capitalist control." Alain Badiou, *Philosophy for Militants* (London: Verso, 2012), 41–44.

49. Roland Barthes, *Mythologies* (New York: Hill and Wang, 1972), 116.

50. Leonard Freed, *Black in White America* (Los Angeles: Getty Publications, 2010), 3.

51. Albert Murray, "White Norms, Black Deviation," in *The Death of White Sociology: Essays on Race and Culture*, ed. Joyce A. Ladner (New York: Random House, 1973), 97.

52. Regarding the alleged naiveté of African American positions in the international arena, Brenda Plummer writes: "That increasing numbers of African Americans embarked on such trips to such places as Israel and the Soviet Union does not mean that the African-American foreign policy interest is based on naiveté, as certain scholars have snidely implied. In the search for power, all parties have their interests at heart, although the resources at their disposal to realize their goals may vary." See Brenda Gayle Plummer, *In Search of Power: African Americans in the Era of Decolonization, 1956–1974* (Cambridge: Cambridge University Press, 2013), 149.

53. Quoted in Maria Höhn and Martin Klimke, *A Breath of Freedom: The Civil Rights Struggle, African American GIs, and Germany* (New York: Palgrave Macmillan, 2010), 54. One reviewer of Smith's novel wrote: "There is a disturbing parallel between the attitudes of these soldiers—who when they were abroad felt the breath of the only kind of freedom they long for—and the people behind the Iron Curtain in Europe and Russia who see in the West political and intellectual emancipation." Harrison Smith, "Land of Freedom?" *Saturday Review*, August 28, 1948, 14–15.

54. Frederick Taylor, *Exorcising Hitler: The Occupation and Denazification of Germany* (New York: Bloomsbury Press, 2011).

55. For a more surrealist or expressionist drama of race and slavery set in the American South, see Fassbinder's enigmatic film *Whity* (1970), which

centers on an obsequious mulatto servant who serves his white master (and illegitimate father) to the point of murder.

56. Höhn and Klimke, *Breath of Freedom*, 1–3.

57. See "Angela Davis: Black Soldier," and Milton White, "Self-Determination for Black Soldiers," *Black Scholar* 2, no. 3 (November 1970): 1, 40–46.

58. Richard H. King, *Race, Culture, and the Intellectuals, 1940–1970* (Baltimore: Johns Hopkins University Press, 2004); Newton quoted in Carol Anderson, "The Histories of African American Anticolonialism during the Cold War," in *The Cold War in the Third World*, ed. Robert J. McMahon (Oxford: Oxford University Press, 2013), 182. For example, Huey Newton, cofounder of the Black Panther Party, "alerted the Communist guerillas in South Vietnam that the Panthers 'would . . . recruit an African American unit to fight with the National Liberation Front,' the Vietcong, against the U.S. armed forces." Yet as Anderson notes, "For all the revolutionary bravado on display, the reality was decidedly more mundane. Detroit, Newark, and the scores of other cities ablaze in the late 1960s were not training grounds for guerillas-in-waiting or boot camps for black commandos on their way to Angola and Vietnam to fight for colonial liberation" (183). Rather, the radical ferment in these blighted cities expressed the economic disfranchisement, police brutality, and decaying educational and social institutions that African Americans found increasingly intolerable in the 1960s and 1970s.

CHAPTER 2 Our Totalitarian Critics

1. See *To Secure These Rights: The Report of the President's Committee on Civil Rights*, 148, http://www.trumanlibrary.org/civilrights/srights1.htm.

2. In a special message to Congress on February 2, 1948, President Truman outlined several civil rights initiatives. Truman instructed the Congress that the "position of the United States in the world today" makes the matter of civil rights "especially urgent." As the Cold War gains momentum, the "peoples of the world are faced with the choice of freedom or enslavement." Appearing in Harlem on October 29, 1948—during the middle of his election campaign and after his executive orders to desegregate the nation's military and federal workforce—Truman said, "Today the democratic way of life is being challenged all over the world. Democracy's answer to the challenge of totalitarianism is its promise of equal rights and equal opportunities for all mankind." Truman, Address in Harlem, New York, upon Receiving the Franklin Roosevelt Award, http://www.trumanlibrary.org/publicpapers/index.php?pid=2016.

3. Consider one passage, not necessarily exemplary, from the report:

> At the same time we are afraid that the "reason" upon which [Thomas] Jefferson relied to combat error is hampered by the successful effort of some totalitarians to conceal their true nature. To expect people to reject totalitarians, when we do not provide mechanisms to guarantee that

> essential information is available, is foolhardy. These two concerns go together. If we fall back upon hysteria and repression as our weapons against totalitarians, we will defeat ourselves. Communists want nothing more than to be lumped with freedom-loving non-Communists. This simply makes it easier for them to conceal their true nature and to allege that the term "Communist" is "meaningless." Irresponsible opportunists who make it a practice to attack every person or group with whom they disagree as "Communists" have thereby actually aided their supposed "enemies." At the same time we cannot let these abuses deter us from the legitimate exposing of real Communists and real Fascists. Moreover, the same zeal must be shown in defending our democracy against one group as against the other. (*To Secure These Rights*, 49)

I adapt these examples of Truman and Eisenhower's civil rights initiatives from Mary L. Dudziak, *Cold War Civil Rights: Race and the Image of American Democracy* (Princeton, NJ: Princeton University Press, 2000).

4. "Third World states could help to validate one or the other of those rival ideologies when they opted to embrace either democratic capitalism or Soviet-style socialism as the true path to modernist transformation. . . . For a mélange of reasons, consequently, Soviets and Americans alike came to envisage vast stretches of the Third World as more than just instrumental in maintaining the overall balance of military, economic, and political power in the international arena." Robert J. McMahon, ed., *The Cold War in the Third World* (Oxford: Oxford University Press, 2013), 2–3.

5. Kenneth A. Osgood, "Words and Deeds: Race, Colonialism, and Eisenhower's Propaganda War in the Third World," in *The Eisenhower Administration, the Third World, and the Globalization of the Cold War*, ed. Kathryn C. Statler and Andrew L. Johns (Lanham, MD: Rowman and Littlefield, 2006), 3–4.

6. Michael R. Adamson, "'The Most Important Single Aspect of Our Foreign Policy'? The Eisenhower Administration, Foreign Aid, and the Third World," in Statler and Johns, *Eisenhower Administration, the Third World, and the Globalization of the Cold War*, 47–72.

7. Quoted in Dudziak, *Cold War Civil Rights*, 139–140.

8. With respect to desegregation, evocations of the "totalitarian threat" cut both ways. In a discursive twist, Southern reactionaries also invoked the term in response to the federal government's deployment of troops in Little Rock, and even to legislation such as the antidiscrimination Fair Employment Practice Committee bill. See Dudziak, *Cold War Civil Rights*, 136; and Ira Katznelson, *Fear Itself: The New Deal and the Origins of Our Time* (New York: Liveright Publishing, 2013), 189.

9. Sheila Fitzpatrick and Michael Geyer, eds., *Beyond Totalitarianism: Stalinism and Nazism Compared* (Cambridge: Cambridge University Press, 2009), 1–37. For another comparative volume, more ideologically committed to the Nazism-Stalinism equation, see *Stalinism and Nazism: History and Memory Compared*, ed. Henry Rousso (Lincoln: University of Nebraska Press, 2004).

10. Albert Memmi, *The Colonizer and the Colonized* (Boston: Beacon Press, 1991), 62–63: "What is fascism, if not a regime of oppression for the benefit

of a few? The entire administrative and political machinery of a colony has no other goal. The human relationships have arisen from the severest exploitation, founded on inequality and contempt, guaranteed by police authoritarianism. There is no doubt in the minds of those who have lived through it that colonialism is one variety of fascism. . . . This totalitarian aspect which even democratic regimes take on in their colonies is contradictory in appearance only."

11. See *Le livre noir du colonialisme: Xvie–xxie siècle; De l'extermination à la repentance*, ed. Marc Ferro (Paris: Robert Laffont, 2003). *The Black Book of Communism* is a global compendium of state-sponsored communist crimes—summary executions, torture, enforced famines, psychological devastation, deportations, liquidation of entire classes or groups—composed mainly by former French communists and fellow travelers. See *The Black Book of Communism: Crimes, Terror, Repression*, ed. Mark Kramer (Cambridge, MA: Harvard University Press, 1997).

12. For a summary of and a series of contributions to this debate, see Volker Langbehn and Mohammad Salama, eds., *German Colonialism: Race, the Holocaust, and Postwar Germany* (New York: Columbia University Press, 2011), iv–xxxi. Proponents of the continuity thesis credit Arendt's theory of totalitarianism, with its lengthy discussion of the Scramble for Africa in its "Imperialism" chapter, as the inspiration for this argument. For a challenge to this interpretation of Arendt, see A. Dirk Moses, "Hannah Arendt, Imperialisms, and the Holocaust," in Langbehn and Salama, *German Colonialism*, 72–92.

13. See Moses, "Hannah Arendt, Imperialisms, and the Holocaust," 85; and Michael Rothberg, *Multidirectional Memory: Remembering the Holocaust in the Age of Decolonization* (Stanford, CA: Stanford University Press, 2009).

14. Fredric Jameson, *Valences of the Dialectic* (London: Verso, 2010), 215–216.

15. Ibid., 219–220. Jameson continues: "Other groups' experience of fear is occasional, rather than constitutive: standpoint analysis specifically demands a differentiation between the various negative experiences of constraint, between the *exploitation* suffered by workers and the *oppression* suffered by women and continuing on through the distinct structural forms of exclusion and alienation characteristic of other kinds of group experience."

16. Ralph Ellison, "Remembering Richard Wright," in *The Collected Essays of Ralph Ellison* (New York: Random House, 1995), 659–675.

17. See Dudziak, *Cold War Civil Rights*, 47–55.

18. In 1968, Richard M. Dalfiume was among the first scholars to recognize that the Second World War spurred black militancy and "planted the seeds" for "the civil rights revolution of the 1950s and 1960s." See Dalfiume, "The 'Forgotten Years' of the Negro Revolution," *Journal of American History* 55, no. 1 (June 1968): 90–106.

19. One historian argues that Walter White, in his capacity as secretary of the NAACP, abandoned his anticolonial solidarity and embraced liberal anticommunism at the behest of U.S. State Department officials, who promised him greater influence—later reneged upon—in the formulation of domestic

race relations policy. See Kenneth R. Janken, "From Colonial Liberation to Cold War Liberalism: Walter White, the NAACP, and Foreign Affairs, 1941–1955," *Ethnic and Racial Studies* 21, no. 6 (November 1998): 1074–1095. For a similar discussion centered on the United Nations delegate Edith Sampson, invited by Walter White and the State Department to join its worldwide Voice of America tour, see "Symposium: African Americans and U.S. Foreign Relations," in *Diplomatic History* 20, no. 4 (Fall 1996): 531–650, especially the following essays: Helen Laville and Scott Lucas, "The American Way: Edith Sampson, the NAACP, and African American Identity in the Cold War," 565–590; Gerald Horne, "Who Lost the Cold War? Africans and African Americans," 613–626; Carol Anderson, "From Hope to Disillusion: African Americans, the United Nations, and the Struggle for Human Rights, 1944–1947," 531–564; and Brenda Gayle Plummer, "'Below the Level of Men': African Americans, Race, and the History of U.S. Foreign Relations," 639–650.

Horne criticizes Laville, Lucas, and, to a lesser degree, Anderson for understating the profound political losses that Africans and African Americans sustained with the end of the Cold War. Without the field-leveling presence of the Soviet Union and the support of a robust international left, Horne argues, Africans and African Americans effectively surrendered political strength despite numerous civil rights concessions granted by the U.S. government. The decline of the secular left, Horne observes, also created a vacuum filled by religious "fundamentalism" in Africa and, in the U.S. context, restricted the previously outspoken NAACP from assailing racial injustice—the price to be paid for a closer rapprochement with the State Department. Anderson, however, asserts that the NAACP did not merely abandon anticolonial for domestic concerns; instead, it "mastered the arcane rules and power relationships at the State Department, the United Nations, and the White House to undermine the global legitimacy of colonialism and white supremacy." Carol Anderson, "The Histories of African American Colonialism during the Cold War," in McMahon, *Cold War in the Third World*, 184. For an essay on the domestic repudiation of Martin Luther King Jr.'s critique of U.S. foreign policy, especially his denunciation of the Vietnam War, see Thomas J. Noer, "Martin Luther King Jr. and the Cold War," *Peace and Change* 22, no. 2 (April 1997): 111–131. For a recent summation of this field, see John Munro and Ian Rocksborough-Smith, "Reframing Black Internationalism and Civil Rights during the Cold War," *Journal of American Studies of Turkey* 29 (2009): 63–78.

20. "In the face of anticommunist repression domestically, liberal African American leaders in the NAACP and other black political organizations retreated from any form of militant anticolonialism." Erik S. McDuffie, "Black and Red: Black Liberation, the Cold War, and the Horne Thesis," *Journal of African American History* 96, no. 2 (Spring 2011): 241.

21. Jan-Werner Müller, "Fear and Freedom: On 'Cold War Liberalism,'" *European Journal of Political Theory* 7, no. 1 (2008): 47.

22. Ibid., 45–64. Müller continues:

> It was concerned with fear in two senses: it was a minimal or negative liberalism, or, as others have put it, a "liberalism without illusions" that was fearful of ambitious programmes advanced by those who felt absolutely certain in their convictions and sure about their political prescriptions. But it also was based on the insight that many political evils and pathologies ultimately originated in fear itself: Popper, for instance, spoke of the typical "fear of admitting to ourselves that the responsibility for our ethical decisions is entirely ours and cannot be shifted to anybody else." This kind of fear was then said to be crucial in motivating the plunge into totalitarian ideology. (47–48)

For a literary account of Cold War liberalism, see Amanda Anderson, "Character and Ideology: The Case of Cold War Liberalism," *New Literary History* 42, no. 2 (2011): 209–229. Anderson draws attention to the neglected character traits and affective states—such as optimism, irony, and pessimism—that attend descriptions of Cold War liberalism. Similarly, we might note a corollary set of traits characterizing totalitarian leadership: obsessive suspiciousness, lust for power, fear and anxiety over the status of his regime, and so on.

23. Paul Robeson, *Here I Stand* (Boston: Beacon Press, 1988), 81–82.

24. See Penny Von Eschen, *Satchmo Blows Up the World: Jazz Ambassadors Play the Cold War* (Cambridge, MA: Harvard University Press, 2004).

25. Brenda Gayle Plummer, *In Search of Power: African Americans in the Era of Decolonization* (Cambridge: Cambridge University Press, 2013), 27.

26. Richard Iton, *In Search of the Black Fantastic: Politics and Popular Culture in the Post–Civil Rights Era* (Oxford: Oxford University Press, 2008), 48.

27. "Ironically," Von Eschen observes, "many of [Dizzy] Gillespie's ties to Brazilian and South American artists were built partly through his State Department tours." Yet these ties did not necessarily "ironically" undermine the state's objectives. Brian Russell Roberts seizes the crucial point here: "Gillespie's race-based ties to South American musicians would have contributed to what one US official described as public diplomacy's effort to 'provide the United States with . . . stable cultural bridges to Latin America.' I would suggest, then, that the irony Von Eschen notes in Gillespie's situation is more a function of the present-day critical default position that sees color-based transnationalism as official internationalism's subversive counterdiscourse." Roberts's point is astute, as U.S. officials promoted precisely these forms of intercultural, race-based collaborations in order to bolster national interests—but in later decades, it is also the case that these delegations were viable to the extent that they did not lead to anticolonial or left internationalist projects deemed inimical to these interests. Von Eschen, *Satchmo Blows Up the World*, 127; see also Roberts, *Artistic Ambassadors: Literary and International Representation of the New Negro Era* (Charlottesville: University of Virginia Press, 2013).

28. Barbara Foley, *Wrestling with the Left: The Making of Ralph Ellison's* Invisible Man (Durham, NC: Duke University Press, 2010). For an argument

that *Invisible Man,* rather than capitulating to Cold War ideology, gave voice to the black radicalism of the 1940s, see Christopher Z. Hobson, "*Invisible Man* and African American Radicalism in World War II," *African American Review* 39, no. 3 (2005): 355–376.

29. Arnold Rampersad, *Ralph Ellison: A Biography* (New York: Knopf, 2007), 244–245.

30. "She customarily gives the impression," Wald writes, "that her work at the *People's Voice* was merely a paying job on a traditional newspaper, or she confines her Harlem journalistic experience to the *Amsterdam News.*" Alan M. Wald, *Trinity of Passion: The Literary Left and the Antifascist Crusade* (Chapel Hill: University of North Carolina Press, 2007), 116.

31. Ann Lane Petry, "The Novel as Social Criticism," in *The Writer's Book,* ed. Helen Hull (New York: Harper Brothers, 1950), 31–39. Petry continues: "This particular label has been used so extensively in recent years that the ghost of Marx seems even livelier than that of Hamlet's father's ghost or at least he, Marx, appears to have done his haunting over more of the world's surface" (33). In a new appraisal of Petry, Farah Jasmine Griffin remarks of this essay that "most certainly, during the Cold War, even the most right wing of readers would not argue with the importance of biblical injunctions." Griffin, *Harlem Nocturne: Women Artists and Progressive Politics during World War II* (New York: Basic Civitas, 2013), 115–117.

32. Carol Anderson, "The Histories of African American Anticolonialism during the Cold War," in McMahon, *Cold War in the Third World,* 180.

33. "Certainly by August of 1939," writes Thomas Hill Schaub, "a great many liberals, social democrats, socialists, and communists had long ago separated themselves from Stalinist communism, developed loyalties to Trotsky or other communist and socialist alternatives, or had turned their backs on communism altogether. Their decisions were invariably accompanied by narratives of maturation and realism, of awakening to a more sober and skeptical perception of political reality and human nature." Schaub, *American Fiction in the Cold War* (Madison: University of Wisconsin Press, 1991), 6–7.

34. Yet it is important to acknowledge here the contribution of Alan Wald's trilogy on the U.S. antifascist literary left, especially the last volume, *American Night.* Against the conventional wisdom that postwar American literature capitulated wholesale to the trend toward postwar liberalism, his study delineates the debates and permutations, publishing ventures and aesthetic experiments of a wide (if somewhat obscure) array of leftist writers and intellectuals who were still very active during the early Cold War years. See Alan M. Wald, *American Night: The Literary Left in the Era of the Cold War* (Chapel Hill: University of North Carolina Press, 2012). For an account of postwar American fiction that concentrates on writers who substituted sociology and class struggle for psychology and interiority, or Marx for Freud, see Morris J. Dickstein, *Leopards in the Temple: The Transformation of American Fiction, 1945–1970* (Cambridge, MA: Harvard University Press, 2002). What differentiates Dickstein's account from similar arguments is his focus on emergent black and Jewish writers as "outsiders," inspired by Dos-

toyevsky's underground, whose success eventually transformed American fiction by propelling their marginal protagonists to the cultural center.

35. Irving Howe, "Black Boys and Native Sons," *Dissent* 10 (Autumn 1963): 353–368. For a reappraisal of this debate, see Darryl Lorenzo Wellington, "Fighting at Cross-Purposes: Irving Howe vs. Ralph Ellison," *Dissent* 52, no. 3 (Summer 2005): 101–105.

36. "Liberalism and the Negro: A Roundtable Discussion," *Commentary* 37, no. 3 (March 1964): 31.

37. Ibid., 39.

38. Walter Laqueur, "Is There Now, or Has There Ever Been, Such a Thing as Totalitarianism?" *Commentary* 80, no. 4 (October 1985): 29–35. "No idea in our time has provoked more impassioned debate than the idea of totalitarianism," writes Laqueur. "Used indiscriminately by some as a synonym for fascism, or Communism, or both, it is abhorred and denounced by others as a source of deliberate confusion and a propaganda weapon. . . . But behind seemingly semantic hair-splitting are some of the key issues facing U.S. foreign policy—in particular, how to conduct relations with the Soviet bloc and the Third World" (29).

39. For the argument that Shaka Zulu embodies totalitarian traits, see John L. Stanley, "Is Totalitarianism a New Phenomenon? Reflections on Hannah Arendt's Origins of Totalitarianism," *Review of Politics* 49, no. 2 (Spring 1987): 177–207. For the interpretation of Plato's thought as totalitarian, see Karl Popper, *The Open Society and Its Enemies*, vol. 1, *The Spell of Plato* (Princeton, NJ: Princeton University Press, 1971).

40. For historical accounts of how Nazi Germany and the Soviet Union merged into an image of totalitarianism in U.S. culture, see Les K. Adler and Thomas G. Paterson, "Red Fascism: The Merger of Nazi Germany and Soviet Russia in the American Image of Totalitarianism, 1930s–1950s," *American Historical Review* 75, no. 4 (April 1970): 1046–1064; see also Benjamin L. Alpers, *Dictators, Democracy, and American Public Culture: Envisioning the Totalitarian Enemy* (Chapel Hill: University of North Carolina Press, 2003).

41. "Cruelty per se," writes Stanley Elkins, "cannot be considered the primary key to this [childlike conformity exacted from the plantation slave and the camp inmate]; of far greater importance was the 'closedness' of the system, in which all lines of authority descended from the master and in which alternative social bases that might have supported alternative standards were systematically suppressed." Elkins, *Slavery* (Chicago: University of Chicago Press, 1976), 128.

42. See *African Slavery in Latin America and the Caribbean*, ed. Herbert S. Klein and Ben Vinson III (Oxford: Oxford University Press, 2007).

43. In the American context, slaves—like Nazi camp inmates—had what Elkins calls only one "significant other": the slave master (or the S.S. guard). If perhaps underrating the authority of slaveholders in Latin American slavery, Elkins notes that in that context the slave had multiple and often competing significant others. Though the master of course remained dominant, other primarily religious figures, such as the friar, the priest, the "jealous

Jesuit," and (in the secular order) the local magistrate, constituted significant others who supervised practices of slavery and liaised between master and slave. Elkins, *Slavery*, 135–136.

44. Critics differ over whether to employ the term *Shoah* or *Holocaust* in reference to the destruction of European Jewry under Nazism. As Kirsten Fermaglich and others have noted, "Far from occupying a sacred space in American culture, 'the Holocaust' did not . . . exist in Americans' vocabulary until the late 1960s." Fermaglich, *American Dreams and Nazi Nightmares: Early Holocaust Consciousness and Liberal America, 1957–1965* (Waltham, MA: Brandeis University Press, 2006), 1–2. In addition to retaining the uniquely anti-Semitic character of this atrocity, the term *Shoah* also has the advantage over the idea that *the* Holocaust trumps and overshadows other barbarisms committed in the twentieth century and in modernity generally. See William F. S. Miles, "Third World Views of the Holocaust," *Journal of Genocide Research* 6, no. 3 (September 2004): 371–393.

45. For a discussion of how Elkins's thesis gets conscripted into 1960s arguments about the injurious effects of slavery and segregation on the black psyche—otherwise known as the "damage thesis"—see Daryl Michael Scott, *Contempt and Pity: Social Policy and the Image of the Damaged Black Psyche, 1880–1996* (Chapel Hill: University of North Carolina Press, 1997).

46. For a balanced reappraisal of Elkins's *Slavery* and the debates it ignited, see Richard H. King, *Race, Culture, and the Intellectuals, 1940–1970* (Baltimore: Johns Hopkins University Press, 2004), 151–172. King recalls Eugene Genovese's observation that "an individual slave might display a capacity for resistance *and* for acquiescence, might act an Uncle Tom at one minute and a Nat Turner the next. There was a variety, a 'doubleness' to use the Du Boisian concept, within the individual slave as well as the slave population." Ibid., 160. See also Eugene D. Genovese, "Rebelliousness and Docility in the Negro Slave: A Critique of the Elkins Thesis," in *The Debate over Slavery: Stanley Elkins and His Critics*, ed. Ann Lane (Urbana: University of Illinois Press, 1971), 43–74.

47. The influence of Elkins's thesis is evident in the following remarks on the Chinese gulag from David Brion Davis, a leading intellectual historian of slavery: "As late as the 1990s, testimony from former political prisoners in China has proved once again how torture, constant surveillance, and a near-starvation diet can transform human behavior. Students of slavery should at least be aware that strong-minded men and women admit that in the Chinese camps they fawningly tried to ingratiate themselves with guards, stole food from one another, informed on friends, and finally became convinced that it was their own fault that they were dying from starvation." Davis, introduction to *A Historical Guide to World Slavery*, ed. Seymour Drescher and Stanley L. Engerman (Oxford: Oxford University Press, 1998), xi.

48. Elkins, *Slavery*, 105.

49. Ibid., 113.

50. Surprisingly, Elkins discusses Douglass's role as an abolitionist and his relationship to Garrison but neglects his narrative.

51. Frederick Douglass, *Narrative of the Life of Frederick Douglass: An American Slave, Written by Himself* (Boston: St. Martin's, 2003), 52.

52. Ibid., 53–54.

53. In language that anticipates Elkins, Ralph Ellison continues: "The primary technique in its enforcement is to impress the Negro child with the omniscience and omnipotence of the whites to the point that whites appear as ahuman as Jehovah, and as relentless as a Mississippi flood. Socially it is effected through an elaborate scheme of taboos supported by a ruthless physical violence, which strikes not only the offender but the entire black community." Ellison, "Richard Wright's Blues," *Antioch Review* 50, nos. 1–2: 61–74.

54. Cedric Robinson, *Black Marxism: The Making of the Black Radical Tradition* (Chapel Hill: University of North Carolina Press, 1983), 290.

55. Regarding naturalism, there's no doubt that Wright saw value in its purportedly "scientific" ambition to produce objective descriptions of material and social reality, but Wright's commitment to symbolic narrative, in my view, overtakes the purely descriptive impulse. In this respect, Jameson's remarks on Lukács and naturalism are instructive here: "[One] always needs to insist, not merely on Lukács's own understanding of his work on realism as a *critique* of Stalinist aesthetics, but also on the code-word function of the negative term 'naturalism' as a tactical euphemism in the Moscow of the 1920s, very precisely for 'socialist realism.' Something may even be gained . . . by insisting on his constitutive identification of realism with narrative and storytelling. 'Photographic realism,' what he called naturalism, is in his aesthetic disparaged very precisely on the basis of its non- or anti-narrative structure, on the symptomatic formal influence within it of the sheerly descriptive." Jameson, *Valences of the Dialectic*, 203.

56. George Orwell, "Arthur Koestler," in *The Complete Works of George Orwell*, ed. Peter Davison, vol. 16, *I Have Tried to Tell the Truth, 1943–1944* (London: Secker and Warburg, 1998), 392.

57. For a brilliant exploration of the relation between total war and totalitarianism, see Ira Katznelson, *Desolation and Enlightenment: Political Knowledge after Total War, Totalitarianism, and the Holocaust* (New York: Columbia University Press, 2003).

58. Orwell, "Arthur Koestler," 393.

59. Richard Overy, "The Concentration Camp: An International Perspective," *Eurozine* 25 (August 2011), http://www.eurozine.com/articles/2011–08–25-overy-en.html.

60. See Benjamin Madley, "From Africa to Auschwitz: How German South West Africa Incubated Ideas and Methods Adopted and Developed by the Nazis in Eastern Europe," *European History Quarterly* 35, no. 3 (2005): 429–464; and Casper W. Erichsen and David Olusoga, *The Kaiser's Holocaust: Germany's Forgotten Genocide and the Colonial Roots of Nazism* (London: Faber and Faber, 2010).

61. Richard Wright, *Black Boy (American Hunger): A Record of Childhood and Youth* (New York: HarperCollins, 1993), 196–197.

62. Abdul. R. JanMohamed, *The Death-Bound Subject: Richard Wright's Archaeology of Death* (Durham, NC: Duke University Press, 2005), 2.

63. Ellison, "Richard Wright's Blues," 62.

64. Wright, *Black Boy*, 196–197.

65. Ibid., 189–190.

66. Leszek Kolakowski, "Totalitarianism and the Virtue of the Lie," in *My Correct Views on Everything* (South Bend, IN: St. Augustine's Press, 2005), 70.

67. Consequently Wright's works are known for their portrayals of disfigured black subjectivities, or of what Daryl Michael Scott calls the "damage thesis" saturating postwar representations of black life. But less attention has been devoted to Wright's imagining of the consequences for racism among whites. See Scott, *Contempt and Pity: Social Policy and the Image of the Damaged Black Psyche, 1880–1996* (Chapel Hill: University of North Carolina Press, 1997).

68. Ellison, "Richard Wright's Blues," 65.

69. On these self-consciously literary elements of *Black Boy*, see Amy Hungerford's lecture: https://www.youtube.com/watch?v=Twb_APQpzkk&list=PLE177272031E69808.

70. Wright, *Black Boy*, 73–74.

71. Jan Mohamed, *Death-Bound Subject*, 2.

72. On the fascist dimensions of Wright's characters, especially Cross Damon of *The Outsider*, see Mark Christian Thompson, *Black Fascisms: African American Literature and Culture between the Wars* (Charlottesville: University of Virginia Press, 2007), chapter 6.

73. King, *Race, Culture, and the Intellectuals*, 143.

74. Richard Wright, "How 'Bigger' Was Born," *Saturday Review of Literature*, June 1, 1940, 3–4.

75. George F. Kennan, "Totalitarianism in the Modern World," in *Totalitarianism: Proceedings of a Conference Held at the American Academy of Arts and Sciences, March 1953*, ed. Carl J. Friedrich (Cambridge, MA: Harvard University Press, 1954), 19. On this passage from Kennan, as well as the racial inflection of antitotalitarian and anti-Soviet discourse, see William Pietz, "The 'Post-Colonialism' of Cold War Discourse," *Social Text* 19/20 (Autumn 1988): 55–75.

76. Czeslaw Milosz, *The Captive Mind* (New York: Vintage, 1990).

77. With the phrase "unknowing"—signifying modernist destabilization of spatial and temporal certainties embedded in realist protocols—I refer to Phillip Weinstein's luminous study. See Weinstein, *Unknowing: The Work of Modernist Fiction* (Ithaca, NY: Cornell University Press, 2005).

78. Badiou, *The Century* (Cambridge: Polity Press, 2007), 54–56.

79. "For Lenin," Badiou writes, "the instrument of victory is theoretical and practical lucidity, in view of a decisive confrontation, a final and total war. The fact that this war will be total means that victory is victorious indeed. The century therefore is a century of war." Alain Badiou, "One Divides Itself into Two," in *Lenin Reloaded: Toward a Politics of Truth*, ed. Sebastian Budgen, Stathis Kouvelakis, and Slavoj Žižek (Durham, NC: Duke University Press, 2007), 9. See also Etienne Balibar, "The Philosophical Moment in

Politics Determined by War: Lenin, 1914–1916," in Budgen, Kouvelakis, and Žižek, *Lenin Reloaded*, 207–221. See also the illuminating new revisionist biography of Lenin by Lars T. Lih, *Lenin* (London: Reaktion Books, 2011).

80. Žižek views the term *totalitarian* as purely ideological and political, and the term *totality* as philosophical, Hegelian. He indicts the "postmodern deconstructionist Left" for rehabilitating, unwittingly, and updating the wisdom of liberals like Isaiah Berlin when they invoke totalitarianism. When they do so,

> "[totalitarianism]" is thus elevated to the level of ontological confusion; it is conceived as a kind of Kantian paralogism of pure political reason, an inevitable "transcendental illusion" which occurs when a positive political order is directly, in an illegitimate short circuit, identified with the impossible Otherness of Justice—*any* stance that does not endorse the mantra of contingency/displacement/finitude is dismissed as potentially "totalitarian." The philosophical notion of *totality* and the political notion of *totalitarianism* tend to overlap here, in a line that stretches from Karl Popper to Jean-François Lyotard: the Hegelian totality of Reason is perceived as the ultimate totalitarian edifice in philosophy. (Žižek, *Did Somebody Say Totalitarianism?* [London: Verso Books, 2002], 6)

81. For a critical survey, see Martin Jay, *Marxism and Totality: The Adventures of a Concept from Lukács to Habermas* (Berkeley: University of California Press, 1986).

82. Jameson, *Valences of the Dialectic*, 207. An "aspiration" and an "intention," totality, according to Jameson, is "not a form of knowledge, but rather a framework in which various kinds of knowledge are positioned, pursued, and evaluated." And on the "level of political strategies and tactics, 'totalization' means nothing more forbidding than alliance politics and various avatars and variants of popular fronts and hegemonic blocks, including the dilemmas and the failures of those complicated and delicate enterprises." Jameson, *Valences of the Dialectic*, 211, 213.

83. Michel Foucault, *"Society Must Be Defended": Lectures at the Collège de France, 1975–1976* (London: Penguin Books, 2004), 6. For Foucault's additional remarks on totalization, see his penultimate lecture on March 10, 1976; for his analysis of race purity and state racism, see his fourth lecture on January 28–29, 1976; for his analysis of biopolitics, biopower, and racism vis-à-vis Nazism and Socialism, see his final lecture on March 17, 1976.

84. On the other hand, as suggested earlier, feminist theorists have profitably assimilated this conception of totality in the form of "standpoint theory," which according to Jameson "now enables a principled relativism, in which the epistemological claims of the various groups can be inspected (and respected) for their 'truth content' (Adorno's *Wahrheitsgehalt*) or their respective 'moments of truth.'" Jameson, *Valences of the Dialectic*, 215.

85. See Katznelson, *Desolation and Enlightenment*, 17; and Gerhard L. Weinberg, *A World at Arms: A Global History of World War II* (Cambridge: Cambridge University Press, 1994), 1–2. For Weinberg, the Second World War was unequivocally a European war, so that in his judgment Italy's invasion of

Ethiopia and Japan's aggression against China, "however grim for the participants, and especially for the Chinese and Ethiopians, those wars, too, belonged in a prior framework." Yet he stops short of explaining what this "framework" might be, suggesting only that the Ethiopian case was "a colonial war in the tradition of earlier seizures of African territory" by other European powers. My sense is that neither of these invasions belongs in the margins of the global conflict to come.

86. Katznelson, *Desolation and Enlightenment*, 18.

87. "Ludendorff," Lindqvist continues, "belonged to a nation without empire. He saw quite clearly the connection between the total war that the peoples of Asia and Africa had endured and the total war that now awaited Europe. The difference between Ludendorff and Oppenheimer was that the same 'totality' which according to the lawyer made total war a crime, in the eyes of the general gave it moral justification." Sven Lindqvist, *A History of Bombing* (New York: The New Press, 2001), 68.

88. Kimoto analyzes a series of sessions among the Kyoto School philosophers, the first of which was held on November 26, 1941, just thirteen days before Japan attacked Pearl Harbor. The last session culminated in a major theoretical statement, "The Philosophy of Total War," that articulated a philosophical basis for the war but also named the raison d'etre for the whole symposium. Takeshi Kimoto, "Antinomies of Total War," *positions* 17, no. 1 (2009): 104.

89. Ibid., 104–105.

90. An important statement by Kōsaka Masaaki during the opening session encapsulates the collective's vision of total war: "When man becomes indignant, his indignation is total. He is indignant in mind and body. This is the case with war: both heaven and earth become indignant. In this way, the soul of humanity comes to be purified. This is why it is war that determines the crucial turning points in world history. Hence world history is purgatory." Quoted in Kimoto, "Antinomies of Total War," 104.

91. On interwar Japan's sense of being "overcome by modernity" and its resultant effort to "overcome modernity," see Harry D. Harootunian, *Overcome by Modernity: History, Culture, and Community in Interwar Japan* (Princeton, NJ: Princeton University Press, 2001), especially chapter 2.

92. Ibid., 108. For a meditation on the concept of wartime, see Mary L. Dudziak, *Wartime: An Idea, Its History, Its Consequences* (Oxford: Oxford University Press, 2012).

93. "The major Western Allies—Britain, France, Italy, and the United States—each had five seats in the plenary. So did Japan, despite its relatively minor contribution to the war effort; as Britain's main ally in East Asia, and with Lloyd George's support it, too, was recognized as a major power. . . . The Chinese, as we will see, strongly protested their relegation to the ranks of the small nations, especially given Japan's recognition as a major power. Their protests, however, were ignored." Erez Manela, *The Wilsonian Moment: Self-Determination and the International Origins of Anticolonial Nationalism* (Oxford: Oxford University Press, 2007), 57.

94. "Japanese militarism," writes Katznelson, "controlled much of the Pacific and the Asian mainland, having conquered the Philippines, Burma, Hong Kong, Malaya, Singapore, and the Dutch East Indies. Australia was threatened by invasion. China seemed quite likely to yield to Japanese force." Ira Katznelson, *Fear Itself: The New Deal and the Origins of Our Time* (New York: W. W. Norton, 2013), 41.

95. For example, in a 1933 editorial, "Japan and Ethiopia," Du Bois writes: "It is now reported . . . that Japan and Ethiopia have entered into an economic treaty by which Japan is to receive 16,000,000 acres for Japanese colonization and Ethiopia is to be repaid by Japanese ingenuity, trade, and friendship. If this is true, we shall be extremely pleased. . . . We have no illusions about the Japanese motives in this matter. They are going to use Ethiopia for purposes of profit. At the same time the treatment of Ethiopia by England and Italy and France has been so selfish and outrageous that nothing Japan can do can possibly be worse." Du Bois, "Japan and Ethiopia," in *W. E. B. Du Bois on Asia: Crossing the World Color Line*, ed. Bill V. Mullen and Cathryn Watson (Jackson: University of Mississippi Press, 2005), 75. Of course, Du Bois was writing two years before Italy's ghastly invasion of Ethiopia.

96. For an excellent collection of Du Bois's writings on Asia, see Mullen and Watson, *W. E. B. Du Bois on Asia*. For a pathbreaking account of Du Bois's views on China, Japan, and Asia in the context of his and Shirley Graham's evolving Maoism, see Yunxiang Gao, "W. E. B. Du Bois and Shirley Graham Du Bois in Maoist China," *Du Bois Review* 10, no. 1 (2013): 59–85.

97. See also David Williams, *Defending Japan's Pacific War: The Kyoto School Philosophers and Post-White Power* (New York: Routledge, 2005); Gerald Horne, *Race War! White Supremacy and the Japanese Attack on the British Empire* (New York: New York University Press, 2005); and Marc Gallicchio, *The African American Encounter with Japan and China* (Chapel Hill: University of North Carolina Press, 2000). Regarding Williams, who opposes the branding of Kyoto School thought as "fascist," Kimoto charges that he takes "these philosophers' wartime discourse at face value," insisting "that despite Japan's defeat, they proposed and anticipated the formation of a 'post-white' world in which western supremacy comes to an end. Provocative as this thesis may be, Williams's basic standpoint remains in several ways extremely confused and problematic." First, he disputes the idea that the Kyoto School philosophers would employ "such a racial metaphor as 'post-whiteness.'" Second, regarding Williams's inattention to how the Kyoto School discourse apparently supported Japan's war effort, Kimoto asks: "Is this not ultimately a rather 'orthodox' view of the school, one that ignores the role of imperial Japan as victimizer? Third, and above all, Williams does not criticize but indeed actually admires the Kyoto School's imperial nationalism." Finally, he notes that "Williams professes a high regard for the German writer Ernst Jünger's essay on total mobilization, which lies at the heart of fascist thought. One might thus be tempted to suspect that Williams's revisionism is actually a desperate attempt to rescue American imperialism by way of its former enemy." Kimoto, "Antinomies of Total War," 102–103.

98. Kolakowski, "Totalitarianism and the Virtue of the Lie," 66.

99. Tvetan Todorov, *Hope and Memory: Lessons from the Twentieth Century* (Princeton, NJ: Princeton University Press, 2003), 1.

100. Yet one then wonders why it is in 1990s France (especially between Furet's *The Passing of an Illusion* in 1995 and *The Black Book of Communism* in 1997) that many of the strongest, or at least most internationally visible, denunciations of communism have emerged.

101. Tzvetan Todorov, *The Totalitarian Experience* (Chicago: University of Chicago Press, 2009), 51–64.

102. Here Todorov recounts an episode from his book *A French Tragedy*, in which "the role of the rescuers is played by the mediators who attempt to liberate hostages from the two groups at war. During the Algerian War, Germaine Tillion, who had been in the German death camps and was not unaware of the violence of Soviet repression, had in turn chosen that role for herself, refusing to take the side of either warring party. 'I refuse to kill one to save the other,' she said. I might add that the attitude of the rescuer does not belong to a national tradition or a social milieu; it is an individual choice." Todorov, *Totalitarian Experience*, 17–18.

103. Alain Badiou, *Communist Hypothesis* (Cambridge: Polity Press, 2007), 13. Versus Badiou's "passion for the real," as well as against the zealous denunciations of communism, Todorov stakes out a firm but less impassioned position: "The passion, habitually shown in debating this question [of the conceptual validity of totalitarianism]," he writes, "seems excessive to me but corresponds to the intensity of reaction to the events themselves that are linked to one or the other of these regimes. In my opinion, the usefulness of the comparison is obvious, whether on the structural or historical level. The force with which this idea is sometimes rejected arises from a misunderstanding of comparison: while indicating a belonging to a common genus, comparison, far from establishing identity, enables one to grasp differences." Todorov, *Totalitarian Experience*, 25. Of course, this notion of a "common genus" between fascism and communism cuts to the core of the Marxist objection: thinkers within this tradition are more inclined to see liberal democracy and fascism, "for all their differences," as belonging to a common genus.

104. These attitudes explain, I think, the opposite regard in which each thinker holds the value of historical memory. For Todorov, "Memory can serve as a remedy against evil only if we seek to find the reasons for it deep within ourselves, and not just in other people conceived as rigidly different from us." By contrast, Badiou asserts in a footnote: "What is not subjected to thinking endures. Contrary to what is often said, it is thought that forbids repetition, not memory." Todorov, *Totalitarian Experience*, 44–45; Badiou, *Century*, 203.

105. Giorgio Agamben, *State of Exception* (Chicago: University of Chicago Press, 2005), 2. For Agamben, the link between the state of exception and the camp is inextricable: "One cannot overestimate," he writes, "the importance of this constitutive nexus between state of exception and concentration camp

for a correct understanding of the nature of the camp. . . . *The camp is the space that opens up when the state of exception starts to become the rule.*" Agamben, *Means without End: Notes on Politics* (Minneapolis: University of Minnesota Press, 2000), 38–39, and *Homo Sacer: Sovereign Power and Bare Life* (Stanford, CA: Stanford University Press, 1998), 119–188.

106. Agamben, *Means without Ends*, 38. With respect to the Boer War, in the late 1970s Thomas Pakenham argued that, contrary to the contemporaneous view of the Boer War as a "gentleman's war" and a "white man's war," "no generalization could be more misleading." He writes: "From digging in the War Office Files, and talking to war veterans, one comes to realize what an important part in the war was played by Africans. . . . By the end of the war, nearly ten thousand Africans were serving under arms in the British forces. Many non-combatants were flogged by the Boers or shot. . . . In general it was the Africans who had to pay the heaviest price in the war and its aftermath." Pakenham, *The Boer War* (New York: Perennial, 1991), xxi.

107. See the essays collected in Simone Bignall and Marcelo Svirsky, eds., *Agamben and Colonialism* (Edinburgh: Edinburgh University Press, 2012). For critics of Agamben who question the historical basis of his theories, see Mark Mazower, "Foucault, Agamben: Theory and the Nazis," *boundary 2* 35, no. 1 (2008): 23–34; Phillippe Mesnard, "The Political Philosophy of Giorgio Agamben: A Critical Evaluation," *Totalitarian Movements and Political Religions* 5, no. 1 (Summer 2004): 139–157; and Ichiro Takayoshi, "Can Philosophy Explain Nazi Violence? Giorgio Agamben and the Problem of the Historico-Philosophical Method," *Journal of Genocide Studies* 13 (May 2011): 47–66.

108. As Archie Brown commonsensically observes, the Second World War "had a different starting date in different countries—as late as June 1941 in the case of the Soviet Union." See Brown's magisterial history, *The Rise and Fall of Communism* (New York: HarperCollins, 2009), 4. Scholars and writers have begun to pose this question (of the periodization of the Second World War) anew. Writing in a historical and theoretical mode, Mary Dudziak asks, "When Was World War II?" See Dudziak, *Wartime*, 33–62. Similarly, Sven Lindqvist asks rhetorically:

> When did the Second World War actually begin? Was it on September 18, 1931, when the Japanese attacked China and turned the northeastern province into the Japanese vassal state Manchuko? Or was it March of 1932, when the Japanese air force suddenly bombed Shanghai and caused several thousand civilian deaths? Or perhaps in 1933, when the Japanese occupied northern China all the way down to Beijing and Tientsin? The Japanese called the war "the China Incident." From the European perspective, all of that happened much too far away to be considered world war. The world was in Europe. But when the Japanese attacked the railway station in Nantao on August 26, 1937, and not only killed hundreds of civilian Chinese, but also wounded the British ambassador, Sir Hughe Knatchball-Huggesson, it did make an impression. (Lindqvist, *History of Bombing*, 71)

109. Carol Anderson, "Rethinking Radicalism: African Americans and the Liberation Struggles in Somalia, Libya, and Eritrea, 1945–1949," *Journal of the Historical Society* 11, no. 4 (December 2011): 385–423.

110. David Atkinson, "Encountering Bare Life in Italian Libya and Colonial Amnesia in Agamben," in Bignall and Svirsky, *Agamben and Colonialism*, 156. As Laqueur writes with some justification, "While the Italians 'invented' totalitarianism as a theoretical concept, however, their practical contribution to the form was quite modest: of all the great dictatorships of our time, Italian fascism was the least totalitarian." But of course this view depends on the omission of Ethiopia and Libya from Italy's fascist image. See Laqueur, "Is There Now, or Has There Ever Been, Such a Thing as Totalitarianism?," 29.

111. As with many aspects of Agamben's thought, the entwinement of the state of exception with the concentration camp is hazy, especially where their enactment in different political regimes is concerned. It's true that an insufficient differentiation of the scale and management across concentration camps across national contexts comes at the expense of Agamben's philosophical inquiry into their logic in modernity. As Mark Mazower writes, "For Agamben—and not only for him—the camps constitute a warning from history. . . . But maybe the camps also provide a warning of a different kind. There are, in the first place, camps, and then there are camps. In the summer of 1939, there were probably about 1.5 million prisoners in the Soviet Gulag; at the time, the figure for the Third Reich was 21,400. So point one: the term *totalitarianism* hides more than it reveals—in this case, vast divergences between the Nazi and the Communist camp experiences." But then Mazower notes the exponential rise in Nazi camp *inmates* during the war, which had increased to 115,000 by August 1942, and then had swollen to over 700,000 by early 1945. He then draws a pertinent question: "How far is it legitimate to ignore this astonishing growth in favor of the static image of a frozen 'concentration camp universe'?" Mazower, "Foucault, Agamben," 30. As is likely already evident, my project wrestles with but does not resolve a similar problem of historical differentiation.

112. Agamben, *Homo Sacer*, 121.

113. Nikhil Pal Singh, "The Afterlife of Fascism," *South Atlantic Quarterly* 105, no. 1 (Winter 2006): 79.

114. See Domenico Losurdo, *Liberalism: A Counter-History* (New York: Verso, 2011).

115. Singh, "Afterlife of Fascism," 79.

CHAPTER 3 The Twilight of Empire

1. Robert Lucas, "Jess Simple 'Speaks His Mind' in Langston Hughes' New Publication," *Chicago Defender*, March 25, 1950, 2. On the significance of the Simple character, see Donna Sullivan Harper, *Not So Simple: The "Simple" Stories by Langston Hughes* (Columbia: University of Missouri Press, 1995); and Brian Dolinar, *The Black Cultural Front: Black Writers and Artists*

of the Depression Generation (Jackson: University Press of Mississippi, 2012), 71–124.

2. There are good reasons, according to Laura James, to doubt this legendary version of Nasser at Suez.

> Unfortunately, the legend surrounding this defining moment in modern Egyptian history tends to obscure the actual sequence of events. The summer of 1956 is often described like a slow-motion table tennis match. President Nasser, offended by Western hostility as expressed through the "Omega" plan, granted diplomatic recognition to communist China on 16 May. In response, the United States decided to withdraw its offer to help fund the Aswan High Dam. This was finally made clear in a meeting between the US Secretary of State, John Foster Dulles, and the Egyptian Ambassador to Washington, Ahmed Hussein, on 19 July. Unsurprised but deeply offended, Nasser's knockout riposte was a highly dramatic speech at Alexandria a week later, nationalising the Suez Canal Company in the teeth of the Western powers, in order to use the revenues to pay for the Dam. It is a compelling tale, but it raises more questions than it answers. For example, when was the decision to nationalise the Suez Canal actually made, and who was involved? (Laura M. James, *Nasser at War: Arab Images of the Enemy* [New York: Palgrave Macmillan, 2006], 22)

James usefully challenges this standard account. But for the purposes of this chapter, the legendary version remains indispensable, since the contemporaneous narratives of Nasser and Suez—however apocryphal—that colonized onlookers received, reimagined, and disseminated in their own media resonate strongly with the mythical account. Ibid.

3. Horace Cayton, "World at Large," *Pittsburgh Courier*, November 24, 1956.

4. "Anticolonial struggle and civil rights insurgency," writes Plummer, "brought to the fore actors who, though historically connected to the past, altered the political agenda of the respective constituencies in new ways." Brenda Gayle Plummer, *Rising Wind: Black Americans and U.S. Foreign Affairs, 1935–1960* (Chapel Hill: University of North Carolina Press, 1996), 257. With respect to British colonial rule in Africa and Asia, anticolonial activists, by the 1950s, increasingly rejected what Dipesh Chakrabarty identifies as the historicist element in liberal colonial ideology. As Chakrabarty argues, the British Empire, in accordance with Enlightenment and liberal principles articulated by John Locke and John Stuart Mill, justified colonial rule on historicist grounds, the idea that non-Western peoples were *not yet* sufficiently civilized for self-rule. In (liberal) theory, all nations and peoples were entitled to freedom and self-government, but not all were ready for independence. After an unspecified period of enlightened despotism and colonial tutelage, however, such peoples could hope to attain the measure of civilization requisite for self-rule; colonial historicism, then, was a "recommendation to the colonized to wait." This argument, defended most eloquently in John Stuart Mill's essays "On Liberty" and "On Representative Government,"

consigns the non-Western world to what Chakrabarty calls the "waiting room of history." Chakrabarty, *Provincializing Europe: Postcolonial Thought and Historical Difference* (Princeton, NJ: Princeton University Press, 2000), 8. With respect to the U.S. foreign policy debate on decolonization, as one historian writes, there "was in the long run very little debate over the goal of the policy; after World War II, the inevitability of decolonization was an accepted fact in nearly every corner." One of the central questions, however, involved "the timing and speed of decolonization. This later became the key issue in the debate, and thus was the point that exhibited the greatest degree of change over the period [from 1952 to 1962]." Steven Metz, "American Attitudes toward Decolonization in Africa," *Political Science Quarterly* 99, no. 3 (Fall 1984): 517.

5. John Prados, "The Central Intelligence Agency and the Face of Decolonization under the Eisenhower Administration," in *The Eisenhower Administration, The Third World, and the Globalization of the Cold War*, ed. Kathryn C. Statler and Andrew L. Johns (Oxford: Rowman and Littlefield, 2006), 37.

6. See Immanuel Wallerstein, "What Cold War in Asia? An Interpretive Essay," in *The Cold War in Asia: The Battle for Hearts and Minds*, ed. Zheng Yangwen, Hong Liu, and Michael Szonyi (Leiden, NL: Brill, 2010), 17. On the Cuban Missile Crisis, Wallerstein writes:

> Castro nonetheless ran into great difficulty with the US government, which sought to overthrow his regime. So Castro announced that he had been a communist all his life. . . . The Fidelistas then took over the Cuban Communist Party, and this forced the Soviet Union, in the logic of the Cold War, to defend the Cuban regime against any US invasion. When the Cuban Missile Crisis occurred, the US did not send troops to Cuba. Rather, the US and the Soviet Union negotiated a de facto truce, thereby avoiding military conflict. Thus the Chinese and the Vietnamese and the Cubans all used the Soviet Union to achieve political changes to the status quo which they desired. It was not the other way around. It was not the Soviet Union that used the Chinese, the Vietnamese or the Cubans. Indeed, the Soviet Union was the reluctant ally. (Ibid., 23)

Defending a similar view of the global South's agency in the Cold War, Thomas Borstelmann writes: "Both Africans and African Americans were determined to make the U.S. government take sides in struggles that seemed to them utterly clear in their moral justice and world historical in their political significance. This was their 'Cold War,' replete with the same full measure of righteousness and clarity that Kennedy and other Cold Warriors saw in their own conflict with Communism." Borstelmann, "'Hedging Our Bets and Buying Time': John Kennedy and Racial Revolution in the American South and Southern Africa," *Diplomatic History* 24, no. 3 (Summer 2000): 435.

7. Eric Hayot, "Against Periodization; or, On Institutional Time," *New Literary History* 42, no. 4 (Autumn 2011): 747. Despite the assortment of challenges to periodization in literary studies over the past few decades, argues Hayot, conventional periods remain intransigently fixed in our intellectual,

institutional, and pedagogical practices. Rather than dispense with periodization, however, Hayot proposes the creation of new periods organized around times "that cross or combine our existing ones," "cross national boundaries . . . [and] borrow for their logic some non-national principle of social or cultural coherence," and use "telescopic models that lead from the small to the large, rather than the reverse," among other innovations.

8. Certainly, an uncritical interface with globalization is not the only or even primary concern with transnational inquiry: intellectual and methodological concerns—proficiency in other languages and cultures, access to archives, reliance on secondary sources outside one's field—abound. The scholarship on transnational American studies is growing at a rapid rate; for a few programmatic statements, see Shelley Fisher Fishkin and her respondents: Fishkin, "Crossroads of Cultures: The Transnational Turn in American Studies; Presidential Address to the American Studies Association," *American Quarterly* 57, no. 1 (2005): 17–57; Alfred Hornung, "Transnational American Studies: Response to the Presidential Address," *American Quarterly* 57, no. 1 (2005): 67–73; Mae N. Ngai, "Transnationalism and the Transformation of the 'Other': Response to the Presidential Address," *American Quarterly* 57, no. 1: 59–65; and Winfried Flück, "A New Beginning? Transnationalisms," *New Literary History* 42, no. 3 (Summer 2011): 365–384.

9. Frantz Fanon, *The Wretched of the Earth* (New York: Grove Press, 1963), 76–77.

10. Giorgio Agamben, *Homo Sacer: Sovereign Power and Bare Life* (Stanford, CA: Stanford University Press, 1998), 24.

11. On nonalignment, Mark Atwood Lawrence writes: "For its champions, nonalignment meant nothing less than a 'third way' for young nations that had little to gain by siding with the Communist East or the capitalist West and no stake in the East-West military rivalry. Viewed within the context of the global history of the twentieth century, nonalignment seems an eminently sensible response to Cold War binaries by poor nations that had suffered under colonial domination and sought to enjoy independence free of domination by new foreign masters." A few pages later, Lawrence writes: "Perhaps the best evidence of the momentum that nonalignment had gathered by the early 1960s is the seriousness with which the global powers viewed the phenomenon and worked—mostly unsuccessfully—to influence it." Lawrence, "The Rise and Fall of Nonalignment," in *The Cold War in the Third World*, ed. Robert J. McMahon (Oxford: Oxford University Press, 2013), 139–155. Nonalignment provided an independent space for the Third World to condemn racism, nuclear proliferation, the protection of local cultures, and economic development. "Far more perplexing," Lawrence notes, "are the reasons why nonalignment did not take root and thrive more than it did." Ibid., 140; see also Christopher J. Lee, "Between a Moment and an Era: The Origins and Afterlives of Bandung," in *Making a World after Empire: The Bandung Moment and Its Political Afterlives*, ed. Christopher J. Lee (Athens: Ohio University Press, 2010), 1–42.

12. "Though strongly opposed to local communism," writes Salim Yaqub, "Nasser insisted that the Arab states refrain from aligning with

either of the two Cold War blocs and instead pursue productive relations with both. In 1955 Egypt concluded a barter agreement with the Soviet Union (via Czechoslovakia), acquiring over $200 million worth of sophisticated weapons in exchange for surplus cotton. Over the next three-and-a-half decades, Moscow would conclude numerous other arms and aid agreements with left-leaning (but almost always non-Communist) Arab regimes." Yaqub, "The Cold War and the Middle East," in *The Cold War and the Third World* (Oxford: Oxford University Press, 2013), 15. As one historian notes, Nasser "demonstrated consummate skills in the politics of the cold war by winning American support to persuade Britain to withdraw from the British military base in Suez in 1954 while also obtaining arms from the Soviet Union through Czechoslovakia in 1955." Peter G. Boyle, "The Hungarian Revolution and the Suez Crisis," *History* 90, no. 300 (October 2005): 553. For a broader overview of how the Cold War, especially the U.S. role, shaped the Middle East and precipitated post–Cold War tensions in the region, see Rashid Khalidi, *Sowing Crisis: The Cold War and American Dominance in the Middle East* (Boston: Beacon Press, 2009).

13. Langston Hughes, "Simple's World of Black and White," *Chicago Defender*, January 15, 1958, 10.

14. See Wilson J. Moses, *The Golden Age of Black Nationalism, 1820–1925* (New York: Oxford University Press, 1988).

15. As one Egyptian political activist, Saadedine Ibrahim, recalls: "One of the very early phrases that Nasser coined was addressing the common man: 'Raise your head fellow brother, the end of colonialism has come.' And that is the kind of language, message that echoed very deeply with the average man, because it was a simple language and people who were downtrodden, people who were beaten, mistreated, felt worthless, began to gain that kind of confidence, spirit that they didn't have before." Ibrahim, "Arab Unity: Nasser's Revolution," *Aljazeera;* in English at http://www.aljazeera.com/focus/arabunity/2008/02/200852517252821627.html.

Scholars continue to debate the legacy of Nasserism in Egypt and the Arab world. For an overview of previous models and new approaches, see *Rethinking Nasserism: Revolution and Historical Memory in Modern Egypt*, ed. Elie Podeh and Onn Winckler (Gainesville: University Press of Florida, 2004). For a polemical treatment of Nasser's legacy, which traces Nazi encroachments into Egypt and their influence on Nasser, see Paul Berman, *The Flight of the Intellectuals: The Controversy over Islamism and the Press* (New York: Melville House, 2010), 66–113. Berman's account relies heavily on Jeffrey Herf, *Nazi Propaganda for the Arab World* (New Haven, CT: Yale University Press, 2009). For a scholarly and thorough account of Egyptian responses to fascism and Nazism in the 1930s, which argues that intellectual and public opinion in Egypt largely rejected totalitarianism, see *Confronting Fascism in Egypt: Dictatorship versus Democracy in the 1930s*, ed. Israel Gershoni and James Jankowski (Stanford, CA: Stanford University Press, 2010).

16. Fanon, *Wretched of the Earth*, 46.

17. "Gossip might seem to be a perfect instance of public discourse," writes Warner.

> It circulates widely among a social network, beyond the control of private individuals. It sets the norms of membership in a diffuse way that cannot be controlled by a central authority. For these reasons, a number of scholars have celebrated its potential for popular sociability and for the weak-group politics of women, peasants, and others. But gossip is never a relation among strangers. You gossip about particular people and to particular people. What you can get away with saying depends very much on whom you are talking to and what your status is in that person's eyes. . . . Intensely personal measurements of group membership, relative standing, and trust are the constant and unavoidable pragmatic work of gossip. An apparent exception is gossip about public figures who do not belong to the official social network made by gossiping, especially when official or unofficial censorship makes scandal unreportable by more legitimate means. About such people it is possible to gossip among strangers, and the gossip often has both reflexivity ("People are saying . . ."; "Everybody knows that . . .") and timeliness (hot gossip versus stale news). (Michael Warner, *Publics and Counterpublics* [Brooklyn, NY: Zone Books, 2002], 78–79, especially chapters 2 ["Publics and Counterpublics"] and 3 ["Styles of Intellectual Publics"])

18. For a moving biopic that captures mass Egyptian sentiment following Nasser's nationalization of Suez, see *Nasser 56* (1996), directed by Mohamed Fadel and written by Mahfouz Abd Al Rahman. For an analysis of this film and the biopic genre in Egypt, see Joel Gordon, "Film, Fame, and Public Memory: Egyptian Biopics from *Mustafa Kamil* to *Nasser 56*," in *International Journal of Middle East Studies* 31 (1999): 61–79. For accounts of Nasser and Suez ("through Egyptian eyes") by one of his close associates, a figure dubbed by the journalist Gamal Nkrumah "the Arab world's foremost political writer," see Mohamed Hassanein Heikal's *The Cairo Documents: The Inside Story of Nasser and His Relationship with World Leaders, Rebels, and Statesmen* (New York: Doubleday, 1973); and *Cutting the Lion's Tail: Suez through Egyptian Eyes* (London: André Deutsch Limited, 1986).

19. "In fact," as Carol Anderson writes,

> this battle to dismantle empires of racism in the midst of the Cold War reveals something of the possible. This struggle, frankly, should have been stillborn given the disproportionate financial, political, and technological power arrayed by the Europeans and Americans. It should have been an exercise in futility because of the ideological straightjacket of East and West that construed challenges to that discourse as traitorous. And, it should have been impossible given the geographical dispersion of racial allies spread across three continents with limited access to the technologies that revolutionized communications. Yet in the end, African Americans found ways to circumnavigate around those challenges and work with and for those whom they saw as waging a similar struggle. (Anderson, "The Histories of African American Anticolonialism during the Cold War," in McMahon, *Cold War in the Third World*, 179)

20. Michael Hanchard, "Afro-Modernity: Temporality, Politics, and the African Diaspora," *Public Culture* 11, no. 1 (1999): 248.

21. "Proudly We Can Be Africans," editorial, *Baltimore Afro-American*, April 6, 1957, 4.

22. One exception to this shift is the case of Pauli Murray, whose sojourn to Ghana during that nation's independence movement provided an occasion to dis-identify with Africa and to reaffirm her American identity. Nonetheless, the fact of Murray's—and numerous skilled African Americans'—involvement in Ghana's nation-building efforts in the 1950s signaled a focus on continental Africa as a site of revolutionary change and collaboration. For Murray's account of her experience in Ghana, see Murray, *Pauli Murray: The Autobiography of a Black Activist, Feminist, Lawyer, Priest, and Poet* (Knoxville: University of Tennessee Press, 1989), 318–358. On Murray's politics in Ghana, see Kevin Gaines, *American Africans in Ghana: Black Expatriates and the Civil Rights Era* (Chapel Hill: University of North Carolina Press, 2007), 110–135. On Countee Cullen's "Heritage," Aric Putnam writes: "The poem's use of Africa is not an indictment of that continent or of the poet's African ancestry. Rather, it is a lamentation over how little of its memory survives in the present. In Cullen's poem, Africa endures as metaphor; it has been charged with 'meaning but not memory.' Africa the concept has shaped the poet's identity, but Africa the continent is absent." By the 1950s and 1960s, Africa is decidedly *present*, and its status as a source of identity for the diaspora is alternately reinforced or beside the point. Putnam, *The Insistent Call: Rhetorical Moments in Black Anticolonialism, 1929–1937* (Amherst: University of Massachusetts Press, 2012), 2.

23. See John Cullen Gruesser, *Black on Black: Twentieth-Century African-American Writing about Africa* (Lexington: University of Kentucky Press, 2000). One possible exception to this one-way discourse (that is, discourse that does not involve Egyptian interlocutors) is Shirley Graham Du Bois, who at least wrote for *The Egyptian Gazette* and drew on interviews and first-hand accounts while resident in Cairo for her biography of Nasser. But in my research I have been unable to locate, say, Egyptian reviews of her biography, to say nothing of more substantive exchanges between African Americans and Egyptians on the Suez Crisis.

24. For a reappraisal of Eisenhower's containment strategies in Egypt, Morocco, and Tunisia, see Egya N. Sangmuah, "Eisenhower and Containment in North Africa, 1956–1960," *Middle East Journal* 44, no. 1 (Winter 1990): 76–91. See also Salim Yaqub, *Containing Arab Nationalism: The Eisenhower Doctrine and the Middle East* (Chapel Hill: University of North Carolina Press, 2004), 23.

25. U.S. ambassador George McGhee, for instance, referred to Lumumba's Congolese regime as "obscurantist, arbitrary, primitive, totalitarian, willful, and irresponsible." Quoted in Odd Arne Westad, *The Global Cold War: Third World Interventions and the Making of Our Times* (Cambridge: Cambridge University Press, 2005), 141. Regarding Bella's Algerian Liberation Front, historian James D. Le Sueur writes: "For [Jacques] Soustelle," the French governor general in Algeria in the mid-1950s, "the Muslims' offensive

aggression and what he considered to be the politics of Cairo and the CRUA [Comité révolutionnaire d'unité et d'action] (controlled, he argued, by Gamal Abdel Nasser, the exterior head of the Algerian nationalist movement) constituted something very similar to the Hitlerian threat." Le Sueur, *Uncivil War: Intellectuals and Identity Politics during the Decolonization of Algeria* (Lincoln: University of Nebraska Press, 2005), 35.

26. *Reassessing Suez 1956: New Perspective on the Crisis and Its Aftermath*, ed. Simon C. Smith (Hampshire, UK: Ashgate, 2008), 2–4.

27. "Al-Ghitany, who was jailed for half a year during the regime of President Gamal Abdel Nasser, has firsthand experience of the horrors of totalitarianism," writes Ahmed El Shamsy. Al-Ghitany's 1974 novel, *Zayni Barakat*, is imagined as a parable of Nasserism set in 1517 Egypt, following the Ottoman conquest. "On the surface," El Shamsy continues, "the novel's depiction of state terror, its nefarious and debilitating effects on society, and the country's subsequent defeat by a foreign power (the Ottomans, standing in for Israel) allow the novel to appear as an indictment of the totalitarian trajectory of post-independence Egypt."

Yet for El Shamsy, a fundamental ambiguity lies at the heart of *Zayni Barakat*, given what he perceives as the author's "evasive treatment of the enigmatic Barakat [the novel's protagonist and stand-in for Nasser]." "As a result," he continues, "the critique of Nasser and Nasserism in *Zayni Barakat* remained half-hearted and incomplete." He attributes this ambiguity, retrospectively, to the novelist's latent desire for the fulfillment of Nasser's promise, despite his own suffering under the regime; El Shamsy traces al-Ghitany's recent militarist proclivities in Egypt's twenty-first-century revolution to this novel's ambiguity. "Four decades have passed since Nasser's death and [General Abdul-Fattah al-Sisi's] rise, and it is al-Ghitany and his generation of Egyptian intellectuals who seem to yearn in their old age for a repetition of what they were part of as young men: the elating days of Nasserite optimism and common purpose, which somewhere, inexplicably, took a wrong turn and ended in the dark dungeons of the security police." Ahmed El Shamsy, "Sisi, Nasser, and the Great Egyptian Novel," *Muftah*, October 15, 2013, http://muftah.org/sisi-nasser-the-great-egyptian-novel/#_ftn1. See also Samia Mehrez, *Egyptian Writers between History and Fiction: Essays on Naguib Mahfouz, Sonallah Ibrahim, and Gamal al-Ghitani* (Cairo: American University in Cairo Press, 2005), especially chapter 5.

28. Alain Badiou, "The Destruction of the European Jews and the Question of Evil," in *Polemics* (London: Verso, 2006), 173.

29. Fanon, *Wretched of the Earth*, 41.

30. Arguing that Eden undertook a far more determined effort to control the British press than previous historians of Suez have acknowledged, Shaw writes:

> [Eden's] aim throughout was to use the newspapers to create and maintain a climate of opinion at home in favour of war, whilst simultaneously obscuring his hatred of Nasser, and the true scale and nature of the military preparations for that war. By encouraging the press to advocate the

> need for force on the grounds of the dangers posed to Britain and the Middle East by Nasser, and yet at the same time giving the impression that it was itself surprisingly moderate, the government hoped it could justify a progressively aggressive policy by claiming that it was merely yielding to public opinion as manifested in a "free" and "independent" press. This, in turn, would increase the pressure on the Egyptian president, who was known to be a voracious reader of the British and American press.

Tony Shaw, *Eden, Suez, and the Mass Media: Propaganda and Persuasion during the Suez Crisis* (London: I. B. Tauris, 1996), 10–14.

31. "The longer the crisis went on," Shaw continues,

> and the more opposed to intervention the US administration became, the greater the emphasis put by Eden on appealing over the heads of President Eisenhower and Secretary of State Dulles to the American people themselves. Consequently, the Foreign Office school of thought which argued that the route to US foreign policy was through American public opinion came increasingly to the fore. . . . With the American public particularly in mind, Nasser was portrayed as a Soviet "stooge" whose dangerous antics could threaten US interests in the Middle East and ultimately lead to war in this most unstable, but strategically and economically vital, region. Finally, in addition to all this, Britain and France had to depict themselves as the policemen of the Middle East, as the only powers physically capable of enforcing "international law" in that region. (Shaw, *Eden, Suez, and the Mass Media*, 11–12)

32. In its 1975 obituary for Mollet, the *New York Times* begins, notably, with his role in Suez: "Guy Mollet, the French socialist leader who, as Premier, ordered French troops to join with those of Britain and Israel in the ill-fated invasion of Egypt in 1956, died of a heart attack yesterday at his Paris home." Though alluding to his socialist background (he "was a tough-minded Marxist-Socialist . . . but despised Stalinism") and his time spent as a war prisoner under the Nazis, the article focuses on his role at Suez and the controversies surrounding his decision to send French conscripts to Algeria to squelch the rebel movement. "Mr. Mollet's immediate reaction [to Egyptian nationalization]," the obituary notes, "was to say that France would join armed intervention, if necessary, to protect France's oil lifeline to the East." But the article concludes with Mollet's claim that to "the end he maintained that his chief reason for getting France into the war was to stop the Egyptians from providing aid to the Algerian rebels." "Guy Mollet Is Dead at 69; Led France in Suez Crisis," *New York Times*, October 4, 1975, 30. Articles like this attest to how powerfully the memory of Suez—and connected events like the French-Algerian War—shadowed the "fiasco's" European architects, often decades after the event.

33. As one scholar writes recently about *The Philosophy of the Revolution:*

> Long before the revolution, Europe or "the West" had become a common concept that featured in political discourse in Egypt. . . . In *The Philosophy*, however, the West is given little attention. Where Nasser discusses the powers opposing the revolution, he mentions three groups, all internal:

the big landowners, the "old politicians" and a large number of government officials. In fact, nowhere in *The Philosophy* does Nasser choose to discuss specific Western countries. Instead, only a short reference to imperialism points out that the revolution has enemies abroad. (Robert Woltering, *Occidentalisms in the Arab World: Ideology and Images of the West in the Egyptian Media* [New York: I. B. Tauris, 2011], 73–74)

34. But curiously, other rhetorical strategies, contradictory with the totalitarian imagery, circulated in British media. According to Christopher Hitchens, Nasser also "was being denounced on British radio as a 'secret Zionist and also a secret Freemason.'" Hitchens, "Hungary, Suez, and Hannah Arendt," *World Policy Journal* 23, no. 4 (Winter 2006–2007): 89. Adapted from a lecture, Hitchens's text provides no documentation for this claim.

35. Karl Jaspers, *The Future of Mankind* (Chicago: University of Chicago Press), 91, 150.

36. For an account of British and American competing interests in the Middle East, oil politics, and the creation of the international monetary system, see Steven G. Galpern, *Money, Oil, and Empire in the Middle East: Sterling and Postwar Imperialism, 1944–1971* (Cambridge: Cambridge University Press, 2009).

37. Historians Jeffrey Herf and Matthias Küntzel have shown how Nazi leadership, seeking to gain alliances during the war, established a rapprochement with leaders in Egypt, Iraq, and other Arab countries, influencing leaders like the Palestinian Haj Amin al-Husseini as well as Sayyid Qutb and Hassan al-Banna, forerunners of the Muslim Brotherhood in Egypt. Herf shows how in the years 1939 to 1945, Nazi and Arab leaders broadcasted Nazi propaganda, via shortwave radio transmitters near Berlin, in Persian in Iran and in Arabic throughout the Middle East and North Africa. Translations of *Mein Kampf* and *Protocols of the Elders of Zion* then appeared in Arabic. As Herf observes, this convergence encouraged Nazi leadership to revise their doctrinal anti-Semitism because, as their Arab mediators pointed out, Arabs were also Semitic peoples; consequently Nazi officials redefined their anti-Semitism to apply only to Jews and to exempt other Semitic peoples of the region. Jeffrey Herf, *Nazi Propaganda for the Arab World* (New Haven, CT: Yale University Press, 2009); Matthias Küntzel, *Jihad and Jew-Hatred: Islamism, Nazism, and the Roots of 9/11* (New York: Telos Press, 2007); see also the exchange between Richard Wolin and Jeffrey Herf, "Herf's Misuses of History" and "'Islamo-Fascism': An Exchange," *Chronicle of Higher Education*, November 22, 2009. See also Ian Baruma and Avishai Margalit, *Occidentalism: The West in the Eyes of Its Enemies* (New York: Penguin Press, 2004); and Paul Berman, *Terror and Liberalism* (New York: W. W. Norton, 2003) and *The Flight of the Intellectuals* (Brooklyn, NY: Melville House, 2010). In the exchange between Herf and Wolin, the central historiographical question animates an urgent political question, insofar as the debate turns on whether a genuine archival discovery—evidence of Nazi traffic in the Arab world—ought to serve as an explanation of contemporary events, namely those assembled under the sign of Islamo-Fascism.

38. For these and other films, including *Suez in Perspective*, see the online archive at Colonial Film: Moving Images of the British Empire, http://www.colonialfilm.org.uk.

39. Compared, these films on Suez and Nigeria project "good" and "bad" modes of decolonization analogous to Mahmoud Mamdani's analysis of the "good" and "bad" figures of Islam originating during the Cold War. See Mamdani's *Good Muslim, Bad Muslim: America, the Cold War, and the Roots of Terror* (New York: Three Leaves Press, 2004).

40. Zachary Karabell, *Parting the Desert: The Creation of the Suez Canal* (New York: Alfred A. Knopf, 2003), 26–27. Among other sources, my summary of the canal's creation draws on Karabell's informative if triumphalist account. See also John Marlowe, *World Ditch: The Making of the Suez Canal* (New York: Macmillan, 1964).

41. Karabell attributes this poem to "Enfantin or one of his followers." Karabell, *Parting the Desert*, 51–52.

42. María Josefina Saldaña-Portillo tidily summarizes another scholar's work on the feminization of nature: "As Evelyn Fox Keller has argued, the Enlightenment subject's quest for scientific mastery proceeded according to the discursive practice of feminizing nature as its object. This feminization of nature 'solidified the polarization of the masculine and the feminine that was central to the formation of early industrial capitalist society.'" Saldaña-Portillo, *The Revolutionary Imagination in the Americas and the Age of Development* (Durham, NC: Duke University Press, 2003), 300.

43. Ibid., 32.

44. "Latest—From the Sphinx" (author unattributed), quoted in *Archives of Empire Volume 1: From the East India Company to the Suez Canal*, ed. Barbara Harlow and Mia Carter (Durham, NC: Duke University Press, 2003), 615–616.

45. Ferdinand's father, Mathieu, was a diplomat to Egypt, where he had befriended the ruthless and charismatic leader Muhammad Ali, the Albanian pasha under Ottoman sovereignty; foreign minister Charles Maurice de Talleyrand-Périgord mentored Mathieu; Mathieu's brother, Barthélemy, also served in challenging roles in Egypt; Ferdinand's grandfather Martin and his great uncle Dominique had both been in the Diplomatic Service. Karabell describes Ferdinand:

> Ferdinand de Lesseps was a potent combination of vision, pragmatism, and will. Without vision, Lesseps could never have turned a hundred-mile stretch of barely inhabited desert with no source of fresh water into a canal connecting the Mediterranean to the Red Sea. He could not have mobilized the leaders of Egypt, the financial elites of Europe, Napoleon III, and millions of French citizens to support his improbable scheme. He could never have dodged the opposition of the British government and its wily prime minister, Lord Palmerston, or the animosity of the Ottoman sultan and his ministers in Constantinople. Without pragmatism, Lesseps could never have organized a venture that required the largest jetty ever constructed and a decade of labor by tens of thousands of workers. He could not have convinced engineers to design machines to dredge the soil; he

> could not have set up a company to oversee the excavation of seventy-five million cubic meters of sand; he could not have maneuvered through the diplomatic shoals that constantly loomed. And without will, he could not have fended off others who wanted to claim the idea for themselves. (Karabell, *Parting the Desert*, 7)

46. An American observer wrote in 1869:

> "J'ai pour principe de commencer par avoir la confiance," said M. de Lesseps recently to an English engineer, who was complimenting him on the almost insuperable difficulties he had to overcome in the prosecution of his great enterprise, which is to be completed on the first of October, 1869. And in this speech we find the keynotes, at once to the character and the success of the man, who has made that great work not only a possibility, but an actuality; who has reopened the communication between East and West, by cutting the Siamese ligature of the Isthmus of Suez, excelling the work of the Pharaohs in the sixth century BC, and of Amrou the Arab conqueror in the seventh century after. ("Ferdinand de Lesseps and the Suez Canal," *Putnam's Magazine* 3, no. 18 [June 1869], 647)

Lesseps "has Spanish blood in his veins, and partakes in character and disposition many of the higher traits of that race, which ignorant persons consider inferior to the Anglo-Saxon in genuine manhood." Ibid., 648.

47. "La vieille idée du percement de l'Isthme de Suez va devinir un fait pratique. L'Europe s'agite pour apporter son concours à l'entreprise; le temps de la persuasion théorique est passé, le temps de l'execution positive commence." Ferdinand de Lesseps, prefatory note dated November 9, 1858, in Friedrich Szarvady, *Der Suez Kanal* (Leipzig: F. U. Brodhaus, 1859), v.

48. "C'est donc pour moi le moment de vous exprimer, et d'exprimer par vous, au journalism de l'Allemagne les sentiments de reconnaissance que m'inspire, la part important prise par la presse allemande, dans les luttes préliminaires. Elle a sans cesse soutenu notre project, elle l'a defend, expliqué; elle a démasqué des adversaires malveillants et convaincu les esprits bienveillants; elle a exposé l'immense utilité du canal des deux mers pour la civilisation, pour l'avenir social et commercial du monde entire. Des publicists distingués ont defend notre cause avec chaleur, avec enthousiasme, avec esprit et sagacité. Je ne m'étonne pas que ces adhesions soient venues de l'Allemagne, car cette nation, plus cosmopolite que toute autre se préoccupe moins de ses intérêts particuliers et personnels que de l' intérêt general de l'humanité." De Lesseps, prefatory note.

49. See Saree Makdisi, *Romantic Imperialism: Universal Empire and the Culture of Modernity* (Cambridge: Cambridge University Press, 1998).

50. "The attempt to control from Cairo the agricultural wealth of the Nile valley was in itself nothing new," Mitchell continues:

> What was new in the nineteenth century was the nature of control. Earlier kinds of power, however centralised, were never continuous. They operated intermittently, typically in the form of levies, obligations and extortions imposed upon certain less powerful households, which in turn

> imposed levies on those less powerful around them, and so on. . . . From the nineteenth century for the first time political power sought to work in a manner that was continuous, meticulous and uniform. The method was no longer simply to take a share of what was produced and exchanged, but to enter into the process of production. By supervising each of its aspects separately and without interruption, political power attempted to discipline, coordinate and increase what were now thought of as the "productive powers" of the country. (Timothy Mitchell, *Colonising Egypt* [Berkeley: University of California Press, 1988], 34–39)

51. Harlow and Carter, *Archives of Empire Volume 1*, 575.

52. Martin Heidegger, *The Question Concerning Technology and Other Essays* (New York: Harper and Row, 1977), 129–134.

53. Karabell, *Parting the Desert*, 118.

54. Gautier's "own map of Cairo, he explained, 'built with the materials of *A Thousand and One Nights*, arranges itself around Marilhat's *Place de l'Ezbekieh*, a remarkable and violent painting. . . .' The attentive European, wrote Flaubert in Cairo, '*re*discovers here much more than he discovers.'" Mitchell, *Colonising Egypt*, 30.

55. On Lesseps and the map, see Karabell, *Parting the Desert*, 78; and Joseph Conrad, *Heart of Darkness: Case Studies in Contemporary Criticism*, 3rd ed., ed. Ross C. Murfin (Boston: Bedford, 2010), 22.

56. Richard Wright, *The Color Curtain*, in Wright, *Black Power: Three Books from Exile: Black Power; The Color Curtain; and White Man, Listen!* (New York: HarperCollins, 2008), 504.

57. Percy Hetherington Fitzgerald, *The Great Canal at Suez: Its Political, Engineering, and Financial History; with an Account of the Struggles of Its Projector, Ferdinand de Lesseps* (London: Savill, Edwards, 1876), vii.

58. *Suez*, dir. Allan Dwan (Twentieth Century Fox Film Corporation, 2012).

59. Steve Morewood, "The Prelude to the Suez Crisis: The Rise and Fall of British Dominance over the Suez Canal, 1869–1956," in Smith, *Reassessing Suez 1956*, 13–15.

60. See J. C. Hurewitz, "The Historical Context," in *Suez 1956: The Crisis and Its Consequences*, ed. Wm. Roger Louis and Roger Owen (Oxford: Clarendon Press, 1989), 20.

61. In the opening speech at the Bandung Conference of Asian and African nations in Bandung, Indonesia, 1955, President Sukarno recalled an earlier "public analysis of colonialism," in which he "then drew attention to what I called the 'Life-line of Imperialism.' This line runs from the Straits of Gibraltar, through the Mediterranean, the Suez Canal, the Red Sea, the Indian Ocean, the South China Sea and the Sea of Japan." "Speech by President Sukarno of Indonesia at the Opening of the Conference," in *Asia-Africa Speaks from Bandung* (Ministry of Foreign Affairs, Republic of Indonesia, 1955), 21.

62. Smith, *Reassessing Suez 1956*, 2.

63. As one article in the *Baltimore Afro-American* records, African Americans were eager to gain "inside" information about the Suez Crisis from local

"specialists": "Mr Saadat Hasan, midwest director of the Arab Information Center, in an address before the Windy City Press Club here Thursday, defended the Egyptian government's effort to nationalize the Suez Canal." "Information Specialist Gives 'Inside' Suez Info," *Baltimore Afro-American*, August 18, 1956, 6.

64. Dominick LaCapra, *History, Literature, Critical Theory* (Ithaca, NY: Cornell University Press, 2013), 2.

65. Charles P. Henry, *Ralph Bunche: Model Negro or American Other?* (New York: New York University Press, 1999), 167.

66. Barbara Foley, *Radical Representations: Politics and Form in U.S. Proletarian Fiction, 1929–1941* (Durham, NC: Duke University Press, 1993), 65.

67. W. E. B. Du Bois, "Suez," *Masses & Mainstream* 9, no. 11 (December 1956): 42–43.

68. "Even at the time of the Suez War," writes Scott Lucas, "'collusion' was suspected by Members of Parliament, journalists, and the Oxford University Union in Britain and by the Eisenhower Administration in the United States." W. Scott Lucas, "Redefining the Suez 'Collusion,'" *Middle Eastern Studies* 26, no. 1 (January 1990): 88.

69. W. E. B. Du Bois, "The Winds of Time," *Chicago Defender*, May 15, 1948; and "The Case for the Jews," *Chicago Star*, May 8, 1948.

70. Melani McAlister, *Epic Encounters: Culture, Media, and U.S. Interests in the Middle East since 1945* (Berkeley: University of California Press, 2001), 85. The question of Israel's "collusion," as W. Scott Lucas argues, is complex: though there is no doubt that Britain, France, and Israel agreed that the latter would invade the Sinai Peninsula, upon which the former two powers would intervene to "separate" the bordering nations—all as a pretext for regaining the canal—many accounts of this collaboration leave unanswered several pressing questions, particularly with respect to "the influence of the Arab-Israeli frontier dispute upon all events concerning the Middle East, including the Suez controversy." Lucas, "Redefining the Suez 'Collusion,'" 88–112.

71. According to Badiou, a "point is a moment within a truth procedure (such as a sequence of emancipatory politics) when a binary choice (do this *or* that) decides the future of the entire process." Alain Badiou, *The Communist Hypothesis* (London: Verso, 2010), 38.

72. W. E. B. Du Bois, "Superior Race," *Smart Set* 70 (January–April 1923): 55–60.

73. As one scholar notes, it is difficult to formulate a precise definition that would encompass all acts of propaganda, and only propaganda, across history. In the seventeenth century, when the term emerges from the Pope's establishment of a mission charged with propagating the Christian faith, propaganda had no negative connotation; not until the birth of methods employed during World War I had the term acquired a pejorative meaning. "Propaganda," Peter Kenez writes, "is nothing more than the attempt to transmit social and political values in the hope of affecting thinking, emotions, and thereby behavior. . . . To rail against propaganda is useless, for it is an integral part of the modern world." Kenez, *The Birth of the Propaganda State: Soviet Methods of Mass Mobilization, 1917–1929* (Cambridge: Cambridge University Press, 1985), 4.

74. "Egypt Nationalizes Suez Canal Company; Will Use Revenues to Build Aswan Dam," *New York Times*, July 27, 1956, 1.

75. One contemporary observer of Suez, a Foreign Service official stationed in Laos, wrote about Dulles's role:

> The British and French found it expedient to put much of the blame for the big mess on America's Dulles, who had precipitated Nasser's anger by his abrupt decision to withdraw from the Aswan dam deal. Dulles also, after Nasser's seizure of the canal company, had talked London and Paris out of taking strong measures, thus bestowing triumph upon Nasser. That the British and French should dare imply that any part of the whole jumble was Dulles's fault generally produced outcries of protest and indignation among Americans, especially most of those who assembled late every afternoon near my room in the barracks building to inform each other vociferously of their latest thoughts on current issues. (Jack Nixon, "Variations on the Suez Crisis," American Diplomacy: Foreign Service Dispatches and Periodic Reports on U.S. Foreign Policy, http://www.unc.edu/depts/diplomat/archives_roll/2003_04–06/nixon_suez/nixon_suez.html)

76. *The Eisenhower Diaries*, ed. R. H. Ferrell (New York: W. W. Norton, 1980), 319.

77. Robert R. Bowie, "Eisenhower, Dulles, and the Suez Crisis," in Louis and Owen, *Suez 1956*, 191.

78. Diane B. Kunz, "The Importance of Having Money: The Economic Diplomacy of the Suez Crisis," in Louis and Owen, *Suez 1956*, 215–232. See also Galpern, *Money, Oil, and Empire in the Middle East*.

79. The African American communist Doxie Wilkerson, who allegedly resigned from the party in 1957 after Khrushchev's revelations about Stalin (a topic discussed in Chapter 4), foresaw this reconfiguration of the "special relationship" as early as 1941, when he joined a group of intellectuals debating the question of racial minorities and World War II. He quotes the economist Virgil Jordan ("leader of finance and industry, able spokesman of American Big Business"), who says in a prophetic address to a convention of investment bankers:

> Whatever the outcome of the war, America has embarked upon a career of imperialism, both in world affairs and in every other aspect of life. . . . Even though, by our aid, England should emerge from this struggle without defeat, she will be so impoverished economically and crippled in prestige that it is improbable she will be able to resume or maintain the dominant position in world affairs she has occupied so long. At best, England will become a junior partner in a new Anglo-American imperialism, in which the economic resources and the military and naval strength of the United States will be the center of gravity. (Wilkerson, "Russia's Proposed New World Order of Socialism," *Journal of Negro Education* 10, no. 3 [July 1941]: 396)

80. McAlister, *Epic Encounters*, 32–35.

81. Yaqub, *Containing Arab Nationalism*, 73.

82. Ibid., 23.

83. Prados, "The Central Intelligence Agency and the Face of Decolonization," 38.

84. Yaqub, "The Cold War and the Middle East," 16. For a fuller elaboration of the Eisenhower Doctrine in the Arab world, see Yaqub's *Containing Arab Nationalism*.

85. See Edward Said, *Orientalism* (New York: Pantheon Books, 1978), 49–73.

86. John S. Badeau, "The Middle East: Conflict in Priorities," *Foreign Affairs*, January 1958. Astutely, Badeau notes: "In recent months there has been a good deal of interest in the application of international law to the free use of the Suez Canal and freedom of navigation in the Gulf of Aqaba. But international law represents largely the practice of the Western world in its diplomatic relationships; yet we approach the Middle East with the assumption that this body of Western experience has a universal validity. The fact is that the Muslim world in medieval times developed its own 'international law' and had its own principles of diplomacy." Ibid., 233.

87. Roderic H. Davison, "Where Is the Middle East?," *Foreign Affairs*, July 1960, 669. Though the phrase "Middle East" gains currency in 1890 (though it may have originated in the British mid-nineteenth century) with the publication of American naval officer Alfred Thayer Mahan's *The Influence of Sea Power upon History*, its geographical referents fluctuated over the next half century according to American perceptions of events and interests in the region.

88. Dwight D. Eisenhower, Second Inaugural Address, January 21, 1957, http://www.eisenhower.archives.gov/all_about_ike/speeches/1957_inaugural_address.pdf.

89. Mary L. Dudziak, *Cold War Civil Rights*, (Princeton, NJ: Princeton University Press, 2011), 115–151; Dulles quotation, 131.

90. Horace Cayton, "World at Large," *Pittsburgh Courier*, November 24, 1956.

91. I have not located documentation to verify Cayton's claim, though Soviet support for the Bandung Conference is widely discussed. "In April 1955, shortly before the Geneva Conference," writes Gordon Barrass, "Moscow backed the conference of almost thirty African and Asian nations, held at Bandung in Indonesia. It was there that Zhou En-Lai, the Chinese foreign minister, promoted the idea of 'peaceful coexistence.' Most delegates thought this meant live-and-let-live, while in fact it meant promoting normal relations between countries while the communists sought to extend their influence abroad and prevent foreign influences from affecting their own societies." Barrass, *The Great Cold War: A Journey through the Hall of Mirrors* (Stanford, CA: Stanford University Press, 2009), 105.

92. See Shaw, *Eden, Suez, and the Mass Media*.

93. Fanon, *Wretched of the Earth*, 78–79.

94. Mystery still enshrouds the death of Lumumba. See Ludo De Witte's *The Assassination of Patrice Lumumba* (New York: Verso, 2001) and the exchange

between Brian Urquhart and De Witte in Brian Urquhart, "The Tragedy of Lumumba," *New York Review of Books*, October 2, 2001; and De Witte and Colin Legum, reply by Brian Urquhart, "The Tragedy of Lumumba: An Exchange," *New York Review of Books*, December 20, 2001. For a recent commentary by a former staff director of the U.S. House of Representatives' Subcommittee on Africa, see Stephen R. Weissman's "What Really Happened in Congo: The CIA, the Murder of Lumumba, and the Rise of Mobutu," *Foreign Affairs* 93, no. 4 (July–August 2014): 14–24.

95. The Bulganin communiqué of November 5, 1956, continues: "We are fully determined to crush the aggressors and restore peace in the East through the use of force. We hope at this critical moment you will display due prudence and draw the correct conclusions from this." Quoted in W. Scott Lucas, *Divided We Stand: Britain, the US, and the Suez Crisis* (London: Hodder and Stoughton, 1991), 290. On this communiqué, see also Keith Kyle, *Suez* (New York: St. Martin's Press, 1991), 456–460. For two studies that advance different interpretations of Israel's response to the Czech-Egyptian Arms Deal, a question that bears on Israel's comportment toward Egypt and collaboration with France and Britain in the lead-up to Suez, see Motti Golani, "The Historical Place of the Czech-Egyptian Arms Deal, Fall 1955," *Middle Eastern Studies* 31, no. 4 (October 1995): 804–827; and Guy Laron, "'Logic Dictates that They May Attack When They Feel They Can Win': The 1955 Czech-Egyptian Arms Deal, the Egyptian Army, and Israeli Intelligence," *Middle East Journal* 63, no. 1 (Winter 2009): 69–84.

96. Despite the international shockwaves Khrushchev's speech generated, critics then and now debate the accuracy of Khrushchev's revelations and his own role in that repression, as well as his attribution of responsibility to Stalin as a maniacal leader rather than to the system that sustained Soviet repression for a quarter century. For an indictment of Khrushchev's speech in the broader context of Marxism's "breakdown," see the third volume of Leszek Kolakowski's *Main Currents of Marxism* (New York: W. W. Norton, 2005). See also his "My Correct Views on Everything: A Rejoinder to E. P. Thompson," in *My Correct Views on Everything* (South Bend, IN: St. Augustine's Press, 2005), 3–26.

97. Dipesh Chakrabarty, "The Legacies of Bandung: Decolonization and the Politics of Culture," in Lee, *Making a World after Empire*, 50.

98. See W. E. B. Du Bois, "Lenin and Africa," in *W. E. B. Du Bois on Africa*, ed. Eugene F. Provenzo Jr. and Edmund Baraka (Walnut Creek, CA: Left Coast Press, 2012), 253–259. Originally published in the Soviet journal *Sovremennyi vostok*, no. 4 (1959).

99. See Kate Baldwin, *Beyond the Color Line and the Color Curtain: Reading Encounters between Black and Red, 1922–1963* (Durham, NC: Duke University Press, 2002), 149–201.

100. As Diane B. Kunz shows, Dulles proposed the Suez Canal Users' Association as a way to mediate Egyptian and European interests in the canal. "Premised on the assumption that the Egyptians could not run the Canal, from beginning to end [the users' association] made no substantive sense. It did,

however, meet two American requirements. The first was that it was consistent with Eisenhower's conviction that 'this was not the issue upon which to try to downgrade Nasser.' The second was that it would keep the British and French occupied, which was important because the Administration believed that 'the passage of time was working in favour of a compromise.'" Nasser summarily rejected the proposal. Kunz, "Importance of Having Money, 221–222.

101. George Schuyler, "The World Today," *Pittsburgh Courier*, October 31, 1959, A6. This theme recurs throughout the black press. See also Zaki Salama, "Egypt Hosts Nasser's Six Year Rule, Applauds Gains," *Chicago Defender*, August 2, 1958, 2; "May Be Doubtful but It's a Fact," *Chicago Defender*, September 3, 1966, 5; and "Nasser's Still Boss 10 Years after Suez," *Chicago Defender*, October 22, 1966, 4.

102. Langston Hughes, "Simple Discusses Rocks," *Chicago Defender*, October 18, 1958.

103. See John Stuart Mill, *Considerations on Representative Government* (Amherst, NY: Prometheus Books, 1991), especially chapter 18, "Of the Government of Dependencies by a Free State."

104. "Sweat and Blood," *Baltimore Afro-American*, August 18, 1956, 20.

105. Jawalharlal Nehru, who had been appointed to mediate discussions between Egypt and England, did not applaud Nasser's action. Nehru believed that in spontaneously nationalizing the Canal Nasser was acting in an angry and intemperate fashion. But once England, France, and Israel invaded Egypt, Nehru quickly sided with Nasser, writing that he "could not imagine a worse case of aggression. . . . The whole future of the relations between Europe and Asia hangs in the balance." Sarvepalli Gopal, "India, the Crisis, and the Non-Aligned Nations," in Louis and Owen, *Suez 1956*, 185.

106. Jawalharlal Nehru, *Asia-Africa Speaks from Bandung* (Jakarta: Ministry of Foreign Affairs, Republic of Indonesia, 1955).

107. On collaborations between African Americans and Indians, see Gerald Horne, *The End of Empires: African Americans and India* (Philadelphia: Temple University Press, 2008); and Nico Slate, *Colored Cosmopolitanism: The Shared Struggle for Freedom in the United States and India* (Cambridge, MA: Harvard University Press, 2012).

108. "Nehru Says Egypt Rightfully Seized Suez Canal under Laws," *Baltimore Afro-American*, August 18, 1956.

109. Gopal, "India, the Crisis, and the Non-Aligned Nations," 173.

110. "Nehru Says Egypt Rightfully Seized Suez Canal."

111. "Nehru Greatly Shocked by Aggression in Egypt," *Baltimore Afro-American*, November 17, 1956; "India Fights Colonialism," *Chicago Defender*, December 30, 1961, 8.

112. J. A. Rogers, "History Shows," *Pittsburgh Courier*, August 9, 1958, A9.

113. The question is followed with England's stake: "In 1955, 8,630 tons went through the canal. Oil bound for England equaled 20,543 tons." More substantive analyses followed. Journalist Louis Lautier, the first black American voted into the National Press Club, wrote articles on Middle East oil

politics, focusing on tax revenues generated for the U.S. Treasury via American oil producer Aramco, jointly owned by Saudi Arabia. Lautier, "Suez Canal Crisis Linked with Colonialism, Egypt's Equality," *Baltimore Afro-American*, October 20, 1956, 13; and "Capital Spotlight: Cites Figures, Facts about Oil," *Baltimore Afro-American*, March 2, 1957, 4. "Although the U.S. claims to be neutral in the dispute over the Suez," opines the *Defender*, "plenty of American ships use the Canal and the U.S. plan to subsidize ships with extra oil to re-route them around the Cape of Good Hope is a long and expensive operation which may even threaten the domestic oil supply." "Trap for Nasser," *Chicago Defender*, September 29, 1956, 2. For a recent account of the political and economic collaborations and tensions between England and the United States concerning Middle Eastern oil, see Galpern, *Money, Oil, and Empire in the Middle East*.

114. Louis E. Martin, "Dope and Data," *Chicago Defender*, November 17, 1956, 9.

115. Harold L. Keith, "Patriot or Thief? Egyptian Action after Suez Sets an Example for Others to Follow," *Pittsburgh Courier*, February 23, 1957.

116. "Our Opinions: Dangerous Diplomacy," *Chicago Defender*, August 11, 1956, 9.

117. Gordon, "Film, Fame, and Public Memory."

118. Regarding Israel, Cayton writes:

> Israel has invaded Egypt and by this action has precipitated the most potent political crisis since Korea. Why should a small nation of less than two million attack that Arab nation and throw the entire world into danger of war? Her behavior seems hard to understand, for it was an act of violent desperation. . . . The fact of the matter is that Israel is fighting for her life. Egypt and the rest of the Arab countries have openly avowed their purpose of destroying the country. Our foreign policy under the present administration has been to make friends with the Arabs at the expense of Israel. With the rise of Nasser and the seizing of the Suez Canal, it became apparent that the next step of the enraged Arabs would be the liquidation of Israel. (Horace Cayton, "World at Large," *Pittsburgh Courier*, November 10, 1956, A6)

Like many commentators, however, Cayton modified his views when it became apparent that Israel had colluded with Britain and France in the invasion of Egypt. Ibid. On this score, Benjamin Mays writes: "It will be difficult to convince the world that England and France did not give Israel the nod to invade Egypt. . . . When the English military left Suez in 1954, the agreement was that if the waterways were attacked and if Egypt was attacked, the English would again guard the canal. [Israel's] invasion of Egypt made it possible according to [the] agreement for the British to return." Mays, "Crisis in the Middle East," *Pittsburgh Courier*, November 24, 1956, A4.

Though tending to identify Egyptians and Palestinians as colonial subjects, many writers in the black press also supported the nascent state of Israel. See, for example, Max Fine, "Israel Celebrates 10th Independence Anniversary,"

Chicago Defender, May 3, 1958, 2. Invoking Jewish American sociologist Louis Wirth's (pre-Israel) prognostication that an independent Jewish state would simply ghettoize diaspora Jewry, Louis E. Martin counters: "Today, however, I doubt that there are many Jews who do not feel that Israel represents the best hope for the future and who do not glory in its remarkable progress and development in so little time." Martin, "Dope and Data," 9. In a letter to the editor, a reader commends the one journalist's dissent from the valorization of Nasser: "I would like to thank Mr. Strother for agreeing with me that Nasser is a dictator. . . . I have talked to many colored people about Israel. They feel as I do, that Israel's struggle for survival and her fight for democracy is also their fight." Al Loewenthal, "Defends Israel," *Chicago Defender*, February 23, 1957, 10.

119. Horace Cayton, "World at Large," *Pittsburgh Courier*, August 15, 1959, B6.

120. Horace Cayton, "World at Large," *Pittsburgh Courier*, August 2, 1958, A8.

121. For an account of black and white Americans' appropriations of ancient Egypt, see Scott Trafton, *Egypt Land: Race and Nineteenth-Century American Egyptomania* (Durham, NC: Duke University Press, 2004).

122. "U.S. Student in Egypt Mistaken for an Arab," *Chicago Defender*, May 6, 1961, 5. Another student, "unable to study medicine in the U.S. after graduating from Howard," claims that he "sang his way to Egypt, where he explained his plight to President Nasser." A sensation in Egypt, the student was an emcee in a music competition that "created the first popular enthusiasm for American music since the Suez incident began." "Howard Grad Doing U.S. Goodwill Job in Egypt," *Baltimore Afro-American*, June 8, 1957, 18.

123. Echoing a remark made in a previously cited column, Langston Hughes writes: "Then there is Nasser, who seems to be the Adam Clayton Powell of the Arab countries, tall, dark, handsome, and loud." See Hughes, "Colored Peoples in World News Last Year," *Chicago Defender*, January 19, 1957, 9. "Egyptian President, Gamal Abdel Nasser, who looks like Thurgood Marshall of the NAACP, does not seem to understand that he is supposed to take off his hat when white folks enter the room," writes Louis E. Martin. Martin, "Dope and Data," 9.

124. Horace Cayton, "World at Large," *Pittsburgh Courier*, November 24, 1956, A6. In a report from Brussels, J. A. Rogers interviews "colored folk in Europe" who "seem to be solidly behind Nasser [whom Rogers calls a 'mulatto, a very common type in Cairo']. I have asked many—Africans, West Indians, Americans, North Africans—what they thought, and everyone said he was glad." Rogers, "History Shows," *Pittsburgh Courier*, October 6, 1956, A4.

125. "Scanning the Horizon," *Chicago Defender*, December 15, 1956, 2.

126. See "Marguerite Cartwright," in *African American National Biography*, vol. 2, ed. Henry Louis Gates Jr. and Evelyn Brooks Higginbotham (Oxford: Oxford University Press, 2008), 201–203.

127. Marguerite Cartwright, "Essays on Nasser: The Last Time I Saw Nasser," *Pittsburgh Courier*, October 27, 1956, A5.

128. “Oral History Interview with Henry Byroade,” Harry S. Truman Library and Museum. Byroade continues: “Later on he got involved in Yemen and all over the Arab world and so on. But in the beginning we weren’t really having any trouble with Nasser. I talked to him hundreds of hours on the Arab-Israeli problem. In a way he was more reasonable than any Arab leader at the time. Now, there’s a reason for this. Until that attack, which happened the day after I got there, Egypt and Israel had never had any border problems really. They were a little farther away, and we didn’t have that kind of public opinion problem.” http://www.trumanlibrary.org/oralhist/byroade.htm.

129. Bunche, quoted in Brian Urquhart, *Ralph Bunche: An American Odyssey* (New York: W. W. Norton, 1998), 279, 281–282.

130. Fanon, *Wretched of the Earth*, 77. Insofar as such portraits say more about the observer than the observed, Bunche’s description also reflects his own powerful position within the precincts of the U.S. foreign policy establishment. At the same time, Bunche’s place within this establishment was ambiguous. Though he seemed to benefit diplomatically from his fair complexion, he also endured racial slights from white colleagues and, during the Communist witch-hunt of the 1950s, would be called to account for his early radical views and associations. See Urquhart, *Ralph Bunche*, especially chapter 18.

131. Apparently in normal circumstances when Nasser addressed Egyptians via transistor radio, his speeches were subdued. Consider this lyrical description by one Lebanese political scientist, Iliya Harik:

> Nasser’s speeches contained no fiery rhetoric; they were monotonous, flowing slowly and incessantly like the great Nile. His words were pronounced with deliberation; his pauses and repetitions were frequent. His style was not ornate; rather, he spoke in a colloquial, conversational manner. The villagers sat listening as if at a séance. Nasser took them into his confidence, or seemed to do so, by explaining affairs of state in uncomplicated language. . . . He congratulated himself for what he had done for them, called on their patience for hardships that had to be endured, and lectured them on socialism. The villagers were entertained, moderately enlightened, and above all, flattered. (Quoted in Podeh and Winckler, *Rethinking Nasserism*, 17)

132. Kevin Gaines and other critics have attributed this form of liberal citizenship to certain black intellectuals writing on Third World politics. On Pauli Murray’s turbulent stint in Ghana, Gaines writes: “Murray’s ideological sparring with the Ghanaian government was informed by a dominant, ostensibly color-blind American liberalism that in effect banished an independent black political identity to a Siberia-like realm of otherness, its racialized logic accusing African American dissenters of ‘thinking like blacks’ instead of ‘like Americans.’ ” Gaines, *American Africans in Ghana*, 117; and Kevin Gaines, “E. Franklin Frazier’s Revenge: Anticolonialism, Nonalignment, and Black Intellectuals’ Critiques of Western Culture,” *American Literary History* 17,

no. 3 (Fall 2005): 506–529. See also the aforementioned symposium, "African Americans and U.S. Foreign Relations," in *Diplomatic History* 20, no. 4 (Fall 1996): 531–650.

133. Scholars like Edward Said, Melani McAlister, and Michael Shapiro have adumbrated overlapping definitions of the term *moral geography.* Adapting Shapiro's version, McAlister defines the term in the following way: "cultural and political practices that work together to mark not only states but also regions, cultural groupings, and ethnic or racial territories. Moral geographies shape human understandings of the world ethically and politically as well as cognitively; they consist of a 'set of silent ethical assertions' that mark connection and separation. Different moral geographies can coexist and even compete; each represents a different type of imaginative affiliation linked to certain ideas about significant spaces." McAlister, *Epic Encounters*, 4.

134. The Aswan Dam, a high dam near the Egyptian-Sudanese border, "was designed to transform Egypt's economy and society by adding over 850,000 hectares to the area of cultivable land, rendering the Nile navigable as far south as Sudan and generating the electricity necessary for industrialization." Shaw, *Eden, Suez, and the Mass Media*, 3.

135. Shirley Graham Du Bois, "Egypt Is Africa," *Black Scholar* 1, no. 7 (May 1970): 22.

136. See Laila Morsy, "The Military Clauses of the Anglo-Egyptian Treaty of Friendship and Alliance, 1936," *International Journal of Middle East Studies* 16 (1984): 68. Morsy quotes a speech by Egyptian opposition leader Nahas Pasha: "Britain Defends the Independence of Abyssinia, But Does Not Hesitate to Encroach on Egypt's Rights." Ibid., 67. As Morsy suggests, the "stationing of British troops in Egypt had been the bone of contention in all previous negotiations," but apparently factions within both sides agreed that at least some British military presence there served both nations' interests. The question involved the magnitude of that presence, its location, and what interests it served, Ibid., 73.

137. Shirley Graham Du Bois, *Gamal Abdel Nasser: Son of the Nile: A Biography* (New York: Third Press, 1972), 48.

138. "All peoples," continues Graham Du Bois, "have come to the Valley of the Nile—the Assyrians, the Phoenicians, the Persians, the Mongols, the Turks, the Greeks, the Romans, the Arabs, the British. The great ones came to rule—but in time they passed away. British armies and fleets came—intending to stay forever. But Gamal Abdul Nasser rid the country of them and seized the Suez Canal—built with the sweat and blood and tears of Egyptians. From all would-be conquerors, Egypt absorbed something, shaped and molded what they wanted for their needs, without losing the essence of their being." Graham Du Bois, "Egypt Is Africa," 32.

139. Graham Du Bois, *Gamal Abdel Nasser*, 60–61.

140. Ibid.

141. "Nasser Says UAR Led Freedom Fight," *Pittsburgh Courier*, February 11, 1961, A2.

142. In his *Philosophy of History* (1837), Hegel writes:

> *Africa* must be divided into three parts: one is that which lies south of the desert of Sahara—Africa proper—the Upland almost entirely unknown to us, with narrow coast-tracts along the sea; the second is that to the north of the desert—European Africa (if we may so call it)—a coastland; the third is the river region of the Nile, the only valley-land of Africa, and which is in connection with Asia. Africa proper, as far as History goes back, has remained—for all purposes of connection with the rest of the World—shut up; it is the Gold-land compressed within itself—the land of childhood, which lying beyond the day of self-conscious history, is enveloped in the dark mantle of Night. (Hegel, *The Philosophy of History*, 109–114, http://libcom.org/files/Philosophy_of_History.pdf)

143. Graham Du Bois, *Gamal Abdel Nasser*, 49.

144. Fanon continues: "Taking the continent as a whole, this religious tension may be responsible for the revival of the commonest racial feeling. Africa is divided into Black and White, and the names that are substituted—Africa South of the Sahara, Africa North of the Sahara—do not manage to hide this latent racism. Here it is affirmed that White Africa has a thousand-year-old tradition of culture; that she is Mediterranean, that she is a continuation of Europe, and that she shares in Greco-Latin civilization. Black Africa is looked on as a region that is inert, brutal, uncivilized, in a word, savage." Fanon, *Wretched of the Earth*, 160–161.

145. See Leopold Senghor, *The Foundations of "Africanité" or "Négritude" and "Arabité"* (Paris: Présence Africaine, 1967); and Cheik Anta Diop, *Precolonial Black Africa* (Chicago: Lawrence Hill Books, 1987).

146. Gamal Abdel Nasser, *The Philosophy of the Revolution* (Cairo: Mondiale Press, 1955), 54.

147. Arnold Rivkin, "Israel and the Afro-Asian World," *Foreign Affairs*, April 1959, 487.

148. "As early as 1953," Muehlenbeck continues, "the government-affiliated periodical *Al-Akhbar* editorialized, 'We look for a power which will protect Africa and play the same role as the United States *vis-à-vis* the American continent. We see no one but Egypt. It is the greatest African power with a personality that is universally recognised. It is necessary for Egypt to pursue one African policy, the enfranchisement of the Continent.'" Philip E. Muehlenbeck, *Betting on the Africans: John F. Kennedy's Courting of African Nationalist Leaders* (Oxford: Oxford University Press, 2014), 123.

149. Graham Du Bois, "Egypt Is Africa," 30.

150. Ibid., 33; Nasser, *Philosophy of the Revolution*, 52–67.

151. Nasser, *Philosophy of the Revolution*, 70.

152. A reviewer from the American University of Beirut noted in 1957: "It should be admitted that the English translation of this book is extremely poor and leaves one wondering how responsible authorities in Egypt permit its sale. In its present form it stands as poor propaganda for Egyptian scholarship." Several English translations, but no scholarly editions, have been

published of *The Philosophy of the Revolution*. I want to acknowledge Dr. Hope Ishak, my Arabic teacher, for her help in translating this passage and identifying the English mistranslation. For the version cited here, see *The Philosophy of the Revolution*, with an introduction by Dorothy Thompson; publication of this version is attributed to the General Organisation for Government Printing Offices, Cairo, Managing Director Mohamed El-Fateh Omr—but includes no date, translator, or other information. Other published versions (several exist, though some rely on identical or similar English translations) lack attribution altogether.

153. Graham Du Bois, *Gamal Abdel Nasser*, 64. Of course, Graham's assumption that the United States dropped the atomic bombs "after Allied victory was assured" is debatable and still a contentious subject.

154. Richard Wright, "The Psychological Reactions of Oppressed People," in *Black Power: Three Books from Exile*, 683.

155. Wallerstein, "What Cold War in Asia?," 17.

156. Wright, *Color Curtain*, 468.

157. Jacques Soustelle, "The Wealth of the Sahara," *Foreign Affairs*, July 1959, 626. A *Time* magazine profile of Soustelle opens with a luxurious, if incongruous, scene at Hassi-Messaoud:

> It was a scene to gladden even the most jaded cruise director. The open-air movie was filled to capacity with a bronzed, relaxed audience. In the swimming pool near by, energetic types were splashing away at water polo. From the "Bikini" bar came the clink of glasses and the hum of bar babble, and in the soft glow cast by indirect neon lighting, palm leaves fluttered.
>
> Only one thing marred the luxury-liner atmosphere that hung last week over the self-contained little world called Hassi Messaoud (Blessed Well): the waves that billowed around it were of sand, not of water. Hassi Messaoud, the Dawson City of the great French oil rush of 1959, lies deep in the barren wastes of the Sahara, 400 miles (or three days by truck) south of Algiers.
>
> Four years ago Hassi Messaoud was simply an abandoned water hole, a navigational reference point for voyagers across the vast sea of sand and stone that the Romans called leonum arida nutrix—the arid nurse of lions. Today it has 5,000 inhabitants, sprawls over nearly 60 square miles of desert. Hassi Messaoud still has no women, no children, no church, no mosque. But it does have three hotels (650 rooms in air-conditioned cottages), two movie theaters, two swimming pools, an airport big enough to handle Caravelle jets, and 124 private firms, including an automatic laundry and a lemonade factory. Between the buildings green lawns grow in topsoil trucked in from Algiers. In its three staff dining rooms white-jacketed waiters serve meals worthy of a three-star Paris restaurant, from pate to four kinds of cheese. (*Time*, August 17, 1959, 28)

158. On the fallout of Suez for French politics and the Algerian war, see Maurice Vaïsse, "Post-Suez France," and Adam Watson, "The Aftermath of

Suez: Consequences for French Decolonization" in Louis and Owen, *Suez 1956*, 335–346.

159. "The Visionary," *Time*, August 17, 1959, 28–36.

160. David Harvey, *Cosmopolitanism and the Geographies of Freedom* (New York: Columbia University Press, 2009), 40. In chapter 2, Harvey draws on, and challenges, postcolonial critiques of liberalism principally by Uday Mehta and Dipesh Chakrabarty. See Mehta, *Liberalism and Empire: A Study in Nineteenth-Century Liberal Thought* (Chicago: University of Chicago Press, 1999); and Chakrabarty, *Provincializing Europe*. See also Chakrabarty and Mehta's interlocutor, Bhikhu Parekh, "Superior People: The Narrowness of Liberalism from Mill to Rawls," *Times Literary Supplement*, February 25, 1994, 11–13.

161. Soustelle, "Wealth of the Sahara," 627.

162. Immanuel Wallerstein, *World-Systems Analysis: An Introduction* (Durham, NC: Duke University Press, 2004), 10.

163. On Eisenhower's "atoms for peace" campaign as part of a broader cold war of ideas, see Kenneth Osgood, *Total Cold War: Eisenhower's Secret Propaganda Battle at Home and Abroad* (Lawrence: University Press of Kansas, 2008), 153–180.

164. Fanon, *Wretched of the Earth*, 81–82.

165. Ibid., 82.

166. Danielle Endres defines nuclear colonialism as a "system of domination through which governments and corporations disproportionately target and devastate indigenous peoples and their lands to maintain the nuclear production process." Endres, "The Rhetoric of Nuclear Colonialism: Rhetorical Exclusion of American Indian Arguments in the Yucca Mountain Nuclear Waste Siting Decision," *Communication and Critical/Cultural Studies* 6, no. 1 (March 2009): 39–60.

167. Jean-Marc Regnault, "France's Search for Nuclear Test Sites, 1957–1963," *Journal of Military History* 67 (October 2003): 1226. Though French officials publicly tended to downplay the Algerian revolution in their Saharan projects, privately they acknowledged the difficulties the war posed. Renault cites General Charles Ailleret, France's commanding general of the Special Weapons Section, who wrote to another colonel in charge of the technical division for building and fortifications: "We cannot rule out the possibility that the external circumstances will in the near future force us to give up the test firing range in the Sahara—either a general moratorium on tests which might contaminate the globe with radioactivity, or an internationalization of the Algerian conflict, or instability in North Africa, which would create conditions that would no longer permit tests in the Sahara to be carried out conveniently." Ibid., 1228.

168. Gaines, *American Africans in Ghana*, 104–105.

169. Gamal Nkrumah, "A Tale of Two Canals," *Al-Ahram Weekly*, no. 1213 (September 11, 2014), http://weekly.ahram.org.eg/News/7188/32/A-tale-of-two-canals.aspx.

170. Eric Waldron, *Tropic Death* (New York: Liveright, 2013), 67–68.

171. Jennifer Brittan, "The Terminal: Eric Walrond, the City of Colón, and the Caribbean of the Panama Canal," *American Literary History* 25, no. 2 (Summer 2013): 300. "Focusing on the informal canal economy, unofficial labor, and neighborhoods famed as the very frontier of debauchery," Brittan writes, "Walrond highlights the elements of the city [Colón] that Zone administrators worked tirelessly to expel" (304).

172. Julie Greene notes that the replacement of French failure with U.S. initiative on the Panama Canal transformed into a narrative of American exceptionalism—during the time of the canal's construction and since. For this contemporary view, she cites the remarks in 2005 by David McCullough, who published the bestselling *The Path between the Seas* in 1977: "I think often about why the French failed at Panama and why we succeeded. One of the reasons we succeeded is that we were gifted, we were attuned to adaptation, to doing what works, whereas they were trained to do everything in a certain way. We have a gift for improvisation." Greene, *The Canal Builders: Making America's Empire at the Panama Canal* (New York: Penguin Press, 2009), 3.

173. As Julie Greene notes, this system of compensation was exceedingly complex:

> The [Isthmian Canal Company] used a complex pay scale for its silver workers that differentiated them not on the basis of the job they did but according to their race, ethnicity, and nationality. Unskilled West Indians were categorized as "Laborer A" and paid the equivalent of ten cents U.S. currency per hour; Colombians, Panamanians, and other Latin Americans were classified as "Laborer B" and paid thirteen cents per hour (West Indians were explicitly excluded from this category); "Laborer C" received sixteen cents, and the category was reserved for a "European or other white laborer or black American laborer" who came to this Canal Zone on his own, that is, without an official [Isthmian Canal Company] labor contract; Europeans with a contract were classified as "Laborer D" and received twenty cents per hour." (Greene, *Canal Builders*, 164)

174. Ibid., 8–9.

175. Louis Wirth, "Is a Hitler Defeat Essential to the Preservation of Democracy in the Western Hemisphere?" *Journal of Negro Education* (July 1941): 421.

176. Eric Williams, "The Impact of the International Crisis upon the Negro in the Caribbean," *Journal of Negro Education* (July 1941): 536, 541.

177. "Suez Shift Boon to the Panama Canal," *New York Times*, January 4, 1958, 30.

178. Memorandum of conversation between Dulles and Eisenhower, vol. 16, Suez Crisis (July 26–December 31, 1956), doc. 71, http://history.state.gov/historicaldocuments/frus1955–57v16/d71.

179. Anthony Eden, *Full Circle: The Memoirs of Anthony Eden* (Boston: Houghton Mifflin, 1960), 557.

180. "Rescue Not Desired," *Baltimore Afro-American*, May 20, 1961, 4.

181. "Suez and Panama," *Baltimore Afro-American*, September 29, 1956, 4.

182. "Horizon: Rev. Mr. Dulles," *Pittsburgh Courier*, August 18, 1956, A4. Regarding the supposed influence of Dulles's religious beliefs on his foreign policy decisions, Salim Yaqub observes: "Dulles's rigid moralism, though real, was specific and limited. Some scholars have seen Dulles's international approach as an extension of his unwavering Protestant faith, but a more convincing interpretation treats the legal profession as the overarching model for his diplomacy." Yaqub, *Containing Arab Nationalism*, 28.

183. Prattis writes: "We drew up a treaty based upon our willingness to buy [the Isthmus of Panama, then under Colombian control]. In this treaty we insisted upon taking over a zone, five miles wide on either side of the proposed canal. The Colombian Senate balked on that. Know what happened then? The Panamanians decided to 'revolt.' When the Colombians moved in to quell the 'revolt,' they found Uncle Sam waiting for them with a great big gun." P. L. Prattis, "Rev. Mr. Dulles," *Pittsburgh Courier*, August 18, 1956, A4.

184. "Showdown in Panama," *Baltimore Afro-American*, November 21, 1959, 4.

185. "Courts of World Opinion: Trying the Panama Flag Riots of 1964," *Diplomatic History* 28, no. 1 (January 2004): 83–112.

186. "Get Out of Panama," *Baltimore Afro-American*, January, 25, 1964, 13.

187. In his September 7, 1977, speech on the signing of the Panama Canal Treaty, Jimmy Carter said:

> Under these accords, Panama will play an increasingly important role in the operation and defense of the canal during the next 23 years. And after that, the United States will still be able to counter any threat to the canal's neutrality and openness for use. . . . Many of you seated at this table have made known for years through the Organization of American States and through your own personal expressions of concern to my predecessors in the White House, your own strong feelings about the Panama Canal Treaty of 1903. That treaty, drafted in a world so different from ours today, has become an obstacle to better relations with Latin America. ("Statement on the Panama Canal Treaty Signing [September 7, 1977]," Miller Center of the University of Virginia website, http://millercenter.org/president/speeches/detail/3928)

188. Benjamin L. Hooks, "Time to Return Panama Canal We 'Stole,'" *Baltimore Afro-American*, October 1, 1977, 5.

CHAPTER 4 The Right to Fail

1. Recent appraisals include Kate Baldwin, *Beyond the Color Line and the Iron Curtain: Reading Encounters between Black and Red, 1922–1963* (Durham, NC: Duke University Press, 2002); Joy Carew, *Blacks, Reds, and Russians: Sojourners in Search of the Soviet Promise* (Piscataway, NJ: Rutgers University Press, 2010); Yunxiang Gao, "W. E. B. and Shirley Graham Du Bois in Maoist China," *Du Bois Review: Social Science Research on Race* 10, no. 1 (Spring 2013): 59–85; Gerald Horne, *Black and Red: W. E. B. Du Bois and the Afro-*

American Response to the Cold War, 1944–1963 (New York: State University of New York Press, 1985); and Eric Porter, *The Problem of the Future World: W. E. B. Du Bois and the Race Concept at Midcentury* (Durham, NC: Duke University Press, 2010).

2. Regarding Du Bois's affinity for Stalinism, Porter adds: "Yet we must avoid the problem of making leftist ideas and affinities overly determinative of his thought during these years in either positive or negative ways. Du Bois might have praised Stalin, for example, but he was not a Stalinist in any systematic way." Yet it is unclear how many independent intellectuals of this era could be described as "a Stalinist in any systematic way." In some measure, this chapter is in pursuit of precisely these overly determined leftist ideas and affinities. Porter, *Problem of the Future World*, 10.

3. Few have considered the influence of the writer and activist Shirley Graham on Du Bois's postwar thought or her own contribution to the transnational black literary left, a subject explored in Chapter 5. Not surprisingly, though, the question of influence remains a matter of contention and a difficult one to disentangle. Who influenced whom, and how? What is more illuminating than the question of reciprocal influence is the path each writer traveled en route to a synthesis of communism, Pan-Africanism, and Maoism as an alternative to the Cold War consensus. By "consensus" I do not mean that this period, roughly from 1945 to 1968, was not marked by diverse and sometimes vigorous modes of contestation to Cold War ideological regimes. Some critics read this period as one, for example, when former leftists enacted self-reflexive or aesthetically and ideologically hybrid recompositions of former leftist commitments. By "Cold War consensus," I simply mean to recall the incorporation of anticommunism into a broader national mission increasingly identified with centrist liberalism, one that alienated blacks and whites alike from the Soviet experiment and created a system in which the perception of an individual's deviation from that national mission often resulted in significant consequences, including incarceration, detention, travel restriction, and public trials, among other punitive measures.

4. David Levering Lewis, *W. E. B. Du Bois: The Fight for Equality and the American Century, 1919–1963* (New York: Henry Holt, 2000), 229.

5. As the Cold War mounted, William E. Cain observes, Du Bois defended peace and civil liberties against right-wing assault while assailing inequality, segregation, and colonialism. "But he spoke and acted as a Stalinist. This is the most troubling fact about his extraordinary career." Cain notes, rightly, that it is inadequate "to call Du Bois a socialist and anti-imperialist: this makes him too easy to locate and comprehend." Cain, "From Liberalism to Communism: The Political Thought of W. E. B. Du Bois," in *Cultures of U.S. Imperialism*, ed. Amy Kaplan and Donald E. Pease (Durham, NC: Duke University Press, 1993), 456–473. Similarly, John Carlos Rowe writes: "Rightly condemning U.S. imperialism around the globe and Cold War ideology, he would nevertheless rationalize stubbornly and blindly Stalinist oppression both within and outside the Soviet Union, ignoring the fact that state communism had been as corrupted in practice in

the Soviet empire as democracy was corrupted by Western capitalism." John Carlos Rowe, *Literary Culture and U.S. Imperialism: From the Revolution to World War II* (Oxford: Oxford University Press, 2000), 215.

Each of these critical assessments captures some truth about Du Bois's appropriation—to some degree ironic, notes Ira Katznelson—of Stalinism. Yet collectively they define this trajectory as a twisted arc "from liberalism to communism," a narrative that conceals an idiosyncratic unity of Du Bois's thought that is most in evidence in his work during the 1940s and 1950s. Moreover, this narrative shrinks the conceptual space for the geopolitical alternative to liberal capitalist hegemony that he strived to engender. Katznelson adds: It "was not just his decision to exit [the United States for Ghana] but also his late-life Bolshevism, even his ironic approbation of Stalin, that signify just how bruising America's racial order and Cold War persecutions proved to be. . . . Du Bois's early liberalism did not, perhaps could not, survive 93 years of persistent racism." Katznelson, "Du Bois's Century," *Social Science History* 23, no. 4 (1999): 463.

6. W. E. B. Du Bois, *Dusk of Dawn: An Essay toward an Autobiography of a Race Concept* (Oxford: Oxford University Press, 2014), 16.

7. David Levering Lewis uncovers a revealing anecdote from one conversation between Du Bois and a Soviet official, Ovid Gorchakov, who apparently was "absolutely amazed by the breadth of his culture, his grasp of events, his vast erudition." As the two had apparently developed a rapport, Gorchakov wanted to confide in Du Bois about Stalin's regime but soon realized that "Du Bois 'excused Stalin's terror' and that he was not at all disposed to discuss (wisely enough) the continuing imperfections of the Soviet system." Levering Lewis, *W. E. B. Du Bois: The Fight for Equality and the American Century*, 561.

8. Baldwin, *Beyond the Color Line and the Iron Curtain*, 154.

9. On the concept of the "new man" in Stalinism and Nazism, see Peter Fritzsche and Jochen Hellbeck, "The New Man in Stalinist Russia and Nazi Germany," in *Beyond Totalitarianism: Stalinism and Nazism Compared*, ed. Michael Geyer and Sheila Fitzpatrick (Cambridge: Cambridge University Press, 2008), 302–344.

10. Fredric Jameson cites Theodor Adorno, Susan Sontag, and George Steiner as the principal exponents of this criticism. Theodor W. Adorno, *Notes to Literature*, vol. 2 (New York: Columbia University Press, 1992); Susan Sontag, *Against Interpretation and Other Essays* (New York: Picador, 2001); George Steiner, *Language and Silence: Essays on Language, Literature, and the Inhuman* (New Haven, CT: Yale University Press, 1998).

11. Bill V. Mullen, *Un-American: W. E. B. Du Bois and the Century of World Revolution* (Philadelphia: Temple University Press, 2015), 25.

12. Gordon S. Barrass, *The Great Cold War: A Journey through the Hall of Mirrors* (Stanford, CA: Stanford University Press, 2009), 106–107.

13. See Konstantin Azadovskii and Boris Egorov, "From Anti-Westernism to Anti-Semitism," *Journal of Cold War Studies* 4, no. 1 (Winter 2002): 66–80; Joshua Rubenstein and Vladimir P. Naumov, eds., *Stalin's Se-*

cret Pogrom: The Postwar Inquisition of the Jewish Anti-Fascist Committee (New Haven, CT: Yale University Press, 2005); and Jonathan Brent, *Stalin's Last Crime: The Plot against the Jewish Doctors, 1948–1953* (New York: Harper Perennial, 2004). One telling anecdote concerning Stalin's anti-Semitism involves the revelation of Lenin's own Jewish ancestry. When Lenin's elder sister Anna disclosed in a letter in the early 1930s to Stalin that Lenin's great-grandfather, Moishe Blank, was a Jew, and that publicizing this fact could "help combat anti-Semitism," Stalin staunchly refused and insisted she keep this knowledge to herself. See Lars T. Lih, *Lenin* (London: Reaktion Books, 2011), 20; and Dmitri Volkogonov, *Lenin: A New Biography* (New York: Free Press, 1994), 8–9.

14. Brent Hayes Edwards, *The Practice of Diaspora: Literature, Translation, and the Rise of Black Internationalism* (Cambridge, MA: Harvard University Press, 2003), 245.

15. W. E. B. Du Bois, *Color and Democracy: Colonies and Peace* (New York: Harcourt, Brace, 1945), 118.

16. Maurice Merleau-Ponty, *Humanism and Terror: An Essay on the Communist Problem* (Boston: Beacon Press, 1990), xiii–xv.

17. Levering Lewis, *W. E. B. Du Bois: The Fight for Equality and the American Century*, 260.

18. One might note in this context the involvement of Mao's China in African American affairs, including, of course, Mao's celebrated statements of support for the black revolution in 1963 and 1968. But the Chinese role differed for at least two reasons. First, the Chinese, as subjects of British imperialism, considered themselves part of the colonized Afro-Asian world and thus regarded themselves experientially allied with black Americans and other racially dominated groups. Second, China during this period was weak relative to the rival superpowers (though few serious observers denied the country's potential) and neither desired nor could afford to intervene internationally on the scale of the Soviet Union. Compared with Western nations, or with Japan, China remained relatively insular and far less likely to become entangled in a foreign nation's—especially America's—domestic affairs. Robeson Taj Frazier writes that Du Bois and Graham's two-month journey through China in 1959 widened "their perceptions of the process of galvanizing less-developed, formerly colonized nations toward economic sufficiency and social values of selflessness, sacrifice, and collective toil." Taj Frazier, *The East Is Black: Cold War China and the Black Radical Imagination* (Durham, NC: Duke University Press, 2015), 40.

19. This point is not to deny reciprocal efforts conducted by the U.S. government concerning, for example, Soviet Russia's own repressed groups or occupied foreign nations such as East Germany or Hungary or Soviet Central Asia.

20. Blakely dates this interest to Lenin, who in a 1900 article, "Capitalism in Agriculture," referred, passingly, to the emancipation of American Negroes, but the communist preoccupation with the Negro question most likely dates earlier, beginning with Marx and Engel's extensive commentaries on

the subject during the 1860s. Allison Blakely, "Recent Soviet Interpretations on 'The Negro Problem,'" *Black Scholar* 10, no. 6/7 (March/April 1979): 59–63. See also Karl Marx, *The Civil War in the United States* (New York: International Publishers, 1937); Gerald Runkle, "Karl Marx and the American Civil War," *Comparative Studies in Society and History* 6, no. 2 (January 1964): 117–141; and *An Unfinished Revolution: Karl Marx and Abraham Lincoln*, ed. Robin Blackburn (London: Verso, 2011).

21. John William Van Zanten III, "The Soviet Evaluation of the American Negro Problem, 1954–1965: A Study of Ideology and Propaganda" (PhD diss., Yale University, 1966), 2.

22. In addition to the superb efforts of Cloutier and Edwards in authenticating this manuscript, I wish to acknowledge Bryan Wagner, whose invitation to Berkeley in 2012 presented me an opportunity to discuss McKay's manuscript along with his colleagues. I want also to thank Nadia Ellis, Steven Lee, Michael Cohen, and Keith Feldman for their perspicacious contributions.

23. Mullen, *Un-American*, 32.

24. I adapt this definition of politics from Faisal Devji, *Landscapes of the Jihad: Militancy, Morality, Modernity* (Ithaca, NY: Cornell University Press, 2005), 3–4.

25. John Henrik Clarke, review of *Black Bolshevik: Autobiography of an Afro-American Communist*, by Harry Haywood, *Black Scholar* 10, nos. 6–7 (March–April 1979): 56.

26. Harry Haywood, *A Black Communist in the Freedom Struggle: The Life of Harry Haywood* (Minneapolis: University of Minnesota Press, 2012), 135–136.

27. For an account of McKay, Du Bois, Haywood, Robert Robinson, and black American fellow travelers to the USSR, see Carew, *Blacks, Reds, and Russians.*

28. Levering Lewis continues: "In contrast to [Paul] Robeson, who found the exposure of Stalinist horrors, whose enormities he had tried not to know, psychologically devastating, Du Bois adjusted the Russian casualty tables in light of the Atlantic slave trade, the scramble for Africa, the needless First World War, Nazi death camps, and the color-coded poverty and wage-slavery raging within and beyond North America. To Du Bois, the degradation of the communist ideal in Soviet Russia was philosophically irrelevant to the expiation of the sins of American democracy, whose very possibility he now deeply doubted." Levering Lewis, *W. E. B. Du Bois: The Fight for Equality and the American Century*, 557.

29. Melvyn P. Leffler, *The Specter of Communism: The United States and the Origins of the Cold War, 1917–1953* (New York: Hill and Wang, 1994), 21.

30. Baldwin, *Beyond the Color Line and the Iron Curtain*, 150.

31. Archie Brown, *The Rise and Fall of Communism* (New York: HarperCollins, 2011), 122–123. Concerning the approved "criticism and self-criticism," Gide wrote:

> It is not the Party line which is discussed or criticized, but only the question whether a certain theory tallies or not with this sacred line. No state

> of mind is more dangerous than this, nor more likely to imperil real culture. Soviet citizens remain in the most complete ignorance of everything outside their own country and—what is worse—have been persuaded that everything abroad is vastly inferior to everything at home. On the other hand, although they are not interested in what prevails outside their country, they are very much interested in what foreigners think of them. What they are very anxious to know is whether they are sufficiently admired abroad. . . . What they want from them is praise and not information. (Quoted in Brown, *Rise and Fall of Communism*, 122–123)

32. Michael Denning, *The Cultural Front: The Laboring of American Culture in the Twentieth Century* (London: Verso, 2011). I want to acknowledge Nathaniel Landry, whose research has enhanced my understanding of this genre.

33. On *Russia and America*, Kate Baldwin writes: "Du Bois's work, then, poses a challenge: to tread the fine line between overidentifying Du Bois with the ruin of the Soviet empire—and hence assigning to his idealism a necessarily 'tragic' fate—and underidentifying or not appreciating the ways in which Du Bois allied himself with the Soviet Union through a consciousness of outsider status and thus as a counter to what he insisted were the monolithic goals of a post–World War II Americanization." Baldwin, *Beyond the Color Line and the Iron Curtain*, 153.

34. W. E. B. Du Bois, *Russia and America: An Interpretation, 1950*. W. E. B. Du Bois Papers (MS 312), Special Collections and University Archives, University of Massachusetts Amherst Libraries, 19. In-text page citations to this work are in parentheses.

35. Cited in Alan Wald, *American Night: The Literary Left in the Era of the Cold War* (Chapel Hill: University of North Carolina Press, 2012), 57.

36. Alain Badiou, *The Communist Hypothesis* (London: Verso, 2010), especially 1–40. In-text page citations to this work are in parentheses.

37. Ibid., 2.

38. John Roberts, *The Necessity of Error* (London: Verso, 2011), 9. In a discussion of "error and enlightenment," Roberts writes:

> For let us be clear: the theorization of the error has had a strange half-life, that is, although it is ubiquitous—in passing—as a knotty site of problems in philosophy, the philosophy of science, psychoanalysis, art theory, and political praxis, it nonetheless remains a subfusc, shadowy presence theoretically. In this sense there is no systematic, materialist and synoptic analysis of the productiveness of the error across these domains. This is not surprising, because the status of the error has represented a profound problem for Marxism in the twentieth century, in so far as the thing that truth is designed to expunge or challenge has continually mocked Marxism's claims to reason; Marxism has seemingly been a home to a thousand (unproductive) errors and the hubris of scientific objectivity. (Ibid., 5–6)

39. Badiou, *Communist Hypothesis*, 6. According to Badiou: "My examination of the particularities of the notion of failure in politics represents an

attempt to define the generic form taken by all truth processes when they come up against obstacles that are inherent in the world in which they operate. The underlying formalization of this problem is the concept of 'point' described in Book IV of my *Logics of Worlds*. A point is a moment within a truth procedure (such as a sequence of emancipatory politics) when a binary choice (do this *or* that) decides the future of the entire process." Ibid., 38. For a thorough account of Badiou's political thought, see Bruno Bosteels, *Badiou and Politics* (Durham, NC: Duke University Press, 2011). Since Badiou's "reactivation" of the communist hypothesis in the wake of the global economic crisis, there have been numerous responses, pro and contra, to his intervention.

40. See Alain Badiou, *Ethics: An Essay on the Understanding of Evil* (London: Verso, 2001).

41. Shirley Graham Du Bois, "Greetings from Cairo, Egypt to the Pan-African Students Organization," unpublished draft dated May 17–20, 1970. Shirley Graham Du Bois Papers, Schlesinger Library, Harvard University.

42. Mullen, *Un-American*, 88.

43. Slavoj Žižek, *Did Somebody Say Totalitarianism? 5 Interventions in the (Mis)Use of a Notion* (New York: Verso, 2001), 33.

44. Ibid., 119–120.

45. Consider this passage:

> But it is the organized capital of America, England, France, and Germany which is chiefly instrumental in preventing the realization of the Russian workingman's psychology. It has used every weapon to crush Russia. It sent against Russia every scoundrel who could lead a mob and gave him money, guns, ammunition; and when Russia nearly committed suicide in crushing this civil war, modern industry began the industrial boycott, the refusal of capital and credit which is being carried on today just as far as international jealousy and greed will allow. . . . On the other hand, so long as the most powerful nations in the world are determined that Russia must fail, there can be but a minimum of free discussion and democratic difference of opinion in Russia. (Du Bois, *Russia and America*, 39)

46. "Du Bois introduces doubts about triumphs of the Soviet experiment. He describes as 'savage' Stalin's attacks in January 1933 on the kulaks who resisted liquidation, some of whom 'had to be dealt with summarily.'" Mullen, *Un-American*, 88.

47. On the Soviet rejection of whiteness, see Baldwin, *Beyond the Color Line and the Iron Curtain*, 149–201.

48. Du Bois writes: "By 1885, the United States had adopted its basic philosophy: Life was Business and Business was Life; Civilization was the product of Industry and Industry was seed and product of Human Culture. Without profitable Industry nothing worthwhile was possible and Science, Art and Religion were the gracious gifts of the Merchant and his Banker. . . . Americans lied, stole, murdered, lynched and mobbed. Their untrammeled

exploits became world legends. But wages rose, comforts multiplied and the national standard of living increased. . . . This was white supremacy." Du Bois, *Russia and America*, 161.

49. George F. Kennan, *The Charge in the Soviet Union (Kennan) to the Secretary of State* (the "Long Telegram"), February 22, 1946 (National Security Archive, George Washington University).

50. Thomas Borstelmann, *The Cold War and the Color Line: American Race Relations in the Global Arena* (Cambridge, MA: Harvard University Press, 2001), 50.

51. Richard Wright, *Black Power: Three Books from Exile: Black Power; The Color Curtain; and White Man Listen!* (New York: Harper Perennial Modern Classics, 2008), 467, 537–538.

52. Du Bois's sense of Stalin's importance to world history and global socialism went beyond his role in the Second World War. In *Russia and America*, he exalts the Georgian's leadership in the Lenin-Stalin-Trotsky troika:

> Stalin escaped from Siberia in the turmoil marking the opening of the Russo-Japanese war and went back to the Caucasus, where he helped in the oil workers' strike which anticipated the Petersburg Revolt of 1905, and which resulted in the first collective agreement between workers and employers ever signed in Russia. The Czarists let the Black Hundred [an ultranationalist movement in Russia, known for its extreme xenophobia and anti-Semitism, that staunchly supported the reigning monarchy] loose on Socialists and Jews and soon had the Caucasus writhing in interracial feuds. Here Stalin learned his great and never to be forgotten lesson of the dangers of race hate, which stood him in great stead during the years when he was Commissar of Nationalities. (Du Bois, *Russia and America*, 61)

"The World Revolution the Communists hoped for did not materialize. Even Lenin had doubted if a single Socialist agricultural state could stand alone in a capitalistic industrial world: and Trotsky had insisted that the Russian Revolution could succeed only if it was prelude to a European uprising. *Only Stalin, slowly but with ear to ground, came to believe that Russia not only could but must prepare to stand alone in the world as a socialist state.*" Ibid., 65.

53. W. E. B. Du Bois, "On Stalin," in *W. E. B. Du Bois: A Reader*, ed. David Levering Lewis (New York: Henry Holt, 1995), 796–797.

54. See Williamson Murray and Allen B. Millett, *A War to Be Won: Fighting the Second World War* (Cambridge, MA: Harvard University Press, 2000).

55. Levering Lewis, *W. E. B. Du Bois: The Fight for Equality and the American Century*, 462.

56. Lauren McConnell frames her discussion of Robeson in the same manner as scholars have addressed Du Bois's Soviet experience: "What was unusual about this [interest in the USSR] was not Robeson's interest in the ideals of socialism and his attraction to the 'great social experiment' taking

place in the Soviet Union, for many people had a similar interest, but the fact that he remained a supporter of Stalin and the USSR in the face of mounting evidence that the great experiment had gone terribly wrong." Versus interpretations that view Robeson as relatively ignorant about Soviet repression, or as deliberately uninquisitive on the subject so that he could enjoy elite privileges, McConnell adopts an anthropological approach that centers less on what Robeson knew than on how he knew (or did not know) it: "Robeson was deeply affected by his 'lived experiences' in the Soviet Union, especially his visits in the 1930s, so much so that the positive 'experience near' knowledge he acquired through physically interacting with the Soviet people outweighed, in his mind, the negative 'experience distant' knowledge about the Soviet Union he read about or was told about later on." McConnell, "Understanding Paul Robeson's Soviet Experience," *Theatre History Studies* 30 (2010): 138–153.

57. W. E. B. Du Bois, "The Real Reason behind Paul Robeson's Persecution," in Levering Lewis, *W. E. B. Du Bois: A Reader*, 798–799.

58. Throughout Redding's career, writes Lawrence Jackson, he agonized over the racial obligations imposed on black artists as much as the vagaries of relationships with white publishers and liberal responses to racial inequality. By the early 1950s, amid the fits and starts of desegregation, Redding "wished more deeply than ever to liberate himself from the obligations of racial duty. He chose to involve himself in the maintenance of national identity." Jackson, *The Indignant Generation* (Princeton, NJ: Princeton University Press, 2011), 404.

59. "During the Truman years," writes Mary Dudziak, "in no country was the focus on American race relations of greater importance than in India. Chester Bowles discovered in 1951, early in his tenure as U.S. ambassador to India, that 'the number one question' in Asia about the United States was 'about America's treatment of the Negro.' Bowles took Indian concerns very seriously because he believed India to be of great strategic importance to the United States." Dudziak, *Cold War Civil Rights: Race and the Image of American Democracy* (Princeton, NJ: Princeton University Press, 2011), 33.

60. Jackson, *Indignant Generation*, 404. Concerning *An American in India*'s mainstream reception, Jackson writes: "The mainstream press looked favorably on his efforts. *Time* magazine, one of the nation's leading weekly news magazines, and unused to news coverage of Negro Americans, did its best to make Redding palatable for its audience. . . . He has told the startling truth about India in a calm, clean book." Though *Time* referred to Redding as a "good-looking Negro professor of English at Hampton Institute," what was of greater concern, writes Jackson, was "his politics, his views that could be shaped into a chastisement of India's policy of neutrality toward China and the Soviet Union and then also of India's left-leaning intellectual class. 'Redding likens the Reds to wild dogs that run in packs all over India,' was *Time*'s quick synopsis of the book. In the year in which the Supreme Court struck down the laws upholding racial segregation, Redding put on the togs of a cold warrior." Jackson, *Indignant Generation*, 405.

61. "It seemed impossible," Redding writes,

> for these Indians to conceive of a dark-skinned American as being other than the enemy of white, or of having a loyalty that goes beyond color. I was asked more than once whether the Negro community of America would join with the colored peoples of the world in a war against the white man. If the question was plainly theoretical and diagnostic, the color-consciousness in which it was conceived was not. . . . I think it was as much this as an urge for abstract social justice that threw them on the side of the Tunisians, the Arabs, and the natives and "coloreds" of South Africa. (Saunders Redding, *An American in India: A Personal Report on the Indian Dilemma and the Nature of Her Conflicts* [New York: Bobbs-Merrill, 1954], 114–115)

62. William B. Davis, "How Negroes Live in Russia," *Ebony*, January 1960, 65–73.

63. Davis notes that the indefatigable Robinson had produced no fewer than twenty-seven "industrial inventions" employed by the Soviet government and at the time held a position as a senior engineer at a Moscow ball-bearing plant with more than a quarter century's service to his credit. Davis, "How Negroes Live in Russia," 66. See also Robert Robinson, *Black on Red: My 44 Years Inside the Soviet Union; An Autobiography by Black American Robert Robinson* (Washington, D.C.: Acropolis Books, 1988).

64. Davis writes: "There are about 300 Egyptian students at the University of Moscow [in addition to about 30 students from other African countries like Ghana, Sudan, Uganda, and Cameroon]. The Russian government is investing a great deal in these African students. For example, Russia pays for the transportation of these students from Africa to Moscow. On arrival they receive 3,000 rubles ($300) as an allotment for the purchase of winter clothes." He notes that each student receives 900 rubles a month—whereas the average Russian worker earns only 800 rubles—in addition to a summer stipend, a 1,500-ruble bonus for spending money, and a biannual fund for two-way transportation between the students' home country and Moscow. Davis, "How Negroes Live in Russia," 68.

65. *Soviet Propaganda: Russia's Animated Propaganda War: American Imperialists and Fascist Barbarians*, Odeon Entertainment, 2007.

66. *Mister Twister* (1933), *Soviet Propaganda: Russia's Animated Propaganda War* (disc one, "American Imperialists"), Odeon Entertainment DVD.

67. See Terry Martin, *Affirmative Action Empire: Nations and Nationalism in the Soviet Union, 1923–1939* (Ithaca, NY: Cornell University Press, 2001).

68. Richard Wright, *Black Boy: A Record of Childhood and Youth* (New York: Harper Perennial Classics, 2007), 335.

69. Du Bois, *Russia and America*, chapter 3, 2; my italics.

70. Redding, *American in India*, 147.

71. Some critics adopted firm antiwar positions. In a deeply idealistic address, Robert M. Hutchins, then president of the University of Chicago, advances one of the most stridently antiwar arguments in the volume. Hutchins, "America and the War," *Journal of Negro Education* 10, no. 3 (July 1941): 435–441. In-text page citations to this work are in parentheses.

72. Usefully, Hutchins employs the phrase "democratic community" rather than the generic "democracy." "To have a community men must work together. They must have common principles and purposes. If some men are tearing down a house while others are building it, we do not say they are working together. . . . The aims of a democratic community are moral. United by devotion to law, equality, and justice the democratic community works together for the happiness of all the citizens. I leave it to you the decision whether we have yet achieved a democratic community in the United States." Hutchins, "America and the War," 438–439. Hutchins's notion of democratic community has an almost utopian resonance, but his argument is that something close to moral perfection is necessary. Such a moral order is necessary for legitimate military intervention, he argues, since the present regime of class and racial inequality leaves us "a good deal short of that level of excellence which entitles us to convert the world by force of arms." Ibid., 437.

73. Ralph Bunche, "The Negro in the Political Life of the United States," *Journal of Negro Education* 10, no. 3 (July 1941): 583–584.

74. Ralph Bunche, "Africa and the Current World Conflict," in *Ralph J. Bunche: Selected Speeches and Writings*, ed. Charles P. Henry (Ann Arbor: The University of Michigan Press, 1995).

75. W. E. B. Du Bois, "Neuropa: Hitler's New World Order," *Journal of Negro Education* 10, no. 3 (July 1941): 385. In-text page citations to this work are in parentheses.

76. An illuminating introduction to Du Bois's writings on Nazi Germany is Werner Sollors, "W. E. B. Du Bois in Nazi Germany: A Surprising, Prescient Visitor," *Chronicle of Higher Education*, November 12, 1999, http://chronicle.com/article/WEB-Du-Bois-in-Nazi/1896/.

77. Hortense Spillers, "The Idea of Black Culture," *New Centennial Review* 6, no. 3 (2007): 7–28.

78. Du Bois, "Neuropa," 383–384. "It may well be that the real fight," he intones, "which is dividing the world today, is the question as to how much of human action must by the laws of science be subject to scientific control; and on the other hand, how large a section of life, about the absolute necessities of health and subsistence, can be reserved as the area of human freedom for individual action, creative thought, and artistic taste." Ibid., 385.

79. Regarding collaboration between W. E. B. Du Bois and Shirley Graham, Kate Baldwin observes that "*In Battle for Peace* is the only published book of Du Bois's in which he consciously shares authored space with a woman." But this form of coauthorship was far from equal, with Graham supplementing Du Bois's account with marginal commentary. "In spite of their shared space of authorship, Du Bois and Graham offer quite different perspectives on their own function as author. At no point in his text does Du Bois express awareness of his wife's presence beside him as a commentator or an intellectual equal. Rather, her presence is always beside him as a loving support, confidant, and nurturing supplicant." Baldwin claims that "the superficial effect of her commentary is to largely compound the marginalization of women to anecdotal asides." Baldwin, *Beyond the Color Line and the Iron Curtain*, 190–191. Baldwin's observation is correct, though critics have

also perpetuated this marginalization by neglecting Graham's own large corpus of work. Chapters 3 and 5 seek to redress this neglect.

CHAPTER 5 From Nkrumah's Ghana to Nasser's Egypt

1. Percival L. Prattis, letter to Shirley Graham Du Bois, July 17, 1958, Shirley Graham Du Bois Papers, Schlesinger Library, Harvard University.

2. Ibid.

3. Lorenz M. Lüthi, *The Sino-Soviet Split: Cold War in the Communist World* (Princeton, NJ: Princeton University Press, 2008), 46–53.

4. Ronaldo Munck, review of *The Revolutionary Imagination in the Americas in the Age of Development*, by Mara Josefina Saldaña-Portillo, *American Historical Review* 9, no. 3 (June 2004): 876–877.

5. Erica R. Edwards, *Charisma and the Fictions of Black Leadership* (Minneapolis: University of Minnesota Press, 2012), xv.

6. Ann Douglas, "Periodizing the American Century: Modernism, Postmodernism, and Postcolonialism in the Cold War Context," *Modernism/Modernity* 5, no. 3 (1998): 84.

7. Kevin Gaines, *American Africans in Ghana: Black Expatriates and the Civil Rights Era* (Chapel Hill: University of North Carolina Press, 2006), 7. Gaines rejects the zero-sum choice foisted upon U.S. blacks between American and African diaspora sensibilities, a binary that "suggests the persistence of the dominant view that the American Negro was strictly American, an assertion whose political intent was the delegitimization of Afro-diasporic solidarities." Ibid., 9.

8. Aleksandr Furensenko and Timothy Naftali, *"One Hell of a Gamble": The Secret History of the Cuban Missile Crisis* (New York: W. W. Norton, 1998), 73.

9. Shirley Graham Du Bois, "Egypt Is Africa," *Black Scholar* 2, no. 1 (September 1970): 30.

10. Gerald Horne, *Race Woman: The Lives of Shirley Graham Du Bois* (New York: New York University Press, 2000), 19.

11. There are some exceptions to this general neglect. Russ Castronovo's *Beautiful Democracy*, for example, contains a section on "organized propaganda" in the context of lynching, aesthetics, and Du Bois's editorial work at *The Crisis*. Castronovo, *Beautiful Democracy: Aesthetics and Anarchy in a Global Era* (Chicago: University of Chicago Press, 2007).

12. Stephen Best and Sharon Marcus, "Surface Reading: An Introduction," *Representations* 108 (Fall 2009): 3.

13. Jameson's *The Political Unconscious* remains exemplary in this regard. See Fredric Jameson, *The Political Unconscious* (Ithaca, NY: Cornell University Press, 1981).

14. Jonathan Auerbach and Russ Castronovo, "Thirteen Propositions about Propaganda," introduction to *The Oxford Handbook of Propaganda Studies*, ed. Auerbach and Castronovo (Oxford: Oxford University Press, 2013), 2.

15. Auerbach and Castronovo, "Thirteen Propositions about Propaganda," 1–15.

16. Horne, *Race Woman*, 174. Horne continues: "She developed a sort of 'left nationalism' that eventually led her to Maoism and disaffection from some of her allies in the U.S. Communist Party." Ibid. Beyond crediting Shirley Graham Du Bois with bringing her husband, more than three decades her senior, into wider contact with multiracial communist and leftwing circles, few commentators have considered the influence of writer and activist Graham on Du Bois's postwar thought or her own contribution to the transnational black literary left. Horne, however, doubts that she strongly influenced Du Bois politically.

17. J. Saunders Redding, *An American in India: A Personal Report on the Indian Dilemma and the Nature of Her Conflicts* (Indianapolis: Bobbs-Merrill, 1954), 262.

18. See Paul Michael McGarr, "'Quiet Americans in India': The CIA and the Politics of Intelligence in Cold War South Asia," *Diplomatic History* 38, no. 5 (2014): 1046–1082.

19. See Lawrence P. Jackson, *The Indignant Generation: A Narrative History of African American Writers and Critics* (Princeton, NJ: Princeton University Press, 2011), 266.

20. Ann Petry, "The Novel as Social Criticism," in *The Writer's Book*, ed. Helen Hunt (New York: Harper Brothers, 1950), 33.

21. Czeslaw Milosz, introduction to *"The Trial Begins" and "On Socialist Realism,"* by Abram Tertz, trans. Max Hayward (Berkeley: University of California Press, 1982). The pseudonymous author of this text refers to the definition of socialist realism codified by the Union of Soviet Writers: "Socialist realism is the basic method of Soviet literature and literary criticism. It demands of the artist the truthful, historically concrete representation of reality in its revolutionary development. Moreover, the truthfulness and historical concreteness of the artistic representation of reality must be linked with the task of ideological transformation and education of workers in the spirit of socialism." Tertz, *On Socialist Realism*, 148.

22. Tertz, *On Socialist Realism*, 167.

23. Carol Anderson, "The Histories of African Americans' Anticolonialism during the the Cold War," in *The Cold War in the Third World*, ed. Robert J. McMahon (Oxford: Oxford University Press, 2013), 180.

24. To this list he adds a fourth characteristic "of the true partisan," which he calls the "telluric." Schmitt specifies the figure of the partisan against expansive "re-interpretations" of the concept, symptomatic of the Nazi period, that foreground "the illegal resistance fighter and underground activist" as the true type of partisan. For Schmitt, the inclusion of these types risks dissolution of the concept since, ultimately, "any individualist and non-conformist can be called a partisan, without any consideration as to whether he would even think of taking up arms." Carl Schmitt, *Theory of the Partisan* (New York: Telos, 2007, 18–20).

25. Ibid., 21.

26. Horne, *Race Woman*, 38.

27. In French:

> Ces lignes proviennent d'un ouvrage publié en 1952, et qui avait pour auteur W. E. B. DuBois—écrivain noir américain et "pére du panafricanisme." L'ouvrage de DuBois s'intutulait *In Battle for Peace—The Story of My 83rd Birthday*, et décrivait la lute de l'essayiste d'*Ames Noires* contre les tribunaux maccarthystes. Ce livre était assorti de "Commentaires" de la second femme de DuBois, Shirley Graham. C'est à cette dernière que le department de la justice, malgré la recommandation contraire du department d'Etat, vient de refuser l'accès du territoire des Etats-Unis, lui interdisant ainsi de prendre la parole à l'université Fisk, dans le Tennessee, et de render visite à des membres de sa famille. Depuis 1963, comme son mari, Shirley Graham—aujourd-hui âgée de soixante et onze ans—avait pris la nationalité ghanéenne. ("*Correspondence*" segment in *Le Monde*, May 9, 1970, Graham Du Bois Papers)

28. Shirley Graham Du Bois, "Comment," in W. E. B. Du Bois, *In Battle for Peace: The Story of My 83rd Birthday* (Oxford: Oxford University Press, 2007), 3.

29. "En avril 1970, une commission d'enquête sur les sources de l'agitation dans les universities américaines, preside par M. Sol M. Linowitz, ancien ambassadeur auprès de l'Organisation des Etaits américaines et ancient directeur general de la firm Xerox, metait en cause MM. Agnew *['Les remarques de vice-président ne sont pas constructives.']* et Reagan." (Ibid.)

30. Raymond Farrell to the Honorable Phillip Burton, May 27, 1970, Graham Du Bois Papers.

31. Horne, *Race Woman*, 19.

32. Shirley Graham Du Bois to Richard P. Stevens, April 29, 1970, Graham Du Bois Papers.

33. David Levering Lewis, *W. E. B. Du Bois: The Fight for Equality and the American Century, 1919–1963* (New York: Henry Holt, 2000), 556. "Significantly," writes Levering Lewis, "under oath, he stated flatly that he was not a Communist, but Judge Alexander Bix jibed that the witness was 'a fella who would decide who and what was a Communist for himself.' " Ibid.

34. Ibid., 565.

35. Horne observes that this "plan would not go down well with those who could easily view it as a dangerous precedent for other nations to emulate, thus disrupting a traditional and steady profit stream for those in 'the West' who controlled programming. Strikingly, after her ambitious plans were mentioned in the trade publication Variety, she received an immediate letter of inquiry from the U.K. office of the U.S. programming firm Desilu, which had been started by the television star Lucille Ball and her then husband, Desi Arnaz." Horne, *Race Woman*, 176–177.

36. U.S. officials were also most likely intrigued by Graham Du Bois's role in "the effort to establish the Ghana State Publishing House, which would print books to be circulated continentally. This latter venture was

'being built and equipped by advisors from the German Democratic Republic,' that is, Communist-ruled East Germany. These investments in communications media were strategic components of Nkrumah's Pan-African vision of a united continent." Horne, *Race Woman*, 175.

37. Ibid, 177.

38. Shirley Graham Du Bois, "Radio Report to Japan," March 14, 1964, Graham Du Bois Papers.

39. Mohamed H. Heikal, *Cutting the Lion's Tail: Suez through Egyptian Eyes* (London: André Deutsch Limited, 1986), xiii.

40. Richard Wright, *Black Power: A Record of Reactions in a Land of Pathos* in *Black Power: Three Books from Exile: Black Power; The Color Curtain; and White Man, Listen!* (New York: HarperCollins, 2008), 418.

41. Graham Du Bois, "Radio Report to Japan."

42. Ibid.

43. Frantz Fanon, *The Wretched of the Earth* (New York: Grove Press, 1963), 47.

44. Graham Du Bois, "Radio Report to Japan."

45. Shirley Graham Du Bois, letter to Kwame Nkrumah, June 30, 1965, Graham Du Bois Papers.

46. James H. Robinson, letter to Shirley Graham Du Bois, February 3, 1966, Graham Du Bois Papers.

47. Michael Hayward, letter to Shirley Graham Du Bois, May 13, 1965, Graham Du Bois Papers.

48. Pauli Murray, *The Autobiography of a Black Activist, Feminist, Lawyer, Priest, and Poet* (Knoxville: University of Tennessee Press, 1989), 318.

49. Ibid.

50. Ibid., 321–323.

51. Dipesh Chakrabarty, *Provincializing Europe: Postcolonial Thought and Historical Difference* (Princeton, NJ: Princeton University Press, 2001), 7.

52. Murray, *Autobiography*, 328.

53. Indeed, she was so assiduous in her efforts that her supervision of Ghana Television apparently caused some conflict with her Ghanaian colleagues. In a letter branded confidential, one representative from Ghana Information Services wrote Shirley Graham with consternation about what he saw as the poaching of talented staff (cameramen, photographers, technicians) from Information Services to her Television Department.

54. Shirley Graham Du Bois, "To the African Nation," *Freedomways* 3, no. 4 (Fall 1963): 564.

55. "Thus it was that the stern tutelage forced upon a dedicated, young revolutionary leader," Graham writes of Nkrumah, "developed that political sagacity and insight which today combines with wide knowledge of the modern world to produce a statesman of dynamic action, a spokesman of African aspirations whose words carry powerful impact." Ibid., 565.

56. Horne, *Race Woman*, 207. "Others," Horne continues, "including some Communists and others on the Left, did not altogether agree; this upset her tremendously and was a factor pushing her away from her erstwhile U.S.

Communist comrades and toward Maoist China." Ibid. Though Horne does not elaborate on his perception of Graham Du Bois's politics, it is possible to gather from other remarks that he sees her affinity for sundry (and indeed sometimes conflicting) forms of "left nationalism," combined with her often dogmatic writings, as signs of her lack of political sophistication.

57. "Jews and Israelis," *Pittsburgh Courier*, December 29, 1956.

58. Shirley Graham Du Bois, "Cairo: Six Months after the Blitzkrieg," Graham Du Bois Papers. Graham does not date the manuscript, but we can infer that she composed it approximately in December of 1967, if we credit her title "Six Months after the Blitzkrieg" (namely, the Israeli attacks on Arab states in June 1967). These notes reveal that Graham derives much of her information about Egyptian and Middle Eastern politics from Mohamed H. Heikal, Nasser's close confidante.

> These developments [fractures within and challenges to Nasser's leadership] are being made clear to the people of Cairo. No attempt has been made to deny that grievous mistakes have been made in the past. Inquiries and review of the past are being made not so much to determine who was to blame for mistakes as to find out what was to blame. Early in September Mohamed Hassanein Heikal, editor of Cairo's Al Ahram, a leading Arabic newspaper in this part of the world, began a series of informative articles. Heikal is always regarded as the authentic spokesman for the Government and his weekly articles appearing each Friday, appear in translation in the English and French press, on Saturday. Heikal's article of October 20th, discussing "the military aspects of the setback" is brutally frank. He plunges headlong into the subject by posing the question: How did the enemy handle his resources in order to achieve what he has? (Ibid.)

59. Ali A. Mazrui, "Black Africa and the Arabs," *Foreign Affairs*, July 1975, 728.

60. "After escaping Ghana," writes Horne,

> Graham Du Bois faced the dilemma of where she should live. This was a trying episode in her life. "Every day" became "a real battle to 'keep going!'" . . . [Graham Du Bois] had to be quite careful in moving around the globe. Not only was there the constant danger of extradition to Ghana, but right after the coup Ghanaian officials kidnapped a Guinean delegation to an international conference when the plane on which they were traveling made an intermediate stop in Accra. Since Guinea had given refuge to Nkrumah, relations between the two West African states had deteriorated. . . . This kind of fearful uncertainty caused her to consider residing in sites as diverse as Tanzania, East Germany, France, Mexico, and Algeria. During the final eleven years of her life she visited all of these places and others, though she resided for the most part in Cairo, with long stints in Guinea, China, and the United States. (Horne, *Race Woman*, 209–210)

Immediately after the coup, she spent some time in East Berlin, where she visited the political cartoonist Ollie Harrington, who, after years in Paris, had been living in the German Democratic Republic since the erection of the Berlin Wall.

61. Ibid., 208.

62. A contemporaneous reviewer of Nasser's *Philosophy* notes that "Muhammed Naguib, the ex-president of Egypt, was ousted because his policy of slow and evolutionary reform clashed with Nasser's forceful philosophy of whipping Egypt into the consciousness of a modern state. In view of this policy a good comparative study can be written on Nasser and Ataturk." Elie Salem, review of *The Philosophy of Revolution*, by Gamal Abd El-Nasser, *Journal of Politics* 19, no. 1 (1957): 150. For the Free Officers of the Egyptian Revolution—a group made up, as Vijay Prashad observes, "of old-school nationalists of the Wafd Party, members of the Muslim Brotherhood, Communists, and also aristocrats who had lost faith in King Farouk"—the "ideology of Pan-Arabism and the secular Turkish lineage of Kemal Ataturk appealed to their ideas about Egyptian modernity." Vijay Prashad, *The Darker Nations: A People's History of the Third World* (New York: New Press, 2007), 51.

63. This summation derives from Elie Podeh and Onn Winckler, introduction to *Rethinking Nasserism: Revolution and Historical Memory in Modern Egypt*, ed. Podeh and Winckler (Gainesville: University of Florida Press, 2004), 1–4. The authors continue: "Some scholars assert that the term *Nasserism* (al-Nasiriyya) is a Western invention. Others suggest that Nasser's adversaries coined the term." Arab intellectuals and politicians, they suggest, have adopted the suffix reluctantly, since the term's supposedly Western origin undercuts the movement's anticolonial edge; and for others it ascribes too much significance to the personality of Nasser, at the expense of other agents. "Gradually, however, the term *al-Nasiriyya* did enter into Arab discourse, appearing in encyclopedias, books, and articles. With the de-Nasserization process gaining momentum in Egypt and the Arab world in the early 1970s, the term became negative and its supporters were politically marginalized." Ibid., 5.

64. Toni Morrison has commented on this passage in Bernal's work, and I find illuminating the interspersing of her quotation from *Black Athena* with commentary on Morrison's own debt to that work.

> What struck me in his analysis were the *process* of the fabrication of Ancient Greece and the *motives* for the fabrication. The latter (motive) involved the concepts of purity and of progress. The former (process) required misreading, predetermined selectively of authentic sources, and—silence. . . . I have quoted . . . from Bernal's text because *motive*, so seldom an element brought to bear on the history of history, is located, delineated, and confronted in Bernal's research and has helped my own thinking about the process and motives of scholarly attention to and an appraisal of Afro-American presence in the literature of the United States. (Toni Morrison, "Unspeakable Things Unspoken: The Afro-American

Presence in American Literature," October 7, 1988, http://tannerlectures.utah.edu/_documents/a-to-z/m/morrison90.pdf)

65. Ilan Pappé, *The Ethnic Cleansing of Palestine* (Oxford: Oneworld Publications, 2006), 7.

66. "Between early 1964 and the outbreak of the Six-Day War in June 1967," writes one commentator, "a significantly new relationship emerged, one that expanded with Israel's decisive victory. Policies toward Israel developed into a special patron-client relationship and an unwritten security guarantee, one that identified Israel as a critical strategic Cold War asset to counter Soviet involvement in the region." Arlene Lazarowitz, "Different Approaches to a Regional Search for Balance: The Johnson Administration, the State Department, and the Middle East, 1964–1967," *Diplomatic History* 32, no. 1 (January 2008): 25.

67. According to Schmitt, this antagonistic situation imbues ordinary language such that all political terms assume a polemical character anchored in concrete, recognizable conflicts. Words such as "state, republic, society, class," writes Schmitt, "as well as sovereignty, constitutional state, absolutism, dictatorship, economic planning, neutral or total state, and so on, are incomprehensible if one does not know exactly who is to be affected, combated, refuted, or negated by such a term." Without grounding in specific situations, these terms slip into the realm of "empty and ghostlike abstractions." Carl Schmitt, *The Concept of the Political*, trans. George Schwab (Chicago: University of Chicago Press, 1996), 28–31. Schmitt's translator renders *Freund und Feind gruppieren* as "friend and enemy antithesis."

68. Shirley Graham Du Bois, "Friends and Enemies," *Egyptian Gazette*, October 23, 1967.

69. Shirley Graham Du Bois, "Balance or Threat?" *Egyptian Gazette*, July 25, 1968.

70. Ibid.

71. Shirley Graham Du Bois, "Soviet Power," *Egyptian Gazette* (undated; copied in tandem with another column, "Arab South," dated November 8, 1967).

72. Khaled Diab, "Hope for the Egyptian Nubians Damned by the Dam," *Guardian*, April 21, 2012, http://www.theguardian.com/commentisfree/2012/apr/21/egypt-nubians-dam; and Ayah Aman, "Egypt's Nubians Demand Rights on Aswan High Dam Anniversary," *Al Monitor*, June 9, 2014, http://www.al-monitor.com/pulse/originals/2014/06/egypt-nubians-demand-rights-displacement.html#.

73. Schmitt, *Concept of the Political*, 32.

74. Shirley Graham Du Bois, "The Lesson of the Eilat," *Egyptian Gazette*, October 25, 1967.

75. Shirley Graham Du Bois, letter to Dr. Richard Stevens, Lincoln University, Graham Du Bois Papers.

76. W. E. B. Du Bois, "The Case for the Jews," in *W. E. B. Du Bois: A Reader*, ed. Eric J. Sundquist (Oxford: Oxford University Press, 1996), 461.

77. Ibid., 462–464.

78. Ibid., 462.

79. Alex Lubin, *Liberation Geographies: The Making of an Afro-Arab Political Imaginary* (Chapel Hill: University of North Carolina Press, 2014), 1–77. According to Lubin, "Du Bois's support for Zionism put him at odds with many of the Jewish intellectuals, activists, and donors who helped organize the National Association for the Advancement of Colored People (NAACP). The most influential donors to the NAACP, a list that included Louis Marshall, Franz Boas, Melville Herskovits, and the Springarns, all opposed Zionism because they were politically committed to the notion of complete Jewish assimilation." Ibid., 45. Du Bois's backing of Zionism also exceeded the support for this movement expressed by his NAACP colleagues, suggesting to Lubin that Zionism could be seen as a leftist internationalist movement similar to Pan-Africanism. The case of Du Bois implies, then, that the powerful historical analogy between these movements mattered more than Jewish support for black American causes.

80. W. E. B. Du Bois, "The Negro and the Warsaw Ghetto," in Sundquist, *W. E. B. Du Bois*, 472.

81. Du Bois's unimpeachable point was that Nazism had rendered Zionism no longer an "academic" matter, as the destruction and dispersal of European Jewry urgently necessitated the provision of a secure, sovereign territory. "What had been a theoretical demand for a Zion," Du Bois writes, "now became a necessity for more than a million displaced and homeless Jews. There was actually no other place on earth for them to go." Du Bois indicts Britain for reneging on its previous commitment during the First World War and capitulating to economic and industrial needs—namely, oil production—with an abandonment of Zionism after the Second World War. He also charges Truman, "*after having promised to stand by the founding of Zion*," with "*inexplicably*" going "*back upon his word*" and refusing "*to permit arms to be given to the beleaguered Jews in Palestine and since then has been trying to straddle the fence and make any efforts of the United Nations ineffective and impossible.*" Du Bois, "Case for the Jews," 463.

82. Ibid., 462.

83. Du Bois, "Negro and the Warsaw Ghetto," 473.

84. Ilan Pappé, *The Idea of Israel: A History of Power and Knowledge* (London: Verso, 2014), 33–34. Pappé continues:

> At the same time, Palestinians were also becoming a subject of academic inquiry. Following the 1967 war, the production of knowledge within Israel about the Palestinians was primarily a project of "know thy enemy" and of military intelligence gathering. For that reason, both Israeli academics and Israeli media commonly used the term "terrorism" when referring to any kind of Palestinian political, social and cultural activity. "Palestinian terrorism" was depicted as having been present from the very beginning of the Zionist project in Palestine and still being there when academic research into it began in earnest. This characterization was so comprehensive and airtight that it assigned almost every chapter in Palestinian history to the domain of "terrorism" and absolved hardly any of the organizations and personalities that made up the Palestinian na-

> tional movement from the accusation of being terrorists. The government, academic, the media, the army, and the NGOs of civil society all took part in constructing the negative image of the Palestinians. (Ibid.)

I cite Pappé with awareness of the controversy generated by his work. For one of his critics, see Benny Morris, "The Liar as Hero," *New Republic*, March 17, 2011, http://www.newrepublic.com/article/books/magazine/85344/ilan-pappe-sloppy-dishonest-historian.

85. Shirley Graham Du Bois, "Confrontation in the Middle East," *Black Scholar*, 5, no. 3 (November 1973): 32–33.

86. Ibid., 33–34.

87. "Latest reports from the United Nations," she writes, "indicate that the Security Council members are finding it difficult to arrive at an agreed upon formula to deal with the latest Israeli aggression against Jordan at El Salt on August 4. This is true despite the obvious course which lies open to the Security Council, on the basis of its past declarations and decisions, and in accordance with the UN Charter, to take really effective, firm and concrete measures against Israel." Shirley Graham Du Bois, "Why So Difficult?," *Egyptian Gazette*, August 14, 1968.

88. "The ultimate result of the 1967 War was Resolution 242," writes one historian recently, "which remains the operative document defining prospective peace talks between Israel and Arab neighbours. Another consequence of the war was the general acceptance in the scholarly literature that the war established a 'special relationship' between Israel and the United States that still exists." Charles D. Smith, "The United States and the 1967 War," in *The 1967 Arab-Israeli War: Origins and Consequences*, ed. Wm. Roger Louis and Avi Shlaim (Cambridge: Cambridge University Press, 2012), 166.

89. Wm. Roger Louis, "Britain: The Ghost of Suez and Resolution 242," in Louis and Shlaim, *The 1967 Arab-Israeli War*, 241. On the resolution's obscureness, see *U.N Security Council Resolution 242: A Case Study in Diplomatic Ambiguity* (Washington, DC: Institute for the Study of Diplomacy, Georgetown University, 1981).

90. The Spanish *los* is a definite plural article; in this sentence, the French *des* is a "déterminant," equivalent roughly to a determiner in English but an "article indéfini" in French. In German, which is not an official UN language, the sentence in Resolution 242 reads: "Rückzug der israelischen Streitkräfte aus (den) Gebieten, die während des jüngsten Konflikts besetzt wurden"; the *den* in parentheses is followed by an asterisk, which refers readers to the English ("from territories") and French ("des territoires") phrases. "Revolution 242 (1967) vom 22. November 1967," Vereinte Nationen Sicherheitsrat (United Nations Security Council), Vereinte Nationen Deutscher Übersetzungsdienst (United Nations German Version), http://www.un.org/depts/german/sr/sr_67/sr242-67.pdf.

91. Louis and Shlaim reach a different conclusion regarding the French version, based on an interpretation of *des territoires* and their view that de Gaulle strongly favored Israel's withdrawal: "When the UN Security Council voted in favour of Resolution 242, the French translation called on Israel to

withdraw from 'the territories' and not 'territories occupied in the recent conflict.' The definite article implied total withdrawal. There could be no mistake about French intent." Louis and Shlaim, introduction to *1967 Arab-Israeli War*, 18.

92. "Caradon believed there could be no doubt: 'Since the resolution was a British resolution it is of course the British text which prevails.'" Note that Caradon refers to the resolution as a "British," rather than English, text. Louis, "Britain," 242.

93. Ibid. Louis continues: "If not in the tradition of perfidious Albion, the draft resolution in its various phases eventually seemed, to the Arabs at least, to be reminiscent of the contradictory promises made during World War I. Or, to use a phrase that comes to mind when describing assurances given by Caradon to the Arabs, to some extent he may have fudged it—but it should be added that Kuznesov [the Soviet deputy minister of foreign affairs who in the Security Council advocated full withdrawal] and Goldberg as well as Caradon assumed at the time that there would be complete withdrawal except for minor border adjustments." Ibid.

94. Eugene Kontorovich, "Resolution 242 Revisited: New Evidence on the Required Scope of Israeli Withdrawal," *Chicago Journal of International Law* 16 no. 1 (Summer 2015): 127–150. Kontorovich writes:

> One interpretation holds that Resolution 242 requires a complete Israeli withdrawal from all the territories that came under its control during the Six-Day War. This is consistent with, but not mandated by, a straightforward reading of the language and the French text. . . . Yet the drafting history of the provision tells a different story. The British and U.S. diplomats involved in framing the resolution specifically omitted a "the" before "territories" to leave the extent of the required withdrawal open for future negotiations between Israel and its neighbors. Indeed, over several months of deliberations in the [UN Security] Council, the U.K. and U.S. rejected attempts by the Arab-aligned nations to explicitly require withdrawal from "all" or "the" territories. The Western states insisted that it would be both unreasonable and unrealistic to require complete Israeli abandonment of Jerusalem's holy sites." (Ibid., 129–130)

95. Graham Du Bois writes: "In other words the UAR is not prepared to submit to blackmail. Israel and the US know full well that the acquisition of territories through aggression is in violation of the United Nations Charter to which they are both signatories. They know full well that the minimum condition which must precede any and all other moves in the Middle East toward a normalization of the situation is the withdrawal of Israeli forces to positions they held prior to June 5." Shirley Graham Du Bois, "Political Play-Acting," *Egyptian Gazette*, November 1, 1967.

96. Shirley Graham Du Bois, "Suemed Pipeline," *Egyptian Gazette*, October 2, 1968. "Despite the prediction made at that time by imperialist circles in the West that the Canal would 'fall into ruin under Egyptian admin-

istration,'" she writes, "the world has seen instead steady improvement and constantly growing capacity under Egyptian administration."

97. "The real danger [in achieving UN agreement on the 242 draft] came from the Indian delegation," writes Wm. Roger Louis. "An Indian draft resolution proved to be 'more Arab than the Arabs' and had considerable support because of growing indignation against Israel. Only through the supreme effort of Wilson, writing directly to the Indian Prime Minister, did the British manage to get the Indian resolution withdrawn." Louis, "Britain," 240.

98. Shirley Graham Du Bois, "For Victory at the Polls," *Egyptian Gazette*, October 18, 1968.

99. Shirley Graham Du Bois, "Political Play-Acting," *Egyptian Gazette*, November 1, 1967.

100. Shirley Graham Du Bois, "A Letter to My Brothers in America" (unpublished), February 25, 1974, Graham Du Bois Papers.

101. Graham Du Bois, "Why So Difficult?" "As early as 1953," she continues, "following the Israeli slaughter and destruction in the Jordanian village of Quibya (population 2,000, which buried 66 dead following the massacre), Zionist pressure forced Mr John Foster Dulles, then Secretary of State, to reverse his decision to cut off aid to Israel as an act of censure, only three days after the cut-off was announced."

102. Graham Du Bois, "Why So Difficult?" "As long as the United Nations and the world community," continues Graham, "fail to put teeth into its condemnations and censures of Israel for its continuing aggression, the Palestinian people will be justified in concluding that they have only one road open to redress their twenty-year grievance, the road of armed resistance from within."

103. Smith, "United States and the 1967 War," 167. Smith continues: "The strongest support for his Great Society programs that legislated equal rights for blacks had come from associates who were Jewish, some of whom joined him in backing Franklin D. Roosevelt's 'New Deal' programs during the late 1930s. Many of these Jewish liberals now openly criticized Johnson's escalation of America's military forces in Southeast Asia. Acutely aware of their views, Johnson approved a military aid package for Israel, far more ambitious than Kennedy's, leading up to the 1964 presidential elections." Ibid.

104. Avi Shlaim, "Israel: Poor Little Samson," in Louis and Shlaim, *1967 Arab-Israeli War*, 29.

105. Without promising U.S. backing of Israel in the war, Johnson eventually signaled his administration's support of its ally in the Middle East. Persuasively, William B. Quandt designates this tacit support the "yellow light" thesis: Johnson gave Israel neither the "green" nor the "red" light to attack its Arab adversaries; instead, as tensions escalated and Israeli appeals to Washington increased, his administration eventually flashed Israel a "yellow" light. "The only realistic means of convincing Israel not to act on its own," writes Quandt, "would have entailed unilateral US military action to reopen the Strait of Tiran. This, Johnson was not prepared to undertake, in large

measure because of Congress. As a result, the president acquiesced in Israel's decision to launch a preemptive war and made sure that the Israelis knew in advance that, while he was in office, there would be no repeat of the US pressure on Israel similar to that imposed during the Suez crisis in 1956. In brief, in the crucial days before Israel undertook the decision to go to war, the light from Washington shifted from red to yellow." Quandt, "Lyndon Johnson and the June 1967 War: What Color Was the Light?" *Middle East Journal* 46, no. 2 (Spring 1992): 199.

106. The Six-Day War also endowed Israelis with new confidence, but one that seemed to foster intensifying domination of the Palestinian population as Israel struggled to administer its newly acquired territories. Did the enhanced U.S.-Israel relationship after 1967—and increased U.S. aid to Israel—contribute to this entwinement of confidence and domination? For Graham, the relationship was crystalline, an indication of Johnson's willingness to sacrifice Palestinians—whom she regarded as a colonized, racially persecuted group—for the sake of electoral support. Though she may not have realized that Johnson was a sincere supporter of the Jewish state, Graham was incisive in her identification of electoral politics as the president's central concern: shaping a foreign policy that satisfied Israel and American Jews but did not proffer unqualified support for military operations—while continuing to appear to uphold a public commitment to impartial support of all nations involved.

107. For a critical account of the Palestinian struggle attentive to failures of its various leaders and movements, see Rashid Khalidi, *The Iron Cage: The Story of the Palestinian Struggle for Statehood* (Boston: Beacon Press, 2006).

108. "It is ludicrous in the extreme for the [Democratic] Party platform to talk of 'defence' in the case of Israel when from its very inception it has been the aggressor," she writes. "The 1948 war of terrorism and extermination to drive Arabs out of occupied Palestine, the 1956 tri-partite aggression, the June, 1967, aggression and continuous lesser acts of aggression against Arab states are evidence of this fact. It has been the Arab states and the Arab peoples who have required the means of defence against the expansionist, military offensives of Israel, and not the other way around." Shirley Graham Du Bois, "Phantoms for Israel," *Egyptian Gazette*, August 29, 1968.

109. Shirley Graham Du Bois, "One More Unity Link," *Egyptian Gazette*, September 4, 1968.

110. Shirley Graham Du Bois, *Egyptian Gazette*, March 26, 1968 (draft).

111. "The decisive factor in triggering the crisis that led to the Six-Day War was inter-Arab rivalries," writes Avi Shlaim. "It may sound perverse to suggest that the war owed more to the rivalries between the Arab states than to the dispute between them and Israel, but such a view is warranted by the facts. The Arab world was in a state of considerable turmoil arising out of the conflict and suspicions between the so-called progressive and the reactionary regimes." Avi Shlaim, "Jordan: Walking the Tight Rope," in Louis and Shlaim, *1967 Arab-Israeli War*, 104.

112. One historian argues recently that Israeli officials initially viewed the conflict as a defensive war of national security, not as an offensive effort, but that Israel's leadership—buoyed by its military triumph and (ambivalent but solid) U.S. support—eventually sought to preserve the territorial gains the nation reaped from the war. "In all of [Israel's military] plans," writes Avi Shlaim, "the capture of territory was intended not for retention but for bargaining purposes after the guns fell silent. The Egyptian challenge, however, rekindled an expansionist streak that had been largely dormant for the best part of two decades." Shlaim, "Israel," 31.

113. Attention to the regional character of this conflict undercuts the image of a life-and-death struggle between Israel and the Nasser-led Arab world as the main cause of war. In support of their claim that inter-Arab rivalries were more decisive in the outbreak of war in 1967 than accounts have acknowledged, Louis and Shlaim note the following developments:

> The Arab world was in a state of turmoil arising from the conflicts and suspicions between the radical and conservative regimes. A militant Ba'th regime rose to power in Syria in February 1966 and started the push for a war to liberate Palestine. President Nasser came under growing pressure to stop hiding behind the United Nations and to come to the rescue of the embattled regime in Damascus. Nasser suspected his Syrian allies of wanting to drag him into a war with Israel, while they suspected that if push came to shove, he would leave them to face Israel on their own. (Louis and Shlaim, introduction to *1967 Arab-Israeli War*, 7)

114. Concerning Egypt, Laura M. James writes: "In Sinai, there was deep confusion; as late as 5 June [Egyptian] officers were still not sure whether their goal was offensive or defensive." James, "Egypt: Dangerous Illusions," in Louis and Shlaim, *1967 Arab-Israeli War*, 66. Regarding Israel, Avi Shlaim writes: "Why did Israel launch a surprise attack on 5 June 1967? What were its war aims? Did they include territorial expansion at the expense of its neighbours? Was this a defensive or an offensive war? Was it a war of choice or a war of no-choice?" Shlaim, "Israel," 23.

115. Gamal Abdel Nasser, *The Philosophy of the Revolution* (Cairo: Mondiale Press, 1955), 55.

116. Philip E. Muehlenbeck, *Betting on the Africans: John F. Kennedy's Courting of African Nationalist Leaders* (Oxford: Oxford University Press, 2014), 123.

117. "U.S. Student in Egypt Mistaken for an Arab," *Chicago Defender*, May 6, 1961, 5. Beyond anecdotes reported in the African American press, information on African and black American student exchanges to Egypt during the Nasser era—in contrast, say, to black diaspora students resident in the Soviet Union—is an underexplored topic.

118. Nasser, *Philosophy of the Revolution*, 69.

119. Ibid., 54.

120. "The relationship between Arabs and black Africans," writes Mazrui, "has always been largely asymmetrical—with the Middle East usually the giver, and black Africa usually the receiver. Throughout the history of their

involvement in black Africa the Arabs have been both conquerors and liberators, both traders in slaves and purveyors of new ideas. Trade and Islam have been companions throughout, with the crescent following the commercial caravan, the muezzin calling believers to prayer from the marketplace." Mazrui, "Black Africa and the Arabs," 725.

121. Regarding Israel's economic forays into Africa, Graham writes:

> Coinciding with the cutting off of Arab oil came the breaking off by African states of all diplomatic and commercial ties with Israel. The Israelis commented bitterly on the ingratitude of Africans! It is true that country had gone all out in extending financial and technical aide [*sic*], know-how, teachers and frequently military advisers to the black countries of Africa. I have seen the luxury hotels they built in Tanzania, Kenya, Senegal and the Ivory Coast. . . . I doubt if there is one black State on the continent which does not have some projects financed and perhaps run by Israelis. They were the most generous [dispensers] of capital (from the United States) to these "struggling" democracies. This policy was meant to neutralize efforts of Arab representatives at the United Nations to expose the aggression, crimes, persecutions and discriminations continually carried on by Israel. It was meant to show the Israelis as the humanitarian, high-minded friends of underdeveloped blacks. (Graham Du Bois, "Confrontation in the Middle East," 34)

122. Wright, *Black Power: Three Books from Exile*, 532.

123. Ibid., 545.

124. Mazrui, "Black Africa and the Arabs," 728. In accounts of this historical moment, the Casablanca group competed with the supposedly more conservative, pro-Western Monrovia group comprising Nigeria, Senegal, Togo, and Liberia—until both factions, in 1963, closed ranks in Addis Ababa and cofounded the Organization of African Unity. Frederick Cooper writes: "If Senghor thought of turning French empire into something other than a series of nation-states, so did Kwame Nkrumah. As his Ghana became independent in 1957, he spoke of creating a 'United States of Africa'. Attempts were subsequently made at forging linkages among like-minded states, some more radical (Casablanca group), some more conservative (Monrovia group), but each state leader was preoccupied with his territorial base. The Organization of African Unity turned out to be more a union of African heads of state than of African people." Cooper, "Possibility and Constraint: African Independence in Historical Perspective," *Journal of African History* 49, no. 2 (July 2008): 177.

125. "Although Nkrumah denied that he had been pressured to sign this communiqué," Mazrui claims, "Ghana's economic relations with Israel remained unchanged for a short while, but the relationship got progressively less warm thereafter." Mazrui, "Black Africa and the Arabs," 728.

126. Graham Du Bois, "Egypt Is Africa," 30.

127. Albert Memmi, "The Impossible Life of Frantz Fanon," trans. Thomas Cassirer and G. Michael Twomey, *Massachusetts Review* 14, no. 1 (Winter 1973):

13. Memmi writes: "Nor has there been much questioning about the profound significance of this extraordinary adventure, as if the political correctness of a line of conduct accounted for its motivations, as if it went without saying that a Black West Indian intellectual could some day become an Algerian patriot, with so absolute a self-sacrifice that he would die from it, refusing to spare his meager declining strength, in spite of the objurgations of his own comrades-in-arms." Ibid. In-text citations to this work are in parentheses.

128. Graham Du Bois, "Egypt Is Africa," 24.

129. Ibid., 31–32.

130. Ibid., 23.

131. Ibid., 31.

> When, therefore, you read of the empire established by the Arabians' astonishing drive "out of their remote peninsula" between 640 AD to 732—consider the part Africans played in that drive. It ushered in the Arabs' Golden Age, when the libraries, scholastic centers and scientific studies of Cordova, Alexandria and Baghdad illumined thinking in Europe. It was from this Arabian-African influence in Spain and southern France that music and art in Europe took on new life—that the Renaissance was born. It was during this Golden Age that Timbuctoo on the Niger River in West Africa became an important center of learning and a commercial port—that over a thousand years ago Cairo was founded and Cairo's largest Mosque was transformed into Al Azhur University—now the oldest existing university in the world. Today Al Azhur graduates women students—includes in its curriculum studies of all the major African languages: Swahili, Hausa, Fanti and those of Azania and Zimbabwe. Ponder a moment on these facts. This is what the Arabs and Africans did once—*when they were united!* (Ibid.)

132. J. Gwyn Griffiths, "Hecataeus and Herodotus on 'A Gift of the River,'" *Journal of Near Eastern Studies* 25, no. 1 (January 1966): 57–61.

133. See Michael E. Latham, *Modernization as Ideology: American Social Science and "Nation Building" in the Kennedy Era* (Chapel Hill: University of North Carolina Press, 2000).

134. Muehlenbeck, *Betting on the Africans*, 123.

CHAPTER 6 Bandung or Barbarism

1. There's a ghastly irony to this prescription. "Foreign powers and transnational corporations," writes Wole Soyinka,

> loved to deal with dictatorships—contracts are signed much more quickly, with less institutional overseeing, and it is in the interest of the dictator to help the foreigners "keep the natives in order" while the wealth of the nation is siphoned out, the land is degraded through mineral explorations, eternal gas flares from petroleum destroy fauna and environment, traditional fishing ponds are polluted, the birds drop dead from the air

> while toxic and pulmonary diseases sap the vitality of the people. Thus enters the rationalization of both military takeovers and their mimic one-party democracies, through recourse to a fictional African past. Democracy, they fictionalize, is foreign to African traditions. The mythology of the "strongman" as a necessary for bringing the continent into the mainstream of a modern world becomes the gospel of trading missions, designating the committed democrats infidels and apostates. (Soyinka, *On Africa* [New Haven, CT: Yale University Press, 2012], 14)

On the other hand, Wright advocated mass education so that "vast populations" could avoid being seduced by "self-seeking demagogues." He then counsels the establishment of "strong, centralized governments in the so-called underdeveloped countries, in the hope that those countries can quickly pull themselves out of the mire and become swiftly modernized and industrialized and thereby set upon the road to democracy, free speech, a secular state, universal suffrage, etc." Richard Wright, "Tradition and Industrialization," in *Black Power: Three Books from Exile: Black Power; The Color Curtain; and White Man, Listen!* (New York: HarperCollins, 2008), 702.

2. Richard Wright, "Tradition and Industrialization," in Wright, *Black Power: Three Books from Exile*, 723. Against an unremitting backlash against the Enlightenment, critics in recent years have challenged conventional understandings of this period as the secular Age of Reason, observing that the metaphor of enlightenment itself derives from Christian and other religious sources. Critics have also questioned the view that the Enlightenment formed the intellectual basis for European imperialism and racism, or the idea that its secularizing impulse dissolved the moral pillars that religion had traditionally sustained. For a defense of the complexity of Enlightenment thought against postmodern challenges, see Louis Dupré, *The Enlightenment and the Intellectual Foundations of Modern Culture* (New Haven, CT: Yale University Press, 2004); for a discussion of postmodern critiques of the Enlightenment in relation to contemporary culture wars in the United States, see David A. Hollinger, "The Enlightenment and the Genealogy of Cultural Conflict in the United States," in *What's Left of Enlightenment? A Postmodern Question*, ed. Keith Baker and Peter Reill (Stanford, CA: Stanford University Press, 2001).

3. The sense of freedom—the basis of the idea of negative liberty, an anchor of the liberal tradition—signifies the absence of obstacles or constraints: freedom from arbitrary power, superstition, and the vicissitudes of nature and material want. See the classic essays on negative liberty by Isaiah Berlin, *Four Essays on Liberty* (Oxford: Oxford University Press, 1990). My use of the terms *enlightenment* and *the Enlightenment* adheres to the usage employed by midcentury intellectuals like Wright, who associated the term with ideas about the priority of the rational individual and society, universal freedom and equality, historical progress, natural rights and the state of nature, secularization and the disenchantment of the world, and, in some cases, notions of human perfectibility and perpetual peace, but also of racial hierarchies and European superiority.

4. Richard Wright, *The Color Curtain*, in Wright, *Black Power: Three Books from Exile*, 535. In-text page citations to this work are in parentheses.

5. Max Horkheimer and Theodor W. Adorno, *Dialectic of Enlightenment: Philosophical Fragments* (Stanford, CA: Stanford University Press, 2002), xi. On Weber's theory of rationalization, the work of Alan Sica remains an indispensible guide. See Sica, *Weber, Irrationality, and Social Order* (Berkeley: University of California Press, 1990) and *Max Weber and the New Century* (New Brunswick, NJ: Transaction Publishers, 2004). On the relationship between Weber's theory of rationalization and barbarism, see Asher Horowitz and Terry Maley, eds., *The Barbarism of Reason: Max Weber and the Twilight of Enlightenment* (Toronto: University of Toronto Press, 1994). For a Weberian interpretation of twentieth-century barbarism as derivative of modernity's quest for order, efficiency, and bureaucratic rationalization, see Zygmunt Bauman's works *Modernity and Ambivalence* (Cambridge: Polity Press, 1991) and *Modernity and the Holocaust* (Ithaca, NY: Cornell University Press, 2001). Claiming the nineteenth-century dialectical heritage of Marx against more pessimistic twentieth-century Frankfurt-style critiques, Marshall Berman balances attention to the exhilarating dimensions of modernity with its alienating and destabilizing effects. See Berman's celebrated *All That Is Solid Melts into Air: The Experience of Modernity* (New York: Penguin Books, 1988).

6. Achille Mbembe, "Necropolitics," *Public Culture* 15, no. 1 (2003): 13–14.

7. For a positive appraisal of the Third World project and its legacy, see Vijay Prashad, *The Darker Nations: A People's History of the Third World* (New York: The New Press, 2008). For David Scott's reading, via C. L. R. James, of the postcolonial era as tragedy, see Scott, *Conscripts of Modernity: The Tragedy of Colonial Enlightenment* (Durham, NC: Duke University Press, 2004).

8. Richard Wright, "The Psychological Reactions of Oppressed People," in Wright, *Black Power: Three Books from Exile*, 652.

9. Wright, *Color Curtain*, 519.

10. For Wright, Western whites were also, if less vulnerably, "anchored in tradition and habit," insofar as they were unable to comprehend the relentlessly skeptical attitude of black intellectuals like Wright who "were never allowed to blend, in a natural and healthy manner, with the culture and civilization of the West." The consolidation of whiteness deprived Westerners of what Wright called "double vision": the ability to "understand the West" as well as the "non- or anti-Western point of view." Naturally, Wright's notion of "double vision" invites comparison with Du Boisian "double consciousness." Both terms are premised on a sense of the bifurcated identity or consciousness of black Americans; both claimed an epistemic advantage, along with some measure of alienation, as a consequence of this division. But Du Bois's conception betrays a romantic resonance, a sense that this mode of consciousness both represented a point of entry for blacks onto the stage of world history and conjured the magic of Negro cultural expression. Wright's notion is more individuated and less grandly historical in scope. "Double vision" seems to refer primarily to a facility for arbitration, a privileged (but

not neutral) vantage point from which to adjudicate claims made on behalf of the Western and non-Western worlds. See Wright, "Tradition and Industrialization," 705.

11. Gates continues: "[Wright] was emphatic that, however venal the motivation, the European colonizers 'could not have done a better job of liberating the masses of Asia and Africa from their age-old traditions.'" "Today a knowing black, brown, or yellow man can say: 'Thank you, Mr. White Man, for freeing me from the rot of my irrational traditions and customs.'" Henry Louis Gates Jr., "Third World of Theory: Enlightenment's Esau," *Critical Inquiry* 34 (Winter 2008): 191–205.

12. Wright, "Tradition and Industrialization," 702.

13. Manthia Diawara, *In Search of Africa* (Cambridge, MA: Harvard University Press, 1998), 59–76. "I have recently encountered Africans and African Americans," Diawara writes, "who are willing to discuss *Black Power* openly, without being too self-conscious about it. The end of the Cold War has provided an opportunity for us to discuss the advantages to Africans of discipline, punctuality, the inner organization of the personality solidarity, focus, and perseverance, and stalwartness, which are the meanings intended by Wright's statement, 'African life must be militarized.'" Richard H. King highlights Wright's willingness to champion "the secular universalism at the heart of the modernizing vision he proposed" against the supposedly particularist claims of Negritude and other ethnocentric imaginaries. King, *Race, Culture, and the Intellectuals: 1940–1970* (Baltimore: Johns Hopkins University Press, 2004), 209.

14. As Che Guevara records in his *Pasajes*, once he, Guevara, was "promoted to commander of his own platoon, it becomes *his* duty to instill discipline, dispense love, and administer justice. Castro sends Guevara's platoon to an adjacent region to extend the liberated zone: 'Together with our newfound experience of independent life came new problems for the guerillas. It was necessary to establish a rigid discipline, to designate ranks, and establish a General Command to ensure victory in upcoming battles. This was not an easy task given the poor discipline of the troops' (*Pasajes* 80)." María Josefina Saldaña-Portillo, *The Revolutionary Imagination in the Americas and the Age of Development* (Durham, NC: Duke University Press, 2003), 81.

15. Gabriel A. Almond, *The Appeals of Communism* (Princeton, NJ: Princeton University Press, 1954), 7.

16. Ibid., 9–13.

17. Ibid., 113–114.

18. Ibid., 60.

19. Ibid., 104–105.

20. Even Wright's literary efforts to reconcile or to cope with his communist past were seen as incongruent with the national mission and therefore necessitous of surveillance. As Mary Helen Washington writes, "The 'equation between the red and the black' [that is, between communism and civil rights activism] was so fixed in the mind of J. Edgar Hoover that he recommended that the writer Richard Wright be kept on the Security Index

because 'his militant attitude toward the Negro problem' signified a weak commitment to anticommunism." Washington, *The Other Blacklist: The African American Literary and Cultural Left of the 1950s* (New York: Columbia University Press, 2014), 3.

21. Guy Reynolds, *Apostles of Modernity: American Writers in the Age of Development* (Lincoln: University of Nebraska Press, 2008), 105.

22. Ibid., 55–56.

23. Wright, *Color Curtain*, 477. In these remarks one finds a remarkable anticipation of twenty-first-century discourses that characterize Islamism and the transnational jihad as a new totalitarian threat on the global stage. Yet Wright identifies the exact opposite dynamic in the 1950s from that found in contemporary debates: whereas today's pundits frame debates about "Islam and the West" in terms of a split Muslim subjectivity, alienated and prone to extremism, Wright sees the "Moslem mind," despite colonization, as relatively whole and unfazed by Western normativity. On the contemporary framing of Islamism as a totalitarian threat, Anson Rabinbach writes: "The terrorist attacks of September 11, 2001, and the debate over the American war in Iraq, revived talk of totalitarianism among liberals and leftists thinking about radical Islamists and Middle East dictatorships." Rabinbach, "Totalitarianism Revisited," *Dissent Magazine* (Summer 2006), http://www.dissentmagazine.org/article/?article=660. Walter Laqueur identifies some early, occasional precursors to the representations of Islamic totalitarianism and Islamo-fascism in the decades from 1960 to 1990. See also Laqueur, "The Origins of Fascism: Islamic Fascism, Islamophobia, Antisemitism," Oxford University Press blog, October 25, 2006, http:/blog.oup.com/2006/10/the_origins_of_2; and Richard Shorten, "The Failure of Political Argument: The Language of Anti-Fascism and Anti-Totalitarianism in Post–September 11th Discourse," *British Journal of Politics and International Relations* 11, no. 3 (2009): 479–503.

24. Wright, *Color Curtain*, 524–525.

25. For a crisp definition and critique of the concept of historicism, see Dipesh Chakrabarty, *Provincializing Europe: Postcolonial Thought and Historical Difference* (Princeton, NJ: Princeton University Press, 2000), 6–16.

26. For example, Wright writes: "I'm numbed and appalled when I know that millions of men in Asia and Africa assign more reality to their dead fathers than to the crying claims of their daily lives: poverty, political degradation, illness, ignorance, etc." In response to the staggering infant mortality rate in Accra, Wright "shivers" at the explanation,

> The children did not wish to stay. Their ghost mothers called them home. . . . And when I hear that explanation I know that there can be no altering of social conditions in those areas until such religious rationalizations have been swept from men's minds, no matter how devoutly they are believed in or defended. Indeed, the teeming religions gripping the minds and consciousness of Asians and Africans offend me. I can conceive of no identification with such mystical conceptions of life that freeze millions in static degradation, no matter how emotionally satisfying such

> degradation seems to those who wallow in it. (Wright, "Tradition and Industrialization," 706)

27. Wright, "Psychological Reactions of Oppressed People," 676.

28. Richard H. King, *Race, Culture, and the Intellectuals* (Baltimore: Johns Hopkins University Press, 2004), 214.

29. On this point, Wole Soyinka argues that

> both Christianity and Islam had been guilty not merely of physical atrocities on African soil, including enslavement of the indigenes, but of a systematic assault on African spirituality in their contest for religious hegemony. Therefore the claims of either religion to mutual tolerance, I proposed, were still limited to the binary insularity of the world's incorrigible hegemonists, since they have proved incapable of taking into consideration the rights of other religions to equal respect, equal space, and tolerance. Still—as frankly championed between these covers—I offered that, for that very reason, those "invisible" religions of the world occupied a unique position to act as neutral arbiters whenever the two rivals went for each other's throats." (Soyinka, *On Africa*, xii)

30. Wright, "Psychological Reactions of Oppressed People," 662.

31. Consider the following paragraph: "The present-day attitude of the national revolutionary in Asia and Africa has the quality of a man who has been put to sleep for centuries and awakens to find the world of which he was a functioning part roaring past him. He is bewildered, hurt, stunned, filled with a sense of self-hate at the trick he feels has been played on him. He and his kind are many; his adversaries are relatively few in number. The world that such a man sees is devoid of meaning." Wright, "Psychological Reactions of Oppressed People," 689.

32. James Baldwin, *The Fire Next Time* (New York: Vintage, 1993), 46.

33. Wright, "Psychological Reactions of Oppressed People," 656–657.

34. Kevin Gaines, "Revisiting Richard Wright in Ghana: Black Radicalism and the Dialectics of Diaspora," *Social Text* 19, no. 2 (Summer 2001): 84.

35. As Richard H. King reminds us, "Historically the discipline of sociology originated in the attempt to describe and explain the process of modernization. . . . In the United States, modernization has referred to the transformation of an agricultural into an industrial economy and of a rural, folk culture into a secular, urban culture. In contrast with the Marxist vision of a classless society, liberal modernization theory assumed that, though role differentiation and even social stratification would increase, the importance of race and ethnicity, not to mention religion, would fade as modernization proceeded apace." King, *Race, Culture, and the Intellectuals*, 123.

36. Michael E. Latham, *The Right Kind of Revolution: Modernization, Development, and U.S. Foreign Policy from the Cold War to the Present* (Ithaca, NY: Cornell University Press, 2010), 44.

37. For accounts of JFK's administration and modernization theory, see Michael E. Latham, *Modernization as Ideology: American Social Science and*

"Nation Building" in the Kennedy Era (Chapel Hill: University of North Carolina Press, 2000); and Nils Gilman, *Mandarins of the Future: Modernization Theory in Cold War America* (Baltimore: Johns Hopkins University Press, 2007).

38. Wright, *Color Curtain*, 467, 537–538.

39. John F. Kennedy, "The Alliance for Progress" and "The New Nations of Africa," in *"Let the Word Go Forth": The Speeches, Statements, and Writings of John F. Kennedy, 1947 to 1963*, ed. Theodore C. Sorensen (New York: Delacorte, 1988), 351–369. Many commentators view JFK's commitment to decolonization, especially in Africa, as largely rhetorical but lacking in substance; others regard his development initiatives as part of a Cold War strategy or even neocolonial in their effects. Still other critics argue that JFK's support for African independence was a way to appeal to African American voters without undertaking substantive civil rights reform. On Kennedy's support for African nationalism and African American voters, see James H. Meriwether, "'Worth a Whole Lot of Negro Votes': Black Voters, Africa, and the 1960 Presidential Campaign," *Journal of American History* 95, no. 3 (December 2008): 737–763; and Thomas Borstelmann, "'Hedging Bets and Buying Time': John Kennedy and Racial Revolutions in the American South and Southern Africa," *Diplomatic History* 24, no. 3 (Summer 2000): 435–463. For a contrary view that defends JFK's foreign policy in Africa, see Philip E. Muehlenbeck, *Betting on the Africans: John F. Kennedy's Courting of African Nationalist Leaders* (Oxford: Oxford University Press, 2012).

40. As Michael Latham observes, Lipset argued that developing nations

> would learn a great deal if they sought to acquire the same "key values" of equality and achievement that "stem from our revolutionary origins." As the "first major colony successfully to revolt against colonial rule," the United States had dramatically broken with "traditional sources of legitimacy" and distinguished between "the source of sovereignty and the agents of authority" in a democratic polity. Lipset admitted that these transformations were not always easy ones but optimistically concluded that "the entire Western world has been moving in the American direction. . . . America, which was democratic and equalitarian before industrialization, has merely led the way in these patterns." As far as modernization theorists were concerned, the American past proved that the path through the transitional process was liberal and consensual, not radical or divisive. (Latham, *Modernization as Ideology*, 64–65)

41. Dipesh Chakrabarty, "Legacies of Bandung," in *Making a World after Empire: The Bandung Moment and Its Political Afterlives*, ed. Christopher J. Lee (Athens: Ohio University Press, 2010), 52.

42. Talcott Parsons, *Essays in Sociological Theory* (New York: Free Press, 1954), 119–123.

43. Kenneth W. Grundy, "Is Totalitarianism Taking Over in Africa?" *Africa Today* 14, no. 3: 12 (italics mine).

44. Ibid., 13–15.

45. At the same time, Grundy cites "additional obstructions to stable, popular government. If the hoped-for modernization is the least bit successful, it can be a politically destabilizing force in weak hands. . . . Modernization begets new elites and greater occupational differentiation." This influx of new, competitive elites with varying allegiances and ideological orientations foments "new tensions" that "continually haunt the ruling party and question its primacy, unity, and omnipotence. In addition the all pervasive economic difficulties facing virtually all underdeveloped lands, the continual pressures from the outside world, and the cultural need to break down centuries-old patterns of life and thought, compound and telescope the tasks of government." Ibid., 13–15.

46. Ibid., 14–16.

47. Wright, *Black Power: Three Books from Exile*, 415.

48. Ibid., 411–413.

49. For Eisenhower's and JFK's deliberations on financing the Volta Dam Project, see Muehlenbeck, *Betting on the Africans*, 18–24, 73–96.

50. Wright, *Black Power: Three Books from Exile*, 418.

51. Wright, "Psychological Reactions of Oppressed People," 666.

52. Ibid., 417.

53. Quoted in King, *Race, Culture, and the Intellectuals*, 213.

54. Gates, "Third World of Theory," 191.

55. Ibid., 195.

56. For Gates, "the anti-imperialist credo has had no more powerful rhetorician [than Edmund Burke]. His campaign against British administration in India, then in corporate/parastatal form, preoccupied him for two decades. Moreover, his was a critique that apprehended fully the violence, both material and cultural, that the political economy of colonialism inflicted upon subject peoples. Nothing was more abhorrent to him than the coercive eradication of India's diverse, indigenous traditions. . . . What mattered to him was enacting a theater, a public spectacle, that would expose the human cruelties of the colonial regime." More important, Burke is credited with a visionary "relativizing imagination," one perhaps better understood as "radically antifoundationalist." Gates, "Third World of Theory," 195–200.

57. This postcolonial critique holds, roughly, that classical liberalism understands itself as a political philosophy that celebrates individuality and diversity; that protects individual rights and freedoms circumscribed within communal or collective limits; that locates sovereignty in the rational, autonomous subject; and that champions progress and the "forward march of history." But in its confrontation with non-European or nonliberal cultures, liberalism regards its others as "dividuals" and holds little esteem for their diverse (namely, nonsecular or nonautonomous) modes of being; considers non-European cultures as irrational and frozen in a state of perpetual childhood (and state of nature), and as in need therefore of liberal tutelage; and consigns non-Europeans, especially the colonized, to the "waiting room of history." See Bhikhu Parekh, "Superior People: The Narrowness of Liberalism from Mill

to Rawls," *Times Literary Supplement*, February 25, 1994, 11–13; and Chakrabarty, *Provincializing Europe*.

Uday Singh Mehta, focusing on liberal paternalism and its inability to tolerate the strange and unfamiliar, contends that "Burke's pragmatism, if it is that, is an expression of his profound humility in the face of a world that he did not presume to understand simply on account of his being rational, modern, or British, and hence a member of the most powerful nation on earth.... By his openness, which is undergirded by humility and a concern with the sentiments that give meaning to people's lives, Burke exposes himself and enters a dialogue with the unfamiliar and accepts the possible risks of that encounter." Mehta, *Liberalism and Empire: A Study in Nineteenth-Century British Liberal Thought* (Chicago: University of Chicago Press, 1999), 1–45. For two studies in contrast on anti-imperialism in Enlightenment thought, see Sankar Muthu, *Enlightenment against Empire* (Princeton, NJ: Princeton University Press, 2003). See also Sunil Agnani, *Hating Empire Properly: The Two Indies and the Limits of Enlightenment Anticolonialism* (Bronx, NY: Fordham University Press, 2013) and "Jacobinism in India, Indianism in English Parliament: Fearing the Enlightenment and Colonial Modernity with Edmund Burke," *Cultural Critique* 68 (Winter 2008): 131–162.

58. Michael Hanchard, "Afro-Modernity: Temporality, Politics, and the African Diaspora," *Public Culture* 11, no. 1: 247.

59. For an account of how this imagined political community, absent state power and territory, manifested in black popular culture, see Richard H. Iton, *In Search of the Black Fantastic: Politics and Popular Culture in the Post–Civil Rights Era* (Oxford: Oxford University Press, 2008).

60. Hanchard, "Afro-Modernity," 248.

61. Frantz Fanon, *The Wretched of the Earth* (New York: Grove Press, 2004). Here I cite the recent translation of *Wretched* by Richard Philcox, rather than the earlier translation by Constance Farrington cited elsewhere in this book. I tend to use the Farrington translation because it captures the historical character of the early 1960s; in this passage, however, the Philcox translation, in my opinion, usefully contemporizes the text. Fanon's passage in French reads:

> Nous avon maintes fois signalé dans les pages qui précèdent que dans les régions sous-développées les responsable politique est toujours en train d'appeler son peuple au combat. Combat contre le colonialisme, combat contre la misère et le sous-développement, combat contre les traditions stérilisantes. Le vocabulaire qu'il utilize dans ses appels est un vocabulaire de chef d'État-Major: "mobilisation des masses," "front de l'agriculture," "front de l'analphabétisme," "défaites subies," "victoires remportées." La jeune nation indépendante évolue pendant les premières annés dans une atmosphère de champ de battaile. C'est que le dirigeant politique d'un pays sous-développé mesure avec effroi le chemin immense que doit franchir son pays. Il en appellee au peuple et lui dit: "Ceignons-nous les reins et travaillons." Le pays, tenacement saisi par une sorte de folie créatrice, se jette dans un effort gigantesque et disproportionné. (Frantz Fanon, *Les Damnés de la Terre* [Paris: Éditions La Découverte/Poche, 2002], 97)

62. Hanchard, "Afro-Modernity," 252. Hanchard elaborates:

> From this vantage point, it should not be difficult to consider the politics of human time affecting these populations. Consequently, what I call racial time became one of the disjunctive temporalities of both Western and Afro-Modernity, beginning with the emergence of racial slavery. Racial time is defined as the inequalities of temporality that result from power relations between racially dominant and subordinate groups. Unequal relationships between dominant and subordinate groups produce unequal temporal access to institutions, goods, services, resources, power, and knowledge, which members of both groups recognize. When coupled with the distinct temporal modalities that relations of dominance and subordination produce, racial time has operated as a structural effect upon the politics of racial difference. (Hanchard, "Afro-Modernity," 252–253)

63. Ibid., 702.

64. Richard Wright, *Pagan Spain* (New York: Harper Perennial, 2008), 3.

65. I borrow the term *illiberal modernity* from Peter Fritzsche and Jochen Hellbeck, who use the term to refer to the construction of a New Man developed by both the Stalinist and Nazi regimes:

> Taken together, the visions and policies of these regimes represented a radical and total rejection of liberalism and its pursuit of the freedoms and rights of the individual. The New Man emerged as a constituent of an insistently collective subject, in the case of the Soviet Union, a classless, Communist society; in the case of the Third Reich, the racial union of Aryans. Although they were illiberal, both regimes were profoundly modern precisely because of their dedication to remaking and redefining the human species. Their project encompassed an alternative, illiberal modernity. (Fritsche and Hellbeck, "The New Man in Stalinist Russia and Nazi Germany," in *Beyond Totalitarianism: Stalinism and Nazism Compared*, ed. Michael Geyer and Sheila Fitzpatrick [Cambridge: Cambridge University Press, 2009], 302)

66. Wright, *Pagan Spain*, 4.

67. Richard Wright, "There Are Still Men Left," quoted in Werner Sollors, *Ethnic Modernism* (Cambridge, MA: Harvard University Press, 2002), 189–190.

68. Thomas Hill Schaub, *American Fiction in the Cold War* (Madison: University of Wisconsin Press, 1991), 6–7.

69. Brenda Gayle Plummer, *In Search of Power: African Americans in the Era of Decolonization, 1956–1974* (Cambridge: Cambridge University Press, 2013), 30.

70. Alain Badiou, *The Century* (Cambridge: Polity Press, 2007), 48–57.

71. Ibid., 19.

72. Richard Wright, "How 'Bigger' Was Born," *Saturday Review of Literature*, June 1, 1940, 3–4.

73. Lorraine Hansberry, review of *The Outsider* in *Richard Wright: The Critical Reception*, ed. John M. Reilly (New York: Burt Franklin and Co.), 219–220.

74. "I stand in the middle of that most fateful of the world's centuries: the twentieth century. Nuclear energy, the center of the sun, is in the hands of men. In most of the land mass of Asia and Africa the traditional and customary class relations of feudal, capitalistic societies have been altered, frequently brutally shattered, by murder and terror. Most of the governments of the earth today rule, by one pretext or another, by open or concealed pressure upon the individual, by black lists, intimidation, fiat, secret police, and machine guns." Wright, *Black Power: Three Books from Exile*, 709.

75. I want to thank Alan Wald for sharing this insight about *The Outsider.*

76. Richard Wright, *The Outsider* (New York: Harper Perennial, 2008), 437.

77. Ibid., 436–437.

78. Ibid., 438.

79. Hansberry, review of *The Outsider,* 220.

80. "Men insofar as they are more than animal reaction and fulfillment of functions are entirely superfluous to totalitarian regimes. Totalitarianism strives not toward despotic rule over men, but toward a system in which men are superfluous. . . . The totalitarian attempt to make men superfluous reflects the experience of modern masses of their superfluity on an overcrowded earth." Hannah Arendt, *The Origins of Totalitarianism* (New York: Harcourt, 1968), 457.

81. Richard Wright, "Psychological Reactions of Oppressed People," 683 (italics mine).

82. Wright, *Black Power: Three Books from Exile*, 518–519.

83. Ibid., 683.

84. Kevin Gaines, *American Africans in Ghana* (Chapel Hill: University of North Carolina Press, 2006), 104–105.

85. Wright, *Outsider,* 484.

86. Eric Hobsbawm, "Barbarism: A User's Guide," *New Left Review* 0, no. 206 (July–August 1994): 45.

87. Ibid.

88. Wright, *Color Curtain*, 514–515.

89. Ibid., 538.

90. Ibid., 515–516.

91. The Cold War inflects *The Color Curtain* in other ways. As Bill Mullen notes, "*The Color Curtain* is fraught with overt and covert markers of Cold War distress: Wright's Indonesian trip and the writing it produced were funded in part by the U.S. Congress of Cultural Freedom, a secret arm of the CIA, and the book weirdly conflates red scare and yellow peril particularly in its portrait of Chou En Lai's restrained performance at Bandung." Mullen, "Discovering Postcolonialism," *American Quarterly* 54, no. 4 (2002): 706.

92. Ibid., 549. For two recent revisionist histories of the United Nations, see Mark Mazower, *No Enchanted Palace: The End of Empire and the Ideological Origins of the United Nations* (Princeton, NJ: Princeton University Press, 2009); and Samuel Moyn, *The Last Utopia: Human Rights in History* (Cambridge, MA: Belknap Press of Harvard University, 2012). Against the view that the United Nations and the postwar proliferation of human rights discourse emerged from the genocides and devastation of the Second World War, Mazower locates the ideological origins of the United Nations in transnational efforts to consolidate imperialist and racialist unity. To illustrate these origins, one needs to look no further than the case of Jan Smuts, the South African premier who helped to draft the United Nations's "stirring preamble." Smuts was also an "architect of white settler nationalism" whom Du Bois assailed for presiding over "the worst race problem of the modern world." Late in their careers, as Samuel Moyn suggests, African American activists like Du Bois, Malcolm X, and Martin Luther King Jr. began to employ human rights language and address antiblack discrimination in the United Nations, but their efforts were exceptional relative to their counterparts in the Third World. According to Moyn, anticolonialism was not a human rights movement, since most leaders in Asia and Africa emphasized national self-determination as the fundamental right of colonized groups rather than the abstract universal subject of international human rights discourse. This focus explains why figures like Vietnam's Ho Chi Minh found inspiration in Woodrow Wilson and V. I. Lenin, advocates of national self-determination, more than in proponents of human rights like Franklin and Eleanor Roosevelt.

93. Wright, *Black Power: Three Books from Exile*, 540.

94. Marguerite Cartwright, "World Backdrop: The Voice of Africa in Conference," *Pittsburgh Courier*, December 27, 1958, A8; and Tillman Durdin, "Richard Wright Examines the Meaning of Bandung," *New York Times*, March 18, 1956.

95. Malcolm X, "Message to the Grass Roots," in *Malcolm X Speaks*, ed. George Breitman (New York: Grove Press, 1994), 5.

96. Olúfémi Táíwò, *How Colonialism Preempted Modernity in Africa* (Bloomington: Indiana University Press, 2010), 22.

Conclusion

1. See *McCarthyism: The Great American Red Scare, A Documentary History*, ed. Albert Fried (Oxford: Oxford University Press, 1997), 85–88.

2. William Worthy, "McCarranism and a Free Press," *Freedomways* 3, no. 2 (Spring 1963): 191–193.

3. Benjamin J. Davis, "The McCarran Act and the Negro Freedom Movement," *Freedomways* 3, no. 2 (Spring 1963): 198.

4. Bill V. Mullen, *Un-American: W. E. B. Du Bois and the Century of World Revolution* (Philadelphia: Temple University Press, 2015), 171–172. About the McCarran Act, James writes:

> The political organization of Modern Europe has been based upon the creation and consolidation of national states. And the national state, every single national state, had and still has a racial doctrine. This doctrine is that the national race, the national stock, the national blood, is superior to all other national races, national stocks and national bloods. This doctrine was sometimes stated, often hidden, but it was and is there, and over the last twenty years has grown stronger in every country of the world. Who doubts this has only to read the McCarran Immigration Bill of 1952, which is permeated with the doctrine of racial superiority. (C. L. R. James, *Mariners, Renegades, and Castaways: The Story of Herman Melville and the World We Live In* [Hanover, NH: Dartmouth College Press, 2001], 13)

5. James Baldwin, *The Fire Next Time* (New York: Vintage International, 1993), 82.

6. On the gendered inflection of paranoia, Sianne Ngai writes: "The disposition to theorize thus finds itself aligned with paranoia, defined here not as mental illness but as a species of fear based on the dysphoric apprehension of a holistic and all-encompassing system." Some feminist writers have adopted paranoiac modes of criticism; for "the feminist critic, however, it remains important simply to recognize the way in which conspiracy theory seems intimately tied to the hermeneutic quests of male agent-intellectuals, in contexts ranging from *Critical Inquiry* to Fox Television." Ngai, *Ugly Feelings* (Cambridge, MA: Harvard University Press, 2005), 299–300.

7. Ollie Harrington, *Why I Left America and Other Essays*, ed. M. Thomas Inge (Jackson: University Press of Mississippi, 1993). In his introduction to Harrington's essay collection, *Why I Left America*, M. Thomas Inge writes: "He illustrated the first installments of a serialization of Richard Wright's *Native Son* beginning in the first issue, until the series was cancelled due to readers' complaints about the profanity used by Wright's characters. This was the first and only collaboration between the two men who later would become the closest of friends in Paris." Ollie Harrington, *Why I Left America and Other Essays*, ed. M. Thomas Inge (Jackson: University Press of Mississippi, 1993), xx.

8. John A. Williams, *The Man Who Cried I Am* (Woodstock, NY: Overlook Press, 2004), 262. In-text page citations to this work are in parentheses.

9. "Add to these facts the recent furor over detention camps still in existence and the growing suspicion of the CIA and the FBI, and it is not surprising that a black critic such as David Henderson should approach the book as a social document, a part of the protest school of black writing, which points out and documents real examples of racial prejudice and persecution." Robert E. Fleming, "The Nightmare Level of *The Man Who Cried I Am*," *Contemporary Literature* 14, no. 2 (Spring 1973): 186. For the critic referenced by Fleming, see David Henderson, "*The Man Who Cried I Am:* A Critique," in *Black Expression*, ed. Addison Gayle Jr. (New York: Weybright and Talley, 1969), 365–371.

10. "Each of America's iconic industries—agriculture, oil and gas, cosmetics, plastics, pesticides, tobacco, medicine, construction, military—has undoubtedly led to tens of millions of cancer deaths," writes S. Lochlann

Jain. Cancer's unique enmeshment with these industries and its nearly ubiquitous presence in the United States "makes it central to the growth of both the industry and the illness, in short, to the existence of the United States as we know it." Jain, *Malignant: How Cancer Becomes Us* (Berkeley: University of California Press, 2013), 5–6.

11. Williams, *Man Who Cried I Am*, 25.

12. Ibid., 209.

13. For a critique of persistent ideas about black particularity, see Kenneth W. Warren's *What Was African American Literature?* (Cambridge, MA: Harvard University Press, 2011), 44–80.

14. Harrington, *Why I Left America*, 12.

15. Williams, *Man Who Cried I Am*, 221–222.

16. See Ronald Judy, *Disforming the Canon: African-Arabic Slave Narratives and the Vernacular* (Minneapolis: University of Minnesota Press, 1993).

17. E. Franklin Frazier, *The Negro Family in the United States* (Chicago: University of Chicago Press, 1939), 15. Regarding Du Bois's well-known remarks about his African ancestry, Frazier writes: "Du Bois, of mixed blood, has woven the slender bond between himself and Africa from a romantic story of a Bantu ancestress." Ibid., 11.

18. "Perhaps the most indisputable of these rock-bottom 'truths,' and the most peculiar (since it is hard to believe it could be maintained for any other language), is that Arabic as a language is a dangerous ideology." Edward Said, *Orientalism* (New York: Vintage, 1994), 320–321.

19. Williams, *Man Who Cried I Am*, 13.

20. Ibid., 14. Why, Max asks, couldn't Michelle allow Harry's body to remain out in the open for a while, so people could come and look at him? "He'd like that."

21. Williams, *Man Who Cried I Am*, 77. The historian Tyler Stovall describes this document:

> Most of all, the American army tried to restrict contacts between black soldiers and the French population, as far as possible. Like blacks, many white Americans believed that the French were relatively color-blind, and feared that African Americans in France would grow accustomed to being treated as equals, and would then want the same treatment when they returned home. To prevent this expectation, in August 1918 the army drew up guidelines to explain to the French how they should treat black soldiers. Called "Secret Information Concerning Black American Troops," this document instructed French military and civilian officials in the finer points of American race relations. It noted that whereas many French were inclined to be friendly toward blacks, in America it was imperative to maintain strict separation of the races in order to prevent "mongrelization," and that white Americans saw such friendliness as offensive. Implicit was the threat that American aid might be withheld if the French did not learn the proper way of dealing with blacks. In particular, the document warned against intimacies between blacks and Frenchwomen. (Stovall,

Paris Noir: African Americans in the City of Light [New York: Houghton Mifflin, 1996], 14)

22. Quoted in Maria Höhn and Martin Klimke, *A Breath of Freedom: The Civil Rights Struggle, African American GIs, and Germany* (New York: Palgrave Macmillan, 2010), 54.

Acknowledgments

As Edward Said taught us, the question of beginnings—of a nation, a literary text, a language—is a fraught and difficult type of inquiry. Even when it comes to acknowledging those who helped me to write this book, I don't know where to begin. That's because so many uncommonly generous people have nurtured my work at every step of the way.

But maybe I can begin with one individual: Dr. Lettie Jane Austin. Dr. Austin joined the English faculty at Howard University in 1947, rose to full professor in 1968, and taught at Howard until her passing in 2008. If you asked students in the English Department about taking a class with Dr. Austin—who possessed three master's degrees and two doctorates—most advised you not to. A wiser few, however, said *absolutely* take her class; I'm glad I listened to them. On my first essay assignment, Dr. Austin issued me a C+ and changed my life. I treasure the gift of her friendship and her investment in my potential. Beyond Howard, Dr. Austin led many professional lives, but she remained foremost a teacher—a master teacher. Early on, she taught me by example that education is one powerful way of doing politics. I dedicate *Race and the Totalitarian Century* to her memory. I'm also indebted to Howard University's other dedicated faculty and administrators, who ignited my interest in African American literature and, more important, unabashedly treated their students like family.

Many of the ideas contained in this book evolved during my graduate career at the University of Chicago, where I was privileged to explore multiple humanistic disciplines and eventually to find my intellectual way. My Chicago story begins in the summer of 1999, when I came to the university to conduct research under the auspices of the Summer Research Opportunity Program. I'm sure Jim Chandler and Saree Makdisi had better things to do that summer, but they took on my research project on Joseph Conrad with verve and patience and convinced me that Chicago was the place for me. Chicago also brought me within the orbit of talented artists and cherished friends Sonny Arthur, Adam Carter, and Rocky Russell, whose creativity introduced me to new ideas and modes of expression.

Some of the discussion in Chapter 1 was first developed in my essay "The 'Lost Years' or a 'Decade of Progress'? African American Writers and the Second World War," in *A Companion to the Harlem Renaissance*, ed. Cherene Sherrard-Johnson (West Sussex, UK: John Wiley & Sons, Ltd., 2015). Chapter 2 builds upon "*Invoking Totalitarianism: Liberal Democracy versus the Global Jihad in Boualem Sansal's* The German Mujahid," in *Novel: A Forum on Fiction* 47:1 (2014), published by Duke University Press.

Writing in his book's acknowledgments, one sociologist calls Lauren Berlant one of the world's great close readers. I imagine her reputation in this respect is well established. But it ought to be known that she is just as superb a close reader for her many students who, like I once did, approach her with merely the kernel of an idea—or a dense pack of kernels, like an unpopped bag of popcorn. Lauren Berlant makes them pop. No one I know is better at exfoliating inessential layers to find the heart of an intellectual production. I remain in her debt.

From my first graduate seminar with him, Ken Warren has been an incisive critic, sage counselor, and unfailing proponent of my work. Ken modeled, among other things, the art of prolepsis and disciplined argumentation. I thank him for his friendship and intellectual camaraderie. In addition to lending morale, Debbie Nelson asked me all the right questions and taught me a great deal about post-1945 American culture.

I would like to express my deep gratitude to the humanities center of the University of Pittsburgh, an epicenter for intellectual dialogue on topics of humanistic inquiry. Under Jonathon Arac's elegant leadership, Pitt's Humanities Center awarded me a one-year postdoctoral fellowship that allowed me to complete portions of this book. I want to thank Jonathon and Sabine Von Dirke for being such magnanimous hosts and expansive humanists. I'd also like to thank Bill Scott for reading and providing detailed feedback on a chapter draft and for sharing with me his own archival research. In addition to reading a chapter draft, April Womack was a great interlocutor and friend to me in Pittsburgh.

I want to thank Harvard University Press's executive editor for the humanities, Lindsay Waters, for his unflagging commitment to this book. I'm endlessly grateful for his determination to see this book through. I also want to thank Amanda Peery, assistant editor at Harvard, whose diligence, thoroughness, and optimism earned my complete confidence. I owe a special debt to the two anonymous reviewers of my manuscript, whose exquisite reports exemplify scholarly generosity and the summum bonum of the peer review process. In an era when everyone is overcommitted, these reviewers invested extraordinary effort and shared their deep erudition in their reports. I hope they see their invaluable input reflected within these pages.

I'd like to thank the expert librarians and staff at the Schlesinger Library at Harvard University, the Schomburg Center for Research in Black Culture, the Beineke Library at Yale University, and the Moorland-Spingarn Library at Howard University. I want to acknowledge particularly the Moorland-Spingarn's chief curator, Joellen ElBashir, whom I've known since my undergraduate days and whose family is also my family. I send my love to the whole ElBashir-Hill clan, especially to Anthony—my brother and general counsel in all matters—and to his wife, my friend, Hanadi.

Special gratitude is owed to Chris Freeburg—the (fiercely protective) big brother I always wanted—whose inimitable good humor, sound advice, and constructive criticism helped me to navigate the terrain of the academic profession. For their encouragement and suggestions over the years, I would like to express my gratitude to friends and colleagues from various institutions: Nancy Armstrong, Daphne Brooks, Erica Edwards, Eddie Glaude, Bill Gleason, Yogita Goyal, Tom Guglielmo, Gene Jarrett, Saikat Majumdar, Rolland Murray, M. Lee Pelton, Imani Perry, Therí Pickens, Steven Sohn, Bryan Wagner, Ivy Wilson, and Richard Yarborough, among many others. As a newly minted PhD, I was lucky enough to benefit from the guidance and wisdom of Elizabeth Alexander, Glenda Gilmore (who pointed me to the work of Shirley Graham Du Bois), Jonathon Holloway, Darnell Hunt, Gordon Hutner, Jim Miller, Gretchen Flesher Moon, Ken Nolley, Caleb Smith, Hortense Spillers, Alan Wald, and Michael Warner (whose behind-the-scenes advocacy has not escaped my notice).

At Stanford University, I have been embarrassingly fortunate to work with supportive and virtuoso colleagues. In the Department of English, I wish to thank John Bender, Eavan Boland, Terry Castle, Ken Fields, Shelley Fisher Fishkin, Denise Gigante, Blair Hoxby, Claire Jarvis, Nick Jenkins, Adam Johnson, Michelle Karnes, Andrea Lunsford, Mark McGurl, Stephen Orgel, Pat Parker, Peggy Phelan, Judith Richardson, Nancy Ruttenburg, Elizabeth Tallent, Blakey Vermeule, Toby Wolf, and Alex Woloch. The unparalleled mentorship of Michele Elam, Gavin Jones, and Ramón Saldívar means the world to me. A perspicacious interlocutor and cherished friend, Paula Moya is a joy to work with. Sianne Ngai is the kindest, smartest, and most genuine colleague one could hope for. Her crucial feedback improved this book and elevated my spirit. The department's administrators, past and present—Christina Ablaza, Alyce Boster, Nicole Bridges, Judy Candell, Dagmar Logie, Laura Ma, Katie Oey, Nelia Peralta, Vivian Sana, and Maile Yee—provide skilled support and make our department fun and efficient in equal measure.

In Stanford's Center for Comparative Studies in Race and Ethnicity, I want to thank H. Samy Alim, Ralph Banks, Jennifer Brody, Cheryl Brown, Al Camarillo, Jim Campbell, Prudence Carter, Jennifer Eberhardt, Harry Elam, Corey Fields, Duana Fullwiley, Allyson Hobbes, Héctor Hoyos, Alvan Ikoku, Tomás Jiménez, Hazel Markus, David Palumbo-Liu, José David Saldívar, Gary Segura, and Matt

Snipp—all exemplary scholars and marvelous colleagues. In addition to providing a singular space for the multidisciplinary study of race and ethnicity, the faculty and students of CCSRE have created a community defined by collegiality, scholarly engagement, and mutual support. Special recognition is due to Al Camarillo for his indomitable leadership in Stanford's Faculty Development Initiative.

In Stanford's Center for African Studies, I've enjoyed abundant conviviality and intellectual stimulation. I want to thank Laura Hubbard, Grant Parker, and Richard Roberts for their efforts in sustaining, and growing, this unique environment. In Stanford's Division of Literatures, Languages, and Cultures, I'm indebted to Russell Berman for sharing his vast experience in higher education and his wide, deep knowledge of modern culture and politics. I can't thank him enough for his support of my research.

My students at Stanford University have challenged, taught, surprised, and delighted me with their ideas and engagement with the most pressing dilemmas of our world. In particular, doctoral students Aku Ammah-Tagoe, Calvin Miaw, J. D. Porter, and Chris Suh have inspired me with their own cutting-edge research. I also want to acknowledge the brilliant, hardworking students in my Concepts of Modernity II seminar—Cynthia Garcia, Elise Huerta, Matthew Mason, Juan Pablo Melo, and Paul Wallace—who engaged imaginatively and rigorously with many of the ideas I was contemplating during the late stage of writing. I was energized, also, by the scope and promise of their projects.

When I taught in Germany on a Fulbright award during 2008 and 2009, the faculty in the American Studies Department at Humboldt University of Berlin—Eva Boesenberg, Markus Heide, Renate Hof, Reinhard Isensee, Suncica Klass, and Martin Klepper—treated me like a true colleague and a long-lost friend. I miss everyone at Humboldt Amerikanistik and hope our paths cross again soon.

The scholars associated with the Post45 collective represent the forefront of post–World War II U.S. literary studies. I've profited immeasurably from my affiliation with these scholars. I'd like to acknowledge the contributions to my thinking of Andrew Hoberek, Amy Hungerford, Colleen Lye, Deak Nabers, Scott Saul, and Michael Szalay.

I send all my love and thanks to my entire family, especially my wonderful and doting parents, Gary and Wendy Rasberry, who are unbreakable pillars of support. More now than ever, I appreciate that they always trusted my judgment and valued my aspirations. Their boundless love moves and motivates me. To my beloved grandparents—Thomas and Dolores Rasberry and Edward and Eunice Davis—I strive to make them proud and only wish that I could have seen their faces with my book in their hands.

My wife, Tatyana Marisol—my *consigliere*, inspiration, and co-architect and love of my life—I thank for her reliably brilliant insights, sage advice, and creative input. I'm grateful that she kept me buoyant during the arduous process of completing a book. Her loving presence during this time imbued the process with a sublime meaning I could never have anticipated. And I send lots of love and thanks to my new family—Sonia, Sheriff, Anastasia, Eric, Kimberly, *Abuela* Estelle, and many more—who have embraced me with open, loving arms.

Memory is a reservoir and a sieve. If my memory has failed me in these acknowledgments, I hope that all who have contributed to this book, in any way, find their imprint within its pages and accept my sincerest thanks.

Index

Page numbers in *italics* indicate illustrations.